PEARSON CUSTOM PUBLISHING

Politics of the British Isles

Compiled from:

Politics UK
Seventh Edition
by Bill Jones and Philip Norton

The New British Politics
Fourth Edition
by Ian Budge, David McKay, Kenneth Newton and John Bartle

Exploring British Politics
Second Edition
by Mark Garnett and Philip Lynch

PEARSON

Harlow, England • London • New York • Boston • San Francisco • Toronto • Sydney • Auckland • Singapore • Hong Kong
Tokyo • Seoul • Taipei • New Delhi • Cape Town • Sao Paulo • Mexico City • Madrid • Amsterdam • Munich • Paris • Milan

Pearson Education Limited
Edinburgh Gate
Harlow
Essex CM20 2JE

And associated companies throughout the world

Visit us on the World Wide Web at:
www.pearsoned.co.uk

ISBN 978 1 78134 705 8

Printed and bound in Great Britain.

Contents

Topic 1: Introduction

1 Politics in perspective
Bill Jones 1

Topic 2: Ideology and Ideas

2 Political ideas: the major parties
Bill Jones 17

3 Political ideas: themes and fringes
Bill Jones 37

4 Ideology and the liberal tradition
Bill Jones 65

Topic 3: Political Parties

5 Political Parties and Party Factions
Ian Budge/David McKay/Ken Newton/John Bartle 79

6 Party Ideologies and Political Representation
Ian Budge/David McKay/Ken Newton/John Bartle 107

7 Political parties
Richard Kelly 133

Topic 4: Elections and Electoral Behaviour

8 Elections
Mark Garnett 153

9 Elections and Voting
Ian Budge/David McKay/Ken Newton/John Bartle 173

10 The 2010 Election: The End of New Labour
Bill Jones/Phillip Norton 205

Topic 5: Pressure Groups

11 Pressure Groups
Ian Budge/David McKay/Ken Newton/John Bartle 225

12 Participation beyond elections
Mark Garnett 249

Topic 6: Media

13 The mass media and political communications
Bill Jones 273

Topic 7: Policy Process

14 The policy-making process
Bill Jones 297

Topic 8: Prime Minister and Cabinet

15 The Prime Minister, the Cabinet, and the Core Executive
Ian Budge/David McKay/Ken Newton/John Bartle 321

16 Ministries, Ministers and Mandarins: Central Government in Britain
Ian Budge/David McKay/Ken Newton/John Bartle 343

Topic 9: Parliament

17 The House of Commons
Philip Norton 363

18 The House of Lords
Philip Norton 409

Topic 10: Devolution

19 Devolution
Russell Deacon 443

Index 467

Topic 1:
Introduction

Politics in perspective

Bill Jones

There has never been a perfect government, because men have passions; and if they did not have passions, there would be no need for government.

Voltaire, *Politique et legislation*

The love of power is the love of ourselves.

William Hazlitt

I love fame; I love public reputation; I love to live in the eye of the country.

Benjamin Disraeli

Learning objectives

- To establish some understanding of the discipline of politics so that the subsequent contents of the book can be absorbed within its context.

- To explain and illustrate the concept of politics.

- To discuss the nature of politicians and the reasons why they choose their profession.

- To explain the importance of certain key concepts.

- To provide a brief overview of topics covered in the book.

From Chapter 1 of *Politics UK*, 7/e. Bill Jones and Philip Norton. © Pearson Education 2001–2010. All rights reserved.

■ The concept of politics defined and discussed

Politics is far from being a popular area of activity; politicians rank below those modern bêtes noire, estate agents, in some opinion polls. They are often held to be, among other failings: self-serving, venal, dishonest, power-obsessed people who are more likely to be a danger to society rather than its salvation. Politics and its politicians have changed over the years, both in its practices and the way it is regarded. Originally, it is fair to say, politicians were mostly people who had seized control by force and exercised it in their own interests. **Power** was often used merely to reflect the will and the glory of the chief conqueror and the changing nature of his whims.

Since those days a number of changes have occurred:

1 Rulers who are interested only in power for themselves, have become a recognised phenomenon against whom society must protect itself. Aristotle, the Greek philosopher argued that 'man is by nature a political animal' who required a robust system of law to be kept in check.

2 He also argued that government was best undertaken by a relatively disinterested group of well educated men, in effect a stratum of cultured gentlemen.

3 Two groups, long assumed to be excluded from the governing class – the very poor (originally slaves) and women – are no longer regarded as beyond the pale, though neither are as well represented as their numbers might justify.

4 Democracy – or a system whereby every citizen is entitled to some kind of say in their own government – has become widely accepted as desirable, especially in developed countries in Europe, North America and increasingly large parts of the rest of the world.

Defining politics

What precisely did Aristotle mean when he said man is by nature a *political* animal? The word is much used and most people think they know what it means but usually they cannot give a clear explanation. A typical reply might be that it's concerned with: 'Political parties, you know, Labour and Conservatives'.

Clearly this is factually correct but it does not take us very far towards a definition as many things have connections to political parties. No, to extract a clear definition we have to examine what things occur when 'politics' is definitely present.

For example, the following made-up news items can all be said to involve 'politics' at some level:

1 Father seeks to influence soccer manager to give his son a place in the team.

2 Chancellor ignores union claims for increased salaries.

3 Oil prices continue to rise as war spreads in Middle East.

4 Thousands demonstrate in favour of climate change measures.

The first example illustrates that politics operates at a 'micro' level; we speak of the 'politics' of the family or 'small groups'. The second is drawn from the mainstream of what we regard as 'political': a government minister taking a decision on something.

From these and the other two examples it can be seen that 'politics' entails:

■ a strong element of conflict and its resolution;

■ a struggle for scarce and finite resources;

■ the use of various methods of persuasion or pressure, to achieve a desired outcome.

So, if we can move towards a definition, it might be constructed as:

Politics is a process that seeks to manage or resolve conflicts of interest between people, usually in a peaceful fashion. In its general sense it can describe the interactions of any group of individuals, but in its specific sense it refers to the many and complex relationships that exist between state institutions and the rest of society.

■ Politicians and their ambition

'Politics is a spectator sport', writes Julian Critchley (1995: 80). An enduring question that exercises us spectators is 'Why are they doing it?' Dr Johnson, in his typically blunt fashion, said politics was 'nothing more nor less than a means of rising in the world'. But we know somehow that mere self-interest is not the whole truth. Peter Riddell of

BOX 1.1 IDEAS AND PERSPECTIVES

What does government do?

If politics is largely about government then what are the things that governments do? Anthony Giddens, in his *The Third Way*, provides the following analysis:

- provide means for the representation of diverse interests;
- offer a forum for reconciling the competing claims of those interests;
- create and protect an open public sphere, in which unconstrained debate about policy issues can be carried on;
- provide a diversity of public goods, including forms of collective security and welfare;
- regulate markets in the public interest and foster market competition where monopoly threatens;
- foster social peace through the provision of policing;
- promote the active development of human capital through its core role in the education system;
- sustain an effective system of law;
- have a directly economic role, as a prime employer, in macro and micro intervention, plus the provision of infrastructure;
- more controversially, perhaps, have a civilising aim – government reflects the widely held norms and values, but can also help shape them, in the educational system and elsewhere;
- foster regional and trans-national alliances and pursue global goals.

Source: Giddens (1998: 47–8)

The Times, in his wonderfully perceptive book *Honest Opportunism*, looks at this topic in some detail. He quotes Disraeli, who perhaps offers us a more rounded and believable account of his interest in politics to his Shrewsbury constituents: 'There is no doubt, gentlemen, that all men who offer themselves as candidates for public favour have motives of some sort. I candidly acknowledge that I have and I will tell you what they are: I love fame; I love public reputation; I love to live in the eye of the country.'

Riddell also quotes F.E. Smith, who candidly gloried in the 'endless adventure of governing men'. For those who think that these statements were merely expressions of nineteenth-century romanticism, Riddell offers the example of Richard Crossman's comment that politics is a 'never ending adventure – with its routs and discomfitures, rushes and sallies', its 'fights for the fearless and goals for the eager'. He also includes Michael Heseltine, whom he once heard, irritated, asking at one of Jeffrey Archer's parties in 1986: 'Why *shouldn't* I be Prime Minister then?'

The tendency of politicians to explain their taste for politics in terms of concern for 'the people' is seldom sincere. In the view of Henry Fairlie this is nothing more than 'humbug'. William Waldegrave

agrees: 'Any politician who tells you he isn't ambitious is only telling you he isn't for some tactical reason; or more bluntly, telling you a lie – I certainly wouldn't deny that I wanted ministerial office; yes, I'm ambitious.' As if more proof were needed, David Owen once said on television that 'Ambition drives politics like money drives the international economy.' Ambition, of course, is good for society only if it works for the general good; if it is purely self-inclined we end up with the likes of Saddam Hussein. As Edmund Burke noted: 'Ambition can creep as well as soar.' Politics is also an all-consuming obsession for some people. Writing in *The Guardian*, 11 March 2006, Michael Heseltine, that famously ambitious Conservative politician who narrowly missed gaining the top prize, probably spoke for all those bitten by the political bug when he said: 'Politics is a life sentence. It's an obsessive, all demanding, utterly fascinating, totally committing profession – stimulating, satisfying, stretching.'

Riddell goes on in his book – now dated but important as it discerned an important trend – to analyse how the ambitious political animal has slowly transformed British politics. He follows up and develops Anthony King's concept of the 'career politician', observing that a decreasing number of

---

BOX 1.2   The Hubris Syndrome

Symptoms of the 'hubris' syndrome are as follows:

- A narcissistic propensity to see one's world primarily as an arena in which to exercise power and seek glory.
- A disproportionate concern with image and presentation.
- A messianic manner.
- Excessive confidence in one's own judgement and contempt for advice.

- Exaggerated self-belief, bordering on omnipotence.
- A belief that one is accountable solely to history or god.
- Loss of contact with reality; often associated with progressive isolation.
- Restlessness, recklessness and impulsiveness.

Extracted from Sarah Boseley's 'A Doctor Writes: Politicians' Pride is a Medical Disorder', The Guardian, 28 March 2009

MPs had backgrounds in professions, or 'proper jobs' in Westminster parlance, compared with those who centred their whole lives on politics. The jobs of these people were of secondary importance, merely anticipating or supporting the Westminster career. In 1951 the figure was 11 per cent; by 1992 it was 31 per cent. By contrast, the proportion of new MPs with 'proper jobs' fell from 80 per cent to 41 per cent.

Many of this new breed begin life as researchers for an MP or in a party's research department, then proceed to seek selection as a candidate and from there into parliament and from then on, ever onwards and upwards. The kind of MP who enters politics in later life is in steep decline; the new breed of driven young professionals has tended to dominate the field, proving firmer of purpose and more skilled in execution than those for whom politics is a later or learned vocation. The kind of businessman who achieves distinction in his field and then goes into politics is now a rarity rather than the familiar figure of the nineteenth century or the earlier decades of the twentieth century.

affected by the perception that he was an arrogant man, impatient with views with which he did not agree. So his 2007 book *The Hubris Syndrome: Bush, Blair and the Intoxication of Power* (he also wrote a paper on the same subject for the journal of the Royal Society of Psychiatrists in March 2009), made interesting reading for students of politics. He identifies the tendency to be intoxicated with power as an occupational hazard in politics and names as 'sufferers', Lloyd George, Neville Chamberlain, Thatcher, Blair and George Bush.

Owen, who admits to have exhibited elements of the syndrome himself, believes he has discerned a medical condition:

I have seen the isolation – this extraordinary pressure under which leaders in business or in politics live, with shortages of sleep – a generally very high-pressured existence. I'd liken it to . . . a long-distance runner. You go through a pain threshold and something changes. The public are way ahead. The man in the street starts to say the prime minister has 'lost it'. They put it all down to adrenaline. They see these people as supercharged.

■ Ambition to hubris: a short journey?

Lord David Owen trained as a doctor and became an MP in 1966. He was made Labour Foreign Secretary at the precocious age of 38. His subsequent resignation from the party and involvement in the short-lived Social Democratic Party, denied him the senior role in government which many had predicted. There is little doubt his career was adversely

■ Are politicians viewed generally with too much cynicism?

Certainly politics and its practitioners, according to many opinion polls, are seen in the present day, variously, as untrustworthy, self-seeking, power mad or cynical manipulators. My own view is that the cynicism has been excessive. Most politicians are quite decent people, trying hard to make a difference for the better. One of the problems is that in a 24-7 news age the media know that negative stories about political transgressions, whether sexual, financial or merely concerning incompetence, will attract great interest. The public loves to have someone to blame for things they do not like – high prices, poor public services, inflation, or whatever – and too often politicians are on the receiving end.

For example, Labour Home Secretary Jaqui Smith received a terrible press in late March 2009 when it transpired her husband had bought two 'blue' movies and charged them to his wife's Parliamentary expenses. The media really went to town; the minister was not directly involved but was at the same time embroiled in another well publicised dispute as to which was her 'main home' for expenses purposes. The accumulation of such stories tends to construct a default negative image of MPs, garnished perhaps by a national tradition or habit of sometimes savagely non-deferential, satirical criticism of our rulers. There is much evidence to suggest we are excessively cynical about our politicians but the history of their own behaviour makes it clear that they should be treated with, at minimum, a cautious discrimination. I think the closest to the truth I have found was encapsulated by Estelle Morris, a Labour Education Secretary who resigned in 2002. Upon being elevated to the Cabinet she asked a colleague what its members were 'really like' and received the reply:

The good news they are just like all the rest of us; but the bad news is . . . they are just like all the rest of us.

■ Key concepts in the study of politics

What is a concept?

A concept is usually expressed by a single word or occasionally by a phrase. Concepts are frequently general in nature, representing a specific function or category of objects. For example, the word 'table' usually refers to an individual human artefact, but it also embodies the whole idea of a table, which we might understand as a flat platform usually supported by legs and designed to have objects rested upon it. Without this definition a table would be a meaningless object; it is the concept that gives it purpose and function. As Andrew Heywood (1994: 4) explains:

a concept is more than a proper noun or the name of a thing. There is a difference between talking about a chair, a particular and unique chair, and holding the concept of a 'chair', the idea of a chair. The concept of a chair is an abstract notion, composed of the various features which give a chair its distinctive character – in this case, for instance, the capacity to be sat upon.

It follows, therefore, that the concept of a 'parliament' refers not to a specific parliament in a given country but to the generality of them – the abstract idea underlying them. By the same token, as we grow up, we come to attribute meaning and function to everyday objects through learning the appropriate concepts – plates, cups, windows, doors and so forth. Without these concepts we would be totally confused, surrounded by a mass of meaningless phenomena. In one sense concepts are the meaning we place on our surrounding world, impose on it, to enable us to deal with it. Similarly, we come to understand the political world through concepts that we learn from our reading, the media and our teachers. Over the years we come to extend them and refine them in order to achieve a sophisticated understanding, to become 'politically literate'. To use a slightly different analogy, concepts are like the different lenses opticians place in front of us when attempting to find the one that enables us to see more effectively. Without them we cannot bring a blurred world into focus; with them we achieve, or hope to achieve, some clarity and sharpness.

Power and authority and other ideas

These are two central ideas in the study of politics and need to be understood from the outset.

Power In essence this means the ability to get someone else to do what they otherwise would not have done. This could be achieved through direct coercion: threatening or delivering violence; pointing a gun at someone. While this relationship might be widely reflected in relations between states, it is rare, except in brutal tyrannies, for it to occur within organised states. Here there is a system for the management of disputes and usually this precludes the use of force or coercion, except as a background resort if all else fails.

Bachrach and Baratz (1981) argued that power is more subtle than this: decisions made by politicians not to do things were just as important as those actually made. If a matter is marginalised or ignored completely through the ability of someone or a group to exclude it, then considerable power is being exercised. Marx argued that those with control over wealth and its production effectively ruled society as they were able, through their control of the main institutions of society, to permeate it with the values upon which their own power rested. Thus, in his view, rich capitalists were able to win acceptance for their economic system as unarguable 'commonsense'.

Authority is the acceptance by someone of another's right to tell them what to do, for example a policeman or a judge. In other words this is power with the crucial added ingredient of legitimacy. For it to work the means whereby authority is granted – a process of discussion in an elected parliament – the related institutions must also be regarded as legitimate and authoritative. Few governments can survive without this characteristic.

Interests This term relates to what politicians are concerned to achieve. It could be more resources for a specific group in society, or more generally a class of people. It could be the reversal of a political decision – for example withdrawal from the EU – or it might be the obtaining of a place of status and power in government or merely an honour like a knighthood or a peerage. George Orwell in his dystopic novel, *Nineteen Eighty-Four*, suggests politicians are basically concerned to accumulate power, often for its own sake (see above, Politicians and their ambition). Certainly history can offer up any number of despots and tyrants – Hitler, Stalin, Saddam Hussein – who would fit this bill, but in a democracy, to some extent an antidote to political tyranny, safeguards are usually built in to prevent such a leader from gaining power.

Actors This term is often used to describe people who participate in politics: the *dramatis personae* of the process, which has often been likened to a performance or a game. Indeed senator Eugene McCarthy once wittily suggested that:

Being in politics is like being a football coach. You have to be smart enough to understand the game and dumb enough to think it's important.

Legislature This is the element of government in a democracy which is usually elected by a society to discuss and pass the laws by which it wishes to be governed. It is the election which provides the democratic authority the government needs to govern effectively. So in the case of the UK, it is Parliament, comprising the Commons, Lords and the Queen. It hardly needs saying that, at the time of writing, only the first element is democratically elected.

Executive This element is responsible for implementing the policies and laws produced by the legislature. In the Westminster model of government, the government is formed by the party winning a majority at a general election. In the US model, the President is elected separately and has a legitimacy similar to that of the legislature, producing a relationship between them which is essentially one of conflict and cooperation through negotiation.

Judiciary This is the part of government which interprets the laws, running the legal system of courts and the machinery of justice. It also handles appeals against alleged miscarriages of justice and rules whether laws are compatible with EU law which, since 1972, has taken precedence over domestic law by virtue of the terms of the Treaty of Paris.

Some political concepts are merely descriptive, for example 'election', but others embody a 'normative' quality – they contain an 'ought'. Such a concept is:

Democracy This notion of citizen involvement in government goes back to the Greeks who pioneered it in their city states. Churchill famously said of democracy that:

No one pretends that democracy is perfect or all wise. Indeed, it has been said that democracy is the worst form of government, except for all the others that have been tried from time to time.

In Britain it evolved out of conflicts between an absolute monarchy and an advisory council-cum-parliament reflecting the wealth all monarchs needed to rule. After centuries of gradually emerging authority the latter refused to endorse the royal will and a short but bitter civil war – in which parliamentary forces took the field under Oliver Cromwell against royalist armies – saw the king deposed and executed in 1649. In 1660 the monarchy was restored but had lost its supremacy to Parliament which was now set on a trajectory of increasing and decisive control over government business. The 1832 Reform Act laid the foundations for the democratic representation that has continued to evolve to the present day.

There can be no doubt our system is flawed:

1 Most voters are bored by current affairs and are functionally politically illiterate.

2 There is currently widespread distrust of politicians in the UK, scarcely allayed by the continuing behaviour of some of them.

3 Rousseau pointed out that the British electorate only has power on election days; once they have voted power is virtually immune from popular influence.

4 As Robert Michels observed with his 'iron law of oligarchy' outwardly democratic forms are usually subverted by small elites who come to control all the major institutions.

5 Voters' willingness to participate has been weakened by the complexity of some modern issues, for example, whether the UK should join the euro.

6 The media now dominates the conduct of democratic politics and politicians, with their media manipulators or 'spin doctors' have been able to disguise and obfuscate the real issues when it has suited them.

Representation This is another normative idea, central to democracy in that it enables large societies to be ruled to a degree, admittedly tenuous when few are interested in politics, by every citizen. The authors of the American Revolution adopted Reverend John Mayhew's resonant 1750 phrase – 'No Taxation without Representation' – as the banner of their cause because they believed the right to levy taxes could legitimately be obtained only through the consent of the American peoples' elected representatives.

Precisely what form representation takes is another matter as there is more than one possibility.

1 Altruistic: here someone will seek to protect and advance the interests of those represented. Whether such stated objectives, for example by MPs, are genuine, however, will always be a matter of judgement for voters.

2 'Delegate representative': this is when someone is obligated to represent voters' views in a defined way.

3 'Judgement representative': this version, wholly antithetical to item 2 above, is forever connected to the orator and theorist, Edmund Burke who, in 1774, told his electors in Bristol:

Your representative owes you, not his industry only, but his judgement; and he betrays, instead of serving you, if he sacrifices it to your opinion.

This approach risks being elitist in that it assumes the representative better knows what is good for his/her electors than they do.

4 'Revolutionary or "class" representative': this is usually associated with Marxist notions that bourgeois capitalism so blinds voters to the fact of their own exploitation, that only those revolutionaries who are aware of the proletariat's genuine interests can truly represent them.

5 'Educated representative': this is the view that voters require substantial knowledge of current affairs before they can properly vote. But if education is to be the criterion for representation, then why not select those who excel in competitive exams to represent us in government, like the mandarins of imperial China? (see Heywood 1994: 178–9).

6 Representation as microcosm: American President John Adams (1735–1826) argued that the legislature should be as exactly as possible 'a portrait in miniature of the people at large, as it should think, feel, reason and act like them'. This is a rather narrow view, however, which suggests a man cannot represent a woman or someone of one social class represent a voter from another.

In the British system representation is accepted as a fundamental requirement but no single interpretation is entrenched. Rather – perhaps in tune with Britain's pragmatic traditions – aspects of several of the above can be discerned. Apart from the occasional exceptions, British politicians are relatively non-corrupt and take their representative duties seriously; Tony Benn has argued for the delegate approach to representation, but for his fellow parliamentarians the Burkean view is the more accepted; the revolutionary approach has never been widely supported in Britain; and, while most MPs are well educated, it is not thought that a high level of education is an essential prerequisite either for an MP or for a voter.

Human nature This idea is central to the study of politics, that how human beings behave depends on their essential natures, so philosophers have speculated upon its essence. Thomas Hobbes, for example, was pessimistic: he felt that without the protective constraints of civilised society, the selfish nature of human beings would make life 'solitary, poor, nasty, brutish and short'. There would be no security of property, 'no thine and mine distinct; but only that to be everyman's, that he can get; and for so long as he can keep it'. Others did not agree. Rousseau argued that it was the evils of modern society which were responsible for its own dysfunctions. Karl Marx too was an optimist on this topic, arguing that mankind was much better than it appeared because of the corrupting effects of the harsh economic system of privately owned capital. Marx believed that human nature was a rogue product of a sick society asserting: 'Environment determines consciousness'. It followed that changing the social environment for the better would improve human nature too.

Charles Darwin's theory of evolution encouraged some, like Herbert Spencer to argue that this notion of the 'survival of the fittest' justified capitalism as the way in which the species was developing itself and to argue against government interference with the 'natural order' of things. But then came Sigmund Freud.

Freud argued that man is driven by instinctual urges underlying the desire to experience pleasure and the, often conflicting, need to adjust to social reality. To live any kind of ordered life excludes the continuance of the pleasure principle, so drives are repressed and sublimated into socially useful activities like work and achievement:

Sublimation of instinct is an essentially conspicuous feature of cultural development: it is what makes it possible for the higher psychical activities, in [the] scientific, artistic or ideological, to play such an important part in civilised life.

Herbert Marcuse agreed with Freud about repression but argued that modern society, especially class differences, generated too much of it and that a revolution was needed to correct the imbalance.

Nationalism It would be wrong to assume that nationalism has always been around. The extension of loyalty to a common ethnicity within a common territory, all sharing a common history and culture, including struggle against common foes arrived around 250 years ago and was facilitated greatly by industrialisation and modern economies. In the case of England it probably arrived earlier, around Elizabethan times; in Shakespeare's *Henry V* we have the king exhorting, 'Cry God for Harry, England and St George!'

The French Revolution allied the notion that everyone is endowed with certain natural rights with the right to self-determination for a national 'community' of people and this helped breath fire into a number of national movements in the nineteenth century including those of Belgium, Greece and Poland, not to mention the unifying nationalism of Italy and Germany. England, and its wider expression, Britain, has tended to pride itself on not

---

BOX 1.3   IDEAS AND PERSPECTIVES

Human nature – Milgram's experiment

The experimental psychologist Stanley Milgram conducted a historic experiment which suggested that – even though we might think it's the last thing we might do – everyone is capable of being sadistically cruel in response to presumed authority. He set up a situation in which people, more or less at random, were invited to join an alleged test involving someone tied to a chair. The participant was asked by a man in a white coat who appeared to have scientific authority to ask the pinioned person some questions and to administer electric shocks if the answers were wrong. The subject of the test was, in fact, an actor who shouted and writhed in response to the shocks. The participant, however, was told to continue with the shocks notwithstanding the subject's screams right up to an allegedly fatal level of 450 volts. Most of them did so without serious complaint. This experiment, essentially into human nature, showed, somewhat bleakly, that most of us are capable of behaving like guards in concentration camps if we accept the authority of the person directing us to apply the sadistic or even fatal force.

being especially nationalistic and on this side of the Atlantic, American patriotism is often seen as rather too overt and crude. Yet fierce sentiments do exist just below the surface, as the raucous support for the national football team and the 'Euro-scepticism' expressed towards the EU demonstrate.

Class Every society becomes stratified sooner or later into those with power and those without. The Greeks and Romans had slaves; Saxon and Norman nobility in England had serfs and peasants working their estates; and by the nineteenth century there were great masses of people working in factories owned by a small group of super-rich business men. For Karl Marx the formation of different classes and the consequent conflict between them was the motive force of history, constantly changing the present society into the future one. Studying British society in the industrial era, he discerned a small property-owning middle class (or *bourgeoisie*) controlling the lives of a vast new working class (or *proletariat*). His analysis was so profound, detailed and acute he immediately influenced thinking on society all over Europe, yet he did much more.

Marx believed the duty of a philosopher was not just to study society but to *change* it. He went on to argue that in the age of capitalism the rich would so exploit the poor that in the end the latter would rise up, cast off their shackles and commence a process whereby members of the working class would seize control of their own destinies. It followed, according to Marx that the duty of progressive people everywhere was to assist this historical process and help provide the vanguard of the working-class revolution.

Today the working class has halved in size since the early twentieth century and the middle class has burgeoned. John Major, when he became Prime Minister in 1990, tried to argue that Britain was now 'classless', but few accept this complacent analysis which so favours the group in power. Andrew Adonis and Stephen Pollard, in their book *A Class Act* (1997), show how a new 'super class' has emerged on US-style salaries and how another group – sometimes called an 'underclass' – has emerged at the bottom, living in poverty. Attempts by New Labour since 1997 to remove class inequalities have entailed massive expenditures on welfare services but the evidence is that the inequalities remain huge: only the rate of change has been arrested. Class is still very much a live political issue in the UK.

Freedom This elusive concept divides into 'freedom from' and 'freedom to': negative and positive freedom. It is imperative that people are free from the fear, persecution and imprisonment of a tyrannical regime but also important that people are not prevented by circumstances – birth, education, poverty – from having the chance to realise their potential as human beings. While both left and right can agree on the avoidance of the former, they differ sharply over the latter.

It was the liberal philosopher T.H. Green (see Wemde 2004) who first argued, in modern times, for 'positive freedom'. He believed that anyone prevented from realising his or her full potential was in a real sense unfree. He defined freedom as the ability of people to 'make the best and most of themselves'. If they were not able to do this then they were not free. This definition, so attractive to socialists, in theory opened up the whole field of government intervention, especially via welfare services. Such a formulation of the concept also carries with it the clear implication that wealth should be redistributed to give more chances to more people.

Opponents of this approach, echoing classical liberals, claim that it is self-defeating: the government takes away the individual's freedom to improve his or her lot; it takes away the freedom of employers to employ workers at rates the market requires; it is part, in fact, of a subtle, incremental tyranny. In the twentieth century, Friedrich Hayek (2001) and the economist Milton Friedman (1962) argued this case passionately, insisting that such a position was the 'road to servitude'. Sir Keith Joseph, a disciple of both thinkers, stated flatly that 'poverty is not unfreedom'.

Defenders insist that unless individuals are empowered to realise their personal potential, then they are not truly free. They also argue that the kind of freedom right-wingers and classical liberals want is the freedom of the strong to dominate the weak, or, as R.H. Tawney (1931) vividly put it, 'the freedom of the pike is death to the minnows'.

Equality This is another two-pronged concept, comprising 'equality of opportunity' and 'equality of outcome'. The left prefer the latter, the right the former. Both agree on the need for equality of opportunity and both sign up to it in respect of the law, gender, race and career choices; the problem lies with the 'outcome' bit. The right maintain that we already have full equality in respect of all the items mentioned. They cite the fact that anyone can proceed educationally, whatever their circumstances, provided they are dedicated and put in the effort. The left counter that the claim is disingenuous in that, while the odd one or two might manage to climb to the top from very humble beginnings, the majority fail miserably.

Meanwhile, those born in comfortable and supportive middle-class families, not only do much better in terms of education and career but also in terms of gaining positions of power in society: director's boardrooms, senior ranks of the armed forces, journalism, civil service and academe not to mention Parliament and the Cabinet. If the analogy of a race is used children from poor backgrounds, with less caring parents, start it from some distance behind those from privileged backgrounds.

Left-wingers have argued that the 'playing field' should be level for everyone and have urged more equal salaries or redistribution via taxation and state benefits. This wins the right-wing riposte that such actions remove incentives: if people can survive easily on benefits, they will not feel the need to work and improve themselves. In consequence society will be the poorer and those who have worked hard will see their reward highly taxed so that the lazy can benefit.

Social justice Who should get what in society? This concept causes as much disagreement and very similar debate as that over equality. Marx's ideal communist society was supposed to deliver: 'From each according to his ability, to each according to his needs.'

At the heart of this notion of social justice is that large accumulations of wealth, juxtaposed by poverty and ill health, are not justifiable. It follows, according to this approach, that wealth should be redistributed in society and, indeed, between nations. On the other hand, even left-wing theorists agree that some economic inequality is necessary to make the economic system work, so the real debate concerns how much redistribution is needed to achieve justice.

One influential thinker on the Left has been John Rawls, whose book *A Theory of Justice* (1999) has occasioned much debate. He asked us to consider what distribution of goods we would endorse if we were rational people planning a society but, crucially, were unaware of our own capacities. In this way it would be possible to prevent people from

favouring their own talents and strengths, for example preventing a clever person from advocating a meritocracy or a physically strong person a free-for-all society. This ensures that any decisions reached would be neutral. Rawls argues that all would agree on the greatest possible degree of liberty in which people would be able to develop their talents and life plans. In addition, however, Rawls posits the 'difference principle', whereby he maintains that social and economic inequalities – differences in wealth, income and status – are only just if they work to the advantage of the most disadvantaged members of society and only if they can be competed for fairly by all. Rawls argues that in such a situation rational people would choose, through a sense of insecurity, a society in which the position of the worst-off is best protected; this would be a market economy in which wealth is redistributed through tax and welfare systems up to the point when it becomes a disincentive to the economic activity. (It has to be said, however, that some poor people oppose high taxation and the benefits public expenditure can give to the poor because they hope one day to be rich and do not wish their bounty to be reduced by the depredations of the taxman.)

On the right Robert Nozick (1974) has been an influential theorist, arguing that wealth is justifiable if it is justly acquired in the first place (for example has not been stolen) and has been justly transferred from one person to another. He goes on to argue that if these conditions have not been met the injustice should be rectified. Nozick rejects the notion of 'social justice', the idea that inequality is somehow morally wrong. If transfers of wealth take place between one group in society and another, it should be on the basis of private charity, made on the basis of personal choice. But Nozick's views do not necessarily bolster right-wing views on property as the rectification principle could imply the redistribution of much wealth, especially when it is considered that so much of the wealth of the West has been won at the expense of plunder and slavery in Third World countries.

■ Analysing the political process

To illustrate some of the concepts used in the understanding of the political process a hypothetical situation is posited below and its implications considered.

BOX 1.4   BRITAIN IN CONTEXT

Conceptual dissonance

The former publisher and infamous fraud, Robert Maxwell, once wrote a series of hagiographic studies of East European leaders which sold extremely well in their own countries but showed a strange disinclination to fly from the shelves anywhere else. In the book he wrote about the notorious Romanian leader, Nicolae Ceauşescu, Maxwell, in an interview incorporated into the text, asks 'Mister President, tell me, why do your people love you so?' This question and its unperturbed reply illustrate the fact that different people have different takes on commonly understood ideas. Maxwell, driven by self-interest, probably knew the man was a vicious autocrat; Ceauşescu in turn probably genuinely believed he was loved, as his famous look of incomprehension indicated when crowds in front of his palace began angrily to interrupt one of his interminable speeches in 1989, a short time before he was deposed and shot. Both men, totally absorbed in their own false worlds, no doubt perceived the world differently from the people they exploited. But such 'conceptual dissonance' tends to occur between nations as well as between different kinds of people.

In many cases this flows from the vastly different histories experienced by countries. France, for example, has never quite recovered from its 1789 revolution founded upon the great ideas of 'Liberty, Equality and Fraternity'. Consequently, new arrivals to France have become citizens of the republic on an equal standing with everyone else. Such legal even-handedness is wholly admirable, one might think, but in the autumn of 2005 its limits were exposed when French leaders, especially Jacques Chirac, seemed to refuse to believe that the young men of the Muslim faith, many of North African provenance, who were rioting in the suburbs of Paris and other big cities, suffered from severe racial discrimination and disproportionate economic hardship. So deeply ingrained was this belief in equality that no separate social statistics were available regarding France's constituent minorities. They were just the same so there were no separate figures.

Another example of conceptual dissonance is provided by the difference between Western and Muslim societies. In the West free speech is a hallowed principle, defended even if it offends some people holding deep religious beliefs. For fundamentalist Muslims such tolerance is not possible. Anything which reflects what they see as disrespect for the prophet Mohammed they interpret not as merely a difference of viewpoint or maybe satirical humour, but as unforgivable blasphemy. The case of the Danish cartoons published in a right-wing newspaper in November 2005 well illustrated this difference in perception, only one of many between the two cultures.

In Japan, still influenced by its ancient culture, the world is also perceived in a different way from in the West. For example, social hierarchy is deemed in some situations to be as important as equality, so that people seated at a dinner table will place the person believed by a group to be the most senior and important in the place of honour while other guests will be placed according to their perceived rank and place in society.

The USA, created in the heat of a revolution against the perceived tyranny of George III, places huge stress on the need for democracy. This helps explain why the USA elects far more public officials than the UK; for example, dog and rat catchers, as well as mayors and sheriffs, are elected in America but not in the UK. It might also explain why President George W. Bush and his advisers believed so passionately in disseminating democracy in the Middle East. They believed it would lead to greater moderation, acceptance of the West and happiness for the Arab citizens concerned. For a long while it seemed this assumption had tragically misfired in the case of Iraq, invaded in 2003, whereupon it descended into chaos for several years. At the time of writing (2009) Iraq seems relatively peaceful but the cost has arguably been prohibitive.

The Mother of Parliaments: a model for many other legislatures
Source: Steve Allan/Brand X Pictures

A major national newspaper breaks a story that Kevin Broadstairs, a Conservative cabinet minister, has been having an affair with an actress. The PM issues a statement in support of his colleague and old friend from university days. However, more embarrassing details hit the front pages of the tabloids, including the fact that the same actress has also been carrying on with a senior member of the Opposition. The 1922 Committee meets, and influential voices call for a resignation.

This not unfamiliar situation can be analysed as follows:

■ *Interests*: The PM needs to appear above suspicion of 'favouritism' but also needs to show that he is loyal and not a hostage to either groups of backbenchers or the press. Broadstairs obviously has an interest in keeping his job, retaining respect within his party and saving his rocky marriage. The governing party needs to sustain its reputation as the defender of family values. The press wishes to sell more newspapers.

■ *Actors*: In this situation are potentially numerous: the PM, Broadstairs, the actress, her former lovers, backbench MPs, editors, television producers, the Opposition, Mrs Broadstairs and (unfortunately) her children, the Church, feminists and anyone else willing to enter the fray.

■ *Power*: The power relationship in these circumstances is naturally influenced by the ability of each side to enforce threats. The PM has the power of political life or death over the minister but would like to show his strength by resisting resignation calls; Broadstairs effectively has no power in this situation and is largely dependent on the PM's goodwill and possible press revelations.

- *Authority*: No one questions the PM's right to sack Broadstairs. However, the press's right to force resignations is very much resisted by politicians. The ultimate authority of the governing party to call for the minister's head is also not questioned.

- *Political process*: Will Broadstairs survive? Our minister in this situation is a hostage to the discretion of his mistress and other people either involved or perceiving an interest in the affair.

The outcome will depend on the following:

- *Political will*: How prepared are the PM and Broadstairs to stand firm against resignation calls? How long could he hold out once the 1922 Committee has given the thumbs down? How long would this committee stay silent as it saw the issue eroding voter support? How effective would Broadstairs' enemies in his own party be in hastening his downfall?

- *Influence*: How much influence does the PM have in Fleet Street? The evidence suggests that political sympathies of a paper count for nothing when a really juicy scandal is involved. Even right-wing papers carried full coverage of sleaze stories relating to John Major's government. Does Broadstairs have a body of support on the back benches, or is he a 'loner'?

- *Manipulation*: How good is the minister at coping with the situation? Can he make a clean breast of it, like Paddy Ashdown regarding his extramarital affair in January 1992, and survive with reputation arguably enhanced? Can he handle hostile press conferences and media interviews (as David Mellor did with aplomb – though much good it did him)? Can the minister call up old favours on the back benches?

Let's suppose that things quieten down for a few days, the PM defends his friend at Question Time and the wife says she'll stand by her man. If this was all there was to it, Broadstairs would survive and live to fight again, albeit with his reputation and prospects damaged. We saw that in the somewhat similar David Mellor case the revelations kept on coming (much to public amusement and his embarrassment), but the crucial revelations concerned acceptance of undeclared favours by the minister. After this, backbench calls for a resignation and an excited press ensured that Mellor had to go.

The political process in this case is a little haphazard and depends to some extent on each day's tabloid headlines. It will also depend on the PM's judgement as to when the problem has ceased to be an individual one and has escalated to the point when his own judgement and the political standing of his party are in question. Alastair Campbell, Blair's famously powerful press secretary, reckoned that if public criticism of a minister continued after fourteen days then, even if blameless, the minister would have to resign as such publicity prevents the minister from functioning as the government requires. Once that point has been reached it is only a matter of time before the minister's career is over. There was much in ex-Prime Minister Harold Wilson's tongue-in-cheek comment that 'much of politics is presentation, and what isn't, is timing'.

Plan of the book

This opening chapter has discussed the meaning of politics, the nature of politicians and key concepts in the study of politics. The rest of the book, organised in six parts, follows directly from the definition we adopted on page 4.

Politics is about conflicting interests: Part 1 provides the historical, social and economic contexts from which such conflicts emerge in Britain; Part 2, on ideology, examines the intellectual basis of such conflicts. Politics is centrally concerned with how state institutions manage or resolve conflicts within society: Parts 3, 4 and 5 deal respectively with the representative, legislative (law making) and executive (law implementing) processes whereby such management takes place or is attempted. Finally, Part 6 examines how these institutions handle the major policy areas.

Chapter summary

This introductory chapter has explained that politics is about the management and resolution of conflicts by what people want to do and achieve. The study of the subject focuses on how this process is performed, especially the way individuals relate to the state. Key concepts in the study of politics are explained: power, authority, equality, representation, democracy and social justice.

Discussion points

■ Why do you think people go into politics and make it their life's work?

■ Think of a typically political scenario and analyse it in the way demonstrated in the chapter.

■ Which interpretation of equality and social justice seem most appealing to you?

Further reading

Crick's classic work (2000) is essential reading, as is Duverger (1966). Leftwich (1984) is worth reading as an easy-to-understand initiation, and Laver (1983) repays study too. Renwick and Swinburn (1989) is useful on concepts, though Heywood (1994) is by any standards a brilliant textbook. Axford *et al.* (1997) is also well worth looking into. Riddell (1993) is both highly perceptive and very entertaining – a must for anyone wondering if the subject is for them. O'Rourke (1992) is a humorous but insightful book. Oliver (1992) is an amusing collection of silly quotations from politicians. Michael Moran's book (Moran 2005) offers a subtle and authoritative introduction.

Bibliography

Adonis, A. and Pollarch, S. (1997) *A Class Act: The Myth of Britain's Classless Society* (Hamish Hamilton Ltd).

All, A.R. and Peters, B.G. (2000) *Modern Politics and Government* (Macmillan), Chapter 1.

Axford, B., Browning, G.K., Huggins, R., Rosamond, B. and Turner, J. (1997) *Politics: An Introduction* (Routledge).

Bachrach, P. and Baratz, M. (1981) 'The two faces of power', in F.G. Castles, D.J. Murray and D.C. Potter (eds) *Decision, Organisations and Society* (Penguin).

Crick, B. (2000) *In Defence of Politics* (Continuum).

Critchley, J. (1995) *A Bag of Boiled Sweets* (Faber and Faber).

Dearlove, J. and Saunders, P. (2000) *Introduction to British Politics* (Polity Press), Chapter 1.

Duverger, M. (1966) *The Idea of Politics* (Methuen).

Friedman, M. (1962) *Free to Choose: A Personal Statement* (Secker and Warburg).

Gamble, A. (2000) *Politics and Fate* (Polity Press).

Giddens, A. (1998) *The Third Way* (Polity Press).

Hague, R., Harrop, M. and Breslin, S. (2000) *Comparative Government and Politics* (Palgrave).

Hayek, F.A. (2001) *The Road to Serfdom* (Routledge Classics).

Healey, D. (1990) *The Time of My Life* (Penguin).

Heywood, A. (1994) *Political Ideas and Concepts* (Macmillan).

Jones, B. (2005) *The Dictionary of British Politics* (Manchester University Press).

Kingdom, J. (1999) *Government and Politics in Britain* (Polity Press).

Lasswell, H. (1936) *Politics, Who Gets What, When, How?* (McGraw-Hill).

Laver, M. (1983) *Invitation to Politics* (Martin Robertson).

Leftwich, A. (1984) *What is Politics? The Activity and its Study* (Blackwell).

Minogue, K. (2000) *Politics: A Very Short Introduction* (Oxford University Press).

Moran, M. (2005) *Politics and Governance in the UK* (Palgrave).

Nozick, Robert (1974) *Anarchy, State and Utopia* (Blackwell).

Oliver, D. (1992) *Political Babble* (Wiley).

O'Rourke, R.J. (1992) *Parliament of Whores* (Picador).

Orwell, G. (1955) *Nineteen Eighty-Four* (Penguin).

Owen, David (2007) *The Hubris Syndrome: Bush, Blair and the Intoxication of Power* (Politicos).

Rawls, John (1999) *A Theory of Justice* (Revised edn) (Belknap).

Renwick, A. and Swinburn, I. (1989) *Basic Political Categories*, 2nd edn (Hutchinson).

Riddell, P. (1993) *Honest Opportunism* (Hamish Hamilton).

Robins, S. (2001) *The Ruling Asses* (Prion).

Tawney, R.H. (1931) *Equality* (Unwin).

Wemde, Ben (2004) *T.H. Green's Theory of Positive Freedom: From Metaphysics to Political Theory* (Imprint Academic).

Zakaria, F. (2004) *The Future of Freedom* (Norton).

Useful websites

British Politics page: www.ukpol.co.uk

Euro Consortium for Political Research: www.essex.ac.uk/ecpr

International Political Science Association: www.ipsa-aisp.org/

Political Science resources: www.socsciresearch.com/r12html

UK Political Studies Association: www.psa.ac.uk

Blogs

Bill Jones's blog: http://skipper59.blogspot.com/

Norman Geras: http://normblog.typepad.com

Guido Fawkes: http://5thNovember.blogspot.com/

Topic 2:
Ideology and Ideas

Political ideas: the major parties

Bill Jones

Party spokesmen say not what they mean but what they have agreed to say.
Michael Portillo, *The Observer*, 2 March 2003

Learning objectives

- To explain the provenance of Conservatism and the ideology of capitalist free enterprise, to explain the difference between 'one nation' and neo-liberal Conservatism, and to assess the impact of Margaret Thatcher on her party's ideas.

- To trace the origins of Labour thinking to the rejection of nineteenth-century **capitalism**, to describe its maturing into corporate **socialism** and revisionism plus the left-wing dissent of the 1970s and 1980s, and to analyse the impact of Labour's rapid move into the centre and the apparent embrace of neo-Thatcherite and communitarian ideas by Tony Blair.

- To sum up the message of the Liberal Party over the years, including its alliance with the SDP and its evolution into the Liberal Democrats.

From Chapter 5 of *Politics UK*, 7/e. Bill Jones and Philip Norton. © Pearson Education 2001–2010. All rights reserved.

Introduction

I n the aftermath of the Second World War, some commentators felt that the two major political parties in Britain were 'converging' ideologically. Daniel Bell, the American sociologist, wrote of 'the end of ideology', and in the 1970s a postwar 'consensus' was discerned between the two parties on the desirability of a welfare state and a mixed economy. Britain's relative economic decline inclined both parties to adopt more radical remedies that drew on their ideological roots. Margaret Thatcher swung the Conservatives violently to the right, while Labour went radically to the left in the early 1980s. Once Thatcher had gone, Major adopted a less overtly ideological stance, while Labour, following the failed experiment of Michael Foot as leader, successively under Neil Kinnock, John Smith and Tony Blair moved rapidly into the centre. This chapter analyses the evolution of the ideas of the major parties and brings up to date their most recent changes.

■ The Conservative Party

Source: Courtesy of the Conservative Party
(www.conservatives.com)

Key elements of Conservatism

Lord Hailsham (1959) has described 'Conservatism' as not so much a philosophy as an 'attitude'. However, it is possible to discern a number of key tenets on which Conservative policies have been based:

1 *The purpose of politics is social and political harmony*: Conservatives have traditionally believed that politics is about enabling people to become what they are or what they wish to be. They also believe in a balance, a harmony in society, a measured **pragmatism** that has always kept options open. Like Edmund Burke, they have tended to believe that 'all government . . . is founded on compromise'.

2 *Human nature is imperfect and corruptible*: This quasi-religious notion of 'original sin' lies at the heart of Conservatism, leading its supporters to doubt the altruism of humankind beyond close family, to perceive most people as more interested in taking rather than giving, and to see them as fairly easy to corrupt without the external discipline of strong government.

3 *The **rule of law** is the basis of all freedom*: Law restricts freedom, yet without it there would be no freedom at all, but instead – given humanity's selfish, aggressive nature – anarchic chaos. Accepting the authority of the law is therefore the precondition of all liberty.

4 *Social institutions create a sense of society and nation*: Social and political institutions help to bind together imperfect human beings in a thing called society. Living together constructively and happily is an art, and this has to be learned. At the heart of the learning process lies the family and the institution of marriage. The royal family provides an idealised and unifying 'micro-model'. At the macro level is the idea of the 'nation', ultimately a cause worth dying for.

5 *Foreign policy is the pursuit of state interests in an anarchic world*: States exhibit all the dangerous characteristics of individuals plus a few even more unpleasant ones of their own. A judicious defence of national interests is the best guide for any country in the jungle of international relations.

6 *Liberty is the highest political end*: Individuals need freedom to develop their own personalities and pursue their destinies. Conservatives agree with Mill that it should entail freedom from oppression and be allowed to extend until it encroaches upon the freedom of others. It should not embrace the 'levelling' of wealth, as advocated by socialists, as this redistribution would be imposed upon a reluctant population by the state (see also Chapter 1).

7 *Government through checks and balances*: 'Political liberty', said Lord Hailsham, 'is nothing else than the diffusion of power.' This means in practice institutions that divide power between them, with all having a measure of independence, thus preventing any single arm of government from being over-mighty.

8 *Property*: Conservatives, like David Hume, believe that the right to property is the 'first principle of justice' on which the 'peace and security of human society entirely depend'. Norton and Aughey (1981) take this further, arguing that it is an 'education. It enlightens the citizens in the value of stability and shows that the security of small property depends upon the security of all property' (p. 34). The Conservative policy of selling council houses reflected this belief in that it is assumed, probably rightly in this case, that people will cherish their houses more once they enjoy personal ownership.

9 ***Equality of opportunity*** *but not of result*: Conservatives believe everyone should have the same opportunity to better themselves. Some will be more able or more motivated and will achieve more and accumulate more property. Thus an unequal distribution of wealth reflects a naturally unequal distribution of ability. Norton and Aughey (1981) maintain that the party is fundamentally concerned with justifying inequality in a way that 'conserves a hierarchy of wealth and power and make[s] it intelligible to democracy' (p. 47). To do this, Conservatives argue that inequality is necessary to maintain incentives and make the economy work; equality of reward would reward the lazy as much as the industrious.

10 *One nation*: Benjamin Disraeli, the famous nineteenth-century Conservative Prime Minister, added a new element to his party's philosophy by criticising the 'two nations' in Britain, the rich and the poor. He advocated an alliance between the aristocracy and the lower orders to create one nation. His advice was controversial and has come to be seen as synonymous with the liberal approach to Conservatism.

11 *Rule by élite*: Conservatives have tended to believe the art of government is not given to all; it is distributed unevenly, like all abilities, and is carefully developed in families and outside these most commonly in good schools, universities and the armed forces.

12 *Political change*: Conservatives are suspicious of political change as society develops organically as an infinitely complex and subtle entity; precipitate change could damage irreparably things of great value. Therefore they distrust the system builders such as Marx, and the root-and-branch reformers such as Tony Benn. But they do not deny the need for all change; rather they tend to agree with the Duke of Cambridge that the best time for it is 'when it can be no longer resisted', or with Enoch Powell that the 'supreme function of a politician is to judge the correct moment for reform'.

The impact of Thatcherism

This collection of pragmatic guides to belief and action was able to accommodate the postwar Labour landslide, which brought nationalisation, the managed Keynesian economy, close cooperation with the trade unions and the welfare state. The role of Harold Macmillan was crucial here. In the 1930s he wrote *The Middle Way*, a plea for a regulated laissez-faire economy that would minimise unemployment and introduce forward economic planning. He was able to accept many of the reforms introduced by Labour and reinterpret them for his own party.

The postwar consensus continued with little difference over domestic policy between Macmillan and Gaitskell, Wilson and Heath. But when the economy began to fail in relation to competitors in the late 1960s and early 1970s a hurricane of dissent began to blow up on the right of the Conservative Party – in the person of Margaret Thatcher. She had no quarrel with traditional positions on law, property and liberty, but she was passionately convinced of a limited role for government (although not necessarily a weak one); she wanted to 'roll back' the socialist frontiers of the state. She was uninterested in checks and balances but wanted to maximise her power to achieve the things she wanted. She was opposed to contrived 'equality' and favoured the functional inequalities required by a dynamic economy. She had scant respect for the aristocracy as she admired only ability and energy, qualities she owned in abundance. She was not in favour of gradual change but wanted radical alterations, *in her lifetime*. She was a revolutionary within her own party, which still, even in 2010, had not stopped reverberating from her impact.

Thatcherite economics

1 Margaret Thatcher was strongly influenced by Sir Keith Joseph, in turn influenced by the American economist Milton Friedman. He urged that to control inflation it was merely necessary to control the supply of money and credit circulating in the economy.

2 Joseph was also a disciple of Friedrich von Hayek, who believed that freedom to buy, sell and employ, i.e. economic freedom, was the foundation of all freedom. Like Hayek, he saw the drift to collectivism as a bad thing: socialists promised the 'road to freedom' but delivered instead the 'high road to servitude'.

3 Hayek and Friedman agreed with Adam Smith and the classical liberals that, if left to themselves, market forces – businessmen using their energy and ingenuity to meet the needs of customers – would create prosperity. To call this 'exploitation' of the working man, as socialists did, was nonsense as businessmen were the philanthropists of society, creating employment, paying wages and endowing charities. When markets were allowed to work properly they benefited all classes: everyone benefited, even the poor: 'the greatest social service of them all', said Thatcher, 'is the creation of wealth.'

4 Thatcher believed strongly that:

(i) state intervention destroyed freedom and efficiency through taking power from the consumer – the communist 'command' economies were inefficient and corrupt, protecting employment through temporary and harmful palliatives, and controlling so much of the economy that the wealth-producing sector became unacceptably squeezed, and that

(ii) state welfare was expensive, morally weakening in that it eroded the self-reliance she so prized, and was, in addition, monopolistic, denying choice as well as being less efficient than private provision.

5 Trade unions were one of Thatcher's bêtes noires. She saw them as undemocratic, reactionary vested interests that regularly held the country to ransom in the 1970s. She was determined to confront and defeat them.

6 Her defence of national interests was founded in a passionate patriotism, which sustained her support for the armed forces and the alliance with the USA. During the Falklands War she showed great composure and courage in taking risks and ultimately triumphing. The reverse side of this was her preference for the US link over the European Union, which she suspected of being a Trojan horse for German plans to dominate the whole continent.

Margaret Thatcher therefore drove a battering ram through traditional Conservatism, but economically it was a return to the classical liberalism of the early to mid-nineteenth century (see Chapter 4). Many claimed to have been converted to her ideas, but the 1980s witnessed a tough internal battle, which the Prime Minister eventually won, between her and the so-called 'wet' wing of the party, which still hearkened back to the inclusive 'one nation' strand of the party's thinking.

The Major years

When John Major succeeded Margaret Thatcher following the virtual 'coup' in November 1990, many thought he would be the best hope of stern and unbending Thatcherism, but he seemed much more conciliatory, more concerned with the un-Thatcherite aim of achieving unity even at the cost of compromise. As the years passed, however, it became apparent that this initial analysis is far away from what happened. Major's government was almost wholly circumscribed by the ideas of his predecessor. As Heywood has pointed out, the Major government accepted her ideas; there was no conflict with 'wets', and even Heseltine, Clarke and Patten had accepted the unchallenged supremacy of markets by the mid-1990s. Moreover, he took her ideas further even than she dared in her day, privatising British Rail and introducing the market principle into many hitherto forbidden areas of the welfare state. The changes were in style rather than substance. In the 1980s, Thatcherism adopted a 'heroic' mode, smashing socialism and the power of the trade unions; it was like a continuous war or revolution as the Prime Minister tried to change 'the hearts and minds of the nation'. Major replaced that style with a 'managerial' version. However, he also added another element: a return to 'neo-conservatism' with a renewed emphasis on morality (the 'back to basics' campaign), obligation and citizenship. Conservatives have long been worried by the downside of market forces: growing inequality, the emergence of an underclass, insecurity at work and the loss of the 'feel-good factor', or the sense of the nation 'being at ease with itself' to use Major's phrase. There was a feeling in the mid-1990s that the nation's social fabric was in dire need of repair. Added to this market individualism plus neo-conservatism had been a shift towards a 'Little Englandism'. Most commentators did not believe Major was this kind of politician by instinct, but that he was forced to adjust his position on Europe quite drastically by the determined Eurosceptic minority, which, through his tiny majority, held the balance of power.

Major was criticised from many parts of the party: 'poor judgement and weak leadership' (*The Sun*); 'drifting with the intellectual tide' (Thatcher); 'He is not a natural leader, he cannot speak, he has no sense of strategy or direction' (Lord Rees Mogg); 'a nice bloke but not up to the job' (Kenneth Clarke); and, the cruellest cut, 'the government gave the impression of being in office but not in power' (Norman Lamont).

Hague's new start

As soon as the Conservatives lost the 1997 election so calamitously Major resigned and a contest was held for a new leader. In the end, genial ex-Chancellor Kenneth Clarke was judged too pro-EU and MPs chose the relatively unknown and untested William Hague. He was at least, for those who regretted the demise of Thatcher, firm on the subject of Europe: he would have very little of it and would not join the emergent European single currency for at least a parliamentary term, if ever. Those who mocked this narrow, Little England perspective were checked when his party won the European elections handsomely in June 1999. Subsequently Michael Portillo, the right-winger many felt would have won the leadership had he not astonishingly lost his huge majority to novice Labour candidate Stephen Twigg, had effectively reinvented himself as the quintessence of the 'Compassionate Conservatism' its leaders now claimed to embrace. However, this flirtation with a softer image did not last for the party as a whole; the Conservative High Command – alarmed by polls flat-lining at one-third of the vote – were worried that the party's core vote was about to crumble. In October 1999 Hague unveiled his 'Commonsense Revolution', a bundle of right-wing measures focusing on five 'guarantees': to cut taxes as a share of the national income; to keep out of the single currency

until at least the end of the next parliamentary session and to demand opt-outs on measures not in the national interest; a 'parents guarantee' whereby inefficient heads could be dismissed; a 'patients guarantee' setting maximum times for treatment; and a get-tough guarantee on work dodgers, who would lose all benefit if refusing work after eight weeks. In fact the conference represented a surprising swing back towards Thatcherism. The lady herself appeared and was cheered to the echo by the ageing delegates as well as praised in speeches that pointedly and hurtfully ignored the contributions made by the premier of seven years, John Major. Most of the right-wing press applauded the party's rediscovery of its identity – being right-wing, Eurosceptic and proud of it. But others were not so sure. That shrewd commentator Peter Riddell wrote that

The more William Hague roused his party faithful in Blackpool, the more he led them away from power . . . [his] main achievement . . . may have been to deepen the divisions within his own party and to reduce still further its chances of winning the next election.

(*The Times*, 12 October 1999)

BIOGRAPHY

William Hague (1961–)

English Conservative politician. Made his debut with a precocious speech at the 1977 conference. After Oxford, he worked as a management consultant and then became MP for Richmond in his native Yorkshire. He was seen as suitably opposed to Europe in 1997 and was preferred to Kenneth Clarke as leader. His early years were difficult with successes inside the Commons but rarely in the country. In the election of 2001 he stuck to his Eurosceptic guns throughout the campaign but could only persuade the nation to return one more Conservative MP. He resigned, with remarkably good grace, shortly after the election defeat. After that he busied himself with after-dinner speaking, an acclaimed biography of the Younger Pitt and occasional broadcasting. David Cameron, however, in December 2005 summoned him back to his party's front bench as Shadow Foreign Secretary and unofficial Deputy Leader.

Riddell, not for the first time, proved remarkably prescient: in June 2001 Labour's second landslide occurred. Hague resigned and a contest for the leadership of the Tories took place amid some acrimony. According to the new rules for electing a leader, the parliamentary party held a series of ballots to find the two candidates between whom the party faithful would choose. Portillo soon fell by the wayside, foundering, it seemed, on his admission of a homosexual experience when a student at Cambridge. It was left to Kenneth Clarke, again, to battle it out with the inexperienced right-winger Iain Duncan Smith. The latter's Euroscepticism, tough line on crime and general Thatcherite orthodoxy proved much more attractive, in the judgement of the ageing party membership, compared with the liberal one-nation approach of Clarke – despite his obvious political gifts – who lost by a two-to-one majority.

The Iain Duncan Smith effect

'IDS', as he is known, began his tenure as leader by striving to make an impression in the Commons, but Blair proved too dominant and his opponent too unsure of his ground to 'win' even a few of the weekly Prime Minister's Question Time encounters. What made it worse was that so many of the well-known Conservatives either had retired (e.g. Tebbit, Baker, Fowler), had not been keen on serving under Duncan Smith (e.g. Clarke, Hague), or were still stigmatised by association with the 'bad old days' of the Conservative's eighteen years in power (e.g. Howard, Gummer). Despite his defeat for the leadership, Portillo's influence remained as a voice calling for 'modernisation' of the Conservative message: a more inclusive attitude to women, gays and ethnic minorities; a distancing from anything resembling racism on immigration policy; an acceptance of the need to modernise and improve public services; and a less dogmatic hostility to all things European. Once again the dead weight of lumpen party opinion on key policy issues served to retard any progress. Duncan Smith's ineffectual orthodoxy was soon found to be out of touch in the polls, and in the spring of 2002, at the party's Harrogate conference, IDS effected a neat volte-face on policy, calling for a compassionate attitude towards the 'vulnerable' in society, a decentralisation of power to the regions and a supportive attitude towards the public services. However, shifting towards a new policy position is one thing; communicating it, via an unknown Shadow Cabinet, is another: the polls still flat-lined

at just over 30 percentage points. The new leader faced immense difficulty in convincing voters that his party was not, as he complained, 'nasty, extreme and strange' (*Observer* 2 July 2002). At the party conference later in the year, the new party chairman, Theresa May, urged the party to lose its 'nasty' image: evidence of her support for the modernisation camp. However, the *éminence grise* of this tendency featured again in February 2003 when Michael Portillo complained bitterly at the peremptory sacking of the chief executive of the party, Mark MacGregor. The outbreak of war against Iraq the following month enabled Duncan Smith to occupy familiar Conservative territory – pro-armed forces and pro-USA – although such a position precluded political exploitation of Prime Minister Blair's discomfort in prosecuting a war unpopular in the country and even more so in his own party; Kenneth's Clarke's backing of an 'anti-war' horse over Iraq scarcely helped to strengthen the embattled leader's position. Discontent with IDS grew in the run-up to the 2003 party conference and soon afterwards he lost a crucial party vote of

BIOGRAPHY

Michael Portillo (1953–)

Conservative politician. Educated at Cambridge. Worked for the Conservative Research Department, 1976–9, and as junior minister in various departments until he became a Cabinet minister in the early 1990s. Was defeated in the 1997 election and missed his chance to lead the party then. Worked hard at being an advocate of 'caring Conservatism' before becoming adopted as a candidate in the safe seat of Kensington. Made Shadow Chancellor in late 1999. 'Re-invented' himself as a caring, inclusive one-nation Conservative with speeches, television programmes and an admission of student-day homosexual experience. This last caused trouble with older Conservatives; when Portillo stood for the leadership after Hague's resignation, Norman Tebbit made a thinly veiled attack on his sexuality, and the modernisers' hope was defeated at the Commons stage (according to the new procedure) before party members were able to vote on the two nominees.

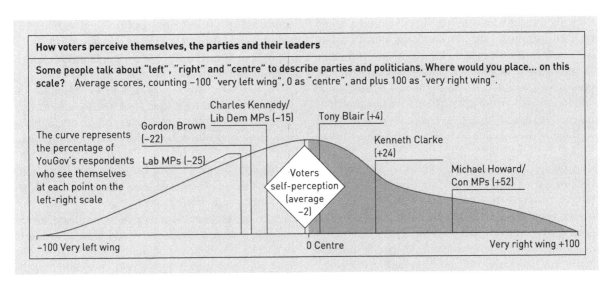

Figure 5.1 How voters perceive themselves, the parties and their leaders
Source: From Policy Exchange (2005) *The Case for Change*, May 2005. Reproduced with permission

confidence. Michael Howard, the right-wing former Home Secretary, was selected in his place.

The era of Michael Howard

On Thursday 6 November 2003 the man who came sixth in the 1997 leadership challenge was, remarkably, elected unopposed to the leadership of his party. Despite his reputation for being a right-winger, Howard stressed his desire to continue IDS's emphasis on social justice with policies aimed at helping the disadvantaged. This was accompanied by calls for zero tolerance policing, more spending on drug treatment for addicts and an increase in the basic state pension. His concerns regarding Europe were underlined by renewed calls for a referendum on the proposed new constitution for the EU.

From the outset, Howard proved reasonably effective at Prime Minister's Questions but found it hard to resist the need to bolster up the core vote and did little to move the party into the electorally crucial centre ground. The party continued to languish in the polls as the general election approached in 2005. The party continued to lack a distinctive message right up to polling day on 5 May and duly paid the price when the votes were counted. The Conservatives won 33 more seats but had to sit back and watch an unpopular government led by a gifted but mistrusted Tony Blair maintain its hold on the Commons to the extent of an overall majority of 66. Howard, the old professional, seasoned politician, had hoped to lead a renaissance of Toryism but had proved to be merely a stop-gap leader of a party

which some perceived to be in terminal decline. Howard resigned quite soon but stayed on to preside over the election of his successor. This period – May to October – saw much soul searching during which most party members came to realise that drastic change was necessary. The Conservative Policy Exchange think tank produced a devastating report on the party highlighting its unpopularity, lack of contact with modern society and hopeless image as a party favouring middle-class people in the shires and the south-east. Figure 5.1, drawn from the report, reveals how people viewed their own political position on the left–right continuum and then superimposed their estimates of where leading politicians stood. Inevitably the majority of people occupy the centre ground, indicating where any party wishing to win an election needs to project its messages. Howard was perceived as being quite far to the right – his MPs also. Kenneth Clarke, on the other hand, was seen as substantially closer to the centre. Gordon Brown was located slightly to the right of Labour MPs and to the left of Charles Kennedy. And Tony Blair? His brilliant sense of where the centre of political gravity lies enabled him to sit astride the middle of the graph, four points to the right of dead centre.

The election of David Cameron, December 2005

The Conservative Party conference in October 2005 at Blackpool indicated that the party had finally realised that major change to the party and its thinking was necessary before an election win could be contemplated. The declared leadership candidates were able to address the delegates and make an initial pitch. Howard had influenced his own succession by placing members of the new young liberal or 'moderniser' group in his party to major positions in the Shadow Cabinet – George Osborne (34) to Shadow Chancellor and David Cameron (39) to Education – and allowing them to make an impression before the leadership contest in the autumn. Osborne, it seemed, had already decided not to run but to manage the campaign of his old Etonian friend, Cameron. Parallels with Tony Blair's rise to power were already being made before Cameron delighted the conference with a speech he had learnt by heart and delivered, apparently spontaneously, without notes. David Davis, the former minister in his mid-50s, who had assembled what many thought to be an impregnable lead among declared MPs, tried to follow suit but, compared with the sparkling, inspiring rhetoric of his rival, appeared lacklustre and dull. Cameron went on to win easily the MPs' ballot and then to win over the party for the membership ballot on 5 December which he won by a margin of two to one. On 6 December he took on Blair at PMQs and, in an excellent, witty debut performance, told him 'you were the future once'.

Cameron seeks to 'rebrand' and move into the centre ground

Cameron, while copying the informal, media-friendly style of the younger Tony Blair, was careful to steer clear of specific policy commitments, though it was clear his period in power would see a jettisoning of the party's much beloved positions on a number of issues. Cameron and his coterie of 'Notting Hill Set' colleagues were very keen to change the brand image of the party. During the 2005 election, focus groups had revealed that members who liked a policy position when it was explained to them changed their mind when they discovered it was a Conservative party policy. Concerted efforts were made to banish the notion of the 'nasty party', the idea of a bigoted, intolerant group of richer, older people who wanted power merely to advance their own interests and outdated way of life. Consequently Cameron let it be known his name was not David but 'Dave'; that he cared deeply about special-needs childcare (his NHS-cared-for disabled son, Ivan, died in February 2009); that he cared about the environment (cycling to the Commons, appointing environmentalist Zac

Goldsmith to an advisory position); that he cared about world poverty (Bob Geldof's turn to be included); and that the party no longer hated gays and opposed civil partnerships.

In late December Oliver Letwin declared his party favoured redistribution of wealth, and shortly afterwards Cameron shifted its position on immigration from opposition to qualified support for those incomers essential to the economy. Cameron also addressed the key area of tax cuts. It seemed Conservatives now would basically accept the 4 per cent increase in basic taxation since 1997 as necessary to sustain public services at requisite levels. He also declared that cuts would have to come in the wake of economic stability, a reversal of the Thatcherite view that the latter is a condition for the achievement of the former. And the party would no longer be the natural adjunct of the free enterprise economy: henceforward, the party would 'stand up to as well as for business'.

The new boy was careful, however, to keep the core vote onside with a judicious dash of Euro-scepticism. True, he wished to bury the party's civil war over the EU, which he deemed irrelevant now that the proposed new constitution had been rejected by France and Holland. But he nevertheless wanted the Conservative party to end its membership of the European People's Party, a right-wing grouping which nevertheless favoured rather too much integration. Perhaps his biggest break with the past, however, was to declare that the litmus test for social policies should be what they could do for the disadvantaged: many older Tories must have felt a twinge of apoplexy at that.

Like Blair in the mid-90s he set up a number of study groups to review policy areas. Opinion polls almost immediately registered a lead for Labour, albeit a slender one at that early stage. Blair must have realised at once that the political situation had been drastically changed and that he no longer could expect a free ride in his domination of the centre ground. But Cameron too did not face an easy ride; right-wing commentator, Melanie Phillips, writing in the *Daily Mail*, believed his prospectus 'leaves millions of natural conservatives effectively disenfranchised – and even worse demonized as dinosaurs by the party that is supposed to represent them'.

Wise old commentators judged such opposition to be precisely what Cameron needed. Blair had risen to public prominence over his brilliant defeat of party traditionalists over Clause 4. Lacking any similar dragons to slay, Cameron needed to overcome opposition from the older cohorts as represented,

Bob Geldof helps accelerate the Conservatives' new momentum by agreeing to become a consultant for them on world poverty
Source: Copyright © David Parkins. From the *Guardian*, 29 December 2005. Reproduced with permission

for example, by Lord Tebbit, one of Thatcher's most loyal and true-blue Conservative followers; it would be by overcoming such opposition that his party would be seen to have changed. As the 2010 election approached Cameron and his advisers sought to position themselves on the major questions of the day:

1 The need drastically to reduce government debt of £175 bn in 2009 so that international markets would not lose faith in the UK's ability to repay what it owed and increase interest rates for any future lending.

2 The political aim was to blame Labour for the recession triggered by the US banking crisis in 2007.

3 To offer protection for the NHS and education but to insist on deep cuts in public spending elsewhere to reduce debt and the size of the state.

4 Policy on the EU was made difficult by the insistence of the party rank and file on a referendum on the Lisbon treaty which they saw as strengthening moves towards a federalist Europe. On this issue Cameron faced a dilemma once the Lisbon Treaty had become ratified by all EU members and become a fait accompli. He solved it by abandoning the referendum idea.

The Labour Party and socialism

Source: Courtesy of the Labour Party (www.labour.org.uk)

Socialism

Socialism developed as a critique and alternative to capitalism and its political expression, Conservatism. It focused on economics as the key activity, but the full sweep of its message provided guidance on virtually all aspects of living.

Critique of capitalism

Socialism asserted that capitalism 'exploited' the working masses by selling the fruits of their labour, taking the lion's share of the revenue and paying only subsistence wages. This produced huge disparities in income between the suburban-living rich and the urban-based poor. Because the ruling capitalists dominate all the institutions of the state, argued Karl Marx, whose analysis was more influential in Britain than his prescriptions, they subtly intrude their values into all walks of life, and a complex web of mystifications produces a 'false consciousness' in which the working class believes wrongly that its best interests are served by supporting capitalist values. Capitalist championing of 'individualism' and 'freedom' are mere cloaks for the exploitation of the weak by the strong. The ruthlessness of the system induces similar qualities within society. Wage labour merely relieved employers of any residual obligations they might have felt towards their workers. By living in large urban settlements working men were alienated from each other, while the automating of industry denied workers any creative satisfaction. A final criticism was that capitalism with its booms and slumps was inevitably inefficient and inferior to a planned economy. Socialists argued that two large antagonistic classes emerge in capitalist societies: a small wealthy ruling class and a large impoverished proletariat, living in the cities, which actually created wealth.

Underlying principles of socialism

Socialism developed out of this critique of nineteenth-century capitalism. The principles underlying the new creed included the following:

1 *Human nature is basically good*: People wish to live together peacefully and cooperatively, according to this view; it is only the selfish competitive economic system of capitalism that distorts it.

2 *'Environment creates consciousness'*: It followed from this Marxist axiom that a superior environment will create a superior kind of person.

3 *Workers create the wealth*: They are entitled to receive the full fruits of their efforts and not the small fraction that the rich, bourgeois factory owners pay them.

4 *Equality*: Everyone has the right to start off in life with the same chances as everyone else; the strong should not exploit their advantage and impose themselves on the weak.

5 *Freedom*: The poor need more resources for the playing field of life to be level and thus be truly free.

6 *Collectivism*: Social solidarity should take the place of selfish individualism.

The Labour Party

Labour in power

Labour held power briefly in the 1920s and began to formulate a more pragmatic, less emotional and more coherent version of socialism. During the 1930s and the war years socialist thinkers such as Hugh Dalton (1887–1962) and Herbert Morrison (1888–1965) developed what has since been called 'corporate socialism', comprising:

1 *Keynesian economics*: Management of the economy, using investment to cure slumps and squeeze out unemployment.

2 *Centralised planning of the economy*: This was the corollary of the Keynesian approach; it had worked brilliantly during the 1939–45 war and would do the same for the peace, promised Labour.

3 *Nationalisation*: Morrison devised this approach based on bringing an industry out of private and into public control via a board accountable to Parliament. Once in power, Labour nationalised 20 per cent of the economy, including the major utilities.

4 *Welfare state*: Labour established the National Health Service and expanded universal social services into a virtual 'welfare state' in which the state had obligations to citizens 'from the cradle to the grave'.

5 *Mixed economy*: The extent of nationalisation was not defined but, unlike the Soviet command economies, it was intended to maintain a private sector, albeit one subordinate to the public.

6 *Socialist foreign policy*: The trauma of two world wars convinced Labour that a new approach was needed based on disarmament and international collective security. The USSR, however, proved resistant to fraternal overtures from a fellow left-wing government, and ultimately Labour's combative Foreign Secretary, Ernest Bevin (1881–1952), was forced to encourage the USA into the NATO alliance.

Revisionism

Anthony Crosland (1918–77), along with others like Gaitskell, Healey and Jenkins, was not content, like Morrison, to declare that 'socialism is what the Labour government does'; in his *The Future of Socialism* (1956), he asserted that Marx's predictions of capitalist societies polarising before revolutions established left-wing government had been proved hopelessly wrong; the working class had ignored revolutions and had been strengthened by full employment. The business class had not fought the advance of socialism but had been *tamed* by it. Crosland argued that the ownership of the economy was no longer relevant, as salaried managers were now the key players.

He attacked another sacred cow by maintaining that nationalisation was not necessarily the most effective road to socialism and that other forms of collective ownership were more effective. He concluded that Labour should now concentrate its efforts on reducing inequality through progressive taxation and redistributive benefits and – the key proposal – reducing class differences through an end to selection in education. In practice, revisionism was Labour's policy for the next thirty years, but when in government in the 1970s its fatal flaw was exposed: it was dependent on an expanding economy, and when this fell into decline public expenditure cuts became inevitable.

The left wing of the party, however, never accepted revisionism, and first Aneurin (Nye) Bevan, then Michael Foot, opposed the new drift towards a diluted ideology. In the 1960s, Wilson defied the Left in the parliamentary party, but when it teamed up with the trade unions trouble was in store for the 1970s administrations under both Wilson and Callaghan. Led by Tony Benn, the Left now offered an alternative economic strategy based on workers' control, extended state control of the economy, **participatory democracy** at all levels of national life, fresh injections of funds into the welfare state, encouragement of extra-parliamentary activity,

and unilateral abandonment of nuclear weapons. The revisionist leadership tried to ignore the Left, but when the 1979 general election was lost to a new and militantly ideological leader, Margaret Thatcher, the Left insisted that a similar return to the roots of socialist ideology was necessary. With the revisionist leadership defeated and discredited, the Left made its move, managing to translate its candidate, Michael Foot, into leader in 1980, plus imposing a radically left-wing set of policies on the party, which resulted in the 1983 manifesto being dubbed by Gerald Kaufman 'the longest suicide note in history'. More significantly, the Left's ascendancy led to the defection of an important centre-right section of the party to form the Social Democratic Party (see Box 5.1). The conventional view is that the new party split the anti-Tory vote and helped to keep Thatcher in power for a decade. However, the party's history as written by Ivor Crewe and Anthony King (1995) concluded that this transient new force, if anything, reduced the Tory majority.

Neil Kinnock, elected as Foot's successor, was a child of the Left but soon recanted, dismissing its prescriptions as 'Disneyland thinking'. He assiduously began to nudge his party towards the centre ground via a series of policy reviews, which essentially accepted the 'efficiency and realism' of the market as the best model of economic organisation. It was implicit in this new analysis – although hotly denied – that socialism was no longer relevant; even the word disappeared from party policy documents. When he lost the crucial 1992 election, he resigned and John Smith continued this 'desocialising' work. When Smith died tragically of a heart attack in May 1994, Tony Blair was elected leader and soon placed his stamp on a party denied power for nearly fifteen years.

Views of Labour leaders

As for Tony Blair, I still think, as I thought when I first met him, we're lucky to have him – both the Labour Party and the nation. He might have gone off and joined the Social Democrats and no-one would have heard of him again.

Michael Foot, *The Observer*, 6 September 1996

My view of Christian values has led me to oppose what I perceived to be a narrow view of self-interest that Conservatism – particularly in its modern, more right-wing form – represents.

Tony Blair, September 1995

BOX 5.1   Social Democratic Party

On 1 August 1980 Shirley Williams, David Owen and Bill Rodgers published their famous 'Gang of Three' statement: an open letter in the *Guardian* 'rejecting class war, accepting the mixed economy and the need to manage it efficiently'. After the Wembley conference of 1981 which passed rule changes strengthening the power of left-wing activists over candidate selection and the party leadership, the Gang of Three joined Roy Jenkins to form the Social Democratic Party (SDP). Over the next few months over two dozen Labour MPs made the same journey, joined by a solitary Conservative. The SDP fought the 1983 election in 'Alliance' with the small Liberal Party, garnering 26 per cent of the vote but less than 4 per cent of the seats. The much wished for breakthrough in 1987 failed when they mustered only 22 per cent. A formal merger of the two parties was delayed by personality problems posed largely by David Owen but by 1988 the future Liberal Democrats had emerged, albeit for a while with a defiant Owenite rump. The SDP was formed in a blaze of publicity and 'breaking the mould' rhetoric, but a genuine alternative was probably not on offer. In one sense its message represented an amalgam of policies picked up across the political spectrum. Decentralisation was close to the Liberal, Bennite and Green position; SDP views on the market economy and trade unions were close to Margaret Thatcher's position – she actually praised Owen for being 'sound' on both – and on social policy and defence the SDP was close to the position of the Callaghan government, to which the SDP leaders had once belonged. This is not to say that the SDP lacked a carefully worked out and detailed programme, merely that it lacked a distinctive alternative or even radical quality. History will judge the SDP as a party of protest with a limited appeal outside the middle classes.

Having already abandoned its former policies of opposition to the European Community/Union, unilateral nuclear disarmament and nationalisation, Blair shifted the party even further to the right by attacking the power of trade unions in the party. He waged a spectacularly successful war against the 'collective ownership' Clause Four in the party's constitution, drafted by Sidney Webb in 1917:

To secure for the workers by hand or by brain the full fruits of their industry and the most equitable distribution thereof that may be possible upon the basis of the common ownership of the means of production, distribution, and exchange, and the best obtainable system of popular administration and control of each industry or service.

Clause Four rewritten

The iconic clause, so fundamental that it was inscribed on membership cards, was replaced in April 1995 at a special conference by a massive majority. The new clause endorsed a 'dynamic economy, serving the public interest'; a 'just society which judges its strength by the condition of the weak as much as the strong'; 'an open democracy, in which government is held to account by the people'; and where 'decisions are taken as far as practicable by the communities they affect'.

Not content with this Blair later drew the party away from the social democratic heartland of full employment and welfare spending: it was deemed that the requisite high taxation would never be endorsed by middle-class voters – remember that Labour was caught out badly by the Conservatives over tax in 1992 – and it was believed that the world's economy had changed. With modern technology the economy has become globalised so that flows of capital can break companies and even currencies in minutes. To maintain policies of high taxation, it was believed, risks massive withdrawals of capital by speculators and investors from any economy contemplating such socialistic measures.

There was now no alternative to Thatcher's economics; 'New Labour' had effectively embraced tax cuts, low inflation, a market economy plus encouragement of entrepreneurial activity and some privatisation. Tony Blair flirted for a while with the idea of a 'stakeholder society', that everyone, individuals and groups, should have some investment in society, and everyone should feel part of their community at all levels, economic, cultural and social; the idea withered through business opposition to any wider role. The other biggish idea supported by Blair was constitutional reform; Labour embraced devolved assemblies for both Scotland and Wales plus reform of the House of Lords and a referendum on the electoral system. However, the changes were pitted with flaws, none more so than the unresolved, so-called 'West Lothian question', whereby Scottish MPs would have the ability to vote on English issues but English MPs do not have the ability to reciprocate as the internally elected assembly would assume this role (see Chapter 14). The Lords reform agenda stalled after the virtual abolition of hereditary peers and the chamber continued in its half-reformed way. As for reforming the voting system, the results of the Jenkins Report continued to gather dust as the party swung against the idea.

Blairism

The massive endorsement of New Labour in the general election of 1 May 1997 was fulfilment of the strategy conceived and implemented by Tony Blair and his close collaborator Peter Mandelson to move the Labour Party into a position where it embraced the market economy and removed the fear of old-style socialism felt by the middle-class occupants of 'Middle England'. 'Blairism' was vaguely expressed and lent itself to wide interpretation, but some commentators disagreed and claimed that Blairism boasted a coherent philosophical framework and was a well worked-out 'project'. Socially it is based on the idea of communitarianism. At university, Blair was very interested in the ideas of John McMurray, a Scottish philosopher who took issue with the modish idea of 'individualism', that the individual has choices and freedoms and is an autonomous unit. McMurray argued the contrary, that, as Adams puts it:

People do not exist in a vacuum; in fact, they only exist in relation to others. The completely autonomous self of liberal theory is a myth. People's personalities are created in their relationships with others, in the family and the wider community. By pursuing the interests of society as a whole we benefit individuals including ourselves.

Adams (1998: 148–9)

Blair argued that people should build communities based on the idea of responsibility, a sense of duty towards others maybe less fortunate and a recognition that one's actions have repercussions and may require reparation. Old Labour tended to see poor people as 'victims of the system'; to speak

of them having responsibilities is to borrow from another right-wing lexicon. Blair has also subscribed to the idea of a *Third Way*. Apart from being an alternative to socialism and pro-capitalist ideology, it was never clearly defined. Another participant has been the eminent sociologist Anthony Giddens, highly regarded by Blair, who has written a book, *The Third Way: The Renewal of Social Democracy*. This argues that the old definitions of left and right are obsolete (see Chapter 4) and that in the world of globalisation a new approach is required. He defines the overall aim of Third Way politics as helping citizens to:

pilot their way through the major revolutions of our time: globalisation, transformations in personal life and our relationship to nature . . . One might suggest as a prime motto for the new politics, 'No rights without responsibilities'.

Giddens (1998: 64–5) (see also Box 5.2)

Blair in power

For the first two years in power, Gordon Brown kept the brake firmly on expenditure but after the 2001 election, Labour embarked in 2002 on the spending of over $100 billion over the following years, marking for many a welcome return to Old Labour orthodoxy. However, the event that transformed Labour during the early months of 2003 was the war on Iraq. Tony Blair had decided to stand 'shoulder to shoulder' with George W. Bush after the horrific attacks on the World Trade Center on 11 September 2001, but the extent of his loyalty to a right-wing president advised by Republican hawks was anathema to many Labour MPs. When it proved impossible to muster a United Nations Security Council majority for the war in March, 139 MPs supported a hostile motion and Robin Cook resigned from the Cabinet. Left-wing critics spoke of a leadership contest. Such speculation proved premature but Blair's blind support for US foreign policy was squeezing support in his own New Labour power base (see also Chapter 28).

Blair's legacy

As it became obvious there was not much time left, Blair seemed to obsess with leaving a lasting 'legacy'. While he would have loved it to include a shiny new health and education service, polls showed voters relatively unimpressed and Labour

BOX 5.2   IDEAS AND PERSPECTIVES

How 'new' is New Labour?

A number of scholars have considered this question but the approach of Steven Fielding of Salford University (2003) is perhaps the most useful for this chapter's purposes. Fielding argues that New Labour is in reality part of the continuous development of social democratic thinking over the last century and a half. He denies the claim, associated with Roy Hattersley for one, that New Labour was a kind of 'coup' involving Blair, Mandelson and Gould and also denies the idea that New Labour was, in fact, all that new. His case is that New Labour was less to do with high-profile personalities and more to do with social democratic adaptations to the constantly fluid nature of international economics. As he sees it New Labour was an attempt to reconcile a system which produced winners and losers with the ideas of equality, justice and efficiency. This last was the crucial lacuna in socialism as Attlee's nationalisation produced overmanned loss-making state behemoths. Labour began to view the economy not so differently from Conservatives as something where growth and productivity had to be encouraged.

When this apparent attempt failed in a welter of strikes in 1979, the left swung back to bedrock and a right-wing Conservative government was elected. When voters rejected the left in 1983 and 1987 new thinking was set in train which nudged ever closer to an acceptance of market forces and a capitalist economy.

Writing some years into Labour's period in power, Fielding concluded:

The party at the start of the twenty-first century may be a highly cautious social democratic organization; but recognizably social democratic it remains. If the state has advanced modestly and in novel ways since 1997 Labour's purpose in office is the same as it ever was: to reform capitalism so that it may better serve the interests of the majority.

Source: Fielding (2003: 217)

---

critics furious at his encouragement of private sector invasion of such public sector citadels. For so many people, whatever their party loyalties, the debacle of the Iraq war will be emblazoned on Blair's grave. But this would be unfair. His tireless efforts in Northern Ireland, arguably proved crucial in winning an admittedly fragile settlement which saw a new Executive formed before he left office. Secondly, Blair caused the Conservatives to desert the aridities of Thatcherism. He had stolen Tory clothes to an extent but had subtly re-attired his party as liberal, tolerant and dedicated to improving the place of the less well-off majority. As leader followed leader the Conservatives finally got the message: they would have to change, just as Labour did from the mid-80s. David Cameron was the result. Now the litmus test for a new policy is, ostensibly at least, what it can do for the disadvantaged. Homophobia is out; environmentalism is very much in; pro-business yes, but at a distance; tax cuts maybe but not until the economy can sustain them.

Already the signs of Blair's greatest legacy perhaps are evident in our present politics: Thatcher finished off left-wing socialism but Blair has put paid to right-wing Conservatism: a legacy of which any left-leaning politician can be proud.

Gordon Brown's period in power

Brown's period as Prime Minister lasted only from June 2007, so he did not have much time to implant any characteristic elements. Indeed his critics claimed he lacked any real vision of what his party should offer the country.

Economy

Their voices were partially stilled by his reaction to the banking crisis of 2007 and the subsequent recession. He took confident strides in a Keynesian direction, channelling huge amounts of money into the banking system as a 'fiscal stimulus' to ensure the threatened collapse did not occur. There is some justification for believing his claim that other nations followed his lead. The problem with such a policy was that it built up huge levels of debt which imposed heavy interest repayment obligations. In the run up to the election Labour argued that continued investment in the economy was necessary to avoid an even deeper recession. His arguments were undermined to an extent, in autumn 2009, when it became clear the UK economy was not emerging from recession like other developed nations like the USA, Germany, France and Japan. Labour argued strongly that they were not to blame for the recession and that the expenditure cuts proposed by the Tories would cause a fragile recovery to collapse into even deeper recession.

Public expenditure

Labour insisted in late 2009 that it would maintain public spending to sustain recovery and protect recipients of services. This was undermined however by Treasury plans indicating severe cuts in planned Labour expenditure from 2011 onwards.

Foreign policy

Labour took a positive view on the EU, supporting the Lisbon Treaty and seeking to ridicule Conservative hostility. On Afghanistan they offered continued support to the war but were damaged by accusations that British troops had not been properly equipped to fight the Taliban.

Long period in power: 1997–2010

As for the Tories in 1997, Labour suffered from the fact that they had been in power for three terms (over 12 years) and voters were tired of them. Frequent examples of poor or incompetent government received considerable publicity and fuelled fears of a major rejection at the 2010 election.

■ The Liberal Democrats

Source: Courtesy of the Liberal Democrats Party (www.libdems.org.uk)

After the war the Liberal Party continued to decline politically but still offered an alternative to voters in the centre of political ideas. At heart the party still adhered to the ideas of 'new liberalism' covered in Chapter 4, with emphases on individual liberty, equality, a mixed economy, a developed welfare state and a reformed, democratised system of government. Under the skilful successive leaderships of Jo Grimond, Jeremy Thorpe and David Steel, the party survived the postwar decades but hardly prospered. Then in 1981, as we have seen, it joined forces with the breakaway SDP to form the 'Alliance'. It was not difficult to unite on policies, which were very close; rather it was personalities who caused the foundering of this short-lived collaboration (see Box 5.1). In 1987, the two elements of the Alliance formally merged and fought the 1992 election as the Liberal Democrats. Its manifesto, *Changing Britain for Good*, called for a shift of power to the consumer and ordinary citizen, the development of worker shareholding and a market economy in which the market is the 'servant and not the master'. In addition, the party repeated the traditional call for reform of the voting system and **devolution** of power to the regions. Following the 1992 general election its new leader, Paddy Ashdown (elected in 1988), made steady progress with a replacing of 'equidistance' between the two big parties with a policy of open cooperation with Labour; in 1996, a joint Labour/Lib-Dem committee was set up to liaise on constitutional reform.

BIOGRAPHY

Paddy Ashdown (1941–)

Former leader of Liberal Democrats. Formerly captain in the Marines, he saw active service in Borneo. He also learned to speak Mandarin Chinese as part of the diplomatic corps 1971–6. Won Yeovil in 1983 as a Liberal and became leader of merged party in 1988. He worked hard to build a close relationship with Labour. Lib-Dems won 46 seats in the 1997 general election, after which Ashdown retired as leader. Charles Kennedy took over in 1999. Ashdown was appointed by the UN as International High Representative in Bosnia in May 2002.

The strong showing by the Liberal Democrats in the 1997 general election buttressed the claim of that party to be the de facto left-of-centre conscience of the new Blair order regarding constitutional reform and the nurturing of the welfare state, especially the educational system. The Lib Dems joined a Cabinet committee tasked with studying the future of constitutional reform – a tempting whiff of power perhaps for a party starved of it since the paltry sniff provided by the Lib–Lab pact of 1977–9. In 1999, Paddy Ashdown stood down after a distinguished period as leader of Britain's third party. His successor was the amiable Charles Kennedy, popular on quiz shows and a witty, clubbable man. He rejected suggestions to take up a left of Labour stance as the kind of *cul de sac* that had ruined Labour in the early 1980s. Instead he chose a 'business as usual' policy of 'constructive opposition' to Tony Blair with a view to replacing the Conservatives as the official opposition to the Labour government. In an interview with the US magazine *Talk*, Blair said that his biggest mistake in May 1997 had been not to ask Ashdown to join his Cabinet, although with such a huge majority it was politically impossible to deny even a single post to his own party.

In the 2005 election Kennedy fought his usual relaxed campaign, offering an anti-war stance over Iraq, increased taxation for the very rich, and no tuition fees for university students. This worked well in constituencies where Labour was the Lib-Dem target, and twelve seats were won in this way. However, what attracted former Labour voters did not work the same magic in the close Lib-Dem–Conservative seats: only three were won while five were lost.

This election of 62 MPs, though welcome, still carried a sense of feeling of a missed opportunity; in addition there developed sense that the party was losing what momentum it had gained at the election and all this contributed towards a whispering campaign against Kennedy. Complicating the situation, by the time of the autumn party conference a new wing was identified in the expanded 62-strong ranks of the Lib Dems: a group leaning more to the right, epitomised by *The Orange Book* of essays written by MPs and activists favouring a greater acceptance of market forces. Kennedy found his attempts to keep both factions happy were failing and by November senior party colleagues were said to be briefing against him.

Kennedy finally admitted the chief accusation against him – that he had a drinking problem – and a few days later, when the pressure did not abate, stood down in early January 2006. In the resultant, chaotic contest Simon Hughes and Chris Huhne waged a lively campaign, but the veteran Sir Menzies (Ming) Campbell won quite easily in the end, March 2006. When he in turn proved unable to offer a new direction and higher poll ratings, he too resigned in October 2007. Another contest took place and this time the young, good-looking Nick Clegg was the choice. He too had difficulty making an impact but he led the way in his 2008 conference in suggesting tax cuts; a nudge perhaps in the direction likely to win seats in the south-east from the Conservatives However, the Lib Dems have much for which to hope and fight; psephological predictions of a hung parliament in the 2009–10 election raised much talk of which side he would swing in any resultant coalition negotiations. The political positions of the Lib Dems have never seemed to matter very much as power has always seemed so far away. However, the possible prospect of a hung parliament, made their evolving policy positions for once into matters of intense interest.

■ The financial crisis of 2008

The worldwide financial crisis signalled by the collapse of the prestigious Lehman's investment Bank, in September 2008, presaged a desperate time in which leading governments tried a variety of remedies to a patient well into intensive care. It soon became apparent that a divide was opening up in party political reaction to the crisis. Prime Minister Gordon Brown, sought to blame the 'subprime' mortgage selling of US banks in the early years of the new century as the cause of the crisis and argued forcefully for a massive Keynesian 'fiscal stimulus' of borrowed money to kick start the world economy back into life. The Lib Dems, led by their formidable finance spokesman, Vince Cable – popular for his prescience in foreseeing the crisis and his wit in analysing it – tended to offer critical support to this approach. The Conservatives however, decided more lavish borrowing to solve a crisis caused by unwise borrowing was to take out a mortgage on the nation's future which our children will have to repay. In the wake of the G20 summit in London, 2009, the world could see that injections of vast funding saved the banking system but could not prevent a deep recession in most Western economies.

BOX 5.3   BRITAIN IN CONTEXT

Mainstream ideas and the political spectrum

As explained in Chapter 4, the political spectrum is usually represented from left to right, with unregulated free enterprise on the right and an anarchic or a communally owned economy on the left. Many of the ideas on the fringes – anarchism on the left or fascism on the right – would be regarded as extreme in the present day and unlikely to hold centre stage. Ideas likely to feature in the 'mainstream' of politics will usually be in the centre ground, that group of ideas which at any one time represents the general consensus of what people believe to be reasonable or legitimate political objectives.

Objectives which fall outside the mainstream are not automatic lost causes: repeated advocacy or changed circumstances can draw them into the centre – like anti-union legislation and privatisation during the early 1980s in the UK. During that same period the political spectrum was at its broadest in Britain with a near command economy being urged on Labour's left and a minimalist free enterprise state on the Thatcherite right. Since then ideological differences have narrowed significantly but they are still wider in Britain than in the USA.

Naturally right-wing pro-capitalist ideas are powerful in the USA, often seen as the 'headquarters' of world free enterprise thinking. By the same token 'left-wing' ideas, together with the US mainstream, are further to the right than in the UK. Americans have traditionally regarded any left-wing idea as the thin end of a communist wedge and therefore to be resisted as 'unpatriotic', not sufficiently 'American'. So even state-funded health services, commonplace in Europe, are seen from across the Atlantic as 'socialist' and therefore slightly sinister. Some theorists explain the weakness of US left-wing thinking as the consequence of 'hegemonic'

right-wing ideas: ideas so deeply ingrained and powerful they squeeze the life out of any alternatives. It is certainly true that both major parties in the USA stoutly support free enterprise economics: even the Democrats urge economic growth and support business, though not with the passion of the true believing Republicans.

Within Europe political spectrums, as in Britain, have tended to shift rightwards. Capitalism was no longer seen as a system which necessarily disadvantages large groups of people, but rather as the motor of dynamic economic growth from which all can benefit. Consequently communism faded away in the wake of the Cold War and most brands of left-wing socialism tended to follow suit. Former communist countries display a fascinating mix of ideas in their spectrums. During communism, as in most authoritarian regimes, the political spectrum was very narrow, containing virtually no options for genuine change.

But once the old pro-Moscow regimes imploded they were replaced by volatile new democracies in which, as in Russia, wild nationalism was present together with some surviving residual old-style communism. Many Russians, relieved at the passing of communism, were alarmed by their new combustible democracy and associated social dislocation. They gratefully accepted the promise of security which the former KGB chief Putin offered as president, even if political choices were once again heavily circumscribed. It would seem to be the case that a wide political spectrum, offering the chance of usually limited change at any particular time, is a characteristic of democracies. Authoritarian regimes do not tend to offer much choice and seek to shrink their spectrums into an unchanging narrowness.

Chapter summary

Conservatism is more than mere pragmatism in the ruling interest but includes a concern for unity, harmony and balance in a society based on property, equal opportunity, élite rule and gradual change. Margaret Thatcher gave major prominence to the neo-liberal strand in Conservatism, which stressed the primacy of markets in economics. Major returned to the rhetoric of 'one nation' Conservatism but contained the practice of Thatcherism. Labour began as a socialist party dedicated to the replacement of capitalism by a collectively owned economy, but in government translated this into nationalisation, a policy of doubtful success. In opposition during the 1980s it gradually shed its socialist clothes and donned those of the free market and restricted public spending: in effect a compromise with Thatcherism. Liberal Democrats inherited the 'new liberal ideas', of the early twentieth century to which they added an initial disposition to work with the Labour Party in office, something which faded after the invasion of Iraq in 2003.

Discussion points

■ To what extent was Margaret Thatcher a Conservative?

■ Did John Major contribute anything distinctive to Conservative thinking?

■ Did Labour sell out its principles during the 1980s?

■ Is there room for a distinctive third set of political ideas in Britain, and do the Lib-Dems offer them?

Further reading

Andrew Heywood's *Political Ideologies* (1998) is a valuable source, as is the similar book by Ian Adams (1998). The Giddens book, *The Third Way*, has been criticised as too vague, but it is chock full of interesting ideas and more than repays a careful reading.

Bibliography

Adams, I. (1998) *Ideology and Politics in Britain Today* (Manchester University Press).

Ashbee, E. and Ashford, N. (1999) *US Politics Today* (Manchester University Press).

Beer, S.H. (1982) *Britain Against Itself* (Faber).

Crewe, I. and King, A. (1995) *SDP: The Birth, Life and Death of the Social Democratic Party* (Oxford University Press).

Crosland, C.A.R. (1956) *The Future of Socialism* (Jonathan Cape).

Driver, S. and Mantell, L. (1998) *New Labour: Politics after Thatcherism* (Pluto Press).

Field, F. (1995) *Making Welfare Work* (Institute of Community Studies).

Fielding, S. (2003) *The Labour Party* (Palgrave).

Foley, M. (1994) *Ideas that Shape Politics* (Manchester University Press).

Foote, G. (1997) *The Labour Party's Political Thought* (Manchester University Press).

Giddens, A. (1998) *The Third Way: The Renewal of Social Democracy* (Polity Press).

Gould, B. (1989) *A Future for Socialism* (Jonathan Cape).

Gould, P. (1998) *The Unfinished Revolution* (Little, Brown).

Hailsham, Lord (1959) *The Conservative Case* (Penguin).

Heywood, A. (1998) *Political Ideologies*, 2nd edn (Macmillan).

Howell, D. (1980) *British Social Democracy* (Croom Helm).

Hutton, W. (1998) *The Stakeholding Society* (Polity Press).

Kelly, R. (1999) 'The Third Way', *Politics Review*, September.

Kelly, R. (1999) *British Political Parties Today* (Manchester University Press).

▶

Marshall, P. and Laws, D. (2004) *The Orange Book: Reclaiming Liberalism* (Profile Books).

Norton, P. and Aughey, A. (1981) *Conservatives and Conservatism* (Temple Smith).

Policy Exchange (2005) *The Case for Change* (Policy Exchange).

Russell, A. (2004) *Neither Left nor Right – the Liberal Democrats and the Electorate* (Manchester University Press).

Smith, C. (1998) *Creative Britain* (Faber and Faber).

Tressell, R. (1965) *The Ragged Trousered Philanthropists* (Panther; first published 1914).

Tucker, K. (1998) *Anthony Giddens and Modern Social Theory* (Sage).

Whiteley, P. and Seyd, P. (1992) *Labour's Grass Roots: the Politics of Party Membership* (Clarendon).

Useful websites

Centre for Policy Studies: www.cps.org.uk/

Conservative Party: www.conservatives.com/

Institute of Economic Affairs: www.iea.org.uk/

Institute of Public Policy Research:
   www.ippr.org.uk

Labour Party: www.labour.org.uk/

Liberal Democrats: www.libdems.org.uk/

Political ideas: themes and fringes

Bill Jones

Learning objectives

- To explain and put into context the themes of:
  - feminism;
  - national identity;
  - environmentalism.

- To identify, analyse and elucidate the political fringe on the far left and far right.

- To explain the intellectual source of ideas characterising the political fringe.

From Chapter 6 of *Politics UK*, 7/e. Bill Jones and Philip Norton. © Pearson Education 2001–2010. All rights reserved.

Introduction

The first three chapters in this section looked at ideology, political concepts and party political ideas. This fourth chapter addresses three major themes – **feminism**, **national identity** and **environmentalism**. This is followed by the rarefied world of the political fringe, represented by a colourful assemblage of small parties that are not always easy to identify; they may be seen selling their newspapers on the street or taking part in street demonstrations or even contesting national elections. However, their intellectual roots are often connected to major philosophical themes and are therefore of interest.

■ Gender issues

Any woman whose IQ hovers above her body temperature must be a feminist.

Rita Mae Brown, author

In 1980, a United Nations report stated:

While women represent 50 per cent of the world's population, they perform nearly two-thirds of all working hours, receive one-tenth of world income and own less than 1 per cent of world property.

Despite the existence of a worldwide feminist movement, the position of women worldwide has improved very slightly, if at all, since the dawn of feminism in the late eighteenth century. The rights of women were implicit in the recognition of the rights of 'men', but thinkers such as Locke did not include women in their scheme of things. Rousseau did, however (while treating his own wife very badly), and in 1792 Mary Wollstonecraft's *A Vindication of the Rights of Women* (see Wollstonecraft, 1967) articulated their rights explicitly (see Biography) just as the French Revolution was asserting the rights of oppressed people everywhere. Whether women were 'oppressed' or not was a moot point. Most men assumed that women existed to perform domestic roles: producing and rearing children and caring for their husbands as well as doing all the household chores. Probably most women at the time would have agreed, had they ever thought themselves important enough to be consulted. They had no possibility of pursuing careers, voting or participating in public life. Their consolation was the power they exercised through this domestic role, influencing their menfolk, maybe even dominating them, behind the scenes. But the legal position of women at this time was dire: they had no right to divorce (unlike their husbands); they had no right to marital property; and their husbands could beat them quite legally – even rape them should they wish. Moreover, men regularly used prostitutes while preaching fidelity for their wives and divorcing them when this failed, on their side, to be upheld. In 'exchange' women were praised for their femininity and sensitivity and were idealised by the notion of romantic love. An unequal relationship indeed.

Emergent socialist ideas supported the position of women. Friedrich Engels argued in his book *The Origin of the Family, Private Property and the State* (1884) that the pre-historical position of

BIOGRAPHY

Mary Wollstonecraft (1757–97)

Mary Wollstonecraft was an Anglo-Irish writer and is often cited as the first modern feminist. At the age of 28 she wrote a semi-auto-biographical novel, *Maria*. She moved to London to become the 'first of a new genus' of women, a full-time professional writer and editor specialising in women and children. She was closely associated with the group of radical reforming writers called the English Jacobins, where she met her future husband, the philosopher William Godwin. In her book *A Vindication of the Rights of Women* (1792) she argued for equal rights for women in society, especially regarding educational opportunities. Her daughter with Godwin was Mary Shelley, the author of *Frankenstein*.

women had been usurped by men so that property now was passed on through the male line instead of the female because men wished to pass on property to their sons. The exploitative relationship between the propertied class and the proletariat was mirrored within the family by the relationship between men and women. A socialist revolution would sweep away private property and remove the economic basis of the exploitative monogamous marriage.

During the nineteenth century the women's movement, such as it was, concentrated on gaining the vote, the belief being that, once this citadel had fallen, the other injustices regarding the imbalance of political and legal rights compared with men would soon be remedied.

To an extent these early feminists were operating with the grain of history, as the franchise for men was being progressively extended at this time. Nevertheless, it took a bitter and militant struggle for the 'suffragettes', led by Emmeline and Christabel Pankhurst, to win through: in 1918 women received the vote, but only if they fulfilled certain educational and property qualifications and were, bizarrely it now seems, over the age of 30. They finally achieved equal political rights in 1928, but this did not automatically transform their position, or make any difference at all in the short and medium term. The women's movement subsided for a number of decades, but the impact of another world war, where women once again played leading roles on the home front, advanced their claims for better treatment. Simone de Beauvoir's *The Second Sex* (1952) attacked the asymmetry whereby men were defined as free independent beings and women merely in terms of their relationships with men.

But the so-called 'second wave' of feminism began with Betty Friedan's *The Feminine Mystique* (1963). This major work rejected the myth that women were different and were happy being the domestic adjuncts of their men. Having nominally equal rights did not deliver real equality in a world controlled by men and discriminating against women. In the late 1960s and 1970s, the work of Germaine Greer (*The Female Eunuch*, 1971) and Kate Millett (*Sexual Politics*, 1969) moved the focus of debate from the wider world of career and public life to the micro-worlds that we all inhabit. Greer developed some of the ideas of Herbert Marcuse (1964, 1969a, 1969b), who argued that Western society was sexually repressed. She suggested that women had absorbed the male idea of

their sexuality as soft and yielding – a kind of sex image stereotype – while their true and possibly quite different nature was not allowed to be expressed and fulfilled. Concomitant with this went an assertion of lesbianism as a socially demonised activity. Instead of their living out expected roles, Greer was insisting that people could be true to themselves, being 'male' or 'female' according to their own natures. Millett's emphasis was on how women are brainwashed into accepting a given image of themselves regarding their role and even their appearance. This image, according to her, was a reflection of 'patriarchy': constructed by men with their interests in mind. What was attributed to gender roles was in fact no more than a socially constructed role that women were induced to accept from birth via a battery of socialising agencies, including family, tradition, law, the media and popular culture. Women were forced to accept a narrow, constricting role of being gentle, caring mother figures whose job was to tend their men. Alternatively, they were seen as whores and temptresses, equally subservient but this time more dangerous. Millett also directed attention at the family and home, pointing out that here was the most important arena in which the male controlled the key sexual relationship, dominating the female; following from this is the key feminist phrase, that 'the personal is the political'.

In the 1970s it was observed that liberal feminists, who believed that reform and a high degree of equality were possible in society as it is, coexisted with socialist feminists, who believed that the main inequality was still between classes and not the sexes. They believed that major changes to the

BIOGRAPHY

Germaine Greer (1939–)

Australian feminist, author and journalist. Educated at Melbourne and Cambridge Universities. Lectured at Warwick University but best known for her book *The Female Eunuch* (1971), which attacked the institution of marriage as a form of slavery and the way women's sexuality was misrepresented and denied by males. She modified her militant position in later life but is still an active advocate for women's rights.

BOX 6.1   IDEAS AND PERSPECTIVES

Sexual inequality at work

According to LSE research reports in February 2000 and January 2001, a woman earns on average £250,000 less than a man during a lifetime. This is partly because women workers tend to be concentrated in low-paid jobs but also because they are paid less than men for doing the same work and routinely denied access to bonus payments and pension schemes. Figures released in autumn 2008 revealed the gap is getting wider with men earning on average £15.54 an hour and woman £12.88; this makes a gender pay gap of 17.1 per cent, up from 17 per cent a year earlier; the TUC point out the gap is 21 per cent in the private sector.

economy and society were necessary before women could be truly free. A third group soon emerged: the *radical* feminists. For them the problem lies not in society or the economy but in human nature, more precisely, male human nature. The problem with women, in other words, is men. In *The Dialectic of Sex* (1980, originally published 1971), Shulamith Firestone perceived a fundamental oppression of women by men as a result of their biological role. Sexual domination therefore both precedes and exceeds economic exploitation. What she advocates is a 'sexual revolution much larger than – inclusive of – a socialist one' to 'eradicate the tapeworm of exploitation'. She argues for a restructuring of society through science, whereby children would be produced artificially and looked after communally so that women's physical and psychological burdens would be removed and they would be free for the first time in history.

Susan Brownmiller – *Against our Will* (1975) – shifts the focus to the violence that men use to threaten women; the fear of rape is used to maintain male dominance, and rapists act for all men in demonstrating the consequences of non-compliance. Other feminist writers, such as Andrea Dworkin and Dale Spender – often called 'supremacists' – assert female moral superiority and argue that the world would be better if women were in control. Often this type of feminist will be separatist in relation to men; their lesbianism consequently has a political quality to it. For them men are not necessary for women, and women who live with men are 'man identified' instead of being 'woman identified'.

It is often said that since the 1970s the women's movement has lost momentum. Certainly the tone has become milder; Greer (1985) and Friedan (1982) have both disappointed radicals by writing approvingly of domesticity and childrearing. The New Right in the USA and UK, moreover, have

reinforced 'traditional values' of women's roles and the desirability of marriage (and by implication the subversive effects of one-parent families) to hold society together. In their book *Contemporary Feminist Politics* (1993), Lovenduski and Randall applauded the progress made by the women's movement in permeating institutions and professions and in disseminating feminist values so effectively that they have become widely accepted as orthodoxies. However, they lament the failure to replace activists when they bow out of activity, and the internecine squabbling and fragmentation that have weakened the movement. A report covered by *The Observer* (7 November 1999) questioned whether women have made much progress at all. The American Psychological Association's study concluded that 'even though the fight for equal rights widened opportunities for many, it failed to give women control over their lives'. Experts cited in the article suggested the same could be said of the UK too; two-thirds of the 1300 receiving electro-convulsive therapy each week for depressive illnesses are women. The strong showing of women candidates in the 1997 general election – women MPs virtually doubled from 62 to 120, most of them Labour – cheered campaigners for more female representation and those who defended the special Labour measures to favour women candidates in winnable seats. However, some feminists have criticised 'Blair's babes', as they have been dubbed, as performing a decorative but non-feminist role in the governing party. Comparisons are made on the Labour side with the fiercely effective Barbara Castle and on the Conservative side with the legendary Thatcher. Boxes 6.2–6.4 provide chapter and verse on employment and political life in the UK showing that, while much has been achieved in the recent past, women are still at a definite disadvantage compared to men.

BOX 6.5   IDEAS AND PERSPECTIVES

Feminist debates

This is a schematic summary of the main strands of feminist thought. It is important to understand that these strands are not rigidly separate, that some writers could be entered in more than one category, and that in recent years there has been a significant convergence of apparently competing approaches.

Type of feminism	Key concepts	Goals	Key writers
Liberal	Rights, equality	The same rights and opportunities as for men, with a focus on the public sphere	*Classic:* Mary Wollstonecraft, John Stuart Mill *Recent:* Betty Friedan, Naomi Wolf, Natasha Walter
Radical	Patriarchy, 'the personal is political', sisterhood	Radical transformation of all spheres of life to liberate women from male power. Replace or displace men as the measure of human worth	Kate Millett, Andrea Dworkin, Catherine MacKinnon, Germaine Greer
Socialist and Marxist	Class, capitalism, exploitation	An economically just society in which all women and men can fulfil their potential	*Classic:* William Thompson, Friedrich Engels, Alexandra Kollontai, Sylvia Pankhurst *Recent:* Michelle Barrett, Juliet Mitchell, Sheila Rowbotham, Lynne Segal, Anne Phillips
Black	Interactive and multiple oppressions, solidarity, black	An end to the interconnecting oppressions of gender, 'race' and class	*Classic:* Maria Stewart, Julia Cooper *Recent:* Patricia Hill Collins, bell hooks, Angela Davis, Heidi Mirza
Postmodern	Fragmentation, discourse, deconstruction, differences	Overcoming binary oppositions. Free-floating, fluid gender identities. However, the idea of a final goal is rejected in principle	Judith Butler, Julia Kristeva, Joan Scott, Denise Riley, Michelle Barrett

Source: Valerie Bryson (2003) 'Feminist debates, ideology: feminism', *Politics Review*, Vol. 12, No. 4, April 2003. Reproduced with permission from Philip Allan Updates

felt a thrill of pride in seeing the 1950s map of the world coloured with so much red had soon to adjust to a much more humble role.

Along with imperial decline came its economic concomitant: a slow sinking of Britain from 'work-shop of the world' to 'sick man of Europe'. During the seventies the sour mood of the times infected a workforce which became increasingly uncooperative and demanding of higher wages just when the country could no longer afford them. The result

English football fans display their support for the national team
Source: Action Plus Sports Images / Neil Tingle

was a major upsetting of the postwar settlement whereby agreed increased taxes funded a welfare state and included trade unions as a valued partner of government. Margaret Thatcher set about enthroning the role of markets, removing the inefficient nationalised industries, curbing the overpowerful unions and rolling back the role of the state. But the effects of this harsh medicine on Scotland and Wales gave added power to the arguments for independence in these countries. When Tony Blair was elected in 1997 the stage was set for the partial dismantling of the constitution – devolution – posing a number of questions about the concept of Britain. 'England' is no longer synonymous with 'Britain' now new identities have been assumed by the nations of the Celtic fringe, each with their separate assemblies.

At the same time there is an internal questioning of identity caused by the inflow of immigrants, initially from the empire and Commonwealth after 1945, and latterly by economic and political refugees from poorer and strife-torn countries during the latter part of the century. This growing

band of ethnic minorities has changed the nature of British cities and arguably made the country a 'multicultural' society. But there are evident strains, sometimes violent, between immigrants and their British neighbours; many resist this loss of their old identity and argue that such people are at heart 'foreigners'. Lord Norman Tebbit controversially demanded that, when cricket teams arrived from their home countries, Commonwealth immigrants should support the English side. In practice, immigrants and their descendants now tend to assume a dual identity of 'black British' or 'British Asian'.

Yet another thread in this complex reworking of identities is the European Union. At the 'Congress of Europe' in May 1948 Winston Churchill made the chairman's address, including the words: 'I hope to see a Europe where men and women of every country will think of being European and wherever they go in this wide domain will truly feel, "I am at home".' The truth is that neither he nor Ernest Bevin, Labour Foreign Secretary from 1945 to 1951, actually believed all the warm words they said about a united Europe. Like US diplomats, they recognised a degree of unity as necessary to resist the Soviet threat and were not opposed to a closer coming together should the nations concerned wish it; the problem was that Britain, when it came down to it, did not.

Bevin had explained in 1946 that Britain saw herself as a 'great power', adding that 'the very fact we have fought so hard for liberty, and paid such a high price, warrants our retaining that position' (Gamble 2003: 189). So Europe was seen as something separate from Britain, which still sat at the 'big boys' table. When the European Iron and Steel Community was established in 1950 – the organisational template, as it turned out, for the later European Community – Britain loftily stood aside, refusing to allow any mere Europeans to decide how these nationalised concerns should be run. The same thing happened with the developments up to 1957 when the Treaty of Rome established the new experiment in supranationalism. Clement Attlee summed up a dominant British political class view of Europe when he said:

The so-called Common Market of six nations. Know them all well. Very recently, this country spent a great deal of blood and treasury rescuing four of 'em from attacks by the other two.

It is no surprise that Britain initially was not interested but then the devastating American rebuff of Suez, plus the signs that British capitalism was unable to keep pace with the new dynamic customs union based in Brussels, brought about a dramatic change of emphasis and potential allegiance. Britain applied in 1959 and received another rebuff, this time courtesy of General De Gaulle who repeated the trick in 1967. Running behind the bus trying to catch it and then being thrown off when we did was not the best early experience to have of this economically integrated Europe. We finally made it in 1972 when the General had left the stage and a staunchly Europhile Ted Heath was able to manufacture a majority Commons vote for entry.

But dissent was by no means stilled. At first it was the Labour left which cavilled at this 'capitalist club' but under Thatcher it was the right-wing Conservatives who gave full expression to an anti-European position. They could not begin to accept that the British identity, forged by a thousand years of history, a worldwide empire and heroic struggles against tyranny, could be meekly subsumed into what Margaret Thatcher liked to call 'The Belgian

Empire'. Against what proved to be her better judgement she acceded to measures of greater integration but then, after leaving office, became an avid and bitter cheerleader for the Eurosceptic cause. Polls showed that upwards of a third of Britons tended to agree with her.

The dilemma for Britain's changing sense of identity now emerged starkly during the 1980s and 1990s. The Tory right preferred America to Europe: the American attitude to economics, welfare and, indeed, the management of world order. When Labour entered government many felt this identification would swing back towards our partners in Europe. Certainly Blair subscribed to the Social Chapter upon which Conservative sceptics had poured so much vitriol and joined in the EU (as it was called after Maastricht in 1992) summits, but his desire for Britain to join the common currency, the euro, was prevented by his Chancellor Gordon Brown to whom Blair had conceded virtual control of the economy. So entry into the EU's inner counsels was prevented; EU opponents were pleased and hoped Labour would maintain the pro-American bias favoured by many Conservatives. Brown, in any case, is a warm admirer of the American economic model and had tried hard to keep employment 'flexible', unlike many EU countries where pro-worker employment laws hold down productivity. But the biggest shifting of Gamble's 'four spheres' occurred after the 9/11 attack on the World Trade Center in New York (see Figure 6.1).

At this point, when the world stood back in horror, Blair was quick to offer his 'shoulder to shoulder' support for the USA. Other EU partners expressed outrage but none could match the fervour of Blair's support. Later Blair sent in troops to Afghanistan and then, much more controversially, to Iraq. British public opinion was similar to that of most EU countries, even those who supported George W. Bush – very sympathetic to the USA in the wake of the 9/11 attack but two-thirds of voters were not prepared to envisage an invasion against Iraq, however dreadful its ruler might be. Bush and Defence Secretary Rumsfeld's apparent arrogant disregard for multilateral solutions alienated much of European and British opinion. Blair refused to be drawn towards the EU consensus and remained true to his earlier position, matching Bush's rhetoric with his own. But Blair did have an idea of the role his country should perform; as he said in January 2003: 'We can help to be a bridge between the US and Europe.' The problems associated with such a route

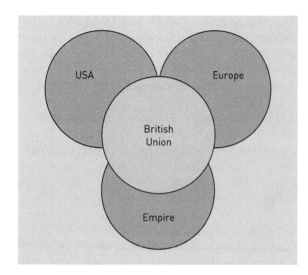

Figure 6.1 The Four Circles of England: in his *Between Europe and America* (2003), Andrew Gamble (pp. 30–4) quotes Churchill's view that Britain lay at the touching point of three circles – Empire, Europe and America. Gamble argues that since devolution, a fourth, that of the 'British Union', should be added

to a new identity were threefold. Firstly, Blair had shown a heavy bias towards the US, philosophically in terms of economic systems and politically in terms of its world role as a hyper-power. Secondly, Europe's two biggest and leading countries, France and Germany, both leaders and voters, were not as enamoured of the US as Tony Blair. Thirdly, on the major issues like Iraq, British public opinion was closer to America's European critics than to Blair's enthusiastic and uncritical support.

'Britishness'

Linda Colley (2005), in her book, *Britons: Forging the Nation 1707–1837*, argues that British people, known as such since the Act of Union 1707 with Scotland, tend to have a 'layered' sense of being British plus an often even closer identity like Scottish, Welsh, Northern Irish, Asian or Caribbean; oddly perhaps 'English' is more often regarded as interchangeable with 'British'. Some polling evidence suggests that the 'British' layer has given way to the connecting identity, so that many now feel more English, Scottish and so forth than the composite 'British'. Gordon Brown was clearly seeking to minimise his Scottishness by emphasising the importance of 'Britishness'. In January 2006 he even suggested a national day for 'Britain', explaining he

wished to 'recapture the union flag from the far right'. In a reference to the 7/7 bombings he added:

We have to face uncomfortable facts that while the British response to July 7th was remarkable, they were British citizens, British born apparently integrated into our communities, who were prepared to maim and kill fellow British citizens irrespective of their religion.

■ Green thinking

The ecological perspective rejects philosophies of the right, left and centre as more similar than dissimilar. Sir Jonathon Porritt (a senior environment adviser to the Blair government) characterises them collectively as '**industrialism**': this 'super-ideology . . . conditioned to thrive on the ruthless exploitation of both people and planet, is itself the greatest threat we face' (Porritt 1984). Conservatives, socialists and centre politicians argue about rival economic approaches – individualism versus collectivism and how the cake of national income should be sliced up and distributed – but they all agree that the size of the cake should be increased through vigorous economic growth. This is the central proposition that the Greens most emphatically reject. 'Industrialism', they say, is predicated on the continuous expansion of the goods and services and on the promotion of even more consumption through advertising and the discovery of an increasing range of 'needs'. It creates great inequalities whereby a rich and envied minority set the pace in lavish and unnecessary consumption while a substantial number – in many countries a majority – are either unemployed or live in relative, perhaps dire poverty. The Conservatives have presided over an increase in income differentials but have offered economic growth as a panacea: more for the rich and more for the poor. Porritt observes:

If the system works, i.e. we achieve full employment, we basically destroy the planet; if it doesn't, i.e. we end up with mass unemployment, we destroy the lives of millions of people . . . From an industrial point of view it is rational to . . . promote wasteful consumption, to discount social costs, to destroy the environment. From the Green point of view it is totally irrational, simply because we hold true to the most important political reality of all: that all wealth ultimately derives from the finite resources of our planet.

Porritt (1984: 46–7)

The Green view goes on to adduce a number of basic principles:

1 *A world approach*: All human activity should reflect appreciation of the world's finite resources and easily damaged ecology.

2 *Respect the rights of our descendants*: Our children have the right to inherit a beautiful and bountiful planet rather than an exhausted and polluted one.

3 *Sufficiency*: We should be satisfied with 'enough' rather than constantly seeking 'more'.

4 *A conserver economy*: We must conserve what we have rather than squander it through pursuit of high-growth strategies.

5 *Care and share*: Given that resources are limited, we must shift our energies to sharing what we have and looking after all sections of society properly.

6 *Self-reliance*: We should learn to provide for ourselves rather than surrendering responsibility to specialised agencies.

7 *Decentralise and democratise*: We must form smaller units of production, encourage cooperative enterprises and give people local power over their own affairs. At the same time, international integration must move forward rapidly.

Porritt maintains that this amounts to a wholly alternative view of rationality and mankind's existence. He contrasts the two world-views of industrialism and ecology in Table 6.1.

Inevitably, the other major parties have done all they can to climb aboard the Green bandwagon, cloaking their policies in light green clothes

Table 6.1 Two worlds: industrialism versus ecology

Industrialism	Ecology
The environment	
Domination over nature	Harmony with nature
Environment managed as a resource	Resources regarded as strictly finite
High energy, high consumption	Low energy, low consumption
Nuclear power	Renewable sources of energy
Values	
An ethos of aggressive individualism	Cooperatively based communitarian society with emphasis on personal autonomy
Pursuit of material goods	Move towards spiritual, non-material values
Rationality and packaged knowledge	Intuition and understanding
Patriarchal values, hierarchical structure	Post-patriarchal feminist values, non-hierarchical structure
Unquestioning acceptance of technology	Discriminating use and development of science and technology
The economy	
Economic growth and demand stimulation	Sustainability, quality of life and simplicity
Production for exchange and profit	Production for use
High income differentials	Low income differentials
A free-market economy	Local production for local need
Ever-expanding world trade	Self-reliance
Employment as a means to an end	Work as an end in itself
Capital-intensive production	Labour-intensive production
Political organisation	
Centralisation, economies of scale	Decentralisation, human scale
Representative democracy	Direct democracy, participative involvement
Sovereignty of nation-state	Internationalism and global solidarity
Institutionalised violence	Non-violence

Source: Adapted from Porritt (1984) *Seeing Green*, pp. 216–17

47

and shamelessly stealing the rhetoric of the environmentalists.

As it currently stands, the Greens' political programme is unlikely to fall within the 'art of the possible' (see below). It has established some support among students, and in 1994 it gained four council seats, but its best parliamentary performance was in 1989, when it managed 6.1 per cent of the vote in Lambeth, Vauxhall. In May 2003 Greens won seven seats in the Scottish Parliament. In 2005 the Greens fielded 202 candidates but not one got elected. Hardly a launching pad for power, but as Malcolm Muggeridge once pointed out, 'utopias flourish in chaos', and if global warming continues unchecked accompanied by more environmental chaos, it may well be the Greens who inherit politically what is left of the Earth, if it is not already too late by then.

BOX 6.6   IDEAS AND PERSPECTIVES

Global warming

Of all the many dangers facing the world's environment, it has been the problem of global warming that has most exercised environmentalists and governments in recent years.

The scientific argument on 'greenhouse' gases

It is an obvious fact that the earth receives its warmth from the sun. However, certain gases within the earth's atmosphere have been crucial in helping retain the sun's heat over the billions of years life has been evolving. Some of the sun's heat is reflected back into space but the retention of a portion of this heat, absorbed by the gases, has enabled the earth to achieve a temperature ideal for supporting life. Indeed, without such gases the average temperature of the world would have been −15°C instead of +18°C.

The first person to make the link between climate and greenhouse gases was the Swedish scientist Svante Arrhenius in 1898. He calculated that a doubling of CO_2 would increase world temperatures by 5–6°C. Other scientists observed that volcanic eruptions of sulphur dioxide into the atmosphere, which reflects sunlight, causes a degree of cooling. Some have attributed global warming to the lack of volcanic activity in the twentieth century. In 1988 the UN established the Intergovernmental Panel on Climate Change. The IPCC's latest estimate is of a warming of between 1.4 and 5.8°C by 2100 depending on what is done to curb gas emissions (IPCC 2001). Other studies suggest even higher rates of warming.

Consequences of global warming

The earth's temperature has provided the conditions in which humans have evolved and flourished, but rapidly rising temperatures would cause deforestation, the loss of fishing stocks, the collapse of many crops, outbreaks of many more destructive tropical storms, the melting of vast permafrosted areas (which would also release massive new stored reserves of CO_2) and the gradual melting of the ice-caps, causing catastrophic rises in sea level amounting to over 200 feet.

The developing world

The surging economies of China and India – often using CO_2-rich emitting energy production methods – hugely increase the threats, but it is hard for the developed world to insist that poorer countries forego the benefits and comforts which the West has enjoyed for many years. Awareness of the dangers grew throughout the latter half of the twentieth century, and in 1997 an agreement was reached at Kyoto whereby signatories agreed to reduce emissions to 5 per cent below the 1990 levels by 2010; in practice this means a reduction of 29 per cent in all greenhouse gases. Developing countries were excluded from this requirement, but the biggest problem lay with the reluctance of the USA to ratify the agreement.

With only 5 per cent of the world's population, the world's biggest economy emits a quarter of the world's CO_2. Energy lobbies in the USA vigorously disputed the thesis that the planet's climate is heating up.

George W. Bush, originally an oil man and advised by many more, refused to accept the Kyoto Protocol. One of his advisers, Myron Ebell, attacked the statement of David King, Britain's Chief Scientific Officer, that global warming was more of a threat to the future of the world than terrorism, on the grounds that King did not have the scientific expertise. He also claimed the whole global warming story was a scare tactic created by Europe to enable their ailing economies to compete more effectively against the USA. Barack Obama, elected in 2008, basically accepts the arguments and has pledged to reverse Bush's policy on this issue.

Scepticism about global warming remains despite the fact that 99 per cent of scientists in this area of study insist it is a fact. Some people argue that climate has always varied, with the Thames regularly freezing over in the Middle Ages, and Ice Ages occurring not infrequently. Scientists riposte that of the warmest 20 years ever experienced, 16 have happened during the last quarter-century and match almost precisely increases in CO_2 as a proportion of the atmosphere. Temperature increases of that kind are unprecedented and are conclusive evidence that we do have an acute problem which could conceivably lead to the ending of all human life.

The United Kingdom
The UK was an enthusiastic signatory of Kyoto and at first made good progress towards the agreed goal, assisted by a switch of power stations from coal to gas. The 2005 Labour manifesto set a target of 20 per cent, well above the required Kyoto level, but as the deadline has approached performance has declined. On 28 March 2006, Margaret Beckett, the then environment secretary, announced that reductions were likely to be in the range 15–18 per cent instead, blaming increased economic growth and the rise in oil prices which had caused many power stations to return to coal use. Since then recession-affected economic shrinkage will probably reduce emissions in the UK and worldwide. (See also Chapter 26.)

■ The political fringe

The political fringe is the name given to those small factions and groups that often do their political work outside the conference halls of the main parties rather than within them. Those who belong are often determined ideologues, given to regular argument in groups prone to splits and factions. They do have some intrinsic interest, however, as microcosms of political ideas and conflicts. It must also be remembered that in the early part of this century the Labour Party was just such a small faction, snapping around the heels of the Liberal Party. Yet within a couple of decades it was actually in power and destined to be there – with a huge majority – as the new millennium started.

Far left

Marx, Lenin and Stalin

Most far left groups owe their intellectual debts to Karl Marx. He argued that under a capitalist economy rich property owners would so drive down wages in pursuit of profits and a competitive edge that a vast army of impoverished workers would eventually rise up and sweep away the whole corrupt system. Once private property had been abolished, working people would begin to live new and better lives in an economy in which people would work willingly for each other and not reluctantly for an employer. It did not quite work out that way.

After the Marxist takeover of power in Russia in 1917, a period of great hardship and economic instability followed. Lenin established a political system based on centralised control supported by a network of secret police. He believed in the need for a 'vanguard party' of professional revolutionaries to lead the masses – who were deluded by agencies of capitalism into a 'false consciousness' – when the time came. There had to be rigid discipline and acceptance of the vanguard party's 'dictatorship of the proletariat' while it implemented socialism. Communists claimed that this was the transitional stage the USSR had achieved by the early 1920s, when Lenin died.

49

Joseph Stalin (1879–1953)

Soviet dictator. Trained as a priest before becoming a revolutionary in Georgia, Russia. Was secretary to Lenin's Communist Party and after his death deviously manipulated his enemies out of power while placing his own supporters in key positions. Became unchallenged dictator in 1930s and tried to neutralise Hitler by doing a deal with him. Hitler broke the agreement and attacked the USSR in 1941. After initial reverses the Soviets fought back under Stalin's leadership and defeated Hitler. Despite his brutal behaviour Stalin won friends on the left in Western countries, who persisted in believing his propaganda and seeing him as a force for progress.

USSR. Members managed to survive the astonishing volte-face when Stalin ceased to oppose Hitler as first priority and signed a deal with him in 1939 to partition Poland. Once Hitler had invaded Soviet Russia in 1941, British communists breathed a sigh of relief; they were at last able to luxuriate in a vast amphitheatre of approving views as the whole country applauded the heroic Soviet effort. After the war, the party won two seats – Mile End and West Fife – but Stalin's expansion into Eastern Europe, his blockade of Berlin in 1948 and the crushing (after his death) of the Hungarian rising in 1956 by the Soviet military machine, not to mention Khrushchev's denunciation of Stalin in his secret speech to the 20th Party Congress, substantially disillusioned communists and Moscow 'fellow travellers' alike. The Cold War effectively ruined the chances of communist parties achieving power anywhere in Europe, and they began to wither and atrophy.

Trotsky – advocate of 'worldwide revolution' – was Lenin's heir apparent, but the dogged, apparently un-intellectual Joseph Stalin, Secretary of the Party, was cleverer than his brilliant colleague. He urged 'socialism in one country' rather than working for an unlikely international conflagration; he out-manoeuvred his rivals and plotted ruthlessly, succeeding in presenting Trotsky as a traitor to the revolution. Stalin eventually drove Trotsky into exile in Mexico, where his agents succeeded in assassinating him in 1940 (see Biography).

Stalin, by then, had become a brutal dictator, both paranoid and obsessed with power, claiming to be implementing **communism** but in reality imposing industrialisation, collective farming and his own tyrannical rule on a reluctant and starving peasantry. Anyone less than obsequiously worshipful of their leader was imprisoned, exiled or shot. Overseas communist parties were employed essentially to assist the development of the 'home of socialism', and any deviation from the party line was punished by expulsion or worse.

This is the legacy inherited by extreme left-wing parties in Britain. The Communist Party of Great Britain (CPGB) was founded in 1920 and became the willing tool of Moscow's message in this country, interpreting all the shifts in the official line and condemning anyone perceived as an enemy of the

Leon Trotsky (1879–1940)

Leon Trotsky was a Russian Jewish revolutionary politician born in the Ukraine. He was arrested for being a Marxist at the age of 19 but escaped from Siberia in 1902. After teaming up with Lenin, he became president of the first soviet in St Petersburg after the abortive 1905 revolution. He escaped to the West but returned to Russia in March 1917 to assist Lenin in organising the Bolshevik Revolution in November of the same year. He conducted peace negotiations with the Germans and led the Red Army of five million men in the ensuing civil war. An inspiring and charismatic leader as well as brilliant intellectually, Trotsky should have succeeded Lenin in 1924, but his theories of permanent world revolution were less well suited to the times than Stalin's pragmatic 'socialism in one country'; he was eventually exiled in 1929, being assassinated in Mexico with an ice pick in 1940 by Ramon del Rio, an agent of Moscow. His ideas live on, but mostly on the radical intellectual fringe in developed countries.

In the 1970s and 1980s opposition to communism in Eastern Europe intensified, and the accession of the liberal Mikhail Gorbachev to power in Moscow was the signal for bloodless revolutions throughout the former communist bloc, with only China, Cuba, Vietnam and Laos being spared. The CPGB split into a hard-line pro-Moscow rump and a liberal 'Euro-communist' wing, with the latter seizing control. It tried to transform itself into 'an open, democratic party of the new pluralistic and radical left'. In 1991 it ceased to be the CPGB and renamed itself the Democratic Left, though with little public support. Some of its former supporters, however, stuck with the party paper, *The Morning Star*, and founded the Communist Party of Britain – to little political effect: it has never fought a parliamentary election.

Trotskyism

A number of Trotskyite bodies sprang up during and after Trotsky's lifetime, calling for worldwide revolution. Ted Grant, a South African, was involved with some of them, such as the Militant Labour League, in the 1930s. With Peter Taafe, Grant set up the *Militant* newspaper and adopted the tactic of 'entryism', the idea being to infiltrate members of a 'Militant Tendency' (notice only a 'tendency' and not a separate party, which would have breached Labour rules) into the decaying structure of the 1960s Labour Party. The idea then was to seize leadership at the grass-roots level and, in theory, the country once the time for revolution arrived. The Tendency virtually controlled Liverpool City Council in the 1980s, and two members, Dave Nellist and Terry Fields, were elected MPs, plus Pat Wall for Bradford in 1987 (died 1990). They advocated a number of radical measures, including nationalisation of the top 200 companies, extension of state control over the whole economy, workers' control in state-owned industries, nationalisation of the media, a slashing of defence spending, withdrawal from the EC and abolition of the House of Lords. In 1992, the Tendency expelled its guru Ted Grant, ending its policy of entryism; the movement gave way to Militant Labour, still attempting to influence the Labour Party, but most of the prominent members had faded away and the MPs not only lost their seats but were first expelled from the party. However, Militant MPs, while exercising little influence during their time in the Commons, did impress with their dedication, hard work and refusal to accept more salary for themselves than a skilled worker.

The Workers' Revolutionary Party

Another Trotskyist thread into the colourful tapestry of the far left was provided by 'The Club', a grouping, led by Gerry Healy, which left the Revolutionary Socialist Party in 1947 to infiltrate the Labour Party. Healy was soon expelled from Labour for his Trotskyite views and put his energies into a new party to express and promote the views of his hero. The idea, as with all such parties, is to build up battle-hardened cadres to seize power when capitalism collapses, as it must, in its view. Its newspaper, *Newsline*, was rumoured in the seventies to be funded by Libya's Colonel Qadhafi. Membership was never high and suffered from Healy's imperious and eccentric leadership style, which led to the WRP actually splitting into two versions in the eighties and to his finally being deposed shortly afterwards. Celebrity members such as Vanessa Redgrave and her brother Corin, who stood as candidates in 1974 and 1979, gave the party a high media profile. The WRP still exists, led by Sheila Torrence, and still publishes *Newsline*.

The Socialist Workers' Party

Tony Cliff, who founded the Socialist Workers' Party, left the Labour Party at the beginning of the 1960s. His party has concentrated on international revolution, and international links are stressed. Paul Foot (1938–2004), nephew of Michael and a national columnist, was a high-profile and persuasive member. The SWP prints a newspaper, *Socialist Worker*, touted by young converts in many British cities and towns. It was also behind the Anti-Nazi League, set up to fight the growth of European Nazism in the 1970s and then revived in 1992 after the rise of the BNP in Britain. These initiatives won an influx of new members; since that heyday it has shrunk though remains active in fighting its causes and supporting Respect (see below) in local elections.

The Socialist Labour Party

This was formed in 1996 by miners' leader Arthur Scargill following his failure to prevent the rewriting of Clause Four at Labour's conference in 1995. 'We recognise only two classes in society, both of which are recognised by their relationship to the means of production', he explained. 'Our problems are the result of a rotten capitalist system.' Accordingly, his party favours common ownership of the economy,

Socialist Worker

www.socialistworker.co.uk

80p | No 1995 | 8 April 2006

THE DAY TO BURY BLAIR

MAY 4

SR

THE SOCIALIST REVIEW

MAGAZINE WITH SOCIALIST WORKER THIS WEEK

● **Strike to save our pensions**
● **Vote Respect in the local elections**

TONY BLAIR hopes he can ride out the storms of protest over the murderous war in Iraq. He hopes he can brush aside the resistance to the government's plunder of workers' pensions and the plans to make us all work longer.

He hopes he can insert private companies at the very centre of the NHS and schools before he leaves 10 Downing Street.

But on Thursday 4 May we can all do something to bring Blair down sooner rather than later. In the local elections we can campaign and vote for Respect.

If Respect councillors sweep into town halls it will be one of the most powerful weapons to pitch Blair out of office.

And trade union activists are pushing for 4 May to be part of a two-day strike that would

repeat and extend the electrifying success of the 28 March strike over pensions.

We cannot afford to let Blair survive a day longer. Victories for Respect and massive strikes over pensions can make 4 May a day from which he never recovers.

**Pensions action >>page 2
Respect election campaign >>page 5**

Egypt's year of resistance
Pages 8&9

Anne Alexander speaks to three women who took up arms against imperialism in 1956

A dirty little secret exposed
Page 3

Simon Basketter reveals the blacklists of union militants held by construction bosses

France at the crossroads
Pages 4&16

François Chesnais, Jim Wolfreys, Danièle Obono, Pierre Khalfa and Basile Pot report on days of hope in France

Beckett: a lust for despair?
Page 13

Sinead Kennedy looks at the life and work of the radical Irish playwright

US lied to cover-up massacres in Iraq

THE US has been caught trying to lay the blame for a massacre of Iraqi civilians on the resistance. The revelations come as reports of two new attrocities have surfaced.

The US claimed that one soldier and 15 Iraqi civilians—including seven women and three children—were killed by an insurgent attack on the town of Haditha in November.

But an investigation by Time magazine exposed the story as a lie. Time discovered that US troops went on the rampage through the town in revenge for the death of a Marine earlier that day.

Soldiers then tried to cover up the murders by claiming the civilians were killed by an insurgent bomb.

The revelation comes after the killing of 37 worshipers on

26 March during a US raid on a Shia Muslim mosque in eastern Baghdad.

The US claimed the men were killed after they fired on troops. But locals say that the men were executed by an Iraqi death squad under the control of a US officer.

The attack on the mosque came the day after Iraqi police published an official report on a massacre in the village of Abu Sifa, 37 miles north of Baghdad.

In that attack, which took place on 15 March, 11 civilians were killed, including four children and a six month old baby.

The report states, "US forces gathered the family in one room and executed 11 people, including five children, four women and two men, then they bombed the house, burned three vehicles and killed their animals."

A bad day out for Condi and Jack >>page 6

Trotskyist left urges voters to dump Blair.

Source: Courtesy of *The Socialist Worker*

full employment, a four-day week, a ban on non-essential overtime, retirement at 56, restoration of union rights, abolition of the monarchy, House of Lords and public schools, and withdrawal from the EU. Only 500 attended the launch in May 1996. Scargill fought for the seat of Newport East against Alan Howarth in 1997 and for Hartlepool against Peter Mandelson in 2001 but polled negligibly.

The Socialist Alliance

This was a novel 'umbrella' organisation of left-wing parties that fought the 2001 general election. It was chaired by Dave Nellist, the former Militant MP, and its manifesto was both a scathing critique of New Labour as no better than Thatcherism and a hard-won (far left groups find it hard to agree) common

---

BOX 6.7   IDEAS AND PERSPECTIVES

The strange case of *Living Marxism*

This magazine, a descendant of the CPGB's *Marxism Today*, morphed into the more modern-sounding *LM* in the late 1990s when it published an article accusing ITN of fabricating the discovery of an apparently emaciated Muslim in a detention camp which in reality was a haven for such refugees. The magazine was sued, lost the action and was forced to close. But it is the provenance of the magazine and the movement it subsequently set in train which are so interesting for students of the far left. The story is traced to 1974 when a Trotskyist faction split from the International Socialists (now the Socialist Workers' Party) – which, in the words of David Pallister and colleagues (*Guardian*, 8 July 2000), 'used to spend most of its time in textual agonizing over the third volume of *Das Kapital*' – to form the Revolutionary Communist Group.

The RCG saw its role as training a 'vanguard elite to storm the citadels of capitalism'. However, Trotskyist groupings are notoriously both fickle and factional, and in 1976 one of the group's thinkers, David Yaffe, led out a like-minded section (broadly in favour of collaborating with certain other far left groups) called the Revolutionary Communist Tendency, later Party, or RCP. *Living Marxism* was its mouthpiece and, as such, it attracted notice for its intellectual energy and creativity. New RCP members were often recruited in 'up-market' places like Oxbridge and Covent Garden and after a period of 'political education' were encouraged to enter the professions, often those associated with the media or academe, and then donate a proportion of their salaries to the party.

In the wake of the Cold War's demise came a change of direction: the RCP was disbanded and *Living Marxism* became *LM*, the *raison d'être* for which was held to be 'freedom' – freedom to challenge, to offend, to say what one wanted. Under the influence of two thinkers, Frank Furedi (Professor of Sociology at the University of Kent) and former social worker Claire Fox, *LM* waged war on what was held to be government-manufactured panics over issues like GM foods, child rearing, AIDS as a heterosexual disease, and much else besides.

'The spirit of *LM*', in Furedi's words, 'is to go against the grain: to oppose all censorship, bans and regulations and codes of conduct; to stand up for social and scientific experimentation; to insist that we have the right to live as autonomous adults who take responsibility for our own affairs.'

The mission of the '*LM* Group' was alleged by some to be a permeation of the opinion-forming professions; Fox's Institute of Ideas and *LM* magazine were two facilitating agencies to these ends, organising seminars and conferences, involving 'Establishment' bodies like the Institute for Contemporary Arts and intellectuals like Blake Morrison, Lisa Jardine and Linda Grant.

This philosophy of 'ban nothing, question everything', unsurprisingly, found supporters on the libertarian right. Pallister *et al.* suggest that the grouping of right-wing **think tanks** and research institutes in the US known as the 'Freedom Network' offered a source of like-minded ideas, support and, indeed, quite possibly finance. So, we see a slightly weird evolution here of an extreme left faction morphing into new forms, imploding and then becoming a broader cultural movement which joined hands with groups that are sufficiently far to the right to make poor old Leon Trotsky revolve in his grave (see also Box 4.2 on Libertarianism for links with the far right, in Chapter 4).

agenda for an 'alternative to the global, unregulated free market'. However, the results did not augur well for future growth and success. The candidates who stood received very low percentages of the vote and the Alliance seemed to have closed down in 2005 but its website promises it is 'coming back'.

Respect: The Unity Coalition

This body was set up in 2004 as a result of collaboration between George Galloway, the SWP and members of the Muslim Association of Britain to campaign principally against the ongoing war in Iraq. Galloway was formerly the talented but maverick MP for a Glasgow constituency, expelled from Labour in 2004 for calling on British troops to disobey orders. He fought a clever, though much criticised, campaign in Hackney and Bethnal Green against the sitting MP, Oona King, and won a sensational victory. Apart from its anti-war stance, Respect offers a left-wing socialist prospectus including the end of privatisation and 'the bringing back into democratic public ownership of the other public services'.

John Callaghan, the authority on the far left, judges that 'far left politics is dying in its Leninist form and has moved into Green and anti-globalisation movements and has involved former militants from Muslim communities' (e-mail to author, 8 April 2006). But he makes a shrewd point when he points out that far left politics often act as an apprenticeship for future mainstream politicians, citing Alan Milburn and Stephen Byers (former Trotskyists) and John Reid (former member of the CPGB).

Far right

Fascism

This set of ideas, developed by Benito Mussolini in the 1920s and supplemented by Adolf Hitler in the 1930s, was founded on xenophobic nationalism and total submission to the state. Democracy was scorned as the language of weakness and mediocrity; a one-party totalitarian state led by a charismatic leader was the preferred alternative. The leader and his team were seen as the result of an evolving process whereby the best people and ideas won through. It followed that the same thing happened when nations fought; war was the means whereby nations grew and developed. Hitler added a racial twist: the Aryans were the founding race of

BIOGRAPHY

Adolf Hitler (1889–1945)

German dictator. Was originally an Austrian who tried to make a living as an artist. Fought in the First World War and set up the racist, expansionist Nazi movement in the 1920s. Came to power in the early 1930s and set about dominating Europe via threats, invasions and finally all-out war. In 1942 he dominated the continent but his decision to invade Russia and to declare war on the USA eventually proved his downfall. Still retains his admirers on the political fringe.

Europe, a race of conquerors, and the Germans their finest exemplars; all other races were inferior; the Jews in particular were lower than vermin and should therefore be destroyed. In the stressful inter-war years, racked by economic depression and unemployment, these unwholesome ideas seemed attractive and full of hope to many who faced despair as their only alternative. It is emotionally satisfying perhaps to blame one's troubles on a single group in society, especially one that is quite easily recognisable physically and very successful economically and culturally. It has also to be said that such ideas flourished in the fertile soil of a German culture sympathetic to anti-Semitism.

In Britain, Sir Oswald Mosley founded a party that evolved into the British Union of Fascists, offering himself as the strong charismatic national leader who would end the party bickering and lead the country into new successes. Mosley proposed that employers and workers should combine in the national interest and work in harmony; strikes and lock-outs should be banned; all major elements in the productive process should work together to plan the economy (corporatism). Moreover, he argued that the British Empire would provide all the things the country needed, and imports that could be made in Britain would be banned. Parliament and the old parties would be reformed and MPs would be elected according to occupational groups. Once elected, Parliament would pass on power to the leader to introduce the 'corporate state'. Parties and Parliament would be ended; everyone and everything would be 'subordinated to the national purpose'. Mosley's anti-Semitism was disguised in Britain, but his coded references to 'alien influences' were clear enough to most Britons; he favoured sending all the Jews in the world to a barren reservation. When it was revealed that Hitler's remedy to his self-invented 'Jewish problem' had been genocide of the most horrifying kind, a revulsion set in against fascist ideas. But they have proved unnervingly resilient and still appear in the present time in a different form.

The National Front and the BNP

In 1967 the National Front (NF) was formed. Its central message was a racist one, warning against dilution of the British race via intermarriage with other races of different colour which it believed would produce an inferior breed of Briton. Repatriation of black Britons was the answer offered. At the level of theory, however, the Jews were offered as the main threats, being characterised as an international conspiracy to subvert Western economies and introduce communism before setting up a world government based in Israel. This side of the NF and its utter contempt for democracy was disguised in public expressions, but it exercised considerable appeal to young men with a taste for violence and racial hatred. It later changed its name to the National Democrats. In 1983 the 'New' NF – later the British National Party – was born; this is dedicated to infiltration and is more secretive, having many contacts with neo-Nazi groups abroad and many terrorist groups too. Football supporters are often infiltrated by NF members, and in 1994 a friendly football match between Ireland and England was abandoned following thuggish violence instigated by the NF. A related body called Combat 18 (the number in the name relates to the order in the alphabet of Hitler's initials: AH) openly supports Nazi ideas and embraces violence as a political method.

The BNP at the 1997 general election

As previously, the general election of May 1997 saw the usual multicoloured rainbow of fringe joke candidates. But for the far left and far right as well as the pranksters the result was widespread loss of deposits; voters may flirt with the fringe from time to time, but when the election arrives they revert, perhaps fortunately, to 'sensible' voting. In May 2002, the BNP won three council seats in Burnley –

the biggest electoral victory for the far right in two decades. The party's new leader, Nick Griffin, with his articulate style and Cambridge education (see quotation from the *Observer* below), gave the party a credibility with arguments that exploited the feelings of poor indigenous voters that somehow immigrants were not only changing the nature of their localities but also receiving favoured treatment. This was argued with particular success in respect of asylum seekers, an issue much loved by the tabloids. These developments worried the mainstream parties, which were keen to nip this electoral upturn in the bud.

The BNP has deliberately become increasingly sophisticated in the last few years to ensure ballot box success. . . . The irony is that it's New Labour who have shown us how to do it; we learnt from them that a party could change without losing its support base. New Labour dropped Old Labour in much the same way as we've moved on from the so-called 'skin head' era. We realized that the type of recruit we needed in the modern world was completely different to the sort we needed when we were engaging in street level activities.

Kevin Scott, North-East Director BNP, quoted in the *Observer*, 20 April 2003

The same issue of *The Observer* also published the facts that:

- Thirteen of the BNP's twenty-eight regional directors or branch organisers in 2002 had criminal records for offences that included assault, theft, fraud, racist abuse and possession of drugs and weapons.

- Two thousand racial attacks were recorded by the Home Office up to 2003 after the dispersal programme for asylum seekers began in 2001.

- In 2003, 221 seats were targeted by the BNP, including councils in Lincolnshire, Cumbria, Surrey, Hampshire, Somerset, Wiltshire, Devon and Cornwall. In the event, on 1 May 2003 the party won thirteen seats nationwide, including eight in Burnley; however, Nick Griffin lost his fight for a seat, and his party won no seats in Sunderland despite fielding twenty-five candidates.

- In 2004 a BBC undercover reporter recorded a speech in Keighley by Nick Griffin in which he said: 'These 18-, 19- and 25-year-old Asian Muslims are seducing and raping white girls in this town right now.' He continued: 'It's part of their plan for conquering countries. They will expand into the rest of the UK as the last Whites try and find their way to the sea. Vote BNP so the British people really realize the evil of what these people have done to our country.' This speech, and a similar one by a former Leeds City Council candidate, both faced charges of behaviour likely to incite racial hatred in January 2006, but both defendants were sensationally acquitted when the cases came to court in 2006.

The BNP in 2009

The history of British fringe politics might well make 2009 a 'breakthrough year' for the far right. Immigration issues still rankled among those made unemployed by the recession of that year and the BNP benefited from the widespread backlash of distrust of politics. In the Euro-elections of June

Labour came third behind UKIP but more worrying for many in the party was the fact that the lower turnout in the north-west had enabled the BNP to win two MEPs and therefore take a place of sorts on the national stage, rather than occupying its usual fringe position.

Following this the BBC felt obliged to invite the BNP leader Nick Griffin to participate in *Question Time*, the popular BBC show which provides something of a national showcase for different political viewpoints. The decision was fiercely contested by the likes of Peter Hain who claimed a 'clueless BBC is giving the BNP the legitimacy it craves' and quoted Griffin's own claim that his party aimed to 'defend rights for Whites with well-directed boots and fists'.

But it is hard to deny the BBC were acting within the democratic traditions of the country. In the event, the programme, on 22 October 2009, provoked much interest. Griffin was attacked by panel members (including Jack Straw and Chris Huhne) and the

BNP leader Nick Griffin celebrates his election as one of eight MEPs (Members of the European Parliament) for the north-west of England
Source: Getty Images / AFP

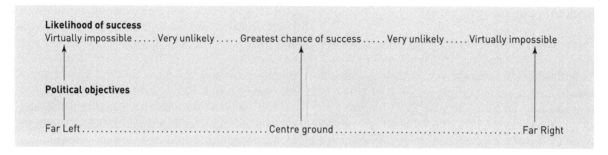

Figure 6.2 The art of the possible

The art of the possible

audience, and was generally felt to have been exposed as a second-rate politician. But his party had received a major publicity boost and it remains to be seen how beneficial it might prove to be.

Politicians on the fringe have made a conscious or unconscious decision regarding the 'art of the possible', Bismarck's acute definition of politics. As Figure 6.2 illustrates, political objectives on the extremes have little chance of success; the best chances exist in the political centre. It is the big mainstream parties that tend to set the agenda and to go on to achieve items upon it. Changing Labour's Clause Four on common ownership was held to be beyond the art of the possible for a long time after Gaitskell's attempt failed in the late 1950s. Later, Callaghan referred to the issue as 'theological', but Blair decided that such a change was necessary to convince the public that Labour was no longer dangerously radical. His brilliant campaign in 1994 to change the clause to some extent redefined the art of the possible (Figure 6.2) in the Labour Party. Items on the far left or right are either unattainable or achievable only if circumstances change radically and, usually, rapidly.

Parties on the fringe have two possible strategies to pursue. First, they can eschew any real chance of winning power and seek merely to change the hearts and minds of citizens to provide the context in which radical change can occur. Early socialists effectively performed this role until the creed became a credible alternative in the mid-twentieth century. Even so, it took over 100 years for socialism to win an electoral victory in Britain, so activists of this type have to be genuinely dedicated to change in the future; few are so patient. Alternatively, the less patient can seek to short-circuit the normal process of propagandising and winning over opinions by manipulating the democratic process. The really extreme activists on the right and left seek to set a revolutionary set of events in train and to seize power rather as the Bolsheviks did in Russia in 1917. As people usually need a substantial period to change their minds completely, this strategy usually requires the use of force, with all its attendant unpredictability and dangers. The early British communists and the Militants sought to reach the same objective through 'entryism': to drive their Trojan horse into a big party, Labour, and to win power through subterfuge. Seemingly underhand, this is not too disreputable a strategy given that the right-wing Conservatives led by Thatcher in the 1970s managed to achieve something similar by using the democratic machinery and then steering the party in a radical direction. Left-wing Labour tried a similar exercise in the early 1980s but was rebuffed so sharply by the electorate in 1983 that it left the way open for New Labour, maestros of the centre ground. So the radical socialist journalist Paul Foot sought to pursue the 'long haul' route of gradually changing social attitudes through education and exhortation. His uncle, Michael, also a fiery left-winger in his youth, decided to compromise a little and became a mainstream politician in the 1970s with a seat in the Cabinet and later a period as party leader. Time alone will tell how successful the agitators of the present will prove in the future, though those who articulate a 'green' perspective have seen their ideas move rapidly from the extreme left to somewhere much closer to the centre ground in a matter of only two to three decades. Moreover, the local and devolved assembly elections on 1 May 2003 saw one-in-eight voters casting their vote for parties on the political fringe, provoking the thought that maybe some of those groups on the fringe are destined in the near future to join the mainstream.

Radical Islam

This branch of 'fringe' thinking has come into sharp focus since 9/11 and the 7/7 bombings in London. Radical Islam sees it as the will of Allah to establish a world caliphate, to convert unbelievers either by persuasion or force. While such ideas seem to find little purchase in the USA, the 7/7 bombers were all second-generation immigrants to Britain from the Leeds area and ostensibly seemed well integrated into British society. It seems economically deprived areas of immigrant settlement nourishes radicalism with converts – like the Shoe Bomber, Richard Reid – particularly likely to take the extremist road.

Al Muhajiroun was a 1986 group led by Omar Bakri Muhammad which praised the 9/11 attacks and was banned under the 2006 Terrorism Act with Bakri expelled from the UK; however, it is believed the also banned *Saviour Sect*, is essentially a reformed version of *al Muhajiroun*. Abu Hamza al-Masri, a convicted terrorist, founded the Islamic Council of Britain, 11 September 2002, with the goal of 'implementing sharia law in Britain'. Other radical groups often are UK branches of transnational Islamic bodies like *Hizb ut-Tahrir*, an ostensibly peaceful grouping which some have claimed is a breeding ground for those who go on to adopt more extremist convictions.

BOX 6.8 BRITAIN IN CONTEXT

Themes and fringes

Box 5.3 in the last chapter focused on the political spectrum, my case being that in the USA it is not especially wide with very little support for left of centre positions or, indeed, for those right of centre as well. However, this should not be taken to imply that there are no groups occupying positions substantially to the left and right. Far from it.

The Socialist Party of America was born at the turn of the nineteenth century. Its leader, Eugene Debs, not only went to jail for his beliefs but stood for President on more than one occasion, yet never quite managed to poll a million votes. He was succeeded by Norman Thomas, a graduate of Princeton and a lay minister who also stood for the highest office but did no better than Debs in the end.

During the 1930s Roosevelt's New Deal, with its extensive government intervention in the economy, was implicitly socialist, but after the Second World War the backlash began with any left-wing idea being associated with communism and 'un-American' activities. The resultant McCarthyite witch hunts of the 1950s further weakened the left, but the socialist tradition survives in the form of The Socialist Party of the USA – not a major force, with affiliates in only 18 states. The Communist Party of the USA is even smaller and more ineffective. But there is, at the present time, the Progressive Coalition of House of Representatives

members, numbering about sixty, who subscribe to a socialistic set of ideas. However, the only real force on the left is the Democratic Party, and this tends to deter those tending to the left from switching support to a small party with no chance of achieving power. Almost certainly, however, the groups on the far right are more powerful than those on the left.

One variety of socialism, the National Socialist Movement (NSM), is in fact on the far right, being admirers of Nazi Germany and the policies of Hitler. But the main blanket term for the far right is the 'Patriot Movement'. This takes in the militias which operate in well over half of the states together with the rifle clubs and survivalist clubs. These groups, many of them steeped in ultra-nationalism and anti-Semitism, were influential in motivating John McVeigh, the Oklahoma Bomber. The worrying aspect of such right-wing groupings is that they reject the *legitimacy* of government, its right to issue laws and levy taxes. Similarly, groups representing the Afro-American minority in the 1960s and 1970s, like the Black Panthers and the Weathermen, refused to accept government authority and were prepared to use violence as a method.

Another characteristic of US society not reflected to the same degree in the UK is the 'culture wars' within it. Here we see groups who believe that a changing society which includes a large number of single-parent families, a variety of races and people of contrasting sexual preferences requires a more liberal and flexible set of values, especially towards sexuality and abortion. Other groups, however, often motivated by religious convictions, hotly resist such a move and are determined, for example, to reverse the Supreme Court ruling which makes abortion legal.

Often supported by their churches, a large section of American society feel that family values are under severe attack and need to be defended against the compromised attitudes of current urban life, reinforced by the media and popular music. Almost 40 per cent of Americans regularly attend church and, under George W. Bush, such leanings have acquired political significance. In Britain only about 5 per cent of people attend church and religion generally has scant influence.

Chapter summary

Feminism is concerned with the unequal position of women in society and falls into liberal, socialist and radical categories. Nationalism emerged in the nineteenth century and, while it is now contested by internationalism, still retains much of its destructive force. Green thinking applies environmentalism to politics, calling for a revolutionary change in the way developed societies live. Far left fringe groups tend to draw on the ideas of Marx and Trotsky; their relevance has declined since the anti-communist revolutions, but many followers still keep up the struggle. Far right groups tend to be neo-fascist and racialist; their support is small but their influence subversive.

Discussion points

■ Has feminism achieved any major victories, and if so what are they?

■ What problems are there in defining the British identity?

■ Is nationalism more dangerous than terrorism?

■ What chance is there of the Greens ever winning power in the UK?

■ Why do you think people join fringe political groups?

Further reading

Lovenduski and Randall (1993) is a thorough review of feminism in Britain; the political ideas books by Adams (1993) and Heywood (1992) have good sections on nationalism; and Dobson (1990) and Porritt (1984) are good on ecology. An excellent study of totalitarianism is Arendt

(1951). On fascism, also recommended is Cheles et al. (1991); Thurlow (1986) is a history of British fascism to the present day.

Bibliography

Adams, I. (1993) *Political Ideology Today* (Manchester University Press).

Adams, I. (1998) *Ideology and Politics in Britain Today* (Manchester University Press).

Arendt, H. (1951) *The Origins of Totalitarianism* (Allen and Unwin).

Bentley, R., Dorey, P. and Roberts, D. (2003) *British Politics Update 1999–2002* (Causeway Press).

Brownmiller, S. (1975) *Against our Will: Men, Women and Rape* (Simon and Schuster).

Bryson, V. (2003) 'Feminist debates, ideology: feminism', *Politics Review*, Vol. 12, No. 4, April 2003.

Callaghan, J. (1987) *The Far Left in British Politics* (Blackwell).

Cheles, L., Ferguson, M. and Wright, P. (1991) *Neo-Fascism in Europe* (Longman).

Colley, L. (2005) *Britons: Forging the Nation 1707–1837* (Yale University Press).

de Beauvoir, S. (1968) *The Second Sex* (Bantam; first published 1952).

Dobson, A. (1990) *Green Political Thought* (Unwin Hyman).

Dowds, M. and Young, J. (1996) *13th British Social Attitudes Survey* (SPCR).

Engels, F. (2010) *The Origin of the Family, Private Property and the State* (Penguin Classics; first published 1884).

Equal Opportunities Commission (2006) *Sex and Power: Who Runs Britain? 2006* (Equal Opportunities Commission).

Ferguson, N. (2003) *Empire* (Allen Lane).

Firestone, S. (1980) *The Dialectic of Sex* (Women's Press).

Friedan, B. (1963) *The Feminine Mystique* (Norton).

Friedan, B. (1982) *The Second Stage* (Norton).

Gamble, A. (2003) *Between Europe and America* (Palgrave).

Giddens, A. (1998) *The Third Way* (Polity Press).

Greer, G. (1971) *The Female Eunuch* (Granada).

Greer, G. (1985) *Sex and Destiny* (Harper and Row).

Heywood, A. (1992) *Political Ideologies* (Macmillan).

House of Commons (200) *Weekly Information Bulletin*, 18 December 2004 (HMSO).

Hussein, E. (2007) *The Islamist* (Penguin).

Intergovernmental Panel on Climate Change (2001) *Climate Change 2001*, United Nations.

Lovenduski, J. and Norris, P. (2003) 'Westminster women: the politics of presence', *Political Studies*, Vol. 51, No. 1, March.

Lovenduski, J. and Randall, V. (1993) *Contemporary Feminist Politics* (Oxford University Press).

Marcuse, H. (1964) *One Dimensional Man* (Beacon).

Marcuse, H. (1969a) *An Essay on Liberation* (Penguin).

Marcuse, H. (1969b) *Eros and Civilisation* (Sphere).

Millett, K. (1969) *Sexual Politics* (Granada).

Nozick, R. (1974) *Anarchy, State and Utopia* (Blackwell).

Paglia, C. (2006) *Break, Blow, Burn* (Vintage).

Porritt, J. (1984) *Seeing Green* (Blackwell).

Reid, J.R. (2004) *The United States of Europe* (Penguin).

Thurlow, R. (1986) *Fascism in Britain* (Blackwell).

Wolf, A. (2006) 'Working girls', *Prospect*, April.

Wollstonecraft, M.A. (1967) *A Vindication of the Rights of Women* (Norton; originally published 1792).

Useful websites

Anti-Nazi League: www.anl.org.uk/campaigns.html

Green Party: www.greenparty.org.uk

National Democrats:
    www.netlink.co.uk/users/natdems/

Searchlight Magazine:
    www.searchlightmagazine.com/default.asp

Socialist Alliance: www.socialistalliance.net

Socialist Workers' Party: www.swp.org.uk

Workers' Revolutionary Party: www.wrp.org.uk

And another thing . . .

The long-term impact of the banking crisis on British politics – the optimistic and pessimistic scenarios

Steve Richards

Gordon Brown felt most at ease as Prime Minister for a few weeks in the autumn of 2008 when the economy went into meltdown. Suddenly he started to enjoy himself as he appeared to get a grip on the financial crisis. This was no time for a novice, he told the Labour conference in September of that year at a point when some in his cabinet were scheming to remove him. Shortly afterwards Brown was not only secure in his job, but the beneficiary of a bounce in the polls. The banking crisis had at least resolved for the time being the separate crisis over his leadership.

At last Brown had discovered a populist language to describe what he was doing. For months prior to the crisis he had admitted privately that he could not find accessible phrases and themes to convey his political purpose. That was partly because the purpose had become so ill defined that no phrase was available to capture the policies shaped increasingly by insecure expediency.

But by the end of September 2008 Brown was declaring with a robust self-confidence that the government would do whatever it took to help people in recession. He and other senior allies who had agonised for years over how to make the case for the state as a benevolent force were now doing so on every media outlet. Brown, Ed Miliband and Ed Balls all declared in interviews that this was a crisis that demanded a progressive response in which the government would be on the side of the people in the face of chronic market failure.

The mood at the Labour conference in the autumn of 2008 was on the whole even more euphoric. Fringe meetings were a noisy din of celebratory declarations about the crisis marking the end of Thatcherism and the beginning of social democracy. Brown made his moves accompanied by an uncharacteristically bold Bank of England. Banks were saved at great cost. International summits were called. Interest rates fell. David Cameron and George Osborne, normally self-assured and accomplished political artists, appeared to be thrown by the ideologically challenging events. One moment they declared they would support the government in a blitz-like spirit of national consensus. The next they were attacking Brown with a renewed intensity. Their lead in some opinion polls narrowed to a few points.

That brief period, which opened with Labour's conference in Manchester and ended with the pre-budget report delivered by the Chancellor, Alistair Darling, in December 2008, highlights the dangers of predicting the political consequences of the crisis. Those few weeks had a curiously unreal feel at the time and look even more dream-like in retrospect. There was always something slightly odd in the assumption that a government that had been in power for more than a decade would be the main political beneficiary of the biggest economic crisis since 1945. Of course there were precedents to back up the fleetingly giddy optimism of some ministers. John Major won amid economic gloom in 1992 and lost as the economy showed signs of booming in 1997. But with Brown having served as a uniquely dominant Chancellor for more than a decade explaining away steep decline was always going to be a challenge rather than an electoral opportunity.

The other optimistic scenario, as expressed by many senior figures in Labour and the Liberal Democrats, about the opening of a new progressive era also looks to be seriously misjudged, at least in the short term. The financial crisis brought about the end of lightly regulated markets, but the consequences of the reckless era mean that the government is broke. Darling's budget in April 2009 confirmed that public spending will be cut more drastically than it was in the 1980s.

For the next few years there will be no link between higher taxes and improvements in public services as there was in 2003 when Brown as Chancellor raised National Insurance Contributions to pay for higher levels of investment in the NHS. The budget in 2003 was the nearest Britain has come to dancing openly to the tunes of social democracy. The night before Brown announced the NIC rise I bumped into one of Tony Blair's most influential advisers who told me he thought the proposal would lose Labour the next election. In fact the budget proved to be the most popular Brown delivered in his eleven years in the Treasury. In the aftermath of the recession taxes will rise and services will decline, not exactly a vote-winning proposition.

There is though a cause for optimism about the likely nature of the political debate that will follow the recession. There will be an unavoidable focus on the role of the state. Such a debate should be welcomed across the political spectrum. New Labour never dared to instigate any public exchanges on the state partly because it had no fixed position of its own. My shelves creak with speeches by Blair and Brown on a thousand policy areas, but you will search in vain for defining comments on the size of the state and its purpose. They had famous and unresolved internal rows about the best way of delivering public services. Blair and Brown could never resolve the conundrum: how or why should central government hand over responsibility to local providers while taking the political and economic risks of raising taxes to pay for the provision of those services? But this is a secondary issue compared with the even bigger questions about what the state can and should be doing.

As the axe falls the debate will start. Will there be co-payments for NHS treatments? Is the private sector really more efficient in providing some public services? Should Britain rather pathetically seek to punch above its weight internationally by fighting wars and renewing trident when it cannot run a modern train service and still struggles to reach European standards in other public services, not surprisingly as funding has only come close to the EU average recently after decades of stinginess?

The recession will change British politics profoundly, but the change will be sluggish. In one of his last interviews before he died the former Labour prime minister, James Callaghan, told me that his generation had been slow to realise that the challenges of the 1970s demanded a different response to the ones they had been conditioned to give.

We were brought up politically in the 1930s when unemployment was the great social and economic evil. This included some Conservatives too. I think Ted Heath, Harold Wilson and I all felt we should do anything to prevent unemployment from rising. But we did not appreciate the global changes that limited what a government could do to insulate a country. We were too slow to appreciate that there would be jobs in new industries even if some of the less productive sectors in Britain would close. But we were working to avoid a repeat of the 1930s.

When Callaghan famously detected a 'sea change' in British politics during the 1979 election he was referring to a current which had been flowing for several years.

Callaghan, Wilson and Heath are not alone. When faced with tidal waves political leaders tend to stick with the strokes they learnt when they were younger. Brown's responses to the collapse of Northern Rock in 1997 were defined by what had happened in the 1970s and 1980s, his politically formative decades. He was terrified of nationalising the bank out of a fear of appearing to be 'old Labour'. Even when the *Economist* and the *Financial Times* advocated state ownership Brown resisted. Before he became prime minister he was tormented above all by taunts from the Conservatives and some internal critics that he would return to 'old Labour' policies. He resolved with his usual dogged determination to prove his opponents wrong, and in doing so landed himself in even more difficulty refusing to recognise that when ardently free-market magazines are calling for nationalisation it is politically safe to act.

The government's response has been slightly behind the curve throughout the crisis. Even Brown's widely hailed recapitalisation of the banks that took place in the autumn of 2008 was a confused initiative. The taxpayer was backing the banks, but the banks retained the freedom to do more or less what they liked. Only the Liberal Democrats' Treasury Spokesman, Vince Cable, has put the case for the temporary ownership of more banks in order to guarantee the flow of credit once more into the economy. The deification of Cable is illuminating. On one level he has the luxury of commenting from the sidelines, unburdened by power. But in his own quiet unassuming way he plays the role of Sir Keith Joseph in the 1970s, challenging orthodoxies that had been accepted for the previous two decades. In contrast David Cameron and George Osborne have tended to look to the 1980s for guidance, but as Callaghan and Brown discovered the past is a treacherous route map.

Political change will be shaped by the recession rather than the other way around. At some point a visionary will surface, or a political realignment will take place. The trigger will be the debate about the state as it was in different ways in 1979 and 1945.

Ideology and the liberal tradition

Bill Jones

Learning objectives

- To clarify the concept of ideology.

- To trace the transition of new ideas from their 'revolutionary' inception to accepted orthodoxy.

- To show how classical liberalism developed into new liberalism, the creed that set the social agenda for the next century.

From Chapter 4 of *Politics UK*, 7/e. Bill Jones and Philip Norton. © Pearson Education 2001–2010. All rights reserved.

Introduction

This chapter begins by discussing what we mean by the term 'ideology'. It goes on to explain how 'liberal' ideas entered the political culture as heresies in the seventeenth and eighteenth centuries but went on to become the orthodoxies of the present age. Classical liberalism in the mid-nineteenth century is examined together with the birth of modern liberalism in the early twentieth century. So-called 'liberal' ideas therefore provide the architecture of our beliefs in a democratic society; we hold our political views views, discuss and debate them within the framework of ideas acquired hundreds of years ago.

■ What is ideology?

For up to two decades after 1945 it seemed as if ideology as a factor in British politics was on the wane. The coalition comradeship of the war had drawn some of the sting from the sharp doctrinal conflicts between the two major political parties, and in its wake the Conservatives had conceded – without too much ill grace – that Labour would expand welfare services and nationalise a significant sector of the economy. Once in power after 1951, the Conservatives presided over their socialist inheritance of a mixed economy and a welfare state. Both parties seemed to have converged towards a general consensus on political values and institutions: there was more to unite than to divide them. By the end of the 1950s, some commentators – notably the American political scientist Daniel Bell – were pronouncing 'the end of ideology' (see Bell 1960) in Western societies.

However, the faltering of the British economy in the 1960s, exacerbated in the early 1970s by the rise in oil prices, industrial unrest and raging inflation, reopened the ideological debate with a vengeance. A revived Labour Left hurled contumely at their right-wing Cabinet colleagues for allegedly betraying socialist principles. Margaret Thatcher, meanwhile, Leader of the Opposition after 1975, began to elaborate a position far to the right of her predecessor Edward Heath (Prime Minister, 1970–4 – see Biography). The industrial paralysis of the 1978–9 'winter of discontent' provided a shabby end for Jim Callaghan's Labour government and a perfect backcloth against which Thatcher's confident assertions could be projected. From 1979 to 1990, ideology in the form of Thatcherism or the New Right triumphed over what has subsequently been labelled the 'post-war consensus'.

BIOGRAPHY

Edward Heath (1916–2005)

Conservative Prime Minister. Educated at Oxford in the 1930s, when he was deeply concerned about unemployment and the threat of fascism. He fought with distinction in the war and entered politics in its wake. He was a prominent younger member of Macmillan's governments and became leader of the Conservatives a year after their defeat of 1964. He became Prime Minister in 1970 on a right-wing ticket but resorted to 'left-wing' reflation when unemployment began to soar. During his four years in power, his greatest achievement was taking the country into Europe. He was replaced by Margaret Thatcher as leader in 1975 and could not hide his resentment at her 'disloyalty' (i.e. to him) or her extreme right-wing policies. He remained a bitter critical figure, defending his record and Europe, attacking his successor until the end of his career.

Ideology as a concept is not easy to define. Perhaps it is helpful to regard ideology as 'applied philosophy'. It links philosophical ideas to the contemporary world, it provides a comprehensive and systematic perspective whereby human society can be understood, and it provides a framework of principles from which policies can be developed.

Individuals support ideologies for a variety of reasons: moral commitment – often genuine, whatever cynics might say – as well as self-interest. It is entirely possible for a businessman, for example, to believe quite genuinely, that a pro-business set of policies by a party is good not only for him but for the nation as a whole. Clearly, ideology will mean more to political activists. It has to be recognised that most people are ill-informed on political matters, nor especially interested in them. But the broad mass of the population is not completely inert. During election campaigns they receive a crash course in political education, and leaving aside the more crass appeals to emotion and unreason, most voters are influenced to some extent by the ideological debate. The party with the clearest message that seems most relevant to the times can win elections, as Labour discovered in 1945, the Conservatives in 1979 and Labour again in 1997.

■ Classifying ideologies

This is a difficult and imperfect science, but the following two approaches should help to clarify it.

The horizontal left–right continuum

Left	Centre	Right

This is the most familiar classification, used and abused in the press and in everyday conversations. It arose from the seating arrangements adopted in the French Estates General in 1789, where the aristocracy sat to the right of the King and the popular movements to his left. Subsequently the terms have come to represent adherence to particular groups of principles. Right-wingers stress freedom, or the right of individuals to do as they please and develop their own lives and personalities without interference, especially from governments – which history teaches are potentially tyrannical. Left-wingers believe that this kind of freedom is only won by the strong at the expense of the weak. They see equality as the more important value and stress the collective interest of the community above that of the individual.

The implications of these principles for economic policy are obviously of key importance. Right-wingers champion free enterprise, or capitalism: the rights of individuals to set up their own businesses, to provide goods and services and to reap what reward they can. Left-wingers disagree. Capitalism, they argue, creates poverty amid plenty – much better to move towards collective ownership so that

workers can receive the full benefit of their labour. Politicians in the centre dismiss both these positions as extreme and damaging to the harmony of national life. They tend to argue for various combinations of left and right principles or compromises between them: in practice a mixed economy plus efficient welfare services. The left–right continuum therefore relates in practice principally to economic and social policy.

Left	Centre	Right
Equality	Less inequality	Freedom
Collectivism	Some collectivism	Individualism
Collective ownership	Mixed economy	Free enterprise

The vertical axis or continuum

The inadequacies of the left–right continuum are obvious. It is both crude and inaccurate in that many people can subscribe to ideas drawn from its whole width and consequently defy classification. H.J. Eysenck suggested in the early 1950s that if a 'tough' and 'tender' axis could bisect the left–right continuum, ideas could be more accurately plotted on two dimensions. In this way ideological objectives could be separated from political methodology – so tough left-wingers, e.g. communists, would occupy the top left-hand quarter, tough right-wingers, e.g. fascists, the top right-hand quarter, and so on.

The vertical axis can also be used to plot other features:

1 An authoritarian–libertarian axis is perhaps a more precise variation on the tough and tender theme.

2 A status quo–revolutionary axis is also useful. The Conservative Party has traditionally been characterised as defending the established order. However, Margaret Thatcher was a committed radical who wanted to engineer major and irreversible changes. It was Labour and the Conservative 'wets' who defended the status quo in the 1980s.

Political parties and the left–right continuum

Despite its inadequacies, the left–right continuum is useful because it is commonly understood (though see Box 4.1). It will be used as a guide to the

BOX 4.1   IDEAS AND PERSPECTIVES

Left and right discussed

In his book *The Third Way* (1998), Anthony Giddens suggests left and right are less than adequate terms. He points out that what was once left can now be right – such as nineteenth-century free-market views. He quotes the Italian writer Bobbio, who argues that politics is adversarial and that 'left and right' encapsulates the familiar idea of bodily opposites, i.e. the left and right arms. He goes on to say that when ideas are evenly balanced most people accept the dichotomy, but when one ideology seems 'the only game in town' neither side finds the terms suitable. The strong ideology seeks to claim it is the 'only' alternative, while the weaker tries to strengthen its position by absorbing some elements of the stronger side and offering them as its own, producing a 'synthesis of opposing positions with the intentions in practice of saving whatever can be saved of one's own position by drawing in the opposing position and thus neutralising it'. Both sides then present their views as beyond the old left/right distinction and as something totally new and exciting. Giddens comments that 'the claim that Tony Blair has taken over most of the views of Thatcherism and recycled them as something new is readily comprehensible from such a standpoint'. Giddens insists that the 'left' is not just the opposite of 'right': the core of the former is concerned with social justice or 'emancipatory' politics, while the right has shifted to anti-global and even racist positions.

He goes on to accept that socialism is no longer valid as a 'theory of economic management' and that in consequence the right/left distinction has lost relevance. Now people face 'life politics' decisions such as those connected with nuclear energy, work, global warming, devolution and the future of the EU, none of which fits easily into the old dichotomy. By talking of the 'radical centre', Giddens suggests that 'major gains' can be derived as it 'permits exchange across political fences which were much higher'. So to look at welfare reform, it is not merely an argument about high or low spending but comprises 'common issues facing all welfare reformers. The question of how to deal with an ageing population isn't just a matter of setting pension levels. It requires more radical rethinking in relation to the changing nature of ageing.'

Source: Giddens (1998: 37–46)

following sections, but first a word on the way in which political parties relate to the political spectrum.

For most of the postwar period, the major ideological divisions have not occurred between the two big parties but within them. The Labour Party has covered a very wide spectrum from the revolutionary Left to the cautious social democrat Right. Similarly, two major Conservative schools of thought developed in the late 1970s: traditional ('wet') conservatism and the New Right or Thatcherite conservatism. The centre ground was dominated for many years by the Liberal Party, but during the 1980s it was first augmented by the Social Democratic Party (which split off from the Labour Party in 1981) and then was fragmented when the merger initiative following the 1987 general election resulted in the awkward progeny of the Social and Liberal Democrats plus the rump Social Democratic Party led defiantly by David Owen until May 1990, when the party formally folded.

■ The liberal tradition

Since then, like so many other political labels coined as forms of abuse ('tory' was once a name given to Irish outlaws), the word 'liberalism' has lost its derogatory connotations and fully traversed the ground between vice and virtue. Now liberalism denotes opinions and qualities that are generally applauded. Most people would like to think they are liberal in the sense of being open-minded, tolerant, generous or rational. This is partly because the ideas of the English liberal philosophers from the mid-seventeenth to the mid-nineteenth centuries became accepted as dominant elements in our political culture. These were the ideas that helped to create our liberal democratic political system in the late nineteenth century and since then have provided its philosophical underpinning.

Interestingly, in the USA the term came to assume a pejorative meaning in the early 1980s, when the Republicans successfully linked it to being 'soft on communism' and therefore anti-American (see Box 4.2); in March 2006 the film actor George Clooney's statement that he was indeed a 'liberal' consequently contained a note of defiance.

An important distinction clearly has to be made between liberal with a small 'l' and the Liberalism associated with the party of the same name until the 1987 merger. The Liberal Party always claimed a particular continuity with liberal philosophical ideas; but so deeply ingrained have these views become that most political parties also owe them substantial unacknowledged philosophical debts. For their part, liberals have made contributions to political, social and economic thinking that have been hugely influential and have been plundered shamelessly by other parties. It makes sense, therefore, to begin with some consideration of the liberal tradition of both the philosophical 'l' and party political 'L' variety.

Philosophical liberalism

Bertrand Russell attributes the birth of English liberal thought in part to the French philosopher René Descartes (1596–1650). His famous proposition 'I think, therefore I am' made 'the basis of knowledge different for each person since for each the starting point was his own existence not that of other individuals or the community' (Russell 1965: 579). To us such propositions seem unexceptional, but in the mid-seventeenth century they were potentially revolutionary because they questioned the very basis of feudal society. This relied on unquestioning acceptance of the monarch's divine right to rule, the aristocracy's hereditary privileges and the Church's explanation of the world together with its moral leadership. Feudal society was in any case reeling from the impact of the Civil War (1642–9), the repercussions of which produced a limited constitutional monarchy and the embryo of modern parliamentary government. Descartes had inaugurated a new style of thinking.

BIOGRAPHY

Bertrand Russell (1872–1970)

British philosopher and mathematician. *Principia Mathematica* was his most influential philosophical work but he wrote many popular books as well, including *The History of Western Philosophy* (1946). A radical member of the Liberal Party, he opposed the new creed of communism and after the Second World War threw himself into opposing nuclear weapons as a passionate pacifist.

Rationality

John Locke (1632–1704) did much to set the style of liberal thinking as rational and undogmatic. He accepted some certainties, such as his own existence, God and mathematical logic, but he respected an area of doubt in relation to most propositions. He was inclined to accept differences of opinion as the natural consequences of free individual development. Liberal philosophers tended to give greater credence to facts established by scientific enquiry – the systematic testing of theories against reality – rather than to assertions accepted as fact purely on the basis of tradition.

Toleration

This lack of dogmatism was closely connected with a liberal prejudice in favour of **toleration** and compromise. Conflicts between crown and Parliament, Catholicism and Protestantism had divided the country for too long, they felt: it was time to recognise that religious belief was a matter of personal conscience, not a concern of government.

Natural rights and the consent of the governed

This idea emerged out of the 'contract' theorists of the seventeenth and eighteenth centuries. These thinkers believed that each individual had made a kind of agreement to obey the government in exchange for the services of the state, principally 'security' or protection from wrong-doing. It was not suggested that anything had actually been signed;

the idea was more of an application of the legal concept of rights to the philosophical realm. It was all a far cry from Sir Robert Filmer's doctrine that the divine authority of monarchs to receive absolute obedience could be traced back to Adam and Eve, from whom all monarchs were originally descended.

Individual liberty

The idea of natural rights was closely allied to the concept of individual **liberty**, which had already been established by the eighteenth century: freedom for arbitrary arrest, search and taxation; equality before the law; jury trials, freedom of thought and expression, freedom to buy and sell.

Such liberties in practice were protected by constitutional checks and balances, limited government and representation. John Stuart Mill established the classic liberal view on liberty when he argued that anyone should be free to do as they wish unless their actions impinge on the freedom of someone else (see Box 4.2).

Constitutional checks and balances

Locke argued something destined to influence all future democratic government: that to ensure that executive power was not exercised arbitrarily by the monarch, the law-making or legislative arm of government should be separate, independent and removable by the community. This doctrine of the 'separation of powers' informed liberal enthusiasm for written constitutions (although, ironically, Britain has never had a written constitution or, indeed, an effective separation of powers).

Limited government

Instead of the absolute power that Filmer argued the monarch was free to exercise, liberal philosophers, mindful of past abuses, sought to restrict the legitimacy of government to a protection of civil liberties. It was held to be especially important that government did not interfere with the right to property or the exercise of economic activity.

Representation

It followed that if the legislature was to be removable then it needed to be representative. Many liberal Whigs – inclined to support parliament rather than the monarch – in the eighteenth century believed that Parliament was generally representative of the nation, even though the franchise was small and usually based on a highly restrictive property qualification. However, such positions were destined to be

---

BOX 4.2   IDEAS AND PERSPECTIVES

Libertarianism

For some people the central aim of political activity should be the defence of freedom, that everyone owns their own body, life and property and has the right to do as they please with them. This is essentially the J.S. Mill position, but the assertion of the individual right to freedom above all else leads to some unusual political positions. For example, some argue that the state needs to defend the freedom of others to certain rights – welfare support, for example – but for libertarians this involves an unacceptable imposition of taxes by the government, demands backed by force.

They also argue against any kind of censorship, the military draft, the minimum wage, laws on sexual behaviour, drug use and immigration controls while supporting free trade and prostitution. Robert Nozick's much admired 1974 work, *Anarchy, State and Utopia*, elaborated some of these positions including the view of taxation as 'forced labour'. Translated into the more conventional political world, libertarianism appeals partly to the anarchic left who resent any controls but perhaps more powerfully to the right and, because it implicitly entails disobedience to the law and a complete 'rolling back' of the state, the far right. In the USA some groups have established themselves as libertarian enclaves in conventional society, seeking to be true to their visions and in the process rejecting the whole concept and machinery of government with its controls, regulation and impositions. At this point left-wing anarchism and right-wing libertarianism meet in a variety of intriguing ways.

eroded by the inherent logic of natural rights: if everyone had equal rights then surely they should have an equal say in removing a government not of their liking?

The influence of the liberal philosophers perhaps seems greater in retrospect than it was because they were often seeking to justify and accelerate political trends that were already well under way. Nevertheless, such liberal notions were of key importance and provide ideas still used as touchstones in the present day.

Some commentators, such as Eccleshall (1984, 1986) and Gamble (1981), see liberalism as providing the philosophical rationale for modern capitalist society. Certainly the idea of individual freedom, property rights and limited government suited the emergent entrepreneurial middle classes destined to come of political age in the next century. However, liberal views on government have enjoyed a general acceptance not just in Britain but also in the USA, Western Europe and elsewhere. They have provided the commonly accepted ground rules of democratic behaviour, the 'procedural values' of toleration, fair play and free speech that Bernard Crick, the great modern advocate of citizenship, argued should be positively reinforced in our society via our classrooms. They have provided in one sense an 'enabling' ideology that all major parties have accepted. Indeed, it is in some ways surprising that a creed originating in an agrarian, largely non-industrialised country should have provided a political framework that has survived so tenaciously and indeed triumphantly into the present day.

Classical liberalism

The American and French Revolutions applied liberal principles in a way that shocked many of their more moderate adherents. The Napoleonic interlude caused a period of reaction, but during the mid- to late-nineteenth century classical liberalism took shape. Claiming continuity with the early liberals, this new school was based on the economic ideas of Adam Smith and the radical philosophers Jeremy Bentham, James Mill and his son John Stuart Mill. Liberalism with a capital 'L' then took the stage in the form of the Liberal Party, a grouping based on the Whigs, disaffected Tories – the group in the eighteenth-century parliament which supported the king – and the Manchester Radicals led by Richard Cobden and John Bright.

Classical liberalism was characterised by the idea of the independent, rational and self-governing citizen as the basic unit of society. For liberals, this concept now represented a goal or vision to be worked for. Liberals hoped that through the erosion of aristocratic privilege and the moral transformation of the working class, social differences would give way to a new society of equals.

Human nature

The liberal view of human nature was fairly optimistic. John Stuart Mill, for example, doubted whether working for the common good would induce citizens to produce goods as efficiently as when self-interest was involved. His awareness of human selfishness perhaps underlay his advice against too rapid a rate of social progress. However, at the heart of liberal philosophy was a belief in the potential of human nature to change into Locke's civilised reasonable human being, capable of being educated into responsible citizenship. Many liberals felt that such an education would take a great many years but that it was possible, especially through direct involvement of citizens in the economy and the political system.

BIOGRAPHY

John Stuart Mill (1806–73)

British philosopher. Influenced by his father, James, he became a leading advocate of representative government. Sat as an MP in the 1860s and supported votes for women. Wrote *Principles of Political Economy* (1848), *On Liberty* (1859), *Representative Government* (1861) and *Utilitarianism* (1863).

Freedom

Classical liberalism retained the emphasis on freedom. In his essay *On Liberty*, for example, Mill felt: 'It was imperative that human beings should be free to form opinions and to express their opinions without reserve.' The only constraint should be that in the exercise of his freedom, an individual should not impinge upon the freedom of others.

Utilitarianism

Jeremy Bentham (1748–1832) took the rationality of liberal philosophy to new levels with his science of utilitarianism. His approach was based on what now seems an extraordinarily simplistic view of human psychology. He argued that human beings were disposed to seek pleasure and avoid pain. While they sought what was best for themselves they frequently made mistakes. The role of government therefore was to assist individuals in making the correct choices, in enabling the achievement of the 'greatest happiness for the greatest number'. While Bentham embraced the *laissez-faire/capitalist* economic system as highly utilitarian, he believed that most laws and administrative arrangements reflected aristocratic privilege and therefore were in need of reform. His ideas were criticised as simplistic and his Panopticon – a model prison based on his philosophy – was generally seen as risible by other philosophers, but he had a pervasive influence on Liberal legislators in the nineteenth century.

Minimal government – middle-class values

Bentham's influence paradoxically led to far-reaching legal and administrative reforms: for example, the regulatory framework for mines and factories. However, other liberals were strongly opposed to such regulation both as a violation of laissez-faire principles and as an interference in the moral education of the poor. Liberals such as the social Darwinist Herbert Spencer (1820–1903) argued that welfare provision was wrong in that it sheltered the poor from the consequences of their behaviour. 'Is it not manifest', he argued, 'that there must exist in our midst an immense amount of misery which is a normal result of misconduct and ought not to be dissociated from it?' State support for the poor was therefore a dangerous narcotic likely to prevent the right lessons being learned. The stern lesson that classical liberals wished to teach was that the poorer classes would face the penalties of poverty unless they adopted the values and lifestyles of their economic superiors: thrift, hard work, moderate indulgence and self-improving pastimes.

Representative government

Bentham and James Mill (1773–1836) introduced arguments in favour of representative government. Bentham dismissed the natural rights argument as 'nonsense on stilts'. His own utilitarian reasoning was that such a form of government was the most effective safeguard for citizens against possibly rapacious rulers or powerful 'sinister interests'. As both men believed individuals to be the best judge of where their own interests lay, they favoured universal franchise (although Mill sought to restrict it to men over 40). His son, J.S. Mill (1806–73), is probably the best-known advocate of representative government. He urged adult male and female suffrage, but to guard against a 'capricious and impulsive' House of Commons he advised a literacy qualification for voting and a system of plural voting whereby educated professional people would be able to cast more votes than ill-educated workers. Mill also believed that a participatory **democracy** and the sense of responsibility it would imbue would contribute towards the moral education of society: 'Democracy creates a morally better person because it forces people to develop their potentialities.'

Laissez-faire economics

Laissez-faire economics was predicated on the tenet of individual freedom: it asserted that the ability to act freely in the marketplace – to buy and sell property, employ workers and take profit – was central to any free society. Adam Smith's (1723–90) broadsides against the trade protection of the eighteenth-century mercantilist system provided the clearest possible statement of the case for economic activity free from political restrictions. According to Smith, producers should be allowed to supply products at the price consumers are willing to pay. Provided that competition was fair, the 'invisible hand' of the market would ensure that goods were produced at the lowest possible price commensurate with the quality consumers required. Producers would be motivated by selfish pursuit of profit but would also provide social 'goods', through providing employment, creating wealth and distributing it in accordance with the energy and ability of people active in the economic system. Smith believed that government intervention and regulation would impede this potentially perfect self-adjusting system. Liberals were not especially worried by the inequalities thrown up by laissez-faire economics or claims that employers 'exploited' employees. Classical liberals were opposed to inherited financial advantages but not so concerned with the differences created by different performances in relation to the market. They favoured the meritocracy of the market: they were the high priests of capitalism.

Peace through trade

Liberals, especially the so-called Manchester Radicals, also applied their free-trade principles to foreign affairs. Richard Cobden, for example, regarded diplomacy and war as the dangerous pastimes of the aristocracy. His answer to these perennial problems was 'to make diplomacy open and subject to parliamentary control', eliminate trade barriers, and encourage free trade worldwide. Commerce, he argued, was peaceful and beneficial, and it encouraged co-operation and contact between nations. If the world were a completely open market, national economies would become more integrated and interdependent and governments would be less likely to engage in conflicts or war.

The new liberalism

The emphasis of classical liberalism was on laissez-faire, wealth production, toleration of inequality, minimal welfare, individual responsibility and moral education. Towards the end of the nineteenth century, however, liberals themselves began to move away from their own ascetic economic doctrines. John Stuart Mill had argued that government intervention was only justified to prevent injury to the life, property or freedom of others. To some liberals it appeared that capitalist society had become so complex and repressive that the freedom of poor people to develop their potential was being restricted: even if they were inclined to emulate their middle-class betters their capacity to do so was held back by poverty, poor health and education, and squalid living and working conditions. Liberal thinkers began to shift their emphasis away from 'negative' freedom – freedom from oppression – towards providing 'positive' freedom – the capacity of people to make real choices regarding education, employment, leisure and so on.

State responsibility for welfare

T.H. Green (1836–82) helped to initiate this movement for positive action to assist the poor by calling for a tax on inherited wealth. Alfred Marshall (1842–1924) believed that capitalism now provided such material plenty that it had the capacity to redistribute some of its largesse to the disadvantaged so that they would be able genuinely to help themselves to become self-reliant. But it was L.T. Hobhouse (1864–1929) who perhaps marked the key shift of Liberals towards paternalism:

The state as over-parent is quite as truly liberal as socialistic. It is the basis of the rights of the child, of his protection against parental neglect, of the equality of opportunity which he may claim as a 'future citizen'.

Hobhouse insisted that his version of paternalism should not be oppressively imposed; he favoured a basic minimum standard of living that would provide 'equal opportunities of self-development'. He followed Green in proposing taxation to finance such welfare innovations as health insurance and pensions. The great Liberal victory of 1906 enabled the government to implement many of these new measures. Thereafter Liberals became firm advocates of **welfarism**; in 1942, the Liberal William Beveridge produced his famous blueprint for the postwar welfare state.

The mixed economy: Hobsonian and Keynesian economics

Government intervention of a different kind was proposed by J.A. Hobson (1858–1940). He was the first major liberal economist (he later became a socialist) to argue that capitalism was fatally flawed. Its tendency to produce a rich minority who accumulated unspent profits and luxury goods meant that the full value of goods produced was not consumed by society. This created slumps and, indirectly, the phenomenon of economic imperialism. Capitalists were forced by such under-consumption to export their savings abroad, thus creating overseas interests with political and colonial consequences. Hobson argued that the state could solve this crisis with one Olympian move: redirect wealth from the minority to the poor via progressive taxation. The section of society most in need would then be able to unblock the mechanism which caused overproduction and unemployment, thus making moral as well as economic sense.

J.M. Keynes (1883–1946) (see Biography) completed this revolution in liberal economic thought by arguing that demand could be stimulated not by redistribution of wealth to the poor but by government-directed investment in new economic activity. Confronted by a world recession and massive unemployment, he concentrated on a different part of the economic cycle. He agreed that the retention of wealth by capitalists under a laissez-faire economic system lay at the heart of the problem, but he believed the key to be increased investment, not increased consumption. Instead of saving in a crisis,

John Maynard Keynes (1883–1946)

Born in Cambridge, Keynes was the son of an academic. He was educated at Eton and King's College, Cambridge, where he mixed in avant-garde intellectual circles, such as the 'Bloomsbury group', and taught sporadically. He served in the India Office (1906–8) and later wrote his first book on this subject. In the First World War he advised the Treasury and represented it at the Versailles Treaty negotiations but resigned over the terms proposed. His essay *The Economic Consequences of the Peace* (1919) brought his powerful radical intellect to the notice of the country's ruling élite. He attacked Churchill's restoration of the gold standard in 1925, and the unemployment caused by the Depression inspired his most famous work, *A General Theory of Employment, Interest and Money* (1936). His views won support on the left and in the centre as well as helping to inspire the New Deal policies of Roosevelt in the USA.

Keynes married a Soviet ballerina and with her father founded the Vic-Wells ballet. In 1943 he established the Arts Theatre in Cambridge. In the same year he played a leading role in the Bretton Woods agreement, which set up a new international economic order, the establishment of the International Monetary Fund and negotiations following the ending of lend-lease (a financial agreement whereby aid was channelled to the UK during the war) after the war to secure a major loan to help Britain to survive the rigours of the immediate postwar world. Most people achieve only a fraction in their lifetimes of what Keynes managed to do. He was one of the truly great figures of the century, and his influence lives on today.

governments should encourage businessmen to invest in new economic activity. Through the creation of new economic enterprises wealth would be generated, consumption increased, other economic activities stimulated and unemployment reduced. He envisaged a mixed economy in which the state would intervene with a whole range of economic controls to achieve full employment and planned economic growth. Keynes was not just concerned with the cold science of economics: his view of the mixed economy would serve social ends in the form of alleviated hardship and the extension of opportunity. But while Keynes was unhappy with capitalism in the 1930s he did not propose to replace it – merely to modify it. He was no egalitarian, unlike socialist economists, and disagreed with Hobsonian calls for wealth redistribution, which he felt would adversely affect the incentives to achieve that human nature required: 'for my own part I believe there is social and psychological justification for significant inequalities of income and wealth' (Keynes 1985: 374).

Internationalism

Radical liberals such as J.A. Hobson, Norman Angel, E.D. Morel, C.R. Buxton, H.N. Brailsford, Lowes Dickinson and Charles Trevelyan produced an influential critique of the international system, arguing that the practice of secret diplomacy, imperialist competition for markets, haphazard balance-of-power policies and the sinister role of arms manufacturers made war between nations tragically inevitable. The First World War appeared to vindicate their analysis and encouraged them to develop the idea of an overarching international authority: the League of Nations. The idea was picked up by political parties and world leaders, including the US President, Woodrow Wilson, and through the catalyst of war was translated into the League of Nations by the Versailles Treaty. Most of the radical liberals joined the Labour Party during and after the war, but the Liberal Party subsequently remained staunchly internationalist and in favour of disarmament proposals throughout the interwar period. Despite the failure of the League, Liberals passionately supported the United Nations which emerged in the wake of the Second World War.

Further development of democratic government

The New Liberals were no less interested than their predecessors in the development of representative democracy through extension of the franchise and the strengthening of the House of Commons. Lloyd George's device of including welfare proposals in his 1909 Budget – a measure that the House of Lords had traditionally passed 'on the nod' – precipitated a conflict between the two chambers that resulted in the House of Lords' power being reduced from one of absolute veto over legislation to one of delay only. In the early 1920s, the Liberal Party gave way to Labour as the chief opposition party, returning 159 MPs in 1923, 59 in 1929 and only 21 in 1935. The dramatic decline in the party's fortunes coincided with its support for a change in the electoral system from the 'first-past-the-post' system, which favoured big parties, to alternatives that would provide fairer representation to smaller parties, such as the Liberals, with thinly spread national support.

This chapter has sought to emphasise the centrality of the liberal (note small 'l') tradition in the evolution of modern British political thought. In the eighteenth century, it helped to establish reason,

---

BOX 4.3   BRITAIN IN CONTEXT

Liberal values

It is seductively easy to believe that the beliefs underpinning one's own system of government are somehow 'natural', 'universal' and superior to those of other cultures. Probably the most famous statement of liberal values is enshrined in the Declaration of Independence made by the 'thirteen united states of America' in 1776, beginning:

We hold these truths to be self-evident, that all men are created equal, that they are endowed by their Creator with certain unalienable Rights, that among these are Life, Liberty, and the pursuit of Happiness. That to secure these rights, Governments are instituted among Men, deriving their just powers from the consent of the governed.

These few words embody much of the liberal thinking of Hobbes (his views were a mixture of the liberal and illiberal), Locke, Paine, Rousseau and other thinkers associated the impending French Revolution. 'Life, liberty and the pursuit of happiness' were considered to be 'self-evident' truths, reflecting universal rights owned by all humans. At the time, when it was believed monarchs ruled with the authority of God who had decreed a natural order and social hierarchy, such views were wholly unorthodox and revolutionary; as much as the armies of Napoleon they unseated the established order in Europe and set the movement towards democracy in train.

As the new order took shape, what once was heretical became at first acceptable and then, by degrees, the new unchallenged orthodoxy. Citizens in Britain and the USA do not question these 'inalienable rights' which are enshrined in law and constitution; though in the USA the term 'liberal' has acquired pejorative overtones through the efforts of Republicans to identify Democrats with 'Un-American' (and hence unpatriotic) socialist ideas.

However, elsewhere in the world, such liberal values did not pass unchallenged. Communist countries claimed such beliefs were merely one of the means whereby property-owning capitalists fooled the exploited working classes into accepting gross inequalities. In more recent times fundamentalist Muslim movements have condemned Western liberalism as a sign of the West's decadence and corruption. They do not subscribe to notions of free speech but believe government should be a direct extension of their religion. This has given birth to a 'theocracy' in Iran, powerful internal movements in Muslim states and worldwide movements like al-Qaeda which seek to destroy the West; all this reinforcing the analysis of Samuel P. Huntington's exceptional book *The Clash of Civilizations and the Remaking of World Order* (Touchstone Books, 1997).

We should not, therefore, assume that liberal values are automatically right, and we should remember that:

1 Even cherished values – such as freedom of speech – are not absolute; Western countries all legislate to place limits of some kind.
2 Some Muslim countries do not accept liberal values but regard religious values as absolute, thus producing powerful conflicts with secular views of government (read Orhan Pamuk's novel *Snow* for excellent insights into these conflicts).
3 Before we reject such opposing views we should remember that even in 1776 (our Christian) God's name was invoked as the source of liberal values.

toleration, liberty, natural rights and the consent of the governed in place of religious dogma, feudal allegiance and the divine right of monarchs to rule. In the nineteenth century, it added representative, democratic government with power shared between various elements. Having provided key guidelines for our modern system of government, classical liberalism argued for minimal government intervention in social policy and an economy run essentially in harmony with market forces.

The New Liberals, however, engineered a new intellectual revolution. They argued for government intervention to control an increasingly complex economy that distributed great rewards and terrible penalties with near-random unfairness. They also saw commerce not as the healing balm for international conflicts but as the source of the conflicts themselves. The irony is that the Liberals Keynes and Beveridge proved to be the chief architects of the postwar consensus between Labour and Conservatives, while, as we shall see, Margaret Thatcher wrought her revolution not through application of traditional conservatism but through a rediscovery of classical liberalism.

■ Fukuyama and the end of history

No account of the development of the liberal tradition in politics can end without some reference to Francis Fukuyama, the formerly obscure official in the US State Department who argued in articles and a book (1992) that the liberal tradition had developed to the extent that, allied to free-enterprise economics, it had eclipsed all its rivals on the left and right – communism, fascism, socialism – thus producing the 'universalisation of Western Liberal democracy as the final form of human government'.

He founded his reasoning on the Hegelian notion that civilisations successively develop, resolve internal conflicts and change for the better. The 'end of history' is when a point is reached whereby conflict is eradicated and the form of society best suited to human nature has evolved.

The importance of the article lay partly in its timing. The British Empire took a couple of decades to expire, but Stalin's collapsed in a few years at the end of the 1980s. The intellectual world was deafened by the crashing of rotten regimes and astonished by the apparent vibrancy of their democratic successors. Moreover, after decades of defending liberal values against a grey and predatory communist bloc, the Western intelligentsia responded warmly to a thesis that appeared to say 'we've won'. Fukuyama's bold thesis fitted the facts and suited the mood of the times. Even in Britain the triumph of Thatcher in three successive elections between 1979 and 1987 seemed to reflect the thrust of the argument and her stated resolve to destroy socialism in her country. However, Fukuyama's thesis seems to ignore the exponential forces for change that are transforming society at breakneck speed: computer technology and the information revolution; the huge pressure on finite world resources; the spread of nuclear weapons; and the increasing concentration of wealth in a few hands, leading to the huge and growing gap between rich and poor. Who is to say that these forces will not undermine the liberal consensus and positions and possibly usher in a new authoritarianism? Moreover, as Samuel P. Huntington's book, *The Clash of Civilizations and the Remaking of World Order*, suggested, the world could now be engaged in a struggle between the values of the West and the more traditional and narrow values of Islam.

To assume that the liberal underpinnings of many of the world's political systems will survive can be seen as at best naive and at worst complacent.

Chapter summary

Ideology is a kind of applied philosophy. It can be classified on the right–left continuum, a flawed but still much-used form. The liberal tradition, based on rights, freedom and representation, developed from the seventeenth century and set the ground rules for political activity during the nineteenth and twentieth. Classical liberalism elevated the market economy, but the New Liberalism, which was concerned to protect society from its excesses, still provides the rationales for the welfare state and the mixed economy.

Discussion points

- Are there better ways of classifying ideology than the left–right continuum?

- What are the grounds for thinking that all human beings have rights?

- Should government resist interfering in the economy?

- Have the Liberals been exploited/robbed in ideological terms by the other two big parties?

- Defend the Fukuyama thesis that the evolution of political systems has reached its end-point in liberal democratic free enterprise.

Further reading

Two excellent books are available that introduce politics students to ideology: Adams (1999) is well written and subtly argued, while Heywood (1998) is also essential reading. Useful in general terms are Eccleshall (1984) and Gamble (1981). Plant (1991) is more difficult but no less rewarding. On utilitarianism and liberalism, the texts by J.S. Mill (1971, 1975, 1985a, 1985b) are as good a starting point for understanding liberalism asany. Eccleshall (1986) lays some claim to be the definitive text, but Arblaster (1984) and Manning (1976) address wider readerships. Fukuyama (1992) elaborates the 'end of history' theory. Fareed Zakaria's *The Future of Freedom* (2004) is a quite brilliant book on threats to liberal democracy.

Bibliography

Adams, I. (1999) *Political Ideology Today*, 2nd edn (Manchester University Press).

Arblaster, A. (1984) *The Rise and Fall of Western Liberalism* (Blackwell).

Bell, D. (1960) *The End of Ideology* (Free Press).

Eccleshall, R. (1984) *Political Ideologies* (Hutchinson).

Eccleshall, R. (1986) *British Liberalism* (Longman).

Fukuyama, F. (1992) *The End of History and the Last Man* (Hamish Hamilton).

Gamble, A. (1981) *An Introduction to Modern Social and Political Thought* (Macmillan).

Giddens, A. (1998) *The Third Way* (Polity Press).

Hattersley, R. (1989) 'Endpiece: nous and nostalgia', *The Guardian*, 30 September 1989.

Heywood, A. (1998) *Political Ideologies: An Introduction*, 2nd edn (Macmillan).

Huntington, S.P. (1996) *The Clash of Civilizations and the Remaking of World Order* (University of Oklahoma Press, also in paperback published by Touchstone Books, 1997).

Keynes, J.M. (1971) *The Economic Consequences of the Peace*, Vol. II of his *Collected Works* (Palgrave Macmillan; first published 1919).

Keynes, J.M. (1985) *A General Theory of Employment, Interest and Money*, Vol. VII of his *Collected Works* (Macmillan; first published 1936).

Manning, D.J. (1976) *Liberalism* (St Martin's Press).

Mill, J.S. (1971) *Utilitarianism* (Everyman; first published 1863).

Mill, J.S. (1975) *Representative Government* (Oxford University Press; first published 1861).

Mill, J.S. (1985a) *On Liberty* (Penguin; first published 1859).

Mill, J.S. (1985b) *Principles of Political Economy* (Penguin; first published 1848).

Nozick, R. (1974) *Anarchy, State and Utopia* (Blackwell).

Pamuk, O. (2004) *Snow* (Faber and Faber).

Plant, R. (1991) *Modern Political Thought* (Blackwell).

Russell, B. (1965) *The History of Western Philosophy* (Unwin).

Sutherland, J. (1999) 'How Blair discovered defeat by definition', *The Guardian*, 25 October 1999.

Zakaria, F. (2004) *The Future of Freedom* (Norton).

Useful websites

http://libertarianism.com

Topic 3:
Political Parties

Political parties and party factions

The parties, particularly the Conservatives and Labour, link together all the political processes and organisations we have examined up to this point. Their influence is obvious in elections, where they provide the alternatives for voting and stimulate popular participation. But they also form a central focus for the media, which they continuously try to influence to their advantage. The ultimate aim of parties is to control the government, so as to inject party policies and personalities into the decision-making process. In government the parties interact with civil servants, business and pressure groups in the ways already described.

The parties' external relations with other political institutions are the subject of almost every chapter of this book. Here we concentrate on the parties' internal structures and relationships, leaving party ideology to Chapter 17.

We look at internal relationships because we cannot take party unity and discipline for granted. Parties have to unite to win elections and run the government. But as the deep Conservative divisions on Europe have shown, internal disputes can give rise to factions and tendencies within a party. For most of the time these groups can live together; otherwise they could not form a party. If disagreements become too extreme, however, disaffected factions may split off to form a new party. This is far from being a remote possibility. It has happened in recent memory. In 1981 former Labour MPs founded the Social Democratic Party (SDP) and fatally split the vote on the centre-left.

We consider the history of party factionalism in this chapter, along with the ways in which party organisations and structures have adapted to counter it and put overall control in the hands of the leadership.

This chapter therefore covers:

- the functions of political parties
- the evolution of the modern parties
- factions and factionalism within the parties
- how they are organised.

Functions of parties

The evolution of modern parties cannot be understood without an appreciation of their general role. Democratic parties are associations of generally like-minded people who, by means of election, compete for state power to further their common goals. A unique characteristic of parties is that they serve the dual function of government and representation. As instruments of the government they form an

From Chapter 16 of *The New British Politics*, 4/e. Ian Budge, David McKay, John Bartle and Ken Newton.

Party

An organisation of ideologically like-minded people who come together to seek power – often to fight elections with a view to gaining representation in decision-making bodies.

executive that seeks to steer the state. They recruit and train politicians, they implement policies and they mobilise popular support. As instruments of representation they promote the interests and values of sections of the electorate, translate their demands into policies and give them a sense of place within the wider society. Most important of all, they form the government or the opposition, the 'ins' or the 'outs', thereby rendering the government ultimately accountable to the electorate. In elections voters can choose to either 'kick the rascals out' or 'give them another chance to put things right'.

As instruments of the government and representation the major parties therefore perform a third function: political integration. To win elections parties must attract support from many different groups. By aggregating distinct group interests parties identify and create consensus across large segments of the population. They must also respond to expectations or persuade electors to modify them, by altering ideas about what government can do. Horizontally, parties link many groups; vertically, they act as a link between citizen and state and are one of the few instruments for public education about what the government can achieve.

Parties have to concern themselves with interests and needs beyond those of their core voters, because they need to attract other voters. They also aim to form governments that will make policy for the country as a whole. They cannot just pursue a narrowly sectional programme but have to reach out to many groups by varying their appeals. The need to adapt to new circumstances and new challenges, however, makes internal disputes an ever-present possibility. To be national and representative parties have to be coalitions of interests; but political interests invariably conflict. We can see how this has worked out by looking at the growth of British parties from the mid-nineteenth century onwards.

Party unity and internal dissent: Conservatives, Liberals and Labour, 1868–1979

Emergence of modern parties: Whig and Tory, Conservative and Liberal

Like most other political institutions in Britain parties took on their modern form in the mid-nineteenth century. The shift produced by the Second Reform Act of 1867–8 from a small, restricted electorate to a large one numbered in millions meant that local 'notables' could no longer rely on their own resources to secure the election of themselves or their nominees. Central party organisations emerged that fostered local organisations in every constituency and provided supporters for local campaigns. Members were no longer drawn into these organisations by personal ties to a candidate but by support for the national party's principles and policies, which local MPs pledged to support in Parliament. Soon it became immaterial whether the candidate was a local person or not. Just about anyone pledged to the national leadership and policy was acceptable because the job of an MP was to support and serve the party. MPs thus owed their election to their endorsement by the central organisation and were dependent on leadership approval for (re)election. This became a powerful factor enforcing party discipline in Parliament.

The newly emerging Conservatives defined themselves as defenders of traditional institutions such as the Crown and Church, and as supporters of the empire. At the same time they cast themselves as social reformers concerned to improve the lot of the poor. Both these goals were justified by appeals to national unity but also served to attract the votes of the newly enfranchised working class.

The Liberals emphasised free trade at home and abroad, and were not much interested in the empire. They advocated political reforms, particularly those opening careers to the expanding lower middle class, Nonconformists and Roman Catholics. Since most Catholics originated in Ireland, the Liberals sought an alliance with the Irish Nationalist Party in Parliament, which led them to advocate 'Home Rule' (a form of devolution) for Ireland in 1886. This measure split the party, driving out manufacturers who saw it as a step to dissolving the empire and old Whig aristocrats who viewed it as an attack on Irish property rights.

The early twentieth century: Conservative, Liberal and Labour

The Conservatives suffered a split in 1905 when the new influx of Unionist businessmen supported tariffs to protect British markets. The Liberal Party united around the Irish Home Rule project and a programme of social reform, aiming to attract Catholic working-class voters and their political representatives, the Irish Nationalists and the Labour Party. With their support the Liberals passed legislation setting up a rudimentary Welfare State; the power of the House of Lords to delay legislation was limited to three years, and Irish Home Rule was pencilled in for 1914. The latter was largely overtaken by the First World War, which split the Liberals over military strategy. A section of the party, led by David Lloyd George, formed a coalition with the Conservatives (1916–22). The resulting split in the Liberal Party was never completely healed.

Liberal divisions provided an opportunity for the new Labour Party, which had struggled to make an impact. Unlike the other parties, Labour was not formed by parliamentarians seeking a mass base, but by bodies outside Parliament seeking parliamentary representation. The trade unions allied with existing socialist parties, which had a constituency-based organisation, to form the Labour Representation Committee in 1900. This became the Labour Party in 1906. From its very beginning Labour was a coalition of ethical (largely Christian) socialists who wanted to abolish capitalism and replace it with a society based on cooperation rather than competition, the Fabians who were pragmatic reformers who wanted to replace capitalism with a more rational system and trade unions who simply wanted to improve the lot of their members. The party attracted many – though by no means all – in its 'natural' working-class constituency, further eroding the Liberals' electoral base. In 1918 Labour adopted an explicitly 'socialist' commitment to public ownership. The weakening of both Liberal and Conservative parties resulting from continuing divisions between 'coalitionists' and 'anti-coalitionists' helped Labour form minority governments in 1923–4 and 1929–31 and establish itself as the main opposition to the Conservatives.

The 1929–31 Labour government coincided with the financial crisis of 1931 caused by the world depression. The Labour Party split over the question of cutting unemployment benefit as part of a package of orthodox financial measures to restore confidence. Four members of the Cabinet, including the Labour leader Ramsay MacDonald, joined a national government dominated by the Conservatives and supported also by a Liberal **faction**, the 'National Liberals'. MacDonald's actions were regarded as betrayal by the majority of the party and haunted Labour throughout the 1930s.

The national government introduced policies to ameliorate the worst effects of the depression in the 1930s, including trade protectionism and increased government intervention in the economy. The outbreak of the Second World War in 1939, however, required the government to intervene even more extensively. The political mood shifted decisively leftwards: favouring collective (state) action, government intervention and the provision of welfare.

Labour's participation in the coalition from May 1940 onwards provided many within the party with experience of government and this helped Labour appear less dangerously radical. The party secured a sweeping electoral victory in 1945

Factions

Enduring (and often organised) groups within parties that share common attitudes or place particular emphasis on certain parts of a party's core beliefs.

81

and carried out many radical reforms: creating the National Health Service, founding the Welfare State along the lines advocated by the Beveridge Report (1944), experimenting with Keynesian policies to sustain high levels of employment and nationalising many industries (including coal, gas, electricity). Most of these policies were accepted by their Conservative opponents. In just six short years the terms of political debate had altered: all the major parties accepted that the state would act to solve economic and social problems.

Post-war developments: Conservative, Labour and Liberals 1945–79

While Labour remained reasonably united on its social reforms, it became increasingly divided by two issues during the 1950s. The first was the building of British nuclear weapons (a decision taken by the 1945–51 Labour government). A left faction wanted Britain to engage in 'unilateral nuclear disarmament', chiefly for moral reasons. A right faction, on the other hand, argued that the deterrent should not be surrendered without multilateral agreements. The second issue related to 'nationalisation'. Clause 4 of the party's constitution committed Labour to the public ownership of industry, but left the precise scope of the commitment unclear. The 'Keep Left' group, led by Aneurin Bevan, wanted to extend nationalisation to large parts of private enterprise. The **social democrats** on the right, such as Tony Crosland, wanted to play down the party's commitments to public ownership and focus on promoting equality.

Social democrats

'Moderate' socialists who emphasise the pursuit of equality rather than nationalisation as the goal of the Labour Party

Labour divisions in the 1950s were exacerbated by Conservative electoral success. The popularity of the Labour government's reforms gave the upper hand within the Conservative Party to the 'one-nation' tendency in the Conservative party led by R. A. Butler and Harold Macmillan, who argued that national unity and stability depended on reasonable living conditions for the lower classes, through government intervention if necessary. This led to acceptance and extension of the Welfare State, though the party was less keen on nationalisation and returned some enterprises to the private sector in the 1950s (later known as 'privatisation').

The limited privatisation that took place under the Conservative government (1951–64) was not enough to challenge the 'social democratic consensus' that existed between the dominant factions in both major parties, and among the Liberals. Harold Wilson, Labour Prime Minister 1964–70 and 1974–6, papered over his party's divisions by extending economic planning and promising to harness technology to solve Britain's problems. Labour's experiment with planning, however, proved a failure. In 1967 it was forced to 'devalue' the pound and this badly damaged its reputation for economic competence. Its faith in technology also proved misplaced. Many technological projects, including the supersonic Concorde aircraft, either failed or proved too costly.

The Wilson governments, followed by the Callaghan administration (1976–9), lapsed into pragmatic crisis management; especially after the recessions produced by the oil price shocks of the early 1970s. Inflation and unemployment grew rapidly and the government's attempt to control both via a prices and incomes policy, negotiated with the unions, failed. Many workers sought large pay rises in the expectation that inflation would erode their value. The number of strikes, particularly unofficial strikes called without a ballot, increased rapidly. The various crises came to a head in 1978–9, the so-called 'winter of discontent', when a series of strikes led to shortages of basic products and rubbish piling up in the streets. Labour's reputation as the party that could control the unions and govern competently was left in tatters and not restored for many years.

Plate 16.1 The Winter of Discontent. A series of strikes in the winter of 1978/9 led to Mrs Thatcher's election in 1979 and shattered Labour's reputation of economic competence

Source: Empics

BRIEFINGS

16.1 The social democratic consensus, 1950–79

This covers the ideas that the mainstream sections of all parties broadly shared between 1950 and 1979. Factions of both major parties always stood outside this consensus and, even where there was agreement by the parties on fundamentals, disagreement remained on details and emphasis. The consensus consisted in:

■ acceptance of a 'mixed economy', consisting both of private companies and of nationalised industries (especially where there was a 'natural monopoly' of supply as in the electricity and gas industries)

■ a Keynesian economic policy aimed at striking the right balance between inflation and unemployment

■ acceptance of the powers and roles of the main pressure groups (particularly business and trade unions)

■ acceptance of the steady expansion of the Welfare State and the National Health Service

■ a managed withdrawal from colonies and overseas territories

■ support for NATO in the Cold War with Russia, while seeking to reduce confrontation (détente).

The 'New Right' under Mrs Thatcher broke dramatically with aspects of the consensus in the 1980s. However, even after 18 years in power the proportion of national income in the public sector (NHS, Welfare State and education) had not altered dramatically. Mrs Thatcher failed to wean the public off their reliance on the state.

The Conservative Party was also divided by the mid-1970s. The defeat of the 'one-nation'-dominated party in the election of 1964 prompted a reassessment of its ideas. The Heath government (1970–74) briefly experimented with radical right-wing policies; removing government subsidies for 'lame duck' companies and introducing legislation to reduce union power. When unemployment grew and the trade union legislation failed, however, Heath proved just as pragmatic as Wilson. In a dramatic 'U-turn' his government bailed out struggling companies and tried to engage trade union and business in planning the economy; actions that many on the right regarded as a betrayal.

The oil price shocks of the early 1970s dramatically increased the power of the unions. In 1974 the miners called a strike to increase their pay and industry was limited to a 'three-day week'. This strike precipitated, and contributed to, Heath's defeat in the February 1974 election. Shortly after, Margaret Thatcher success-fully challenged Heath for the leadership. Her supporters became known as 'the dries' or '**the New Right**'. They included Neo-Liberals (associated with the Adam Smith Institute, the Institute of Economic Affairs or Centre for Policy Studies) who advocated the free market and a reduction in state power and Neo-Conservatives, who were concerned about the erosion of order and self-discipline and wished to reassert the authority of the state. The dries were initially outnumbered by '**One Nation Tories**' or 'wets' (associated with the 'Tory Reform Group', which was formed in 1975), who were sceptical about New Right solutions.

The New Right

Comprise both Neo-Conservatives who are concerned to preserve order, authority and discipline and Neo-Liberals who emphasise a free market economy.

One Nation Conservatives

Moderate Conservatives who emphasise the need for pragmatic policies to promote social stability rather than adherence to any ideological (particularly free market) principles.

Factions and factionalism since 1979

Although many wets hoped that their new leader would prove more pragmatic when in office, they were disappointed. Instead, the 1979 general election became one of the few 'watershed' elections of the twentieth century and marked an end to the presumption that the state would automatically intervene to solve social or economic problems.

Margaret Thatcher's governments prioritised the control of inflation ahead of unemployment, introduced strict controls on government spending, privatised many state industries, introduced laws to control unions, cut local government spending and reduced the size of the Civil Service. She faced down opponents in the Falklands War (1982) and the miners' strike (1984–5). Defeat of the miners, as did the defeat of the Argentinians, had enormous symbolic importance for Mrs Thatcher. She took it as an indication that only a 'resolute' approach would solve Britain's problems.

Although Mrs Thatcher and her supporters were in a minority in both Cabinet and party, she was often able to get her own way and obtain reforms more radical than her colleagues thought were wise. The Cabinet was sometimes 'bounced' into accepting radical policies. She also appealed over the heads of colleagues for the support of party members at Conservative conferences. At other times she publicly committed the government to contentious policies. Many wets were appalled at the massive increase in unemployment, social divisions and riots in the inner cities, but at a loss to know what to do. If they removed her, they risked dividing the party and letting the Labour Party (socialists) in. Moreover, many of their own preferred solutions had been discredited under Heath. The 'wets', therefore, largely failed to mobilise. 'One Nation' groups such as Centre Forward, founded by Francis Pym, a former Foreign Secretary, had little impact. Most of the parliamentary party were, moreover, loyalists and concerned with ensuring election victory. Her run of election successes gave her the prestige and authority to rid herself of some of the 'wets' from her Cabinets and win over others. Thus, by the end of the 1980s the 'wet–dry' opposition had been largely superseded. Most Conservatives accepted

'Scientists think they might one day be able to produce two Conservatives who agree about Europe'

the principle of the 'free market and strong (but slimmed-down) State' that Thatcher proposed.

Though she largely won the party over on economic policy, Mrs Thatcher began to lose support as a result of her increasingly hostile attitude to Europe. In 1986 her Neo-Liberalism led her to sign the Single European Act and accept an end to the British veto over large swathes of policy. Later, however, her Neo-Conservativism, and in particular her belief in the nation state, led her to express concerns about social and political integration. She made an increasing number of speeches or off-the-cuff comments that either cast doubt on or simply contradicted Cabinet policy. In a famous speech at Bruges she linked her belief in markets with a desire to preserve the nation state, 'We have not successfully rolled back the frontiers of the state in Britain, only to see them reimposed at a European level with a European super-state exercising a new dominance from Brussels.' It was her refusal to accept further European integration, coupled with her association with an unpopular new system of financing local government (the poll tax) that brought about her downfall in 1990. Sir Geoffrey Howe, the Deputy Prime Minister, resigned in protest at her attitude to Europe and called on someone to challenge her leadership. Michael Heseltine, a leading wet, stood against her. Abandoned by many Cabinet colleagues, she resigned and was replaced by John Major who tried to unite the party in the run-up to the next election.

The Conservative Party's election victories in the 1980s were due as much (if not more) to splits within Labour as to the attractions of New Right policies. It won only around 42 per cent of the vote in the 1980s. Its large parliamentary majorities were a result of a divided opposition and the 'first past the post' electoral system (see Chapter 15). The split in Labour occurred because the left, led by Tony Benn (a former minister), claimed that Labour governments had failed to implement socialist policies. The left succeeded in persuading many of the trade unions who dominated the party to support proposals, including massive increases in spending and taxation, withdrawal from Europe without a referendum, the repeal of the Conservatives' 'anti-trade union' laws and unilateral nuclear disarmament. These proposals were incorporated in the party's manifesto for the 1983 election – known as 'the longest suicide note in history'! At the same time, groups such as the Campaign for Labour Party Democracy and the Labour Coordinating Committee campaigned for reforms to the party's constitution to increase the activists' control of the Parliamentary Labour Party and ensure that a future Labour government would not renege on its commitments.

The right of the Labour Party felt threatened by these developments. Uneasiness with policy extremism, the power of left-wing activists and the shift in trade union support for left-wing policies provoked a major split involving some of the most prominent figures on the right of the party including Roy Jenkins (a former Chancellor of the Exchequer), Shirley Williams, David Owen and Bill Rodgers. This 'Gang of Four' founded the Social Democratic Party (SDP) in 1981. The new party aroused enthusiasm for its commitment to a reformed social democratic consensus as an alternative to the dogmatic policies of the left and right. The new SDP was a natural ally of the Liberals who, after 20 years of drift, gradually recovered from 1959 onwards with a non-doctrinaire but radical reform programme. The 'SDP-Liberal Alliance' formed between the two parties gained a quarter of the vote in 1983, driving Labour down to 27.6 per cent.

The Alliance held on to most of its ground in the election of 1987, winning 22.6 per cent of the vote to Labour's 30.8 per cent. By that time, however, bitter clashes between the leaders and disagreements about policy, coupled with electoral failure, led many in both parties to conclude that it was time to merge and create a new party, the Liberal Democrats, in 1988. After initial hiccups, the new party inherited the mantle of the Alliance and many, though not all, of their former supporters.

The Social Democratic secession, and the miserable performance of the party in the 1983 election, prompted a reappraisal among many on the left of the Labour Party. The 'soft left', many of whom – like Gordon Brown and Tony Blair – were members of the Tribune Group, cooperated with right-wing Labour MPs who were members of another group called Solidarity to elect a compromise leader with a left-wing past, Neil Kinnock (1983–92) and a deputy leader with right-wing (social democratic) credentials, Roy Hattersley (1983–92). In time the old distinction between left and right was replaced by a division between the parliamentary leadership and a small and weak left faction, organised around the Socialist Campaign group.

Kinnock was convinced that the only way for Labour to recover was to offer moderate policies and assert strong leadership. The party slowly shed left-wing policies and accepted many of the reforms introduced by the Thatcher governments. It dropped its proposals to leave the European Community and subsequently became an enthusiastic pro-European party (something made easier by Mrs Thatcher's increasing hostility to Europe). After a long internal struggle it also abandoned unilateralism. Strong internal leadership was also seen as a necessary element of party 'modernisation'. The party introduced reforms to purge itself of 'entryists' such as the hard-left Militant Tendency and shifted the balance of power from activists and trade unions to ordinary party members. Although this strategy was successful Labour gained votes only gradually. The party received 30.8 per cent in 1987 and 34.4 per cent in 1992.

These disappointing results were seen as pointing towards even further moderation in terms of accepting financial and, above all, fiscal orthodoxy, with restraints on government spending and direct taxation. After its fourth consecutive defeat in 1992 Labour elected John Smith as the new leader. Smith sought to consolidate Kinnock's reforms and wait for the Conservative Party to make mistakes. His death in May 1994 led to the election of Tony Blair as leader and a reappraisal of Labour's strategy.

Blair's approach was very different from that of Smith. In a bold first step he launched a campaign to drop its commitment to public ownership and replace it with an updated statement of beliefs. This was accepted in a ballot of the membership in 1995. 'New Labour' essentially sought to reassure voters that Labour no longer represented a risk to their standards of living. Working closely with his colleague, Gordon Brown, Blair continually emphasised the importance of a market economy and his reluctance to intervene in it. There was a new emphasis on education and

Plate 16.3 Tony Blair's New Labour learned many lessons from Mrs Thatcher's governments (1979–90)

Source: Empics

training to equip people for the global economy and a desire to reform the Welfare State to encourage people to work. In order to help expunge memories of the 'winter of discontent' Blair warned the trade unions that they could expect 'fairness, not favours' from a Labour government. In order to further reassure middle-class voters in England ('middle England') that Labour no longer constituted a threat, Gordon Brown announced in 1997 that there would be no increases in the basic or top rates of income tax. These changes, coupled with commitments to increase spending on the NHS, helped transform Labour into a modern social democratic party that largely left the market to produce wealth, but accepted that the state would modestly redistribute it via public spending.

The party also adopted an increasingly 'tough' approach to law and order issues, promising to marry a concern for social justice with a determination that everyone should play by the rules. This approach was summarised by Blair's soundbite that Labour would be 'tough on crime, tough on the causes of crime'. This shift in emphasis not only appealed to voters in 'middle England' – it also appealed to the authoritarian instincts of many of its working-class voters.

'New Labour' neatly avoided many of the difficult issues associated with wealth redistribution and government intervention in the economy. The party's electoral successes in 1997 and 2001 were undoubtedly aided by the Conservative Party's weaknesses, but gave Blair great personal authority. Large parts of his party, however, remained committed to more 'Old Labour' policies and wanted the government to spend more and be more sympathetic to the trade unions. Labour remained an uneasy alliance of disparate groups, welded together by history and a desperate desire to win.

Thatcher's legacy to the Conservative Party was to leave it more ideological than it had ever been before, especially in relation to Europe. The tensions between the free European market and national sovereignty came out into the open and produced a confrontation between '**Eurosceptics**' and '**Europhiles**' and led both to organise into factions. Eurosceptics, such as members of the Bruges Group and Fresh Start, believed in defending British sovereignty, either by limiting the powers of the EU to what they were in the early 1980s, before the Maastricht Treaty or the SEA, or if necessary by withdrawing altogether. Europhiles, who were members of the Centre for Europe and the Positive European Group, believed that it was in the national interest to remain at the heart of Europe. They maintained that Britain

Eurosceptics

Those who are not generally well disposed to the further integration of Europe, at least within the framework of the European Union.

Europhiles

Those who are generally well disposed to the further integration of Europe within the framework of the European Union.

THE ONE COMMANDMENT

Plate 16.4 Tony Blair's New Labour demonstrated a determination to win that was uncharacteristic of the old Labour Party

Source: Daily Telegraph

could not stand aside from currency union because it was already so heavily involved in the single market (a position that agreed with many of the business interests that have traditionally supported the Conservatives). The Major government (1990–7) steered an uneasy course between these extremes, but was continually denounced by both sides.

The role of the European issue in Mrs Thatcher's downfall also soured relations within the party. Those who admired her could never forgive the parliamentary party for removing her from office and saw every subsequent treaty as a betrayal. A small group of MPs were suspended from the parliamentary party for refusing to support the government on a vital vote on the Maastricht Treaty in 1993. In 1995 Major tried to resolve the conflict by resigning the leadership. In the subsequent election he defeated the Eurosceptic John Redwood, but even this did not stop open warfare. Many activists joined the Referendum Party, which fought the 1997 election demanding a referendum on British membership of the European Union. Others joined the United Kingdom Independence Party (UKIP), which proposed that Britain leave the European Union.

After the 1997 general election the Europhiles found themselves in an increasing minority in the party. Three successive leaders: William Hague, Iain Duncan Smith and Michael Howard were all confirmed Eurosceptics. In order to resolve the European issue Hague proposed that Britain stay out of the single currency for two parliamentary terms. This policy was overwhelmingly supported in a ballot of members in 1998. In the 2001 election the Conservatives campaigned to 'Save the Pound', but went down to yet another defeat. Polls suggested that, although most voters opposed the single currency, the issue was not very important to them and the party appeared 'obsessed' with the issue. Duncan Smith and Howard, therefore, played down the European issue.

While Europe most obviously divided the Conservative Party at the start of the twenty-first century, it also remained divided about other aspects of the Thatcher inheritance, especially the role of the public sector. Neo-liberals wished to continue with a tax-cutting agenda and extend the market to the public services by using the private sector. 'One Nation Tories' wished to reassure voters that the public services would be safe in their hands by matching Labour's spending commitments. In 2001 and 2005 the party fudged the issue by promising to fund tax cuts by reducing waste; a proposition that voters found difficult to believe and which made it easy for opponents to accuse them of secret plans to cut services.

The Conservatives remain divided on moral issues. 'Modernisers', including many Neo-Liberals, wanted the party to be less critical of those who lived alternative lifestyles (single-parent families, homosexual couples and so on) and more supportive of women who wanted to work. They were concerned that the party's emphasis on 'traditional' families (married, heterosexual couples) made them appear to be hostile to increasing sections of the public (unmarried couples, single-parent families and homosexual couples). Neo-Conservatives, on the other hand, opposed civil partnerships for homosexual couples and other policies that undermined 'family values'. They also supported immigration controls. Though such policies were not necessarily motivated by racism, they did little to encourage ethnic minorities to join the party.

On becoming leader, David Cameron appeared to advocate a 'compassionate' conservatism and accept parts of the New Labour agenda. He played down tax cuts and sought to reassure voters that the party would spend as much as Labour on the key public services: especially the NHS and education. Cameron has also tried to re-position the party by focusing on issues such as the environment and global poverty and also by welcoming those who had alternative (chiefly homosexual) lifestyles.

Plate 16.5 David Cameron, the new Conservative leader, is trying to re-position the party at the centre and foster a new image

Source: Empics

More traditional Conservatives, such as Norman Tebbit, expressed outrage but their influence in the party appears to have waned as a result of successive defeats.

'New Labour' represented both a threat and an opportunity for the Liberal Democrats. Labour's moderation attracted many former supporters. But the apparent ideological closeness of the two parties also made it easier for both party supporters to cooperate to keep the Conservatives out. 'Tactical voting' in 1997 and 2001 increased the centre party's haul of seats, even though its vote hardly altered. Disillusion with Labour added to their vote in 2005.

In Labour's first term, the Liberal Democrats cooperated in introducing Labour's constitutional reform package; but were disappointed by the failure to hold a referendum on electoral reform. In the second term, the Liberal Democrats became more critical of the government, especially in relation to Iraq, civil liberties and reform of the public services. Despite their continued success in 2005, there were calls for their leader, Charles Kennedy, to stand down. The immediate cause of concern was Kennedy's personal performance as leader and, in particular, his self-confessed drinking problem. There were deeper tensions, however. Those MPs who followed the old Liberal tradition believed that the party had become too 'statist' in its attempt to appeal to disappointed former Labour voters. They were concerned that the more socially liberal Conservative Party which appeared to be taking shape under David Cameron would attract many former Liberal Democrats. In the event, Kennedy was forced to stand down and Sir Menzies Campbell became leader. Many in the party expected that the next election would produce a 'hung Parliament', which might provide them with an opportunity to achieve electoral reform (see Chapter 15).

The Labour Party has also had to face internal problems in recent years. Just as in the 1950s the divisions have related to both domestic and foreign policy. 'Old Labour' MPs opposed some of Blair's plans to reform the public services; in particular contracting out, self-governing hospitals and schools reform (see Chapter 18). It was Blair's decision to support the 'war on terror' and to go to war in Iraq, however, that most bitterly divided his party. Blair's commitment to fight terrorism at home by increasing police powers and introducing national identity cards also alarmed many libertarians. In late 2005 the government was defeated in the Commons on proposals to detain suspects for up to 90 days.

Plate 16.6 The Liberal Democrats faced strategic difficulties after their success in the 2005 general election. They replaced Charles Kennedy with Sir Menzies Campbell

Source: Empics

By the end of 2005 all the major parties appeared to be competing on the 'centre ground'. It remains to be seen whether David Cameron can broaden the Conservative Party's appeal, whether Menzies Campbell can forge a new position for the Liberal Democrats and whether a new Labour leader, such as Gordon Brown, can succeed in appealing to both 'middle England' and Labour's core voters.

Party structure and organisation

Factional disputes are capable of destroying parties' hopes of election victory. They are obviously situations leaders would like to avoid. One way of controlling or dampening confrontations is through organisation. We have already noted how Kinnock and Blair rooted out 'extremists' in constituency Labour parties by tightening central control. In this section we examine how British party organisations usually enable the party to function and how they allow leaders to exercise control.

BRIEFINGS

16.2 Michels and McKenzie: The iron law of oligarchy and British political parties

In 1911 the German sociologist Robert Michels published *Political Parties* (New York: Dover Publications, 1959), in which he formulated the 'iron law of oligarchy'. This states that mass organisations cannot be democratic, by their very nature, and will always be controlled by a small elite group ('the oligarchy'). There are two reasons for this. First, leaders know all the business of their organisation. They control internal communications and have greater political skills than ordinary members. Second, the 'masses' are incompetent. Few know much about policy matters, or turn up to meetings. Most feel the need for 'direction and guidance' provided by leaders. A culture of deference is thus encouraged.

According to Michels leaders develop their own particular interests and goals, which differ from those of members. They control organisations, and use them for their own purposes, not those of the members. Leaders of mass movements inevitably become members of the power elite.

Robert McKenzie applied Michels' analysis to the Conservative and Labour parties in the 1950s in his classic *British Political Parties* (London: Heinemann, 1955). He began by noting that the Conservative Party was not formally democratic and vested a great deal of power in the leader. The Labour Party, on the other hand, liked to think of itself as democratic, in that the party conference was the sovereign body of the party and the leader merely a 'servant' of the conference. McKenzie argued, however, that for most practical purposes power was distributed in the same way in the two parties. One reason was simply that the trade unions sided with the leadership in their battles with their activists in local parties. He also argued that leaders were accountable to the wider electorate rather than their 'members'. In short, Michels' general argument was correct because the British constitution trumped the Labour's Party's constitution.

Things changed after McKenzie's book was written. The left reduced the power of the leader by making MPs subject to regular reselection by local activists. It was hoped that the threat of 'deselection' would make them more sensitive to the activists and less concerned to please the leader. The left also obtained reforms of the method of electing the leader, giving the trade unions and constituency activists a share of the vote in an electoral college. They failed, however, to make the National Executive Committee (NEC, a body elected by annual conference) responsible for drafting Labour's election manifesto. Had they succeeded, the leadership would have been severely constrained and have found it very difficult to 'modernise' its policies, as eventually happened under Neil Kinnock's leadership.

Under Kinnock's (1983–92) and John Smith's (1992–4) leadership the principle of one member one vote was extended to election of the party leader and selection of candidates in an effort to bypass the activists. Just as Michels suggested, this group was more likely to defer to party leaders. Thus, while formal power appeared to pass to members, in reality it returned to the parliamentary leadership.

As we shall shortly demonstrate, party organisations reflect both the origins and the ideologies of the parties. However, since the ultimate purpose of most parties is to gain power and since elections are a competitive business, they often learn from successful parties both at home and abroad. (New Labour learned a great deal from observing Bill Clinton's New Democrats in the United States.) It is hardly surprising, therefore, that the party organisations resemble each other.

The organisational ladder contains four main rungs:

1. At the top is the leadership, a group of 20–30 MPs occupying, or hoping to occupy, senior government positions as Cabinet ministers. Their primary interest is in winning the next election.

2. A little further down is the parliamentary party of elected MPs and members of the House of Lords, from whom the leadership is drawn. They too place enormous importance on electoral success, but their priorities are subtly different from the leadership. Most MPs represent safe seats and have more to fear from deselection by local parties or from an unfavourable redrawing of their constituency boundaries than from an adverse national swing against the party.

3. Much further down the ladder is the party in the country – the unpaid officers and active members of local associations – many of them elected councillors on the local authority. For most activists the reward is not career advancement – indeed there are no tangible rewards at all – but furtherance of the party's broad goals, on which they tend to take a more principled stand than leaders and MPs.

4. On the bottom rung is the 'party in the electorate': stalwart supporters (or 'party identifiers') who, while not formally members, can be relied on to vote for the party in elections and to accept the party line on most political issues.

All major parties can be examined in these terms. However, the precise nature of the party organisation depends on their origins and ideology.

The impact of origins and ideology

The Conservative Party began in the nineteenth century as a party formed in Parliament; after the extension of the franchise it organised in the country in order to mobilise support. It was always assumed, however, that the members would defer to their parliamentary leaders. Historically there has been little pretence that Conservative party members 'decide' policy or that the party is democratic. Members have simply wanted their leaders to win in order to keep their (socialist) opponents out!

The Labour Party, on the other hand, was formed in order to gain greater working-class representation in Parliament. It was part of a wider 'labour movement' that consisted of an 'industrial' and a 'political' wing' (the trade unions and the party respectively). Since the unions provided most of the money, personnel and organisation, they insisted on having formal rights over policy, but reserved the right to govern their own affairs according to their own rule books. Labour is a **'federal' party**. It was the union organisations, rather than individual union members, that affiliated to the party. Trade union members paid a 'political levy', which went to a 'political fund'. The union executive decided how many members should be affiliated to the party. The more members the unions affiliated, the more votes they acquired at conference. These votes were, moreover, cast in a single **bloc** to maximise their impact, rather than divided in order to reflect divisions of opinion within the union. From its birth through to the early 1990s the unions had around 90 per cent of votes at conference and dominated its committees. Not surprisingly, critics called Labour a 'wholly owned subsidiary' of the unions.

These differences in origins were accentuated by differences in ideology. Conservatism regards leadership and deference from members to leaders as natural. Socialist ideology, on the other hand, claims that all are equal and have an equal right to be listened to in policy making. The very idea of leadership is, therefore, often regarded with suspicion by socialists. These differences have important implications for party competition. The Conservatives have a natural impulse to allow the leader enough policy discretion to win elections. Labour's equally natural impulse is to constrain the leader and reduce their discretion.

The concentration of power in the hands of the Conservative Party leader has helped it continually adapt to changing circumstances. In the Labour Party, by contrast, the dispersion of power in its affiliates and continual demands for wider participation in policy making has made it more difficult for the party to adapt. The Conservatives have historically tended to be both less 'ideological' and more pragmatic than Labour. The party has, therefore, been able to adapt more quickly to changed circumstances. Labour, on the other hand, has continually struggled to reconcile '**modernisation**' with its core principles and has agonised over what these core principles were. In recent years these roles have arguably been reversed. New Labour has been less ideological (some would say unprincipled) while the Conservatives have been more ideological (some would say dogmatic), especially in relation to Europe.

The leadership

At the apex of the party organisation stands the party leader or, since political parties are teams of like-minded politicians, the leadership. The leaders of both parties were, until 1983, elected by fellow MPs. From 1983 the Labour leader has been elected by an electoral college consisting of MPs (and MEPs), the trade unions and ordinary party members. From 2001 the Conservative leader has been elected by party members in a national ballot after the parliamentary party has whittled a field of candidates down to two. (There was no national ballot in 2003 because Michael Howard was the only candidate.)

The leader of the Conservative Party has enormous powers over policy and senior appointments. Indeed the leader is the only person with formal responsibility for policy; a position that was unaltered when the party adopted a new constitution in 1998. The Conservative leader nominates a colleague to write the party's manifesto (in 2005 Michael Howard appointed David Cameron). The leader can also appoint members of the shadow Cabinet, a party chairman (who is responsible for the operation of Conservative Central Office), deputy chairmen, the party treasurer and several members of the party's board of management, which assumes responsibility for party organisation reviewing the annual accounts, appointing senior staff, administering the national membership list, maintaining a list of approved candidates and resolving disputes.

The leader of the Labour Party, by contrast, has far fewer powers. The party's constitution declares that the annual conference is the 'sovereign body', which implies that it can both change the constitution and make policy. According to that constitution, the Labour manifesto is drawn up by a joint committee of the Cabinet (or shadow Cabinet) and the National Executive Committee (NEC). The leader and deputy leader of the party are ex officio members of the NEC. Historically, the NEC itself also had a policy-making role between party conferences and often produced policies that were at odds with the parliamentary leadership. When in opposition there are annual elections among Labour MPs to select members of the shadow Cabinet and the leader must appoint these in his first Cabinet. The party's general secretary is appointed by the NEC, while the party treasurer is elected by annual conference, as is the NEC itself.

Labour's penchant for elections had one unintended (and undesirable) consequence: together with the ideological pluralism that characterises the party, it encouraged organised groups to emerge in order to compete for office. Conflict within the party became 'institutionalised'. Party members were just as likely to view 'politics' as a battle between one Labour faction and another as they were to think of it as a competition with the Conservatives. The annual conferences in the 1970s were the scene of heated debates between the factions. The Conservative Party, by contrast, allowed the leader to make such appointments as (s)he deemed necessary to achieve a 'balance' between the various parts of the party. Conservatives were, moreover, less ideological. While there were policy differences between individuals in the leadership, these were less intense and did not become the focus of elections. The Conservative Party was, therefore, a party of *tendencies* rather than *factions*. Not surprisingly, it used to be said that 'unity' was the Conservatives 'secret weapon', but it could equally have been said that 'disunity' was Labour's not so secret handicap.

> **'Tendencies'**
>
> Individuals who share common attitudes or place particular emphasis on parts of a party's ideology but who are not organised.

On paper the Conservative leader appears to be far more powerful than the Labour leader. Yet the formal 'powers' set out on paper are not the same as 'power', defined simply as the ability to get one's way. The power of the leader depends, among other things, on the positions of other senior colleagues (or 'big beasts'), the party's position in the polls and the leader's political skills. Edward Heath (1975), Margaret Thatcher (1990) and Iain Duncan Smith (2003) were all ousted from office when they lost the confidence of colleagues.

Leaders have more time, resources and expertise than most other figures in the party. They can, in addition, usually rely on party members to defer to them. In recent years, both parties' leaders have appealed to members over the heads of the leadership and activists by holding referendums. Success is not inevitable, however. Conservative activists failed to provide the two-thirds support Michael Howard required to abolish their role in the election of the leader in 2005.

In practice Labour leaders have often been in just as strong a position as their Conservative counterparts, since they could invariably rely on the support of the trade unions. Indeed, it was only when Labour leaders lost this support that they became much weaker than their Conservative counterparts and more constrained. Once a Labour leader became prime minister, he acquired all the powers of that great office, including extensive powers of appointment, control of honours and so on. Tony Blair is a good case in point.

The parliamentary parties

All members of the Conservative Parliamentary Party who take the Conservative whip are members of the 1922 Committee, which meets once a week to discuss all matters affecting the party. This committee elects a chairman (who has formal responsibility for organising the parliamentary round of the leadership election) and an executive committee.

When the Conservative Party is in government ministers regularly attend meetings of the 1922 Committee to exchange views with their backbenchers. A failure to impress the audience may have an adverse effect on a minister's career and even lead to resignation. The Conservative Parliamentary Party is capable of exhibiting great loyalty to the leader. Even those 'wet' MPs who were privately bitterly critical of Mrs Thatcher in the 1980s couched their criticism in moderate language. Yet as more and more MPs have become professional politicians and the personal cost of losing elections has risen, deference has weakened and the pressure on leaders to produce electoral success increased. Backbench MPs became more restless under John Major in response to concerns about developments in Europe and lingering bitterness about Mrs Thatcher's removal from office.

The Parliamentary Labour Party (PLP) is organised in a similar way to that of the Conservative Party. It has its own standing orders, which were revised before the party came to power in 1997 to give it greater power to discipline MPs. The chairman of the PLP is elected by MPs and chairs its weekly meetings. Labour MPs did not rebel much in the first term, but became much more likely to do so in the second term (see Chapter 18).

Both parliamentary parties have a team of 'whips' who are responsible for MPs from certain regions. They relay information from the front to the backbenches, try to ensure that the party's vote is maximised and monitor the performance of MPs and ministers. Occasionally, they try to get an MP to follow the official party line by threatening to write to the local Conservative association or Constituency Labour Party (CLP) accusing them of disloyalty. Local parties, however, are sometimes immune to such pressures and reward MPs for taking an 'independent' line. Attempts to make sure that MPs stay 'on message' by providing them with pagers and mobile phones have often failed because MPs switched them off! Party cohesion in Parliament depends much more on instinctive loyalty than threats of deselection and the patronage of the Prime Minister. A backbench MP, who has good relations with his local party and does not want high office or honours, is unlikely to be successfully bullied by the party hierarchy.

The national headquarters

Conservative Central Office and Labour Party headquarters serve several functions:

- keeping national membership lists (vital for membership ballots and financial appeals)
- advising the local parties on policy
- providing training for campaigns
- providing advice on regulatory matters
- producing campaign materials (standardised leaflets)
- commissioning party election broadcasts
- supplying the parliamentary party with additional research.

The Conservative chairman is appointed by the leader and regarded as the leader's man (or woman) in Central Office; Labour's general secretary is appointed by the National Executive Committee and regarded as a servant of the party. In practice, however, the general secretary forges a close working relationship with the leader.

The party in the country and party conferences

Local parties

The major British parties are organised in similar ways at a local level. A Conservative association or CLP exists in each parliamentary constituency on the mainland and, where support is strong enough, in each ward making up the constituency. In the 1950s local parties served a social function and many joined them to get access to sporting facilities or simply to meet people. As leisure opportunities have increased the parties have lost this function and membership has declined dramatically. Their main function now is to contest elections by raising campaign

BRIEFINGS

16.3 Why has party membership fallen?

Party membership has fallen dramatically in recent years. In the mid-1950s the Conservative Party claimed over 2 million members and Labour around 800,000. By 2005 membership stood at around 320,000 for the Conservatives, 215,000 for Labour and 75,000 for the Liberal Democrats. While there have been occasional increases in membership (there was a net increase of 100,000 Labour Party members when Blair became leader) there has been a general decline. There are a number of possible reasons for this:

- Some of the decline is more apparent than real. Historically, membership records were inaccurate and local parties tended to 'over-claim'. Conservative associations often included many of those who attended Conservative clubs for social reasons rather than those who paid subscriptions, while CLPs had to pretend that they had at least 1,000 members in order to send delegates to conference. Rule changes and computerisation has improved the accuracy of records.

- Increased leisure opportunities. People no longer need to join parties for social reasons.

- Organisations closely associated with the parties have declined. (The trade unions in the case of Labour and the Church of England in the case of the Conservatives.)

- The real cost of party membership has increased.

- Ideological convergence. The sharp divisions between the parties have been much reduced. There is less incentive to join parties.

- The decline of 'tribal' loyalties. More people have mixed characteristics that weaken party attachments.

- Politics is structured around new issues (such as the environment) that are less relevant to the major parties, which were based on class and left–right ideological divisions.

- Parties do not need members as much. National elections are fought on television and do not need campaigners (except in marginal seats).

- The leadership of parties can often raise funds by appealing directly to the public or a few rich individuals.

- Voters are smarter. They realise that they have little influence over party policy and are not taken seriously by the leadership.

The decline in membership may matter. Research has demonstrated that local campaigns do influence voters. A party without 'foot soldiers' may be unable to mobilise its vote on election day. The decline in membership may also lead a party to rely on a few rich individuals for finance. (It is easier to ask one individual for £10 million than a million members for £10 each!) Unless this money comes with 'no strings attached' there is a risk that rich individuals will gain excessive influence.

funds, engaging in electioneering and, most important of all, selecting the candidate who, in the safe seats, will become the MP. In most parties political agreement is taken for granted and politics is not discussed much!

Conservative associations have traditionally enjoyed autonomy over their own affairs (electing their own officers, having their own finances, selecting their own candidates, fighting campaigns and imposing discipline). Although some associations are enormously wealthy, they are reluctant to make contributions to Central Office, accusing it of waste and bureaucracy. They also jealously guarded their rights to select candidates and resisted attempts to select more socially representative individuals (women, ethnic minorities and openly homosexual candidates have not found it easy to be selected for 'safe' seats).

This autonomy has been eroded in recent years, though members have acquired the right to elect members of the board of management, the right to expect a certain level of service and the right to participate in the election of the party leader. Each local association used to have its own constitution. The new constitution adopted in 1998 produced 'model rules' and made it clear that every association is subject to national rules and the authority of the leader. Local associations are required to report regularly on their activities and forward subscription money to Central Office. Members can also now join the party nationally. Money is automatically deducted before being forwarded to the constituencies, making it much easier to fund the central organisation. In addition, there is a national membership list, so leaders can now communicate directly with members without relying on local associations. There are even provisions for the national party to take over those local parties that do not meet performance criteria relating to recruitment and campaigning. The constitution also introduced a new Ethics and Integrity Committee that has the power to expel members for conduct likely to bring the party into disrepute. In February 2002 the committee expelled Jeffrey Archer, after his conviction for perjury.

The new constitution did not alter the method by which candidates are selected. Central Office keeps a list of approved candidates and offers training to potential candidates. Attempts to influence the type of candidate have met with little success. In late 2005 it was announced that a 'priority list' would be drawn up consisting of a wider range of the 'best' in British society and that associations will be encouraged to involve non-party members in the selection process. It remains to be seen whether this will make the parliamentary party more representative of the party as a whole. In the past associations have resisted attempts to produce a 'politically correct' list of candidates.

Constituency Labour Parties have always been subject to a great deal of central control by the NEC, who were anxious to keep their left-wing activists in check. In the 1970s and 1980s the general management committees of the CLPs, which dominated the local parties, became dominated by left-wing activists. The NEC has extensive powers to interfere in the operation of CLPs and impose candidates. The party experimented with 'all women' short-lists before the 1997 election, but this was declared illegal by the courts. The *Sex Discrimination (Candidate Selection) Act, 2002* made the practice legal for a short time. The tactic backfired spectacularly in Blaenau Gwent in 2005 when Peter Law stood as an independent, defeating the official female Labour candidate.

Annual conference and policy making

Conservative associations have the right to send members to attend the annual conference that takes place in the autumn of each year. Those who attend act as representatives and are expected to make up their minds in light of the debate. Unlike the Labour equivalent, the conference has no formal policy-making powers, rarely votes and often does little more than provide senior party figures with a platform for expressing their current thinking. The conventional wisdom, therefore, has been that while Labour conferences decide, Conservative conferences confer.

The conventional wisdom probably underestimates the influence that Conservative members have over policy. Although most attention is focused on the annual conference there is a thriving conference system with special conferences for women, youth sections, councillors and the Welsh and Scottish parties. The Conservative leadership is often sensitive to the mood in the party and is anxious to please members. Certainly there is a great deal of evidence that senior party figures take their conference speeches seriously, not just because they wish to address the nation but because they wish to please the 'party faithful'.

It is difficult to measure influence with precision because there are so few votes. Most of the influence undoubtedly takes place in private meetings outside the conference halls. There are, however, clear cases of influence. In the 1950s the Conservative conference pressured the leadership to increase targets for house building, while in the 1970s the conference persuaded the party to adopt a more restrictive immigration policy. Such influence does not always produce popular policies, however. In the late 1980s ministers were persuaded to introduce the massively unpopular poll tax as a result of pressure from the grass roots, who wished to avoid increases in the old tax (domestic rates). The results were disastrous and the new tax was both introduced and abolished in the 1987–92 Parliament!

The Labour Party's constitution declares that the annual conference is the 'sovereign' body of the party; suggesting that it is the place where all the great matters are decided. It provides its members (the trade unions, constituency parties and other affiliated organisations) with formal voting rights. Those attending conference are 'delegates' who are mandated (instructed) how to vote on each motion or proposal. This makes it less easy for the party to achieve a compromise at the conference. Delegates have, however, enjoyed some discretion because motions produced by various parts of the party on the same issue have had to be collected together in 'composite' motions, which – by definition – cannot have been discussed beforehand.

Traditionally the large trade union delegations would get together before conference and cut deals that were mutually beneficial to their members and supportive of the leader. Labour leaders looked to the unions and their bloc votes to protect them from the CLPs. Yet as the unions moved to the left in the 1970s the Labour leadership found itself increasingly at odds with both conference and the NEC. Harold Wilson and James Callaghan regularly ignored conference decisions or invoked the rule that since a motion had not been carried by a two-thirds majority it could not be put in the party's programme for office and could not be included in the manifesto. This continual flouting of the spirit of conference decisions caused resentment and led to demands to increase the constraints on the leader and make him the servant of the conference. In the late 1970s the CLPs launched a successful campaign to introduce an electoral college for the election of the Labour leader. This was made up of trade unions (40 per cent of vote), CLPs (30 per cent) and MPs (30 per cent). The unions, however, were not obliged to ballot their members and most general secretaries or executives took it on themselves to decide how their bloc vote would be cast without consulting their members. The initiative in leadership elections, therefore, lay with a few union leaders who could provide any candidate with momentum by promising their votes. In effect a few union leaders decided who would be the Labour leader in 1983 (Kinnock) and 1992 (Smith). At around the same time a system of 'mandatory reselection' was introduced that obliged parties to hold a reselection meeting and made it more likely that the MP or candidate would be deselected. Unsurprisingly, the leadership felt compelled to accede to the demands of the conference and the 1983 Labour manifesto contained many of the policies the left wanted. Perhaps equally unsurprisingly, the party went down to its worst defeat since 1918, gaining just 28.6 per cent of the vote.

The road from the 1983 manifesto to the New Labour landslide of 1997 was a long one because the leadership had to carry the case for organisational and policy 'modernisation' to each and every part of the party. Neil Kinnock, in particular, devoted a great deal of time and energy to persuading the unions to support change. Continued electoral failure added to the pressure for the unions to cede power. In 1993 their share of the vote in the electoral college was reduced to just one-third and they were required to ballot their members in Labour leadership elections. This reform meant that the initiative shifted back to the PLP. A candidate could build momentum by securing the support of MPs (who could announce their intentions without consulting anyone if they wished). The unions' share of votes at conference was reduced from 90 to 70 per cent in 1993 and to under 50 per cent in 1995 and they were allocated a smaller proportion of seats on the NEC. Both these changes were designed to counter claims that Labour was 'in the pockets of the unions'. Both, however, carried another risk. As the unions lost their share of the vote, the CLPs gained accordingly. Unless something was done to change matters, the conference and NEC might shift to the left.

In order to prevent this the leadership also acted to reduce the power of the NEC and annual conference. The NEC was increasingly required to focus on organisation and campaigns rather than policy. The annual conference was neutered by reforming policy making. This process had actually begun in the late 1980s when the party used joint committees of the shadow Cabinet and NEC to formulate policies, thus increasing the leadership's ability to control decisions. In the mid-1990s Labour introduced more new policy-making mechanisms. A National Policy Forum (NPF) was established, made up of around 180 members elected by the various party 'stakeholders' (unions, CLPs and socialist societies). This meets two or three times a year behind closed doors and out of the media spotlight. Labour's divisions have, as a direct consequence, become much less evident. Beneath the NPF are around six policy commissions covering specific areas. These are required to formulate policy over a two-year period, taking evidence from all parts of the party, commissioning research papers and producing draft reports that are circulated among the various parts of the party. The policy commissions are jointly chaired by a member of the NEC and ministers. Informal consultations are usually chaired by specially trained facilitators at regional conferences. The whole policy process is guided by a Joint Policy Committee (JPC), chaired by the Prime Minister and comprising the NEC and members of the government.

The new policy-making process is designed to be more 'deliberative' than in the past and increase the role of the leadership. The briefing papers are often produced by the leadership, ministers and their advisers. Policy papers are discussed, comments collated and revisions drafted. The final proposals do not formally become party policy until they are voted on at conference. Formally, conference remains 'sovereign'. It is very difficult, nevertheless, for opponents of the leadership to mobilise opposition at this late stage. Annual conference has, in effect, become a mere rubber stamp, a 'showcase' for the leadership and an opportunity to project a new 'modern' image to the electorate.

Labour conferences are less entertaining than in the past, but there is little doubt that the conference system (comprising the NPF, JPC and Policy Commission) is more effective at making electorally popular policy.

The party in the electorate

The Conservative Party has traditionally been attentive to the needs of the wider electorate and largely eschewed a narrow ideological approach to politics. In the 1950s it claimed a massive membership of around 2 million that could not only be relied on to vote and sometimes to campaign for it, but also to provide a useful gauge of public opinion. This may have been one of the factors that allowed it to rapidly accept the social democratic consensus from 1945.

Ironically the Labour Party, the self-styled 'People's Party', has often been inattentive to the wider electorate and has instead turned in on itself, focusing on internal battles rather than the need to reach out to voters. The party often pursued an ideological approach to politics that made it difficult to 'modernise'. Since it has always been able to rely on the trade unions to provide affiliated members, moreover, it has never had a genuinely mass membership and its members are politically unrepresentative of both its voters and potential voters.

The principal architects of New Labour were all too aware of the party's tendency to turn in on itself and focus on internal battles rather than focus on the battle with the Conservatives. They eagerly used opinion polls and focus groups to keep in touch with popular opinion. The process began in the early 1980s but speeded up under New Labour, which invested heavily in such methods. Philip Gould, Blair's focus group 'guru', produced streams of memos, keeping the leadership informed about what ordinary people were saying and advising them what words to use in making their appeals. Such research also found its way into the new National Policy Forum and various Policy Commission discussions. Revealingly, one party document warned that, 'for the government to stay in tune with the party, the party must stay in tune with the nation' (the Labour Party, *Partnership in Power*). In 2003 the party also launched the so-called 'Big Conversation' in which it canvassed members' and voters' opinions on a range of subjects.

Some regarded the use of such techniques as anti-democratic, since they diminish the role of party members and vastly increase the power of the strategic community of professionals around the leader who have responsibility for collecting such data. Others cast doubt on the usefulness of the information, alleging that the findings were inevitably distorted to comply with the leadership's positions. It could be argued, however, that market research methods improve democracy by making parties more responsive to the wider electorate. As party membership continues to fall members are likely to become increasingly unrepresentative of the electorate as a whole. It is essential that all parties listen to the wider electorate if they are to adapt or modernise. The danger, however, is that if ordinary party members feel that their opinions count for just as much (or less) than focus group members, there is less incentive for them to join. Some have seen the new techniques of political marketing as contributing to a massive drop in party membership.

Summary

Commentators sometimes depict political parties as disciplined armies moving in perfect order on the political battleground. The reality could hardly be more different. As with all voluntary organisations, people join with dissimilar objectives and protest or quit if these are not met. Parties have an inner life, marked by ideological divisions, personal rivalries and tensions between the leadership and members. All parties are uneasy coalitions.

This is clearly evident in the recent struggles within both Conservative and Labour parties and goes back a long way, as shown by our earlier discussion and by the Milestones section that follows. We have emphasised not only party divisions, however, but also the way in which leaders can use their organisational advantages to pull the party together and stake out a winning position that endures over a considerable period of time. Besides covering internal disputes this chapter has charted the overall development of the parties and their internal structure. Specifically it has discussed:

■ inner tensions and ideological developments from 1868 to 1979;

■ factional and leadership initiatives of the 1980s and 1990s;

■ the way in which parties link grass roots and leadership through their organisational structures;

■ the leverage this gives to party leaders in pulling the party together.

MILESTONES

Milestones in the development of British political parties

Conservatives		Liberals		Labour	
1867–8	Second Reform Act transforms franchise from a small, propertied basis to a mass electorate				
1870s	Primrose League promotes mass organisation of party, with a branch in every constituency. Party promotes Empire, monarchy and social reform	Joseph Chamberlain and the 'Birmingham Caucus' pioneer a mass party organisation emulated in other parts of Britain			
1868–86	Alternation of Conservatives and Liberals in government				
1886	Accession of Liberal Unionists initiates 20-year dominance of Conservative Party in national politics	Gladstone's First Home Rule Bill for Ireland splits Liberal Party			
				1900	Labour Representation Committee brings together socialist parties and trade unions
1905	Under influence of Liberal Unionists, party advocates imperial preference and protection, is defeated in the general election, and remains divided	1905–14	Liberal governments introduce social reforms and push for Irish Home Rule Parliament Act 1911, National Health Insurance Act 1911, Irish Home Rule Bills 1912, 1913, 1914	1905–14	Labour supports reforming Liberal governments
				1914–18	Labour internally divided over whether Britain should fight First World War
1922	Break-up of coalition. Bonar Law propels Conservatives to office	1922–9	Liberals split between 'Lloyd George' and 'Asquith' Liberals	1923–4	First minority Labour government legislates for public housing programmes
				1929–31	Second minority Labour government
1926	General strike broken by Conservative government with implicit support of Liberals and Labour				
1931	Financial crisis related to world slump leads to split in Labour and Liberal parties, and formation of Conservative-dominated 'national government'				
1932	Government intervenes to impose protection, tariffs, industrial mergers and rudimentary planning	Split between mainstream opposition and 'National Liberals' who are absorbed by Conservatives		1932	Split between mainstream Labour and 'National Labour' who are absorbed by Conservatives
1940–5	Wartime coalition government, in which Labour basically runs home affairs				
1946–51	Conservatives accept Welfare State and most nationalisations	Liberals drift without clear leadership			Reforming Labour governments establish 'Welfare State', nationalise large industries and decolonise India
1951–59	They win elections of 1951, 1955 and 1959 on basis of abolishing controls and freeing economy	1959	Grimond provides strong leadership that reverses vote decline	1951–64	Party divides increasingly between left and right

Milestones in the development of British political parties continued

Conservatives		Liberals		Labour	
1962–4	Government shifts to idea of indicative economic planning	1964	Gain votes with advocacy of electoral reform, civil rights and European integration	1964–6	Wins 1964 and 1966 elections on basis of 'making planning work'. Devaluation of sterling leads to financially orthodox policies. Trade union reform fails. Strengthening of the left
1965–70	Shift to the right – support for free market and trade union reform				
1970–4	Heath government imposes legal framework on trade unions and joins European Union				
1973–4	'Three-day week' and miners' strike precipitate election, which brings government down	1974	Liberal vote increases to 18–19% at the two general elections that year	1974	Wins elections but with reduced vote. Wage and price controls lead to trade union revolt in 1979 ('winter of discontent'). Loses 1979 election
1975	Margaret Thatcher wins party leadership election on a 'New Right' programme				
1979–90	Margaret Thatcher wins a series of elections on a programme of financial orthodoxy, privatisation of state industry, strict regulation of trade unions, cuts in public expenditure, a cautious attitude to EU and full support of NATO	1983–7	Alliance with Social Democrats nets one-quarter of the vote in general elections of 1983 and 1987	1979–83	Ascendancy of 'hard left'. Alternative economic programme and internal reforms lead to breakaway Social Democrat Party and to heavy election defeat in 1983
				1983	Election of Neil Kinnock as leader. Centralising reforms and adoption of 'Neo-Liberal consensus' fails to avert election defeats of 1987 and 1992
1990	Thatcher ejected as leader to avert election defeat				
1992–7	Split between 'Eurosceptics' and 'pro-Europeans' weakens party by continual controversy. Series of financial and sexual scandals. Go down to record defeat in 1997			1992	Kinnock resigns as party leader
				1992–4	John Smith carries on internal reforms as party leader
				1994	Tony Blair elected party leader, imposes strong central discipline, abolishes Clause 4, loosens ties with the trade unions and evolves image of 'New Labour', which wins 1997 election
		1997	Liberals win 46 seats in Parliament, their largest number since 1929	1997	Government initiates programme of political reform starting with devolution. Cautious pursuit of 'Neo-Liberal consensus' aids stability and economic prosperity

Milestones in the development of British political parties continued

Conservatives		Liberals		Labour	
1998	System for electing party leader changed to include party members	1998–9	Coalitions with Labour in Scotland and Wales		
2001	Eurosceptic, right-wing leader William Hague loses election. He is replaced by the very similar Iain Duncan Smith	2001	New leader Charles Kennedy increases vote and seat numbers	2001	Landslide victory in general election consolidates Tony Blair's leadership
2002	Main party division shifts to efficiency and delivery of public services				
2003	Michael Howard replaces Duncan-Smith				Serious internal dissent over Iraq War
2004					Blair announces intention not to stand for further re-election after 2005
2005	Suffer third consecutive defeat. Howard stands down and is replaced by David Cameron, begins shift to centre		Party makes modest progress but disappointed by results		Labour re-elected for third successive time Government hit by series of revolts in Parliament over plans for new laws on terrorism and education reform
2006			Kennedy is forced to resign and is replaced by Sir Menzies Campbell		

Essays

1. How far are British political parties 'umbrella' organisations covering a loose alliance of factions and tendencies, and how far are they basically united?

2. Does Michels' 'iron law of oligarchy' still hold for British political parties?

3. Are party activists inevitably more extreme than party leaders? Why or why not?

4. In what sense, if at all, is the use of market research and focus groups to inform policy anti-democratic?

Projects

1. Document with examples the major ways in which either the current Conservative or the current Labour leader control their respective parties.

2. Update Robert McKenzie's analysis of power relationships within the Conservative and Labour parties.

3. Imagine that you are asked by a party leader to find out why people do not join their party. How would you go about providing an explanation? What do you think are the most important reasons for the decline in membership?

Further reading

Valuable historical material is contained in R. T. McKenzie, *British Political Parties* (London: Mercury, 1964). The leading book on parties today is Paul Webb, *The Modern British Party System* (London: Sage, 2000). On the Labour Party see Thomas Quinn, *Modernising the Labour Party: Organisational Change since 1983* (Basingstoke: Palgrave Macmillan, 2004). On the Conservative Party see Philip Norton, 'The Conservative Party: is there anyone out there?', in Anthony King (ed.), *Britain at the Polls 2001* (Chatham, NJ: Chatham House, 2002). On the Liberal Democrats see Andrew Russell, *Neither Left nor Right?* (Manchester: Manchester University Press, 2005) and David Denver, 'The Liberal Democrats in constructive opposition', in King, *Britain at the Polls 2001*.

The best account of the internal democratisation of parties is in Paul Webb, 'Parties and party systems: modernisation, regulation and diversity', *Parliamentary Affairs*, **54** (2), 2001, pp. 308–21.

On the Conservative Party see Gillian Peele, 'Towards new Conservatives? Organisational reform and the Conservative Party', *Political Quarterly*, **69** (2), 1998, pp. 141–7; Richard Kelly, 'Farewell conference, hello forum: the making of Labour and Tory policy', *Political Quarterly*, **72** (3), 2001, pp. 329–34; Jennifer Lees-Marshment and Stuart Quayle, 'Empowering the members or marketing the party? The Conservative reforms of 1998', *Political Quarterly*, **72** (2), 2001, 204–12.

On Labour see Thomas Quinn, 'Block voting in the Labour Party: a political exchange model', *Party Politics* (2002), 207–26 and Thomas Quinn, 'Leasehold or freehold? Leadership eviction rules in the British Conservative and Labour Parties', *Political Studies*, **53** (4), 2005, pp. 793–815.

Also see Mark Rathbone, 'The future of the Liberal Democrats', *Talking Politics*, **18** (1), 2005, pp. 14, 16–19 and Peter Joyce, *Realignment of the Left? A History of the Relationship between the Liberal Democrat and Labour Parties* (Basingstoke: Macmillan, 1999); Neal Lawson and Neil Sherlock, *The Progressive Century: The future of the Centre-Left in Britain* (Basingstoke: Palgrave, 2001).

Useful web sites on political parties and party factions

Hot links to these sites can be found on the CWS at www.pearsoned.co.uk/budge. (For further study aids on this subject, please see the self-assessment test for this chapter on *The New British Politics* web site at www.pearsoned.co.uk/budge.)

The main political parties in Britain include, in alphabetical order:

Conservative Party: www.conservative-party.org.uk

Democratic Unionist Party: www.dup.org.uk

Labour Party: www.labour.org.uk

Liberal Democrats: www.libdems.org.uk

Plaid Cymru: www.plaid-cymru.wales.com

Progressive Unionist Party (NI): www.pup.org

Provisional Sinn Fein: sinnfein.ie/index.html

Scottish National Party: www.snp.org.uk

Social Democratic and Labour Party: www.sdlp.ie/sdlp

Ulster Unionist Party: www.uup.org

United Kingdom Unionist Party: www.ukup.org

Other web sites of interest include:

Conservatives: The 'moderate Conservatives' in Conservative Mainstream (http://core1.conservativemainstream.org.uk), the Tory Reform Group (http://core2.trg.org.uk), the Bow Group (www.bowgroup.org), the Eurosceptic Bruges Group (www.brugesgroup.com), the right-wing Monday Club (www. conservativeuk.com).

Labour: The Fabian Society (www.fabian-society.org.uk), the *Tribune* newspaper (http://www.tribweb.co.uk), the *New Labour Renewal* journal (www.renewal. org.uk), the left-wing Campaign Group (www.poptel.org.uk/scgn), Campaign for Labour Party Democracy (http://home.freeuk.net/clpd), the far-left Militant (www.militant.org.uk).

Liberal Democrats: The Liberator (www.liberator.org.uk).

Party ideologies

Parties are at the heart of British politics not only because of the role they perform but because of what they stand for. The last chapter showed how their organisations bridge the various levels of British society, linking members and electors to leaders who form the government or the government-in-waiting.

Parties do not, however, simply seek to run the country for its own sake. They seek to run it along certain lines, either as a free market economy or as a 'mixed' system, in which market competition is regulated and the state intervenes to protect losers. This is only one of the issues that divide the two main parties, but it has been a central one over the past 20 years, and it has deep historical roots.

Other policy differences exist, notably over the European Union. However, parties do tend to shift positions on these issues from time to time. Labour was split on the European Union in the 1970s but is much more supportive today, while the Conservatives totally changed from support to opposition between the mid-1970s and the late 1990s.

On central questions such as the management of the economy, the pursuit of equality and the emphasis on stability, the parties are more consistent in the policies they adopt. This is partly because their position is embedded in their very identity and ideology, as well as in the expectations of its core voters and members. The Conservatives would not be the Conservatives, for example, if they were not sceptical about the extent to which governments can or should directly help people.

This chapter will accordingly:

- examine the concept of 'party families' and the development of party ideologies

- explore the idea of 'left' and 'right' in British politics

- examine party programmes and see how these reflect left–right distinctions

- ask whether ideology is still as important as it was in the past and whether differing party ideologies give voters a real choice

- question the importance of political parties in Britain and ask whether there is an alternative way of running the country.

From Chapter 17 of *The New British Politics*, 4/e. Ian Budge, David McKay, John Bartle and Ken Newton.

Party families

Party families

Groupings of parties with similar beliefs and support groups, even though they operate in different countries.

British political parties are the second oldest in the world (the Americans had them first). But they are not wholly unique. Labour falls into the general 'family' of socialist and social democratic parties, the most numerous of all party families. The Liberals belong to the rather small family of radical liberal parties. In recent years the Conservatives' natural home has been the conservative–liberal, free market grouping.

Even the smaller British parties have counterparts in other countries with whom they form a broad transnational grouping. The Greens, for example, resemble environmental parties elsewhere; and parties such as Plaid Cymru (the Welsh nationalists) and the Scottish Nationalist Party belong to a broad range of minority nationalist parties. The Northern Irish Social Democratic and Labour Party can be classified with the Christian party family, given their roots in Catholicism. Ulster Unionists are in the rather unusual position of being a regional party upholding the central state. Their belief in the indissolubility of the Union groups them with straight Conservative parties elsewhere in Europe.

BRIEFINGS

17.1 Ideology and the concept of 'party families'

'Ideology' is a slippery term that means different things to different people. For present purposes, however, it can be said to be a system of ideas and assumptions that help us understand and interpret the world. It is a set of values and beliefs, factual assumptions and ideas, which indicates the appropriate action to take in given circumstances. The term is often restricted to a fairly explicit, coherent and elaborate set of ideas: a general theory about how the world *is*, how it *should be* ('core beliefs') and how to get from how it is to how it should be ('action principles' or 'predispositions').

Few people have ideologies in this sense, even among the political leadership. But many do subscribe to looser and less explicit ideologies such as liberalism, conservatism or socialism. Parties are built around a few political principles that are roughly compatible (though they may conflict at various times). Moreover, parties in different countries share a similar ideology and can be grouped together as a 'party family' because they share the same beliefs, principles and policies and often win support from the same groups.

Table 17.1 shows the general 'family' to which each British party belongs. It summarises which groups their supporters come from, what their core beliefs and action principles (or policy commitments) are and where they stand on the extent of government intervention in the economy and society, which is the central issue in left–right differences. 'Families' are roughly ordered in left–right terms (the left–right continuum), from radical environmental groupings to socialists and radical liberals to conservative liberals devoted to the free market and as little governmental intervention as possible.

State intervention versus the free market is not the only way in which to think of 'left' and 'right'. The terms are also used to distinguish between internationalist and nationalistic outlooks in foreign and defence policy and between libertarian and authoritarian outlooks on regulating private behaviour. Parties (and individual politicians) can be on the left on one dimension but in the centre or on the right on another. New Labour and Tony Blair, for example, might be described as left of centre on the social and economic dimension but right of centre on many issues touching on the libertarian–authoritarian dimension, such as the introduction of 'tough' anti-terrorism legislation and punishing the use of hard drugs.

British party politics in the twentieth century, however, have largely revolved around the roles of the state versus the market in economic and social affairs. It is, therefore, in these terms that 'left' and 'right' are usually defined. Of course, a summary table like this inevitably simplifies reality. The divisions within British parties have already been described in greater detail in Chapter 16. Nevertheless, the comparison shows what a lot in common they have with European parties, where the same groupings appear.

Table 17.1 European 'party families' and their British members

'Family' ideology	Support groups	Core values	Characteristic policies	Attitudes to government intervention	British 'family member'
Ecological and communitarian	Young, well educated	Environment participation, peace	Encourage sense of community, protect environment, help minorities, disarmament	Support more intervention to achieve objectives	Green Party
Socialist	Workers, public employees in social and service sectors, intellectuals	Equality of wealth and opportunity	Extend welfare protection (health and pensions), regulation of capitalism, peace	Government provision in all areas where market does not provide	Labour Party
Minority nationalist	Territorial minorities	Cultural diversity, regional devolution, autonomy	Decentralisation, devolution and autonomy	Intervention necessary to uphold minority cultures in the modern world	Scottish National Party, Plaid Cymru
Radical liberal	Anti-authoritarian elements of the middle classes, religious minorities, some peripheral regions	Liberty and a minimum standard of living to enjoy it	Safeguards for political and social rights	Against 'big' government but favour intervention to safeguard weaker sectors	Liberal Democrats
Christian democratic	Churches, especially the Catholic Church, the Catholic middle class, country and small towns	Fraternity, community, human dignity	Strengthen traditional morality and family, extend welfare, mixed economy	Intervention where necessary to ensure welfare and family stability	Social Democratic and Labour Party (Northern Ireland)
Conservative	Traditionalists of the State Church, upper and middle class, 'loyal' members of working class, country and small-town areas	Order, security, social hierarchy	Uphold established state structures and national boundaries, maintain armed forces	Intervention as and when necessary to ensure stability	Ulster Unionist Parties, British Conservatives 1868–1979
Conservative (Neo)Liberal	Business and professional middle classes	Liberty, individualism	Freedom from controls, free markets, efficient limited government	Government limited to upholding free market	Conservative Party (post-1979)

Plate 17.1 Advocate of the free market or equality? Tony Blair, like many politicians, combines different ideas

Source: Cartoon Stock

The left–right continuum

A straight line (or dimension) on which it is often convenient to locate parties. It stretches from the left-wing parties that believe in radical or revolutionary change, through the socialists and centre parties, to parties of the moderate right that oppose change, and on to extremist parties espousing a Fascist or Nazi ideology.

The left

Those who generally advocate change in the direction of greater social, political and economic equality. They include Communists, Socialists, Social Democrats, together with some Liberals and Greens.

The right

Those who generally oppose change in the direction of greater social, political and economic equality. They include Fascists, Conservatives and (in the United States) most Republicans.

Party ideologies

The three major British parties clearly differ in terms of all the factors listed in Table 17.1. Labour traditionally drew its members and core supporters from the working class, trade union members and public employees. It elevated 'equality' into a core value and advocated welfare programmes to ensure this. These policies were played down in 'New Labour' manifestos in 1997 and 2001 in favour of 'fairness' or 'equality of opportunity' in order not to scare voters in 'middle England'.

The Liberal Democrats, who are quite radical and reformist by general European standards, come close to Labour on government intervention but are more inclined than Labour to set limits on what governments do. They also have a more enduring concern for protecting individual civil liberties.

The Conservative Party traditionally drew its support from the middle class, members of the Church of England and country-dwellers. It emphasised order, security and the preservation of traditions (including social hierarchy). The legacy of Margaret Thatcher, Conservative leader from 1975 to 1990, was to shift the

Conservative Party decisively. She emphasised the principles of economic freedom and individualism, as represented by the free market, rather than social stability. Traditional Conservatives had often accepted the need for social welfare and economic intervention to maintain political and social order. Mrs Thatcher, however, tried to reduce what she saw as 'dependence' on the state and was prepared to risk creating conflict in order to achieve that goal.

Recent years have thus seen political and ideological shifts on the part of both the New Right and New Labour. How significant are these changes? Are they likely to last? And do they mean that the parties are coming together? Are we seeing both convergence and an end of distinguishing party ideologies?

Ideologies and political cleavages

To answer these questions we need to put today's ideologies in historical perspective. All parties date to the beginning of the twentieth century or earlier and many of the traditional differences between them also derive from that time. Parties adapted their ideology to the needs of particular supporters, both building on and emphasising certain political 'cleavages' in the country. Seeing how they did this helps us appreciate how fundamental **ideology** is to the study of British politics.

The Conservative and Liberal parties trace their origins to the parties (so-called 'cadre' parties) that operated under the very restricted franchise from 1832 to 1867 (when the Second Reform Act enfranchised large parts of the working class). From today's perspective the differences between the leading figures of these two parties do not seem very great. Many (including Gladstone, the dominant figure of nineteenth-century Liberalism) switched between them. Starting from the effective introduction of free trade in 1846–7, however, the Liberals gradually developed more progressive policies, pressing for political reforms and the extension of the franchise. Liberal thinkers, such as T. H. Green (1836–82), began to think of liberty not in terms of 'freedom *from*' monarchical rule, arbitrary government or the tyranny of the majority but 'freedom *to*' develop one's individuality. It was realised that markets failed to provide a clean environment, adequate education

> **Political ideology**
>
> A system of ideas, assumptions, values and beliefs that help us to understand the political world: how it *is*, how it *should* be and how to get from one to the other.

BRIEFINGS

17.2 Social and political cleavages

A political cleavage is made up of three elements:

1. A persistent social (or group-based) division that produces differences in interests, lifestyle and material advantages. Such divisions may be based on differences in class (workers v. employers), religion (Protestant v. Catholic) or geography (urban v. rural).

2. The presence of a set of values common to that group.

3. Party programmes designed to appeal to those group values.

Historically, the franchise was a controversial issue. A first step to the creation of cleavages was often to enfranchise a group so that it could cast votes in favour of a party. Political parties and organisations are, therefore, as important in the creation of cleavages as the objective social divisions themselves. An illustration of this is the fact that the division between town and country never turned into a cleavage in Britain, because all parties lined up with urban interests in accepting free trade after 1850.

For more information on the relationship between cleavages and parties in Western Europe read Seymour Martin Lipset and Stein Rokkan (eds), *Party Systems and Voter Alignments* (New York: Free Press, 1967).

BRIEFINGS

17.3 Classical liberalism

The essence of liberalism (with a small 'l') is the belief that individual rights should be protected by maximising freedom of choice and by limiting the powers of the government. Historically, liberalism represented a rejection of the absolute powers of a monarch, or other ruler, and sought to establish limited government, tolerance and freedom under the law. In Britain classical liberalism was built on the writings of John Locke (1632–1704) and John Stuart Mill (1806–73). In *Two Treatises of Government* (1690) Locke defended the Glorious Revolution of 1688 that established the dependence of the monarch on Parliament and was thus a first step towards limited, constitutional government. In his *Letter Concerning Toleration* (1693) Locke made the case for freedom of religious conscience, and so laid out the case for freedom of thought and belief, which is a fundamental tenet of liberal theory. In *On Liberty* (1859), Mill argued that the only justification for government interference with the liberty of individual citizens is to prevent them doing harm to others (the famous 'harm principle'). His great fear was that majority rule could threaten individual freedom no less than paternalistic or authoritarian government. Classical liberalism was, therefore, opposed both to the despotism of the monarchy and the 'tyranny of the majority'.

Classical economic liberalism is expounded by Adam Smith (1723–90) in his book *The Wealth of Nations* (1776), which argues that the 'invisible hand of the market' succeeds in making individual economic self-interest work for the common good. In this way Smith lays out the arguments for capitalism, individualism and free trade.

BRIEFINGS

17.4 Neo-liberalism

In the twentieth century some of the ideas of classical liberalism have emerged in 'neo-liberal', or 'New Right', form as a reaction to the growth of the state. Neo-liberals place supreme importance on the freedom of the individual and on rolling back the frontiers of the state. They argue that market competition is the best way of guaranteeing both political freedom and economic growth. In *The Road to Serfdom* (1944), for example, F. A. von Hayek (1899–1992) argues that socialism and the Welfare State inevitably lead to loss of individual freedom. The 'Chicago School' of economics, led by Milton Friedman in the 1970s and 1980s, similarly rejects Keynesianism in favour of a form of classical economics that favours competitive markets and low public expenditure. The main economic function of government is to regulate the money supply (monetarism) in order to control inflation. The ideas of Hayek and Friedman influenced Margaret Thatcher. Two right-wing think tanks, the Centre for Policy Studies (established in 1974) and the Adam Smith Institute (established in 1977), produced a steady stream of research arguing that the state was just as (or even more) likely to 'fail' as the market. Such reports provided the intellectual case for reducing the scope of state activity ('state failure').

State failure

The proposition that state intervention in the economy or society invariably leads to a less good social outcome than if the market were left to operate.

and essential needs such as healthcare. It was further argued that state intervention might rectify market failures; though few liberals advocated public ownership. The Liberals' new policies attracted the support of minority groups who felt disadvantaged under the old system: the Scots, the Welsh and religious Nonconformists (both Protestant and Irish Catholic).

With the actual achievement of a mass franchise it became even more important for the Liberals to attract the votes of these groups to gain power. To do so they took up the causes dear to them: removal of state support from the Anglican Church in Ireland and Wales; and wider political reforms, particularly of the patronage system in government appointments and of the Church's hold on education. Representing above all the Nonconformist middle classes of Wales, Scotland and northern and western England, the Liberals could not, however, appear as effective defenders of the working-class interest. This created an opportunity for the Conservatives and the new Labour Party formed in 1906.

BRIEFINGS

17.5 Conservatism

Conservatism (with a small 'c') is a general tendency in politics (or 'a way of thinking') rather than a clearly worked-out ideology such as Marxism. It believes in preserving what is best in traditional society and opposes change (particularly radical change) unless it is vital.

Conservatives believe that society is naturally hierarchical and should be regulated by a strong state. The classical British work of conservative theory is Edmund Burke's *Reflections on the Revolution in France* (1790). This cast great doubt on the capacity of people and governments to plan an ideal society and therefore argued for slow change rather than radical transformation. Old institutions and practices, wrote Burke, often have great, though hidden, virtues, and should be allowed to adapt slowly to changing circumstances. This did not mean, however, that conservatives should resist all change. Conservatives have realised that yielding to reform may prevent revolution. Many Conservatives regarded it as their duty to ward off socialism, but they also regarded it as inevitable. Until the late twentieth century, therefore, most adopted an essentially defensive strategy.

Conservatives have accepted change where necessary and where no change would represent a greater threat to the social fabric. British conservative thought has, therefore, varied over the years. It was strongly opposed to socialist ideas in the first half of the twentieth century, but accepted the 'social democratic consensus' that allowed the National Health Service and Welfare State to expand. The social democratic consensus eroded under the Labour government led by James Callaghan in 1976–9, which introduced policies designed to control the growth of the state. The Conservative government led by Margaret Thatcher in the 1980s was inspired by 'neo-liberal ideas' and tried to reduce both the size of the state and the public's reliance on it to solve problems. Her governments had mixed success in relation to achieving the first goal and little success in the second.

In the mid-nineteenth century the Conservatives, as did other such parties in Europe, defended the traditional state structures – monarchy, army and Church – against reformist Liberals. With the advent of the mass male franchise in 1867–8 they developed an appeal to the new working and lower middle class that built on the themes of national unity, military strength and Empire. The Conservatives consolidated their new support, above all in the south-east and Midlands of England, after the Liberals backed Home Rule (a form of devolution) for Ireland in 1886. The crisis over Irish Home Rule, which the Conservatives opposed, also alienated another traditional group of Liberals (the former Whigs). This left the Liberals more than ever a party of nonconformists on the geographical peripheries and in the urban areas of northern England. While classical liberalism emphasised freedom from arbitrary monarchical government and freedom from the tyranny of the majority, the 'New Liberalism' of the late nineteenth and early twentieth centuries emphasised freedom as the ability to realise one's potential. Many 'New Liberals' began to advocate an enhanced role for the state in order to correct '**market failures**' (such as environmental protection). They also advocated modest redistribution of wealth from the rich to the poor in order both to promote 'national efficiency' and reduce extreme poverty. Liberal governments emphasised the importance of education and promoted 'equality of opportunity' as an alternative to socialist 'equality' of outcome.

The economies of the peripheries were based on manufacturing and so were dominated demographically by the urban working class (Chapters 1 and 2). This left the Liberals vulnerable to a class-based party that could put the interests of this group first, as Labour did from 1906. The final straw for the old Liberal Party, however, was the First World War, which divided the party between those who supported 'total war' and those who clung to more liberal ideals. In the post-war years, the Liberals suffered from a double haemorrhage, losing working-class support to Labour, while the business classes fled to the Conservatives, who offered stronger opposition to demands for greater welfare and trade protection.

Market failure

The proposition that the market, left to its own devices, fails to produce socially optimal outcomes, 'public goods' (e.g. defence, water), to incorporate social costs (e.g. pollution) or to respond to needs (e.g. healthcare).

The consequences were as follows:

- A steady decline in Liberal importance.
- Labour became the main party of opposition to the Conservatives (and attracted many of the 'New Liberals' who favoured an increased role for the state).
- The Conservatives became divided between traditionalists, who were disposed to concede welfare demands for the sake of national unity, security, hierarchy and order, and the ex-Liberal supporters of free trade and the free market.

The ex-Liberals became progressively more influential in the Conservative Party. Of course, free markets depend on the state maintaining order and security. These two sides could compromise on the need for both. But in terms of political priorities, order and security began to take second place to economic freedom, both at home and abroad.

The Labour Party, unlike the Liberals, has always been ambivalent about free trade, and often wanted protection for workers secured by government intervention. It parted company with the Liberals (now Liberal Democrats) on this point. Liberal thinkers developed the argument that to take advantage of economic freedom people needed the resources to implement their choice. To have a choice of medical services, for example, is of no benefit if one cannot afford to buy any of them. However, unlike 'old' Labour, these New Liberals did not see state intervention as a good in itself but as a means to giving individuals economic freedom. As in the case of the other two parties, these ideas spring out of older concerns, modified to fit modern conditions. The question asked later in this chapter is, how far have their older ideas been modified?

First, however, we should comment on the relationship between cleavages and ideologies. The two intermesh because parties aim their appeals at certain social groups in order to gain their support. It is easier to target social groups with identities and interests in common. Trying to appeal to the electorate as a whole on the basis of their common interests is difficult because of the uncertainty about what common interests actually are. Having identified a distinctive social group, politicians can communicate with their leaders who can, in turn, advise their followers to support a particular party.

Of course this is a two-way process because, by appealing to group interests, the party is helping to define them. The working class was much more conscious of itself as a group with distinct and sometimes conflicting interests from other sectors once the Labour Party was launched. The Labour Party also helped develop other organisations to represent them: for example, by strengthening trade unions.

In the books, articles and pamphlets that set out the Labour and working-class case, a systematic analysis of the position of workers in contemporary society appeared, linking together the appeals for more welfare, housing, minimum wages and equality that Labour made at elections. As did other European socialist parties, Labour had the advantage of being able to draw on the work of Karl Marx, who wrote from the mid-nineteenth century onwards, and his intellectual followers; but it drew much more on other traditions, in particular religious nonconformity and radical liberalism such as the Chartism of the 1840s.

Marxist theory sees all events in terms of the class struggle. Nationalism, religion and individualism are simply bourgeois weapons to create 'false consciousness' and delude the workers about where their real interests lie. These are in essence to struggle against their employers, and eventually to overthrow the capitalist system that allows the latter to control the means of production such as factories and land. Their monopoly over the means of production enables them to exploit workers by forcing them to sell their labour (their only resource) very cheaply and thus creates gross inequalities in society.

BRIEFINGS

17.6 Marxism and socialism

The ideology developed by Karl Marx in the mid-nineteenth century is still the best-known political ideology. In contrast with many other socialist parties, however, the British Labour Party was only intermittently influenced by Marxist ideas.

Although it has developed a bewildering number of different branches, Marxism essentially states that economic relations, particularly those between the classes created by the system of production, determine all forms of political and social life. In the late capitalist system there are only two classes of political importance: the capitalists (or property owners or bourgeoisie), who are increasingly rich; and the workers (or proletariat), who are increasingly impoverished. Economic conditions and an informed political leadership encourage workers to develop a revolutionary class consciousness, overthrow the system and, after a period of state socialism, establish a society without either state or property.

According to Marx, history can only be understood in terms of class, and capitalist politics can only be understood as a constant struggle between the bourgeoisie and the proletariat. Other ideas, such as religion or nationalism, might seem important, but are actually manifestations of class interests, which are used by the ruling class to mask political reality and create the false consciousness that conceals the real class struggle. A Marxist, therefore, reacts to events by asking whose class interests are being served. Foreign wars, for example, may appear unconnected with the class struggle but, according to Marxist theory, they are actually a means of promoting capitalist interests.

Few parties in contemporary Europe support all of Marx's arguments. Many in the Labour Party may agree that class relationships are the most important and that the central issues in politics are those concerned with the distribution of resources between classes. But they would argue that the working class – as do others – has an interest in preserving peace and stability. Redistribution achieved through negotiation and argument is much better than imposed solutions supported by force because these can always be reversed by greater force.

Within a broad acceptance of democracy, party ideologies differ from each other in terms of which groups are considered to be the important ones in society and how their interests should be served. Are classes so pervasive and central that the interests of the workers should always come first? Or are workers' interests only part of the national interest, as 'bourgeois' parties tend to argue, and hence better served by strengthening the free market that will create more wealth for all? Or, on the contrary, is economic growth the force that is destroying the natural world in which we all have a common interest, as Greens argue, and so should it be resisted? Should economic growth be resisted because through uncontrolled development it ravages the countryside and threatens the culture of minority groups, which need to be defended by setting up their own institutions, as in Scotland and Ireland?

There is thus rich ground for controversy and argument among the adherents of different ideologies. This is particularly so because no one can say, objectively, which ideology is right. Assertions that class is the most important of social relationships, or that the world would suffer an irreparable loss if Welsh ceased to be spoken, are not subject to decisive proof. They spring out of an identification with or immersion in a particular group in society. One function of an ideology, indeed, is to buttress that identity, as most people belong actually or potentially to many different overlapping groups. For example, is a Polish-born secretary working in north-east England primarily a worker, British, English, Polish, European, Catholic, an immigrant or a woman? In a situation of multiple individual identities parties struggle to make one identity predominant and thus to mobilise support for their policies and general point of view.

Ideologies are thus important not only in telling leaders what to do but in telling voters who they are and so making them receptive to leaders' diagnoses of the

BRIEFINGS

17.7 British socialism and social democracy

British socialism takes from Marxism the ideas of class interest, equality and the Welfare State. It differs from Marxism, however, in maintaining that change can and should be achieved by means of peaceful reform rather than revolution. The Labour Party is a social democratic party, as are the mainstream labour movements in most of Europe.

The Labour Party's 'socialism' drew on a range of traditions, all of which were critical of nineteenth-century industrial capitalism. Ethical (also often Christian) socialists, such as R. H. Tawney (1880–1962), thought that the capitalist system promoted greed and 'uncharitable' behaviour and wanted to replace it with a utopian society. This group brought an evangelical passion to the party. (Less usefully, they also established Labour's reputation as a party of 'bossy do gooders'!) Fabians, on the other hand, stressed that capitalism was inefficient and could be replaced with a more rationally planned system. Sidney Webb (1859–1947), Beatrice Webb (1848–1943) and George Bernard Shaw (1856–1950), believed that the state could act as 'universal problem solver', identifying market failures and removing them by planning, regulation and taxation. With the ethical socialists they believed that revolution was undesirable and that a gradual change to a socialist society was inevitable. The most important influence on Labour's socialism, however, was the trade union movement. While the ethical or Christian socialists supplied Labour with its passion and fervour, the Fabians with its analysis and policy prescriptions, the trade unions supplied the organisation, personnel, resources and its essential pragmatism. Many unions were in no sense socialist, since they wished to improve the lot of their members. The skilled unions, in particular, wanted to maintain 'differentials' with less-skilled workers. The unions ensured that Labour remained focused on practical problems.

Ironically, however, it was John Maynard Keynes (1883–1946), a self-professed Liberal, who had one of the strongest influences on Labour policy. In his book *The General Theory of Employment, Interest, and Money* (1936) Keynes advocated government economic intervention in order to achieve economic stability, growth and full employment. 'Keynesian' demand management and a mixed economy replaced classical 'laissez-faire' (liberal market) economics as the economic orthodoxy between 1945 and 1975. Many claimed that Keynes 'saved capitalism' and that, in accepting his doctrines, Labour had become a party which ameliorated the worst aspects of capitalism rather than a party with a different (socialist) vision of a good society.

In the 1960s British socialist thought went through a period of change under the influence of Anthony Crosland's book, *The Future of Socialism* (1956). This argued that socialist goals of freedom and equality require some government economic planning but a large measure of private economic activity. State control and regulation of key sectors of the economy was necessary, but not further nationalisation. In the 1970s Labour moved sharply to the left as first the activists and then the unions were radicalised by economic failures. The party later moved back to the centre from 1983 onwards eventually abandoning nationalisation (see Chapter 16).

political situation. Ideology is particularly important for political parties, which have to operate across different levels of society. It helps to link up often complex governmental decisions with the broadly defined interests of a party's supporters and voters.

'Left' and 'right' in British politics

Specific party ideologies can be distinguished in terms of how far they are to the 'right' or to the 'left'. This is because differences over the extent of government intervention in society – whether to leave things to the free market or to limit its often disruptive workings – are a central and apparently permanent issue in modern societies. Intervention is sought by all sorts of groups that feel themselves weak in social and economic terms: not just the working class but also ethnic minorities, women and environmentalists. They want the government to restrict the power of the purely economic interests privileged by the market.

BRIEFINGS

17.8 The aims and objectives of the three major parties

The preamble to the Liberal Democrat Constitution (1988)

The Liberal Democrats exist to build and safeguard a fair, free and open society, in which we seek to balance the fundamental values of liberty, equality and community, and in which no one shall be enslaved by poverty, ignorance or conformity. We champion the freedom, dignity and well-being of individuals, we acknowledge and respect their right to freedom of conscience and their right to develop their talents to the full. We aim to disperse power, to foster diversity and to nurture creativity. We believe that the role of the state is to enable citizens to attain these ideals, to contribute fully to their communities and to take part in the decisions that affect their lives. [Continues.]

Conservative Party's proposed aims and objectives (2006)

Our aims:
To improve the quality of life for everyone through:

A dynamic economy, where thriving businesses create jobs, wealth and opportunity.

A strong society, where our families, our communities and our nation create secure foundations on which people can build their lives.

A sustainable environment, where we enhance the beauty of our surroundings and protect the future of the planet.

Our values:
The more we trust people, the stronger they and society become.

We're all in this together – government, business, the voluntary sector, families and individuals. We have a shared responsibility for our shared future.

Clause 4 of the Labour Party Constitution (1995)

The Labour Party is a democratic socialist party. It believes that by the strength of our common endeavour we achieve more than we achieve alone, so as to create for each of us the means to realise our true potential and for all of us a community in which power, wealth and opportunity are in the hands of the many and not the few, where the rights we enjoy reflect the duties we owe, and where we live together freely, in a spirit of solidarity, tolerance and respect [Continues.]

Realism

The view of politics, especially international relations, that emphasises the role of self-interest as a determinant of state policies, and hence the importance of power in these relations.

These differences appear in attitudes to foreign affairs as well as inside Britain. The left-wing parties (Greens, Labour, Liberals) are generally more sympathetic than the right towards supranational bodies such as the EU and UN, designed to regulate what states and multinational corporations do (although the Labour left opposed NATO and the European Economic Community, as it then was, in the 1980s). They tend to be 'idealists' in international terms, with a strong belief in the possibility of peaceful cooperation at the international level and a commitment to building institutions to encourage this.

The fact that all parties take a position on these questions allows us to place them on a single line running from left to right, as shown in Figure 17.1.

Left–right differences are not the only ones that exist between parties, and probably not the most important ones for minority nationalists, for example. They are central to British politics, however, so it is interesting to look at them across the whole political spectrum.

The point that leaps out from Figure 17.1 is that the three main British parties are not, on average, so very distant from each other in terms of the full range of ideological difference that could exist. Labour does *not* want to regulate everything and the Conservatives do *not* want to leave everything to the free market or

BRIEFINGS

17.9 Left–right differences in British politics

The terms 'left' and 'right' originated from the location of supporters and opponents of political change in France at the end of the eighteenth century. Supporters of reform sat on the left of the legislative chamber while supporters of the Crown and established institutions sat on the right. The 'left' today advocates change in the direction of greater political, social and economic *equality*, while the right oppose it. (Note: the right-wing parties often introduce greater changes than left-wing ones but these do not promote equality.)

In the twenty-first century the core distinction is defined in terms of support for more government intervention, on the left, and opposition to it, on the right. Left-wing parties want to extend the Welfare State and increase regulation of the economy. Right-wing parties want the government to refrain from interfering in society and the economy as far as possible, in order to extend individual freedom of choice. However, they do support strong government measures to guarantee law and order and national security. Thus they advocate a strong, but limited, state. In contrast left-wing parties want peace through international cooperation. Left-wing positions have generally developed out of some variant of Marxist ideology.

Centre parties tend to mix these positions and support limited government intervention in most policy areas, but specifically oppose the Marxist analysis of society.

The 'right' adopts 'realist' views, seeing the international arena as a free market, where states and firms pursue their own interests and maximise their well-being. To prevent the pursuit of national interests getting out of hand, however, strong military alliances are necessary to create a 'balance of power' where no one side can dominate. The Cold War of 1948–89, when the US and Soviet alliances confronted each other, was an example of such a balance, where each side deterred the other from taking over the world. Now that the Russians have accepted capitalism and free markets new threats may arise, such as Islamic fundamentalism, which make continuing military preparations necessary. The left tend to be 'idealists' who would be much happier seeing the old alliances dismantled and substituted by supranational bodies.

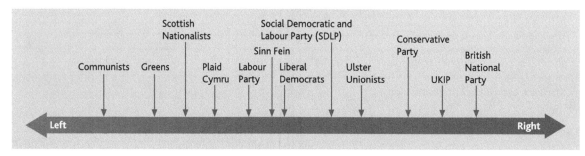

Figure 17.1 Location of UK political parties on the left–right ideological spectrum

(internationally) to only what can be agreed through inter-state negotiations. The Liberals are the most centrist of all, seeking to balance the general efficiency of the free market with government intervention in favour of weaker groups.

The positions set out in Figure 17.1 summarise what the parties have said and done over the 60 years from 1945 to 2005. Of course it is more interesting to ask how they have changed recently: have they moved closer together or drifted further apart? We analyse more precisely what has happened and whether these left–right differences still remain in subsequent sections.

It is also worthwhile looking at the smaller parties' position in these terms. Smaller parties are often thought to be more extreme because they are more 'pure' ideologically than the big parties can afford to be in case they put off voters. However, none of the regional parties takes positions very far (in left–right terms) from those of the main parties. The Scottish Nationalists are a little to the left of Labour. This is a good strategic position to take in Scotland where voters are more

Idealism

The view of politics, especially international relations, that emphasises the role of ideals and morality as a determinant of state policies, and hence the possibility of peaceful co-operation.

sympathetic to state intervention. Plaid Cymru is less radical, partly because it is the Welsh-speaking middle class who form its core voters. The Northern Irish SDLP are even more centrist than the leftist Sinn Fein, and (in left–right terms) are not too far from their local opponents, the Ulster Unionists. The last are traditional Conservatives who believe in order, security and the integrity of the British state. But they support financial aid and government-directed development in Northern Ireland. Further to the right are small single-issue British nationalist and racist parties. The United Kingdom Independence Party defines British nationalism in terms of independence from the European Union and the British National Party in terms of extreme hostility to immigrants and to their descendants, especially Asians and Afro-Caribbeans.

The most extreme left-wing parties are those that have a 'cause' and no regional base, the Communists and the Greens (the party that wants government intervention to save the environment). Both are small parties with limited political support.

The prospects for a genuinely left-wing party have looked dim ever since the downfall of the Soviet Union. The Communist Party of Great Britain has long ceased to contest elections. In 2005, however, a leftist party, RESPECT ('Respect, equality, socialism, peace, environmentalism, community and trade unionism'), contested 26 seats, retaining nine deposits (i.e. obtaining 5 per cent or more of the vote). Its most prominent member, George Galloway, was elected as MP for Bethnal Green. The party owed its limited success to its vociferous opposition to the Iraq War and its appeal among Muslim voters. It seems unlikely to be a permanent feature of British electoral politics. In Scotland, however, the Scottish Socialist Party has gained growing support from traditional Labour supporters disillusioned with New Labour's shift to the centre. In addition, the steady deterioration of the environment, both in Britain and the rest of the world, may well provoke a crisis that will give the Greens more votes and influence. At the moment they are electorally weak, although they won two seats in the 1999 European elections, two seats on the Greater London Assembly in 2004 and environmentalist pressure groups have been effective on many issues (see Chapter 23).

Left–right differences in the major parties' ideologies

In Britain it is the three traditional parties that are the real contenders for power. The next sections examine how they have changed their policies and ideologies over the post-war period. Have they moved closer together recently, or moved further apart, or all moved in the same direction? Seeing how the main parties have changed from election to election, in terms of the left–right differences illustrated in Figure 17.1, provides a way of answering this question.

It is true, of course, that such a 'single-line' representation provides only a very summary idea of the full range of party policies. There is more to political life, and ideology, than just left and right. As Table 17.1 showed, parties on the left have significant differences of opinion among themselves, on the importance of devolution for example, or the primacy of environmental issues. These do not show up in simple left–right terms.

Left–right differences thus do not cover all of British politics. But they are central to them for the following reasons:

■ *Political discussion – in the press, on television, in Parliament – is structured in terms of left and right.* Commentators always ask whether a party is moving towards the centre or the extremes, particularly in the context of elections. A party that has 'seized the centre ground' is usually considered to have a better chance of winning the election, as most electors are thought to be in the 'middle' (somewhere between the left and right poles).

■ *The question of how far governments should intervene – in welfare and the economy above all – is and always has been central to British politics.* Chapter 2 showed how it defined politics in the late nineteenth century and it has remained the crucial dividing line between the major parties ever since.

■ *Because of their centrality, the positions parties take in their election programmes on this range of issues are more likely to carry through into actual government policy than others.* This is important because the measure we use to trace left–right ideological shifts in party positions is derived from the party manifestos.

Elections, manifestos and programmes

A major feature of each general election in Britain is the programme published by each party at the beginning of its campaign (around one month before the election). This is the **party manifesto**. In this document the parties set out their views on how society should develop and how the country should be run for the next parliament. Only parties set out a reasonably detailed overall plan for national development and this distinguishes them from all other political organisations.

A manifesto's practical use is that it gives electors an indication of what would be done if the party were elected as the government, and thus enables voters to choose between them on policy grounds. Manifestos enable voters to exert influence over which policies the incoming government will pursue. The ability of electors to influence government in this way is, however, dependent on the existence of parties with alternative programmes.

If elections simply involved selecting individuals who came together in Parliament after the election in order to form a government, nobody would know in advance what their policy would be and electors would lose their opportunity to influence government policy. It is no coincidence, therefore, that the slow extension of democracy over the last century and a half has been bound up with the consolidation and growth of parties and the intensification of their competition for office.

> **Party manifesto**
>
> The document parties publish at the start of election campaigns outlining the policies they intend to implement if elected to government.

Plate 17.2 Parties are often accused of promising the same things time and time again and failing to deliver
Source: Cartoon Stock

Plate 17.3 Michael Howard launches the Conservative manifesto in 2005
Source: Empics

Democracy in Britain is indissolubly linked to the political parties; and electoral influence over public policy is linked to the programmes the parties offer.

Manifestos are usually prepared under the direction of party leaders (see Chapter 16). But many of the documents on which they are based have been approved by party conferences and other official party bodies. They thus constitute a unique and authoritative policy programme to which the party as a whole is publicly committed.

Despite their importance in setting out a national five-year plan, and offering a choice, party manifestos are not widely read by electors. Their contents are, however, extensively reported in the newspapers and on the television and radio and so they are known to voters, although at second hand. Electors who want to choose between parties in terms of their policies will, in the course of the campaign, be able to acquaint themselves with the main policies the parties lay out.

What do the manifestos actually say? On first reading they seem rather woolly and far from offering a precise programme for government. New Labour was exceptional in 1997 and 2001 in making precise pledges about Scottish and Welsh devolution and about limiting tax increases. Usually the manifesto makes precise commitments in only a few peripheral areas, such as Labour's 1997 commitment to restore trade union rights for employees at GCHQ (the government's intelligence-gathering organisation).

Much of the document consists of rambling discussions of various topics such as 'youth', 'unemployment', 'the economy' and so on. Topics such as these constitute its main sections. Typically the sections state how important the problem is and

Plate 17.4 Tony Blair launches what he promised would be his last manifesto in 2005
Source: Empics

provide an analysis of past developments and of the present situation, stressing party concerns and achievements, but not committing it to very much. This vagueness is due to a well-founded fear by leaders that tying themselves down to specific actions might give too many hostages to fortune. Changed circumstances or a financial crisis might result in their not being able to do what they promised, and thus lead to accusations of bad faith and to their loss of credibility.

From the viewpoint of parties it is better to emphasise the importance of a particular policy area rather than state what exactly it is they will do about it. This does not render the manifesto valueless as a statement of future policy. Its main purpose is to set priorities for action rather than to tie the government in advance to specific things it must do. Talking a lot about a particular area such as 'youth' implies that the party would do more and spend more in the area, without saying exactly what it would do or how much it would spend. Setting priorities in this way makes it easier for electors to choose between the parties on broad policy grounds, rather than having to decide on the feasibility of particular courses of action in areas where they have no expert knowledge.

There is often scepticism about the extent to which parties carry through their programmes in government. Many feel that promises made at the election are simply not kept once the party takes office. Research by Hans Dieter Klingemann *et al.* (*Parties, Policies, and Democracy*, Boulder, CO: Westview, 1994) has shown, however, that not only are the majority of pledges carried through by the winning party but also that the priorities stressed in the manifesto are strongly related to subsequent government expenditure in the different policy areas. Electors choosing between parties on the basis of their policy priorities can thus have some confidence that they will try to put them into effect in government. To paraphrase a recent television advertisement for wood varnish: 'The manifesto [largely] does what it says on the tin'.

Party manifestos and party ideology

Manifestos are programmes for government action so it follows that they are strongly influenced by party ideology. This is apparent from the manifestos issued by different parties at the same election. These often give such dramatically opposed accounts of the situation that one would think they were talking about two quite different countries! Thus in 2005 the Labour manifesto painted a glowing picture of a Britain with an expanding economy and improving public services, while the Conservative document talked of hospital bugs, uncontrolled immigration and excessive regulation stifling private enterprise.

Such differences occur in part because ideologies lead parties to focus on different groups and developments. The Conservative reference point is the English middle class, in particular in the south-east, with their concerns with financial markets, order and opportunity. In recent years Labour has also tried to appeal to 'middle England' while providing something for the peripheries and their problems of economic stagnation, bad housing and health.

Differences in the party programmes also occur because the parties' ideologies and history make them 'proprietors' of different issues. A voter who wants free markets and an emphasis on individual opportunity and law and order knows from what the Conservatives have done and said in the past that it is more likely to provide these than any other party. If these issues are what people think important in an election more are likely to vote Conservative. Education and welfare, however, are 'Labour issues'. Those who think these issues are most important will support that party.

Issues such as these become important partly because of developments outside the political arena. But the parties can also try to focus on them by emphasising 'their' issues in the manifesto and in their campaign. Differences in emphasis thus arise partly from the imperatives of competition, but also build on pre-existing ideological differences between parties and their reputation for competence in different, ideologically defined, issue areas.

Measuring left–right ideology in manifestos

The fact that party programmes stress different kinds of issues according to their ideology gives us an opportunity to measure the ideological distance between them at each election, by assessing the amount of attention each document pays to the characteristic issues of the left and right. The party's position between left and right is not the whole of a party's ideology but it is a major part of it. It covers the most central issues in British politics and the ones on which electors are most likely to assess parties, and governments to take action.

The emphasis parties give to different issue areas can be measured very simply and directly, by counting the number of sentences in each manifesto devoted to each issue area. Table 17.2 shows how the parties differed on the 'top ten' issue areas in the 2005 election, that is, the ten most often mentioned categories in each party manifesto, to which most sentences were devoted. This analysis reveals some agreements and also some differences. After two terms of Labour government it is hardly surprising that all the parties devoted substantial portions of their

Table 17.2 Top ten issues, 2005

Policy areas	Labour		Liberal Democrat		Conservative	
Demographic groups	1	10.2	2	10.7	4	7.3
Health and welfare positive	2	9.9	4	6.0	6	6.1
Government effectiveness	3	9.2	1	15.8	1	18.3
Education positive	4=	9.0	–	–	2	11.0
Law and order	4=	9.0	7	4.5	3	7.6
Culture	6	6.4	–	–	–	–
Internationalism positive	7	4.5	8	4.4	4	7.3
Decentralisation positive	7	4.5	8	4.4	4	7.3
Technology	9	4.2	10	3.8	7	4.1
Incentives	10	3.6	6	5.5	7	4.1
Environmental protection	–	–	3	9.4	–	–
Market regulation	–	–	9	4.2	9	3.1
Agriculture	–	–	–	–	10	2.9

Source: Judith Bara, 'The 2005 manifestos: a sense of déjà vu?', paper presented at the Elections, Public Opinion and Political Parties Conference, September 2005

manifesto to Labour's effectiveness in office. (Labour's manifesto extolling, and the opposition parties attacking, Labour's record.) Labour placed more emphasis on health, welfare and culture than the Conservatives, while the Conservatives placed more emphasis on incentives, market regulation and agriculture. The Liberal Democrats' focus on 'demographic' groups in 2005 stood in marked contrast to their manifesto in 2001 (when this ranked seventh). This change may reflect the centre party's attempt to appeal to certain groups (such as the young and public sector workers) and exploit disillusion with the Labour government.

More revealing than analysis of specific issues is Figure 17.2, which traces the ideological progression of the British parties over the post-war period. We can see how this affects their ideological positions in relation to each other. To do this one can look at left–right differences more directly. All one needs do is group 'left-wing' issues together and add up the percentage of references to them. Then one groups 'right-wing' issues together and adds up their percentage score. Finally one can take the combined percentage for left-wing issues and subtract this from the combined

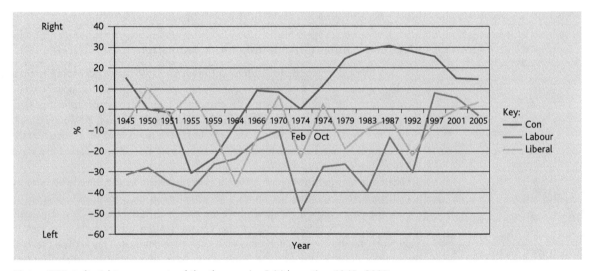

Figure 17.2 Left–right movements of the three major British parties, 1945–2005

Table 17.3 Creating a left–right scale from party manifestos

Negative items (left wing)	Positive items (right wing)
Nationalisation	Free enterprise
Controlled economy	Economic orthodoxy
Welfare: positive	Social services expansion: negative
Regulation of capitalism	Incentives
Economic planning	Freedom
Protectionism: positive	Protectionism: negative
Military: negative	Military: positive
Peace	Effective authority
Education expansion: positive	Constitutionalism: positive
Internationalism: positive	National way of life: positive
Decolonisation	Traditional morality: positive
Labour groups: positive	Law and order
Democracy	Social harmony

Source: Budge *et al.*, Mapping Policy Preferences, Oxford: OUP, 2001, p. 2

percentage for right-wing issues. That gives us a 'scale' running from +100 per cent (all references in a manifesto are to right-wing issues) to −100 per cent (all references in a manifesto are to left-wing issues). In practice, of course, each manifesto will contain references both to left- and right-wing issues, so they will never be totally right wing or totally left wing. Neither will all topics mentioned by parties fit into this particular ideological distinction. This means that on average the main British parties fall near the middle of the left–right space, as we have already seen in Figure 17.1. The positions they take in specific elections vary more, of course, but only within a narrow range of +30 towards the right and −50 towards the left.

Table 17.3 lists left- and right-wing issues. As the essence of the left-wing position is support for government regulation and intervention domestically and the creation of governmental bodies to do the same internationally, the topics picked out as leftist are all the statements that have a bearing on these questions. They include nationalisation (takeover of businesses by government), regulation and control of the economy, provision of welfare and education (again by government) and peace and international cooperation. The right opposes these emphases and puts a stress on freedom from government. The free market needs some government support to keep it going, which is provided by law and order at home and military alliances abroad. All these elements can be seen in Conservative policies up to 1997, which have been characterised as 'free market, strong State'.

Measuring left–right differences in this way enables us to trace the ideological progression of the three main British parties over the whole of the post-war period. In Figure 17.2 left–right positionings are measured on the upright dimension (from +35 – relatively right wing – to −50, relatively left wing). The horizontal dimension is time. Each election can be identified by its particular date: 1945, 1950, 1951 and so on until 2005. This evidence can be used to examine the proposition that there has been 'ideological convergence' among British parties.

Left and right – convergence or divergence?

Differences between the parties were very large in 1945, the post-Second World War election in which Labour won a large majority and started a programme of intervention and reform in all areas. The Conservatives realised that the reforms, particularly the creation of the Welfare State, were popular and that to win elections they had to accept them. By emphasising such left-wing positions they came very close to Labour from 1955 to 1964, the heyday of the social democratic con-

Plate 17.5 'Old Labour' trade unionists, like Arthur Scargill, and left-wingers, like Tony Benn, accused Tony Blair of betraying 'socialism'

Source: Peter Brooks/The Times, 17th September 1996, Centre for the Study of Cartoons & Caricature, University of Kent

sensus. Both parties accepted the Welfare State and a mixed economy, in which the government owned large sectors of industry. However, the convergence was due partly to Labour's own move to the right as it toned down its (increasingly unpopular) emphasis on nationalisation. Meanwhile, the Liberals wandered about between the other two parties with no fixed position.

All this changed after the 1966 election as the Conservatives generally moved to the right; up to 1997, in fact, they remained relatively far to the right. The gap between the two main parties widened as Labour moved dramatically left in 1974 and again in 1983. Only in 1997, as 'New Labour', did it make a dramatic shift to the right, largely by playing down economic intervention while continuing to support welfare and education. This move to the right paralleled that of the Conservatives leftwards in the 1950s: 'If you can't beat 'em, join 'em!' Unlike the earlier Conservative change, the move did not bring Labour close to its main rival as the Conservatives still remained much further to the right. In both 1997 and 2001, the Liberal Democrats were further than Labour. So the 1997 election saw ideological convergence only up to a point. In 2005 Labour moved back to the left and 'passed' the Liberal Democrats as the centre party moved a little to the right. The Conservatives have remained virtually unchanged since 2001. Thus, for the first time since 1992, the parties are in their 'proper' order with Labour on the left, the Liberal Democrats in the centre and the Conservatives on the right. It appears that the 1997 and 2001 elections represented a mild – and temporary – departure from the 'normal' positions of the parties.

The end of ideology?

Ideology is a term with highly negative connotations for many people. It has associations with Marxism and thus with sterile debates among fanatics and extremists about abstract principles. It is also associated with totalitarian regimes that murdered millions in the name of 'racial purity' or 'the victory of the proletariat'. Even when manifested in democratic politics ideology is seen as preventing agreement and maintaining artificial party differences, which get in the way of national unity and successful problem solving.

No wonder, then, that many commentators have predicted an 'end of ideology' at various times in Britain's post-war history. 'Ideology' has been particularly associated with the left. Thus the electoral defeat of Labour in the 1980s and its modification of socialist principles have been seen by many as necessary to creating a more rational and balanced society in Britain.

The positions taken up by the parties, even in 1997 and 2001, were still quite sharply differentiated. It is difficult, moreover, to maintain that there would be no significant differences in Britain today if John Major had won in 1997, if William Hague had won in 2001 or even if Michael Howard had won in 2005. Ideology provides parties with a general course to steer the nation by should they get into power; though progress towards that goal may be as steady as a drunkard's walk.

Past experience suggests that convergence is usually a temporary phenomenon. Convergence in the 1950s was followed by divergence in the early 1970s and early 1980s. Convergence in 2001, for example, was followed by divergence in 2005. There is no 'inevitable' trend towards general agreement. If this did come to pass the parties would lose their identity and with it their separate existence, and would cease to offer alternative choices to electors. A drawing together is always likely to be followed by a drawing apart to traditional policy positions. No 'end of ideology' seems in view, no matter how much party squabbles irritate the public.

The positive contribution of party ideology to electoral choice

Is this necessarily a bad thing? Although 'ideology' has bad connotations it can be regarded as the same thing as holding to firm political principles. Having principled politicians rather than self-servers and office seekers is generally regarded

BRIEFINGS

17.9 Conditions for electoral control over public policy

To summarise the relationship between party representation and electoral choice one can specify four conditions for electoral control over future government policy:

1. Parties must offer voters a choice.

2. Voters need to be aware of the choice.

3. People must vote on the basis of the choice.

4. The party in control of the government follows policies consistent with the options it placed before the electorate (party accountability).

All these conditions require that the parties subscribe to different ideologies to generate policy choices for voters and to give them an incentive to carry through their programme in government.

as good. If the 'end of ideology' amounts to the 'death of principle' this cannot be a good thing.

As the discussion at the beginning of the chapter also indicates, it is impossible to operate in politics without an ideology. People need to have a set of beliefs and assumptions about the way the world works in order to understand it at all. Socialism could only be abandoned by replacing it with another ideology. Neo-liberalism and free market beliefs are in this general sense just as much ideologies as Marxism. Indeed, far and away the most ideological politician in recent British politics has been Margaret Thatcher, the right-wing Conservative Prime Minister from 1979 to 1990.

We cannot escape having ideological parties, so the only question is whether parties should have different ideologies or all share the same one. The general conclusion we can draw from our examinations of party programmes is that they are likely to remain different.

This has positive advantages for the role parties play in representing the views of the British electorate. Consider what would happen if parties did all share the same ideology and offered electors the same policies in their programmes. This would mean that whichever party electors voted into government the same policy would be pursued. Voters would then have no opportunity to choose between policies. Differences in ideology guarantee that different solutions will be offered by different parties and that electors can weigh them up and decide between them with some probability of determining which will actually be pursued.

The doctrine of the party mandate rests on the idea that electors are able to choose between programmes in this way. The core of the argument is that a majority or plurality vote for a party in the general election can also be interpreted as an endorsement of that party's policy programme. This gives the party the authority to put its policies into effect when in government. If all parties offered the same programme governments would lack the authority of a mandate, because no one would know whether electors had really endorsed their programme or had simply been deprived of the opportunity to express an opinion.

BRIEFINGS

17.10 The party mandate

The idea of a party mandate assumes that the party winning most votes in an election will form a government that will carry through its electoral programme, because this has been supported by a majority or plurality of electors. The details of the argument are as follows:

- Electors choose between parties at least in part on the basis of their programme.
- Such programmes are distinguishable from each other, so they offer electors a basis for choice.
- The party that gains most votes forms the government.
- The party or parties that form the next government have a responsibility to carry out their programme in government, because this is a major basis on which they were elected.
- They also have the authority to carry out their programme in government, because it has been selected by the largest number of electors as the best.
- Parties do carry through their programmatic priorities in government.

Ideology has another positive contribution to make in a party democracy such as Britain. It gives parties an incentive to carry through their programme when they get into government. Many voters are cynical about whether governments will actually carry out election promises or will simply ignore their commitments as soon as they take office. The Wilson governments (1964–70, 1974–6) were particularly criticised, having gained office with the promise of economic expansion through state planning and ending by restricting economic activity and creating high unemployment. Their failures prompted a swing to the left discussed in Chapter 16.

In contrast, no one could say that the highly ideological Margaret Thatcher did not vigorously carry through her programme of restricting government and promoting the free market. Thatcher did this because, as well as promising such measures to the electorate, she actually believed in them very strongly.

In theory, governments could be punished retrospectively for breaking earlier election pledges. Some analysts argue that electors would not vote for such a government because they could not trust it to carry through policies they otherwise find attractive. In practice, however, this seems a rather weak sanction because of the lapse of time involved and the many circumstances that will have intervened to make earlier pledges irrelevant or incapable of fulfilment.

While external sanctions or election penalties may be weak, ideological imperatives to carry through the programme may be quite strong, as the case of Thatcher shows. Ideology can thus play a very important role in promoting party accountability. It might be preferable to have 'conviction politicians' saying and then doing what they believe rather than opportunists following the changing whims of public opinion or doing the minimum they think they can get away with.

Alternatives to party democracy

Party democracy

Either (1) the widespread distribution of power within a political party and/or (2) a system of national democracy resting on competitive parties.

At the start of the twenty-first century, parties seem to be exerting a more pervasive influence on general debate than ever. Our evidence shows that they are still divided in ideological terms, and that this situation is likely to continue. It clearly has many advantages in presenting electors with sharp policy choices and guaranteeing that most governments will carry them through.

Many, however, find the constant squabbling between parties deeply dispiriting. It is epitomised by televised debates from Parliament, where Labour and Conservatives appear to shout each other down, with no attempt to debate the merits of the case or to find agreement. Surely things would be better if the good people on all sides came to a problem without party prejudices and found the best solution that genuinely served the national interest? David Cameron, the new Conservative leader, said as much when he accepted the leadership of his party.

The problem lies in discovering what is in the national interest and how best to achieve it. Does it exist at all or is it simply a projection of the interests of one group, for example the City of London or the south-east 'Establishment', at the expense of others? The national interest is perhaps most easily identified in foreign affairs – keeping Britain strong and influential in the world. Even here, however, there has been much criticism of Britain's subservience to the United States and of the costs an overextended world role has imposed on society.

The 'best people' coming together outside their parties would still, therefore, face policy dilemmas, and divide and argue over them. There are no easy or obviously 'best' solutions to political problems. That is why parties and their ideologies have evolved, to ensure that no major interest or grouping in society lacks an advocate to promote its views on any problem about which it is concerned. As Winston Churchill remarked of democracy in general, 'Democracy is the worst form of Government except for all the other forms that have been tried from time to time'. The same can be said of parties and their ideologies. If they did not exist today they would rapidly re-emerge, as they are so essential to democratic debate and choice and to the control of electors over government. In that sense, British democracy cannot do without them, whatever their incidental defects.

Summary

This chapter has examined the different party ideologies that exist in Britain today and how they help maintain party identity and distinctiveness. In particular it has looked at:

- the different 'families' to which British parties belong and how they have evolved over time;

- the way in which party families can be 'placed' in terms of an underlying left–right ideology, centred on differences about the nature and extent of government intervention in society;

- how the left–right positions of the main parties can actually be measured from their election manifestos and used to track changes in their ideological positions over time (Figure 17.2);

- how ideology assists voters as they make choices between alternative programmes for society and to electoral control over government actions, and hence to the general functioning of representative democracy in Britain.

Essays

1. What is ideology? Why is it useful for parties to have one? Or: What are 'political principles'? Why is it useful for parties to have these?

2. What does it mean to say that a party is to the 'left' or to the 'right' in politics?

3. Why is it important that British electors should be presented with different party programmes in an election?

Projects

1. Read three party manifestos without their identifying labels, analyse them and try to guess: (a) which party they belong to; (b) whether they were published at the same election. Give reasons for your judgement.

2. Analyse the reasons for ideological change on the part of the British parties with reference to Figure 17.2.

Further reading

The nature of political ideologies in general is discussed in Andrew Heywood, *Political Ideologies: An Introduction* (Basingstoke: Palgrave Macmillan, 2003); Robert Leach, *British Political Ideologies* (Basingstoke: Palgrave Macmillan 2002). Applications to British election manifestos are made in Ian Budge *et al.*, *Mapping Policy Preferences: Estimates for Parties, Electors and Governments 1945–1998* (Oxford: OUP, 2001) and in Judith Bara and Ian Budge, 'Party policy and ideology: still New Labour?' in Pippa Norris (ed.), *Britain Votes 2001* (Oxford: OUP, 2001) pp. 26–42, reproduced in *Parliamentary Affairs*, **3**, 2001, pp. 590–606. A review of party families and ideologies, as well as of other aspects of British parties, can be found in Paul Webb, *The Modern British Party System* (London: Sage, 2000). Two useful articles on the ideology of New Labour are Michael Freeden, 'The ideology of New Labour', *Political Quarterly*, **70** (1), 1999, pp. 42–51 and J. Buckler and B. Voldwitz, 'New Labour's ideology', *Political*

Quarterly, **71** (2), 2000, pp. 101–4, which criticises Freeden. On the Conservatives, see J. Garnett and P. D. Lynch, 'Bandwagon blues: the Tory fightback fails', *Political Quarterly*, **73** (1), 2002, pp. 29–37. For a comparison of the British party system with other European parties, see Ian Budge *et al.*, *The Politics of the New Europe* (Harlow: Addison Wesley Longman, 1997).

Useful web sites on party ideologies

Hot links to these sites can be found on the CWS at www.pearsoned.co.uk/budge.

In Chapter 16 we provided an extremely comprehensive list containing links to the main political parties as well as the more important party factions.

There are a number of political ideology sites that cover Britain and the world. The Keele Guide to Political Thought and Ideology on the Internet (www.keele.ac.uk/ depts/por/ptbase.htm) is an A–Z guide to political thought, theory and ideologies. In addition to this you can also visit the Social Science Information Gateway (www.sosig.ac.uk/roads/subject-listing/World-cat/polideol.html) for a general introduction to the leading currents in political thought.

In more specific terms, the LockeSmith Institute offers an excellent account of the formative years and historic development of classical Liberalism (www.belmont. edu/lockesmith/); on the same topic, very interesting insights can be found in the Stanford Encyclopaedia of Philosophy (http://plato.stanford.edu/entries/ liberalism/). With regard to neo-liberal theory, a brief historical account of its evolution can be found at www.globalissues.org/TradeRelated/FreeTrade/ Neoliberalism.asp and a more academic approach is available at www.globalpolicy. org/globaliz/econ/histneol.htm. The main trends within Conservatism and its potential evolution are described and critically assessed in www.ukconservatism. freeuk.com. A very insightful analysis of the main currents within Marxism is available from the above-mentioned web site of Keele University.

Concerning the specific ideological features of the main British parties, a good deal of information can be obtained from a careful reading of the political speeches given by their respective leaders.

A complete list of party manifestos since 1945 is available at www.psa.ac.uk/ WWW/elections_uk.htm.

Data collected by the party manifestos project (Budge *et al.*) that codes and counts party policy commitments is available from the book *Mapping Policy Preferences* (Oxford: Oxford University Press, 2001) and its associated CD-Rom.

Political parties

Richard Kelly

Learning objectives

- Elucidate the unpopularity of British political parties.

- Explain the parties' unpopularity, with reference to both internal party politics and wider sociological, ideological and cultural changes.

- Examine the similarities and differences between the main parties' policies.

- Inspect the various ideas concerning the current shape of Britain's party system.

- Assess the implications of economic recession for British party politics.

- Prescribe reforms which may galvanise party politics in the years ahead.

From Chapter 11 of *Politics UK*, 7/e. Bill Jones and Philip Norton. © Pearson Education 2001–2010. All rights reserved.

Introduction

By the autumn of 2007, as Britain moved into a new economic era, it was already clear that British party politics was in a less than robust condition. Indeed, it seemed defined by profound crisis and chronic instability. Events during the next two years only deepened that impression. This chapter will dissect the crisis of British party politics from four related positions:

First, it will examine the relationship between parties and the electorate, highlighting the apparent breakdown between the two. In explaining this breakdown, it will examine the connection between parties and our wider democratic culture, but also touch upon more specific areas such as party organisation, party funding and the seismic journalistic revelations of May–June 2009.

Secondly, it will assess the shifting relationship between the policies of the main parties, particularly since the onset of recession, and ask whether it is still realistic to talk of an inter-party 'consensus'.

Thirdly, it will consider the changing shape of our party system, positing the view that no such 'system' actually exists.

Finally, it will ask whether the current crisis of political parties offers a redemptive opportunity, or whether it leaves the alternative notion – that the major parties are now impotent and redundant – looking grimly irresistible.

■ Disconnection from voters

The symptoms

For at least a decade, it had been plain that there was a widening gap between Britain's major political parties and the electorate. This struck at the heart of our representative democracy, which is dominated by party competition, party policies and party governments. If voters were indeed disenchanted with political parties then, by implication, they were disenchanted with the very basis of our political culture. As the Houghton Report noted as long ago as 1976, 'if the parties fail, then democracy fails' (see Fisher 2008). However, by the first decade of the new century, there were clear signs that the parties were failing chronically in the eyes of voters.

Declining turnout

The most obvious indication of this was diminishing turnout at elections – elections, after all being largely defined by political parties. At the 2005 general election, only 61.5 per cent of eligible voters cast their votes, the second worst turnout since 1918. This meant that the number of voters abstaining was greater than the number voting for any political party – including the party that now governs us. In fact, only 21.6 per cent of eligible voters supported Labour – a record low for a governing party – while the number of people voting Labour in 2005 was lower than in 1987, when Labour lost by a landslide. Among first-time voters, fewer than 40 per cent again chose to vote, while in many urban constituencies only a minority of voters voted. (In Manchester Central, for example, the figure was just 43 per cent.)

Electoral reformers had sometimes argued that low turnout was an indictment not so much of the *party system* as of the *electoral system*, particularly first-past-the-post's tendency to produce 'safe' seats where voting may seem pointless. However, under New Labour a range of new electoral systems have been introduced for various 'secondary' elections; and turnout in these elections has not been impressive either. Turnout in the European elections of 2009 (conducted under the 'party list' system of proportional representation) was just 34 per cent – lower than in 1989 and 1994, when first-past-the-post was still being used. Turnout in the Scottish Parliament and Welsh Assembly elections of 2007 (conducted under the 'additional member system' of PR) was 52 per cent and 43 per cent respectively, while turnout in the various mayoral elections (conducted under 'supplementary vote') has averaged less than 40 per cent. Even in the London mayoral election of 2008, involving an unusual range of colourful and well-known candidates, only a minority of electors (44 per cent) cast their vote. In short, there is no hard evidence as yet that a change of electoral system will energise voters.

Declining identification

Underlying such figures has been a sharp decline in the number of voters who feel an allegiance to any political party. In 1964, 42 per cent of voters 'strongly identified' with a political party, but only 10 per cent did so by 2005 – and this excludes the 39 per cent who did not vote at all. Linked to this has been a growing tendency to support candidates with no party affiliation at all. At the 2005 general election, this was reflected in the election of Richard Taylor in Wyre Forest and Peter Law in Blaenau Gwent – once a Labour fiefdom. Indeed, in the by-elections held in Blaenau Gwent in 2006, independents triumphed in both the Parliamentary and Welsh Assembly contests. In the 25 mayoral elections held between 2000 and 2009, independents triumphed in 10 – and all went on to secure re-election.

This trend towards 'post-party' candidates was exemplified strongly in the local authority elections of 2008. In Wales, independents secured a quarter of council seats and thus constituted a majority on 22 council seats. Likewise, in Barnsley, independents held a third of the council's seats. After these elections, it was often suggested that many of the successful independents were covert Tories, unwilling to disclose their true colours. But, even if that were the case, it is significant that politicians wishing to exploit the governing party's decline are now likely to voice contempt for all parties rather than one in particular.

Declining membership

Meanwhile, party membership has continued to decline. Party leadership contests now provide a useful guide to how many members the parties have, given that all the main ones now enfranchise their grass-root members (it is reasonable to assume that all but the most torpid of party members have some interest in who leads them). In this respect, the three leadership contests since 2005 are revealing.

In the 1950s, Conservative Party membership peaked at over 3 million. Yet, in the 2005 Conservative leadership contest, fewer than 200,000 votes were recorded, despite a lively and well publicised campaign (see Box 11.1). The Liberal Democrats claimed up to 100,000 members during the first 10 years of their existence (1988–1998). Yet, in their 2006 leadership contest, fewer than 42,000 votes were recorded (see Box 11.2). The Labour Party, on coming to power in 1997, claimed around 400,000 members. Yet, in its deputy leadership contest of 2007, fewer than 97,000 votes were registered by its constituency members (see Box 11.3).

BOX 11.1 FACT

The 2005 Conservative leadership contest

David Cameron: 134,466 (67 per cent)
David Davis: 64,398 (32 per cent)
Ballot papers returned: 198,844 (78 per cent)

NB: In the 2 preliminary ballots, confined to Conservative MPs, first Ken Clarke and then Liam Fox were eliminated.

BOX 11.2 FACT

The 2007 Liberal Democrat leadership contest

Nick Clegg: 20,988 (50.6 per cent)
Chris Huhne: 20,477 (49.4 per cent)
Ballot papers returned: 41,465 (65 per cent)

BOX 11.3 FACT

The 2007 Labour deputy leadership contest

Final round[a]

	MPs/MEPs	Constituency members	Affiliated members[b]	Total
Harriet Harman:	15.42%	18.83%	16.18%	50.43%
Alan Johnson:	17.91%	14.50%	17.15%	49.56%
Votes cast:	367 (99%)	96,756 (54%)	215,604 (8%)	312,727 (54%)

[a] There had been four previous rounds of voting, each eliminating the bottom-placed candidate. In order, these had been: Hazel Blears, Peter Hain, Hilary Benn and Jon Cruddas.
[b] Each of the three sections constituted a third of the votes in an electoral college.

As the *Power* report noted in 2006, overall party membership is at just a quarter of its 1964 levels, with only about 2 per cent of voters now members of a political party. The income of the main parties also points to diminishing membership. Fewer members obviously mean fewer subscriptions; and fewer subscriptions mean that the parties become ever more reliant upon institutional funding and the generosity of a few wealthy supporters. By 2006, Labour derived only 8 per cent of its income from member subscriptions, the Conservatives 10 per cent (it had been around 40 per cent fifty years earlier), and the Liberal Democrats 30 per cent. Fewer members also mean a much lower profile in local communities – the number of Conservative Clubs fell by a third between 1980 and 2005, which, in turn, distances parties further from mainstream voters.

The demographic of party membership is also instructive, with the two main parties' youth wings having fewer than 30,000 members between them. It may be an over-gloomy prognosis, and an over-dramatic extrapolation of current trends, but unless the younger generation of voters become enthused by political parties in later life, the concept of 'party membership' could be virtually obsolete by the middle of the century.

Alternative forms of political participation

A further symptom of the party–voter disconnection is the shift from party-based activism to single-issue protest movements and pressure group campaigns. As the *Power* inquiry exemplified, Greenpeace had 30,000 members in 1981 but 221,000 members by 2006; the Royal Society for the Protection of Birds had 98,000 members in 1971 but over a million by 2005 (it is an oft-quoted statistic that membership of the RSPB is greater than that of the three main parties combined). In 2002, over half a million took part in the Countryside Alliance's various demonstrations; in 2003, following the start of the Iraq war, 1.5 m took part in 'Stop The War' protests; in 2005, over 150,000 attended the 'Live8' concert in Hyde Park ahead of the G8 summit. According to the *Power* report, 42 per cent of voters had signed some sort of petition during the previous two years, double the reported number for 1974.

All this points to an alternative, 'post-party' form of political participation, underpinned by a vibrant populism that parties can only envy. Voters have not become disconnected from politics per se; merely the type of politics represented by political parties.

The causes

Social and cultural change

The declining popularity of political parties is a long-term trend, linked to the long-term decline of class alignment upon which the two main parties once thrived. Society is now infinitely more eclectic and diverse, and it may be that a handful of parties cannot reflect the multidimensional society we now have. The multitude of pressure groups may well be a better vehicle for the multitude of interests in modern Britain.

This cultural and sociological shift has been reinforced by the decline of deference and the emergence of a new 'karaoke culture', fuelled by prolonged affluence and a revolution in communications – particularly widespread access to the Internet. These trends have served to empower many voters, while eroding the belief that elites and specialists (including party leaders) somehow 'know best'. Voters with a political interest are now less willing to take their cue from political parties and are more willing to set up their own ad hoc organisations, in which they can play a central role – hence the exponential growth of pressure groups and single-issue campaigns.

Ideological change

Since the end of the Cold War, the growth of pressure group politics has been helped by the demise of the old left–right battle and the subsequent particularisation of political debate. Parties are essentially 'big picture' forms of political activity, addressing the nature of society as a whole rather than its specific elements. Yet parties in the post-Thatcher era have not differed hugely on what that big picture should be – highlighted by a shared acceptance of capitalism plus high public spending, and symbolised by the advent of New Labour after 1994 and David Cameron's 'compassionate Conservatism' after 2005 (Jenkins 2006; Elliott and Hanning 2007). To a large extent, this consensus merely reflected how the bulk of voters felt. Nevertheless, it fuelled their impression that parties are 'all the same' and hastened voters' drift towards forms of political activity with a narrower focus.

Disempowerment

For much of the twentieth century, the cogency of party politics stemmed from an assumption that parties who secured office could, through the implementation of their policies, make a significant difference to society. As already indicated, the emergence of a post-Thatcher consensus has circumscribed that view. However, even if major parties had the *will* to be radically different in power, it is no longer clear that they have the *capacity*. Following the end of the Cold War, the UK economy has been increasingly shaped by global economic forces beyond the governing parties' control, prompting some writers to posit a 'silent takeover' of the British economy (Hertz 2002). By the start of the twenty-first century, any plan by ruling parties to macro-manage the British economy in classic Keynesian fashion – and thus make bold promises to voters – looked archaic and implausible. (Gordon Brown's attempt to alter this impression will be examined at the end of this chapter.)

The globalisation of the British economy was reinforced by the steady Europeanisation of British government. The Single European Act 1986 and the Maastricht Treaty of 1991 had further eroded the autonomy of UK governing parties, while the EU treaties endorsed by New Labour (Amsterdam, Nice, Lisbon) did little to reverse the loss of sovereignty. By 2003, almost four-fifths of the new regulations which annually affected UK voters came not from the policies of the governing party but from decisions made within the EU (Nugent 2003). In areas such as agriculture, fisheries, transport, health/safety regulations, retailing and the environment, a UK party coming into power has limited capacity to alter policies that affected millions of UK voters. By 2009, there was evidence that voters were increasingly aware of this and had formed their own conclusions in terms of the importance of both UK political parties and the elections they contested (*YouGov/Sunday Telegraph*, 16 May 2009).

In theory, this might underline the parties' European elections campaigns. Yet these elections are circumscribed by the limited role of the European Parliament within the EU and the impact of Britain's 72 MEPs (in a Parliament comprising over 600 representatives). This situation might be altered by the emergence of cohesive, pan-European party campaigns. But there were few signs of this in Britain's 2009 European elections, with voters continuing either to treat EU elections sceptically or as an opportunity to protest-vote against the Westminster government.

Reforms by recent governments have further undermined the parties' ability to effect change. The ongoing privatisation programme since 1979 – accelerated by New Labour's Private Finance Initiatives – has left governing parties with far less responsibility for the administration of vital public services. The Government's abdication of routine control of interest rates, transferring it to the Bank of England, has affected parties' ability to shape fiscal policy. And, thanks to legislation in 1998, a governing party's ability to shape human rights has been significantly surrendered to the judiciary. In short, the thesis offered by Richard Rose in 1980 – that parties had only limited scope to 'make a difference' – has been steadily reinforced by subsequent developments.

Party organisation

When explaining the parties' disconnection from voters, the above developments have been compounded by changes to party organisation. At a time when our culture has become less elitist and

---

BOX 11.4 FACT

Selecting Conservative candidates[a]

1 Associations (constituency parties) in 'target' seats with fewer than 300 members must choose Parliamentary candidates via 'primary' ballots open to non-party members.[b]
2 In larger associations, members choose a shortlist, half of whom must be women. The association's executive makes the final selection.[c]
3 An association's executive must consider only applicants from the National Approved List.[d]

[a] These amendments to the selection process were introduced by the Party's Constitutional College in 2006.
[b] This idea was pioneered by the Reading East and Warrington South associations prior to the 2005 general election.
[c] This reverses the previous arrangement, whereby the executive shortlisted and the membership selected. The 'positive discrimination' clause was also introduced in 2006.
[d] The National Approved List comprises about 500 candidates selected by national party officials. Prior to the Bromley and Chislehurst by-election 2006, there was some friction between national and local officials after the latter resisted the advice of the former to choose an A-list candidate.

Source: Conservative Party

---

more democratic, the main parties appear to have become more elitist and less democratic in their own structures.

As Minkin's classic study of *The Labour Party Conference* showed, ordinary Labour members once exercised real influence through the party's various blocs – notably trade unions and constituency parties (CLPs). Yet, during the Blair era, these blocs were diluted by the doctrine of 'one-member-one-vote' (OMOV) which, though anti-elitist in theory, seems to have had the opposite effect in practice: individual members, separated from such blocs, had reduced power to avert and correct the wishes of the leadership (Jackson 2009).

As such, the spread of OMOV inside Labour was accompanied by its rising reputation for autocratic leadership and heavily centralised management – both of which resulted in the demotivation of ordinary members. The *Power* inquiry found that 61 per cent of CLP members had attended no party meetings in a year and, as one CLP member told the *Power* inquiry: 'The power we have locally is negligible, and I don't think we have any say over national policy at all' (underlined by their hostility to the Iraq war). When former MPs Clare Short and Alice Mahon left the Party after 2005, they both cited the erosion of CLP autonomy and the loss of grass-root influence over policy. The present author's study of Labour's 'policy forums' (set up in the late 1990s) found that, in terms of altering Government policy, they were a weak alternative to Labour's conference in the Wilson–Callaghan era (Kelly 2001a).

Despite the introduction of OMOV for its leadership contests in 1998, there have been similar trends within the Conservative Party since 2005 (Denham and O'Hara 2008). Constituency party autonomy in candidate selection has been threatened by the advent of 'A-List' candidates and positive discrimination (see Box 11.4). Constituency party campaigning has also become more centrally controlled following the creation of Lord Ashcroft's 'Marginal Seats Unit' – in return for financing campaigns in such seats, Ashcroft's team has secured much more influence over local Tory parties. Likewise, the 'Conservative conference system', which allowed ordinary members a subtle and discreet influence over policy detail, has been quietly dismantled in favour of the Conservatives' own 'policy forums'. Like Labour's, these seem more open to manipulation by party apparatchiks (Kelly 1989, 2001a).

Redolent of New Labour between 1994 and 1997, Cameron's Conservative Party has thus acquired a 'vanguard' character, driven by a clique of London-based politicians and advisers with an unswerving loyalty to the leader (see Box 11.5). As with Labour's OMOV ballot on its 1997 manifesto, individual Tory members may have been given a vote over broad issues (*vide* the *Fresh Future* reforms of 1998 and the *Built to Last* policy statement of 2006). But, as numerous comments on the *Conservative Home* website testify, they have been stripped of influence over the evolving minutiae of party policy.

There seems to be an 'iron law' here, linking inter-party consensus with elitist party structures.

BOX 11.5 FACT

David Cameron's 'Inner Circle' 2006–9

George Osborne – Shadow Chancellor
Edward Llewellyn – Chief of Staff
George Bridges – Head of Campaigns
Andy Coulson – Head of Press
Steve Hilton – Director of Communications*
Danny Kruger – Chief speechwriter
Desmond Swayne – Cameron's Parliamentary Private Secretary
Oliver Letwin – Head of Policy
Nicholas Boles – Head of *Policy Exchange* (think-tank)

** Coulson resigned in 2007, but retained a 'covert and significant influence' (*Sunday Telegraph*, 25 January 2009).*

This link was identified as long ago as 1955 by McKenzie's seminal study of *British Political Parties*. McKenzie noted that party leaders seeking to woo centrist voters would have to sideline their typically non-centrist members, and thus transform their parties into overt or covert oligarchies. This theory has lately been refined by the importance of political marketing: as both main parties have become more 'market-driven' and 'consumerist', they have further converged in terms of policy (Lees-Marshment 2008).

As Lees-Marshment explained, parties that are evangelical (or 'product-orientated') tend to have a polarising effect on inter-party policy and may end up with a manifesto that is 'exclusive' in the eyes of floating voters (*vide* Labour 1983). But such parties often tend to be quite 'inclusive' in their style of party management. If the party is going to 'evangelise', and seek to 'convert' voters, it makes sense for as many party members as possible to feel a stake in its policies. When Labour in the early 1980s had a decidedly 'product-driven' approach, it also had a reputation for decentralising power from Parliamentary leaders towards extra-Parliamentary activists (Shaw 2007). Likewise, Thatcher's Conservatives after 1983 seemed more inclined to shape rather than reflect public opinion; and this was accompanied by a subtle but steady growth of grass-root policy influence via the party's 'conference system' (Kelly 1989).

However, when a party becomes 'market-driven', the relationship between its leaders and members seems to change. Leaders start to attach less importance to their own members and more importance to

external marketing agencies and voter focus groups, helping them ascertain what voters 'want'. The task of processing the resulting data, and thus interpreting exactly what voters *do* 'want', is often an 'elitist' activity that excludes all but a handful of party members. The task complete, a party's managers wish its members merely to absorb and carry out the 'message'. In such an environment, intra-party discussion becomes nugatory, confined to the communication rather than formulation of policy. The role of party members then becomes ancillary, supporting but not challenging the decisions of 'management'. In our present 'karaoke culture', this sort of role has decreasing appeal to the politically active.

There is further reason why market-driven parties are likely to end up with undemocratic, and potentially unpopular, styles of management. Party leaders who seem to follow, rather than lead, public opinion run the risk of seeming weak and uncertain in the eyes of voters. To compensate for this, there is a temptation for those same leaders to adopt macho forms of intra-party management – 'bravely' clamping down on dissent, 'ruthlessly' driving through their own agenda, 'facing down' those in the party who 'resist change', and generally suppressing party democracy to advertise their 'strong leadership' to voters. Tony Blair's assault on Labour's original Clause IV (1994–5) is probably the definitive example of this, while David Cameron's allies have urged him to find his own 'Clause IV moment', allowing him to crush publicly opposition inside his own party (Heffernan 2007; Jones 2008). Paradoxically, such tactics may only alienate further the 'post-deferential' generation of politicised adults.

Party funding

The way in which the main parties have generated income is another recent example of their self-harming tendencies. During the last decade or so, parties have become increasingly reliant upon the largesse of a few individuals, thus strengthening the idea that they are 'plutocratic' in character and divorced from the wishes of ordinary voters.

In 2006, it emerged that about £14 m of the £17 m Labour spent on its 2005 general election campaign came from about 12 businessmen, while 60 per cent of Conservative costs were financed by about 20 individuals (see Box 11.6). The image this created was made worse by the fact that this funding was often furtive and at odds with the spirit of the 2000 Political Parties, Elections and Referendums Act (Fairclough *et al.* 2007). Although the Act had brought greater transparency to donations given by individuals, parties by 2005 were circumventing it through the acceptance of 'loans' – usually at rates which implied they were nothing more than donations in disguise.

In 2006, Labour Party Treasurer Jack Dromey revealed he had known little about these loans and that party officials had been 'kept in the dark' about Labour's fundraising – a reference to the fact that Lord Levy had been mandated by Blair to solicit huge loans (or de facto donations) for Labour. Labour's rivals seemed far from innocent in this area (see Box 11.6). Details of the Conservatives' own loans were only revealed after an exhaustive inquiry by the Electoral Commission in 2006, when it transpired that some of these loans came from overseas residents – another example of how the spirit of the 2000 Act (which forbade such residents to make donations) was being transgressed.

To compound the problem, such loans were often associated with favouritism. In 2006, it was revealed that Capita – owned by Labour lender Rod Aldridge (see Box 11.6) – had benefited from the Government's public sector contracts, including the management of London's congestion charge. This had clear echoes of the Government exempting motor racing from its ban on tobacco advertising in sport, shortly after Formula 1 chief Bernie Ecclestone gave Labour a hefty donation in 1997.

In 2006, party funding was again brought into disrepute by the 'cash for peerages' scandal, when Scotland Yard investigated claims that senior Labour figures had contravened the Honours (Prevention of Abuses) Act 1925 by promising peerages in return for loans to the party. This led to the arrest of Levy and the possibility that a Labour leader and Prime

---

BOX 11.6 FACT

Substantial loans to the Labour/Conservative parties 2005

Labour

Sir David Garrard	Founder, Minerva property group	£2.3 m
Lord Sainsbury	Chief executive, supermarket dynasty	£2 m
Richard Caring	Clothing magnate	£2 m
Chai Patel	Executive, Priory health group	£1.5 m
Rod Aldridge	Chairman, Capita	£1 m
Nigel Morris	Founder, Capital 1	£1 m
Andrew Rosenfeld	Executive, Minerva	£1 m
Barry Townsley	Stockbroker	£1 m
Christopher Evans	Founder, Merlin Bioscience	£1 m

Conservative

Lord Ashcroft	Former Party Chairman	£3.5 m
Michael Hintze	Hedge fund consultant	£2.5 m
Robert Edmiston	Car dealer	£2 m
Arbuthnot Latham	City banker	£2 m
Johan Eliasch	Sportswear magnate	£1 m

Source: Guardian, 19 September 2006

BOX 11.7 FACT

The reform of party finance: recommendations of the Phillips Report

In March 2006, the Prime Minister commissioned Sir Hayden Phillips to undertake 'the most comprehensive analysis of party funding for over 30 years'. His proposals were published in March 2007.

- **Donations:** Phillips argued that the status quo was 'unsustainable', and agreed with the Conservative Party that donations should be capped at £50,000. Mindful of its narrow but hefty range of donations from trade unions, Labour objected to this proposal.
- **Campaign spending:** Criticising 'excessive and unnecessary' spending, Phillips called for a new cap on campaign spending and agreed with Labour that caps should also apply to constituency spending both during and between campaigns. Mindful of its targeting of marginal seats, the Conservatives objected to this proposal.
- **Further state aid:** Phillips foresaw an extra £25 m of state aid, based on two separate formulae – 'pence per vote' (linking state funding to electoral performance) and 'pence per member' (linking state funding to member recruitment). No party voiced serious objection to this proposal.

The lack of cross-party agreement to these proposals meant they were effectively shelved. According to Matthew Norman, 'The whole exercise was a hopeless waste of time' (*Independent*, 16 March 2007)

Minister would himself be detained by police in the course of a criminal investigation (Levy 2008). Small wonder that, in the wake of Levy's arrest, a *YouGov* poll found that the number of voters who thought the Government 'sleazy and corrupt' was greater than in 1997 – almost 10 years after Labour promised to 'clean up politics', after the last Conservative government had been discredited by 'cash for questions' and other scandals (*Daily Telegraph* 15 July 2006).

The parties might argue that the problems of funding stem from factors beyond their control, particularly the growing number of elections they have to contest. But, here again, voters may not be impressed by this argument, sensing that the parties' lack of income is mainly a result of needless spending. In recent years, parties have financed opulent offices, huge secretariats and lavish campaigns, exemplified by Labour's engorged party payroll (£13 m by 2007), the cost of its 2005 campaign HQ (£3 m compared to its normal HQ costs of £1.6 m), and its spending spree during the year of the 2005 general election (£14.5 m, compared with £2.6 m the year before). The Conservatives have been no less profligate, moving from their old Smith Square Central Office into state-of-the-art offices in London's Millbank without selling or renting Smith Square before leaving, leading to losses of £5.5 m by the end of 2006.

It was hoped by some that the Philips' Report on party finance (2007) would lead to a cleansing of the party funding issue. However, its lack of cross-party support meant that the problem lingered (see Box 11.7). Meanwhile, it later emerged that the parties had become even more reliant upon funding from institutions and a handful of individuals. By May 2009, Labour was again receiving almost 80 per cent of its funds from trade unions, while the Conservatives received over £11 m from just four benefactors (*Daily Telegraph* 27 May).

'Endemic' impropriety

Since the 1990s, the parties' integrity has been generically compromised by scandals affecting numerous party luminaries (Garnett 2008). By 2007, two journalists were able to produce a *Bumper Book of British Sleaze* – a forensic account of how hundreds of party politicians had behaved in a morally questionable way (Morton Jack and O'Rorke 2007).

When dissecting the unpopularity of parties, the *Power* report had avoided any reference to specific individuals, preferring to claim that the problem was 'systemic not personal'. However, a breathtaking piece of investigative journalism carried out by the *Telegraph* newspapers in May–June 2009 – concerning MPs' exploitation of Parliament's Additional Costs

BOX 11.8 FACT

The *Daily Telegraph* investigation of MPs' expenses: a selection of exposures

- *Jacqui Smith* (Lab): Claimed her sister's house was her main home, allowing claim for second home allowance on her family's home in Redditch.
- *Hazel Blears* (Lab): *Geoff Hoon* (Lab, Transport Secretary), *James Purnell* (Lab, Works and Pensions Secretary), *David McLean* (Con): *John Bercow* (Con): Avoided capital gains tax on sale of second homes by telling the Inland Revenue they were main residences.
- *David Chaytor* (Lab): *Elliot Morley* (Lab), *Ben Chapman* (Lab), *Bill Wiggin* (Con): Claimed interest payments on properties no longer mortgaged – a potential breach of Fraud Act 2007.
- *Ruth Kelly* (Lab): Claimed £31,000 of expenses on renovation and repair work on second home (in Bolton), despite much of work being covered by private insurance policy.
- *Shahid Malik* (Lab): Breached ministerial code by renting out second home at below market rate. Forced to resign as Justice Minister.
- *Peter Viggers* (Con): Claimed £1,645 from second home allowance to build floating duck island.
- *Andrew McKay*, *Julie Kirkpatrick* (Con): Husband and wife MPs who simultaneously claimed second home allowances on two different properties.
- *Margaret Moran* (Lab): 'Flipped' second home days before claiming, on new second home, £22,500 for dry rot treatment.
- *Keith Vaz* (Lab): Claimed £75,000 for second home, despite living in family home 12 miles away.
- *Douglas Hogg* (Con): Claimed £2,200 for cost of cleaning moat of second home (a mansion in Lincolnshire).
- *David Davis* (Con): Claimed £5,700 for portico.
- *Cheryl Gillan* (Con): Claimed £4.47 for dog food.
- *Gerry Adams*, *Martin McGuiness* (Sinn Fein): Claimed for second homes in London despite not taking up seats at Westminster.
- *Kitty Usher* (Lab, Work and Pensions Minister): Claimed for cost of removing Artex ceilings for reasons of 'taste'.
- *Charles Kennedy* (Lib Dem): Claimed for cost of sweets and teddy bears.

Source: Daily Telegraph, 11 May–9 June 2009

Allowance – suggested the problem was not so much systemic as endemic, pointing to general amorality on the part of innumerable party figures (see Box 11.8).

By June 2009, the *Telegraph* investigation had inflicted almost terminal damage upon voters' respect for political parties and their MPs. As one voter wrote, 'We are constantly told, by MPs of all parties, that they could earn much more outside politics. I don't think so: they would be in jail.' Another wondered (in respect of MPs' abuse of second home allowances), 'How can we trust political parties to run the country when many of their MPs don't even know where they live' (*Daily Telegraph* 16 May 2009). Britain's representative

democracy – underpinned by party politics – was widely felt to have reached its nadir.

■ Consensus and after

'Avant le deluge': the Thatcher/Blair/Brown settlement (1997–2007)

As indicated earlier, a key reason for voter disenchantment was a sense that parties were 'all the same'. To a large extent, this resulted from the centre-left acknowledging Margaret Thatcher's legacy after 1997 (Shaw 2007; Giddens 2007; Beech and Lee 2008). But the consensus was also shaped by Conservatives conceding aspects of the centre-left agenda, especially in respect of public spending. This 'social market' consensus, underpinning party politics from 1997–2007, is summarised here:

■ There was a general acceptance that only markets and capitalist economics could deliver prosperity. There was a related acceptance that market economics should be extended wherever possible (hence Labour's enthusiasm for PFI schemes) and that the era of greater state ownership was over.

■ There was a general acceptance that low inflation should be the 'holy grail' of economic policy and that monetary discipline (what Chancellor Brown called 'prudence') was the key to achieving it. To this end, there was a general acceptance of Brown's decision to transfer routine control of interest rates to the Bank of England's Monetary Policy Committee, and general support for Brown's Treasury 'rules', supposedly constraining Government borrowing.

■ There was a general acceptance that income tax rates should be much lower than those of the pre-Thatcher era. In his final Budget (2007), Brown made a further gesture to Thatcherism by reducing the basic rate of income tax by 2 per cent.

■ There was a general acceptance that public services should no longer have a 'one-size fits all' character, but instead promote 'diversity' and 'choice'. Labour in power duly rejected comprehensive schools in favour of various educational institutions (city academies, trust schools, specialist schools etc.) and allowed more variation within the NHS via the encouragement of 'foundation hospitals'.

■ There was a general acceptance that the main purpose of economic growth was substantial increases in public spending rather than tax cuts. As the 2005 Tory manifesto stated 'We will increase government spending by 4 per cent a year, compared to Labour's plans to increase spending by 5 per cent a year.' The Conservatives duly promised tax cuts of just £4 bn – seen as 'chicken feed' by some free-market economists (Kelly 2006).

■ There was a general acceptance that Britain's approach to the EU should be one of cautious integration. Labour had come a long way from its

David Cameron: Tory triangulator?
Source: Getty Images/Indigo

1983 position of withdrawal, and had strengthened Britain's links with the EU by incorporating its Social Chapter. The Conservatives, while remaining Eurosceptic, still spoke the language of reform rather than abandonment. Furthermore, neither party showed enthusiasm for the UK joining the EU single currency (although the Liberal Democrats still demanded entry at the earliest opportunity).

Cameron's 'Third Way' (2005–7)

This consensus was strengthened by David Cameron's leadership of the Conservative Party between 2005 and 2007. During his first two years as Opposition leader, Cameron seemed to be 'triangulating' the core principles of Conservatism with the embedded effects of New Labour (Kelly 2008a; Bale 2008). Although this upheld certain aspects of Thatcherism – such as the call for a 'looser and larger Europe' and a pledge to restore marriage tax allowance – it generally tilted towards more liberal-centrist positions. It acknowledged, for example:

- That (*contra* Lady Thatcher's alleged claim) 'there is such a thing as society', and that action was needed to 'mend the broken society'.

- That poverty was an urgent issue and that some wealth redistribution was required.

- That 'stability' was the priority of economic policy – and that it could be threatened by cuts in taxation and government spending.

- That short-term tax cuts would be modest, and that a Conservative government would 'share the proceeds of growth' with increases in public spending.

- That the Conservatives would back New Labour's expansion of higher education by no longer opposing tuition fees.

- That the Conservatives would back New Labour's city academies by shelving their commitment to more grammar schools.

- That 'global warming' and 'carbon footprints' were now key issues for Conservatives (hence the message 'Go Blue, Get Green').

- That crime arose not just from individual wickedness but from socio-economic deprivation (hence journalists' quip that Cameron wished to 'hug a hoodie').

- That same-sex relationships were 'equally valid' and that Labour's civil partnership and 'gay adoption' laws would be respected.

- That Labour's constitutional reforms would be broadly accepted: devolution, the new electoral systems, elective mayors and the quest for a more democratic second chamber would all be continued.

'Apres le deluge': a new polarisation? (2007–9)

Consensus politics are usually the product of prosperity: when most voters are satisfied with the economic status quo, it is hard for an Opposition to be radically different. Conversely, when voters are economically insecure, parties are inclined to offer divergent views as to why things went wrong and how things can be improved. As the economy worsened after 2007, it was therefore unsurprising

that the inter-party consensus became brittle. Indeed, by 2009, some classic left–right arguments had resurfaced.

(i) Public ownership or private ownership?

Having ditched its historic commitment to public ownership in 1994, it seemed during 2007–2008 that Labour was returning to first principles. The failing Northern Rock and Bradford and Bingley building societies were taken under state control, while the Government brokered a merger between the HBOS-Lloyds-TSB banking groups. By 2008, the Government was countenancing the effective nationalisation of the entire UK banking system – a notion once confined to the wildest reaches of the British left.

Though not explicitly opposed to this emergency measure, many Conservatives recognised that they might soon have to re-join the battle for free-market ideas. Interestingly, it was a view shared by Nick Clegg who, after his election as Lib Dem leader, nudged his party away from its left-of-Labour position and towards the free-market liberalism of the party's *Orange Books*, which Clegg and his Treasury spokesman Vince Cable had co-authored a few years earlier (Oaten 2009).

(ii) Keynes or prudence?

Brown's 'prudent' Treasury rules (see above) were meant to show that New Labour heeded Thatcherism's message about the perils of debt and borrowing. The 'sustainable investment rule', for example, stated that Government debt should not exceed 40 per cent of gross domestic product. With hindsight, such rules may have been more about image than reality. National debt had already risen from £350 bn in 1997 to £581 bn in 2007. By 2008, the Institute of Fiscal Studies warned that, when the Government's PFI debts were included, national debt stood at £110 bn, 45 per cent of GDP (Nelson and Hoskin 2008).

By 2009, the Government appeared to be galloping away from neo-liberal economics towards an emphatic form of neo-Keynesianism. Having spent £20 bn on a 'fiscal stimulus' package in November 2008, the Government's Budget of 2009 defied 30 years of economic orthodoxy. Borrowing in 2009–10 alone would rise to £175 bn, with national debt set to reach £1.4 trillion by 2013–14 – an expected 80 per cent of GDP. Conservatives, again

Leader of the Liberal Democrats, Nick Clegg, looks to the delegates as he is applauded after he made his
leadership speech at the Lib Dems Party Conference
Source: Getty Images

backed by Clegg's front bench, attacked the policy, claiming that Labour had 'failed to repair the roof while the sun shone' and ditching their promise to match Labour's spending increases. Baroness Thatcher was said to 'feel very much at home with the new political battle-lines ... though saddened that the lessons of the 1970s must again be learnt' (*Daily Telegraph* 25 April 2009).

(iii) Raise income tax?

Despite Labour's promise in 2005 not to 'raise the basic or top rates of income tax in the next Parliament', the 2009 Budget introduced a new top rate of 50 per cent for those earning £150,000 or more each year. When national insurance increases and personal allowance reductions were included, Britain was left with the highest marginal tax rate of any G7 country. Conservatives again protested and received some support from Clegg and Cable (who had committed their party to a lower standard rate, financed by a £20 bn reduction in public spending).

Although the main opposition parties were guarded about their own remedies, inter-party argument by 2009 thus had a clear ideological flavour. While Labour had re-adopted Keynesian ideas of 'tax, spend and borrow' (with a dose of Clause IV socialism), both Tories and senior Liberal Democrats stayed respectful of Thatcher's legacy, claiming the priority was to reduce debt, cut spending and avert any further tax rises. At the start of 2007, voters were said to be unhappy about the lack of conspicuous differences between the parties: by 2009, they seemed to have been appeased.

■ Which party system?

Given the turmoil of party politics after 2005, it was unsurprising that the shape of our party system remained uncertain. As Box 11.8 shows, it is hard to argue that the classic two-party system still exists. But there is confusion as to what, if anything, has replaced it.

145

BOX 11.9   FACT

The decline of a two-party system

The classic two-party system existed in Britain between 1945 and 1974. It had a number of features, all of which are less applicable today:

- *Duopoly of electoral support*: At the 1951 general election, the Labour and Conservative combined vote was 97 per cent. By the general election of 2005 it was just 67 per cent; in the Euro elections 2009 it was 45 per cent.
- *Duopoly of Parliamentary seats*: At the 1951 general election, all but nine MPs were Labour or Conservative. By 2005 the figure was 92.
- *Parity of electoral support*: Between 1945 and 1974, the average vote gap between the main parties was 3 per cent. Since 1979 it has been 9 per cent.
- *Loyal, class-based support*: Between 1945 and 1974, about two-thirds of the working class and three-quarters of the middle class regularly voted Labour and Conservative respectively. By 2005 a majority of working-class voters did not vote Labour and a majority of middle-class voters did not vote Conservative.
- *A nationwide two-party contest*: In the 1951 general election the Labour and Conservative parties came first and second in all but 12 seats, while both parties won substantial numbers of seats throughout the country. By 2005 one of the parties did not come first or second in over 200 seats, the Conservatives won only one seat in Scotland, while Labour won less than a quarter of the votes in southern England (outside London).

A three-party system?

Liberal Democrats are obviously fond of this claim, pointing out that they too have substantive experience of government. Since the introduction of devolved government in Britain, the party has been part of ruling coalitions in both Wales and Scotland. By 2009, they controlled 23 English councils (such as Stockport and Eastbourne) outright and held over 300 more council seats than Labour. At the 2005 general election, the party was the main opposition to the Conservatives in southern England (outside London) and the most popular party in the south-west. The increased likelihood of a hung Parliament at Westminster, even under first-past-the-post, could copper-fasten the third party's importance, while the political and personal empathy between Cameron and Clegg further increased the chance of a Lib Dem presence in a future coalition.

A multi-party system?

It is not just the Lib Dems who profited from the decline of the two-party system. The advent of proportional representation for many of the UK's elections has accelerated the progress of Britain's other parties. Following the devolution elections of 2007, the Scottish National Party took control of the Scottish executive, while Plaid Cymru became part of the Welsh Assembly coalition. In the 2009 European elections, the United Kingdom Independence Party came second, while the Greens and British National Party each won seats. Indeed, one of the striking features of those elections was the fact that the collapse of Labour's vote did not overwhelmingly benefit the Conservatives: a range of alternative opposition parties – from the SNP in Scotland, to the BNP in northern England and to the Greens in the south – were beneficiaries of the anti-Labour swing.

A dominant party system?

This type of party system, similar to that seen in Japan, involves a plurality of parties contesting elections but only one succeeding – a stark contrast to a two-party system, where each party tastes success regularly. During the last 30 years in Britain, one of the main parties has enjoyed a lengthy spell in power while its main rival crashed to a series of ignominious defeats and looked generally hopeless. The 2009 European elections, when the Government polled just 16 per cent of the popular vote, and was eclipsed even in its traditional heartlands like Wales, seemed to portend an equally long period in the political wilderness for New Labour.

A variable party system?

According to the 'variable' model, Britain has not just one-party system but several party systems working concurrently. In the midlands, for example, there is still a mainly Lab–Con battle; in the south (outside London) a mainly Lib–Con battle; and in northern cities a mainly Lib–Lab battle. In Scotland and Wales, meanwhile, there is a four-way battle involving all three British parties and nationalists. Meanwhile, the 2009 European elections showed that the party battle in England could be complicated further by a resurgent UKIP and BNP.

A defunct party system?

The idea of a 'defunct party system' was first advanced after the 2001 general election (Kelly 2001b). This theory states that any 'system' – political or otherwise – must inherently have a strong measure of consistency and uniformity. Such 'systematic' features certainly existed in the 1950s and 1960s, when a Labour–Conservative battle obtained throughout the country, when tribal class support for the two parties existed in all regions, and when any electoral swing in one seat was replicated in most of the others.

In recent years, however, such clear patterns have been absent. At the 2005 general election, Labour's vote fell by 8 per cent in London, but by 'only' 4 per cent in Scotland; the Conservatives added 2 per cent to their support in the south-east, but lost 2 per cent in the north-east. The pattern of voting behaviour in marginal seats was similarly erratic: for example, the Conservatives enjoyed a swing of 6 per cent in Putney, but suffered a 4 per cent reverse in Cheadle. At the 2009 European elections, Labour added to its support in Leicester, despite catastrophic losses elsewhere.

It may be argued that these figures fit the 'variable party system' thesis described above. However, there are now variations of party support not just *between* but *within* certain areas. In north Wales in 2005, the Conservatives took Clwyd West on a swing of 1.3 per cent – yet their vote fell by 11 per cent in Anglesey. Within Greater Manchester's marginal seats, there was a Lab–Con battle in Bury South and Bolton West, a Lib–Con battle in Hazel Grove and Cheadle, and a Lib–Lab battle in Withington and Rochdale. So, even within a single metropolis, there is nothing 'systematic' about modern party competition.

In summary, today's party battles are marked by trendless voting patterns, irregular swings, infinite fluctuations and large-scale abstentions. The expected effects of the Parliamentary expenses scandal – namely, the growth of support for independents and the targeting of particular MPs – will only strengthen the non-systematic nature of modern elections. The 'British party system' has not just changed: it has apparently ceased to exist.

■ The crisis of political parties: collapse or catharsis?

By the summer of 2009, it was clear that Britain's political parties were in the midst of a serious crisis. This crisis was underpinned by a long-standing disconnection from voters, reinforced by the onset of economic recession, and cemented by disclosures of rapacity (and, in some cases, criminality) among MPs. In the eyes of many voters, at least, Britain's political parties were unfit for purpose.

But what is that purpose? During the twentieth century, one of the supposed functions of political parties was to effect radical and far-reaching change, with Attlee's Labour government and Thatcher's Conservatives usually cited as prime examples. However, by the end of the twentieth century, various factors (globalisation, privatisation, European integration) conspired to suggest that parties could no longer have such a cataclysmic effect. In response to the economic crisis after 2007, Gordon Brown's government aimed to correct this impression, promising to 'save' the country through bold, proactive government and a range of sweeping macro-economic measures.

For a while, left-leaning journals like the *New Statesman* saw such measures as a vindication of state power and, by implication, the governing parties that made it democratically accountable. During the period 2007–9, it was possible to argue that the age of 'particularistic' politics (represented by pressure groups) was waning, while a fresh era of 'generalistic' politics (represented by big government and major

Gordon Brown: re-empowered party government
Source: Getty Images

dramatically, the prospects of avoiding depression were 'slim' (*Financial Times* 22 May 2009). Put another way, unless the governing party pruned its ambitions, the country would suffer; instead of being a cure, hyperactive party government was part of the problem. The pan-continental swing against centre-left parties in the 2009 European elections was, perhaps, an indication that voters sensed this.

It was poignant that the IMF's report came when voters were concluding that the parties' chief spokesmen – their Parliamentarians – were morally ill-equipped to be hyperactive on their behalf. In the midst of the expenses scandal, a *YouGov* poll found a majority of voters thinking all the main parties were 'discredited' and 'could not be trusted' (*Sunday Telegraph* 31 May 2009). With an increasingly self-confident electorate increasingly sceptical of elites, this view had been simmering for some time. But it took a combination of economic and constitutional traumas to bring it powerfully to the surface.

Yet, in the wake of these traumas, it would be wrong to conclude that political parties were now otiose. The parties' most basic task – to govern by aggregating society's diverse interests – remains valid. Indeed, given the complexity of modern society, this task is more pertinent than ever. Nevertheless, if parties are to have enough credibility to carry it out, there will have to be a recasting of party politics, as iconoclastic bodies like *Jury Team* and the *National Union of Voters* were founded to point out.

Some prescriptions

If British party politics is to recover, a number of conditions may be necessary – three of which are considered below.

Localisation/democratisation of government

Although New Labour has extolled 'decentralisation', it is widely felt among voters that the new regional bodies (in Scotland, Wales and London) simply represent another tier of self-serving bureaucracy and inaccessible government. It is telling that, when voters in north-east England had a chance to endorse their own regional assembly (via a referendum in 2004), only 22 per cent did so on a turnout of 48 per cent. It may thus be argued that 'localisation' will not be meaningful unless it substantively empowers bodies that are *actually* local – such as county councils and city-wide authorities. This might be

parties) was about to dawn. The politics of neo-liberalism, reflecting a minimal role for governing parties, was said to be over; the politics of supra-national social democracy, where governing parties had to be radically *dirigiste*, was said to be ascendant.

Yet, by mid-2009, it seemed that a British Government had again overestimated its abilities. The International Monetary Fund's survey found that New Labour's fiscal stimulus had 'not done the trick' and that the Chancellor's projections for renewed growth were 'simply unrealistic'. The IMF warned that, unless UK public spending was cut

Numerous MPs were forced to quit after the expenses scandal
Source: Getty Images/Peter Macdiarmid

followed by greater provision for local referendums and 'initiative' ballots – allowing voters to effect reforms proposed by public petitions – and 'recall' ballots, held if enough voters felt a local public official was unsatisfactory (Carswell and Hannan 2008).

Localisation/democratisation of party structures

The localisation of government might then allow the localisation of political parties. National party leaders would have to eschew any 'control freak' tendencies and accept more federal party organisations, allowing local parties to function in a way that suited local circumstances and empowered local party members. Local members, for example, would no longer have to choose candidates from national party lists, while party policy might also acquire an asymmetrical character.

Within their local organisations, parties might consider enfranchising not just ordinary members but also ordinary voters. 'Primary' elections, in which voters chose party candidates, would therefore become commonplace – and thus mitigate complaints about diminished party membership and 'safe' seats.

An individualistic/intelligible electoral system

By May 2009, some prominent figures (like Labour's Alan Johnson) were suggesting proportional representation as a panacea. But the issue of electoral reform should be handled with care. The two systems of PR now used in England and Wales both incorporate 'closed' party lists, where voters cannot explicitly support or condemn individual party candidates. As such, there have been complaints that PR leads to 'stitch-ups', guaranteeing the election of senior party figures and further alienating voters from the political system (Kelly 2008b). Particularly after the expenses scandal, it is vital that voters feel able to target, negatively or otherwise, individual politicians. A *YouGov* poll found that only a minority of voters saw the expenses crisis as an indictment of our constitutional system, while just a third called for radical constitutional reform. A clear majority thought the crisis was an indictment of individual party MPs – and the priority was for those individuals to be punished (*Daily Telegraph* 1 June 2009).

■ Conclusion: American dream or back to the future?

It could be argued that some of the above ideas – notably dispersed government and looser party structures – point to the Americanisation of our political system. It could also be argued that such an arrangement, while appropriate to a vast democracy like the USA, is less suited to smaller and more homogenous European societies.

Yet there is nothing inherently un-British about such a new constitutional and party system. In fact, it has strong echoes of British politics over a century ago when government was less centralised, parties less regimented and party governments less hubristic in their ambitions. This was a period, in other words, when local government was more significant, variations in local administration more marked, intra-party rules more relaxed and the remit of government more modest and prosaic.

Given the recent economic and constitutional crisis, and with doubts now growing about the efficacy of 'big government', it may be worth considering whether such pre-democratic arrangements could be adapted to a modern, democratic setting. For all their recent difficulties, political parties would be indispensable to such a dramatic upheaval of our polity. In this respect, British political parties – far from being redundant – could be more important than ever in the years ahead.

BOX 11.10 BRITAIN IN CONTEXT

The problems besetting parties in the UK are far from uncommon elsewhere. Indeed, there is a case for arguing they are endemic throughout the world's democratic societies. Fukuyama's 'end of history' thesis (1992) foresaw a narrowing of party differences across the post-Cold War world which has generally served to de-energise voters. Despite Samuel Huntington's warning (1996) that the twenty-first century would be marked by a global 'clash of civilisations', on account of emergent religious fundamentalism, there were few signs by 2009 that this had polarised party debate, or galvanised voters, in most Western polities. In the USA, various studies (e.g. Maisel 2007) have confirmed the long-term trend away from party politics towards pressure group and protest movements, while the 2008 presidential election – featuring perhaps the most charismatic challenger in decades – still failed to raise turnout much above

60 per cent (similar to the figure at the UK general election of 2005, which was widely considered risible). Even more interesting, perhaps, is the limited interest in party politics within the newly democratised European societies (Cular 2005; Wasilewski 2009). Far from providing a contrast to the UK at the 2009 European elections, many of these countries showed even less enthusiasm for party prescriptions. Turnout in Poland, Slovenia and Slovakia, for example, was just 27 per cent, 28 per cent and 20 per cent, while turnout across the EU generally was just 43 per cent. Neither did it seem clear in these elections that party government had been vindicated in the eyes of voters: there was a marked swing against the centre-left, 'big government' parties almost everywhere. In short, one of the key questions posed in this chapter – 'do parties matter?' – continued to receive a globally obtuse response.

Chapter summary

As the first decade of the new century drew to a close, Britain's political parties remained in a state of crisis, stricken by voter disinterest, increasing public hostility, tumbling membership and dubious sources of income. The 2010 general election served to underline this crisis, with the main parties unable to offer the kind of distinctive approaches that once gave party politics traction. The nature of the British party system also stayed unresolved, the traditional two-party system having been succeeded by something altogether more volatile and oblique. However, the depth of the crisis – allied to the onset of recession – also gave parties a redemptive opportunity, encouraging them to reconsider their internal structures, the extent to which they empower their own members, the extent to which they decentralise and their relationship with alternative forms of political activity. It remains to be seen whether the main parties grasp this opportunity – or continue to atrophy in the face of rapid economic, cultural and sociological change.

Discussion points

- Why have UK political parties alienated so many voters?

- In what sense are UK political parties at odds with social, economic and cultural developments?

- Is it now possible to speak of any 'British party system'?

- Is there a post-credit crunch consensus among the main parties?

- Do radical parties like the BNP represent a long-term challenge to the nature of party politics?

- How much can parties in the twenty-first century learn from the those of the nineteenth century?

Further reading

Beech, M. and Lee, S. (eds) (2008) *Ten Years of New Labour* (Palgrave Macmillan).

Beech, M. and Lee, S. (eds) (2009) *The Conservatives Under David Cameron* (Palgrave Macmillan).

Elliott, F. and Hanning, J. (2007) *Cameron: the Rise of the New Conservative* (Harperpress).

Jury Team (2009) *The End of the Party* (JTPublications).

O'Hara, K. (2007) *After Blair: David Cameron and the Conservative Tradition* (Icon Books).

Shaw, E. (2007) *Losing Labour's Soul: New Labour and the Blair Government* (Routledge).

Bibliography

Bale, T. (2008) 'Qualifying the Common Wisdom: David Cameron and Conservative Party Change', *E-Pol* 3,1 www.politicaleducationforum.com.

Baston, L. and Herring, S. (2005) 'The Labour Party' in Seldon, A. and Kavanagh, D. (eds) *The Blair Effect* (Cambridge University Press).

Beech, M. and Lee, S. (eds) (2008) *Ten Years of New Labour* (Palgrave Macmillan).

Broughton, D. (2008) 'Electoral Change in Britain 2005–2008' *E-Pol* 1,1 www.politicaleducationforum.com.

Carswell, D. and Hannan, D. (2008) *The Plan: 12 Months to Renew Britain*, www.Lulu.com.

Cular, G. (2005) *Elections and the Consolidation of Democracy in Croatia* (Zagreb).

Denham, A. and O'Hara, K. (2008) *Democratising Conservative Leadership Selection* (Manchester University Press).

Dorey, P. (2008) 'The Conservatives: from Collapse to Cameron-led recovery', *E-Pol* 1,2 www.politicaleducationforum.com.

Elliott, F. and Hanning, J. (2007) *Cameron: The Rise of the New Conservative* (Harperpress).

Fairclough, P., Kelly, R. and Magee, E. (2007) 'Funding Political Parties: An Intractable Problem' in *UK Government and Politics: Annual Survey 2007* (Philip Allan).

Fisher, J. (2008) 'Party Finance Since 2005', *E-Pol* 1,2 www.politicaleducationforum.com.

Fukuyama (1992) *The End of History and the Last Man* (Penguin).

Garnett, M. (2006) 'Is the Conservative Party conservative?', *Politics Review*, Vol. 15, No. 3.

Garnett, M. (2008) 'Sleaze and British Politics', *E-Pol* 1,1 www.politicaleducationforum.com.

Giddens, A. (2007) *Over To You, Mr Brown* (Polity).

Goodwin, R. (2008) *Innovating Democracy* (Oxford University Press).

Grant, M. (2005) 'Is Labour still a socialist party?', *Politics Review*, Vol. 15, No. 1.

Heffernan, R. (2007) 'Tony Blair as Labour Party Leader' in Seldon, A. (ed.) *Blair's Britain* (Cambridge University Press).

Hertz, N. (2002) *The Silent Takeover: Global Capitalism and the Death of Democracy* (Simon and Schuster).

Huntington, S. (1996) *The Clash of Civilisations and the Making of World Order* (Simon and Schuster).

Jackson, N. (2009) 'All the fun of the seaside', *E-Pol* 2,1 www.politicaleducationforum.com.

Jenkins, S. (2006) *Thatcher and Sons* (Allen Lane).

Jones, D. (2008) *Cameron on Cameron* (Fourth Estate).

Jury Team (2009) *The End of the Party* (JT publications).

Kelly, R. (1989) *Conservative Party Conferences* (Manchester University Press).

Kelly, R. (2001a) 'Farewell Conference, Hello Forum', *Political Quarterly*, Vol. 72, No. 3.

Kelly, R. (2001b) 'The Defunct Party System' *Talking Politics*, Vol. 14, No. 1.

Kelly, R. (2006) 'The Leadership Battle: Turning Point for the Tories?', Fairclough, P., Kelly, R., Magee, E. *UK Government and Politics: Annual Survey 2006*.

Kelly, R. (2008a) 'Conservatism Under Cameron: The New Third Way', *Politics Review*, Vol. 17, No. 3.

Kelly, R. (2008b) 'It's only made things worse: a critique of electoral reform in Britain', *Political Quarterly*, Vol. 79, No. 2.

Kelly, R. (2008c) 'The Battle for the Labour Leadership', Fairclough, P., Kelly, R., Magee, E. *UK Government and Politics*: *Annual Survey 2008* (Philip Allan).

Kelly, R. (2008d) 'The End of Ming' in Fairclough, P., Kelly, R., Magee, E. *UK Government and Politics: Annual Survey 2008* (Philip Allan).

Kelly, R. (2008e) 'The 2008 Elections and the British Party System', *E-Pol* 1,3 www.politicaleducationforum.com.

Kelly, R. (2009) 'Cameron's Third Way: A Redundant Project', *E-Pol* 2,1 www.politicaleducationforum.com.

Lees-Marshment, J. (2008) *Political Marketing and British Political Parties* (Manchester University Press).

Levy, Lord (2008) *A Question of Honour* (Simon and Schuster).

Maisel, L.S. (2007) *American Political Parties and Elections* (Oxford University Press).

McKenzie, R.T. (1955) *British Political Parties* (Heinemann).

Minkin, L. (1978) *The Labour Party Conference* (Allen Lane).

Morton Jack and O'Rourke (2007) *The Bumper Book of British Sleaze* (Foxcote).

Nelson, F. and Hoskin, P. (2008) 'The Great Debt Deceit: how Gordon Brown Cooked the Nation's Books', *Spectator*, 20 September.

Nugent, N. (2003) *The Government and Politics of the European Union* (Palgrave Macmillan).

Oaten, M. (2009) 'Lib Dem Ministers Ahoy?', *E-Pol* 2,2 www.politicaleducationforum.com.

O'Hara, K. (2007) *After Blair: David Cameron and the Conservative Tradition* (Icon Books).

Power Inquiry (2006) *Power To The People* (Rowntree Charitable Trust).

Rose, R. (1980) *Do Parties Make a Difference?* (Macmillan).

Shaw, E. (2007) *Losing Labour's Soul? New Labour and the Blair Government 1997–2007* (Routledge).

Wasilewski, J. (2009) *Political Leadership in Polish Counties* (Warsaw).

Wheatcroft, G. (2005) *The Strange Death of Tory England* (Penguin/Allen Lane).

Webb, P. (2005) 'The Continuing Advance of the Minor Parties', *Parliamentary Affairs*, Vol. 58, No. 4.

Useful websites

www.labour.org.uk

www.conservatives.com

www.conservativehome.blogs.com

www.libdems.org.uk

www.snp.org

www.plaidcymru.org

www.ukip.org

www.greenparty.org.uk

www.bnp.org.uk

www.zyra.org/uk

www.bubl.ac.uk/bublukpoliticalparties

This chapter is dedicated to Rod Martin (1950–2009), founder and Head of Manchester Grammar School's Politics Department, 1977–2009.

Topic 4:
Elections and
Electoral
Behaviour

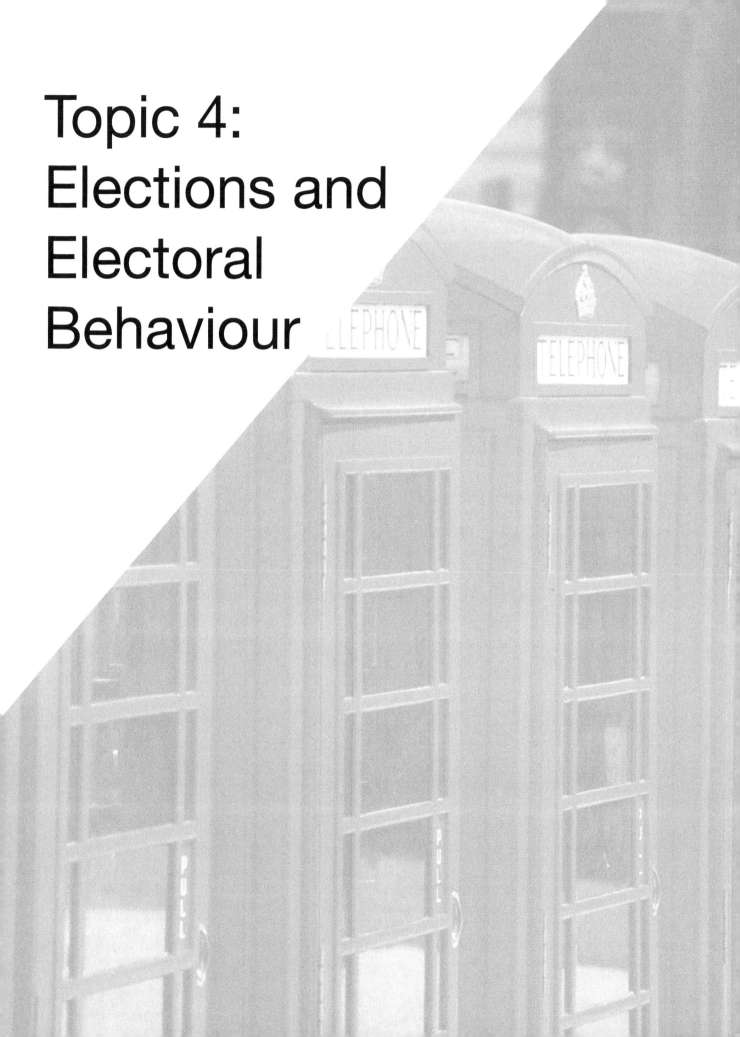

Elections

Mark Garnett

Learning objectives

- To understand the purpose and importance of elections in Britain.
- To evaluate the current voting system used for UK parliamentary elections, and examine the main alternatives.
- To describe recent changes in election campaigns.

Introduction

This chapter begins with a discussion of elections in general, before explaining key details of the voting system ('first-past-the-post' [FPTP], or 'simple plurality', as it is usually called) currently used for elections to the UK parliament. It goes on to outline the perceived problems regarding this system, and speculates about the prospects for change. Finally, it assesses recent changes in campaign techniques, and reforms of the laws regarding campaign finance.

■ The role of elections in liberal democracies

A basic tenet of liberal ideology is that government must be based upon the consent of the governed. This seems to be a fairly simple notion, involving few problems in practice. However, even the greatest liberal thinkers have found it difficult to decide what, exactly, should count as 'consent'. One of the very greatest, John Locke (1632–1704) ended up falling back on the idea of 'tacit consent', arguing that we are in some way expressing our acceptance of the prevailing system of government by merely walking along 'the King's highway'.

For most democrats, the principle of consent demands something much more meaningful than this. In Ancient Athens, citizens represented themselves when key decisions were taken, meeting and voting in a public assembly. This system is known as 'direct democracy'. While the citizen-body as a whole acted as an assembly making key decisions, governmental posts were filled by means of a 'ballot' – in modern parlance, the names of the 'winning' candidates for the necessary jobs were drawn at random out of a hat. In such conditions, office holding was seen as a duty rather than a means of personal advancement or enrichment.

However, in the modern era direct democracy seems wholly impracticable. Some enthusiasts see the Internet as a way of recapturing something approaching the Athenian system. However, the essence of Athenian democracy was that citizens should gather together physically, in a common space, and listen to the various arguments. Deliberations among isolated citizens, using technology rather than direct speech, would seem to be a pale and potentially dangerous imitation, leading to decision-making on the basis of emotion rather than constructive thinking.

Whatever the prospects of a return to direct democracy, most democrats are now reconciled to the idea that key political decisions should be taken by elected representatives. There are, though, two important provisos:

■ Elections should be 'free and fair'; that is, nobody should be prevented from submitting themselves as candidates; no-one should be disqualified from voting, unless for reasons which are themselves subject to common consent; every opportunity should be given to qualified persons to cast their votes; no-one should be subjected to intimidation or bribery; and all voters should have free access to information relevant to their choices, through media which are not subjected to state censorship.

■ Elections should be held at regular intervals, so that representatives can be held to account for decisions taken during their terms of office.

■ Elections in the UK

Until quite recently, few Britons were seriously concerned about the democratic system in the UK. No-one thought that the voting system for the Westminster parliament was perfect, but its verdicts commanded widespread support and the same system was used for all local government elections in Britain. That system is commonly known as '**first-past-the-post**' (**FPTP**, or 'simple plurality'). Under that system, the candidate who receives the most votes is elected – even if he or she is favoured by a relatively small minority of the voters. However, it is not the case that the party which wins the most seats on this basis could automatically form the next government. For that purpose, it is usually necessary

Tony Blair tries to bridge the 'trust gap' in the run-up to the 2005 general election
Source: Copyright © Chris Riddell. From the *Observer*, 20 February 2005. Reproduced with permission from Guardian Newspapers Limited

for a party to win more seats than all of its opponents in combination. In other words, individual seats are won on the basis of FPTP; but only if a party wins an absolute majority (more than 50 per cent) of the seats can it be reasonably sure of being able to form a government. If no single party secures an absolute majority of seats, the monarch as Head of State can become an important power-broker; but by convention he or she has to ask the leader of the party with the most seats if it is in a position to form a minority government, with the active support (or passive approval) of other parties.

The system escaped serious criticism even when it produced apparently anomalous results. Thus, for example, in the general election of 1951 Labour won a greater percentage of the national vote than the Conservatives; but the latter won enough seats to form a majority government, and when it duly did so there were few complaints. The underlying problems began to attract more comment after 1974,

when two general elections were held. In the first (held in February), Labour won fewer votes than the Conservatives, but four more seats. In the second (October), it won almost a million more votes than the Conservatives, and 42 more seats. However, in October 1974 other parties (including the Liberals) won 39 seats between them, meaning that Labour had an overall majority of only three. Labour had campaigned on the basis of a radical election manifesto in both of the elections of 1974, and although the prime minister Harold Wilson did his best to give the impression that he would govern on behalf of the whole nation, his party was heavily dependent on trade union support.

Some of the government's decisions were fiercely opposed by Conservatives, who claimed that the electorate had not given Labour a clear 'mandate' to implement radical policies. Among these critics was Lord Hailsham (1907–2001), who had been Lord Chancellor in the Conservative government

---

BOX 7.1   Britain's road to universal adult suffrage

Until 1832, the British electorate was very small, and its general composition was determined by two characteristics: either the voters were quite substantial property-owners, or they lived in constituencies where (for historic reasons) the monarch had granted a Charter which gave the vote even to relatively poor inhabitants. After many years of agitation, a long process of electoral reform began in 1832 (under the auspicies of the very aristocratic Whig party); but although that measure was hailed as 'The Great Reform Act', it left most males (and all women) disenfranchised. The main landmarks in the gradual move towards universal adult suffrage were as follows:

1832 The 'Great Reform Act' gives the vote to many middle-class property owners, but takes it away from many of the poor people (either in cities or rural areas) who had previously enjoyed the right to vote. Abolishes some seats ('rotten boroughs') which still could return MPs even if hardly anyone lived there any more.

1867 Second Reform Act: Extends the franchise to householders in towns and cities.

1872 Ballot Act: Qualified electors could now vote in secret.

1884 Franchise Act: Extends the vote to rural labourers, so that a quarter of the adult population can now vote.

1918 Representation of the People Act: All men of 21 and over can now vote, along with women of 30 and over. Electorate now more than 75 per cent of adult population.

1928 Representation of the People Act: Voting age equalised for men and women, at 21 years and over.

1948 Representation of the People Act: Abolishes 'plural voting', which allowed people with several properties to vote more than once.

1969 Representation of the People Act: Lowers the voting age to 18, for men and women.

2000 Representation of the People Act: Allows people without a permanent residence in the UK to vote, and opens the door to 'pilot schemes' which could give trial runs to different methods of voting (e.g. all-postal ballots, see below).

(1970–4) led by Edward Heath. In a broadcast lecture of 1976, Hailsham warned that Britain was in danger of becoming an 'elective dictatorship', since a party with very limited electoral support could still contrive to use the democratic forum of parliament to push through divisive policies. Hailsham argued in favour of a strengthened House of Lords which would be elected 'proportionately', as a defence against overmighty and unrepresentative governments (Hailsham 1978: 129). Among his other proposals, Hailsham advocated devolution to Scotland, Wales, Northern Ireland and England; and he urged greater use of referendums to gain an authoritative estimate of public opinion on key issues (see below).

BOX 7.2   Alternative voting systems

A major difficulty facing would-be reformers of the system for parliamentary elections in Britain is that there are several alternatives, none of which can guarantee a perfect symmetry between the preferences of voters and the overall outcome. The scope for disagreement is increased by the fact that the suitability of the different systems varies according to existing political circumstances; thus, for example, while one system is used in Scotland, Wales and Greater London (see below), that method has not been adopted for the Assembly in Northern Ireland. Yet another system is used in elections to the European Parliament.

The **additional member system (AMS)** is best understood as a compromise between first-past-the-post (**FPTP**) and the more proportional systems. It has been adopted for the Scottish Parliament

---

(see Table 7.1), the Welsh Assembly and the Greater London Assembly (GLA), which suggests that it is regarded with some favour by senior politicians – the 'least worst' option in their eyes, perhaps. The system is also used in Germany.

Under AMS, voters can make two choices. The first vote is cast for individual constituency representatives, as in FPTP. These constituency members make up at least half of the resulting assembly. The remaining members are elected on the basis of regional, multi-member constituencies. For this second contest, voters are asked to choose between competing party lists, and the seats are allocated to the successful parties broadly in proportion to the votes they receive. Supporters of the system argue that it retains the link between representatives and their constituents, while also making it less likely that individual electors will consider their votes to have been wasted.

The **single transferable vote (STV)** allows voters to list their choices in order of preference. They can vote for as many candidates as they like. Often, but not always, the constituencies are large and more than one member will be elected. To win a seat, a candidate needs to reach a specified 'quota'. When a candidate reaches this target, his or her remaining votes are redistributed among the other candidates (starting with the second preferences). If no candidate reaches the quota on the first ballot, the candidate with the *least* first preferences is eliminated and his or her votes are redistributed. This process continues until the required number of candidates has reached the quota.

This system is used in the Northern Ireland Assembly, where the quota is set at 14.3 per cent of the overall vote. Since 2007, STV has also been used in Scottish local elections. Supporters claim that the system is roughly proportional, and usually offers voters a very wide choice of candidates (they can, for example, expect to see several candidates from the same party on the ballot-sheet, which means that the outcome is not so tightly controlled by the central party which might favour one candidate over another). However, unlike AMS it does not guarantee a close link between members and a constituency of traditional size.

In the **alternative vote** system **(AV)**, voters also list their choices according to their preferences. The voting takes place in single-member constituencies, and a winner is declared when he or she achieves an overall majority of the votes cast. If no candidate secures more than 50 per cent of the vote when first preferences have been counted, the candidate with the fewest votes is eliminated and his or her second preferences are redistributed. This process continues until someone does achieve more than 50 per cent of the vote.

Supporters of this system argue that it retains the link between constituencies and members. Critics point out that it could lead to anomalies: for example, a candidate who wins clearly on the first ballot, but falls short of an overall majority, might end up being beaten by a rival who was the first preference of far fewer voters. However, it could be argued that this is actually an advantage of the system, since unlike FPTP it could prevent the election of divisive figures, who are loved by a large number of people but actively disliked by the majority.

A closely related system to AV is the **supplementary vote (SV)**. In this system the voter can indicate only two preferences. As with AV, the system is based on single-member constituencies. If no candidate wins an overall majority of first preferences, there is a 'run-off' between the candidates who come first and second. All of the ballots cast for the remaining candidates are examined, and the second preferences redistributed between the top two. At the end of this process, the candidate with the most votes is elected.

This system is used to elect many of England's mayors, including the Mayor of London (see Table 7.2). Like AV, if used in a parliamentary election it would ensure a link between the winning candidate and his or her constituency. However, unlike AV there is little chance than it could lead to a situation in which a candidate with very few first preferences could end up being elected, since only the candidates who come first and second in the initial ballot stand any chance of victory. On the other hand, this does mean that divisive or extravagantly populist figures have a good chance of prevailing.

The **regional list** system is used in the UK for elections to the European Parliament. Voters choose a particular party, rather than specified individuals, in multi-member constituencies. Seats are then allocated in close proportion to the size of the vote – i.e. if a party receives 40 per cent of the votes, it will get something like 40 per cent of the seats. Thus, in the 2009 European elections, the Conservatives won 27.7 per cent of the vote and received 25 of the available seats (in 2009 the UK elected 72 members of the European parliament [MEPs]). In sharp contrast to the situation in FPTP elections, the Liberal Democrats attracted 13.7 per cent of the vote, and were allotted 11 of the 72 seats.

Critics of the regional list system focus on two main issues: first, the constituencies tend to be very large, so that the individual voter feels little attachment to his or her representative; and second, it allows the various parties to decide which candidates are elected (e.g. if a party is allocated one seat on the basis of its electoral support, the party rather than the electorate decides which person should represent them).

Table 7.1 The effect of the additional member system (ams) on the election to the Scottish Parliament, 2007

Party	Share of constituency vote (%)	Constituency seats won	Share of regional list vote (%)	Regional list seats won	Total
Scottish National Party	32.9	21	31.0	26	47
Labour	32.2	37	29.2	9	46
Conservative	16.6	4	13.9	13	17
Lib Dem	16.2	11	11.3	5	16
Green	0.1	0	4.0	2	2
Others	2.0	0	10.6	1	1

Table 7.2 The effect of the supplementary vote (sv) on the London Mayoral election, 2008

Candidate	Party	First preference (%)	Second preferences (from other candidates)	Final percentage vote
Boris Johnson	Conservative	43.2	12.9	53.2
Ken Livingstone	Labour	37.0	15.1	46.8
Brian Paddick	Lib Dem	9.8	32.0	
Sian Berry	Green	3.2	16.6	
Richard Barnbrook	BNP	2.9	6.4	
Alan Craig	Christian Peoples Alliance	1.6	4.0	
Gerard Batten	UKIP	0.9	5.7	
Others		1.3	7.3	

Hailsham did not recommend proportional representation for the House of Commons itself, and after his party won the 1979 general election with a safe majority he seemed less worried about the UK political system. However, during the 18 years of Conservative rule (1979–97) the government's opponents became increasingly concerned. Now that they were in opposition, some Labour supporters suddenly realised that Britain might be an 'elective dictatorship' after all. Mrs Thatcher was able to push through controversial measures despite never coming close to winning an overall majority of votes cast in any of the three general elections which she won (see Table 7.3).

At the 1997 general election the pendulum swung the other way, and Labour began to benefit considerably from the distorting effects of FPTP. In the 2005 general election, Labour needed on average 26,900 votes to secure one MP; for the Conservatives, the necessary total was 44,500 votes. Generally speaking, senior figures in both main parties seemed content to live with these effects, on the grounds that if they did happen to win an election even by a tiny proportion of the vote they were

Table 7.3 Percentage vote share of winning parties at recent general elections (parliamentary majority in brackets)

1979, Conservatives	1983, Conservatives	1987, Conservatives	1992, Conservatives	1997, Labour	2001, Labour	2005, Labour
43.9 (43)	42.4 (144)	42.3 (102)	41.9 (21)	43.2 (179)	40.7 (166)	36.1 (67)

likely to have a 'workable' majority. However, within both Labour and the Conservative Party there were some people who could not forget the days when they had no chance of influencing political decisions even though their parties had won a very respectable share of the national vote. The greatest anger, though, was felt by supporters of the third electoral force – the Liberal–Social Democratic Alliance of the 1980s, which became the merged Liberal Democrat Party in 1988. In the 1983 general election, the Alliance won more than a quarter of the popular vote. Nationally, the gap between the votes for the Alliance and for Labour was less than three-quarters of a million. Nevertheless, thanks to the inbuilt bias of FPTP, the Alliance won just 23 parliamentary seats, compared to 209 for Labour! It was not surprising that Liberals were long-standing critics of the voting system, although this stance was based on principle as well as self-interest since sincere liberals have good reasons to be outraged by a system which places unequal values on the votes of citizens in different parts of the country.

■ The Jenkins Report

Before the 1997 general election, Labour and the Liberal Democrats agreed that a referendum should be held on the UK voting system. Again, cooperation between these parties arose from principle as well as opportunism; the Labour leader Tony Blair felt that the two parties represented 'progressive' politics in Britain, and were thus natural allies against the Tories. However, Blair's commitment to a referendum also reflected his fear that the current system might not deliver a workable majority to his party at the ensuing general election. As it turned out, the impact of FPTP transformed a relatively modest Labour vote into a crushing victory in 1997, so after he took office Blair had much less reason to advocate radical reform.

The former Alliance leader, Lord (Roy) Jenkins, was friendly with Blair and shared his view about the ultimate need for unity among progressive politicians. In October 1997 Blair appointed Jenkins to head a commission on the voting system. Significantly, despite Labour's electoral pledge of a referendum, Jenkins' commission was declared to be 'independent', so that the new government need not feel bound by its conclusions. Accordingly, when Jenkins reported after a year of deliberation, his proposals were quite cautious. He opted for a system under which most MPs (80–85 per cent) would be chosen by the **alternative vote** (see Box 7.2). However, the remaining MPs would be chosen in proportion to the electoral support for their respective parties. This compromise was generally known as 'AV-plus'. On paper, it was a clever idea; the 'AV' MPs would have to secure more than 50 per cent support in their constituencies, and even if they would usually have to rely on second preferences to achieve this proportion, they would still enjoy more legitimacy as constituency representatives than most MPs can currently command. Although the proportional element in Jenkins' system was relatively small, it was likely to act as a corrective to the existing system which gave too much parliamentary weight to the winning party and condemned the smaller parties to irrelevance.

Despite Jenkins' ingenious efforts, Blair could not persuade senior colleagues to endorse his conclusions and the promised referendum has never been held. The fact is that although electoral reform is an engrossing subject to some well-informed people, the average voter is not very interested. If Jenkins had proposed something simple to replace the current system, his chances of success would have been greater. However, he knew that a simple system would have been far too radical for most parliamentarians to accept. Hence, Jenkins decided to opt for complexity, hoping that existing MPs would be persuaded by his logic. It was no surprise that people who had been elected under the present system decided that, with all its undoubted faults, it was far superior to any alternative – especially one which had been proposed by a man who had once hoped to 'break the mould' of two-party politics.

There are, in fact, solid reasons for maintaining FPTP. The most important are:

- FPTP is easy for voters to understand.

- It is based on single-member constituencies, so that voters can identify with the representative of the area in which they live.

- It usually (but not always) produces a clear-cut national verdict, so that the winning party can govern without cutting deals.

- Alternative systems will almost invariably lead to coalition governments, which usually provide weak leadership for the country.

- Many people like to simplify politics into a stark choice between the government and the main opposition party. FPTP encourages two-party politics, and thus gives these voters exactly what they want.

On the other side of the debate, critics of FPTP argue that:

- The system usually gives a thumping majority to parties which have not persuaded a majority of the public that their policies are right.

- Sometimes, though, it leads to a result in which no single party has an overall majority (as in the UK after the election of February 1974). Thus it can lead to political stalemate rather than strong government.

- It encourages irresponsible opposition, since rather than rallying behind a government at a time of national crisis opposition parties will be tempted to make the most out of political difficulties.

- While it can encourage the main parties to exaggerate their differences, at other times it makes them imitate each other, so that voters are deprived of a meaningful choice.

- It depresses electoral turnout, because citizens are less likely to vote in constituencies where their preferred candidates have no chance of winning.

- Although proportional systems might usually result in coalition governments, there is no reason to regard these as necessarily inferior from the democratic point of view to governments which impose policies which do not enjoy backing from a majority of the voting public.

In a democratic state, it would be reassuring to think that the eventual outcome of this debate would be settled by the quality of the arguments on either side – or, perhaps, by an objective review of the effects of different voting systems in Scotland, Wales and Northern Ireland. Regrettably, recent history shows that this is most unlikely to be the case. A system which produces a more 'proportional' outcome – or even one which persuades individual citizens that their votes will not be 'wasted' – is likely to be resisted by both of the main parties while they retain any hope of winning power at Westminster under FPTP. While this situation prevails, both of them will assert that their attachment to FPTP arises from principle rather than expediency. But if there is a closely-fought general election, after which the Liberal Democrats hold the balance of power, it would not be surprising if both Labour and the Conservatives announce a sudden conversion to any one of the various available systems, all of which are more closely compatible with the ideals of liberal democracy. Indeed, in the run up to the 2010 contest Gordon Brown suddenly announced an unexpected 'conversion' to the argument for electoral reform, even though he had been regarded as a stanch supporter of FPTP in the years when Labour's electoral prospects were much brighter.

■ Declining turnout

Whatever critics might say about FPTP, the system of election to the UK parliament does satisfy the basic criteria for the conduct of elections in a liberal democracy. That is, for example, new contests have to be called after a maximum of five years; citizens are free to stand for election (subject to nomination by ten local voters and the payment of a £500 deposit); opportunities to vote (in secret) are plentiful; and the counting of votes almost invariably proceeds without criticism. The task of the Boundary Commission, which makes regular changes to the geographical area of Westminster constituencies in line with demographic changes, is a difficult one. There are significant anomalies – at present constituencies in Wales have an average electorate of 56,000, compared to 70,000 in England. Even so, there have been few major public disagreements about the way in which seats are distributed around the UK.

On this basis, one might argue that the system in Britain has evolved in a fashion which satisfies the criteria of a liberal democracy in *procedural* terms. The remaining question, though, is whether the country is still animated by a democratic *spirit*. The chief concern here relates to the turnout at recent general elections. This is a serious matter, since if political parties no longer attract significant public support the legitimacy of government itself comes into question.

The 1992 general election gave no cause for serious disquiet. Although the Conservatives had been in power for more than a decade, under John Major they secured more votes in 1992 than any British party had achieved at a previous election. Ironically, thanks to the oddities of FPTP (and difficulties within his party) this was not enough to give Major a comfortable parliamentary cushion. By contrast, in 1997 Labour won an overwhelming majority, leading over-excited media commentators to talk of a new political mood in the country. On closer inspection, however, the 1997 general election was hardly a ringing public endorsement of the new government. Turnout was just 71.4 per cent, so that Labour won the support of less than a third of the eligible voters. In the next nationwide poll, the European parliamentary election of May 1999, the turnout slumped to a miserable 24 per cent.

It was just about possible to shrug off the latter statistic, since Britons are notoriously reluctant to vote in European elections. However, there was a dramatic development in the general election of 2001, when turnout was less than 60 per cent – easily the lowest figure recorded since Britain adopted universal suffrage. There was an improvement in the 2005 general election, but still only 61.2 per cent of qualified adults voted despite a steep increase in the number of citizens who cast their vote by post rather than taking the minimal trouble of visiting a polling station.

The political reaction to these disturbing figures was slightly ominous. In public, some ministers expressed concern. They could hardly avoid such comments, since the right to vote had been achieved slowly and painfully, and on paper at least it remained the most important channel through which ordinary members of the public could exercise influence over the political process. But ministers could also fall back on convenient alibis. In 2001, 2005 (and even 1997) the overall outcome of the election had been obvious for some time. This knowledge was likely to act as a serious disincentive to would-be voters – supporters of the opposition parties would be less likely to vote because they were certain of ending up on the losing side, while Labour voters might not take the trouble of voting because they knew their party was going to win regardless of their participation. Thus government supporters were able to claim that the turnout would have been higher if the overall result had been in doubt.

A second, and related excuse was that even people who had a vague attachment to opposition parties were not particularly bothered by the prospect of Labour victories, since the government had tried to avoid controversial decisions. This explanation for the low turnout was particularly convenient for the government, since it would imply that non-voting was actually a testament to its *success* in office. In seizing the 'middle ground' of politics, it might have taken away the fear of defeat which would have driven its own supporters to the polls; but, more importantly, it had deprived its opponents of their traditional incentive to cast a vote. On this view, then, a low turnout was actually a hidden vote of confidence in the government!

Whatever the merits of the Labour governments after 1997, this state of affairs could hardly be comforting to public-spirited Britons. At best, it denoted a general lack of public enthusiasm for elected politicians from all the major parties. Rather than seeing the low turnouts of 2001 and 2005 as evidence that the public was broadly content, it would be more realistic to see the mood of the time as foreshadowing the tidal wave of contempt which engulfed elected politicians in 2009, after revelations of the misuse of parliamentary expenses. In this context, a change in the voting system might not seem an obvious remedy for existing discontent. Alternatively, it could be argued that a new system, which was capable of persuading voters that their ballots would make some difference to the overall result, might encourage wider participation and thus inject a bit more life into a process which seems to be dying on its feet.

■ Election campaigns in contemporary Britain

It can be argued that one reason for the precipitate decline in turnout after New Labour's first term in office was a feeling of election-fatigue among the general public. After his party's 1997 victory, Tony Blair declared that he intended to 'govern as New Labour'. His purpose was to indicate that his government would confound those who hoped (or feared) that Labour was revert back to 'socialism' once the election was out of the way. However, in hindsight Blair's remark can be seen in a different light. Above all, New Labour was primarily an election-fighting outfit; and in government it continued to act as if a new poll was only one step away, for example by trying to ensure that none of its senior spokespeople gave any public expression of dissent.

General elections in Britain have been affected radically by the advent of television in the mid-twentieth century. Television made general elections into national media events, in which party leaders moved fairly rapidly to the centre of the stage. Increasingly, the main business for party strategists is to plan an itinerary for the leader which will showcase his or her strongest attributes; senior colleagues will be expected to tour the country, but their performances will attract limited media coverage (unless, as in the case of John Prescott in 2001, they punch an egg-throwing protestor in the course of their activities).

This focus on the leader at election time is itself of major importance, giving British parliamentary elections something of the flavour of US Presidential campaigns. This impression was reinforced before the 2010 general election by the agreement of the main party leaders to take part in televised debates. It also has a significant spill-over effect; anything that is seen to damage the credibility of the leader *between* elections can be taken by strategists as a blow to the governing party's chances of re-election. Equally, any defects in a party leader's conduct of an election campaign can be used as a reason to change horses afterwards; thus, although Charles Kennedy was a highly popular leader of the Liberal Democrats, during the 2005 election campaign he was accused by colleagues of having been less than sober at media events. Whether or not the public noticed his lapses, members of his party took the view that he was too unreliable to remain as leader, to the widespread bemusement of the voters.

While the party leaders dominate media coverage, important work is still undertaken behind the scenes; and since general elections are won and lost as a result of votes cast in individual constituencies, it would be a mistake to suppose that all meaningful activity is now under the control of the central parties. However, strategists no longer place much value on face-to-face encounters with individual voters. Thanks at least in part to the lack of grass-roots party members, voters tend nowadays to be contacted by telephone or email. The major parties take steps to identify 'target voters', who will be subjected to selling techniques which are more appropriate to the business world. Much of this effort will be directed towards key constituencies, rather than seats which look sure to provide overwhelming majorities for one party or another. Thus while some voters can receive the impression that they are being taken for granted, people living in the most important battlegrounds face almost constant disruption to their lives as senior politicians

BOX 7.3 'Primary' elections in UK politics

In July 2009, the Conservative Party attracted considerable publicity by holding a 'primary' election to decide on its candidate for the Totnes constituency. The Conservative candidacy at Totnes had fallen vacant because the incumbent MP, Anthony Steen, had decided not to contest the forthcoming general election after adverse publicity concerning his claimed expenses. Cynics might say that the circumstances of 2009 made Totnes a seat which the Conservatives could retain, but only if they took a step which 'cleansed' the party's image within the local community. On a less jaundiced view, the idea that local people should choose a party's candidate could only enhance the democratic process. Rather than restricting the vote to party members (or even known Conservative supporters), ballot papers were distributed to *every* eligible voter in the constituency, regardless of their party allegiance. This procedure echoed the system of 'open primaries', used in some US states in the process of selecting party candidates for the national, presidential election. It is inherently risky, since in theory it allows the supporters of opposing parties to cast conspiratorial votes on behalf of the candidate who is least likely to win the ensuing general election. However, in the US open primaries have not been distorted in this way; and certainly after the verdict in Totnes was announced the Conservative leader, David Cameron, seemed to think that the experiment had worked well. The remaining dilemma for the party was whether open primaries would subsequently become the rule rather than the exception; whether they should only be used in unusual circumstances; or whether the 2009 event should be regarded as a one-off expedient, never to be repeated.

parade through their streets in search of photo-opportunities and positive headlines. As such, contemporary campaigning techniques can be regarded as another reason for increased public cynicism about the activities of the major political parties.

■ Reforms of the current system

If the slump in turnout after 1997 was a new development which caught most politicians by surprise, the New Labour years saw the re-emergence (albeit in more urgent form) of a well-established problem in British politics. As long ago as the 1920s, grave suspicions had been raised about an apparent link between the British honours system and the funding of political parties. The central figure in this scandal was the Liberal prime minister David Lloyd George, who amassed an electoral war-chest thanks to some dubious dealings with would-be earls and baronets.

The 1997 general election campaign was the most expensive in British history. Both of the main parties spent more than £25 million, which was a serious strain on their resources. Sources of funding had long provided ammunition for Labour and the Conservatives; the former were accused of being under the control of their trade union paymasters, while the contributions of business leaders to Conservative coffers was equally controversial (even if it attracted less hostile attention in the media).

Soon after the 1997 general election, the Labour government was hit by a scandal from an unexpected quarter. Far from being attacked yet again for its links with the trade unions, the party stood accused of accepting money from rich business-people who had not been known for their previous commitment to socialist values. Among these recent 'converts' to the Labour cause was the Formula 1 supremo, Bernie Ecclestone, who was revealed to have donated £1 million to Labour. Formula 1 had been exempted by the new government from legislation which banned the advertising of tobacco products at certain sporting events. Tobacco firms were important sponsors of Formula 1, so it was natural for Ecclestone to take an interest in the government's decisions on this subject.

In the wake of the Ecclestone affair, the Committee on Standards in Public Life headed by Lord Neill examined the question of party funding. The committee's findings were largely embodied in the Political Parties, Elections and Referendums Act (2000). As they affected elections, the main provisions were:

■ Donations of over £5,000 to political parties at the national level would have to be publicly declared in future, whether the donations were in the form of money or services.

■ The same 'transparency' would apply to donations made to individual constituency parties, above a value of £1,000.

■ Donations from foreign nationals were no longer permissible.

■ 'Blind trusts' (money donated to fund the activities of certain politicians without their direct knowledge) were outlawed.

■ Parties would have to declare their donations either quarterly (at normal times), or weekly (during general election campaigns).

■ Spending by parties would be limited according to a formula which allowed both of the main parties to spend no more than £19.38 million during the calendar year leading up to a general election.

■ The new system would be policed by the independent Electoral Commission.

The new government could claim that the 2000 Act represented a substantial step towards 'cleaner' politics in Britain. In 2005, both major parties spent less than £18 million each on their campaigning activities – well within the limits laid down by the Act.

However, for the main parties the problems were just beginning. Even if campaigns could now be run within the official spending limits, a precipitate decline in contributions from ordinary members left them with inadequate resources. Business-people were the obvious sources of additional supply, and although some of these individuals were undoubtedly philanthropic, others were only bankrolling the parties in the hope of some kind of recompense. This kind of arrangement could still be made because the 2000 Act contained a loophole: although outright donations were more tightly policed, temporary loans were not affected.

In March 2006 the Metropolitan Police began an investigation into charges that honours were being traded in return for loans. The affair cast a shadow over British politics until July 2007, when the Crown Prosecution Service (CPS) finally decided that no criminal charges should be brought. However, several prominent people, including Lord Levy (Labour's chief fundraiser) had been arrested, while Tony Blair himself was interviewed twice by the investigators. It emerged that Labour had raised £14 million in loans for its 2005 election campaign, though the political impact of this news was reduced by the fact that the Conservatives had been even more successful in raising funds on this basis (they received £16 million), while even the Liberal Democrats were unable to boast of a clean bill of health.

State funding?

After the outbreak of the 'cash for honours' affair, the Blair Government established a new inquiry under Sir Hayden Phillips, a respected former civil servant. In March 2007 – before the Crown Prosecution Service had ended its work on 'cash for honours' – Phillips reported findings which were broadly similar to those of an earlier House of Commons committee. He argued that parties should receive up to £25 million per year from the state, depending on their performance. The rules on donations from private sources should be tightened further; the maximum allowed should be £50,000 (a very trifling sum compared to the generous provisions of people like Bernie Ecclestone).

To some observers, Phillips had come up with a reasonable solution to the dilemma of modern political parties, in Britain as elsewhere. On this view, organised parties were essential to the democratic process, but for one reason or another ordinary people were no longer prepared to pay for them on a voluntary basis. The only way round this problem was to get people to pay for them out of taxation. This would allow the state to keep the expense of elections under rigorous control, and to prevent incidents like the Ecclestone scandal from staining the political process in future.

However, the report was unlikely to impress anyone who was already sceptical about the condition of Britain's political parties. In their eyes, the parties had brought their financial problems on themselves, by spending too much on campaigns which were too often dominated by the abuse of opponents rather than constructive suggestions. This style of campaigning had helped to create a mood of serious dissatisfaction with party politics, so that ordinary citizens were no longer prepared to back the established organisations with voluntary donations. For critics of the existing system, state funding could

almost appear as a way of rewarding the political parties for their failure. Thus, while Sir Hayden Phillips had made the best possible case for state funding, the government was never likely to act on his proposals. To have the best chance of carrying public support, the idea of state funding would have to be implemented when parties were once again popular; but if they were truly popular, they would have no need of state support. In view of such considerations, the case for state funding in Britain seemed to be pretty hopeless, especially after the scandals about MPs' expenses which erupted in 2009.

Other proposals for reform

Short of a reform of the voting system itself, other ideas have been canvassed as ways of reviving British democracy:

- *Compulsory voting*: This idea has been implemented in democratic states including Belgium and Australia. Electoral turnout in these countries is indeed much higher than it is in Britain. It could be argued that voting is a duty rather than a right, and (especially if participation is made as easy as possible) it could be argued that no citizen should be excused from taking part in the choice of a government. There are obvious civil liberty issues, but these are seemingly not insuperable: for example, a voter who disliked all of the options could plump for 'none of the above', or even deface the ballot paper. Nevertheless, a reform on these lines might end up disguising the underlying problems of British democracy, rather than solving them.

- *Lowering the voting age*: Some optimistic observers have argued that the process would be healthier if the voting age were lowered from 18 to 16. While this might not increase turnout in the short term, it could pay dividends in the future if young people were allowed to think of themselves as possible participants at an earlier age, thus 'socialising' them into the idea of voting. However, survey evidence has suggested that while young people are interested in politics, they tend on balance to be even more disillusioned with the main parties than their elders. The Electoral Commission's carefully-worded report *Age of Electoral Majority* (2004) endorsed the existing age of 18, although it did recommend that the minimum age of people standing for parliament should be 18 rather than 21.

Michael Howard tries to woo voters of middle England in the 2005 election campaign
Source: Copyright © Chris Riddell. From the *Observer*, 6 March 2005. Reproduced with permission from Guardian Newpapers Limited

All-postal ballots: Between 2000 and 2003, the Electoral Commission oversaw more than 50 'pilot schemes' in which certain local government elections were conducted on the basis of all-postal ballots. This was in keeping with a general drive to make electoral participation as easy as possible: other ideas in this vein included changing the day of general elections to Saturday, rather than the traditional Thursday, or even allowing the polling stations to be set up in supermarkets. Initial trials of the all-postal system seemed promising, but fraud was always likely to be a problem. The resulting scandals meant that postal votes would have to be heavily scrutinised in future, leading to lengthy delays in the declaration of election results. By 2009 it looked as if the government was faced with a new dilemma – either return to the old system, under which postal ballots were only permissible for those who were chronically ill or on holiday, or accept a new situation in which votes could not be counted on election day – an outcome which would reduce the drama of British general elections, and probably reduce the turnout to the miserable level of 2001.

■ Tactical voting, and the rise of the independent candidate

The main parties have fared so badly in their efforts to mobilise public support that one almost suspects a degree of complacency in the face of falling turnout; the only thing that apparently matters to such parties is whether they win or lose, not whether their overall tally of seats reflects a significant degree of public support. The suggested remedies we have examined so far tend to be 'top-down' measures – that is, they have been mooted by

Tony Blair and Gordon Brown present a united front on the campaign trail, despite their well-documented difficulties
Source: Copyright © Peter Nicholls / Pool / Reuters / Corbis

members of the political 'establishment' rather than 'grass-roots' voters. In recent years, however, the voters themselves have tried to take the initiative in ways which have caused a degree of discomfort to the main parties.

Thus, for example, certain individuals (like the musician Billy Bragg) have tried to organise campaigns of 'tactical voting'. In itself, this is a negative comment on the state of British politics, since campaigners have tried to unseat specific candidates rather than promoting the virtues of opposing ones. In particular, before the 1997 general election tactical voting was urged as a way of getting rid of sitting Conservative MPs, by mobilising support behind the candidate best placed to topple them. In a typical case, this would involve Labour supporters voting for a Liberal Democrat – not because such voters actively sought the return of a Liberal Democrat government, but rather because they hated the Tories and a vote for the Liberal Democrats was the best way of getting rid of a sitting Conservative MP. Such campaigns have gone so far as to encourage 'vote swapping', which would entail (for example) a Labour supporter voting Liberal Democrat in a seat where this provided the best chance of removing a Conservative MP, in return for a Liberal Democrat in a different part of the country voting Labour if this promised to produce a similar result.

The overall impact of tactical voting is difficult to estimate with any certainty, but even in the volatile electorate of today it is unlikely to cause a shift in more than a handful of seats. More significant, perhaps, is the tendency of disillusioned voters to reject all of the major parties and seek out alternative candidates. Minor parties (e.g. the Greens in 1989, and the United Kingdom Independence Party [UKIP] in 2004 and 2009) have performed well in European parliamentary elections. But these elections do not attract a high turnout, and are conducted under the **regional** list voting system (see Box 7.2, above) which favours minor parties so long as their support exceeds a minimal level.

In elections to the Westminster parliament, candidates who are (at least formally) independent of *all* parties have caused a greater stir. Thus, in 1997 the former BBC reporter Martin Bell stood as an 'anti-sleaze' candidate in Tatton, Cheshire, and defeated the controversial Conservative MP, Neil Hamilton. In 2001 Dr Richard Taylor won the seat of Wyre Forest on the basis of his campaign to save a local hospital; he won again in 2005. In that election there were other Independent successes, although the father of a soldier killed in Iraq failed to make serious inroads into the majority won by Tony Blair in his constituency of Sedgefield. According to some media speculation, though, an election held in 2010 is likely to see the success of several Independents standing against MPs who have been implicated in various ways in the expenses scandals which hit Westminster in the summer of 2009. However, the candidates most likely to win as Independents tend to be celebrities rather than 'ordinary' citizens like Richard Taylor; and in any case the major parties have been quick to persuade headline-catching expenses offenders to step down at the next election, to create the impression that a new generation of 'clean' candidates is on its way to rescue the flagging system of party competition under FPTP.

■ Referendums

Until the 1970s, the British public enjoyed no formal opportunities to affect political decisions between elections. Other countries held referendums on particular policy issues, but in Britain this device was widely associated with the methods of dictators, who only held such polls in order to give some spurious legitimacy to decisions which they wanted to take, regardless of public opinion. Margaret Thatcher was not alone in using this argument when she attacked Labour's proposal to hold a referendum on continued British membership of the European Economic Community (EEC) in 1975.

However, on that occasion Mrs Thatcher's arguments were unsuccessful. In 1975 the Labour government was seriously divided over EEC membership, and the prime minister Harold Wilson saw a referendum on the issue as a way of resolving the question of membership without incurring any of the electoral penalties which normally affect parties that are seen to be divided. Having secured parliamentary approval for a public vote, he allowed his ministerial colleagues to campaign in accordance with their own beliefs, casting aside the usual restraint of 'collective cabinet responsibility'. In fact, once the better-funded 'Yes' campaign had won the EEC referendum of June 1975, Wilson exploited the opportunity to demote some of those who had campaigned for British withdrawal, notably the Industry Secretary Tony Benn.

The 1975 referendum was not actually the first time that members of the public had been asked for their opinion on a specific issue; but the precedent (the 1973 'Border Poll' held on the subject of the continued existence of Northern Ireland) is not exact, since that was not a nationwide ballot. However, since 1975 referendums have become part of the fabric of British political life – sometimes used, but more frequently refused. The governing principle in the UK is that such polls ought to be called when major constitutional changes are afoot. However, the definition of 'major constitutional changes' is in practice under the control of the existing government. Thus the Maastricht Treaty on European Union was ratified by parliament in 1993, without a referendum, and although Labour held referendums before implementing its policy of devolution to Scotland, Wales and Northern Ireland, it decided not to call votes on proportional representation (see above), membership of the euro-zone, or changes in EU practices arising from the abortive Constitutional Treaty of 2004.

On the face of it, enthusiasts for the referendum as a political device in Britain could be greatly cheered by the record of Labour governments after 1997. However, the evidence gives rise to more cautionary conclusions. Few of Labour's radical constitutional ideas (e.g. its reform of the House of Lords) have been subjected to a public vote. In theory, referendums are only advisory (i.e. parliament could reject the decision of the people if it wanted to); but few governments have actively sought unwelcome advice, and despite its controversial forays in foreign policy New Labour proved to be no exception to this rule.

It could be argued, in fact, that Labour's record actually confirms Mrs Thatcher's warnings back in 1975; that is, referendums have only been called on important questions when the government was confident that the result would be satisfactory, and its use in other cases (e.g. elected mayors outside London) has only been allowed because the government was unlikely to be deeply affected by the verdict. In this respect, the refusal to allow referendums on EU constitutional changes is seen in some quarters as a serious indictment of Labour's commitment to democratic values. Even more significant, perhaps, was the government's breach of its 1997 manifesto commitment to a referendum on electoral reform. From the perspective of those who support a change to a more proportional system of voting, the fact that after the 1997 general election Tony Blair felt strong enough deny the public a chance to endorse a more relevant way of expressing its preferences can only be regarded as the ultimate demonstration of the deleterious effects of FPTP on UK politics.

BOX 7.4 Referendums in the UK since 1973

1973: Border poll in Northern Ireland

A poll, restricted to qualified voters in Northern Ireland, which confirmed that the majority wished to remain part of the United Kingdom (although many members of the nationalist community refused to take part).

1975: Continued UK membership of the European Economic Community

This, the first UK-wide referendum, presented voters with a stark choice: either to stay in, or leave the EEC (later the European Union [EU]). The 'yes' campaign was far better funded, and supported by the majority of mainstream British politicians as well as celebrities. The result was overwhelmingly in favour of continued membership, though critics still complain (with justice) that the 'no' campaign never had a realistic chance to make its case.

1979: Devolution for Scotland and Wales

Voters in Scotland and Wales were asked if they wanted devolved institutions, with limited powers. In Scotland, a slender majority voted 'yes' but this was insufficient since legislation required at least 40 per cent of voters to accept the proposition (in practice the figure turned out to be 33 per cent). In Wales, devolution was rejected by an overwhelming majority.

1997: Devolution for Scotland and Wales

The vote of 1979 was radically revised eighteen years later, although the turnout in both Scotland and Wales was less than it had been first time round. The 'yes' vote in Scotland won 63.5 per cent. In Wales, where the devolved Assembly would have very limited powers, the 'yes' vote was only 50.3 per cent.

1998: Devolution for Northern Ireland

In May 1998 the electorate of Northern Ireland gave a resounding vote of confidence to the previous month's 'Good Friday Agreement', handing back devolved institutions to Northern Ireland after a quarter of a century of direct rule from Westminster. There was also a heavy majority in favour of the Agreement in a poll held south of the border.

2004: Regional assembly for the north-east of England

New Labour wanted to follow up devolution to Scotland, Wales and Northern Ireland with a plan to introduce regional assemblies (with limited powers) in the regions of England. Initially the idea was received with enthusiasm, but this gradually waned amidst fears that the assemblies would be mere 'talking shops'. Ultimately there was a referendum in only one of the regions – the north-east of England, where, significantly, opinion polls had registered high levels of support. In the actual vote, however, the proposal was heavily defeated: more than three-quarters of voters were against the plan.

Since 1998: Elected mayors

In May 1998 a referendum was held in London on the question of a directly-elected mayor and assembly. The proposal was comfortably carried (although turnout was barely more than one third). Labour hoped that many other towns and cities would decide to elect a 'chief executive' in the form of a mayor, but after a fairly auspicious beginning enthusiasm died away. By the beginning of 2008 only 13 mayors (including London's) had been elected; in October 2008 the voters of Stoke-on-Trent decided to scrap the experiment of an elected mayor after just six years.

Local referendums

One interesting aspect of the initiative for local mayors was that it allowed local residents to decide for themselves whether or not a referendum should be held; the poll could be called by the decision of councillors, or if a petition was signed by at least 5 per cent of local residents. Since the Local Government Act 1972, local voters have also enjoyed the power to call a vote on specific issues.

As in national referendums, the result is not officially binding on decision makers; but in practice few councils are prepared to go against a clear-cut decision. This power has been used more frequently in recent years, over things like proposed increases in local taxation, or schemes to alleviate traffic congestion. Thus, for example, in 2005 Edinburgh's citizens voted to reject the council's proposed scheme to levy charges to control city traffic.

BOX 7.5   BRITAIN IN CONTEXT

Although Britain is justly proud of its long history of representative institutions, as we have seen its progress towards universal suffrage was not exactly rapid (although it was not too far behind New Zealand, which became the first major country to give votes to all women as well as men in 1893, and France did not adopt the principle until 1944). Until recently, the general satisfaction with FPTP meant that senior British politicians did not pay much attention when other countries adopted alternative voting systems. If anything, the practical experiences of different systems, especially in European states, were held up as reasons *not* to change the way in which British MPs were elected, because they tended to result in unstable coalitions (Italy), or more stable coalitions in which members of parties with minimal support were able to win an almost automatic place in government (Germany).

However, it is reasonable to argue that the process of 'Europeanisation' has gradually affected opinion in the UK on this matter. All members of the European Parliament are now elected under a proportional system, of one kind or another. By the time the UK held its first European parliamentary election under the regional list system (in 1999),

alternatives to FPTP had already been adopted for the devolved institutions of Scotland, Wales and Northern Ireland. But elections to the European parliament were different because they were held across the whole of the UK. The importance of this change was not widely recognised, because the turnout in these elections was invariably low; few people understood the responsibilities of the parliament; and of the various alternative systems, the regional list arguably has the least attraction for would-be reformers of the Westminster system. Nevertheless, the change at least provided a practical toe-hold within British politics for people who were arguing for more radical reforms.

Another way in which the outside world has affected the conduct of British general elections is the impact of US-style campaigning. The major British parties have freely borrowed techniques from their US counterparts; in particular, critics argue, they have copied the tendency of American parties to concentrated on 'negative campaigning'. However, important differences remain; for example, while candidates for election in the US can buy advertising space on television, legal restrictions prevent this practice in the UK (and other West European states).

Chapter summary

In Britain, the traditional way of electing members of parliament is first-past-the-post (FPTP), where the candidate with the most votes wins the seat. This system has the virtues of simplicity, and of (usually) resulting in a clear overall majority for one party or another. However, the system always distorts public preferences. The Liberal Democrats (and predecessors) have criticised the system for many decades and in recent decades prominent members of the other main parties have echoed their criticisms.

The chapter sets out several alternative systems, which have their own virtues and defects. Overall, however, a chance from the present system seems timely, since it is obvious to most observers that FPTP depresses electoral turnout, because many people feel that their votes will be 'wasted' in one way or another. The logical case for reform seems so strong that the refusal of key politicians to endorse it has almost certainly acted as an additional reason for disillusion with the main parties. There have been some reforms in recent years, including an attempt to make voting as easy as possible; the relative failure of such measures (and the scandals surrounding the use of all-postal ballots) provides another reason for the acceptance of radical change.

On the face of it, since 1973 the referendum has been introduced in Britain as a device which allows members of the public a 'formal' way of influencing key government policies. However, the government, rather than the people, decides when referendums are applicable. Thus the history of the referendum in Britain can be said to lead us back to the initial problem – namely a voting system which hands overwhelming power over decision-making to a party that is unlikely to enjoy overwhelming public support. True, local inhabitants have the right to trigger referendums affecting the policies of their councils, but in a healthy democracy it is difficult to argue that the same right should not be extended to voters at the national level.

Discussion points

■ To what extent does the FPTP system really act as a disincentive to voters in elections to the UK parliament? Has the adoption of alternative systems for devolved institutions encouraged more people to vote?

■ What are the most effective arguments for and against the state funding of British political parties?

■ Under contemporary conditions, would the introduction of a right for British voters to demand referendums on key political issues be a more meaningful reform than any change to the system of voting for the Westminster parliament? If such a right were introduced, what problems might arise?

Further reading

For rigorous and insightful accounts of general elections since 1945, students should consult the 'Nuffield Studies' of each election. The latest of these is D. Kavanagh and D. Butler (eds), *The British General Election of 2005* (Palgrave, 2005). Apart from the Nuffield series, there are other very useful volumes which cover recent general elections; and the books about the election of 2001 are particularly relevant for students of recent trends. P. Norris (ed.), *Britiain Votes 2001* (Oxford University Press, 2001), is particularly recommended, along with J. Bartle, R. Mortimore and S. Atkinson (eds), *Political Communications: The General Election Campaign of 2001* (Frank Cass, 2002).

For rival electoral systems, see especially D. Farrell, *Electoral Systems: A Comparative Introduction* (Palgrave, 2001), and P. Dunleavy and H. Margetts, 'Comparing UK Electoral Systems', in P. Norris and C. Wiezien (eds), *Britain*

Votes 2005 (Oxford University Press, 2005). D. Denver, *Elections and Voters in Britain* (Palgrave, 2nd edition, 2007) provides an admirable introduction for students of the electoral system and voting behaviour in Britain.

Bibliography

Hailsham, Lord (1978), *The Dilemma of Democracy: Diagnosis and Prescription* (Collins).

Useful websites

The key source for this subject is the Electoral Commission's website, www.electoralcommission.org.uk/. Other useful sites relating to electoral reform include www.electoral-reform.org.uk/ and the Constitution Unit's informative site at www.ucl.ac.uk/constitution-unit/.

Elections and voting

Although we may be unclear about the details of media influence, few would deny that it plays a role in shaping the outcomes of elections, and thus the control of the government by one party and ideological tendency of another. Recent general elections have changed the face of British politics by substituting a Labour government for the Conservative one that had ruled for 18 years. After its third election victory in 2005 it looks as if Labour may last almost as long. Television and newspapers derive their power from the influence they are commonly assumed to have over political opinions, which ultimately get translated into votes. As governments have to face elections every four or five years, everything that might affect their chances of winning or losing is important, and that gives them a strong motivation to control journalists or to seek the support of newspaper proprietors.

However, many factors in addition to the media shape election results. Before an election is ever called voters are influenced by their experiences as members of social groups, together with their enduring party loyalties, values and attitudes. After an election is called they may be influenced by the policies they are offered, together with their evaluations of the parties and leaders. The campaign strategies adopted by the party leaderships may therefore have some effect on the outcome.

The exact number of votes a party receives may be less important than the way these votes are 'converted' into parliamentary seats by the counting rules of the electoral system. British governments depend on being able to control Parliament by means of an overall majority of seats in the House of Commons, not on winning a majority (50 per cent) of the popular vote. Labour's historic third victory in 2005 was built on a mere 35.2 per cent of the vote (and just one in five of all eligible voters).

This chapter will review the factors affecting election results. Accordingly it will:

- provide an overview of elections since 1945

- examine the political effects of the current 'first past the post' system for Westminster elections and alternative electoral systems

- analyse the long-term factors that predispose some voters to support the same party and which provide the two major parties with their 'core support'

- analyse the short-term factors that cause votes to change between elections

- explore the reasons for declining turnout in elections and 'disengagement' from the political process.

From Chapter 15 of *The New British Politics*, 4/e. Ian Budge, David McKay, John Bartle and Ken Newton.

Table 15.1 Election results, 1945–2005

Elections	Conservative			Labour			Liberals			Others			Total number of MPs
	Seat nos	Seat %	Vote %	Seat nos	Seat %	Vote %	Seat nos	Seat %	Vote %	Seat nos	Seat %	Vote %	
1945	210	32.8	39.6	393	61.4	48.0	12	1.9	9.0	25	3.9	3.4	640
1950	298	47.7	43.4	315	50.4	46.1	9	1.4	9.1	3	0.5	1.4	625
1951	321	51.4	48.0	295	47.2	48.8	6	1.0	2.6	3	0.5	0.6	625
1955	345	54.8	49.7	277	44.0	46.4	6	1.0	2.7	2	0.3	1.2	630
1959	365	57.9	49.4	258	41.0	43.8	6	1.0	5.9	1	0.2	0.9	630
1964	304	48.3	43.4	317	50.3	44.1	9	1.4	11.2	0	0.0	1.3	630
1966	253	40.2	41.9	364	57.8	48.0	12	1.9	8.6	1	0.2	1.5	630
1970	330	52.4	46.4	288	45.7	43.1	6	1.0	7.5	6	0.9	3.0	630
1974 (Feb)	297	46.8	37.9	301	47.4	37.2	14	2.2	19.3	23[a]	3.6	5.6	635
1974 (Oct)	277	43.6	35.8	319	50.2	39.2	13	2.0	18.3	26	4.1	6.7	635
1979	339	53.4	43.9	269	42.4	36.9	11	1.7	13.8	16	2.5	5.4	635
1983	397	61.1	42.4	209	32.2	27.6	23[b]	3.5	25.4	21	3.2	4.6	650
1987	376	57.8	42.3	229	35.2	30.8	22[b]	3.4	22.5	23	3.5	4.4	650
1992	336	51.6	41.9	271	41.6	34.4	20	3.1	17.8	24	3.7	5.9	651
1997	165	25.0	30.7	418	63.4	43.2	46	7.0	16.8	30	4.5	9.3	659
2001	166	25.2	31.7	413	62.6	40.7	52	8.0	18.3	28	4.2	9.3	659
2005	198	30.7	32.3	356	55.1	35.2	62	9.6	22.0	30	4.6	10.5	646

Notes: [a] Northern Irish MPs are counted as 'others' from 1974; [b] In 1983 and 1987 'Liberal' includes the SDP/Liberal Alliance.

Elections and parties since 1945

Electoral system

A set of procedures for translating votes received by party candidates into shares of parliamentary seats.

British elections register support for the parties, using an **electoral system** that usually, though not inevitably, enables the party with a 'plurality' of the vote (i.e. the largest single vote) to win an absolute majority of seats in the House of Commons and thus form the government on its own. The next chapter will discuss how political parties came to dominate elections in the first place. For the moment, it is important to note that elections involve a choice between party alternatives, not between individual candidates or leaders. In Britain, where one or other of the two main parties normally wins a majority of the seats, elections focus on whether there will be a Conservative or a Labour government. Generally speaking, the Conservatives favour less government intervention in the economy and Labour favours more, so the party choice has implications for policy: do voters want freer markets, more social inequality, lower taxes and lower public spending; or more state intervention, redistribution, taxes and public spending? This is the main ground on which the elections listed in Table 15.1 have been fought.

Elections to Parliament: first past the post

British elections are the result of contests fought in hundreds of different seats from St Ives in Cornwall to Caithness and Sutherland in Scotland (see Map 15.1). In each seat electors cast their vote by placing a cross next to the name of their chosen candidate. In order to win a seat under the **'first past the post'** system a candidate simply needs one more vote than the nearest other candidate. This

Map 15.1 The electoral map of Britain is a common feature of most textbooks but greatly distorts perceptions of party strength (marginal constituencies and safe seats look the same and the Conservative blue in rural seats dominates the map). (Northern Ireland is not shown on this map)

Source: Reproduced with permission of Ordnance Survey. © Crown copyright

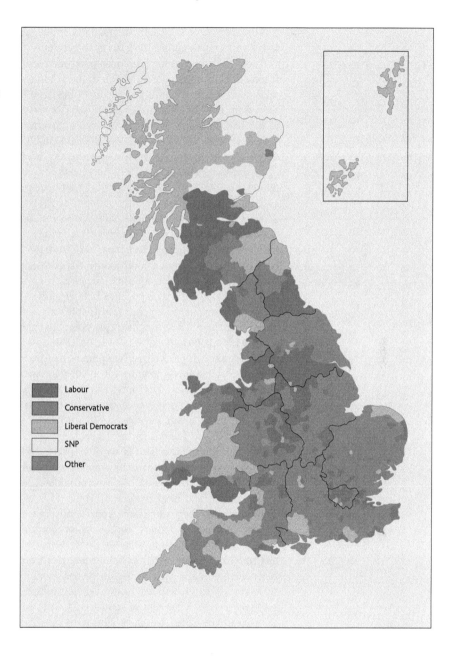

First past the post

Also known as the single-member simple plurality system (SMSP), this translates votes into seats by awarding each seat to the candidate who gets most votes (a plurality) inside a small constituency.

'plurality' rule means that if there are just two candidates contesting a seat the winner would always gain a majority (50 per cent plus 1). If there are more than two candidates, however, a candidate could win with far less than 50 per cent of the vote. In a three-cornered contest a candidate might be elected with 34 per cent of the vote if the other candidates receive 33 per cent each. In a four-sided contest, a candidate could win with as little as 26 per cent.

These are more than mere theoretical possibilities. In the 2005 election only 220 out of 646 (just 34 per cent) of all MPs gained more than 50 per cent of the vote in their constituency!

The plurality rule also has important consequences for parties, the party system and the nature of British politics. The most important consequence for the moment, however, is that it makes it difficult to predict how vote shares are translated into seats in Parliament. Much depends on the distribution of votes across the country.

It is quite possible to imagine that a party could gain a majority even though it has fewer votes than another. The key is to get votes in the 'right' places.

Table 15.1 sets out the relationship between seats and votes since 1945. Several features of this table stand out. First, the winning party has won a proportion of seats that is higher than its proportion of the popular vote. In each of the four elections from 1979 to 1992, for example, the Conservative Party won over 50 per cent of the seats – and thus enough to form a government by itself – even though its vote never rose above 44 per cent. Second, small changes in vote share can produce very significant changes in seat share. For example, the Conservative share of seats between 1979 and 1992 fluctuated between 51.6 and 61.1 per cent, even though its vote share held steady at 42 to 44 per cent. This shows how, under this system, a party's parliamentary strength depends not only on how many votes it gets but also on how its vote – and how the vote of other parties – is spread across constituencies. Small shifts in these distributions can produce large fluctuations in parliamentary majorities. Between 1987 and 1992, for example, the Conservatives' majority fell from a comfortable 100 to a slender 21 even though its share of the vote fell by a mere 0.4 points. The electoral system translated a ripple of votes into a tidal wave of losses because Labour gained votes in the 'right' places.

The third feature to emerge from Table 15.1 is that, despite the distortions produced by Britain's first past the post system, the party that wins the most votes normally wins an outright majority of seats. In this respect the electoral system usually dispenses a rough justice by giving the largest party a bonus of seats large enough to form a stable government over a full parliamentary term. In the 15 elections since 1945 only two – 1950 and February 1974 – have failed to provide the winner with a large enough majority of seats to sustain it in office for a full term. And only two – 1951 and, again, February 1974 – produced the 'wrong' result, in which the Conservative and Labour parties respectively won slightly more seats but slightly fewer votes than their rival. The capacity of the current system to convert a plurality of votes into a majority of seats was illustrated dramatically in the 2005 general election when 35 per cent of the vote provided Labour with 55 per cent of seats.

The fourth and final feature of Table 15.1 is the way in which the Liberal Democrats and their successors consistently fail to receive a 'fair' share of seats (where fairness is defined simply as proportional). In the 1950s the Liberal Democrats obtained a tiny share of the vote (partly because they did not then contest all parliamentary seats). From the late 1950s onwards, however, support for the party increased and they fielded more and more candidates. This further boosted their vote. This growth was, however, not reflected at Westminster. In 1983 the party received 3.5 per cent of seats for 25.4 per cent of the vote, producing a seat to vote ratio of 3.5:25.4 or 0.14. This ratio has increased in recent years, as a result of increased targeting of seats by the party and tactical voting by non-Conservative voters. In 2005 the ratio rose to 9.6:22.0 or 0.44. Nevertheless the Liberal Democrats are still unfairly rewarded (any ratio less than 1 is 'unfair'). As we shall later demonstrate, moreover, the fact that the Liberal Democrats (and other 'national' minor parties) are unlikely to win seats may deter people from voting for those parties in the first place. The current system, therefore, may artificially suppress support for minority parties and increase support for the two major parties.

Proportional representation

A voting system that uses an allocation formula (of which there are many) for distributing seats among parties in proportion to their vote.

The bias in the first past the post system

The British electoral system translated Labour's modest 3-point lead (or 'plurality') over the Conservatives into a comfortable majority of 66 seats because it is currently biased towards Labour. This does not mean that the system is rigged either by or on behalf of the Labour Party. It simply means that the system mechanically operates in Labour's favour.

BRIEFINGS

15.1 Plurality and proportional electoral systems

Free elections are essential to modern democracy. Although at first sight they appear to be a simple matter – expressing a preference for one party over others – they are in fact complex affairs. There are two main types of electoral system (or procedures for translating votes into seats): simple plurality voting and proportional representation.

Simple plurality systems

First past the post (or SMSP)

'First past the post' (FPTP) or 'single member simple plurality' only requires the winning candidate to obtain more votes than any other candidate, no matter how many candidates there are, and no matter how small the winner's share of the total vote is. In a three-way contest the winner may get little more than one-third of the total and, in a four-way contest, little more than one-quarter. Simple plurality voting is usually linked with single-member constituencies (though multi-member constituencies are used in some local elections). In Europe FPTP is used only in the United Kingdom, and outside Europe in the United States and Canada.

Both the act of voting and the method of determining a winner are simple. Locally, the system encourages MPs to serve local constituents in order to build up a 'personal vote'. Nationally, the system invariably produces 'strong' (single-party) government capable of carrying out its 'mandate' and of making 'tough' decisions (in contrast with coalitions, which are supposed to be unable to agree). Thus the link between elections and forming a government is relatively direct. It produces results, however, in which the proportion of seats in the Parliament won by each party does not match the proportion of votes it won in the election. FPTP unfairly penalises some minority parties, including large minority parties such as the Liberal Democrats, which have widespread rather than concentrated geographical support.

Second ballot system

The second ballot system tries to avoid the worst flaws of first past the post by requiring the winning candidate to obtain an absolute majority (50 per cent + 1) of the votes cast in the first round of elections. Failing this, a second (run-off) election is held for the strongest of the first-round candidates. This system is currently used in France for both its parliamentary and presidential elections. It does, however, require voters to go to the polls twice (and turnout is already low under the less demanding SMSP system!).

Additional member system (AMS)

Again this attempts to redress extreme disproportionality in the results from first past the post. Two types of MPs are elected. First, constituency MPs are elected by first past the post. Second, 'top-up' MPs are elected from a 'regional list' in a way which favours parties that lose out in the constituency-based voting. The larger the proportion of list seats the more proportional the overall result. This system preserves the direct link between some MPs and constituencies. It is the system used in Germany for elections to the Bundestag. In the United Kingdom it is used for elections to the Scottish Parliament and Welsh and London Assemblies, where it has reduced but not eliminated the bias in favour of Labour.

Alternative vote system

Another variation on the simple plurality system allows voters to indicate their first and subsequent preferences among candidates, so that if no candidate receives a majority of first preferences second (and subsequent) preferences may be brought into play in second and subsequent counts. The Jenkins Committee on electoral reform (which reported in 1998) recommended a modified version of this system for Westminster elections (called 'AV-plus'). But the Labour government declined to follow their advice.

Proportional representation systems

Proportional representation is not itself an electoral system but a principle by which different electoral systems can be judged. The principle is that the distribution of seats between parties in the elected legislature should correspond to the national distribution of votes cast for the parties in the election. In other words, minorities as well as majorities should be represented in proportion to their voting strength. The main ways of doing this are the party list system and the single transferable vote.

▶

Party list system

This is the simplest way of ensuring that seats are proportional to votes. Parties draw up a list of candidates in order of preference, and the candidates are elected in proportion to the number of votes their party receives in the nation as a whole (as in the Netherlands) or in large regions, starting from the top of the party lists. The party list system is highly proportional. The need for a national list puts a lot of power into the hands of the party leadership, who decide where candidates are ranked (and who is likely to be elected). The system produces no incentives for MPs to serve specific constituents. It is used in most European countries and in UK elections to the European Parliament. In some countries parties must pass a 'threshold' (e.g. 5 per cent of the vote) before they obtain any representation. This is designed to penalise small 'extreme' parties.

Single transferable vote

This system is used in the Irish Republic and for the Northern Irish Assembly and is preferred by the Liberal Democrats for the United Kingdom. It requires multimember rather than single-member constituencies. Voters rank order their preferences for all the candidates, so that their second, third or subsequent preferences can be taken into account. A minimum quota of votes for election to the Parliament is calculated (the quota depends on the number of votes cast divided by the number of members to be elected for the constituency). The first preferences are counted in the initial round of counting. Those candidates who exceed the quota are elected. In the second round the 'surplus votes' (those over the number required by the quota) obtained by candidates elected in the first round are redistributed according to the second preferences of voters for unelected candidates. Once the redistribution of surpluses ceases to elect any further candidates the votes of the least preferred candidate are redistributed according to second and subsequent preferences. Counts continue in this fashion until all seats are filled. There are many minor variations on STV, and different ways of calculating the final result, but the system usually leads to close proportionality at the national level, especially if most of the multimember constituencies elect five or more Members of Parliament. Because voters can rank order all the candidates they do not regard a vote for a minor party candidate as wasted. This system will be used for local elections in Scotland from 2007.

Commentary

The debate about electoral reform is complicated. However, some of the issues can be resolved by careful examination of the evidence. Research into the effect of new electoral systems in the United Kingdom, for example, suggests that there are more spoiled ballots under other systems than under first past the post. But the differences are not very large. Comparative studies across the world suggest that turnout is higher in proportional systems, presumably because voters know that their votes are not 'wasted'. There is, moreover, a great deal of research suggesting that coalition governments can be as stable as single-party governments and deliver more of what voters want. However, in proportional systems the link between elections and the formation of the government is often indirect. In Norway in 1989, for example, the Conservatives lost one in four of their votes and yet managed to move from opposition to government all the same!

The debate about electoral reform, however, may boil down to this: 'Do we want [power] concentrated under the winner-takes-all system of first past the post, or do we want it spread between parties as is probable under any proportional system?' (The Independent Commission on PR, p. 12). Put quite simply, does the greater risk come from a coalition government that is unable to take 'tough but necessary decisions' when needed or a 'strong' government that is all too ready to act by passing hasty, ill-thought-out, ineffective or illiberal legislation?

Since the future is uncertain there is no right or wrong answer to this question. Moreover, one's answer might depend on the way the choice is 'framed'. Someone committed to constituency representation might reject the party list system but accept either AMS or STV (which both preserve the link while ensuring greater proportionality).

The extent of the pro-Labour bias can be illustrated by calculating a 'reverse result' for the 2005 election. The actual result was: Labour 35.2 per cent, Conservatives 32.3 per cent, Labour overall majority of 66. But if the result had been: Labour 32.3 per cent, Conservatives 35.2 per cent, then – assuming a uniform swing – Labour would still have won 62 more seats than the Conservatives (though it would have been 15 seats short of an overall majority).

There are several reasons why the system is biased towards Labour:

- Labour wins many seats with small majorities ('efficiency bias').

- Labour constituencies are smaller (67,000 voters) than Conservative ones (around 73,000). It therefore needs fewer votes to win a seat.

- Labour constituencies have lower turnouts (58 per cent in 2005) than Conservative (65.4 per cent). Labour again needs fewer votes to win seats.

- Liberal Democrat wins come largely at the expense of the Conservatives.

Swing

The simple sum of the change in two parties' share of the vote divided by two. Thus, in 2005 the Tories gained 0.6 points and Labour lost 5.5 points, resulting in a swing of (0.6 + 5.5 = (6.1)/2) 3.05 points to the Conservatives.

The current electoral system produces a significant advantage for Labour and a serious obstacle to the Conservatives. They do not simply need to win more votes – they need to win more votes in the right places. This can be briefly illustrated by considering the effects of a uniform **swing** (where the swing is the same in every constituency). If there is a swing of 1.5 points and the party draws level with Labour at the next election, Labour will still have 115 more seats than the Conservatives and an overall majority of 24 seats. If there is a swing of 4.8 points and a lead over Labour of some 7.1 per cent, the Conservatives will become the largest party in a **hung parliament** and have some claim to form a government (though Labour may still be able to stay in power with Liberal Democrat support). This sort of swing has been achieved only twice by the Conservatives in the post-war period (in 1970 and 1979). In order to gain a slender overall majority of 1 seat (not enough to survive for more than a few months in government) they need a swing of 7.4 points and a lead of 11.9 per cent. This sort of swing has been achieved only twice; both times by Labour (in 1945 and 1997). If history is any guide to the future the Conservatives will have their work cut out to win the next election outright.

Hung Parliament

A situation in which no single party has a majority over all other parties in the House of Commons. In the current 646-member Parliament a party needs 324 seats to gain an overall majority. If no party gains 324 seats there is said to be a 'hung' Parliament.

Targeting seats

The predictions about the sort of swing that the Conservatives need to win an election made above assume that there is a uniform national swing. If recent experience is any guide swing is unlikely to be uniform. Not only do voters in different constituencies behave in different ways, parties behave in different ways in different seats too. In particular, the current system provides incentives for parties to identify those seats that might swing from one party to another and focus their campaign activity on them. If the Conservatives were able to secure a large enough swing in just the most 'marginal' seats, they might be able to win an election with a much smaller swing and a smaller lead over Labour.

Well before each election the main parties assess the electoral battleground and focus their campaigns on '**target' seats**, ensuring that they regularly contact voters in person, by mail or by telephone. Senior party figures regularly visit the targeted constituency in order to gain the attention of local media and raise the party's profile. In the formal campaign itself, moreover, party workers will be directed to these seats in order to mobilise their potential vote and win the seat.

Targeting seats

The process by which parties identify marginal (vulnerable) seats and focus their campaign resources in order to gain or hold that seat.

Targeting of seats is important in an era when party membership is in decline, since parties cannot afford to run a full campaign in every constituency (see Chapter 16). In recent years Labour and the Liberal Democrats have been particularly successful at directing resources (workers, posters and so on) to where they are needed most. Both Labour's traditionally centralised organisation and the Liberal Democrats' focus on 'community politics' have naturally lent themselves to effective local campaigning. By contrast the autonomy (or parochialism) of many Conservative local associations frustrated attempts to direct campaigners to where they were most needed. In 2005 the Conservative campaign was more effective than before. Individual donors were encouraged to support Conservative associations in marginal constituencies and a telephone canvassing operation was put in place that targeted seats. However, the party was still unable to win some highly marginal seats such as Dorset South, which was Labour's most vulnerable seat that year.

Of course all the parties are likely to focus their activities on the marginal seats and the partisan effects are likely to cancel out to some extent. Targeting may, however, have the unintended consequence of reducing turnout in safe seats. If only swing voters in marginal seats (so-called '**golden voters**') are made to feel as if they 'count', core voters in safe seats may be less likely to turn out to vote. In some cases recent election campaigns may have simply bypassed many constituencies. Little wonder then that turnout slumped badly in Labour's safest seats in the north and the inner cities in 2001 and 2005.

Boundary reviews

A special feature of the first past the post system is the importance of constituency boundaries. The 2005 election was (with the exception of Scotland) fought on boundaries introduced in 1995 and without exception based on census data collected in 1990. Changing the boundaries – which is necessary to keep up with shifts of population – can deprive the sitting member by excluding districts with concentrations of supporters or including new districts with concentrations of opponents. The precise boundaries are so important that responsibility for drawing them up is given to an independent Boundary Commission, which is now a special section of the Electoral Commission (see Briefing 15.2).

According to the relevant legislation constituencies should 'as far as is practicable' be of equal size. There is a different notional quota for seats in each of the four parts of the United Kingdom, but it is currently largest in England and Scotland than in Wales, so the latter is 'over-represented at Westminster'. However, the Boundary Commission has to take into account local government boundaries and local ties. This means that it has to strike a balance between these goals. An assistant commissioner, therefore, chairs hearings, receives submissions from the parties and then makes a recommendation. The very public nature of this system largely avoids changes of 'gerrymandering' (altering boundaries to one party's advantage). The final decision on whether to act on these recommendations, however, is made by Parliament itself. In the late 1960s Labour postponed changes that would have lost it seats but still lost the 1970 election!

There is a separate Boundary Commission for Scotland. It advised on the drawing up of new boundaries for the 2005 general election, when the number of Scottish seats was reduced from 72 to 59 in order to reflect the fact that Scotland now has a great deal of autonomy as a result of devolution. This had the effect of reducing the number of Labour MPs by 10, Liberal Democrats by 1 and Scottish Nationalists by 1.

The next Boundary Commission review for England and Wales is due in 2007. There are no plans to reduce the number of seats in Wales, so this will advantage Labour. The review will almost inevitably abolish some of the smaller urban and northern seats in England (held by Labour) and create more rural, suburban and southern seats (which are more Conservative). These changes will probably deprive Labour of about 10 seats; enough to reduce – but not eliminate – Labour's majority.

The impact of new electoral systems

Electoral systems have important consequences for parties, the party system and the culture of politics. The Labour government has introduced new electoral

Golden voters

Swing voters in marginal constituencies. Shifts in their behaviour are amplified by the first past the post system, producing dramatic shifts in the parliamentary strength of the parties.

Boundary reviews

The process of redrawing constituency boundaries in order to ensure constituencies are approximately the same size.

BRIEFINGS

15.2 The Electoral Commission

The Electoral Commission is an independent body created as a result of the Political Parties Elections and Referendum Act 2000. It was established partly as a result of recommendations contained in the fifth report Committee for Standards in Public Life and is accountable to Parliament via a committee chaired by the Speaker of the House of Commons.

The Commission has responsibilities for the following:

■ registering political parties (and party symbols, such as Labour's red rose)

■ registering major donations to political parties (all donations above £5,000 must be registered, spending by third parties is regulated and foreign donations are banned)

■ regulating election campaign spending (limited to around £19 million in the 2005 election)

■ reporting on the conduct of elections

■ reviewing electoral law

■ advising government on changes

■ advising those involved in the regulation of elections and referendums (returning officers and the Association of Electoral Administrators)

■ promoting awareness of electoral systems

■ reviewing constituency boundaries.

The Commission has produced a series of reports on electoral matters, including postal voting, young people and participation, social exclusion and political engagement. It has powers relating to monitoring and investigation of elections, but electoral cases are still dealt with by the courts. (In 2005 several Birmingham Labour councillors were prosecuted for electoral fraud. The judge declared, 'Anybody who has sat through the case I have just tried and listened to evidence of electoral fraud that would disgrace a banana republic would find this surprising.')

The Commission can merely advise the government on changes and may be ignored. In 2004 the government did not accept its recommendation that postal voting should take place in two rather than three regions for the European Parliament, as the government wished. Many believed that Labour declined to accept these recommendations because it believed that a higher turnout in those regions would produce a partisan advantage.

systems in each and every one of the new, devolved authorities (see Table 15.2). By the time of the 2005 general election, everyone in the United Kingdom had been provided with the opportunity to use a system other than first past the post on at least two occasions in elections to the European Parliament. If they lived in the devolved areas of Scotland, Wales and London, they had the experience at least twice more. Voter and party behaviour has already changed as a result, but is likely to alter still further as both respond to new incentives. Across the United Kingdom several large scale experiments in a new form of politics are taking place.

The electoral system had consequences for the relationship between votes and seats. In the European elections of 1994 the Liberal Democrats obtained 17 per cent of the vote but just 2 out of 84 (2.4 per cent) of seats when these were fought under FPTP. In 1999 their vote fell to 13 per cent, but they gained 10 out 84 (12 per cent) seats. In 2003 they got 15 per cent of the vote; but they obtained 12 out of 78 seats (15.4 per cent) under the party list system. The AMS system used in Scotland has had similar results. In the 1997 general election the Conservatives obtained around 18 per cent of the vote north of the border, but did not return a single Scottish MP to Westminster under FPTP. In the elections to the Scottish Parliament held under AMS the party received just 16 per cent of first and second

Table 15.2 Electoral systems in use in the United Kingdom

System	Body elected
Single member first past the post	House of Commons
	Some English/Welsh and all Scottish local authorities until 2007
Multiple member simple plurality	Some English/Welsh local authorities
Additional member system	Scottish Parliament
	Welsh Assembly
	London Assembly
Single transferable vote	Northern Ireland Assembly
	Scottish local elections from 2007
Regional party list	European Parliament
Supplementary vote	London mayor

Source: David Denver, *Election and Voters in Britain*, p. 169

votes, but won 18 out of 129 (14 per cent) seats. The system worked in a similar way in 2003. AMS in Scotland saved the Conservatives from a wipe-out, yet the Conservative Party seems the most hostile to the new systems. It operated in a similar way in Wales.

The same system clearly did *not* benefit Labour in Scotland. The party would probably have won a substantial majority under first past the post, but emerged as merely the largest single party under the AMS system in elections held in 1999 and 2003. It has governed in coalition with the Liberal Democrats since 1999. In Wales Labour was deprived of a majority in the first election, governed as a minority until 2000 and then went into coalition with the Liberal Democrats until 2003. AMS had a similar effect in London, which now has two Green and two UKIP members of the GLA.

The impact of the new electoral systems on voters has been fairly consistent: it has reduced support for the major parties and increased support for the smaller parties. In the 2004 European elections Labour received just 23 per cent of the vote, compared with 35 per cent in the general election less than a year later. Similarly, the Conservatives received just 27 per cent in 2004 compared with 32 per cent in 2005. The party list system allowed voters either to cast a vote according to their real preferences or to experiment with minor parties in relatively unimportant ('**second-order**') **elections**. Support for UKIP in the 2004 Euro-elections (fought under the party list system) rose to 16 per cent, compared with a mere 2.2 per cent just one year later. The AMS system has similarly allowed voters to split their vote in order to reflect their preferences. Around one in five voters appears to have split their votes by voting for one party in the first past the post section and another in the regional list. This has increased the number of minor parties represented at Holyrood; with the Scottish Socialist and Green parties picking up seats that they would not have been allocated under first past the post. In Wales the level of split ticket voting was slightly lower, but still significant.

While first past the post encouraged voters to think of elections as a choice of government between Conservative and Labour, the new electoral systems encourage voters to think more carefully about their preferences and either vote for a minor (or less established) party or split their vote. These developments may have had small 'carry over' consequences in the recent general election. Some of the 1 per cent rise in the vote for minor parties in 2005 may be a 'carry over' from other elections. Voters may be getting used to voting for other parties and, in an era when the major parties appear to be converging, are less worried about the consequences of wasting their vote even under first past the post. These developments

Second-order election

An election to a body other than the national legislature.

will undoubtedly lead some within both major parties to reject any moves to introduce more proportional systems at Westminster. Electoral reform may unleash the 'latent pluralism' and reveal that most voters are 'multi-party' at heart.

A hung Parliament: from first past the post to proportional representation?

Some analysts believe that Labour will continue to lose support at the next general election, either as a result of an economic downturn, failure to improve the public services or as a result of the 'costs of ruling' (see Briefing 15.4). Nevertheless, the electoral system is currently biased in their favour and it seems unlikely that the Conservatives will make enough gains to obtain an overall majority. It is quite possible that the next election will result in a 'hung parliament' in which the Liberal Democrats hold the balance of power and could choose to form a coalition with either of the main parties.

A hung parliament is a real possibility even if the Liberal Democrats lose a substantial portion of the 62 seats they won in 2005. Its parliamentary leadership has suggested that, in these circumstances, they would only be prepared to enter into a coalition on condition that the electoral system for elections to Westminster is reformed. This position is likely to be reinforced by their experience after 1997, when Labour reneged on a manifesto promise to hold a referendum on reform for elections to Westminster. This experience will not necessarily bias the Liberal Democrats against entering into coalition with Labour, but it will almost certainly mean that they will expect legislation on reform of the electoral system to be enacted in the first year of the new parliament.

Given the possibility of a hung parliament, both major parties are likely to cosy up to the Liberal Democrats. Labour will probably stress their commitment to social justice and their record of successful cooperation with that party in Scotland. The Conservatives will stress their belief in freedom and the free markets, their willingness to decentralise the government and the danger of prolonging the Labour government. It remains to be seen, however, whether either Labour or the Conservatives will think it worth taking the risk of introducing a new (more proportional) electoral system. As elections to the European Parliament and devolved institutions make clear, new electoral systems could unleash a dynamic that would destroy their duopoly at Westminster forever.

Explaining individual votes and electoral success

In this section we examine why one party rather than another manages to win more votes. What explains why the Conservatives led Labour by 42 to 35 per cent of the national vote in 1992 but trailed Labour by 32 to 35 per cent in 2005? So many factors can influence voting that the task of selecting the most important to explain the overall result seems almost impossible. However, they include the following:

- long-term social factors (age, race and gender, social class, neighbourhood, religion, housing tenure and so on)
- long-term political factors, party loyalties and values
- short-term 'campaign' issues, policies, evaluations of party competence etc., party and leadership images
- tactical voting considerations.

BRIEFINGS

15.3 Why not ask the voters?

It might be supposed that it would be a good idea to ask voters themselves to explain their own behaviour. Unfortunately, however, there are reasons to be cautious about voters' own explanations.

One problem with 'open-ended questions' ('Why did you vote that way?') is that some voters, particularly the less educated, sophisticated or articulate may not be able to express their reasons. Many may simply respond 'Don't know' because it seems better than embarrassing themselves by making a grammatical mistake or using the wrong word. Yet even if voters are asked 'closed-ended questions' ('Which of the following reasons best explains why you voted?') there are reasons for doubting whether their responses will reveal much:

- Voters may genuinely not know why they vote as they do. Most people are not usually required to explain their actions and may have given them little conscious thought. They may be able to rationalise their behaviour (i.e., tell a plausible story or choose a plausible option) but that may have little to do with the real causes.

- Voters' own explanations will be biased. In particular, they are likely to emphasise the 'immediate' causes of their vote (a campaign event or particular leader) rather than 'deeper' reasons (such as family loyalties or values).

- Voters may be unwilling to reveal to others that they are motivated by socially undesirable (selfish or racist) motivations.

- Voters may not even be willing to reveal to themselves that they are motivated by socially undesirable considerations and may suppress such feelings.

- Voters may be similarly unable to judge the importance of specific factors in their vote decisions.

Most analysts believe that the best way to find out why people vote as they do is to examine the statistical relationship between various social, psychological and political characteristics using responses to structured questions.

A vast amount of research has been done on the relationship between social, economic and political factors and the actual election result. This has identified the central processes that explain both individual vote decisions and the overall election result.

Long-term factors and the vote

Core voters

Those voters who are strongly predisposed to support a party election after election. Parties do not need to persuade their core voters that they are the best party, merely to turn out and vote.

Swing (or floating) voters

Those voters with either weak or non-existent predispositions to support any particular party.

Election outcomes are the result of a large number of decisions arrived at for a large number of reasons. A useful way of thinking about voters, however, is to distinguish between those who support the same party time and time again ('**core voters**') and those who vote for different parties ('**swing voters**').

Core voters provide the major parties with 'all-weather' support. Even in the dramatic landslide election of 1997, some 61 per cent (of all those who voted in 1992) supported the same party as five years previously. Moreover, in the year running up to the 1997 election, fully 82 per cent of those who intended to vote supported the same party. More strikingly still 57 per cent of those who gave a vote intention in each of five successive interviews between 1992 and 1997 indicated support for the same party. For many people at least, political preferences are stable and apparently resistant to change.

One of the main reasons why voters are stable is that they belong to social groups that have developed links with parties. Since these characteristics change only slowly, so do party loyalties.

There are three reasons why groups influence voting behaviour:

1. *Social-psychological*. People seek to understand the world about them. They naturally attach labels to both themselves and the people they meet. They also tend to value people like themselves and seek to gain the acceptance of fellow group members. Membership of a social group, therefore, gives rise to certain 'norms' or 'expectations'. Members of the Church of England are expected to vote Conservative, trade union members to vote Labour and so on.

2. *Rational interests*. Those who share certain characteristics may share similar interests. Public sector workers generally have an interest in increased public spending, while private sector workers have an interest in lower taxes.

3. *Information biases*. Political information is produced in a social context. Members of trade unions are exposed to 'pro-Labour' information, while inhabitants who live in a Conservative area are exposed to 'pro-Conservative' information in their everyday lives.

Table 15.3 briefly summarises the sorts of characteristics that have been associated with Conservative, Labour and Liberal Democrat voting. By far the most important of these characteristics historically has been social class (partly because one party, the Labour Party, styled itself as a class party). Put simply, the middle class have voted Conservative and the working class have voted Labour. In contrast with the rest of Europe, however, religion has played a lesser role in British voting behaviour. There is a tendency for members of the Church of England to vote for the Conservatives – presumably as a result of their association with traditional features of British society, including the monarchy. Catholics are more likely to vote Labour as a result of that party's policies on Ireland and the fact that many Catholics are working class.

Younger voters tend not to vote Conservative. In 1997 they were overwhelmingly Labour, but in 2005 they provided a great deal of support for the Liberal Democrats, possibly because of their opposition to the Iraq War. Black voters,

Table 15.3 Social characteristics associated with party vote

Characteristic	Conservative	Labour	Liberal Democrat
Middle class	X		
Working class		X	
Young voters		X	?
Old voters	X		
Black		X	
White	X		
Church of England	X		
Catholic		X	
Nonconformist		X	X
Higher education			X
High income	X		
Low income		X	
Public sector		X	
Trade union membership		X	
Home owner	X		
Council tenant		X	
Car owner	X		
Reliant on state benefits		X	
England	X		
Scotland		X	
Wales		X	

moreover, provide Labour with strong support. They are more working class and more likely to live in Labour areas. But also Labour has generally been more welcoming of immigrants and supportive of measures to promote equality. Someone with all the characteristics indicated in the Labour column, such as a young, black, working-class, uneducated council tenant, working for a local council and a member of a trade union, is highly likely to be a Labour voter because group norms, material interests and exposure to biased information all push them in one direction.

One thing that stands out from Table 15.3 is that the Liberal Democrats fail to attract the support of any particular group. The only possible exceptions are those who have been in higher education and nonconformists. But these groups spread their support relatively evenly between the parties. Moreover, since neither of these groups is particularly large, the Liberal Democrats have only a small core vote and rely on attracting the temporary support of many voters.

Analyses of voting behaviour usually begin with the relationship between social characteristics and vote for several reasons. First, social characteristics are obvious prior causes of the vote and – unlike political attitudes, opinions and evaluations – are not consequences of vote decisions. (The fact that someone has voted for X might lead them to report 'pro-X' opinions that they do not hold; the fact that someone has voted for X does not alter their race, gender, social class or job!). Second, as we see in Chapter 16, parties develop programmes and policies with certain 'target groups' in mind. Third, analysing social trends enables us to predict whether the size of a party's core vote is increasing or decreasing. The contraction in the size of the working class, trade union membership, the size of the public sector and the number of council tenants in the 1980s, for example, all reduced the size of Labour's core vote and made it necessary to broaden the party's appeal.

Though group memberships influence voting behaviour, they do not determine it. Most people are members of more than one group. This ensures that they are subject to conflicting norms, guided by conflicting interests and exposed to many sources of information. In recent years, moreover, the proportion of the population with either 'pure Conservative' or 'pure Labour' group memberships has fallen dramatically, leaving voters less firmly anchored in the parties and more open to the appeals of others. This has been accentuated by changes in the parties' appeals that have weakened the relationship between group and party. 'New Labour', for example, played down its appeals to the northern industrial and unionised working class in order to attract the expanding middle classes in 'middle England'. Not surprisingly, therefore, social characteristics are poorer and poorer predictors of voting behaviour.

Although these relations tend to endure, the relationship between social characteristics and vote can thus vary over time. This is perhaps best illustrated by exploring how the relationship between social class and party has changed in the post-war period.

Class dealignment

Social class has traditionally been the most significant social influence on the vote in Britain. In the post-war period the Labour Party has invariably attracted the support of somewhere around two-thirds of the 'working class' (those in manual occupations) and the Conservative Party has received the support of a similar proportion of the 'middle class' (those in non-manual occupations). As Figure 15.1 shows, on this simple index of class voting around two-thirds of all voters supported the 'correct' class party in 1945 and 1970 (a degree of 'class alignment' that was very strong by international standards).

From the early 1970s onwards the association between class and vote weakened considerably. Sections of the working class became more prosperous and more

Figure 15.1 Class and voting, 1945–2005

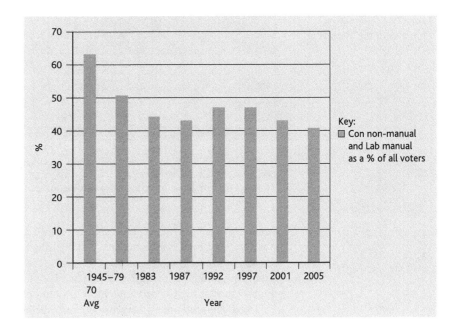

likely to work in the private sector. The middle class became unionised and more likely to work in the public sector. Hence more people were exposed to conflicting norms, interests and less biased sources of information. Thus, as Figure 15.1 shows, by 1979 just 51 per cent of all voters supported the 'correct' class party and by 1987 a mere 44 per cent. This decline in class voting occurred well before the 1997 election, suggesting that 'New Labour' was more of a response to class dealignment than a cause. Although the index increased to 47 in 1997, by 2005 it had fallen to 41 (largely as a result of the greater swing away from Labour to the Conservatives among the working class). Social class has not ceased to be an influence on vote, but its influence has diminished.

Party loyalties

It is widely thought that voters have loyalties to a political party and come to think of themselves as 'being Conservative' or 'being Labour'. These 'party identifiers' tend to support 'their party' in most circumstances and provide their party with 'all-weather' support even when it is undergoing serious internal problems.

One way of estimating a party's 'core' or 'normal' vote is simply to average their vote over a number of elections. Such calculations enable us to judge whether a party's vote is higher (or lower) than average and, accordingly, whether it is likely to fall (or rise) at the next election, other things being equal. While this strategy is simple the problem is that there are many 'averages' that can be calculated and no way of telling which is correct. Table 15.4, for example, shows three possible averages for Labour. The first for 1945–70 is almost 47 per cent. This seems inappropriate because this relates to a period of two-party competition when the centre party almost ceased to exist. The second for 1974–92 at 35 per cent is more plausible. The third average for 1997–2001, however, is 42 per cent and this seems plausible too. Labour's share of the vote in 2005 was 35 per cent. Viewed from the perspective of the earliest and latest period, Labour's performance is poor and seems likely to rise. Viewed from the perspective of the middle period Labour's performance is average and may rise or fall. Thus the average vote method does not produce firm predictions about what is likely to happen to Labour at the next

Table 15.4 Alternative estimates of the 'normal' vote

	Average vote estimate			
	1945–70	1974–1992	1997–2001	2005 Survey[1]
Con.	44.8	41.7	31.2	27.9
Lab.	46.8	35.2	42.0	36.8
Lib. Dem.	7.1	20.0	17.8	13.1
Other	1.3	3.1	9.3	5.1
Floating voters	N/A[2]	N/A	N/A	17.1

Notes: [1] 'Generally speaking do you think of yourself as Conservative, Labour, Liberal Democrat, Nationalist or what?'
[2] It is not possible to estimate swing or floating voters from vote shares.

election. What is fairly clear, however, is that the Conservatives' performance in 2005 was very poor by historic standards and the Liberal Democrats better than average (though how much better again depends on the comparison used). Another problem with this 'method' is that the past may not be a guide to the future if crucial conditions (such as the Conservative Party's traditional thirst for power) have altered.

Given the limitations of the average vote method it is tempting to suggest that we might be able to produce a better indicator of the parties' normal votes if we ask voters directly about their loyalties. It is, however, difficult for voters to distinguish between how they usually think of themselves and how they have actually voted. Different questions produce different indications of core support. (In particular, there is a tendency to bring reported identity into line with vote.) The estimate of the 'normal vote' in the final column of Table 15.4 must, therefore, be treated with caution. Nevertheless, they suggest that in 2005 some 37 per cent of voters 'thought of themselves' as Labour, 28 per cent as 'Conservative' and a mere 13 per cent as 'Liberal Democrats'. Since the actual vote share was 35, 32, 23, Labour seems to have polled under its normal vote, while the Conservatives did slightly better and the Liberal Democrats much better than their normal vote. (This analysis makes the dubious assumption that non-identifiers do not vote.) According to this evidence, however, short-term factors were operating strongly in the Liberal Democrats favour and, to a much lesser extent, the Conservatives.

Further analysis reveals just how complex were the forces influencing vote in 2005. Labour was clearly less good at motivating its potential voters than the Conservatives. Just 75 per cent of Labour identifiers turned out to vote in 2005, compared with 83 per cent of Conservatives. Had Labour been as successful as the Conservatives at mobilising its support its share of the vote would have increased by about 0.6 points. It may be that recent losses in Labour membership, coupled with the reduced enthusiasm on the part of activists in safe Labour seats and the ruthless targeting of marginal seats by the party organisation, contributed to a failure to mobilise Labour's potential vote in 2005 (see Chapter 16).

When they actually bothered to vote Labour identifiers were as loyal to their party as Conservatives were to theirs. However, fully 11 per cent of all Labour identifiers voted Liberal Democrat: some for tactical reasons and many as a result of policy disagreements (Iraq, tuition fees and Blair's unpopularity). It seems likely that many of these votes will return to Labour if the short-term forces that pushed them away (Iraq, the tuition fees controversy and Tony Blair's personal unpopularity) have gone.

Labour won more votes than the Conservatives for the following reasons:

■ It had around a 9-point advantage in terms of party identification.

■ It polled better among non-identifiers (28 to 24 per cent).

■ The party attracted 15 per cent of Liberal Democrat identifiers, compared with just 6 per cent who voted Conservative. Many of these were undoubtedly tactical voters in marginal seats (see below).

The Liberal Democrats received many votes from those who did not think of themselves as belonging to any party. This group made up one in five of all the party's voters and Labour identifiers a further 15 per cent. The Liberal Democrats resemble a small hotel with a high turnover. It has few permanent residents and quite a few temporary visitors.

The main implication of this is that the 2005 election may have concealed Labour's long-term advantage over the Conservatives. However, these loyalties do not represent an insurmountable obstacle to Conservative victory since some loyalists can be persuaded to 'defect' from their normal party. The Conservatives are capable of winning enough votes if the conditions are right (though they may find it difficult to translate these votes into seats!). There has, moreover, been a general weakening of party loyalties, which may work to the Conservatives' advantage.

Partisan dealignment and its consequences

Party loyalties vary in intensity. Some people feel 'intensely' Conservative or Labour while others feel a less intense commitment. This intensity of feeling is itself a predictor of some types of behaviour. Stronger identifiers are more likely to turn out and vote, to vote for their party and be immune to the appeals of other parties. It follows that any decline in the intensity of partisan feeling, other things being equal, will increase the likelihood that voters will temporarily abandon their party if short-term factors are sufficiently strong. As Figure 15.2 shows, long-term party loyalties have weakened. In 1964, 44 per cent of voters thought of themselves as 'very strong' identifiers. By 2005, however, this had fallen to a mere 10 per cent. By this time fully 48 per cent of all electors either felt themselves 'not very strong' Conservative, Labour or Liberal Democrat or had no party loyalties

Figure 15.2 Strength of party loyalties, 1964–2005

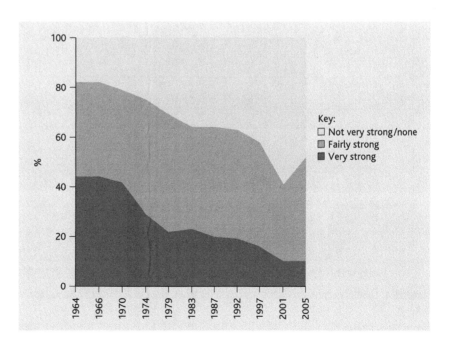

at all. In 1964 a mere 10 per cent of all voters did not think of themselves identifying with any party. By 2005 this figure had risen to 17 per cent.

Figure 15.2 shows that over the course of the last 40 years the pool of weakly aligned or totally uncommitted voters has increased. More and more voters are up for grabs and '**volatile**' (i.e. changeable). Whether or not such voters do swing between the parties depends on the success, or otherwise, of their campaign appeals. We therefore now examine the impact of short-term factors.

Electoral volatility

Large and rapid changes in voting behaviour from one election to another.

Short-term factors and the vote

Political parties can do little to alter the social composition of the electorate or their long-term loyalties in the short term. They must take these factors as 'givens' for any particular election. They can, however, seek to appeal to voters by advocating popular policies, projecting an image of competence, creating a favourable image and persuading people that only they can defeat the least preferred party. (This is why the parties spend so much time and energy creating good relations with the media; they want newspapers, television and radio to carry 'good news stories' about them.) These 'short-term' factors are of great and increasing importance in the determination of the vote.

Policies and positions

Political parties spend a great deal of time formulating policies and drawing up their manifesto proposals in the hope of attracting votes. Yet while some people may take careful note of proposals on issues of particular concern to themselves, their family and group, individual policies rarely have much impact on election

Plate 15.1 Labour's campaign in 2005 extolled its achievements and warned about the consequences of a Conservative victory

Source: Getty Images

BRIEFINGS

15.4 The costs of ruling

One of the most well-corroborated findings of modern voting behaviour research is the tendency of all governing parties to lose support almost irrespective of their performance in office. This finding appears to hold across time and countries. Most calculations suggest that governments lose somewhere around two to three points at each election net of all other factors.

It is possible to treat this as a purely empirical generalisation without worrying about why this phenomenon comes about. However, there are several possible explanations as to why governments lose support:

- **Frustrated expectations** Voters have high expectations of governments and are inevitably disappointed by the reality. (Frustrated expectations may be a consequence of the fact that governments have to make inconsistent promises to different groups in order to win elections.)

- **Ideological distance** Governing parties tend to pursue their own ideological predispositions. Left-wing parties spend more to reduce unemployment and increase the size of the state, right-wing parties spend less to keep inflation and taxes down. By definition these positions are either to the left or the right of the typical voter. The longer they govern the more distant from the average voter they become until they eventually lose. Public opinion thus acts as a 'thermostat', ensuring that governments do not pursue extreme policies.

- **Asymmetrical impact of performance** Voters punish governments for 'bad times' but do not reward them for 'good times'. Evaluations therefore slowly chip away at support for the governing party.

The costs of ruling is an intriguing idea. It suggests that governments will eventually lose elections no matter how good things are: thus democratic competition is sustained. These 'swings' and 'roundabouts' perhaps explain why some politicians adopt a fatalistic approach to elections.

The 'costs of ruling' idea is actually an old one. In the 1960s commentators spoke of 'pendulum politics', referring to the expectation that parties would alternate in office.

outcomes. In 2005 Labour's plans for university 'top-up fees' undoubtedly cost the party some votes among students, first-time voters and some parents of students (or potential students). In general, however, it is the overall direction of policy that seems to have most influence on votes. Whenever one of the major parties has become regarded as 'extreme' they have been punished. In 1983, for example, the Labour Party advocated massive increases in nationalisation, taxation and public spending, withdrawal from the European Union and unilateral nuclear disarmament; policies that were unpopular even among its own voters (see Chapter 17). The party's share of the vote was forced well below its normal vote and it went down to its greatest defeat since 1918.

Performance

Voters are influenced not only by the policies advocated by the parties or the general direction they wish to take the country, but also by judgements of how capable the parties are in achieving consensual goals such as a strong economy, peace and high standards of public life. This is especially true where the parties have converged at 'the centre' and are not offering a radical change. It is generally thought that evaluations of economic competence are particularly important in vote decisions. ('It's the economy, stupid' was a campaign slogan for Bill Clinton in the 1992 presidential election in the United States.) Certainly a government that presided over high unemployment or inflation could expect to be punished, other things being equal. However, the impact of economic conditions might be reduced if the electorate thinks that the government is either not responsible for those

Plate 15.2 The first past the post electoral system makes for exciting election nights as it transforms tiny movements in vote share into dramatic changes in parliamentary representation

Source: Cartoon Stock

conditions (e.g. because they are a result of international factors) or if they think the opposition would do even worse if it were in power.

There is evidence that evaluations of a party's ability to manage the public services (NHS, education and transport) are also of some importance. Moreover, in the wake of the 9/11 attacks in New York and 7/7 attacks in London, it is probably the case that national security considerations are of increasing importance (see Chapter 20). In the 2005 election Labour was given high marks for its management of the economy, but poor marks for its record on the public services and disastrous marks for its record on managing immigration and asylum. These latter issues may have hurt Labour particularly among working-class voters (who swung more heavily to the Conservatives than the middle class).

Assessments of future competence are based in large part on past performance. The Conservative Party was, for example, historically regarded as a competent manager of the economy, while Labour was regarded as incompetent. This made some sense, since Conservative governments were generally associated with economic stability, while Labour governments had been associated with economic crises in the 1930s, 1960s and 1970s. These evaluations were subsequently revised as a result of real events. First, the ERM crisis in September 1992 shattered the Conservatives' reputation for competence. Second, New Labour's adoption of orthodox fiscal and monetary policies, together with its successful management of the economy between 1997 and 2005, did much to revise estimates of Labour's competence. By the time of the 2005 general election 58 per cent of voters thought that Labour would best manage the economy compared with 33 per cent who thought the same of the Conservatives. It was probably this factor, together with Labour's lead in terms of party loyalties, which contributed most to its victory. If Labour were to lose this reputation in the future it might find it very hard to win another election.

Party image

The appeal of political parties is based largely on the appeal of their policy platform and apparent ability to manage the economy and public services. However,

192

Plate 15.3 The ideal politician might need the personal appeal of Santa and the ability to shower gifts on the electorate

Source: Cartoon Stock

"At last, a politician we can trust!"

Plate 15.4 Elections are not necessarily a choice between goods; sometimes voters take the 'least worst' option

Source: Cartoon Stock

"Let's try voting for the greater of the two evils this time and see what happens."

parties can appeal to voters in other ways by projecting a favourable image or otherwise creating a favourable impression. A united party, for example, is more appealing to voters than a disunited party (other things being equal). Similarly, it is an advantage to be thought of as 'caring' rather than 'not caring', 'strong' rather than 'not strong', 'capable of uniting the country' rather than 'dividing the country' and so on.

When voters were asked to state which statement applied most to Labour or the Conservatives in the 2005 general election, voters' responses left no doubt that the Tories had a significant image problem. Respondents in Yougov surveys were asked whether certain statements applied most to the Conservatives or Labour. Those that applied most to the Conservatives included 'it has very little chance of winning this election' (63 per cent), 'it seems to appeal to one section of society rather than the whole country' (48 per cent), 'it seems stuck in the past' (45 per cent), 'it seems rather old and tired' (44 per cent), 'it seems to want to divide people instead of bringing them together' (41 per cent) and 'it seems to chop and change all the time: you can never be sure what it stands for' (35 per cent).

The labels attached to Labour were, by contrast, more positive. They included 'leaders who are prepared to take tough and unpopular decisions' (42 per cent), 'it seems to have succeeded in moving on and left its past behind it' (42 per cent), 'wanting to create the kind of society that is broadly what I want' (40 per cent) and 'even if I don't always agree with it, at least its heart is in the right place' (40 per cent). Thus, for a combination of reasons, most voters simply felt more comfortable with Labour. The Conservatives will undoubtedly wish to alter these perceptions before the next election.

While the Liberal Democrats attracted some voters with their commitments to scrap tuition fees, council tax and NHS targets, they did not seem to convince many voters on important issues such as crime, immigration and the economy. It seems reasonable, therefore, to suggest that part of their appeal lay in their image as a 'nice' and moderate party. While this may be true, it is worth noting that fully 66 per cent of Yougov respondents agreed with the proposition that 'it is easy for the Liberal Democrats to adopt a high moral tone as they have no chance of forming a government'!

Leaders

Most parties choose to build their general election campaigns around their party leaders. The national media similarly treat the election as a gladiatorial contest between the leaders. It is natural, therefore, to assume that many voters are influenced by their assessments of the party leaders (their likeability as a person and their ability to do the job of prime minister). The evidence that leaders do have an impact on voting behaviour, however, is mixed. Most people tend to like the leader of the party that they identify with and/or think the more competent, so knowing how well they like the leader does little to improve our prediction of their vote. Moreover, even when evaluations of the party leaders do have an effect on individual vote decisions, assessments of the party leaders are rarely so favourable to one party that they have a large effect on the election outcome.

If leaders have an effect on the election outcome it is more likely to operate via their impact on the parties' overall position, its policies and evaluations of party competence. William Hague, Iain Duncan Smith and Michael Howard all failed to make their party more attractive not because they were unattractive personalities and implausible prime ministers, but because they failed to reposition their party and craft an attractive image for it.

BRIEFINGS

15.5 Voter Vault

In 2005 the Conservative Party invested £250,000 in a computer programme called Voter Vault to help them identify 'target voters'. The programme used census data, together with 'lifestyle' and credit information, to predict votes and to tailor campaign material that might cause voters to switch.

Liam Fox, the then Tory co-chairman, said: 'This is potentially very significant. In the 2002 mid-term elections in the US, Voter Vault helped the Republicans increase their vote by 4 per cent. This is politics of the margins but this is where elections are won.'

Although great claims are made for such technology it is unlikely that any computer program would have a major impact unless the party also has appeal. In the era of mass membership party local activists would have kept information about the preferences of voters in their heads! Nevertheless, parties are likely to continue investing in such databases in future.

Source: See Nicholas Watt and Julian Borger, 'Tories reveal secret weapon to target voters', *Guardian*, 9 October 2004

Tactical voting

Social characteristics and party loyalties predispose voters to support a particular party most of the time. Short-term factors may lead a voter to prefer one party rather than another in this particular election. The particular strategic position in a constituency, however, may lead someone who prefers A to vote B in order to prevent the least preferred candidate C from winning the seat; especially if that least preferred alternative is intensely disliked. In 1997 and 2001 this factor conspired to deprive the Conservatives of a large number of seats and helped generate some of the 'bias' in the electoral system we have already noted.

The degree of **tactical voting** should not, however, be exaggerated. The majority of voters with an opportunity to vote tactically choose not to do so, either because they are unaware of the tactical situation or because they choose to vote positively for their party of first preference, however hopeless its prospects. Moreover, tactical voting only occurs on a significant scale where supporters of two parties feel much closer to each other than they do to the third. In 2005 around 12 per cent of voters were 'tactical voters', and many voters still thought of Labour and the Liberal Democrats as close to each other. It appears that voters either failed to take account of disagreements between the parties over Iraq or regarded their socio-economic policies as broadly similar. Whatever the case, tactical voting again benefited both Labour and the Liberal Democrats in 2005. It may well be that as intense dislike of the Conservatives declines the motivations for tactical voting may also decline. But that point was not reached in 2005.

Tactical voting

The practice of voting for a candidate who is not one's first preference in order to keep out a less preferred candidate.

Electoral turnout

The vote share received by the political parties is all very interesting but it tells only part of the story about elections. For not only have the major parties received a smaller and smaller share of the vote, fewer and fewer people have bothered to turn out and vote at all. This decline in participation has caused increasing anguish among the political classes. They feel that they need to boost turnout in order to legitimise their actions.

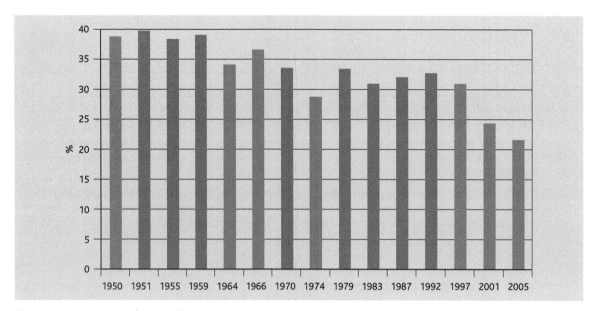

Figure 15.3 Percentage of electoral votes won by governing party, 1950–2005

Table 15.5 Turnout in general elections, 1945–2005

Election	Turnout in UK	Change in turnout
1945	75.5	–
1950	83.6	+8.1
1951	84.0	+0.4
1955	76.8	−7.2
1959	78.7	+1.9
1964	77.1	−1.6
1966	75.8	−1.3
1970	72.0	−3.8
1974 (Feb)	80.9	+8.9
1974 (Oct)	72.8	−8.1
1979	77.9	+5.1
1983	72.7	−5.2
1987	75.3	+2.6
1992	77.7	+2.4
1997	71.4	−6.2
2001	59.4	−12.0
2005	61.4	+2.0

Source: House of Commons Research Paper 05/33
http://www.parliament.uk/commons/lib/research/rp2005/rp05-033.pdf

The low share of the vote won by Labour in 2005 coupled with low turnout means that the proportion of the electorate (including non-voters) which supported the winning party stood at just over one in five of all voters. Moreover, as Figure 15.3 shows, this figure has fallen from around 40 per cent in the 1950s.

The raw data about electoral turnout is displayed in Table 15.5. This shows that the willingness of people to turn out and vote has drifted down from around 84 per cent in the early 1950s to around 60 per cent in the early twenty-first century. Presented in this way the decline does not appear to have been continuous. There were some unusually sharp declines between 1951 and 1955, February and October 1974 and between 1997 and 2001.

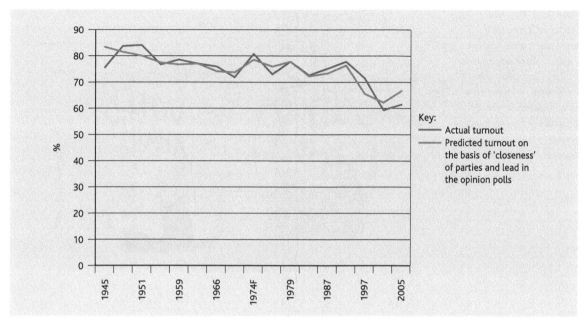

Figure 15.4 Actual and predicted turnout, 1945–2005

Figure 15.4 provides a visual representation of the same data. This strongly suggests that there is an underlying trend downwards in turnout , but that there is some variation around the trend. Thus, any explanation of turnout may have to account for both a long-term trend and short-term deviations from the trend. One obvious cause of variations is the extent to which people think that their vote 'matters'. In particular, the closer they feel the election will be and the greater the difference between the parties, the more likely they are to vote.

It is possible to measure both these factors by gathering data on the 'lead' in the polls prior to the election and the distance between the parties on the left–right

Plate 15.5 While Labour got only 35 per cent of the vote in 2005 they obtained 55 per cent of the seats, partly as a result of tactical voting by 'anti-Conservative' votes

Source: *Manchester Evening News*

Plate 15.6 The new
Electoral Commission
expressed concern about
the lack of participation in
politics (especially among
the young). It launched a
campaign before the 2005
general election to mobilise
voters

Source: Cartoon Stock

"I see disinterest rates are up again".

dimension as estimated by a comparison of the party manifestos (see Chapter 17). It is also possible to capture any long-term effects by including a variable representing the number of years since 1945. Statistical analysis suggests that the following equation provides the best fit to the data:

Turnout = 79.8 − 0.39 (Lead) + 0.12 (Distance) − 0.22 (Years from 1945)

This simple model 'explains' about 70 per cent of the variation in turnout and all three variables contribute to our understanding of trends. The linear trend contributes most powerfully, the further we move from 1945 the lower turnout is. By 2005 this factor alone contributed a 13-point drop in turnout (60 × 0.22 = 13.2). This suggests that there are powerful long-term social and political changes that are reducing turnout. There are, of course, a large number of possible explanations for this trend:

■ The decline of social organisations such as the churches and trade unions, which previously mobilised people to vote.

■ The increasing cynicism of the media.

■ The physical replacement of older cohorts who were socialised into participation and their replacement by increasingly apathetic younger voters. (Older voters valued democracy more because they fought for it between 1939 and 1945!)

The equation also suggests that overall turnout does increase when votes 'count' for more. For example, if Labour's lead had been 10 points rather than 5 in the polls (a difference of 5 points), turnout would have declined by 2 points (5 × −0.39 = −1.95). Distance also had an impact. In 2005 the parties were 8 points further apart from each other than in 2001. Thus, if the parties had been just as close on the left–right scale as they had been in 2001, turnout would have been (8 × 0.12 = 0.96) or 1 point lower. The slight divergence in party positions between 2001 and 2005 boosted turnout marginally.

In 2005 turnout was around 6 points below the level that could have been expected given where the parties stood and Labour's lead in the polls; all of which underlines the fact that 'other factors' were at work in both 2001 and 2005. These may include:

- increased cynicism about the tendency of parties to 'spin'

- the unusual conjunction of small differences in party positions and widespread expectations of a Labour victory

- an Iraq War effect (which may account for the lower turnout among Labour loyalists) (see above)

- increased targeting, which bypassed many voters (see above).

Solutions

Elections are the essential institution of democracy in fulfilling its central purpose of making public policy conform to popular preferences. If fewer than half the people vote, however, the real popular preferences may get distorted or lost. Low turnout may be a sign that many people do not value democratic processes and may be disinclined to defend them if they are threatened. For both these reasons there has been much discussion of how to encourage more people to vote in forthcoming elections. Long-term solutions include:

- increased civic education in schools

- reforming the electoral system to make votes count more

- making it easier to vote (e.g. via the internet or texting).

These measures will probably all help but not enough to raise turnout to over 70 per cent again. The controversial extension of postal voting in 2005 had only a marginal impact on voting. It appears to have allowed committed voters to express their commitment by voting early rather than encouraging non-voters to vote at all.

Political circumstances are likely to play a part – above all if the parties seem to have major policy differences and the election outcome carries important consequences for public policy. Both the major parties' strategies seem to go against this. Labour under Tony Blair (and Gordon Brown) and the Conservatives under David Cameron appear to be playing down differences and seeking to make non-controversial stands. Thus we should not really expect any dramatic rise in turnout in the near future.

CONTROVERSY

Turnout and compulsory voting

One way to stop worrying about turnout percentages would be to legislate for compulsory voting. This might be opposed on the grounds that it restricts freedom of choice. Just as we have to pay taxes however the act of voting could be seen as a civic duty we owe to the democracy we live in. It would not restrict voting choice once we got to the polling booth (or signed in electronically). We could even spoil our ballot paper! But we would have expressed our preferences, which is essential to democracy.

Geoff Hoon, who became Leader of the House of Commons after the 2005 general election, has advocated this for the United Kingdom. He argued that 'international experience points to compulsory voting being the most effective way to increase turnout '. He claimed it was 'the most obvious way to bring those who feel alienated into the political process and the best means to enhance civic participation' and 'bring back the sense that we can all work together'.

Source: See Patrick Wintour, 'Hoon calls for compulsory voting', *Guardian*, 4 July 2005.

Summary

In seeking to explain the results of recent general elections, and the underlying pattern of voting behaviour, this chapter has:

■ shown that Britain's FPTP system has the advantage of usually producing an overall majority in Parliament but the disadvantage of unfairly penalising small parties with widely distributed support, such as the Liberal Democrats

■ pointed out that this makes for strong government but also means that the majority of voters actually vote for other parties than the one which gains office, which may produce cynicism and reduce turnout

■ examined the way other electoral systems work

■ examined the impact of 'long-term' factors that shape the core vote for Labour and Conservatives

■ explained the impact of 'short-term' factors that cause votes to shift between one election and another

■ suggested that the main reasons for the exceptionally low turnout s in 2001 and 2005 were that these elections were foregone conclusions and there seemed to be little at stake.

This chapter's account of elections and voting has focused on the question of which party wins most votes and why. Part of the explanation lies in the parties themselves. In the next two chapters we look directly at the parties and the ways they seek to organise and define themselves, so as to attract voters and members.

MILESTONES

Milestones in post-war elections

1945	Labour wins landslide, helped by army votes, on the basis of an ambitious programme of social reconstruction and promise to demobilise the forces
1950, 1951	Conservatives accept most of Labour's social and economic reforms, including the Welfare State. On this basis, they reduce Labour majority to 6 in 1950 and take over government with majority of 17 in 1951
1955	Conservatives consolidate their majority on the slogan 'Conservative freedom works'
1959	Under Harold Macmillan the Conservatives win a substantially increased majority of 100. In a campaign speech he says, 'Let's face it, you've never had it so good.' The Liberals reorganise and put forward a programme of social reform, doubling their vote. Labour tries to abandon large-scale nationalisation as a policy
1964, 1966	Under its new leader, Harold Wilson, Labour wins a small majority in 1964 and increases it substantially in 1966, with promises of planning for the 'white heat of technology'
1970	Rising price inflation enables the Conservatives under Edward Heath to win the election unexpectedly, with promises of regulating trade unions and letting the 'lame ducks' of industry go bankrupt
1974	Conservatives fight February election in midst of a miners' strike and power shortages (the three-day week) on the slogan 'Who governs Britain?' Inflation, however, is the more important issue for voters. In a hung Parliament Labour forms a minority administration on a promise of 'getting Britain back to work'. In the October election Labour wins small overall majority, promising a 'social contract' with the unions. Liberals and Scottish Nationalists win unprecedented support but few seats
1979	'Winter of discontent' – strikes and industrial unrest – lose election for Labour. Mrs Thatcher becomes Conservative Prime Minister
1983	A Conservative landslide victory of 144, helped by the Falklands War, economic recovery and a divided opposition. Disunited under its left-wing leader, Michael Foot, Labour proposes full-blooded socialism, unilateral nuclear disarmament and withdrawal from the European Economic Community. Its support plummets to a little over one-quarter of the vote. The Liberal/Social Democratic Alliance takes 25 per cent of the vote (but only 23 seats), the best third-party performance for half a century

Milestones in post-war elections continued

1987	Labour's new leader, Neil Kinnock, achieves internal reform but pushes up the Labour vote only marginally. Alliance vote slips slightly. Conservatives retain their vote on the basis of an economic boom and the taming of the trade unions
1992	Conservatives present themselves as a totally new government under John Major and attack Labour as a high-tax party. Labour's attempt to concentrate election campaign on welfare fails. However, they increase their vote to 34.4 per cent while Liberal Democratic support falls
1997	New Labour wins a massive parliamentary majority of 177 with 43.2 per cent of the vote. Conservatives reduced to their lowest share of the vote since 1832. Liberal Democrat seats double to 46, their largest number since 1929, as a result of tactical voting
2001	The results of 1997 are repeated, owing to economic prosperity and irrelevance of Conservative campaign on the euro. Liberal Democrat seats rise to 52. Turnout falls to less than 60 per cent
2005	Labour is returned to office on a sharply reduced share of the vote, as a result of disillusionment with its performance on public services and the Iraq War. The Conservatives make a modest recovery in terms of seats but hardly improve vote at all. Liberal Democrat seats rise again to 62 in a smaller House of Commons. Turnout barely increases despite relaxation of rules on postal voting

Essays

1. Consider the following questions: (a) Why did Labour win the 2005 election? And (b) Why did the Conservatives lose the 2005 election? Are the answers to these questions identical? If not, why not?

2. Is Britain's first past the post electoral system fair?

3. How much do election campaigns affect an election result?

Projects

1. In the light of its three successive defeats what advice would you offer the Conservative Party on how to win the next general election?

2. Write a brief report to either the Labour or Conservative Party leader explaining what the effect of proportional representation might be if it were adopted for elections to Westminster. Where would you gather evidence to support your conclusions? Would reform be an 'unwelcome leap in the dark' or a 'golden opportunity'?

3. Assume that you are a market research company engaged by the Electoral Commission to find out how voters can be persuaded to vote. How would you go about devising your campaign?

Further reading

By far the best book on British voting behaviour is David Denver, *Elections and Voters in Britain* (Basingstoke: Palgrave Macmillan, 2003). Other very useful books on elections are Paul Webb, *The Modern British Party System* (London: Sage, 2000) and Dick Leonard and Roger Mortimore, *Elections in Britain: A Voter's Guide* (Basingstoke: Palgrave, Macmillan, 2005). The best single-volume comparative study of voting in the United Kingdom, United States, France and Germany is Russell J. Dalton, *Citizen Politics: Public Opinion and Political Parties in Advanced Industrial Democracies* (Washington: CQ Press, 2005).

On electoral systems, see David Farrell *Comparing Electoral Systems* (London: Prentice Hall/Harvester Wheatsheaf, 1997); David Denver, 'Whatever happened to electoral reform?' *Politics Review*, **13** (1), 2003, pp. 8–10. On the impact of the new electoral systems see The Independent Commission on PR, *Changed Voting: Changed Politics: Lessons of Britain's Experience of PR since 1997* (London: Constitution Unit, 2003). For an assessment of systems outside the United Kingdom, see Sarah Birch, *Electoral Systems and Political Transformation in Eastern Europe* (Basingstoke: Palgrave Macmillan, 2003).

The 2005 election is reported in Dennis Kavanagh and David Butler, *The British General Election of 2005* (London: Macmillan, 2005) and Pippa Norris and Christopher Wlezien (eds) *Britain Votes 2005* (Oxford: Oxford University Press, 2005). John Bartle and Anthony King (eds), *Britain at the Polls, 2005* (Washington: CQ Press, 2006) contains a useful series of commentaries. Peter Kellner, 'Clearing the fog: what really happened in the 2005 election campaign', *Political Quarterly*, **76** (3), 2003, pp. 323–32 is particularly useful; John Curtice, 'Historic triumph or rebuff', *Politics Review*, **15** (1), 2005, pp. 2–7 and Neil McNaughton, 'The 2005 general election', *Talking Politics*, **18** (2), 2006, pp. 12–15 are also useful. On voting turnout see Pippa Norris, *Democratic Phoenix: Reinventing Political Activism* (Cambridge: Cambridge University Press, 2002).

Useful web sites on elections and voting

Hot links to these sites can be found on the CWS at www.pearsoned.co.uk/budge.

We strongly recommend that you visit the government's Electoral Commission web site (www.electoralcommission.gov.uk). Among other important aspects here you will find an ongoing consultation on the way elections are financed. The UK Politics site (www.ukpol.co.uk) has over 200 pages on election-related material. The British Elections site (www.club.demon.co.uk/Politics/elect.html) maintains coloured maps of Britain depicting its partisan composition across a range of national, local and European elections. The Election Page (www.election.demon.co.uk) offers thorough coverage of all British elections with additional links. As the next general election approaches all the political parties will publish their manifestos on the web (see Chapters 16 and 17 for site details, or consult Richard Kimber's Political Science Resource Pages at www.psr.keele.ac.uk). The Democratic UK site (www.democratic.org.uk) has information on alternative electoral systems, including online election demonstrations for the devolved assemblies.

For more general information on British voting behaviour and public opinion, see Market and Opinion Research International (MORI) (www.mori.com), which includes a digest of polls published by other companies, ICM (www.icmresearch.co.uk) and Yougov (www.yougov.co.uk).

For data sets on British attitudes and public opinion, see the British Election Study (www.essex.ac.uk/bes) and the UK Data Archive (www.data-archive.ac.uk), both at the University of Essex, and the Inter-university Consortium for Political and Social Research (ICPSR) at the University of Michigan (www.icpsr.umich.edu).

For comparative information about elections, voting patterns, electoral systems and electoral administration in other countries, consult the excellent web site of the Institute for Democracy and Electoral Assistance (IDEA) (www.idea.int). See also www.pippanorris.com for papers and data on many aspects of elections and links to other sites, and www.electionworld.org for information on elections in many countries.

http://dodgson.ucsd.edu/lij/, the web site of the Lijphart Election Archive at the University of California, San Diego, has information about elections in 26 countries.

For Scottish elections results and analysis, visit http://election.scotsman.com; for Northern Ireland, www.ark.ac.uk/elections; and for Wales, www.wales.gov.uk.

There are also many sites engaged in analysis and proposals for electoral reform, including Direct Democracy Campaign (www.homeusers.prestel.co.uk/rodmell/index.htm) and Direct Vote (http://myweb.tiscali.co.uk/voter/).

The 2010 Election: The End of New Labour

'The country has spoken but we don't know what they've said.'

Paddy Ashdown, BBC interview, 7 May 2010

'Something did go wrong with the Conservative campaign.'

Michael Portillo, *Daily Telegraph*, 8 May 2010

'Cameron has made the most plausible offer. When he and Clegg meet I would predict a brief but torrid affair.'

Simon Jenkins, *Guardian*, 8 May 2010

'Shimmering on the horizon was the chance of a progressive alliance, a rocket about to take off. Then it crashed to earth.'

Polly Toynbee, *Guardian*, 12 May 2010

Introduction

The election of 2010 was one of the most remarkable in most voters' memories. It produced a 'hung parliament', the first since February 1974, and threw the political parties into an orgy of negotiation, secret meetings and a rather public game of political poker. This chapter aims to cover the prelude to the election and the campaign as well as provide some analysis of the results and their unprecedented consequences.

■ The New Labour Years

In May 1997 Tony Blair ushered out the era of 18 years of Conservative rule and ushered in 'New' Labour. The 'newness' related in part to Labour's embrace of market capitalism and the key role played by the City in Britain's economy. Blair's majority was a staggering 179. His first term was characterised by a buoyant economy but spending restraint, courtesy of Chancellor Gordon Brown, who brashly began to claim he had ended the Tory years of 'boom and bust'. In 2001 Labour won another landslide of 178 but on a much reduced turnout of only 59.2 per cent. After the attack on the Twin Powers in New York on 9/11 (11 September 2001), Blair ranged himself alongside US President George Bush in his 'War on Terror' and in 2003 was a partner in the fateful invasion of Iraq. This war soon proved unpopular as it became a military and political disaster and Labour began to decline in the polls with Blair being accused of mendacity via 'spin' or news management.

His attempts to reform the public services to embrace more private sector elements were not assisted by a Chancellor who believed he should really have been prime minister. According to insider accounts, Brown sincerely believed he had been promised by Blair that he would soon resign to allow him a chance to fulfil his ambition of occupying Number 10. However, this second term saw vast amounts of funding poured into health and education; some argued such spending was unfocused and profligate. In 2005 Blair sought to exclude Brown from his election campaign but was forced to include him to ensure a third victory, this time by a majority of 66, though on only 35 per cent of the vote. Throughout this period the Conservatives had 'flat-lined' in the polls at around 30 per cent and were perceived as a divided party, out of touch with the realities of modern society in all its diversity. In December 2005, old Etonian David Cameron was elected leader and immediately set about rebranding his party and purging it of its extremist 'nasty party' image.

In June 2007, after ten years in power, Tony Blair was finally forced to stand aside for Brown to take over (though without the contest which he once declared he would welcome). Initially Brown enjoyed a 'honeymoon bounce' in the polls as he appeared to handle some minor crises with aplomb. But he fatally allowed speculation about a snap election to extend to the point when it seemed inevitable and then abandoned plans when Tory polls spiked after a conference speech by George Osborne proposing an end to inheritance tax. He denied adverse polls had influenced his decision.

After this turn for the worse – Tories accused him of 'bottling it' – his fortunes never really revived and a succession of disasters attended his government: lost Inland Revenue CDs containing the bank details of millions of people; the failure to deport hundreds of serious overseas offenders who had finished their terms of imprisonment; and his abolition of the 10p tax band in his 2007 budget which, it was revealed, would disadvantage 5.3m of the poorest people in the country. Massive losses in local government elections in 2008 were compounded by by-election defeats and Brown's poll ratings indicated his total failure to win the hearts of voters as his predecessor had once managed.

However, from the autumn of 2008 onwards the banking crisis sparked by the sale of US 'subprime' mortgages began to become desperately serious and Brown was quick to devise a policy of recapitalising British banks; influencing other nations and winning the praise of Nobel prize-winning economist, Paul Krugman. He also tackled the resultant economic recession by the Keynesian solution of injecting substantial amounts of money into the economy. He was also forced to borrow vast sums to maintain his high levels of planned public expenditure: it was calculated that government debt would be in the region of £160–80 billion for a number of years to come. The Conservatives chose to attack Brown's Keynesian approach and argue that expenditure needed to be cut to reduce the deficit and related interest payments. In the spring and summer of 2009 a damaging scandal exploded concerning the way in which MPs exploited their generous expenses. Many MPs were exposed by articles in the *Daily Telegraph* as relying on taxpayers' money to pay for food, regular household upkeep costs, gardening and house repairs. Some had deliberately changed the identification of their 'main residence' to improve flats and houses they subsequently sold on at a profit. Some were even claiming for mortgages which had already been paid off – leading to criminal proceedings. All this induced a powerful 'anti-politics' atmosphere as the election approached.

In the autumn of 2009, despite his spirited attempts to combat the economic crisis, Brown was some 20 points behind Cameron in the polls and the forthcoming election, slated for May 2010, was assumed to be a formality for Cameron by most political commentators. He and George Osborne sought to reinforce their stern message by emphasising how deep cuts needed to be and there was even talk of an 'Age of Austerity' with more specific cuts suggested by Osborne at the 2009 Tory conference. Maybe such talk alarmed voters as the Conservative lead began to narrow and by January 2010 was down to single figures. Labour announced a new 50p in the £ tax on those earning £150,000 and an increase in National Insurance contributions. This set the initial battleground for the election campaign when Brown announced a May election on 6 April. At this point the polls suggested neither Labour nor the Tories would gain an overall majority, with the Liberal Democrats running at 22 or 23 per cent in most polls.

■ The Issues

Economy

Overwhelmingly the issue in this election was the state of the economy. Since 1997 Brown had taunted Tories that he had engineered the end of 'boom and bust' and established a solid economic foundation, exploiting British financial expertise by encouraging the City and super rich individuals to settle in the UK. The banking crisis and the recession in 2008 which saw GDP contract by over 6 per cent, proved Brown had benefitted from a 'boom' and that 'bust', as always, was waiting just around the corner. Brown did his best to argue that these economic travails were the result of events in the USA, and not his responsibility. The Conservatives, however, eager to get their own back, insisted the huge debt mountain was the result of Brown's epic mismanagement of the economy. Given that Conservatives had supported Brown's economic approach and competed to be close friends of the City, this was disingenuous to a degree, but incumbent governments almost always have blame pinned on them for what happens on their watch.

Broken Society

The Conservatives had tried hard to argue that social dysfunction like crime, examples of appalling parenting, and anti-social behaviour were symptoms of a 'broken society' which they alone could fix. To effect this they suggested decentralisation of government, with more local and community control, would improve things immeasurably. In their manifestos Labour suggested a more focussed and benign state, but in theirs the Conservatives essayed the (perhaps) brave idea of the 'Big Society', inviting everyone to join in the running of essential services and take back power from the state. Liberal Democrats argued the 'political' crisis could only be cured by far-reaching reforms to the system and the introduction of a 'new politics'.

Education

It followed, for the Tories, that schools had to be improved, with a proposed adoption of the Swedish practice of allowing parents to form schools and run them on the basis of funding from the state. They supported the expansion of Labour's new 'Academy' schools, a programme they had always thought sensible. Lib Dems also urged decentralisation of power and the encouragement of voluntary energies.

'Playing Field' Changes

The number of seats in the Commons to be contested had been increased by 4 to 650 and a series of Boundary Commission changes had been made creating 13 new seats while 9 disappeared. Rallings and Thrasher of Plymouth University calculated that on the basis of the new boundaries, Labour's majority in 2005 would have been 36 and not 67. This meant that while the Tories would have needed a swing of 2.2 per cent to remove Labour's overall majority, it now became 1.5 per cent. To become the largest single party Cameron needed a swing of 4.6 per cent and to get an overall majority, one of 7.1 per cent; all this assuming a uniform swing across the country. As a result of the expenses scandal a record number of MPs (146) stood down at this election meaning that replacements made the new House, much 'newer' than is usually the case.

■ The Campaign

At the end of March a tanned Tony Blair made a speech in Sedgefield in support of his former friend and bitter rival but it made no special impact. More influential was a televised debate on Channel 4, *Ask the Chancellors*. As the incumbent, Alistair Darling,

addressed what had become the NI debate – Labour wanted to generate £6 billion though raising it, Osborne wanted to abandon such plans – he attacked George Osborne for seeking to have it both ways. By criticising both of them, and raising a couple of laughs, Lib Dem Shadow Chancellor Vince Cable was reckoned to have come off best. Following the official opening of the campaign on 6 April, the wrangle over the NI issue continued. Labour stressed the illogicality of being apparently concerned, initially, about reducing the deficit and then switching to an effective tax cut. Cameron argued NI increases, to be paid by employers too, would be a tax on jobs which would harm the fragile recovery. Brown argued a cut in planned spending would, on the contrary, cause job losses and also threaten the recovery.

These accusations ping-ponged around for some days but Cameron's hand was strengthened by a raft of senior businessmen who publicly came out in support of his line on not imposing the NI increase. Effectively this 'won' the first week for the Conservatives; Labour could not find any point of purchase to attack what was perceived by many as

(Left–right) Chancellor Alistair Darling with Vince Cable and George Osborne in the South Bank Studios in central London for a live televised debate, before the forthcoming 2010 general election
Source: PA Photos.

a postponement of a tax increase: a much more welcome message than the 'austerity' one of the previous autumn.

TV Debates

The second week was transformed by the first televised leaders' debate on 15 April. Ever since the US presidential debates helped John Kennedy win in 1960, there had been pressure for something similar in British elections. To be acceptable there had to be agreement and usually the party expecting to win – e.g. Labour under Blair in 1997 – vetoed the idea to avoid giving a platform to rivals. Perhaps because he had been hounding Gordon Brown so effectively in PMQs, Cameron, despite being the front runner, agreed to a series of three debates on successive Thursdays during the campaign. Inevitably the Liberal Democrats were excited by the prospect as, for the first time, it gave them exposure equal to the two big parties. Commentators discussed the huge pressure on the youthful Nick Clegg to perform and, in the event, he did, above all expectations, finally stepping out from the shadow of his popular deputy, Cable. Cameron found the sombre format, with no audience reactions allowed, much less congenial than the noisy hub-bub of PMQs. Brown's mastery of policy detail enabled this indifferent television performer to exceed expectations, but the revelation was Clegg.

At PMQs, Nick Clegg, tended to suffer the usual fate of Lib Dem leaders in that he was allowed only small interventions; was patronised by both big party leaders; and shouted down by their respective backbench followers. In the calmer atmosphere of the debate Clegg was able to elaborate an approach which sounded fresher and more hopeful than the two big parties. His youthful good looks and television savvy helped to make him the easy 'winner' according to most polls; Cameron came a distant second and Brown third. Over ten million viewers tuned in – a remarkable figure for 90 minutes of dense political debate. On the strength of Clegg's debating skills the poll position of the Liberal Democrats surged to 30 points and over. The debates had created a three-party contest with all three parties gaining poll ratings of about one third of the electorate. Whilst the Conservatives, polling in the mid-thirties, promised to be the biggest party, any hopes of an overall majority seemed to have faded away. Andrew Rawnsley commented (*Observer*, 9 May 2010):

More fluent and comfortable in the format than an unusually constipated Cameron and a stolid Gordon Brown, Clegg grabbed 'change' from the Tory and 'fairness' from Labour.

The result was 'Cleggmania', a theme which the press took up with gusto. Meanwhile the Conservatives rued the day they had thought Cameron's superiority at PMQs would translate to a format restricted by over 70 rules which punished the kind of aggression on which the Commons thrives. However, one consequence of Clegg's success was smear campaigns delivered by the right-wing press and much closer scrutiny of Liberal Democrat policies which many voters found uncongenial (defence and immigration, in particular). Clegg found himself under attack from both sides in the final two debates and, though defending his corner well, saw Cameron – who had quickly adapted to master the new medium – eventually emerge as the overall victor in terms of public perceptions. Interestingly, Cameron did not find much opportunity in the debates to expand on his 'Big Society' approach.

As polling day on 6 May approached, the polls had settled down to the high-twenties for Labour and Liberal Democrats and the low- to mid-thirties for Conservatives. This focused unflattering attention on the first-past-the-post (FPTP) voting system as it appeared possible that a Labour Party which came third in terms of votes cast might still emerge as the winner in terms of seats won. Needless to say, the Conservatives were mortified that what had appeared a 'shoo-in' during the winter of 2008–9, now seemed to be heading for a hung parliament. Whilst the Lib Dems did not balk too much at such a prospect, the Conservatives bent their efforts to suggest such an outcome would provide only weak and indecisive government when strong leadership was required to reassure the international bond markets which controlled the future of UK lending. All three parties were well aware that the crisis in the EU's euro currency, caused by government spending and huge debt in Greece, might spread to other seriously indebted countries like Spain, Portugal and the UK. The shadow of this threat darkened the whole of the campaign and its volatile aftermath.

The rest of the campaign seemed tame by comparison with the innovation of the debates. It comprised the usual hackneyed staged events for all parties, visits to receptive locations plus the predictable photo-ops. All three party leaders took their wives on the campaign trail – something which now may become a regular feature of such events along with the television debates which have increased the US-style 'presidential' focus on the leading personalities. Labour's campaign was especially lacklustre and one event in particular revealed the shortcomings of Gordon Brown as a campaigner.

'Bigotgate'

On 28 April Brown was served up in Rochdale with a widow, grandmother and life-long Labour voter, Mrs Gillian Duffy, for a chat, live for the television agencies. The chat went along predictably with Brown seeking to exercise the charm at his disposal. However, Mrs Duffy asked a question about immigration which Brown found difficult and when he entered his car he declared to aides the meeting had been a 'disaster' referring to that 'bigoted woman'. Unknown to him, his microphone was still live and his private words were recorded. Aghast, he apologised to the lady, later returning to her house to spend 40 minutes doing so again at length. Mrs Duffy refused to accept his apology in

public and when later appearing on Jeremy Vine's BBC radio show, Brown placed his hands over his face in despair – unaware he was being filmed – as the recording of the encounter was played back. It was a PR disaster and cited as further evidence of Brown's poor performance as a candidate for the top job.

However, the damage proved limited as the polls seemed unaffected; maybe voters had already factored in Brown's grumpiness. But the two-faced nature of Brown's treatment of the typical core Labour voter seemed to reinforce a stereotype of politicians who will lie about their feelings to win votes. Brown, however, showed remarkable resilience – a standard feature of his character whatever his misjudgements – in campaigning heroically up to the last minutes of the campaign. Clegg and Cameron also showed great last-minute vigour, with the latter managing a final sustained 36-hour stint. After a campaign transformed by the televised debates, the nation awaited the results on the evening of Thursday 6 May. Interestingly, the poll positions of the three major parties had hardly shifted since

Prime Minister Gordon Brown talks with resident Gillian Duffy on 28 April 2010 in Rochdale
Source: Jeff J. Mitchell/Getty Images

the start of the campaign four weeks earlier. Indeed, the results proved to be quite close to polling six months before the election in November 2009 (see Paul Whiteley, 2010, p7).

■ The Results

The first event in the sequence of results as they fed through into the television companies' elaborate graphic-laden studio sets, was the exit poll, produced jointly by the BBC, ITV and Sky News. It predicted a hung parliament: more particularly 307 seats for the Conservatives, 255 for Labour and only 59 for the Lib Dems. When early returns from Labour seats in the north-west showed swings of 9 and 11 per cent – well above that needed to produce an overall Tory majority – many assumed the exit poll had been wrong (as it was, embarrassingly, in 1992). Tory blogger Iain Dale declared that if it was proved right he would 'run naked down Whitehall' (he later refused to be held to his pledge). Some early swings against Labour, in the north-east exceeded the 7 per cent needed for an overall majority; Cannock Chase even registered 14.2 per cent from Labour to Conservative but other contests showed smaller swings and Scotland even registered a small swing to Labour.

Nevertheless, some Conservatives were confident from their own private polling in the marginals that a pattern would unfold of more and more Tory seats. Yet this did not happen. As the night wore on into the small hours the accuracy of the exit poll became apparent. The final tally of seats is given in Table A1.1.

Table A1.1 The Results

Party	Seats	Poll (%)
Conservative	307	37
Labour	258	29
Liberal Democrats	57	23
Others	28	11

Age

Table A1.2 below shows how age groups broke down for both men and women. It is clear that young men swung heavily to the Conservatives, slightly to

the Lib Dems and away from Labour. Women aged 25–54 deserted Labour in some numbers, and young women seemed to take a shine to Nick Clegg.

Table A1.2 Results by age and gender (2005 figures in brackets)

	Conservatives	Labour	Liberal Democrats	Others
Men 18–24	35 (33)	26 (24)	23 (25)	7
Men 25–34	40 (29)	23 (33)	32 (27)	5
Men 35–54	34 (27)	28 (36)	25 (22)	12
Men 55+	39 (40)	27 (33)	18 (20)	15
Women 18–24	25 (22)	33 (43)	36 (26)	6
Women 25–34	27 (21)	37 (43)	25 (28)	10
Women 35–54	35 (27)	32 (40)	26 (27)	7
Women 55+	44 (41)	30 (34)	19 (20)	8

Source: IPSOS MORI, quoted in the *Observer*, 9 May 2010.

Housing

Table A1.3 below shows how occupiers of different types of housing voted. Owner-occupiers and mortgage-holders backed off substantially, but not dramatically, from Labour; the same could be said about social renters, traditionally a Labour constituency.

Table A1.3 Results by Type of Housing

	Conservatives	Labour	Liberal Democrats	Others
Owner	46 (44)	25 (29)	19 (20)	10
Mortgage-holder	37 (31)	28 (36)	27 (25)	9
Social renter	20 (19)	49 (55)	20 (19)	7
Private renter	35 (27)	25 (36)	27 (28)	12

Source: IPSOS MORI, quoted in the *Observer*, 9 May 2010.

Social Class

Traditionally it is the big social groups of C1 and C2 – together comprising more than half the population – whose movements tend to turn elections; this one was no exception. C1, and especially C2, voters swung markedly from Labour to Conservatives as the figures show in Table A1.4.

The biggest desertion of support can be seen to be in C2 voters – often the group which decides UK elections – where a figure of 40 per cent Labour support in 2005 changed to 22 per cent in 2010.

Table A1.4 Results by Social Class

	Conservatives	Labour	Liberal Democrats	Other
AB (upper middle and middle)	36 (37)	29 (28)	28 (29)	7
C1 (lower middle)	42 (37)	26 (32)	26 (33)	6
C2 (skilled working)	39 (33)	22 (40)	24 (19)	15
DE (working, unemployed, benefits)	28 (25)	44 (48)	15 (18)	13

Source: IPSOS MORI, quoted in the Observer, 9 May 2010.

Paul Richards, a former special adviser to Labour, posted this assessment on his blog of why Labour lost:

Populus found that it was C2 (the 'skilled manual workers') voters who agreed most strongly with the proposition that 'people who play by the rules always get a raw deal'. It was this section of society who deserted Labour on May 6th. It seems like our version of 'fairness' (more women in top jobs) and C2 voters' version of fairness (my daughter being able to afford a house near me) were not the same thing.

Press

Table A1.5 below shows how the right-wing *Mail* and *Telegraph*, already safe Conservative organs of opinion, had edged further to the right since 2005. *The Sun*, meanwhile, which supported Labour in 2005, swung heavily in the direction media moghul owner Rupert Murdoch pointed the newspaper in the autumn 2009 when he threw his weight behind Cameron.

For a full explanation of how the vote was distributed see Table A1.6.

Table A1.5 Newspaper Readership

	Conservatives	Labour	Liberal Democrats	Others	Swing to Conservatives (%)
Daily Mail	61	14	13	12	6
Telegraph	73	10	10	12	5
Guardian	39	45	39	3	2
The Sun	48	25	19	8	17.5

Source: IPSOS MORI, quoted in the Observer, 9 May 2010.

Table A1.6 Distribution of vote

Party	Seats	Gain	Loss	Net	Votes	%	+/–%
Conservative	306	100	3	+97	10,706,647	36.1	+3.8
Labour	258	3	94	–91	8,604,358	29.0	–6.2
Liberal Democrat	57	8	13	–5	6,827,938	23.0	+1.0
Democratic Unionist party	8	0	1	–1	168,216	0.6	–0.3
Scottish National party	6	0	0	0	491,386	1.7	+0.1
Sinn Fein	5	0	0	0	171,942	0.6	–0.1
Plaid Cymru	3	1	0	+1	165,394	0.6	–0.1
Social Democratic and Labour party	3	0	0	0	110,970	0.4	–0.1
Green	1	1	0	+1	285,616	1.0	–0.1
Alliance party	1	1	0	+1	42,762	0.1	+0.0
UK Independence party	0	0	0	0	917,832	3.1	+0.9
British National party	0	0	0	0	563,743	1.9	+1.2
Ulster Conservatives and Unionists – New Force	0	0	1	–1	102,361	0.3	–0.1
English Democrats	0	0	0	0	64,826	0.2	+0.2
Respect-Unity Coalition	0	0	1	–1	33,251	0.1	–0.1
Traditional Unionist Voice	0	0	0	0	26,300	0.1	
Christian party	0	0	0	0	18,623	0.1	
Independent Community and Health Concern	0	0	1	–1	16,150	0.1	+0.0
Trade Unionist and Socialist Coalition	0	0	0	0	12,275	0.0	
Scottish Socialist party	0	0	0	0	3,157	0.0	–0.1
Others	1	1	1	0	319,891	1.1	0.0
After 649 of 650 seats declare				Turnout	29,653,638	65.1	4.0

Source: Sunday Times, 9 May 2010.

■ Regions of the UK

Northern Ireland

The biggest shock here – almost a 'Portillo Moment' in the view of some – was the defeat of the DUP leader, Peter Robinson. He had suffered a major scandal involving his wife having an affair with a teenage lover whom she had also used her influence to help financially. The family's collective tax-funded earnings had also received much unflattering attention and Robinson's loss of Belfast East to the non-sectarian Alliance party caused a sensation. Cameron's hope of a new alliance in the province collapsed as his putative allies, the Ulster Unionists, including their leader Sir Reg Empey, failed to win a single seat. The DUP had to be satisfied with eight seats in the end; Sinn Fein, which does not take up its seats, won five; while the SDLP won three. Sylvia Hermon, who rejected the Tory–UUP alliance, was safely returned to the Commons.

Scotland

This country, as it has tended to over the last few decades, voted to reject Conservatism. Compared to its 28 per cent share of the vote in England, Labour won 42 per cent of the Scottish vote, regaining two seats and registering a small swing to them from the Tories. Labour scooped 42 of the 59 contested seats, Liberal Democrats 11, the SNP 6 and the Tories, a forlorn single seat. Scottish voters also voted tactically to keep out Conservatives, as in Perth and North Perthshire where Labour voters backed the SNP's Peter Wishart. SNP leader Alex Salmond's claim that the nationalists in Scotland and Wales had been dealt a 'mighty hand' proved very wide of the mark once the chance of a 'rainbow coalition' bit the dust.

Wales

The sensation of the night in Wales was the loss by a distraught Lib Dem MP, Lembit Opik, of his Montgomeryshire seat, by a huge swing to the Tories. Labour was pleased to win 16 of the 40 seats in Wales; Conservatives increased from three to eight, and Plaid Cymru had to be satisfied with three.

London

Over 70 seats are determined within London and the Conservatives were probably disappointed not to do better than their tally of 28. Labour did well to defend marginals, for example Sadiq Khan in Tooting and Karen Buck in Westminster North. While the Tories did well in the outer suburban 'ring' they had to concede the south-western reaches to the Liberal Democrats, apart from Richmond, which fell to Cameron's fellow old Etonian, Zac Goldsmith.

England

While Scotland showed Labour garnering 42 per cent of the vote and Wales 36.2 per cent, England managed only 28.1 per cent, with 39.6 per cent to the Conservatives and 24.2 per cent to the Lib Dems. Clearly the results reflected a UK where political allegiances have fractured.

■ Expenses Scandal Impact

Prime 'expenses offenders' for the Conservatives – Sir Peter Viggers, Anthony Steen and Julie Kirkbride – all stood down but, surprisingly perhaps, their successors did not suffer any party political guilt by association as they delivered increased majorities in their respective constituencies. However, those tainted in the Labour Party did less well; for example, Geoff Hoon's successor saw a majority of 10,000 cut to a mere 162, and Kitty Usher's seat was lost as was Sylvia Heal's and Barbara Follett's. The infamous Margaret Moran's replacement managed to win Luton, crushing the 'celebrity' candidate Esther Rantzen in the process. Hazel Blears, a highly publicised 'offender' however, was returned by her Salford constituents though Jaquii Smith, former Home Secretary, was not.

■ Fringe Parties

Much was made of the possible success of fringe parties in the election but generally they did not manage to impress.

BNP

Buoyed up by local government success in Barking, party leader Nick Griffin hoped to do well as a parliamentary candidate. However, he trailed in third in the poll, 18,000 votes behind the winning Margaret Hodge. In another key target seat, Stoke Central, the BNP candidate came in fourth with a desultory 2500 votes. Together with a wholesale loss of local government seats, these results put pressure on party leader Nick Griffin and placed a question mark over the future of the party as a whole.

UKIP

The party urging UK's withdrawal from the EU, had aimed to poll 5 per cent of the vote but managed only a disappointing 3 per cent, and no seats. Its former leader, the acid-tongued Nigel Farage, had stood down as leader to fight Speaker John Bercow in his true-blue Buckingham seat. The tradition is for the Speaker's seat not to be contested but Bercow is unpopular with his colleagues for having reneged on his Thatcherite views and moved close to Labour. With an endorsement from Lord Tebbitt, Farage carried many of his party's hopes for a breakthrough. Shortly before the poll he was aloft in a light plane, trailing a UKIP banner when it became entangled in a propeller and caused a plane crash from which he was extremely lucky to walk away relatively unharmed. From his hospital bed, he must have hoped he had won some sympathy votes; he did not, and came a limp third to a Bercow who coasted home with a 12,000 majority.

Greens

A small party with fervent, but thin, national support fares worse than any from first-past-the-post. Green enthusiasts were delighted in 1989 when they polled 15 per cent of the euro elections vote, but have been frustrated that they could not find support sufficiently concentrated to elect a member of parliament. So the victory of the able Caroline Lucas, the party's leader in Brighton Pavilion, has been met with delight by Greens and their wide spectrum of support on the left.

The End of Big Majorities?

Writing in the *Sunday Times* on 9 May 2010, polling expert Peter Kellner argued the 2010 result suggested the age of 'clear-cut victory may be gone for ever'. The key reason was the inexorable rise of the smaller parties:

Labour and Conservative no longer dominate politics as they once did. In 1951 only nine MPs did not take the Labour or Tory whip; in 1979 the number had climbed to 27, but the 70-seat Conservative lead over Labour delivered Margaret Thatcher a 43-seat overall majority. This time even a 70-seat lead would have been insufficient. As well as the 57 contingent of Liberal Democrats, 28 represented eight smaller parties. To secure an overall majority of just two, the Tories would have needed 86 more MPs than Labour.

Cameron's 'A List'

This 'favoured' list of candidates was invented by Cameron to help change the image of his party as too male, too white and too stuffy. A shining list of hopefuls were assembled – not without criticism from those who were excluded from it – and eased into constituencies where they were thought to have a good chance. In the event voters tended not to take to them: Joanne Cash, Annunziata Rees-Mogg, Shaun Bailey, Helen Whateley, Mal Clarke and the like were all rejected with only Zack Goldsmith and author Louise Bagshawe successfully breasting the electoral tape.

Polling Stations Fiasco

During polling night disturbing tales emerged of scores of voters in some constituencies being denied the right to vote because, despite queuing for some time, their votes could not be allowed after the 10 pm deadline had passed. A total of 1200 voters at 27 polling stations were prevented from casting their votes, according to the Electoral Commission's scathing report on 21 May. Other polling stations found they could not take any more voters as they had run out of ballot papers. Manchester Withington suffered this experience as well as polling stations in Leeds, Liverpool, Milton Keynes, Newcastle and other parts of the UK. It seems that the reason, in most cases, was the sudden surge in turnout after two elections when turnout had been low. At a polling station in Birmingham Ladywood, turnout went up from 18 per cent in previous years to 40 per cent. Critics point out that while turnout was indeed up – to 65 per cent on average – it was still way below levels common in the 1980s and 1990s. It seems exceedingly remiss of returning officers that so many people were denied their basic democratic right to vote. Geoffrey Robertson QC echoed this criticism and predicted those who sue are likely to receive £750 or more in compensation. The Electoral Commission recommended that in future electoral law be adjusted so that people queuing at 10 pm be allowed to vote.

Ethnic Minority MPs

The election saw minority ethnic MPs nearly doubling from 14 to 27. These included: Shabana Mahmood, for Birmingham Ladywood, Labour's first Muslim woman; Helen Grant, for Ann Widdecombe's old seat of Maidstone and the Weald, the Conservatives first black woman; Chi Onwurah, the first African woman to win a seat in Newcastle Central for Labour; and Priti Patel, the first Tory Asian female MP, elected in Witham, Essex.

Women MPs

The UK ranks 73rd in the world for female representation and this election's results did not cause much of an upwards climb. In 2005 women represented 19 per cent of the total number of MPs. On 6 May the percentage increased to 21.5; the result of only another dozen new women being sent to the Commons. Amongst them, however, are some notable additions. Bridget Phillipson for Sunderland South is a council estate girl who made it to Oxford; Luciana Berger, criticised in Wavertree for not being local, managed to increase the Labour majority by 2000; and Ashfield, Geoff Hoon's old seat, narrowly elected GMTV's political correspondent, Gloria del Piero for Labour. However, a slew of well-known women lost their seats: former Labour Home Secretary, Jacqui Smith, prominent Lib Dem Susan Kramer and the former Labour Solicitor General, Vera Baird.

Conservatives' New Intake

With so many MPs retiring before the 2010 election the new intake will do much to provide its character, especially in the case of the winning Conservative MPs. The first thing to note is that the number of female Tory MPs has risen from 17 to 49, with 99 male MPs. Four per cent of all Tory MPs are Asian and 2 per cent Black. Educationally, 5 per cent went to Eton, 35 per cent to private schools (up from 32 per cent in 2005), 36 per cent to state schools and 24 per cent to grammar schools. Almost one third are from Oxbridge universities. Sir Peter Lampl of the Sutton Trust commented: 'These results show clearly that the educational profile of our representatives in the 2010 Parliament does not reflect society at large' (*Daily Telegraph*, 10 May 2010).

Over 40 per cent of MPs have worked in finance, business or management; 13 per cent in law; 13 per cent in the public sector; and 8 per cent in the media or public relations. Overall, over a third of MPs have never served in the Commons before (compared with 18 per cent in 2005).

■ Turnout

On 28 April veteran election analyst Professor David Denver (*Guardian*, 27 April 2010), commenting on the hugely disappointing 59 per cent turnout in 2001, quoted a colleague Professor Anthony King's view: 'Just provide the voters with a closely fought election at which a great deal is at stake and, make no mistake, they will again turn out in their droves.' Denver added: 'If we substitute "respectable numbers" for "droves", I suspect he is about to be proved right.'

The 2005 election had not really provided King's conditions – the turnout had been 61 per cent – but 2010 was shaping up to do so. On average the turnout was 65.1 per cent, a reassuring increase on 2005. However, turnout in rural areas was quite frequently as high as 75 per cent, especially in the southern and south-western parts of England. Urban areas, as usual, reflected much lower turnout figures. Renfrewshire East topped the turnout numbers with 77.3 per cent while at the lower end of the scale, only six seats had less than 50 per cent with Hull and Hessle polling the lowest, a desultory 45.7 per cent. However, over 2 million more voters turned out than in 2005.

Do such figures prove Tony King's prediction? To a degree, yes, but until 1997 turnout of 70 per cent and over was commonplace, so in 2010 even a tight race and key economic bones of contention were insufficient to attract voters out in numbers equal to the later decades of the last century. Denver's expectation of 'respectable numbers' sounds about right, especially when the anti-politics mood caused by the expenses scandal is factored in.

The Aftermath: The Road to Coalition

If Gordon Brown's fate has been to resemble not just one but several Shakespearean tragic heroes – cursed in his relationship with Tony Blair by a jealousy worthy of Othello, racked in the first months of his premiership by the indecision of Hamlet – then today he was Macbeth, seemingly playing out his final act. Like the embattled Scottish king holed up in his castle, watching Birnam Wood march on Dunsinane, Brown sat in No 10 knowing that, a few yards away, enemy forces were gathered, preparing to combine and seize his crown.

Jonathan Freedland, *Observer*, 9 May 2010

Party Outcomes

During Friday 7 May, the exhausted principal players in the election drama must have surveyed their respective positions with a mixture of feelings. All must have been disappointed, though Labour must have felt a combination of emotions. Since mid-2009 most Labour people, apart from the congenitally naive or optimistic, had expected the coming election to end in defeat. Pessimistic supporters feared a wipe-out, Labour perhaps destroyed for a generation. To return 260 seats, therefore, gave substantial reassurance that the party was still in business.

The Conservatives, conversely, had long expected to cruise grandly into office, with a tidy majority. To end up in a hung parliament therefore appeared a disaster to some, a condemnation of Cameron and Osborne's campaign strategy to others. The decision to allow televised debates when well ahead in the polls was especially the object of derision by some disaffected Conservatives. Most of them tended to be of the more traditional variety who thought Cameron's 'Big Society' theme had sounded impractical and was impossible to sell on the doorstep.

But maybe it was the Liberal Democrats who were most keenly disappointed. After steady but unspectacular progress after 1992, the party had played very much a peripheral role in British politics, seeking hard to make an impact and leaning mostly towards support for Labour. Their expectations however had been electrified by the televised debates. From being a 20 per cent polling element in a 'two-and-a-half party system', they suddenly were an equal part of a three-way contest. Of course, the voting system would not deliver them power unless they won over 40 per cent of the vote – almost unthinkable – but a 30-plus share would have given them a slew of more seats and a more powerful moral case to demand voting reform.

The end result however revealed that 'Cleggmania' had delivered virtually nothing: only 1 per cent more of the vote than in 2005 and several seats lost besides. It was 'so unfair and undemocratic' many party members must have raged. But the arithmetic of the election had created a number of intriguing possibilities.

Constitutional rules

In the event of a 'hung parliament', where no party has an overall majority, the rules drawn up, based to some extent on the last time this occurred back in February 1974, lay down that the prime minister *remains* in office while he seeks to form a government which can command the House of Commons.

In practice this means the PM tries to do a deal with another party which will facilitate a majority in the House. In 1974, Tory prime minister Edward Heath – having polled the most votes but still four seats short of Labour's total – tried to persuade Jeremy Thorpe's Liberals to add their weight to the Tories.

Thorpe was interested but when his party insisted on voting reform as a condition, Heath backed off and Labour's Wilson took over at the head of a minority administration. Gordon Brown, therefore – accused of 'squatting' in Number 10 by *The Sun* – was in fact performing his proper role to the letter. But, as he pondered his quandary, the numbers did not look promising for Mr Brown.

Box A1 How Much Difference Would Voting Reform Make?

Much sound and fury after the election focused on reforming the voting system. Alan Travis in the *Guardian*, 11 May 2010, examined the difference various types of voting reform might make.

The Alternative Vote

Would make it possible for voters to rank their preferences among the candidates, ensuring that the winner needs to command the support of over half of all voters. Lib Dems criticise AV as insufficiently proportional and inadequate for fair votes in a proper democracy. Had it been applied in 2010 the results would has been estimated as: Conservatives 281 instead of 307; Labour 262 instead of 258, Liberal Democrats 79 instead of 57 and Others, 28 as under FPTP. Scarcely 'fair voting' from the Lib Dem perspective.

Alternative Vote Plus

This is the system, based on the German model, called the Additional Member System (AMS), and recommended by the 1998 Jenkins Report, which gives voters two votes, one for a constituency MP and another for parties in a 'top-up pool' used to improve proportionality between them. This would have produced results of: Conservatives 275. Labour 234, Liberal Democrat 110 and Others 31.

Single Transferable Vote

This is the system used in Ireland with large multi-member constituencies where candidates are ranked according to preferences and elected when a quota of preferences is achieved. Candidates do not need a majority to be elcted, just the known share of the vote. This is the system favoured by the Lib Dems and would have produced: Conservatives 246, Labour, 207, Liberal Democrats, 162 and Others, 35. It is easy to see why the Liberal Democrats believe this is the system which should be introduced to the UK.

The Post-Election Arithmetic

The figures ended up as: Conservatives, 307; Labour, 258; Lib Dems 57; and Others, 28. This meant that, with no overall majority available to any party, two main options offered themselves: an agreement, ranging from a pact not to vote down major bills to full coalition; or a minority administration in which the Conservatives, as the largest party, sought to pass their major measures, while daring the other parties to precipitate a second election in which they might be punished by the voters for bringing down the government. This feat had been achieved by Wilson in 1974 when his minority government had held on until the autumn when a second election delivered him a small majority of six.

Coalition Options

Conservative–Liberal Democrat

This was easily envisaged as both sets of MPs added up to a comfortable 364, easily able to survive all but the most massive backbench revolts. On the plus side: Clegg and Cameron, both public school and Oxbridge, seemed to get on well personally; both believed in robust approaches to dealing with the deficit; and both shared an antipathy to Labour's record on human rights. Against it however was a formidable list of disadvantages: Lib Dem and Conservative activists, whilst they co-operated on some councils, were frequently at daggers drawn over bitterly disputed local issues; most of the former were naturally closer ideologically to Labour; and many Lib Dem MPs had only been elected through persuading Labour voters to vote for them in order to keep Conservatives *out*, not put them *in*.

Moreover, Lib Dems feared a coalition might absorb their smaller party via a new realignment of centre-left and centre-right – as had happened to the 'National Liberals' in 1931. In addition, the Conservatives were mostly opposed to the EU while the Lib Dems were essentially committed to it. But the most crucial bone of party contention was reform of the voting system. Once again the 'third party' had done badly, garnering nearly a quarter of the popular vote yet winning less than 10 per cent of the seats. Lib Dems were desperate to achieve a more proportional system of voting while the Conservatives, aware that some 60 per cent of voters were left-of-centre, feared such a system would lock them out of power, possibly indefinitely.

Labour–Liberal Democrat

The possibility of a Conservative–Liberal Democrat alignment was too dangerous for Labour to just sit back and watch happen, especially as there was the chance it might become permanent.

Tony Blair and Paddy Ashdown had both wanted such a 'progressive alliance' in 1997 but it had been vetoed by senior figures in Labour's Cabinet. At the end of election night, thirteen years on, a number of Labour Cabinet ministers – such as Business Secretary Lord Mandelson, Welsh Secretary Peter Hain and Home Secretary Alan Johnson – were openly suggesting a deal could be done on voting reform. The Lib Dems knew Labour was more sympathetic than the Tories but were wary of a number of factors: Clegg had declared he did not think he could work with Labour as long as Brown was their leader; a number of Labour's influential figures, like Ed Balls, were not happy about voting reform (Brown, in addition, was believed to have been the main opponent back in 1997); and both parties disagreed on things like ID cards. But the biggest disadvantage lay in the arithmetic.

To assemble a majority, Labour would need to construct a 'rainbow' coalition comprising themselves, the Lib Dems, plus the nationalists and the single Green to achieve a very slim and probably unworkable majority. The DUP might have been persuaded but their natural allies lay in the blue not red corner. Hard-headed realists on both sides doubted if such a coalition could be sustained for long. The SNP would be likely to demand a high price and any major reform of the voting system might have led to revolts in the Labour ranks. Finally, a referendum cobbled together by such an assorted collection of forces might have been perceived as opportunistic and voted down.

Box A2 The Rival Offers

Tory offer to Lib Dems

- Referendum on Alternative Vote for elections to Commons.
- Cabinet seats and other ministerial jobs for Lib Dems.
- Agreement on schools, environment and, possibly, taxation.

Labour offer to Lib Dems

- Guaranteed Alternative Vote for elections to Commons.
- Possible future referendum on 'full PR' of single transferable vote.
- Full coalition with Cabinet seats.
- Broad agreement on deficit reduction.
- New leadership for Labour once binding deal with Lib Dems agreed.

Based on Patrick Wintour, *Guardian*, 11 May 2010

The End Game

The day after a desperately close-fought election campaign must have left Nick Clegg exhausted. And he must have been hugely disappointed when viewing the wreckage of his hopes for a massive increase in seats turned into a net loss of five. But, so baffling and confusing had the whole process been, he suddenly found himself the much courted object of a bidding war. Gordon Brown, still prime minister in Downing St remember, announced he would offer a referendum on the Alternative Vote (AV) system and Cabinet seats to Clegg's party. He said he was prepared to talk to the leaders of 'all parties' and provide civil servant support for any negotiations other parties might pursue.

Cameron countered by announcing a 'big, open, comprehensive offer' to the Liberal Democrats, recognising the differences but emphasising the common ground, plus an 'all-party inquiry into electoral reform'. Clegg had said before the election that if he held the balance of power after it, he would talk to the party with the biggest mandate. Clearly the Conservatives were this party and negotiations ensued with William Hague spokesman on the Conservatives' side. The media interest was intense with 24-hour news channels providing continuous broadcasts. Rumours abounded that the EU and voting reform were proving to be sticking points but Hague and other Tory voices spoke of great good will and a substantial meeting of minds.

The next day the right-wing press were aghast to hear that Clegg had been talking secretly to Labour on Sunday. This was followed by Brown's final attempt to keep Cameron out of what had been his home for the past three years; however, once he realised that a deal with the Lib Dems was not going to happen he announced his resignation as Labour leader, offering to step down after a period of five months once a new Labour leader had been elected by the party. It was rumoured senior figures had urged Brown to stand down with dignity having effectively lost the election. Clegg thereupon announced he would enter into negotiations with Labour, while the country waited on tenterhooks. The day before the *Observer* had followed the likes of Polly Toynbee in Saturday's *Guardian* in urging the negotiation of a 'rainbow coalition'. 'To Seize this Historic Moment, the Lib Dems Must Turn to Labour', cried the Sunday's editorial, backed up by columnists Will Hutton and Nick Cohen.

Leader of the Labour Party, Gordon Brown, with his wife Sarah and children John and James, walk to his car, after he announced his resignation as Prime Minister; Downing Street, on 11 May 2010.
Source: Ben Stansall / AFP / Getty Images.

Clegg carried the hopes of the left-of-centre with him, his ears ringing with cries of betrayal from the Conservatives; though Hague, for one, was careful to withhold criticism of someone he knew might still be his coalition colleague. Hague's caution proved prescient as the talks with Labour soon broke down with both sides blaming the other of not really wanting to come together – both sides were sceptical – and an extraordinary series of attacks on the proposed deal by a number of senior Labour figures, including former Home Secretary John Reid, Lord Falconer, Andy Burnham Diane Abbott, and several others. Their objections ranged from an opposition to changing the voting system to a strong sense that a 'coalition of the losers' would be unstable, undemocratic, short-lived and against the party's long-term interests. Clegg and his colleagues fled to the open arms of his first suitor and a coalition agreement was soon announced.

Perhaps stung by the thought Labour might still capture the prize, Cameron upped his offer on voting reform to a promise of a referendum on the AV system. Shortly afterwards a new coalition Conservative–Liberal Democrat government was announced. Gordon Brown came out of 10 Downing Street to resign with dignity and walked off with his wife and family to return to Scotland before beginning a new life, presumably not so focused on politics.

David Cameron followed Brown to the palace to 'kiss hands' and become Britain's 52nd prime minister. On Wednesday 12 May Cameron and Clegg appeared at a joint press conference in the garden of Number 10 Downing Street, displaying an almost indecent degree of enthusiasm for each other and the new coalition (the *Economist* on 15 May called them a 'startlingly lovely couple').

Prime Minister David Cameron (left) welcomes Deputy Prime Minister Nick Clegg (right) to Downing Street for their first day of coalition government on 12 May 2010.
Source: Matt Cardy / Getty Images.

What did the Liberal Democrats get out of the deal?

Clegg became Deputy Prime Minister with responsibility for political reform – a key part of the deal which is likely to be contentious as the referendum approaches. Four Cabinet posts were given to the smaller party: Chris Huhne became Energy secretary, Vince Cable Business Secretary, Danny Alexander Scottish Secretary and David Laws Chief Secretary to the Treasury.

Coalition Government's Programme

The programme of the new government emerged as including:
1. A five-year fixed parliament which can only be dissolved through a 55 per cent vote in parliament.
2. A mutual agreement to drop increase of inheritance tax threshold to £1 million by Tories and 'mansion tax' by Lib Dems.
3. Abandonment of Labour's planned rise in National Insurance rates but some relaxation of income tax thresholds for the lower paid.
4. Referendum if any further pledging of powers to EU is proposed and no entry to euro during the life of the current parliament.

5. The Tory proposal of £150 marriage tax allowance will go ahead as planned with Lib Dems abstaining.
6. Lib Dems will drop their opposition to the replacement of Trident nuclear missiles.
7. The government deficit to be reduced by £6 billion in 2010.
8. Referendum on AV to be held and a three-line whip applied to coalition MPs.
9. A move to an elected House of Lords.
10. A commission to review party funding.
11. A new 'pupil premium' for children from poor homes to help close gap in school results.

The 55 per cent requirement for the dissolution of parliament caused immediate controversy but at the time of writing, in May 2010, this will surely be only a curtain raiser to the conflicts likely to be caused by cuts in public spending required to solve the problem of the government's massive debt obligations. All political parties will take their time to digest the election results. On the fringe, the BNP has to consider if it even has a future after a disastrous wipe-out of its hopes. Labour has been plunged into a leadership contest with the two Miliband brothers competing against each other and several other candidates. The party will also seek to renew itself and conduct itself as a competent opposition. The Conservative party, in May 2010, was still smarting at being denied its expected easy majority and there were pockets of strong disaffection at the coalition with Nick Clegg. The same could also be said for the Liberal Democrats with some activists claiming the coalition would destroy the party's radical appeal for the foreseeable future. Clegg himself, on 15 May, offered this defence:

There are those on both the left and right who are united in thinking this should not have happened. But the truth is this: there was no other responsible way to play the hand dealt to the political parties by the British people at the election. The parliamentary arithmetic made a Lib–Lab coalition unworkable, and it would have been regarded as illegitimate by the British people. Equally, a minority administration would have been too fragile to tackle the political and economic challenges ahead. (Guardian)

55 Per Cent Rule

Voters and MPs learnt soon after Nick and Dave's 'civil ceremony' that their marriage had a built in anti-divorce device proposed: to dissolve the five-year fixed term a majority of 55 per cent would be required. On the face of it Cameron has relinquished one of the PM's major powers: that of choosing the election date, often criticised as allowing a time to be chosen when the economy is good or can be made to seem so. But the new rule suggests Cameron could be defeated on a vote of no confidence by 51 per cent yet still continue in power to try and form a new coalition. The rationale here is that neither party in the coalition would be able to withdraw, as the Conservatives have 47 per cent and the Opposition plus the Lib Dems 53 per cent. So neither side can pull the rug out within the next 5 years just because, say, they are ahead in the opinion polls and think an election would do them a power of good. 'Sounds good' some thought, but others had their doubts.

Critics argue that whereas previously the PM would have been bound to face the voters if he lost a no-confidence motion, he can now carry on and if MPs want to bring about a vote of no confidence, they have to muster more supporters than the Opposition currently numbers. So, in theory, this 'locks in' the coalition and makes it invulnerable to adverse votes. Many – like David Blunkett, Andrew Adonis and Jack Straw – feel that this is merely a cynical 'fix' to keep Nick and Dave cosy and safe in power. The US government has fixed terms, they say, but if the executive party loses its majority in the legislature, it just has to struggle on as best it can. However, there is a precedent within the UK: the Scottish Parliament has a threshold of 66 per cent, set by the Labour–Lib Dem coalition, and if a new first minister cannot be found within 28 days then an election must be held. Wales has a similar system.

Britain's new coalition Cabinet. Front row (left–right): Work and Pensions Secretary, Iain Duncan Smith; Defence Secretary, Dr Liam Fox; Chancellor of the Exchequer, George Osborne; Foreign Secretary, William Hague; Prime Minister, David Cameron; Deputy Prime Minister, Nick Clegg; Conservative Party Chairman, Baroness Sayeeda Warsi; Welsh Secretary, Cheryl Gillian; Environmental Secretary, Caroline Spelman; Justice Secretary and Lord Chancellor, Ken Clarke; Treasury Secretary, David Laws. Back row (left–right): Chief Whip, Patrick McLoughlin; Home Secretary, Theresa May; Minister for Universities and Science, David Willetts; Minister of State and Policy, Oliver Letwin; Business Secretary, Vince Cable; Minister for the Cabinet Office, Francis Maude; Communities Secretary, Eric Pickles; Leader of the Lords, Lord Strathclyde; Health Secretary, Andrew Lansley; Leader of the Commons, George Young; Education Secretary, Michael Gove; International Development Secretary, Andrew Mitchell; Transport Secretary, Philip Hammond; Energy and Climate Secretary, Chris Huhne; Culture Secretary, Jeremy Hunt; Northern Ireland Secretary, Owen Paterson; Scottish Secretary, Danny Alexander; Attorney General, Dominic Grieve; Cabinet Secretary, Gus O'Donnell. Taken in the garden of Number 10 Downing Street, 13 May 2010.
Source: Andrew Winning – WPA Pool / Getty Images.

Reaction to Coalition from Former Lib Dem Leaders

Former Lib Dem leader Charles Kennedy, could not bring himself to support the deal and so abstained in the vote by fellow Lib Dem MPs on whether to accept the coalition. He regretted the loss of the 'progressive alliance' of Labour and his party which had so attracted Liberal leaders from Jo Grimond onwards. Other former leaders, David Steel and Paddy Ashdown, also expressed severe doubts for similar reasons plus the fear that their smaller group would be 'rolled up' eventually into the bigger right-wing party. However, both the latter finally came down on the side of support on the basis this was the best deal *available*.

Mori Poll Supports Coalition

According to the Mori poll in the *News of the World*, 16 May 2010, the ordinary public had fewer doubts. According to the poll: 59 per cent thought it 'good for the UK'; 72 per cent thought Cameron 'right to form the coalition'; and 66 per cent thought Cameron 'fit to be prime minister'. Moreover, 89 per cent of Tory voters were happy Cameron had formed the coalition, according to the poll.

Whether this coalition of Conservatives with Lib Dems, can survive the challenges of major underlying policy differences, the backlash against inevitably unpopular cuts and the unforeseen crises which affect all governments, remains, tantalisingly, to be seen. The Tantalising prospect for the Conservatives is that, if seen to be successful, the coalition might become permanent and a realignment of British politics occur between the centre right and a major element of the centre left, instead of the re-alignment within the centre-left of which Blair, Ashdown and Kennedy had dreamed. The nightmare downside of such a development for the Lib Dems would be the absorption of their party into the bigger grouping and maybe, in any case, the desertion of their voters to Labour and other parties.

The coalition received its first big hit, 2 June 2010, when David Laws, the brilliant Liberal Democratic Chief Secretary to the Treasury, was forced to resign following revelations he had used £40,000 of public money 2004–10 to pay rent to his male partner. Fellow Liberal Democrat Danny Alexander took over his role but few thought that Laws could be effectively replaced.

Further reading

This chapter has been informed by a wide range of contemporary press articles plus television and radio broadcasts. The following books were also useful:

Callus, G. and Dale, I. (2009) *Total Politics Guide to the 2010 General Election* (Total Politics).

Lee, S. and Beech, M. (eds) (2009) *The Conservatives under David Cameron* (Macmillan).

Maitland, J. (2010) *Jonathan Maitland: The Complete and Utter Guide to the 2010 Election* (Metro).

Paul Whiteley, 'Can Labour Win?, Poliutical Insight, April 2010 pages 5–8.

Rallings, C. and Thrasher, M. (2006) *British Electoral Facts* (Total Politics).

Source: The Sunday Times, © Gerald Scarfe.

Topic 5:
Pressure
Groups

Pressure groups

Although we often read about 'public opinion', there is no such thing. There are a great many public opinions because society is divided into a great many social groups, each with its own set of opinions. Opinions can vary according to age, gender, ethnicity, class, education, religion, region, occupation, history, culture, and social and political values. In order to realise its own rather special set of opinions and goals, each group organises itself into voluntary associations that represent its interests and speak for it on matters of political substance. Since there are a huge variety of social groups and interests there is also a huge variety of voluntary organisations and associations, including charities, community associations, social clubs, youth clubs, churches, educational, scientific and cultural associations, sports clubs and occupational groups for businesspeople, trade unionists and professionals.

Voluntary associations such as these play a vital role in society and politics. They constitute what is often termed 'civil' or 'pluralist' society – an organised sector of society that is outside government and not controlled by it. They are important because they help to give people a sense of belonging and social involvement, and they are a way in which individuals can cooperate with each other to achieve collective goals, whether these are to protect wages and salaries, ban fox-hunting, promote genetically modified foods, play football or grow roses. They are also one of the most important ways that citizens can express their democratic rights to be heard and influence government. Most ordinary citizens do not have any political influence as individuals. To have an impact on politics they must join with others and form pressure groups.

This chapter looks at the role and influence of voluntary organisations and pressure groups in British society and government. It is divided into six main sections:

- civil society and social capital
- voluntary associations, pressure groups, parties and social movements
- how groups operate: tactics and targets
- the impact of groups
- Thatcher, Blair and pressure groups
- pressure groups and democracy.

Civil society and social capital

The idea of **civil society** was important in the classical political theory of the seventeenth and eighteenth centuries, when absolute monarchy was strong and democracy in its infant stages. Its basic claim was that there should be a large area of private and social life which was independent of the state and its rulers. Private groups and associations would provide the foundations for a free society and the

Civil society

The aspects of social and economic life (primarily voluntary associations and private organisations) that are outside the immediate control of the state. A strong civil society based on a large number and wide variety of private associations and organisations is thought to be the basis for democracy.

basis for organised opposition to political tyranny. One of the first things dictators do when they come to power is try to gain control of voluntary organisations, knowing they may be centres of a struggle for freedom and democracy.

The term civil society has come back into common use recently, particularly to describe the social foundations necessary to sustain democracy in central and eastern Europe where, under communism, citizen organisations and associations were closely controlled by the state. Civil society is no less important in established democracies, which are based, it is claimed, on a great diversity of active voluntary associations that are outside the immediate control of the state, even though many of these have little to do with politics most of the time. However, they provide the organisational basis for civic involvement, social participation and forms of collective action that are not regulated by the state.

Some of the basic ideas about civil society are repeated in social capital theory, which also has a long history, going back to the classic work of the French writer Alexis de Tocqueville in *Democracy in America*, published in the mid-nineteenth century. His writings have been reformulated in a more powerful form by the American political scientist Robert Putnam, in his recent research on social capital. Social capital is a mixture of three things:

1. **Trust** Trust between citizens is a powerful social glue that binds society together and makes social, political and economic life easier and more efficient. Those who are socially trusting, it is said, also tend to trust their political leaders and to have confidence in their institutions of government. Social trust between citizens is said, therefore, to be a key to understanding political life.

2. **Norms** The norms of social capital are the cultural expectations of reciprocity (mutual help and respect), civic and community engagement, cooperation and a common appreciation of the public interest. Once again, social life is claimed to have a strong connection with political life.

3. **Social networks** Joining with others (who may be very different socially) in voluntary associations brings people into close relationships with fellow citizens and leads to mutual understanding and tolerance. Networks of civic engagement that develop cooperation and trust help to produce social integration and stability, and a much more efficient and cooperative social and political system.

The bottom line of social capital theory is that a decay of social trust, a decline of voluntary associations and an erosion of community participation and involvement will have a profound effect on political life, causing election turn-out and party membership to fall, political alienation and cynicism to rise, and a mood of low confidence in the institutions of government. In other words, declining social capital, especially voluntary organisation membership, will cause support for politicians, governments and democratic institutions to fall.

We will return to this claim at the end of the chapter when we have looked more closely at the world of voluntary organisations and pressure groups in Britain, how pressure groups are organised, how they work, how they acquire political influence and how they have been treated by recent governments under Thatcher and Blair.

Voluntary associations

Voluntary associations have roots that are deep and widespread in British society. Statistics about them tend to vary from one research report to another, because they depend on how voluntary associations are defined and counted, but most studies show the following:

- Britain has a high density of voluntary associations by western European standards, though by no means the highest (Table 13.1).

- A large proportion of British citizens (40–50 per cent) belong to at least one voluntary association, and a large minority (20 per cent) belong to two or more. According to one recent survey there are about 18 million voluntary group members, 11 million participants and 4 million volunteers (see Table 13.2).

- There are few signs that overall voluntary activity is declining (see Table 13.3), and more signs that it is increasing. While some groups are shrinking, others are growing.

- The number and variety of associations is extremely large and varied. Table 13.4 lists almost 5,800 formally organised voluntary associations in one city alone, and there are likely to be many more that could not be tracked. They cover almost every conceivable sort of human interest and activity. The largest of

Table 13.1 Voluntary associations membership, western Europe, 2002

| | (Percentages of population aged 15 and over) | | | | | |
	France	Germany	Italy	UK	Sweden	Portugal
Sports	32	38	19	36	50	13
Cultural	28	24	15	25	30	6
Consumer	6	29	8	33	38	2
Religious	11	25	11	21	19	12
Trade unions	11	15	14	17	56	7
Humanitarian, social, aid	15	21	15	14	33	7
Social	14	18	8	21	22	7
Environmental	10	15	9	17	14	3
Business	4	9	13	15	10	4
Science	11	9	5	13	14	4
Political	3	6	6	4	10	5
Other	10	9	4	11	13	10

Note: The table shows figures for the four largest countries of western Europe, plus Sweden and Portugal, which tend to be at the high and low ends of organisational membership.
Source: European Social Survey, http://www.europeansocialsurvey.org/

Table 13.2 Voluntary activity

	Percentage	Number (millions)
Member	41	18
Participant	25	11
Volunteer	10	4

Source: C. Pattie, P. Seyd and P. Whiteley, 'Civic attitudes and engagement in modern Britain', *Parliamentary Affairs*, **56**, 2003, p. 625

Table 13.3 Non-members of voluntary associations (percentages)

1959	1977	1983	1987	1990	1998
52	46	42	47	39	47

Source: K. Aarts, 'Intermediate organisations and interest representation', in H.-D. Klingemann and D. Fuchs (eds), *Citizens and the State*, Oxford: Oxford University Press, 1995, p. 232, and Table 13.1

Table 13.4 Voluntary associations in Birmingham, 1970 and 1998

	1970	1998
Sports	2,144	1,192
Social welfare	666	1,319
Cultural	388	507
Trade associations	176	71
Professional	165	112
Social	142	398
Churches	138	848
Forces	122	114
Youth	76	268
Technical and scientific	76	41
Educational	66	475
Trade unions	55	42
Health	50	309
Other	–	75
Total	4,264	5,771

Source: William A. Maloney, Graham Smith and Gerry Stoker, 'Social capital and associational life', in Stephen Baron *et al.* (eds), *Social Capital*, Oxford: Oxford University Press, 2000, p. 220

them are sports clubs, social clubs, consumer groups (especially the AA and the RAC) and churches, but there are also highly specialised associations for science, the arts, hobbies and business interests.

■ Although membership is fairly widely spread in society, 'joiners' tend to be concentrated among the educated, middle and upper class, middle aged and male sections of the population.

Most groups are tightly linked into a pyramid structure, with local branches at the bottom, area and regional associations in the middle and national and international bodies at the top. Cricket clubs, for example, belong to local leagues, which join regional associations, which are brought together by national and international associations. At the same time many local groups are also integrated into a parallel structure of umbrella associations, also in a pyramid that reaches from local associations to national and international headquarters. Cricket clubs are affiliated to local sports councils, which can cover a hundred or more activities

BRIEFINGS

13.1 Political participation in Britain

The most authoritative study of the extent to which people undertake political action shows that, apart from voting, most action is stimulated by social groups. About 14 per cent of adults take part in informal group activity and 11 per cent in organised group activity to do with politics (such as writing letters or distributing leaflets to express concerns). Twenty-one per cent had contacted a local councillor and almost 15 per cent had attended meetings to protest against some policy. Sixty-three per cent had signed a petition.

Most people do not do these things very often: three or four of them are undertaken in a five-year period. When they do, however, it is generally at the prompting of a group that organises the action in the first place. (The percentages are from Geraint Parry, George Moser and Neil Day, *Political Participation and Democracy in Britain*, Cambridge: Cambridge University Press, 1992.)

from angling to yoga, and these also have regional, national and international structures. This complex network of horizontal and vertical links between the same and kindred activities is found among trade unions, professional associations, business associations, charities, churches, sports, women's organisations and environmental groups.

The result of this extensive, overlapping and interlocking network of organisations is twofold: on the one hand, the network helps to integrate and stabilise society; on the other, it can be a formidable and highly organised force if it mobilised politically.

Voluntary associations, pressure groups, political parties and social movements

Pressure groups

Private, voluntary associations that wish to influence or control particular public policies, without actually becoming the government or controlling all public policy.

Many voluntary associations are not at all political. In fact, most organisations try to avoid politics because they are divisive and conflictual, and because they were not formed for political purposes in the first place. They were created so that people could play football, sing in choirs, drink real ale or provide help for the less fortunate. This means that we must distinguish carefully between voluntary associations and pressure groups. Voluntary associations may have any purpose or goal, including political ones, and pressure groups are voluntary associations acting in a specifically political manner. Pressure groups are a type of voluntary association, therefore.

The surprising thing is that a remarkable number of normally non-political voluntary associations become politically involved when their interests are affected. The Football Association is not normally political but the issues of football hooliganism, stadium safety, EU rules on the transfer market and the new Wembley stadium have drawn it into politics on quite a few occasions in recent years. The Rum Importers Association is not political, but became so briefly when the government proposed changes to the weights and measures regulations about the sale of food and drink in 2004. The Violin Teachers Association was not political until public expenditure cuts caused heating in school halls to be turned off early, making it too cold to teach children to play the violin. Government now affects the daily lives of so many people that thousands (if not tens of thousands) of groups are likely to be politically active in national and local politics at any given time.

Political parties are one special kind of voluntary association and similar in important respects to pressure groups. How, then, are we to distinguish between pressure groups and parties? It is not easy because they overlap to some extent, but they also differ in four ways:

1. Parties want to become the government, pressure groups only want to influence government. Action on Smoking and Health (ASH), for example, wants to influence a part of government policy, but does not want to become the government.

2. Parties have broad policy interests, pressure groups generally have narrow ones. The Countryside Alliance has a fairly broad array of interests, but even so it is not involved in most aspects of public policy.

3. Parties are primarily political, many pressure groups are not. The Ramblers' Association becomes involved in politics only when issues arise that are dear to its heart.

4. Parties fight elections, most pressure groups do not because they want to influence not become the government.

There is no clear distinction between parties and pressure groups. Some groups have broad policy interests, for example the Trades Union Congress and the

Plate 13.1 Opposition to the war in Iraq brought together many different groups and organisations to demonstrate in 2003

Source: Topfoto

New social movements

The broad and loose-knit organisations that emerged strongly in the 1970s to influence public policy on such issues as the environment, nuclear energy and weapons, peace, women and minorities. They have wider policy interests than most pressure groups, but are more loosely knit than political parties.

Confederation of British Industries (CBI). Some (e.g. Friends of the Earth, Fathers 4 Justice) are closely tied to politics because they were set up as pressure groups with a political agenda. Some groups fight elections, and a few even win (the Independent Kidderminster Hospital and Health Concern won parliamentary elections in 2001 and 2005), and some sponsor party candidates (the TUC, the National Farmers' Union (NFU)). One thing is clear, however: while there are few political parties, the range, diversity and number of pressure groups is enormous. Although they sometimes overlap we can usually tell the difference between them.

New social movements (NSMs) are another kind of political voluntary organisation. How, then, are we to distinguish them from parties and pressure groups? This is also not easy because all three overlap to some extent, although they also differ in four ways:

1. *Organisationally* they are less bureaucratic and hierarchical than traditional parties and pressure groups, consisting of loose-knit networks of networks. They have been called rainbow alliances.

2. *Ideologically* they often have broader objectives than most pressure groups, but narrower ones than the parties.

3. Their *methods* are often innovative, direct and designed to catch media attention: the opponents of the Newbury bypass who lived in trees and underground tunnels to obstruct building work; Greenpeace, which has sailed its boats into nuclear test zones and the path of whaling ships. They often emphasise direct political action and community involvement.

4. Their *membership* often cuts across normal social divisions of class and left–right politics, bringing together different social groups. 'Crusties' of the anti-road movement have combined with the 'Land-Rover and green welly' country set to defend the countryside.

There is nothing particularly new about 'new' social movements. The most famous in British history is probably the Chartist movement of the mid-nineteenth century, which brought together a broad alliance of liberal, working-class and left-wing interests to press for political reform. However, it is the movements that emerged in the 1970s and 1980s that attract attention now, especially those concerned with women's rights, the environment, peace, minorities, the anti-nuclear movement and animal rights. It was claimed that the new movements would undermine the centralised, hierarchical and bureaucratic parties and pressure groups of conventional politics, so destabilising democracy. New social movements were said to be better adapted to the fluid and fragmented social groupings of postmodern and post-industrial society. This idea was strengthened when the membership of conventional parties and trade unions began to decline in the 1980s and 1990s.

Plate 13.2 Protests against the war in Iraq are still going on in 2006

Source: Alamy/Dominic Burke

231

However, the old parties and many of the old pressure groups proved more resilient than this and responded to the NSM threat. Some had been advocating new social movement goals for a long time (women, peace, minority rights), and they simply responded by making these more prominent in their political agenda and adopting others. Most parties and groups had grassroots organisations and a mass membership already (see Chapter 16) and tried to strengthen them. In fact, community organisation in Britain was not pioneered by new social movements but by the Liberal Party in Birmingham. Its leader in the 1960s, Wallace Lawler, placed a high priority on party organisation in the localities. In the 1990s New Labour tried with some success to forge a new and broad alliance of interests on which to build its revival. There is no doubt that the NSMs have had an impact on British politics, but they have been added to the old system, and changed it rather than transformed it. They operate alongside the parties and pressure groups but have not replaced them.

A last comment on the term 'pressure group' should be made here. Some dislike the term because they think it implies the use of sanctions, coercion, or even illegitimate pressure. They prefer the term 'lobby' or 'interest groups'. Nonetheless, the collective term 'pressure groups' is used for good reasons:

1. Pressure does not necessarily entail illegitimate pressures or sanctions. It may involve nothing more sinister than information or advice.

2. Strictly speaking the term 'interest group' applies to a special kind of pressure group (see Briefing 13.2).

3. The term lobby derives from the idea that pressure groups congregate in the lobby of the House of Commons where they can whisper in the ears of MPs. In fact few pressure groups go near the lobby of the Commons. They use entirely different methods – as we will shortly see.

The pressure group world

The group world has three main features: huge numbers, great diversity and a dense network of groups.

Numbers

There are so many groups that it is virtually impossible to count them. Some are set up for political purposes and continuously active. A few are set up for very specific political purposes and disappear when the issue is decided. A good many are sporadically active in politics when circumstances demand. Between them, they crowd the political arena, pushing and pulling at each other and the government to try to influence public policy.

Diversity and competition

There is a huge variety of pressure groups covering almost every conceivable interest and organised in almost every conceivable way. They are large and small, loose knit and highly organised, strong and weak, rich and poor, conventional and radical. Some support each other, some fight. The Countryside Alliance, the League Against Cruel Sports, the anti-hunt saboteurs and the hunts themselves are all involved in the political struggle about fox-hunting. Similarly issues such as abortion, gun control, road building, joining the euro and Scottish and Welsh independence are fought out between opposing groups and coalitions. It is not true to say that all issues involve two or more opposing groups, but many do.

BRIEFINGS

13.2 Types of pressure group

Pressure groups come in so many shapes and sizes that any attempt to classify them inevitably runs into trouble. For example, interest groups (e.g. the NFU) are primarily concerned with the occupational interests of their members, and cause groups (e.g. the Countryside Alliance) promote a wider range of concerns and values. The problem is that the NFU wants to preserve the rural way of life, as does the Countryside Alliance (a cause group). The concerns of interest and cause groups in the same sector often overlap. Nor is the distinction between trade unions and parties clear in the case of trade unions that are closely aligned with parties. Similarly, the distinction between insider and outsider groups is blurred when some outsider groups move towards the inside (environmental groups). Consequently none of the following categories is watertight but, nevertheless, they are generally helpful in the analysis of the pressure group world.

Interest groups   Interest (or sectional) groups represent the interests of occupational groups, mainly business organisations, professional associations and trade unions. Major examples include the Institute of Directors, the British Medical Association, the Transport and General Workers Union, and the National Union of Students (NUS). They are mainly (not exclusively) concerned with material and economic interests.

Cause groups   Cause groups (promotional or attitude groups) promote a general cause or idea. Membership is not limited to particular occupations, and the range of interests covered is very wide – religion, education, culture and art, leisure, sport, charity and welfare, community, social, youth and science. Major examples include the Royal Society for the Protection of Birds (RSPB), Shelter (a housing action group), the Consumers' Association, animal rights' groups and hunt protesters, and Amnesty International.

New social movements   These have broader concerns than most pressure groups, but are more loosely knit than political parties.

Episodic groups   These are not normally political, but become so when circumstances require (e.g. the Football Association).

'Fire brigade' groups   These are formed to fight a specific issue, and dissolve when it is over (e.g. the Anti-Poll Tax Federation).

Peak associations   Peak associations are 'umbrella' organisations that coordinate the activities of different pressure groups in the same area of interest. Examples include the Confederation of British Industry and the Trades Union Congress, but equivalents exist for many other areas of activity. There are also European peak associations in Brussels (see Chapter 9) and international peak associations (Save the Children, Amnesty International, the Red Cross, the International Labour Organisation) that operate around the world.

Insider groups   Groups with access to government officials and decision makers. Sometimes called established groups, they usually speak for legitimate and mainstream interests in society. Most professional associations have an official standing in policy-making bodies and many are legally entitled to be consulted, for example the National Farmers' Union in the annual farm prices review. Insider groups pay for their privileged status by playing the rules of the Whitehall and Westminster game, which means not being too critical of ministers, and behaving 'responsibly'.

Outsider groups   Outsider groups do not have (easy) access to officials or decision makers. They are kept at arm's length because of who or what they represent. Examples include the Campaign for Nuclear Disarmament (CND), the Animal Liberation Front, and Fathers 4 Justice. Not all groups want greater insider status, because they do not want to become 'domesticated' by being too closely involved with government. Sometimes groups move from outsider to more of an insider status, as environmental groups did in the late 1980s.

Crossbench groups   Some groups are inevitably aligned with a particular party, but most try to maintain party neutrality, knowing that they must deal with whichever party is in power. They are called crossbench groups after crossbench (non-party) members of the House of Lords.

Pyramids of power

Many pressure groups are organised into pyramids in the same way as voluntary associations, with a broad base of local groups, all the way up to a single international peak association. Trade unions, business and trade associations, churches

Plate 13.3 Anti-hunt protestors launch a balloon during the Liberty and Livelihood march, which was organised by the Countryside Alliance in 2003

Source: Topfoto

and professional organisations are notable in this respect but it applies no less to many other kinds of pressure group. Such a tight and well-organised structure can make pressure groups a formidable political force. How powerful they are, however, depends on the tactics they adopt and the targets they are able to aim at in their political campaigns.

How groups operate: tactics and targets

There are two general rules for pressure group operations. First, get into the policy-making cycle as early as possible, when options are being considered, before government takes a position and the political parties draw public battle lines. Second, work at the highest possible level of the political system to which you have access, because that is where the least effort has the greatest influence. These two general rules means there is usually a preferred set of pressure points in the political system.

Civil servants

Much pressure group activity does not concern great policy issues, as many assume. A good deal of group work concerns detailed and technical matters that are usually handled by Whitehall officials. In any case, the policy cycle often starts and ends with the civil servants who draft the early documents and implement final decisions, so successful 'insider' groups develop close working relations with their opposite numbers in Whitehall, and on any given issue are likely to start off a campaign by talking to them. The relationships are sometimes very close indeed because both need each other: groups provide civil servants with technical information and practical advice; civil servants provide groups with inside political information, and channel information to ministers. Early consultation may avoid much trouble later on.

Ministers and the Cabinet

Civil servants cannot 'deliver' their ministers, any more than ministers can guarantee their proposals being accepted by the Cabinet. If an issue is already politicised, as many are, then groups may have to go to Westminster to press their case. They will start with ministers if they can, because this is where the power lies. Insider groups may have access to this high level, where much may be accomplished by small, private meetings in committee rooms or London clubs. Outsider groups do not have such access, so use other methods that tend to be more expensive, time consuming and uncertain.

Westminster

Groups that have no access to high government circles, or cannot convince it of their claims, may turn to the House of Commons, although this is a larger and more uncertain arena than the Cabinet or Whitehall offices. Nevertheless, many pressure groups approach Parliament, and most MPs get mountains of pressure group mail every day. Wealthier groups may employ professional lobbyists with contacts and experience. Groups with a sympathetic MP have been able to take advantage of

BRIEFINGS

13.3 Affecting the detail of legislation

In 1996 a very detailed measure requiring water to be supplied to caravan sites was being considered in a parliamentary standing committee.

It was uncontroversial and the need was not disputed by the parties. The Country Landowners' Association (CLA), however, was concerned about whether landowners or water companies would be responsible for the costs. The CLA was extremely active, using both professional lobbyists and interested MPs (some were members of the association) to influence the committee decision. The water companies had, of course, spotted this possibility, and they also employed consultants and lobbyists. However, more MPs were landowners than shareholders in water companies, so the CLA had the advantage.

This case illustrates several points:

- Even very technical legislation or administration will have consequences for group interests.

- Groups benefiting will often be opposed by groups that might lose, resulting in the push-and-pull of pluralist politics.

- However, the group with more resources has the advantage.

- Given the network of connections between MPs and some pressure groups, there is a very thin line between legitimate 'lobbying' and corruption. There has been a series of scandals in recent years involving MPs, professional lobbyists and personal interests.

private members' bills in the Commons (the laws on abortion and homosexuality have been changed this way), and some well-connected groups can influence legislative details. Some groups can present their views to parliamentary committees, others can influence party backbench committees.

Political parties

Groups with strong links to a political party will use them to try to influence party policy. Trade unions used to be closely connected to the Labour Party and business and trade associations with the Conservatives, but most groups try to maintain a crossbench status so they can work with whichever party is in power.

Local councils

Many pressure groups have purely local objectives: opposition to a new road, support for parking restrictions or traffic controls, better schools. In such cases the natural target is the local council. Even if the issue is a national one, it pays to get the local council on your side. As a democratically elected body it has a legitimate claim to represent local opinion, and resources and expertise to access policy-making circles in central government, even if it does not have much influence. Councils have taken an increasing number of cases to the courts in the 1980s, even as far as the European Court.

Public campaigns and the mass media

Public campaigns are often the last resort of pressure groups, but less so than they were, given the ability of some groups (Greenpeace, Animal Rights Groups, GM opponents, Stop the War in Iraq) to mobilise supporters or attract attention. But in spite of modern mail-shot and advertising techniques, public campaigns tend to be expensive, time consuming and unpredictable. Some groups use advertising firms – also costly – and most try to develop close contacts with journalists. Some groups try to get media coverage by the headline-hitting methods of demonstrations, protests, petitions, sit-ins, civil disobedience or violence against people or property. Email and web site campaigns are increasingly used.

Courts

Some groups have taken their cases to court (equal pay, the abolition of corporal punishment in Scottish schools), including the EU's Court of Justice in Luxembourg and the Council of Europe's Court of Human Rights in Strasbourg. Legal action is often costly and uncertain.

The European Union

The EU is so important that many groups have turned their attention to it, especially to the Commission, and Brussels is now stuffed full of pressure group organisations. Most of them operate in one of four ways. The simplest is to set up an office in Brussels, but this is expensive and often groups look around for partners to share the cost. Second, they can combine with similar interests in other EU states to form a Eurogroup. The EU encourages and officially recognises over 1,000 of them, but they tend to be rather weak and fragmented. Third, groups can form a European pressure group drawing support from EU countries. Fourth, groups can try to work through the British government, or regional governments, which takes us back into the kinds of action outlined earlier.

Policy networks and policy communities

Groups often use a combination of targets, but the most prestigious insider groups work smoothly and quietly with their high-level contacts. Outsider groups have to use the noisier methods of public campaigns. Paradoxically, the quieter the group the greater its influence is likely to be; the more noisy and obstructive its tactics the less influential it is likely to be. In some cases contacts between pressure groups and government are so tight that they form what is known as a **policy community**. The members of such communities are in close and constant contact with each other, and generally agree on the main issues in their policy arena. Policy communities have been formed around food and drink policy, farming, technical education and water privatisation.

The biggest and most powerful policy community in Britain probably centres on the financial interests of the City of London, which reach into the heart of the government through the Treasury and the Bank of England, and into the heart of the national economy through companies and investment. The need to protect the national currency and London's position as a leading financial centre is so obvious to government that the City needs to do little to ensure that its case is heeded by the government.

Sometimes the relationship between Whitehall departments and pressure groups in a policy community is so close that there is a fear that department officials are taken over by the group – the officials 'go native'. This is a danger, of course, because governments and the civil servants are supposed to protect the interests of the public at large, not those of a sectional group. Although it is difficult to say if this actually happens, if only because policy communities are closed circles of influence, the accusation has sometimes been made about decision making in farming, business, the defence industry, the legal system and some areas of health policy. Equally, there is the reverse danger that groups will be 'domesticated' by close and constant contact with government officials. Group leaders are supposed to represent the interests of their members, but if they live in the pockets of officials they may come to lose their autonomy and sell out on group interests.

The twin dangers of domestication and going native are less likely to beset **policy networks**, which are looser, more open and more conflictual than policy communities. Policy networks include not just government and core insider groups, but also a larger and wider range of groups, sometimes even outsider groups. Because a wider variety of opinions is included in networks there is more disagreement, and decision making is more pluralist, spilling over from Whitehall and Westminster into public arenas. Being a group member of a policy network means that groups can retain their autonomy, but equally it also means that they are likely to have less influence over their area of policy interest.

Growth of direct and radical action

The above account emphasises conventional forms of pressure group politics that concentrate on the formal and traditional institutions of government. In recent years the new social movements have used more radical and unconventional forms of direct action. Direct action has a long history, going back at least to Boadicea's attack on the Roman invaders and to Wat Tyler's Peasants' Revolt of 1381. It includes the mass demonstrations of the Chartists (1848), suffragette action later in the nineteenth century, the Jarrow march against unemployment in 1936, and the pitched battles between Fascists and Anti-Fascists in the streets of East London

---

Policy communities

Small, stable, integrated and consensual groupings of government officials and pressure group leaders that form around particular issue areas.

Policy networks

Compared with policy communities, policy (or issue) networks are larger, looser, less integrated and more conflictual networks of political actors in a given policy area.

in the same year. The Campaign for Nuclear Disarmament organised its first Aldermaston March in 1958, and peaceful anti-nuclear civil disobedience was organised by the Committee of 100 in the 1960s. Mass direct action by students, workers and intellectuals spread across large parts of the western world in 1968, and in the 1970s the anti-apartheid movements disrupted sports events against South Africa.

Since the huge publicity given to the demonstrations of 1968, groups seem to have turned increasingly to direct political action in the form of marches, sit-ins, petitions, occupations, civil disobedience and occasional violence. Such methods often get a lot of publicity. Recent examples include:

- **Groups and movements**   The peace movement, environmental groups, women's groups, hunt saboteurs, the anti-poll tax movement, animal rights groups, anti-capitalist groups, People's Fuel Lobby, Farmers for Action, Fathers 4 Justice, Greenpeace, anti-road movements and the Countryside Alliance

- **Forms of direct action**   These include petitions, marches, protests, boycotts, strikes, occupations and sit-ins, most of it peaceful, legal and democratic but sometimes illegal and violent. Greenpeace sailed its boats into nuclear test areas and into the path of whaling ships. The Fathers 4 Action threw purple powder into the debating chamber of the House of Commons and, dressed as Father Christmas, Batman and Spiderman, climbed a balcony of Buckingham Palace, the London Eye and a giant crane. The Countryside Alliance brought an estimated 400,000 people to a protest march in London in 2002, and there 1–2 million demonstrated against a war in Iraq in 2003. Anti-road protestors lived in trees and tunnels to prevent work starting on Twyford Down, poll tax protestors demonstrated peacefully in large numbers (and a few rioted violently), animal rights protestors have demonstrated and petitioned, and some have issued death threats.

Although not new and still not very common, direct and unconventional action is increasing. It has been argued that radical groups and new social movements challenge the traditional structures and organisation of government and tend to destabilise, even threaten, democratic politics. It can also be argued that radical groups may strengthen conventional groups and procedures because, faced with radical action from outsider groups, the government may open negotiations with more conventional and moderate groups to resolve the issue. This is exactly what happened when the Blair government, faced with radical action from farmers, road hauliers and taxi drivers, set up the Fuel Forum in 2000 to solve the fuel tax issue. Direct and radical political action by groups may undermine conventional politics in some ways, but strengthen it in others.

This leads naturally into the questions of the impact of pressure groups, and how and why some are more influential than others.

Impact of pressure groups

So many factors affect the issues surrounding pressure group campaigns that it is difficult to unravel the reasons that lead to groups being successful or unsuccessful. For example, have anti-smoking groups been the power behind the ban on smoking in public places? Quite possibly, but so also might the government take credit, MPs in the new Parliament, scientists who uncovered the link between smoking and passive smoking and cancer, public opinion (which has changed substantially in a few years), foreign governments that have already enacted the same laws, the EU (which banned TV adverts for cigarettes) and the mass media, and quite possibly the poor political tactics of the smoking lobby. How much influence one assigns to anti-smoking pressure groups depends on how much weight you give to the other possible influences that have changed and developed over time. The problem is that so much is going on during pressure group campaigns that it is virtually impossible to be sure about what the causes and effects are.

While it is impossible to pin down the exact influence of any particular group, their political power seems to depend partly on their own group characteristics and partly on the characteristics of the political environment in which they operate.

Group features

- **Membership size and type**   Groups with a large membership can raise money through subscriptions and contributions. With over a million members, a staff of more than 1,300, a gross annual income of £81 million and net assets of £103 million, the Royal Society for the Protection of Birds runs a network of offices and shops around Britain. In 2000 it contributed half a million signatures to a petition to maintain EU bird protection laws.

- **Money**   Some groups are wealthy because of the people and interests they represent. The National Farmers' Union has 132,000 members, an income of £23 million and assets of almost £71 million. Friends of the Earth has total revenues of £5.5 million, net assets of £0.5 million and 2,000 'active' volunteers in the United Kingdom, though 1.5 million members worldwide. This is fairly typical of the difference between many interest and cause groups.

- **Organisational advantages**   Some groups are easier to organise than others. Interest groups are often easily organised at places of work. Cause group sympathisers are often scattered, and potential members difficult to identify and contact. For this reason producer and occupational groups are easier to organise than consumer and cause groups. Doctors are easier to organise than patients, producers easier than consumers, and teachers easier than pupils.

- **Membership density**   A group representing practically all its possible members (e.g. the British Medical Association (BMA) with 100 per cent density) is in a stronger position than a trade union with 50 per cent density.

- **Divided membership**   The BMA speaks for almost all doctors; miners were crucially divided between competing unions in the 1980s. The NFU used to be the only farmers' organisation, but now it competes with Farmers for Action, a more militant group.

- **Internal structure**   Interest groups are often centralised, making political action easier. Cause groups are often more decentralised and participatory, making it more difficult to respond quickly and effectively.

- **Sanctions**   Some groups have powerful sanctions: capital can move easily, labour cannot; professional bodies can withdraw cooperation; some organisations can call on public sympathy. Other groups have few sanctions: the homeless cannot strike, withdraw cooperation or move their investments.

- **Leadership**   A charismatic leader is an asset – e.g. William Wilberforce and the Abolition Society (one of the first pressure groups, and concerned with the abolition of slavery) in the late eighteenth century, and Frank Field (Child Poverty Action Group), Des Wilson (Shelter), and Jonathan Porritt (Friends of the Earth) in recent times.

The political environment

Features of the political environment that might affect the impact of pressure groups include the following:

- **Public opinion** A group with public support is more likely to get a sympathetic hearing; the poor image of students hinders their negotiating power. But public opinion is not always potent; nurses seem to get a more sympathetic hearing in public than in committees that decide their pay.

- **Legitimacy** A group that is thought to speak for legitimate interests – doctors, lawyers, teachers, business – is likely to get a better reception than one which does not – drug addicts, the unemployed, ex-criminals.

- **Insider status** Insider groups are more likely to be successful than outsider groups – but not always.

- **Technical and policy issues** Groups can have more influence on technical issues and details than basic policy matters. On hot political topics they usually have less room for manoeuvre, because the battle lines for these are often fixed.

- **Opposing groups** Some groups operate alone in their field of interest, especially on technical matters that attract little public or political interest. On moral and value issues such as fox-hunting, smoking, abortion and the Iraq war the arenas are crowded with competing groups and attitudes are often inflexible.

- **Institutionalised power** 'Institutionalised power' occurs where the interests of a group are implicitly built into the very structures and cultures of decision making, so that the group often has to do very little to protect its interests. Feminists argue that such an institutional bias results in male supremacy, ethnic minorities talk of institutional racism and workers and trade unionists refer to the 'capitalist system'. The provinces often complain of a built-in bias that favours London.

Because there are so many factors affecting pressure groups' success, it is difficult to estimate their influence in the political system or compare their relative power. The best we can say is that a combination of factors is likely to be important in any given case. Groups with a variety of resources (an insider status, a large bank balance, a mass membership, effective leaders, sympathetic public opinion) are likely to have an advantage in the group struggle. However, things change, and the whole nature and background of pressure groups politics has shifted markedly in the last 25 years in Britain, as we will see now.

Thatcher, Blair and pressure groups

In the earlier post-war era of consensus politics both Conservative and Labour governments cooperated with business and labour organisations to solve economic problems. The National Economic Development Council (NEDC) was created in 1961 in order to institutionalise this three-cornered relationship to take joint action on economic policy. Many similar bodies were created in the 1960s and 1970s, and the practice of officially including insider groups in consultative and decision-making processes was widespread in central and local government. Some writers describe this period as '**corporatist**', though others argue that Britain was never a corporatist state in the way that Austria and Switzerland were. They prefer the term '**tripartite**' to refer to the much looser British system of three-cornered consultation between government, business organisations and trade unions (often described pejoratively as 'beer and sandwiches at No. 10').

Corporatism

A system of policy making in which major economic interests work closely together within government structures to frame and implement public policies. Corporatism requires a formal government apparatus capable of concerting the main economic groups so that they can jointly formulate and implement binding policies on their members.

Tripartism

Tripartism is a looser, less centralised and hierarchical system than corporatism. It brings together three main interests (government, business, unions) to make economic policy. It is a consultative method rather than a binding method of policy making.

Thatcher and pressure groups

The 'winter of discontent' of 1979 effectively brought the tripartite era to an end. When Margaret Thatcher came to power she dismantled or weakened most tripartite practices and institutions. According to her, close cooperation between government and pressure groups was neither democratic nor functional, giving too much political power to private, narrow interests and interfering with the efficient operation of the market. She insisted that her government had been democratically elected to run the country, not private, factional, self-interested pressure groups.

Thatcher confronted many pressure groups, not just trade unions. Business interests, teachers, lawyers, civil servants, doctors, local government, universities, the BBC and the Church of England all felt the roughness of her tongue and the iron of her determination. Official advisory bodies were cut by one-third, and the influence of the rest was reduced. Groups were excluded from the early stages of policy formulation, though less often from the final implementation stages, where cooperation is important for effective policy. In short, the close association between groups and government was broken in the 1980s, and pressure groups often found themselves out in the cold.

Blair and pressure groups

New Labour has tried to establish warmer working relationships with leading groups, but without returning to the old tripartite system:

- It tried to work with the CBI.

- It started quarterly meetings with the TUC in 2000, but these soon came to an end.

- It co-opted group members on to task forces and quangos, although in an ad hoc manner, and as individuals rather than group representatives.

- When a crisis occurred over increases in fuel taxes, it created the Fuel Forum with representatives of the Road Haulage Association, the NFU and the Federation of Small Businesses. This showed a willingness to consult and co-operate with organised groups in order to solve an urgent political problem.

In short, Blair did not try to pick fights with interest groups. But then neither did he encourage them or invite them into the heart of his government. In large part Thatcher and Blair's treatment of groups rests on their different conceptions of democracy – a topic we will take a closer look at now.

Pressure groups and democracy

Thatcher viewed pressure groups as a potential danger to parliamentary democracy. Are they? In theory, groups play an important part in democracy:

- They are an important means of political participation and influence, especially for minorities.

- They collect and sort out group opinions to produce an agreed position (interest aggregation), and argue their case in the political arena (interest articulation).

- Groups inform and educate their members about political issues, and act as channels of communication between citizens, and between citizens and political elites.

- They mobilise citizens politically.

- They serve as pools of talent for recruitment to political office.

- They provide governments with aggregated opinion, technical expertise and practical advice.

In practice, the role of pressure groups has been hotly disputed by competing **pluralist**, elitist and New Right theorists. All democrats agree that freedom of association is crucial, and that rights to assembly and free speech are the hallmarks of democracy, and many would argue that groups have the right to be consulted, at least, on matters affecting their immediate interests. But not all democrats agree on how much power or influence groups should have. Critics of pressure group politics, both left and right wing, point out the following:

- Pressure groups are narrow, sectional, self-interested actors. Governments are democratically elected and accountable to citizens. Therefore governments, not groups, should make policy.

- Too much group power results either in domination by factional interests or in fragmented, confused and unaccountable decision making, what is sometimes called 'hyper-pluralism'.

- Groups can fragment public policy, destroying its unity and any government sense of direction.

- In pursuing its own interest each group forces up public expenditure and expands the scope of public services.

Nonetheless, too little group power means that government is too autocratic. The difficulty, of course, is knowing what is 'too much' and 'too little' power. This seems to be a matter of judgement about the correct balance – too much for some is too little for others.

Whatever conclusion one might reach about the correct role of pressure groups in government, however, there remains the claim that voluntary organisations in general and pressure groups in particular are an essential social basis for democratic politics. This chapter outlined theories of civil society and social capital in the first section, and will return to them now in the last section, since we understand so much more about the group world and how it works in Britain.

Social capital and support for government

There is little doubt that Britain, as do many other western nations, suffers from the same sorts of political malaise that concern social capital theorists so much. Election turn-out and party membership are declining, trust in politicians and confidence in political institutions are at a record-breaking low level, and larger numbers than ever believe that the democratic system is not working well and needs reform. Many are alienated and dissatisfied with British politics and the system of government, and the issue of declining trust is generally acknowledged to be a serious issue.

Is the erosion of civil society and the decay of social capital responsible for declining political support? It seems not. There is little evidence that membership of and activity in voluntary associations has decreased in recent decades, and some evidence that it has increased. Some organisations have declined, it is true, but others have grown. Women's organisations, trade unions and churches have found it difficult to keep their numbers up, but environmental groups, aid and charity organisations and pre-school play groups have expanded. There is no clear sign that

CONTROVERSY

Are pressure groups good for democracy?

The pluralist case

- The greater number and diversity of groups ensures political struggle and competition. As a result (nearly) all issues are contested by competing groups.

- Groups look for allies in the political struggle, which forces them to compromise.

- All groups have some resources to fight battles: money, members, leadership skills, public sympathy or access. Group resources are not distributed equally, but the inequalities are not cumulative. No group is powerless, none all powerful.

- Power is distributed between many different groups. There is no fixed 'power structure'; it depends on circumstances.

- Groups that fail in one arena (Parliament) may succeed in another (the courts, local government, the EU).

- Groups cannot get everything they want. They compromise to get something.

- Many groups have veto power – they can rule out proposals they don't like.

- Pluralist democracy is not perfect, but it works reasonably well, 'warts and all'.

The elitist case

- Group resources are often distributed with cumulative inequality. Just as power in society is unequally distributed, so some groups have few resources, others many.

- Some interests are unorganised, some rely on others to protect them and some are poorly organised – minority groups, children, the mentally ill, the homeless, the poor.

- The group world is dominated by educated, wealthy, middle- and upper-class 'joiners'.

- Groups fight their battles within a political structure and according to rules of the game, which are systematically loaded in favour of middle- and upper-class interests or even a particular sector, such as the City of London.

- Organisations are internally oligarchic. Group leaders are often unelected and unaccountable to members.

- A small national elite controls all important decisions, but leaves smaller issues to pluralist competition.

- The group world reflects and reinforces the political power structure in which the wealthy dominate.

The New Right case

- Groups represent narrow sectional interests; governments are elected by citizens to represent the public good.

- Groups, especially trade unions, distort market operations but so also do professional bodies and some business groups. Their power should be reduced to ensure market competition.

- Groups fragment policy making and prevent government developing a coherent programme.

- In protecting their sectional interests groups slow economic growth, and cause unemployment, inflation and high public expenditure.

- Groups create 'hyper-pluralism' – too many economic and political demands on government. This undermines good economic policy and democracy and creates 'ungovernability' and 'democratic overload'.

- Group leaders are often unelected and unaccountable to their members.

- Government may consult and groups may advise, but government should hold the reins of power.

the number of people belonging to voluntary associations has increased since the 1950s (see Table 13.2). If anything the proportion of non-members has decreased.

A survey by the Institute for Volunteering Research (www.ivr.org.uk) shows that 44 per cent of the adult population was engaged in formal voluntary activity over a 12-month period in 1981, 51 per cent in 1991 and 48 per cent in 1997. The equivalents for informal voluntary activity were 62 per cent, 76 per cent and 74 per cent. This means that about 22 million people were formally volunteering in 1997, and about 33 million were informally volunteering, and that the figures have been fairly stable over a 16-year period. This picture of a generally strong and, if anything, gently rising level of volunteering activity is confirmed by a survey of

40,000 charities carried out by the National Council for Voluntary Associations (www.ncvo-vol.org.uk). It finds evidence of a real growth in the number of organisations and in the number of large charities with incomes of over £1 million. The income of the whole charitable sector increased by £1 billion to £26.3 billion between 2002 and 2003, and it employed 488,000 full-time equivalent staff in 2003. Just under two-thirds of all adults gave money to charities in 2003, and the average monthly donation was £12.32. All these figures suggest a strong voluntary and charitable sector, and one that is growing rather than declining.

It seems that decaying civil society and social capital is not responsible for declining levels of political support in Britain. We have to look elsewhere for an explanation, and one of the prime suspects is the mass media, the topic of the next chapter. Meanwhile we can conclude with some confidence that social capital generated by voluntary associations is not responsible for declining levels of political trust, confidence and support in the United Kingdom.

Summary

- The dense network of voluntary associations in the United Kingdom creates a pluralist or 'civil' society, with indirect and direct consequences for democracy.

- The distinction between pressure groups, new social movements and parties is not clear-cut, but groups usually have a narrower range of policy interests than parties, and want to influence the government, not replace it. New social movements usually have broader interests than groups, but narrower ones than parties, are often more loosely organised and often favour direct action and community organisation.

- The main targets (pressure points) for groups are: top civil servants, ministers and the Cabinet, Westminster, political parties, the mass media and the public, local councils, the courts and the European Union.

- Group influence is impossible to measure but depends on group characteristics (membership size, type and density; income; ability to recruit members; ability to respond quickly to political change; ability to use sanctions; group unity; insider status) and outside factors (public opinion; legitimacy; insider status; whether their issue is politicised; and the power of opposing pressure groups).

- The period of tripartite cooperation in the 1960s and 1970s was ended by Thatcher, who was more inclined to confront and exclude groups from government consultation. The Blair government has tried to work more closely with groups, but has not recreated a tripartite system.

- Pluralist theory places great emphasis on the role of groups in democracy, but elite theory claims that group politics reinforce elite or class power. The New Right argues that groups produce hyper-pluralism, ungovernability and overload.

MILESTONES

Milestones in the development of British pressure groups

1950s	British pressure groups 'discovered' by British and American political scientists
1961	National Economic Development Council set up
1965	Confederation of British Industry formed
1966	Devaluation of the pound postponed for a year by the Labour government because of financial pressures from 'the City'
1968	Demonstrations and direct action by students, workers and intellectuals spread across the western world

Milestones in the development of British pressure groups continued

1969	Trade union pressure forces the Labour government to abandon plans for trade union reform ('In place of strife')
1970s	Rise of the 'new social movements'
1971	The Conservative Industrial Relations Act reduces trade union powers
1974	The Prime Minister (Heath) calls an election, as a result of the miners' strike, and loses
	The Labour government's 'Social Contract' with the trade unions agrees to social legislation and repeal of the Industrial Relations Act in return for a 'prices and incomes policy' but no agreement is struck with business or professional organisations about prices, salaries or profits
	Manpower Services Commission (a tripartite agency for jobs and training) created, followed by 1975 Health and Safety Commission, and 1976 Advisory, Conciliation, and Arbitration Service (ACAS) to deal with industrial relations disputes
1979	Thatcher begins to dismantle the machinery of 'tripartism' and begins a long series of confrontations with a wide range of organised interests and groups
1982	CBI Director-General, Sir Terence Beckett, threatens to 'get the gloves off' with the Thatcher government over its financially orthodox economic policy
1984–5	Miners' strike, the most bitter and prolonged industrial dispute since 1926, lost by miners
1980, 1982, 1984, 1988, 1989, 1990	Employment and Trade Union Acts reducing powers and rights of trade unions
1988	Edwina Currie, Junior Health Minister, is forced out after her statement that eggs are widely infected by salmonella angers egg producers and the NFU
1988–90	Anti-poll tax protests, culminating in demonstrations and riots across the country in 1990
1992	NEDC abolished
1994–6	Payments to MPs and other incidents of sleaze involving pressure groups and lobbyists prompt Nolan Committee to investigate MPs' interests
1997–8	Stronger regulation of MPs' interests by House of Commons
1997	Blair tries to establish working relations with major interest groups, but not under the old tripartite system
1997	The start of a long series of protests by farmers. Countryside Alliance organises demonstration attracting 300,000 people
1998–2000	Destruction of GM crops by Greenpeace
1999	Anti-capitalist and World Trade Organization rallies in London and Seattle become an annual event
2000	Fuel tax protest
2002	Countryside Alliance attracts 400,000 participants in London demonstration. Student protests against top-up fees
2003	Anti-(Iraq) war coalition attracts 1–2 million demonstrators in London

Essays

1. 'Elite theory claims that pressure groups merely reflect and sustain the power structure of modern society.' Discuss.

2. Why do some analysts attach so much importance to civil society, and is Britain such a society?

3. 'Once powerful in Britain, pressure groups have been weakened to the point of powerlessness since 1979.' Is this true?

Projects

1. Collect what information you can from books, articles and newspaper reports about the fuel tax protests of 2000, the campaign against genetically modifed food and the Countryside Alliance. What does this information tell us about the conduct of modern pressure group campaigns?

2. Make a list of all the groups mentioned in this chapter and classify them into their different types listed in Briefing 13.2. What do you learn from this exercise?

3. Carefully read a good national daily newspaper for one week, and list all the pressure groups and pressure group issues mentioned in the news reports. What does this tell you about the pressure group world in Britain?

Further reading

A recent comprehensive book is W. Grant, *Pressure Groups and British Politics* (Basingstoke: Palgrave, 2000). Slightly older is R. Baggot, *Pressure Groups Today* (Manchester: Manchester University Press, 1995). A good study of environmental pressure groups and movements is G. Jordan and W. Maloney, *The Protest Business* (Manchester: Manchester University Press, 1997). On business groups, see W. Grant, *Business and Politics in Britain* (London: Macmillan, 2nd edn, 1993) and, on trade unions, D. Marsh, *The New Politics of British Trade Unions and the Thatcher Legacy* (London: Macmillan, 1992). A good account of European pressure groups is found in S. Mazey and J. J. Richardson, *Lobbying in the European Community* (Oxford: Oxford University Press, 1993).

A review of pressure group politics in 2004 is to be found in W. Grant, 'Pressure politics: a politics of collective consumption?', *Parliamentary Affairs*, **58**, (2), 2005, pp. 366–79. H. Margetts, 'Political participation and protest', in P. Dunleavy *et al.* (eds), *Developments in British Politics* (Basingstoke: Palgrave, 2002) discusses protest politics. Other useful and recent articles include N. Jackson, 'Pressure group politics', *Politics Review*, September 2004, pp. 2–5 and G. Jordan, 'Groups and democracy', *Politics Review*, February 2004, pp. 20–3.

Useful web sites on pressure groups

Hot links to these sites can be found on the CWS at www.pearsoned.co.uk/budge.

Before visiting specific pressure groups' web sites, you might want to log on to www.historylearningsite.co.uk/pressure_groups.htm where you can find basic answers to questions such as: What are pressure groups? How do they influence democratic performance? What is pluralism?

There are tens of thousands of pressure groups in Britain, many of them with web sites, and some with excellent and innovative ones. In the following list you can find samples of those with particularly good web sites and those mentioned in the chapter. Each site will provide basic information about the group, such as its history, objectives, activities and the ways in which you can become involved.

Action on Smoking and Health: www.ash.org

Amnesty International: www.oneworld.org/amnesty/index.html

Animal Concerns: http://animalconcerns.netforchange.com

Black Information Link: www.blink.org.uk

British Medical Association: www.bma.org.uk

Campaign for Nuclear Disarmament: www.cnduk.org

Campaign for an Independent Britain: www.bullen.demon.co.uk

Charter 88: www.charter88.org.uk

Child Poverty Action Group: www.homelesspages.org.uk

Chronicle World (changing Black Britain): www.chronicleworld.org

Commonwealth Foundation: www.commonwealthfoundation.com

Compassion in World Farming: www.ciwf.co.uk

Confederation of British Industry: www.cbi.org.uk

Conservation International: www.conservation.org/xp/CIWEB/home

Country Landowners' Association: www.cla.org.uk

Countryside Alliance: www.countryside-alliance.org

Friends of the Earth: www.foe.co.uk

Greenpeace: www.greenpeace.org/homepage

International Council for Local Environmental Initiatives: www.iclei.org

League Against Cruel Sports: www.league.uk.com

Local Government Association: www.lga.gov.uk

Mind: www.mind.org.uk

National Farmers' Union: www.nfu.org.uk

National Society for the Prevention of Cruelty to Children: www.nspcc.org.uk

National Trust: www.nationaltrust.org.uk

Nexus: www.netnexus.org/nexus

Press for Change: www.pfc.org.uk

Royal National Institute for the Blind: www.rnib.org.uk

Royal Society for the Protection of Birds: www.rspb.org.uk

Shelter: www.shelter.org.uk

World Conservation Monitoring Centre: www.unep-wcmc.org

World Council of Churches: www.wcc-coe.org

Participation beyond elections

Learning outcomes

After reading this chapter, you will:

• Be able to outline the major forms of non-electoral participation in the UK.

• Appreciate the chequered history of referendums in UK politics.

• Understand the complex relationship between pressure groups and liberal democracy.

Introduction

The French philosopher Jean-Jacques Rousseau (1712–78) once jeered that the English people are only 'free' during elections. He meant that these were the only occasions when members of the public could behave like true citizens, and take a meaningful part in making the laws by which they were governed. Even at election time, during the eighteenth century this citizenship was a privilege enjoyed by a few rather than a right extended to all British adults. Women were not allowed to vote, and most men were ruled out by the wide range of qualifications applied in different constituencies. Although there were wide variations, in the typical constituency only the rich could vote.

Despite the very different context of today, Rousseau's remark is still suggestive of a major dilemma for all representative democracies. Elections give citizens a regular opportunity to dismiss unsatisfactory representatives. But normally that judgement can only be delivered at the end of a term of office, by which time many unpopular or damaging decisions could have been made. In the UK, instead of submitting themselves to the electorate as soon as they lose public confidence, governments either call elections when (for what might be transient reasons) their popularity is high, or hang on for as long as possible in the hope that their prospects will improve. There are, though, ways in which citizens can register their feelings between elections. In this chapter we will look at referendums, pressure groups and other forms of participation in the UK, in order to assess whether or not they overcome Rousseau's challenge.

Referendums

Referendum: a mechanism allowing voters to choose between different courses of action in a particular policy area.

Referendums are ballots in which citizens are asked to give their views on specific policies. As such, they can be seen as a return to the kind of direct democracy which was practised in Athens and elsewhere in the ancient world, and which inspired Rousseau (see Chapter 1).

On the face of it, the history in Case study 19.1 suggests that after a slow start the British have become very keen on the referendum, following the long-established practice of many other European countries and the United States. But this impression should be qualified. More than three decades after the EEC poll, this remains the only time that the population of the UK as a whole has been asked to vote on an issue, in spite of strong popular support for the holding of further referendums – particularly on the contentious subject of European integration. The main general principles concerning the suitability of referendums are:

- They can be appropriate ways of deciding constitutional issues of over-riding importance (thus the Labour government initially promised a referendum on an EU constitution, then rejected the idea on the grounds that the terms of the ensuing Lisbon Treaty would not have an impact comparable to the draft EU constitution).
- Although in principle their verdicts can be brushed aside, in practice they have more 'entrenched' status than Acts of Parliament.
- They can be called when an important proposal affects a specific constituency within the UK. In these instances the vote has so far been restricted to the people who are directly affected.

Referendums: for and against

The increasing use of the referendum in the UK gives rise to interesting possibilities at a time of technological change. The Internet and the text-message have been exploited by the media to facilitate instant polls on a wide range of issues. Could these innovations be used by governments – or even make traditional understandings of government redundant? The old ideas of direct democracy (which inspired Rousseau himself) envisaged 'face-to-face' societies where citizens could discuss topical issues in person, without having to appoint an elected intermediary. Might we be able to achieve the same effect in virtual reality?

Referendums in the UK

1973. The 'Border poll' in Northern Ireland

Voters in Northern Ireland were asked if they wanted to remain within the UK. There was an overwhelming 'yes' vote, but this proved very little since opponents of the Union organised an effective boycott. Critics claimed that the referendum was nothing more than a way of confirming what everyone knew already – that the majority in Northern Ireland was Protestant and favoured a continuation of the link with the rest of Britain. In their eyes the real problem was the status of the Catholic minority.

1975. Continued UK membership of the European Economic Community

The first UK-wide referendum was held on 5 June 1975, over Britain's membership of what was then the European Economic Community (EEC). The Labour Prime Minister, Harold Wilson, resorted to the vote chiefly because his party was seriously divided. A 'yes' vote, he hoped, would give him the authority to override the objections of colleagues who wanted the UK to withdraw. On a high turnout (nearly two-thirds) the 'yes' campaign secured what could be presented as a conclusive result. Virtually every region of the UK voted in favour of membership. In England, there was a 69 per cent 'yes' vote. But critics could argue that the poll had been held too late. On a question of such importance, voters should have been asked whether they wanted to join in the first place. By 1975 the 'no' camp was fighting an uphill battle, asking people to overturn a decision which had already been taken. Furthermore, the 'yes' campaign was much better funded and enjoyed overwhelming media support.

1979. Devolution for Scotland and Wales

Voters in Scotland and Wales were asked if they wanted devolved assemblies, with limited powers. In Scotland, the 'yes' campaign secured a very narrow victory – by less than 100,000 votes – on a turnout of less than two-thirds. In practice, this meant that the case for a Scottish assembly had been rejected, because the required level of support had been set by law at 40 per cent of qualified voters. The eventual figure was less than 33 per cent. The Welsh had been offered an assembly without independent law-making powers. The measure was opposed even by some government MPs, like the future Labour leader Neil Kinnock. Only about 20 per cent of those who voted endorsed the proposal, on a turnout of less than 60 per cent. In neither of these abortive attempts to secure popular approval for devolution were English voters asked for their opinions. The failure of the project led directly to the downfall of James Callaghan's Labour government, which was deserted by members of the nationalist parties and defeated on a House of Commons vote of confidence in March 1979 – less than a month after the ill-fated referendums.

1997. Devolution for Scotland and Wales

Eighteen years after the 1979 polls a new Labour government made another attempt to secure approval for devolution. In Scotland and Wales the turnout was even lower than it had been first time round. This was somewhat surprising since opinion was still sharply divided. In Scotland the 'yes' campaign fared better, winning 63.5 per cent of the votes on 11 September 1997. But the Welsh poll, held a week later, was a cliff-hanger; only 50.3 per cent of those who voted said 'yes'. This partly reflected the fact that the powers conferred on the Welsh assembly would be strictly limited, whereas the Scottish people were given a parliament with the authority to make laws and raise additional taxes (see Chapter 12).

1998. Devolution for Northern Ireland

Northern Ireland held its second referendum on 22 May 1998, after the Belfast (or 'Good Friday') Agreement of the previous month. The deal was accepted by more than 70 per cent of those voting (and turnout was exceptionally high, at almost 90 per cent). A resounding 'yes' was also delivered in a similar poll conducted in the Irish Republic. The vote paved the way for a new devolved assembly, which embarked on a somewhat chequered history (see Chapter 12).

2004. Regional assembly for the north-east

New Labour hoped to extend its devolution project to the English regions, proposing that assemblies should be established with strictly limited powers and budgets. Initially there was strong support for the idea; in five regions (the north-east, north-west, the west and east midlands, and Yorkshire and Humberside) a 2002 BBC poll found that almost three-quarters of respondents were in favour. However, by 2004 government confidence in positive outcomes had been sapped. Ultimately only one poll was held, in the north-east in November 2004. In an all-postal ballot nearly 50 per cent cast a vote. The result was almost a mirror-image of the 2002 BBC poll; 78 per cent of voters were against the plan. It was felt that a north-east assembly on the proposed lines would be a 'white elephant' – a talking-shop which increased local taxes without taking any useful action.

Since 1998. Elected mayors

On 7 May 1998 London voters agreed in a referendum to hold elections for a directly-elected mayor and a Greater London Authority. Although the 'yes' campaign secured more than two-thirds of the votes, turnout was miserable at 34 per cent. Other towns and cities have held referendums on the subject of an elected mayor; they can be called either after a majority vote among local councillors, or if a petition is signed by 5 per cent of residents. But by the beginning of 2008 only 13 mayors had been elected (including London's). Even the Prime Minister's constituents in Sedgefield turned down the idea, and in October 2008 the voters of Stoke-on-Trent decided to abolish the mayoralty they had agreed to establish just six years previously. The turnout in the referendums has usually been low (Ealing managed less than 10 per cent when rejecting the proposition in 2002).

Local referendums

Councils sometimes hold local referendums on issues like the level of spending or development projects. As early as 1981 a referendum was held in Coventry on the issue of local taxation. In February 2005 Edinburgh voted against its council's proposed congestion charging scheme to control city traffic. Under the terms of the Local Government Act 1972, voters working through their parish councils are allowed to call local referendums on their own initiative. Only a small number of supporters are necessary. These 'do-it-yourself' referendums are not binding, but councillors would be unwise to ignore clear results on sizeable turnouts. Local polls generated in this way are likely to become more frequent, as people become aware of their regular use in other countries (notably the US). The 2007 Green Paper, *The Governance of Britain* (Cm 7170), referred to the need for greater consultation of local residents, but this initiative was not followed up. One reason why central governments might be wary of local referendums is that they can also be used as ways of generating publicity on controversial national issues – for example, anti-euro campaigners have forced referendums to stop their councils preparing for UK adoption of the single currency.

The subject of e-voting is discussed elsewhere (see Chapter 17). At present, there is no prospect of routine government decision-making being entrusted to voters in this way. More likely, innovations like all-postal ballots, which encourage voter participation, might foster the use of a referendum whenever a reasonable case can be made for one, rather than reserving it for situations which clearly fall into the categories listed above. However, such ballots have already come under suspicion because of allegations of fraud, and in a bitterly and closely-fought referendum the dangers of abuse are obvious. Internet voting would be liable to the same objections. The government has recently introduced a facility whereby citizens can use the Internet to exercise their traditional right of petitioning on specific subjects; the results (see http://petititions.number10.gov.uk) have been mixed at best.

There is much to be said in favour of more frequent referendums. Some issues are clearly too important to be decided exclusively by politicians who may not invariably reflect the views of their constituents, and it can be argued that local residents are the best people to judge proposals which crucially affect their interests. More generally, participation in referendums can enhance the level of public interest in political issues.

However, referendums are still viewed with suspicion in some quarters. Professional politicians tend to regard them as a danger to parliamentary sovereignty. However, this is a difficult case to argue in a democracy, where the legislature is supposed to reflect the views of the public. A more serious point was advanced by Margaret Thatcher (then Leader of the Opposition), when she spoke against the Bill which paved the way for the 1975 referendum on EEC membership. She associated the use of the referendum with dictatorships. There is plenty of evidence to support that view: the referendum (or '**plebiscite**') was a favoured expedient of the Nazis, and in October 2002 Saddam Hussein of Iraq was rewarded with almost unanimous support in a poll on his leadership, despite the fact that his regime was detested in many parts of the country. However, in the context of intimidation, violence and vote-rigging, any supposedly democratic device can be manipulated by an unscrupulous government; the referendum is not really any more susceptible to these abuses than elections.

Plebiscite: a referendum; sometimes used derogatively to refer to referendums held to boost the authority of the government or leader.

In a liberal democracy like the UK some of the obvious sources of manipulation can be avoided. For example, the independent Electoral Commission must inspect the wording of the questions put to voters, to ensure that the referendum options are presented as objectively as possible. The Blair government also accepted many of the recommendations put forward by the 1998 Neill committee, to restrict the official funding which can be provided in referendum campaigns. However, the referendum is still open to abuse even by elected governments which are usually benign. There is an old saying in business that no-one should call a meeting unless the outcome is already known, and the same could be said of the referendum. Critics argued that the 1975 referendum on continued membership of the European Economic Community (EEC) was a cynical exercise on the part of Harold Wilson, who claimed that the UK terms had been significantly improved although in truth negotiations by his government had left them broadly unchanged. Wilson's main motive in calling the referendum was really to appease 'anti-marketeers' within his own party, and he suspended the usual conventions of collective responsibility so that Cabinet colleagues could campaign for a 'no' vote; but given the balance of forces on either side he could always be confident that his own preferred 'yes' option would prevail.

Equally cynical, though, have been more recent decisions *not* to hold referendums. The Blair and Brown governments resisted polls on the two European issues of a single currency and a constitution at least in part because of a fear that the public would defy its wishes. Also, having planned to hold referendums on devolution in four English regions, Labour ended up calling only one – in the north-east, where the opinion polls had indicated that there was the best chance of securing a 'yes' vote (in fact, the government ending up losing even that decision, persuading it to scrap plans to hold the other three; see Case Study 19.1).

Another difficulty with referendums is the question of turnout. Should there be a minimum level which has to be exceeded before the results are binding? Against the wishes of the then Labour government, in 1978 provisions of this kind were

---

Case study: 19.2

Focus groups and citizens' panels

An alternative to the formal referendum is a system of regular consultation with relatively large groups of voters who can be held to be 'representative' of the population as a whole. The Blair governments made considerable use of focus groups which allowed it to monitor public opinion. At Labour's National Policy Forum in November 2003 Blair launched an even more ambitious project: a 'Big Conversation' with British voters, inviting anyone to express their views on the policy choices facing the country. It was hoped that this process would provide ideas for the party's next election manifesto, but the response was disappointing.

Since the late 1990s local councils have also been consulting 'Citizens' Panels' (sometimes called 'Citizens' Juries'), with membership in some cases running to thousands. The panellists offer their views on subjects like the quality of local services. In July 2008 the new prime minister Gordon Brown hailed such bodies as 'Labour's big idea'. But the obvious difficulty is that they are liable to present a distorted view of public opinion. In itself, ironically, being selected as 'representative' figures can make people unrepresentative. In a public setting, faced with determined and eloquent advocates, they might become more inclined to voice opinions which they think will be pleasing to the organisers, or to swallow their personal views when they realise that the general mood is against them. Thus while these consultative bodies can provide political organisations with valuable information, it would be prudent for them to evaluate the findings in conjunction with information unearthed by independent polling companies. The same general objections can be raised against citizen's panels run by pressure groups.

included in the legislation for referendums on devolution for Scotland and Wales. In the case of Scotland, the 'yes' campaign narrowly prevailed when the vote was held in 1979, but it did not secure the necessary level of support in the electorate as a whole. It could also be argued that on issues of far-reaching constitutional significance something more than a simple majority of votes would have to be registered; for example, the proposal might require the support of two-thirds of voters. A more mundane consideration is that referendums are expensive, whatever the method of voting. Against these practical problems, however, is the unquestionable popularity of the referendum among a UK public which has come to see itself as more trustworthy than its elected representatives. Refusal to hold a referendum, against concerted public demands, can be almost as politically damaging as letting the poll go ahead and ending up on the losing side.

Pressure groups

Civil society: the sphere of voluntary activity, where associations can be formed independently of the state. Such organisations (sometimes referred to as 'intermediate institutions') include clubs, pressure groups, political parties and religious organisations. A strong civil society is regarded as an essential element in any liberal democracy.

Referendums and party-run focus groups do allow members of the public to have some say in policy decisions between elections. But in most of these instances the decision to consult the public rests with the politicians. In that sense, for advocates of direct democracy they merely underline the limitations of public influence over the policy process.

By contrast, pressure groups often communicate their opinions when politicians would prefer to be left in peace. There is a wide variety of such groups in the UK, and in recent decades their popularity has been growing (see Table 19.1). Increasing activity of this kind need not be a source of unease; on the contrary, it could be taken as a sign that **civil society** in Britain is healthy, with a highly-motivated citizen

Table 19.1 Pressure group activity in the UK, 2000–2001

A rigorous survey of political participation in the UK found that 62 per cent of respondents claimed to have 'Donated money to an organisation'. Other activities were undertaken by the following proportions:

Signed a petition	42 per cent
Boycotted certain products	31 per cent
Raised funds for an organisation	30 per cent
Worn or displayed a campaign badge or sticker	22 per cent
Contacted a politician	13 per cent
Attended a political meeting or rally	5 per cent
Taken part in a public demonstration	5 per cent
Participated in illegal protest activities	2 per cent

The same survey found that 22 per cent of the population (or around 9 million if the finding was representative of the UK population as a whole) spent 11 or more hours per week involved in a variety of organisations. Some 41 per cent of the population was involved in one or more groups. However, the findings do not necessarily reflect a widespread desire for political participation; a large number of respondents (29 per cent) were members of motoring organisations, which can be involved in serious political issues but which are usually joined by people who want a breakdown service for their cars.

Source: Citizen Audit, Economic and Social Research Council

body, ready to exploit any opportunity to participate in public debate. However, when party membership and voting turnout is declining, the simultaneous rise of pressure groups suggests that people are increasingly dissatisfied with the orthodox political process, and are searching for alternative channels of influence.

The nature of pressure groups

Pressure groups are voluntary organisations which resemble political parties in some important respects. Their growth need not be at the expense of the parties; people can be members of both kinds of organisation. The key differences between parties and pressure groups are:

- One of the main functions of political parties is to contest elections. Pressure groups do not normally put up candidates; if they do so, they are usually aiming to win publicity rather than form a government (or even to win a single seat).
- The goal of pressure groups is to exert influence over office-holders. Political parties seek to hold office themselves.
- Parties develop policies over a wide range of issues. Pressure groups tend to focus on one specific area of policy (although subjects like the environment generate proposals which seriously affect numerous policy areas).

One interesting illustration of these distinctions was the emergence of the Referendum Party which contested 547 seats at the 1997 general election, securing around 2.5 per cent of the UK vote. The party's sole aim was to bring about a referendum on Britain's membership of the European Union (EU), in the hope that this would result in a vote for UK withdrawal. Realistically, its best chance was to force the Conservative Party to adopt this policy. Its members could have attempted to do so by the familiar pressure group tactic of lobbying Conservative candidates, and threatening to vote for their opponents unless they adopted a more Eurosceptic stance. But Sir James Goldsmith, who founded the Referendum Party, was a multi-millionaire who could afford the more dramatic gesture of underwriting a nationwide election campaign. He never had the remotest chance of forming a government – or indeed much realistic hope of winning a single seat under the simple plurality electoral system.

In other words, the Referendum Party is best understood as a pressure group which was able to indulge in a dramatic strategy to advertise its goals. Even though it fared poorly, it outperformed the UK Independence Party (UKIP, founded 1993), which has remained in existence and become more like the older parties by developing policies on a wider range of issues. In the absence of the defunct Referendum Party, UKIP polled well in the 2004 European Parliament elections but lapsed back into insignificance in the 2005 general election, when Europe was barely mentioned as an issue.

The Green Party is another interesting example. Founded in 1973 as the People Party (then renamed the Ecology Party), it fielded only 53 candidates in the 1979 general election and received just 0.1 per cent of the UK vote. However, in the 1989 Euro-elections the Greens secured 15 per cent of the vote. The response of the main parties was to register the popularity of green arguments for the first time, and adopt a more environmentally-friendly stance (at least on paper). Partly as a result (and because of internal disagreements about the political future of the ecology movement) the Greens failed to sustain their momentum in the short term. But the party continued in existence, because it was far more than a single-issue group like the Referendum Party. It developed distinctive policies across a wide range of issues, and under proportional representation has now won seats in the European Parliament, the Scottish Parliament, London Assembly and many local councils. Even though the environmental agenda has become more widely accepted, the British Greens still retain more of the 'pressure group' mentality than their more successful electoral counterparts, like those in Germany (although it is noteworthy that in 2008 the party decided for the first time to follow orthodox UK parties in choosing a leader and deputy leader – Caroline Lucas and Adrian Ramsay).

Insiders and outsiders

Political scientists also distinguish between different kinds of pressure group. For example, an important distinction has been drawn between *insider* and *outsider* groups (see Analysis 19.1). Insider groups work in close cooperation with their target audience (politicians and officials at the most appropriate level). They are accepted as members of **policy networks** (or **policy communities**), and are usually consulted during the preparation of any legislation which might affect them. The outsiders, by contrast, are only consulted by governments if and when this has become unavoidable. While they are excluded from the corridors of power they tend to favour tactics which will win them widespread media coverage.

A long series of discussions between outsider groups and their target organisations can result in a change in their status and behaviour. Over time, they may be accepted as new insider groups, and begin to place less emphasis on public campaigning since they now enjoy private access. The same development is likely to push some former insider groups into the cold. In turn, they can be expected to adopt more vigorous tactics in order to attract publicity and win back their former influence over policy (see Case study 19.3).

The debate on hunting with dogs is a good example of this process at work. Under the Conservative governments of Margaret Thatcher and John Major (1979–97) opposition to hunting was a guarantee of outsider status. Parts of the 1994 Criminal Justice Act were seen as attempts to criminalise even peaceful demonstrations in rural areas. In general, media coverage was unsympathetic to hunt saboteurs. But with the election of the Blair government in 1997 the tables were turned. The previously complacent hunting lobby felt threatened, and formed the Countryside Alliance to uphold what it saw as a key human right. Mass demonstrations in favour of hunting were held in London in 1999, 2002 and 2004. On the latter occasion a group of activists managed to get inside the chamber of the House of Commons before being apprehended. After the government invoked the Parliament Act 1949 to push the ban on hunting with dogs through the House of Lords in November 2004, the Home Secretary David Blunkett announced that the police would not be given extra resources to keep track of illegal hunting, because they could now use the money previously allocated to a crackdown on hunt saboteurs!

Policy networks: made up of ministers, officials and pressure groups which share an interest in a specific policy area. Non-governmental members of a policy network can expect to be consulted on a fairly regular basis, and such groups have 'insider' status.

Policy communities: some groups (e.g. some financial institutions in the City of London) are *always* consulted by governments when their interests are affected. Their relationship with government is so close that they are said to participate in a policy *community*, making it difficult for any other groups to have a meaningful influence.

Analysis: 19.1

Insider and outsider groups

Wyn Grant, a leading academic commentator on pressure groups, has identified sub-groups within the broad categories of insiders and outsiders – see his *Pressure Groups and British Politics* (London: Palgrave, 2000).

Among the insiders, Grant lists the following:

- High profile groups, which enjoy close contacts with the government but are also willing and able to reinforce their position by using the media.
- Low profile groups, which work behind the scenes and try not to advertise their influence.
- 'Prisoner' groups, which can sometimes be taken for granted by governments because they are dependent upon ministerial sympathy.

Grant's outsider sub-categories are:

- Potential insiders, dedicated to winning close contact with the government.
- Outsiders by necessity, excluded from the corridors of power because they lack the necessary importance or skills.
- Ideological outsiders, whose principles cannot be accommodated within the existing political system.

Case study: 19.3

Pressure group tactics

The tactics adopted by a pressure group depend heavily on circumstances. An 'insider' group, which is recognised as a member of a policy network, can operate quietly behind the scenes, attending official or informal meetings with officials and ministers. It will be kept informed of all relevant departmental decisions, and will be given the chance to influence legislation before it is introduced in parliament (or even before the proposal has taken shape). Often such groups will employ professional lobbyists whose sole business is to monitor and influence the thinking of top decision-makers.

'Outsider' groups, by contrast, must try to bring pressure to bear on ministers through activities such as demonstrations and boycotts, or by organising petitions. The recent tendency of groups to perform attention-grabbing stunts shows the perceived power of the media to influence public opinion and thus, indirectly, politicians. But it will also tend to alienate important decision-makers still further. Thus although groups can still move from 'outsider' to 'insider' status, there is a tendency for their initial position to be self-reinforcing. Outsiders will often feel compelled to behave in ways which make it difficult for politicians to speak to them even if they wanted to, while insiders will get to know the key people, thus consolidating their place in the policy network.

Ironically, although evidence had been produced which indicated that hunted animals suffer acute stress, the dramatic reversal of roles in this dispute owed little to new arguments or scientific findings. A party with a long history of opposition to hunting – some of it undoubtedly inspired by class considerations as well as real concern for animal welfare – had won a landslide electoral victory and felt that hunting was one controversial issue on which it could take radical action. Not every supporter of the ban was a Labour MP, and the party included a few passionate opponents of the measure; but the measure always enjoyed an overwhelming majority in the Commons as a whole. In all, MPs passed Bills outlawing hunting with dogs on ten separate occasions (the Lords rejected the measure every time; see Chapter 8). Nearly three hundred hours of parliamentary time were absorbed in these debates; but most of those hours were occupied by arguments which had been heard many times before. The outcome reflected a changed parliamentary situation which itself owed little or nothing to the issue of hunting. Thus the changing fortunes of pressure groups can often be influenced by circumstances beyond their control.

'Sectional' and 'cause' groups

Another helpful distinction can be made between groups which coalesce around some economic interest, and those that campaign for a principle which has no relevance to their material situation. The first of these are usually designated 'sectional' groups, although this label gives the misleading impression that such bodies invariably have a divisive effect on society. Although most 'cause' groups consist of well-meaning activists who just want to make the world a better place, some are quite capable of polarising opinion. The difference is that unlike the sectional groups they are not normally motivated by selfish considerations (although this view is contested by the New Right; see Analysis 19.2 and Chapter 16).

Since sectional groups are generally perceived to fight for their own material interests, wherever possible they try to convince the public that important principles are involved in their struggle. This makes the task of analysis more complicated in practice than the sectional/cause distinction might suggest on paper. It is difficult to

Analysis:	19.2

Pressure groups and the New Right

According to representatives of the New Right, who were prominent among the supporters of Margaret Thatcher, all human activity is self-interested. Thus there can be no distinction between 'sectional' and 'cause' groups. Even if they are not conscious of their real motivation, people who campaign for a moral cause are doing so because they derive some benefit from their activity, even if it is the psychological benefit of being recognised as a 'do-gooder'.

Many representatives of the New Right also deplored the practical effect of pressure groups. They argued that campaigning activity distracts government from the pursuit of the general interest, leading to misguided policy decisions and, all too often, the misuse of taxpayers' money.

Lovers of democracy, enemies of the fox. The Countryside Alliance
speaks out in defence of rural life (© DAN CHUNG/Reuters/Corbis)

categorise an organisation like the Countryside Alliance, whose members support
the freedom to hunt in principle, as well as upholding the economic interests of
people who are employed by hunting. But the Alliance has many unusual features;
it is one group which can probably expect more public support from its 'sectional'
case (avoiding rural unemployment) than its moral 'cause' (upholding the freedom
to do whatever one likes so long as no-one else suffers physical harm). On the other
hand, critics often point out that many successful 'cause' groups, like charities, have
developed 'sectional' interests, with their top personnel commanding high salaries
and seeking to extend their activities for the purposes of self-promotion. This view
has been fostered by the tendency of pressure groups – even 'outsiders' like the
Countryside Alliance – to employ people with grandiose business-style titles, like
Chief Executive. Equally, while many activists have opposed the construction of
new roads or airport developments as a matter of principle, others have betrayed the
so-called 'NIMBY' (Not In My Back Yard) syndrome, feeling far less strongly about
similar proposals which would affect other parts of the UK. These qualifications
mean that students of pressure group politics need to treat the distinction between

Case study:	19.4

Pressure groups, the EU and devolution

The establishment of devolved institutions in Scotland and Wales has provided pressure groups with important new opportunities. Despite the limitations on their powers, they still have the scope to satisfy many pressure group demands within those territories. In themselves, victories in these forums are heartening for pressure groups; but they can also set precedents for action elsewhere. Thus, for example, the Scottish Parliament took action against hunting and smoking before the UK parliament had done so; almost certainly the moves had some influence on the decision-making process at Westminster and Whitehall.

One advantage of the devolved institutions is that, since they are relatively new, they provide opportunities for groups which have been crowded out in London by longer-established 'insider' groups. Employing lobbyists at Edinburgh and Cardiff is therefore a shrewd investment for new groups. UK pressure groups have also been active at Brussels and Strasbourg for many years. This is not just because of the importance of EU law. The EU also actively encourages pressure groups, currently providing support for about a thousand organisations.

cause and sectional groups with some caution, and make informed judgements on the primary purpose of the organisations under review.

One important difference between sectional and cause groups is that the former usually have a specific catchment area from which they can hope to draw support. In other words, they will be able to target their recruitment efforts at people who share the same economic interest (e.g. trade unions can appeal to workers who do similar jobs). The membership of cause groups, by contrast, is usually subject to no such limits. This means that such groups will have to devote much more energy to the task of tracking down potential sympathisers. On the other hand, certain sectional groups have the chance of exerting very serious pressure on a government by virtue of their role in society. For example, in January 2008 more than 20,000 police officers marched through central London in support of a pay claim. Although the government made no immediate concessions, they had to treat this demonstration with far more respect than they would have accorded to a much larger gathering of people who were marching in support of a moral cause. At the same time, complaints from the armed forces about inadequate equipment and medical care arising from the 'war on terror' met with rapid and positive responses from the government.

Some cause groups, of course, are very successful with recruitment. The Royal Society for the Protection of Birds (RSPB) has more than a million members, while the Royal Society for the Prevention of Cruelty to Animals (RSPCA) has attracted around 550,000 activists organised in almost 200 local branches, and can afford to employ 1500 staff. And the difficulty of mobilisation does affect larger sectional groups, like pensioners. Campaigners trying to energise such groups face the problem of the 'free rider' – someone who expects to derive material advantage from a policy change, but abstains from any activity on the assumption that others will make the necessary effort. The difficulty of mobilising large sectional groups sometimes lures a complacent government into disastrous decisions. Thus, for example, ministers were taken by surprise by the furious response to the poll tax after its implementation in 1990, and in 2000 New Labour had to scrap plans for an increase in fuel taxes in the face of mass protests among those, like long-distance lorry drivers, who were most directly affected.

Other distinctions can be drawn in the increasingly crowded cast of pressure groups. Some, like the environmental groups Greenpeace and Friends of the Earth, are transnational in the scope of their activities. Others are strictly local, like the groups that spring up to protest against the construction of a new road or the closure of hospitals and post offices. However, new forms of communication make it easy for such small organisations to liaise with larger, more experienced campaigning groups. The Internet is an obvious channel of communication, and played an important role in the world-wide protests against the war against Iraq in 2003. But cheap air travel also makes it possible even for groups with limited resources to share information face-to-face. For example, in September 1998 environmental campaigners from Sweden, Poland, France and Germany attended a training camp in Staffordshire to learn such skills as tunnelling and tree-house building. The UK animal rights movement is respected by similar groups across the world, and is very happy to give advice to advance the worldwide cause.

'Peak' organisations and neo-corporatism

Sectional groups in the UK were most prominent in the two decades after 1960. During that period, both Conservative and Labour governments consulted closely with representatives from both sides of industry – the employers, chiefly organised in the Confederation of British Industry (CBI, formerly known as the Federation of British Industry) and employees whose trade unions are affiliated to the Trade Union Congress (TUC). Such bodies are described as 'peak' (or 'umbrella') organisations, because they represent a number of groups linked by a similar interest.

Corporatism: a system in which representatives of employers and trade unions are formally incorporated within the policy-making process.

Neo-corporatism: a system in which the government seeks to facilitate agreements between trade unions and employers.

This close government cooperation with key peak organisations is a variety of **corporatism** (see Chapter 3). In its pure form, corporatism is a method of decision-making which overrides democratic institutions, and is associated with the Italian fascist regime of Benito Mussolini. In the UK, the system never came close to that totalitarian state, and is probably best described as 'liberal corporatism' or **neo-corporatism**. Under this arrangement the elected government's role is to act as an 'honest broker' in the national interest, facilitating agreements between trade unions and employers. The key assumption is that decisions are most likely to be accepted by both sides of industry if they are taken in consultation with senior representatives of the most prominent 'peak' organisations.

The key landmark in the history of British corporatism was the formation of the National Economic Development Council (NEDC, or 'NEDDY') by the Conservative government of Harold Macmillan in July 1961. The NEDC provided a forum for regular discussions between the government, the FBI (later the CBI) and the TUC. However, the arrangement never lived up to original hopes, and had broken down by the early 1970s even though NEDDY survived for two more decades. The usual explanation for the failure of neo-corporatism in the UK is that the trade unions became too powerful. After repeated and unsuccessful attempts at reform, successive governments felt compelled to appease the unions, with the result that the British economy came close to collapse. Another explanation is that the 'peak' organisations on both sides were unable to deliver, despite good intentions, because they were unable to command the obedience of their members. Thus, while the TUC as a whole was usually ready to compromise, individual trade unions continued to prioritise the economic interests of their members rather than national goals. Equally, while larger companies within the CBI usually avoided confrontation with the unions for the sake of an easy life, smaller businesses proved more willing to break off negotiations and take the risk of provoking strike action.

The end of corporatism

By the mid-1970s many commentators were worried that the UK was becoming 'ungovernable' (see Chapter 3), largely because of the demands of various sectional groups who were powerful or persuasive enough to win concessions from the government. When Margaret Thatcher came to office in 1979 she was determined to avoid this predicament. She did not abolish the NEDC – that decision was left for her successor John Major – but in opposition she showed no inclination to talk with the TUC, and before the end of her first term in Downing Street she had provoked a public clash with the CBI.

Although she had no love for employers' organisations, Thatcher was on close terms with many influential business figures, and was determined above all to curb the power of the trade unions. Almost every year of her premiership featured a new piece of restrictive legislation. But a more potent weapon was the government's economic policy, which accelerated the decline of the manufacturing industries that were most heavily unionised. In 1979 there were more than 12 million workers affiliated to the TUC; by the time of Thatcher's departure the figure was down to about 8.5 million. However, while it was losing members the trade union movement actually won back much of its old popularity with the general public. But there was no immediate prospect that trade unionists would recover the influence they had enjoyed in their heyday, when their leaders seemed to be at least as powerful as elected politicians.

While Thatcher's critics claim that her attitude towards the trade unions was vindictive and driven by partisan considerations, she proved more than willing to pick squabbles with 'establishment' bodies like the British Medical Association (BMA) and the Bar Council (which managed to fight off most of her proposed reforms of the legal profession: see Chapter 9). Even the Police Federation – previously regarded as an archetypal 'insider group' – was occasionally restive, despite the allegation by left-wing activists that the police had become no more than 'Maggie Thatcher's boot-boys' in return for their favourable treatment in wage negotiations. It was not surprising that by 2008 many police had begun to campaign for the right to take industrial action.

New social movements

Whatever the fate of the neo-corporatist bodies which formerly wielded so much influence, a reasonable case can be made for depicting Thatcher as the inadvertent friend of the pressure group. Many existing bodies were re-activated by the perceived need to oppose her reforms directly, since the electoral process was unable to dislodge her; and others owed their foundation to the impetus of Thatcherite policies. For example, Stonewall was set up to campaign for homosexual rights in the wake of the controversial Clause 28 of the Local Government Act 1988, and the Anti-Poll Tax Federation was created by the Community Charge which became law in the same year. But even before Thatcher's attack on long-established organisations, it was possible to identify a change in the nature of pressure groups and the style of campaigning. Commentators now refer to 'new social movements', which can be distinguished from traditional pressure groups because:

- Their membership tends to be diverse, cutting across old class boundaries.
- They have broad ideological objectives rather than focusing on specific issues.
- Their immediate aim is to win publicity and to bring pressure to bear on decision-makers through the media, rather than engaging in discreet lobbying.
- They build coalitions of different groups with broadly similar objectives, often coming together for single campaigns then diverging without establishing a settled hierarchical structure, or even a formal system of membership.

The first new social movement in the UK is usually taken to be the Campaign for Nuclear Disarmament (CND, founded in 1958). CND tended to attract young, middle-class supporters, who marched every year from the nuclear weapons research facility at Aldermaston, Berkshire, to rallies in London's Trafalgar Square. At that time, CND was widely regarded as a 'subversive' organisation whose activities threatened to leave the West defenceless against the Soviet Union. But in 1960 the Labour Party conference passed a motion endorsing CND's aims, against the fierce opposition of the party leadership. This decision was subsequently reversed, but a similar motion was passed in 1981 and Labour fought the next two elections on an anti-nuclear defence policy.

CND's concern for the future of the planet and its varied inhabitants was shared by members of environmental groups which sprang up in the 1970s, such as Friends of the Earth (1970), Greenpeace (1973), and the Animal Liberation Front (1976). These organisations were far more radical than older groups concerned with the environment, such as the National Trust (1895), the Campaign for the Protection of Rural England (1926), and the League Against Cruel Sports (1926). However, over time the older bodies were themselves influenced to some extent by the new climate of activism; the National Trust, for example, had a long-running and bitter debate in the 1990s about allowing hunting on its land.

Other new groups which arose at this time were inspired by the American civil rights movement of the 1960s. In the second half of that decade the UK's Labour government implemented a series of measures designed to help women, homosexuals and ethnic minorities. The success of these campaigns owed much to the sympathetic stance of Roy Jenkins (Home Secretary from 1965–67). The 1970s saw further legislation, like the Equal Pay Act 1970 and Sex Discrimination Act 1975, which improved working conditions for women, and the Race Relations Act 1976 which tightened previous legislation on racial discrimination. Other groups were founded to campaign on behalf of the poor and the disabled.

SHAC and Huntingdon Life Sciences

On 11 September 2004 around 300 people held an anniversary march in Stamford, Lincolnshire. However, they were not remembering the terrorist attack in New York three years earlier. Rather, they were celebrating the fifth anniversary of a successful mission to release several hundred guinea pigs which had been bred for animal testing.

The demonstrators supported a long-running campaign to close down Huntingdon Life Sciences (HLS), branded by its critics as 'Europe's leading vivisectionist'. The campaign, which began after a Channel 4 documentary in 1997, has made national headlines and inspired the creation of a new police group, the National Extremist Tactical Co-ordination Unit (NETCU). Apart from more orthodox tactics like peaceful marches, workers at HLS have suffered intimidation, and the SHAC campaign has also affected HLS's financial backers and customers in the pharmaceutical industry. Special measures were taken to protect the anonymity of investors, and the government promised financial support. In 2003 HLS took out an injunction against nine named individuals, together with SHAC, London Animal Action and the Animal Liberation Front. It was claimed that less than 50 agitators were endangering the whole of Britain's pharmaceutical industry, worth billions of pounds.

In October 2004 protestors against animal testing dug up the grave of a woman whose relatives bred animals for research. Despite the resulting media outcry, and new legislation designed specifically to curtail its activities, SHAC remains committed to the closure of HLS, and the government clearly regards the case as a trial of strength from which it cannot back down. Sections of the media have given outspoken support to HLS, and it can be argued that far from advancing the cause of animal welfare SHAC's shock tactics have prevented it from winning a fair hearing.

In recent years pressure groups have continued to proliferate and to form alliances of varying duration. In 1991, 250 groups opposing the government's road-building programme were brought together under a loose umbrella organisation, Alarm UK. A similar coalition – 'Plane Stupid' – has coalesced to oppose the expansion of Britain's airports, alongside bodies with more specific objectives like No Third Runway Action Group (NTRAG) which hoped to prevent expansion at Heathrow. UK groups participated in anti-globalisation demonstrations, notably at Quebec and Seattle in 1999, and before the G8 meeting at Gleneagles, Scotland, in 2005. In another relatively new development, although these campaigners do target politicians they acknowledge that governments are increasingly powerless to restrain vast multinational firms. Thus they also direct their activities against giant companies like McDonald's, Esso and Coca-Cola. As well as demonstrating, they try to mobilise the power of the consumer through boycotts.

Until quite recently it was possible to advance persuasive general explanations for the emergence of new social movements. Increasing affluence is usually identified as a factor. The prominence of middle-class activists in the ranks of environmental campaigners, for example, suggests the rise of a 'post-materialist' consciousness among people who enjoy the necessary leisure-time for activism. Such campaigners are likely to be well-educated, and to note with indignation the persistence of anomalous discrimination against women, ethnic minorities and others. The drive to extend rights from humans to animals can partly be explained from the same perspective, since technological change means that animals are no longer essential suppliers of transport and labour-power in industry. Meanwhile, people who give up eating meat on principle can now choose from a wide range of meat-flavoured vegetable products.

On this view, prosperity has generated many of its own critics, who are well-motivated and resourceful enough to use the mass media (which is, of course, another product of the modernity they reject). These activists are difficult to equate with any of the traditional ideologies, and their prominence in pressure groups suggests a degree of disillusionment with the main UK political parties among people who could be expected to channel their energies and ideals through the more traditional institutions if UK democracy was in a vibrant condition.

There is usually an assumption that the members of such movements are 'progressive' or left-wing in the old ideological terminology. However, since the election of the Labour government in 1997 the best-publicised pressure groups have come from a different mould. Hunters, motorists and fathers separated from their children have all used tactics typical of the new social movements, trying to win media publicity with spectacular campaigns which are often planned and coordinated by means of new technology like the Internet and mobile telephones (see also Case study 19.3). Yet all three causes can be said to be reactions *against* the success of new social movements. The pro-hunting lobby has been mobilised by the prospect that animal welfare groups would finally get their way. In 2000 motorists took direct action to oppose fuel taxes which had been advocated by environmentalists. And the pressure group Fathers 4 Justice, which demonstrated inside the House of Commons, at Buckingham Palace and at other famous public buildings including the Big Ben clock tower, could be seen as an indirect product of the feminist movement since its members protested against the alleged tendency of the courts to give the benefit of any doubt to female parents in disputed custody cases.

Clearly the era of new social movements is far from over; people will continue to join together in campaigns for enhanced rights, a safer environment, and

Fathers 4 Justice scale Big Ben in protest stunt, September 2005 (© Bruno Vincent/ Getty Images)

global justice. But while these movements tend to demand positive action from governments, another trend has emerged of campaigning *against* actions which governments have already taken (or are threatening to take). These activists can take heart from the success of the Anti-Poll Tax Federation, which managed not only to secure the abolition of the poll tax but also contributed to the departure of Prime Minister Margaret Thatcher (see also Case study 19.5). While this example lends encouragement to protestors, governments seem more capable of provoking them by taking legislative action in areas, like hunting, which have traditionally been seen as essentially private concerns. And this is not the only source of provocation. The million-strong march in protest against the prospect of war on Iraq in 2003 represented only a small proportion of the widespread opposition to Tony Blair's foreign policy. It encompassed a cornucopia of pressure groups, large and minuscule, many of which had been formed with the specific purpose of opposing UK involvement in the conflict.

Pressure groups and democracy

Positive assessments of pressure group activity usually arise from a pluralist perspective (see Chapter 1). That is, it is assumed that an extensive array of such groups, covering a wide variety of subjects, is a sign of a healthy liberal democracy with an active citizen body. Free competition among such groups is likely to promote good government, because campaigners on all sides of a question can be expected to present evidence in support of their favourite cause. With guaranteed access to a free press, they have reason to hope that the most rational case will win the argument and be reflected in government decisions. Some groups are even set up explicitly to demand a greater role in decision-making for the public as a whole; for example, the 'I Want A Referendum' campaign was established in an attempt to force the government to consult the people on further European integration.

From the pluralist viewpoint, the recent decline of the old sectional pressure groups is a welcome development. While pluralists acknowledge that unions and businesses are important interests in British society, they tended to monopolise government attention, and the voice of the consumer was often neglected in the 1960s and 1970s. The relative decline of these powerful organisations leaves an opening for other groups (like the Consumers' Association, which struggled to make headway when it was founded in 1957, but now commands widespread respect through its magazine *Which?*).

But a more pessimistic view of recent developments is also possible. From the perspective of the New Right (see Analysis 19.2), any increase in pressure group activity is deplorable in itself. Even those who reject the ideological view that pressure group activity only results in increased demands on public expenditure can have similar grounds for questioning the benefits of competition between interested parties. In its most familiar form the pluralist case assumes that there will be something like a level playing field for the competing groups, which ensures that rational decision-makers will tend to accept the most persuasive argument. However, during the 1990s a series of scandals revealed the extent to which privileged access to politicians could be bought, regardless of the quality of the case they were hired to present, or the extent to which it enjoyed public support. Apart from rare cases of direct bribery, well-financed organisations could hire the most skilful and eloquent lobbyists, some of whom obviously gave a higher priority to pleasing their clients than to the cause of good government. This approach would

Case study:	19.5

Recent pressure group successes

Nowadays there are so many pressure groups, many of which oppose each other, that it is rarely possible to say whether their arguments have proved decisive. One should also keep in mind pressure group failures. For example, the Keep Sunday Special campaign could not prevent legislation to allow the extension of Sunday shopping; and despite the popularity of CND, American cruise missiles were sited in British bases in the early 1980s. The Stop the War coalition, which claimed that over a million supporters had marched through London in February 2003, failed to change Tony Blair's policy towards Iraq. The Countryside Alliance also had to accept an end to hunting, at least in its open, traditional form.

However, there are many instances where the work of one or more pressure group has undoubtedly made a difference:

- 1989. The South African government released Nelson Mandela and lifted restrictions on parties opposed to the apartheid system, at least in part because of worldwide boycotts of firms which traded with South Africa. Mandela himself has thanked the people of Britain for their part in bringing down apartheid. Evidently Mandela thought that the pressure groups were more representative of Britain as a whole than their elected prime minister, Margaret Thatcher, who tried hard to prevent effective sanctions against South Africa.

- 1995. Greenpeace protested against Shell's decision to dispose of an oil platform, the Brent Spar, at sea. Despite strong backing from the UK government, Shell capitulated in the face of a Europe-wide boycott.

- 1996. The 'Snowdrop' campaign was formed to press for a ban on privately-owned handguns after the massacre of children and teachers at Dunblane, Scotland, in March 1996. Despite furious protests from the shooting lobby, a total ban on private ownership of handguns was introduced in 1997. Ironically, in the next two years the use of handguns in criminal activities actually increased by more than a third.

- 2000. The government withdrew proposed increases in fuel tax in the wake of mass countrywide protests.

- 2005. The celebrity chef, Jamie Oliver, forced the government to rethink its policy on school meals. While this could be regarded as a success for a one-man pressure group, other bodies had been campaigning for some time on this issue.

- In recent years, environmental groups like Greenpeace have disrupted and delayed the Labour government's plans to permit commercial exploitation of genetically modified (GM) crops. Their stance has a 'celebrity supporter' in the Prince of Wales.

- Senior members of the armed forces (currently serving or retired) have successfully lobbied for improved equipment during the 'war on terror'. If necessary, they have not hesitated to speak out publicly, even when their publicised views seemed critical of the government's foreign policy.

come naturally to 'sectional' groups, which are themselves primarily concerned with the material interests of their members. However, the lasting legacy of lobbying activity in this period was greater public disillusionment with the political system, despite the conclusions of the Nolan Committee (see Chapter 8) which promised tighter regulation of the links between decision-makers and extra-parliamentary organisations.

For pluralists, it can only be an additional cause for concern that the recent growth of pressure group activity has coincided with a fall in more orthodox forms of democratic participation. In their view, government has a crucial part to play in mediating between the different groups; and, ideally, the government at any time should represent a large proportion (if not an overall majority) of the public. However, with electoral turnout falling, political parties can win decisive parliamentary majorities with the support of a relatively modest proportion of the UK electorate. It would be highly dangerous to assume that the low turnout in recent general elections reflects widespread contentment among the public as a whole. The continued popularity of new social movements suggests an increasing number of people who hold beliefs which cannot be accommodated by the main political parties. The marked tendency for movements to spring up in determined opposition to government policies is an indication that discontent is spreading far beyond habitual malcontents who refuse to see anything good in the modern world.

The main worry about the rise of pressure groups is that relatively small, highly-motivated organisations can exercise an influence on government decisions far in excess of their public support. Given the new prominence of pressure groups, it is also pertinent to ask whether their own internal procedures satisfy democratic criteria. In the 1980s Conservative governments criticised trade unions because their leaders were not truly accountable to members; for example, officials like Arthur Scargill, the controversial President of the National Union of Mineworkers (NUM), were elected for life. Legislation was introduced to rectify this situation, and also to force unions to ballot their members before they made financial contributions to the Labour Party. However, the Conservatives seemed less troubled by the extent to which quite secretive business organisations, like Aims of Industry, channelled funds into their own party.

Questions about the democratic credentials of pressure groups extend beyond the most familiar sectional groups. Some organisations, like CND, have actively encouraged the autonomy of local groups rather than trying to coordinate their campaigning from the centre. However, the 'iron law of oligarchy' (see Chapter 15) suggests that there is a tendency for all organisations to fall under the direction of an 'elite' leadership group as they grow larger. This problem is accentuated in the contemporary context, as media outlets try to identify specific individuals who are capable of speaking on behalf of organised groups. Equally, the need to avoid negative publicity provides an incentive to impose discipline on the membership, to the extent of expelling activists who do not toe the 'official' line.

The new dilemmas facing pressure groups in the media age were neatly illustrated in January 2006, when Fathers 4 Justice revealed that they had expelled several members who wanted to take the group's headline-grabbing stunts even further. It was reported that some members had even considered kidnapping Tony Blair's five-year-old son. Such activities are hardly compatible with the healthy democratic activities favoured by pluralists. Fathers 4 Justice recognised this by announcing that it would disband in the wake of the controversy, although it re-formed in the following year and its activities were soon winning renewed media coverage. This example is further evidence that the relationship between pressure groups and democracy is far more complex than many pluralists assume.

Conclusion and summary

The rise in pressure group activity, and the increasing demand for referendums on a variety of subjects, constitute a serious challenge to representative democracy as it has been understood in the UK. Recent developments draw attention to the fact that the current system of representation is a means to an end, not an end in itself. No political system can provide satisfactory outcomes for everyone; but unless representative democracy satisfies a significant majority of the people most of the time, its legitimacy will be called into question.

However, those looking for alternative methods in the referendum and the pressure group are confronted with obvious difficulties. Despite recent technological advances, the referendum is still at best a very cumbersome device. It is also possible to envisage circumstances in which, far from providing authoritative decisions on emotive issues, closely-fought referendums could actually reinforce and inflame existing divisions within society.

Pluralists argue that government can act as an impartial arbiter between competing pressure groups. This idea is more persuasive as a theory than as a guide to actual practice; no government can be wholly impartial. But this does not mean that things would be any better if the existing system of representative democracy was replaced by a parliament of pressure groups. The ideas of such groups often conflict in a way which leaves no room for compromise. Furthermore, pressure groups themselves are not invariably democratic organisations which allow their members a realistic chance of meaningful participation.

Further reading

A useful brief introduction to referendums is E. Magee and D. Outhwaite, 'Referendums and Initiatives', *Politics Review*, Vol. 10, No. 3 (2001), pp. 26–8. I. Horrocks and D. Wring raise questions about technology and participation in 'The Myth of E-thenian Democracy', *Politics Review*, Vol. 10, No. 4 (2001), pp. 31–2. It is still worth consulting D. Butler and U. Kitzinger, *The 1975 Referendum* (London: Macmillan, 1976), which provides a comprehensive and incisive account of the issues involved in the first (and so far, only) UK-wide referendum. M. Qvortrup, *A Comparative Study of Referendums: Government by the People* (Manchester: Manchester University Press, 2nd edition, 2005) compares the UK experience with that of other liberal democracies.

On pressure groups, see W. Grant, *Pressure Groups and British Politics* (London: Palgrave, 2000), and the same author's 'Pressure Politics: The Challenges for Democracy', *Parliamentary Affairs*, Vol. 56, No. 2 (2003), pp. 297–308. B. Coxall's *Pressure Groups in British Politics* (Harlow: Pearson, 2001) is concise and accessible. Although its findings are slightly dated, R. Baggott's *Pressure Groups Today* (Manchester: Manchester University Press, 1995) is still well worth reading. On new social movements, see P. Byrne, *Social Movements in Britain* (London: Routledge, 1997) and, on environmentalism, R. Garner, *Environmental Politics* (London: Palgrave, 2nd edition, 2000). Two special issues of the journal *Parliamentary Affairs* are highly recommended: Vol. 56, No. 4 (2003) focuses on participation and includes articles on pressure groups and protest politics; Vol. 51, No. 3 (1998) looks at new social movements. The Electoral Commission has issued a number of detailed reports on political participation in Britain. The most useful are the regular surveys, *An Audit of Political Engagement* (London: Electoral Commission, 2004, 2005, 2006 and 2008).

Websites

On referendums, see the Electoral Commission website www.electoralcommission.org.uk.

There is a wealth of pressure group material on the Internet. This is only a sample list:

British Medical Association www.bma.org.uk

Campaign for Nuclear Disarmament www.cnduk.org

Child Poverty Action Group www.cpag.org.uk/

Confederation of British Industry www.cbi.org.uk

Countryside Alliance www.countryside-alliance.org

Direct Democracy Campaign www.homeusers.prestel.co.uk/rodmell/index.htm

Fathers4Justice www.fathers-4-justice.org

Friends of the Earth www.foe.co.uk

Greenpeace www.greenpeace.org

I Want a Referendum: Iwantareferedum.com

League Against Cruel Sports www.league.uk.com

National Trust www.nationaltrust.org.uk

Plane Stupid: planestupid.com

Royal Society for the Prevention of Cruelty to Animals www.rspca.org.uk

Royal Society for the Protection of Birds www.rspb.org.uk

Stop Huntingdon Animal Cruelty www.shac.net

Topic 6:
Media

The mass media and political communication

Bill Jones

Learning objectives

- To explain the workings of the media: press and broadcasting.

- To encourage an understanding of how the media interact and influence voting, elections and the rest of the political system.

- To discuss how the pluralist and Marxist dominance theories help to explain how the media operate and influence society.

Introduction

Without newspapers, radio and pre-eminently television, the present political system could not work. The media are so all-pervasive that we are often unaware of the addictive hold they exert over our attentions and the messages they implant in our consciousness on a whole range of matters, including politics. This chapter assesses the impact of the mass media upon the workings of our political system, and some different theories about how they operate in practice.

■ The mass media

The term 'mass media' embraces books, pamphlets and film but is usually understood to refer to newspapers, radio and television. This is not to say that films, theatre, art and books are not important, but perhaps the influence of literature is usually less instant and more long-term. Since the 1950s, television has eclipsed newspapers and radio as the key medium. Surveys indicate that three-quarters of people identify television as the most important single source of information about politics. On average British people now watch over twenty hours of television per week, and given that 20 per cent of television output covers news and current affairs, a fair political content is being imbibed. Indeed, the audience for the evening news bulletins regularly exceeds 20 million. Surveys also regularly show that over 70 per cent of viewers trust television news as fair and accurate, while only one-third trust newspapers.

From the spoken to the written word

Television is now such a dominant medium that it is easy to forget that its provenance has been so recent. During the seventeenth and early eighteenth centuries, political communication was mainly verbal: between members of the relatively small political élite; within a broader public at election times; within political groups such as the seventeenth-century Diggers and Levellers; and occasionally from the pulpit. Given their expense and scarcity at the time, books, pamphlets and **broadsheets** had a limited, although important, role to play; they played a role during the Civil War (1640–49) and at the end of the eighteenth century pamphlets were very important in disseminating radical ideas.

The Industrial Revolution drew workers in from the land into crowded urban spaces where they arguably enjoyed a higher standard of living but were scarcely so contented they were not receptive to reformers and travelling speakers, like Orator Hunt, who delivered inspiring speeches in London and elsewhere including Peter's Fields in Manchester in August 1819, where the crowd was charged by mounted troops in the 'Peterloo Massacre'. The Chartists pursuing similar objectives attracted big audiences and also, like the Anti-Corn Law League, disseminated pamphlets via the new postal system.

Next came the inception of mass circulation newspapers – *The Times, Telegraph, Mail, Express* and *Mirror* – which provided information on current affairs for the newly enfranchised masses. The **Press Barons** – Northcliffe, Beaverbrook and Rothermere – became courted by politicians for the influence they were believed to wield; in consequence they were showered with honours and often given government jobs to further enhance their invariably enormous egos. Table 8.1 provides recent circulation figures for the national dailies.

By tradition the British press has been pro-Conservative. In 1945, the 6.7 million readers of Conservative-supporting papers outnumbered the 4.4 million who read Labour papers. During the 1970s, the tabloid *Sun* increased the imbalance to the right, and by the 1992 election the Labour-supporting press numbered only the *Guardian* and the *Daily Mirror*, with the vast majority of dailies and Sundays supporting the government party: 9.7 million to 3.3 million. However, Major's administration witnessed an astonishing shift of allegiance. It had been anticipated by press irritation with Thatcher's imperious style, continued with the criticism that Major received for being allegedly weak as a leader and insufficiently robust in relation to European issues, and intensified after the disastrous Black Wednesday, 16 September 1992, when Britain was forced out of the Exchange Rate Mechanism.

Table 8.1 Circulation of national dailies, September 2008

	September 2008	September 2007	% change	August 2008	September 2008 (without bulks)	April – September 2008	% change on last year
Sun	3,154,998	3,213,756	−1.83	3,148,792	3,154,998	3,133,776	0.68
Daily Mirror	1,440,651	1,584,742	−9.09	1,455,270	1,440,651	1,461,729	−6.61
Daily Star	731,433	803,726	−8.99	751,494	731,433	735,048	−7.92
Daily Record	380,849	412,332	−7.64	390,197	378,772	389,720	−4.43
Daily Mail	2,241,788	2,365,499	−5.23	2,258,843	2,123,186	2,267,502	−2.88
Daily Express	739,025	814,921	−9.31	748,664	739,025	738,924	−6.42
Daily Telegraph	851,254	890,973	−4.46	860,298	751,971	861,341	−3.43
The Times	638,033	654,482	−2.51	612,779	584,391	620,073	−2.91
Financial Times	429,381	441,219	−2.68	417,570	387,488	435,864	−1.10
The Guardian	348,878	367,546	−5.08	332,587	333,955	345,362	−5.27

Source: Guardian, 10 October 2008

Labour remained defiant despite the withdrawal of support from the *Sun* in the Labour Party Conference in 2009. The *Sun*'s backing of Labour was influential in their landslide victory in 1997
Sources: (Gordon Brown) Getty Images / AFP; (Tony Blair) *Sun* front cover, 30 September 2009, Carl De Souza / AFP,
© News Group Newspapers Ltd

Stalwart Tory press supporters such as the *Mail*, *Times* and *Telegraph* aimed their critical shafts at the government and did not desist even after July 1995 when Major challenged his opponents to stand against him as party leader and won a none-too-convincing victory. In addition to these factors Labour had become **New Labour**, led by the charismatic Tony Blair and shorn of its unpopular policies on unions, taxes and high spending. As the election was announced the *Sun* caused a sensation by

Rupert Murdoch (1931–)

Australian media magnate. Educated at Oxford, where briefly a Marxist. Learned newspaper business in Australia but soon acquired papers in Britain, most famously the *Sun*, the *News of the World*, *The Times* and the *Sunday Times*. His company News International also owns Sky TV, and he owns broadcasting outlets all over the world, including China. Blair and Murdoch seem to get on well and he regularly calls to see the man he helped to elect in 1997. Even during the war in Iraq the *Sun* remained solidly behind Blair.

emphatically backing Blair. Its Murdoch-owned stable-mate, the Sunday *News of the World*, followed suit later in the campaign. It should be noted that by this time a large proportion of the reading public had decided to change sides, and it could be argued that editors were merely making a commercial judgement in changing sides too (see Table 8.2 showing change of allegiances in the 2001 and 2005 general elections).

Table 8.2 Readership allegiances (%) of national daily newspapers, 2005 and (in brackets) 2001

	Labour	Con.	Lib Dem	Swing[a]
Guardian	43 (52)	7 (6)	41 (34)	8 (LD)
Independent	34 (38)	13 (12)	44 (44)	2 (LD)
Times	27 (28)	38 (40)	28 (26)	1.5 (LD)
Telegraph	13 (16)	65 (64)	17 (14)	2 (C)
Financial Times	29 (30)	47 (48)	21 (21)	–
Daily Express	28 (33)	48 (43)	18 (19)	5 (C)
Daily Mail	22 (24)	57 (55)	14 (17)	2 (C)
Sun	45 (52)	33 (29)	12 (11)	5.5 (C)
Mirror	67 (71)	11 (11)	17 (13)	4 (LD)
Star	54 (56)	21 (21)	15 (17)	1 (C)
Election result	36 (42)	33 (33)	23 (19)	3.1 (C)

[a] Percentage swings from Labour to (C) Conservatives, or (LD) Liberal Democrats.
Source: Wring and Deacon (2005)

Quality press and the tabloids

'All the instincts of the working class are Tory: on race, patriotism, you name it. It's just that they happen to vote Labour. Murdoch understands that which is why the Sun *has been so successful'*
(Lord) Bernard Donoughue, quoted in Chris Mullin (2009), *A View from the Foothills*, pp. 397–8

Anyone can see the UK press has 'quality' newspapers like *The Times*, *Telegraph*, *Guardian*, *Financial Times*, *Independent*, with their Sunday extensions, the 'mid-tabloids' like the *Mail* and *Express* and the tabloids like the *Sun*, *Mirror* and *Star*. Each type of product is aimed at and caters for a particular demographic: educated middle class, lower middle class and working class respectively.

Sunday paper sales declined from 17 million to 15 million in the period 1990–8, while dailies declined from 15 million to 13 million. Tabloids, less likely to attract loyal readerships, have tried every possible trick to win readers, from 'bimbos to bingo'. Marketing expert Winston Fletcher, writing in the *Guardian* (30 January 1998), pinpointed the formula, deplored by liberal opinion and politicians alike, that won readers: 'Publishers and editors know what is selling their newspapers with greater precision than ever before. And the figures show it is scandals, misfortunes and disasters.' In other words, 'sleaze sells'. Given the razor-sharp competition for audience share, it is surely regrettable but not so surprising that tabloids seize on scandalous stories like hungry dogs on bones. John Major's travails with sleaze stories have been well documented and helped to bring the Conservatives' eighteen years in power to an end in 1997. But Labour has been by no means immune either to sleaze or to the intrusive style of tabloid reporting which politicians and liberal-inclined opinion deplore but which is eagerly consumed. The foremost victim in recent years was David Blunkett, the remarkable blind Home Secretary who fell in love with a right-wing publisher, Kimberley Quinn, and who then discovered every detail of his relationship being read by the nation over its cornflakes for a number of weeks until evidence of undue favour having been shown to his mistress caused his downfall. After a period of 'purdah' he was brought back into the Cabinet in 2005 only to perish by tabloid once again when his business activities appeared to be in breach of the ministerial code. It is not strictly true to attribute this form of persecution to the tabloids alone; while they often start the process, the quality press watch

Reporters stand by during a typical media frenzy
Source: Rex Features / Nils Jorgensen

closely and join in the feeding frenzy as soon as they think it suitable and advantageous to sales.

But there is more to tabloids than lightweight stories; they sell by the million, and even if a vote is bought through blackening a politician's name, it counts as much as any other on election day. Media experts working for parties read the tabloids very carefully and react accordingly. In elections going back to the 1980s a close correlation was noted between issues run by the Conservatives and lead stories in the tabloids; it was known that certain tabloid editors had close links with Conservative Central Office. Tony Blair had long been convinced of the political importance of the tabloids. In 1997, he even wrote a piece pandering to their Euroscepticism explaining why he had a 'love' for the pound. On May Day 2001, the *Sun* championed the case of a Norfolk farmer who had been imprisoned for shooting an intruder in his house. To counter it Blair personally wrote a 975-word rebuttal during a weekend at Chequers. The *Sun* concluded from this evidence of Blair's respect for the tabloids that he was 'rattled'.

Broadcasting

Hitler, Baldwin and Roosevelt exploited the radio successfully during the interwar years and during the war, Churchill's use of the radio must have been worth quite a few divisions to the war effort so inspiring did it prove. Some politicians, surprisingly including Neville Chamberlain, were adept speaking to the cameras of Pathe News; others, equally surprisingly, like Oswald Mosley, were not. During the war, films like *In Which We Serve*, starring Noel Coward, were effective vehicles for wartime propaganda. Broadcasts of the fledgling television service were stopped during the war and were slow to restart; not so in the USA where television was quickly recruited for political service. None more so than in 1952 when Richard Nixon bought 30 minutes of airtime to clear his name of financial impropriety with his famous 'Checkers' broadcast.

Offering himself as a hard-working honest person of humble origins, he finished his talk by telling viewers how his daughter had received a puppy as a present: he did not care what 'they say about it, we're gonna keep it!' (see quotation below). This blatant appeal to sentiment proved spectacularly successful and confirmed Nixon's vice-presidential place on the Eisenhower ticket. Later on, television ironically contributed to Nixon's undoing through the famous televised debates with Kennedy during the 1960 presidential election contest. Despite an assured verbal performance – those listening on the radio thought he had bested Kennedy – Nixon, the favourite, looked shifty with his five o'clock shadow and crumpled appearance. Kennedy's good looks and strong profile gave him a clear edge. Politicians the world over looked, listened and learned that how you appear on television counts for as much as what you say (see below on 'Television and the image').

Richard Nixon – the 'Checkers' speech

I should say this: Pat doesn't have a mink coat, but she does have a respectable Republican cloth coat. One other thing I should probably tell you, because if I don't they'll be saying this about me too. We did get something, a gift, after the election . . . a little cocker spaniel in a crate all the way from Texas . . . And our little girl, Trisha, the six-year-old, named it Checkers. And you know, the kids love that dog, and I just want to say this right now, that regardless of what they say about it, we're gonna keep it!

Richard Nixon, US Vice-President, in the 'Checkers speech' (cited in Green, 1982)

What they say about the papers

The gallery where the reporters sit has become the fourth estate of the realm.

Lord Macaulay 1828

As a journalist who became a politician . . . I formed rather a different view about the relations between government and the press. What shocked me when I was in government was the easy way in which information was leaked.

Norman Fowler, *Ministers Decide: A Memoire of the Thatcher Years*, 1991

I am absolved of responsibility. We journalists don't have to step on roaches. All we have to do is turn on the light and watch the critters scuttle.

P.J. O'Rourke on the duties of journalists in relation to politics, *Parliament of Whores*, 1992, p. xix

The British Broadcasting Corporation was founded in 1926 as a public corporation. John Reith, its first Director General, set a high moral tone – 'to inform, educate and entertain' – the vestiges of which can still perhaps be discerned. In 1955, however, the BBC's monopoly was broken when ITV came into being, followed by commercial radio in 1973.

The BBC was granted a second television channel (BBC2) in 1964; a second ITV channel (Channel 4) began broadcasting in 1982, and Channel 5 in 1997. In February 1989, Rupert Murdoch's Sky Television began broadcasting using satellite technology. After a quiet start the new technology took hold and was operating at a profit by 1993. Many of the channels offer old films and popular programme repeats from the USA, but Sky News has established itself in the eyes of the public and politicians as a respectable and competent 24-hour news channel which stands comparison with the BBC's equivalent rolling service.

■ Media organisations and the political process

Television has influenced the form of political communication

Broadcasting – especially television – has had a transforming impact on political processes. Two minutes of exposure on peak-time television enables politicians to reach more people than they could meet in a lifetime of canvassing, handshaking or addressing public meetings. Alternatively, speaking on BBC Radio 4's early morning *Today* programme gains access to a largely up-market audience of over one million opinion formers and decision makers (Margaret Thatcher always listened to it and once rang in, unsolicited, to comment). In consequence, broadcasting organisations have become potent players in the political game: the regularity and nature of access to television and radio has become a key political issue; interviewers such as John Humphrys, John Snow and Jeremy Paxman have become important – and controversial – national figures; and investigative current affairs programmes – especially during the Thatcher years – have been the source of bitter political controversy.

In the nineteenth century, it was commonplace for political meetings to entail formal addresses from great orators, such as Gladstone or Lloyd

George, lasting an hour or more. Television has transformed this process. To command attention in our living rooms politicians have to be relaxed, friendly, confidential – they have to talk to us as individuals rather than as members of a crowd. Long speeches are out. On television, orators are obsolete. Political messages have to be compressed into spaces of two to three minutes – often less. Slogans and key phrases have become so important that speech writers are employed to think them up. The playwright Ronald Millar was thus employed and helped to produce Margaret Thatcher's memorable 'The lady's not for turning' speech at the 1981 Conservative Party Conference.

Television and the image

Since the arrival of television, appearances have been crucial. Bruce (1992) quotes a study that suggested 'the impact we make on others depends on . . . how we look and behave – 55 per cent; how we speak – 38 per cent and what we say only 7 per cent. Content and form must therefore synchronise for, if they don't, form will usually dominate or undermine content' (p. 41). So we saw Harold Wilson smoking a pipe to pre-empt what his adviser Marcia Williams felt was an overly aggressive habit of shaking his fist to emphasise a point.

Margaret Thatcher was the first leading politician to take image building totally professionally under the tutelage of her media guru, Gordon Reece. Peter Mandelson, Labour's premier spin doctor of the 1980s and 1990s, commented that by the mid-1980s 'every part of her had been transformed: her hair, her teeth, her nose I suspect, her eyebrows. Not a part of Mrs Thatcher was left unaltered.' Every politician now has a career reason to be vain.

Blair v Brown

These two Labour prime ministers have hugely contrasting images. Blair's was chameleon to a degree; he was so keen to appeal to everyone he tried to be all things to all men: blokey with demotic speech, sipping a cup of tea in photo shoots; serious when reading the lesson at important funerals; aggressive and witty at PMQs; statesmanlike if addressing the UN; and on television he was a natural, able to convey relaxed good humour. He was also a little vain, seeking to dress young in tight jeans and allegedly using fake tan from time to time.

Brown was totally different: shy in public and often dishevelled; unable to project in public the warmth or wit his friends saw in private. At PMQs he was regularly bested by the more Blair-like Cameron and his speaking style, aggressive and incisive in opposition, proved lacklustre and pedestrian in government. Supporters claimed he was honest – not trying to be someone he was not like Blair – and serious in order to address the serious issues of the day. All the polling evidence, however, shows Brown failed to impress, charm or win over the majority of British voters who clearly respond to a little well-crafted wooing, even if it is at times a little obvious.

Broadcasters have usurped the role of certain political institutions

Local party organisation is less important now that television can gain access to people's homes so easily and effectively. However, the message is a more centralised national one, concentrating on the party leadership rather than local issues and local people. The House of Commons has lost some of its informing and educative function to the media. Ministers often prefer to give statements to the media rather than to Parliament – often on the Green just outside the House – and television interviewers gain much more exclusive access to ministers than the House of Commons can ever hope for. Even public discussion and debate are now purveyed via radio and television programmes such as the BBC's *Today*, *Newsnight* and *Question Time*.

The appointment of party leaders

Attlee was famously taciturn in front of the cameras and Churchill never took to it, but Macmillan flirted with television, conducting a stilted 'interview' in Number 10 in the run up to the 1959 election. From hereon, elections became televisual and the ability to shine on it a qualification for the top political jobs. So Wilson was good, Heath not so much so; Callaghan was competent, Thatcher became so. Major was average; Blair was brilliant. Gordon Brown tries hard but cannot overcome some kind of innate shyness and so struggles. David Cameron's 'without notes' speech in the 2006 Tory conference was the launch pad for his campaign and as leader he has proved a very good media performer.

Personnel

Unsurprisingly, the media and politics have become more closely interrelated, with media professionals such as David Steel, Tony Benn, Bryan Gould, Austin Mitchell and Peter Mandelson going into politics, and Robert Kilroy-Silk, Brian Walden, Michael Portillo and Matthew Parris moving out of politics and into the media. The apotheosis of this tendency was represented by former US President Ronald Reagan, who used his actor's ability to speak lines to the camera to compensate, arguably, for other political inadequacies.

Spin doctors

These fearsome-sounding new actors on the political stage focus their energies on ensuring that the media give the desired interpretation of events or statements. Their provenance is usually thought to have been during the eighties when the *New York Times* used the term in an October 1984 article to describe smartly dressed men and women who moved among crowds at political events and sought to explain what their political boss had *really* meant to say. Since then the popular idea is of somewhat shadowy figures moving around and choreographing press conferences or on the phone to television executives cajoling and bullying to get their way. The results are usually believed to be a distortion of the truth and to have fuelled the lack of trust in the political process.

The Labour Party, Tony Blair and 'spin'

For a generation . . . New Labour and spin doctors have been inseparable.

Editorial in the *Guardian*, 17 January 2003

One student of the media quoted a senior Labour spin doctor as saying: 'Communications is not an afterthought to our policy. It's central to the whole mission of New Labour' (Barnett and Gaber 2001: 116). So it is hardly surprising that Labour has been demonised as the party that invests too much in presentation, in 'spin'. Roy Greenslade, writing in the *Guardian* on 6 June 2002, argues that it all began in response to the way Neil Kinnock was treated by the right-wing press during the eighties. He was given no 'honeymoon' when elected in 1983, but from the start was attacked as a 'windbag', weak and incompetent. The *Sun*, *Mail* and *Express* pulled no punches and built up their coverage – much of it

BIOGRAPHY

Alastair Campbell (1957–)

Tony Blair's press secretary. Educated at Cambridge; had a career in tabloid journalism before joining Blair's personal staff. Often referred to as the 'real Deputy Prime Minister', he had constant access to his boss, and his words were held to carry the authority of the PM. He was well known to journalists and he used charm and threats to get his own way. Some Labour voices always believed him too powerful, but his appearance before a Commons Select Committee revealed that he can defend himself with gusto and effectiveness. In 2003 he was incensed when accused via a BBC interview of 'sexing up' the intelligence dossier used to justify the decision to go to war in Iraq. He was exonerated eventually but the ensuing media furore – during which he was accused of vindictiveness against the BBC – proved to be his swansong as he stepped down in the autumn of that year, still defiant and largely contemptuous of the nation's media.

based on no evidence – thoughout the decade. Leading up to the 1992 election, the *Sun*'s editor, Kelvin McKenzie, went to town two days before polling day, devoting nine pages to its 'Nightmare on Kinnock Street' feature. 'It's the *Sun* wot won it' was the triumphant headline following the result.

Maybe the reaction of Mandelson and his colleagues to this onslaught is understandable. Together with Alastair Campbell, Blair's press secretary, he insisted slurs were rebutted and retractions given. The right-wing media soon discovered they were being matched and criticisms of 'New Labour spin' became commonplace. Unfortunately this aggressive media policy continued into government and what had been an asset rapidly became a liability as voters began to doubt the veracity of government statements and statistics.

Mr Campbell lives and breathes for Tony Blair. He is the tough aggressive half of Tony Blair, the side of Tony Blair you never see in public. He writes most of what Tony Blair says. He writes almost everything that appears under Tony Blair's name. So sometimes, when Mr Blair is answering questions in the Commons, I like to watch Mr Campbell as he sits above his boss in the gallery. You sense his face is reflecting what the Prime Minister is thinking but cannot possibly reveal to MPs. When he comes up with a good line, and the loyal sycophants behind him applaud, Mr Campbell beams happily. Sometimes he rolls his head in pleasure at his own jokes. When Mr Blair is worsted, as happens quite a lot these days, Mr Campbell has two expressions. One is merely glum; the other a contemptuous grimace, which implies only a moron could imagine that Mr Hague had scored any kind of point.

Source: Simon Hoggart, 'Commons Sketch': the *Guardian*, 11 November 1999. © Guardian Newspapers Limited 1999, reproduced with permission

Labour tried to claim, after setting up the the Phillis Report in January 2003, that it had relaxed the rules whereby lobby (parliamentary correspondents) rules had been made more transparent but veteran spin doctor Bernard Ingham claimed he was not fooled; he did not believe spin had been banished. 'Spin is still everywhere', he wrote in the *Sunday Times* of 16 March 2003, 'and because of spin, Blair has forfeited the trust of the nation and . . . parliament.' Opinion polls gauging public trust in Blair certainly reinforced such a judgement, and some even attributed the shockingly low turnout in the 2001 election to a collapse of voter belief in what the government was saying.

It would be foolish to accuse New Labour of inventing spin; even before the advent of mass media, governments sought to offer the best possible interpretations of their actions. Yet, for all its expertise, Blair's operation lacked subtlety. Campbell acquired too high a profile as the demonic 'spinner' and even featured as the subject of a televised profile. Blair too once asked in a leaked 2000 memo for 'more eye-catching initiatives' to combat Conservative policy statements. After the non-discovery of Weapons of Mass Destruction in Iraq, after Blair had cited them as the justification for invasion in 2003, the association of New Labour with 'spin' was compounded.

The televising of Parliament

When the proposal that the proceedings of Parliament be televised was first formally proposed in

1966, it was heavily defeated. While other legislative chambers, including the House of Lords, introduced the cameras with no discernible ill effects, the House of Commons resolutely refused, chiefly on the grounds that such an intrusion would rob the House of its distinctive intimate atmosphere: its 'mystique'. By the late 1970s, however, the majorities in favour of exclusion were wafer thin and the case would have been lost in the 1980s but for the stance of Margaret Thatcher. In November 1985, it was rumoured that she had changed her mind, but at the last minute she decided to vote true to form and a number of Conservative MPs – known for their loyalty (or obsequiousness, depending on your viewpoint) – about to vote for the televising of the House instead rushed to join their leader in the 'No' lobby.

Finally, however, after a trial period, on 21 November 1989 the House appeared on television, debating the Queen's Speech. Margaret Thatcher reflected on the experience as follows:

I was really glad when it was over because it is ordeal enough when you are speaking in the Commons or for Question Time without television, but when you have got television there, if you are not careful, you freeze – you just do . . . It is going to be a different House of Commons, but that is that.

The Times, 24 November 1989

In January 1990 the broadcasting restrictions were relaxed: reaction shots of an MP clearly being referred to were allowed, together with 'medium-range' shots of the chamber some four rows behind the MP speaking or from the benches opposite. By the summer of 1990, it was obvious even to critical MPs that 'civilisation as we know it' had not come to an end. On 19 July, the Commons voted 131–32 to make televising of the chamber permanent. However, one unforeseen consequence of the cameras has been the reduction of members in the chamber. Now it is possible for MPs to sit in their offices and do their constituency business while keeping abreast of proceedings on their office televisions.

Television has transformed the electoral process

Since the 1950s, television has become the most important media element in general elections. Unlike in the USA, political advertising is not allowed on British television, but party political broadcasts are allocated on the basis of party voting strength. These have become important during elections and increasingly sophisticated, and some – like the famous Hugh Hudson-produced party political broadcast on Neil Kinnock in 1987 – can have a substantial impact on voter perceptions. More important, however, is the extensive news and current affairs coverage, and here US practice is increasingly being followed:

1 Professional media managers – such as Labour's Peter Mandelson – have become increasingly important. Brendan Bruce, Conservative Director of Communications 1989–91, comments: 'The survival of entire governments and companies now depends on the effectiveness of these advisers yet few outside the inner circles of power even know these mercenaries exist or what their true functions are' (Bruce, 1992, p. 128).

2 Political meetings have declined. Political leaders now follow their US counterparts in planning their activities in the light of likely media coverage. The hustings – open meetings in which debates and heckling occur – have given way to stage-managed rallies to which only party members have access. Entries, exits and ecstatic applause are all meticulously planned with the all-ticket audience as willing and vocal accomplices.

3 Given television's requirements for short, easily packaged messages, political leaders insert pithy, memorable passages into their daily election utterances – the so-called soundbite – in the knowledge that this is what television wants and will show in their news broadcasts and summaries throughout the day.

4 Party Political Broadcasts (PPBs) comprise slots allocated to the parties either on the basis of their voting performance at the previous election or on the number of candidates they are fielding. The first was made by Lord Samuel for the Liberals in 1951 but they were seldom skilfully made until 1987 when Hudson made that film of Neil Kinnock which impressively raised his personal ratings. In 1997 Major vetoed a PPB which represented Blair as a Faust-like figure, prepared to sell his principles for electoral victory. In recent years PPBs have declined further in importance. During the 1980s they averaged nine minutes in length but by 2005 this figure had come down to a mere two-and-a-half minutes.

The media and pressure groups

Just as individual politicians influence the media and seek their platforms to convey their messages, so do pressure groups as they seek to influence government policy. Pressure group campaigners such as Peter Tatchell of Outrage! and Tony Juniper of Friends of the Earth are expert in knowing about and massaging the form in which the press and television like to receive stories. Because it has been so successful, much pressure group activity now revolves around using the media. Anti-blood-sports campaigners use yellow smoke when trying to disrupt hunting events as they know television responds well to it.

■ The mass media and voting behaviour

Jay Blumler *et al.* wrote in 1978 that 'modern election campaigns have to a considerable extent become fully and truly television campaigns'. But what impact do the mass media have on the way in which citizens cast their votes? Does the form that different media give to political messages make any major difference? Substantial research on this topic has been undertaken, although with little definite outcome. One school of thought favours the view that the media do very little to influence voting directly but merely reinforce existing preferences.

Blumler and McQuail (1967) argued that people do not blandly receive and react to political media messages but apply a filter effect. Denver (1992, p. 99) summarises this effect under the headings of selective exposure, perception and retention.

1 *Selective exposure*: Many people avoid politics altogether when on television or in the press, while those who are interested favour those newspapers or television programmes that support rather than challenge their views.

2 *Selective perception*: The views and values that people have serve to 'edit' incoming information so that they tend to accept what they want to believe and ignore what they do not.

3 *Selective retention*: The same editing process is applied to what people choose to remember of what they have read or viewed.

Different media moreover, act in different ways as Table 8.3 suggests.

Table 8.3 The press, television and political influence

Television	Press
Balanced	Partisan
Trusted	Not trusted
Mass audience	Segmented audience
'Passive' audience politically	'Active' audience
Most important source of information	Secondary source

Source: Lecture by David Denver, September 1996

However, the filter-reinforcement thesis seems to accord too minor a role to such an all-pervasive element. It does not seem to make 'common' sense. In an age when party preferences have weakened and people are voting much more instrumentally, according to issues, then surely the more objective television coverage has a role to play in switching votes? Is it reasonable to suppose the filter effect negates all information that challenges or conflicts with established positions? If so, then why do parties persist in spending large sums on party political broadcasts? Some empirical data support a direct-influence thesis, especially in respect of television:

1 Professor Ivor Crewe maintains that during election campaigns up to 30 per cent of voters switch their votes, so despite the surface calm in 1983 and 1987 there was considerable 'churning' beneath the surface. These two elections may have been unusual in any case: the before and after campaign variations were much larger in 1979, 1974 and 1970 although not in the landslide 1997 election.

2 Many studies reveal that the four weeks of an election campaign provide too short a time over which to judge the impact of the media. Major shifts in voting preference take place between elections, and it is quite possible, or even probable that media coverage plays a significant role.

Assessing the effect of the media

Judging the effect of the media on voting behaviour is very difficult, because it is so hard to disentangle it from a myriad of factors such as family, work, region and class that play a determining role. However, it seems fair to say that:

1 *The media do reinforce political attitudes*: This is important when the degree of commitment to a party can prove crucial when events between elections, as they always do, put loyalties to the test.

2 *The media help to set the agenda of debate*: During election campaigns party press conferences attempt to achieve this, but the media do not always conform, and between elections the media, especially the print media, play a much more important agenda-setting role.

3 *It is clear that media reportage has some direct impact* on persuading voters to change sides, but research has not yet made clear whether this effect is major or marginal.

Focus groups

Much has been written about New Labour and focus groups, and a great deal of it has been uncomplimentary. They have been cited as evidence of Labour's concern with the superficial, with adapting policy on the basis of marketing expediency and not principle – in other words, as the thin end of the wedge that Old Labour critics argue has robbed the party of its moral purpose and integrity. This point of view is hotly refuted by the chief enthusiast for the technique in the Blairite party: Philip Gould, former advertising expert, who has written a fascinating book on the evolution of the 'new' party and its march to power (Gould, 1999). In the following extract he explains the technique and his own reasons for having faith in it:

I nearly always conduct focus groups in unassuming front rooms in Watford, or Edgware or Milton Keynes or Huddersfield, in a typical family room stacked with the normal knick-knacks and photos. The eight or so members of the group will have been recruited by a research company according to a formal specification: who they voted for in the last election, their age, their occupation . . . I do not just sit there and listen. I challenge, I argue back, I force them to confront issues. I confront issues myself. I like to use the group to develop and test ideas.
Gould (1999), pp. 327–8

The permanent campaign

In 2000, Ornstein and Mann edited a book entitled *The Permanent Campaign, and its Future*. The provenance of the phrase lay in 1982 with Sidney Blumenthal, who used it to describe the emergent style of media coverage in the USA. Assiduous USA watchers in New Labour's élite seem to have absorbed the new approach and made it their own: 'a nonstop process of seeking to manipulate sources of public approval to engage in the act of governing itself' (Hugh Heclo in Ornstein and Mann, 2000, p. 219). In other words, government and campaigning have become indistinguishable. The tendency now is for parties in government to view each day as something to be 'won' or 'lost'.

BOX 8.1 IDEAS AND PERSPECTIVES

John Lloyd's critique of the media, and a journalist's response

In his book *What the Media are Doing to Our Politics* (Lloyd, 2004), journalist John Lloyd diagnoses a parlous condition in the strained dealings between media and politics in Britain, not to mention other Western liberal democracies. He sees the relationship as one which has evolved from a fractious symbiosis to a damaging struggle for power in which the media have:

Claimed the right to judge and condemn; more, they have decided – without being clear about the decision – that politics is a dirty game, played by devious people who tell an essentially false narrative about the world and thus deceive the British people. This has not been the only, but it has been the increasingly dominant narrative which the media have constructed about politics over the past decade or so and, though it has suffered some knocks, remains dominant.

Lloyd (2004: 35)

In his Reuters lecture in October 2005, Lloyd discerned a 'parallel universe' which his colleagues inhabited and described but which bore little relation to the real world in which the real actors – politicians, corporate executives, trade union leaders, bishops, NGO heads – live and seek to do their jobs. But do these negative assumptions constitute a correct view or are these actors justified in complaining that what the media report is 'deeply inadequate'?

Various journalist reviewers of Lloyd's book were not impressed, but on 10 October 2005, *The Guardian* asked a number of these 'actors' to give their own views. Most felt the charges were justified. Tony Wright MP, academic and chair of the Public Administration Select Committee, felt the media should accept that they too had played a role in 'the collapse of trust in politics and politicians' which newspapers enjoy trumpeting in their pages, because they have helped to '. . . nourish a culture of contempt, engulfing the whole of public life'. Michael Bichard, one-time Permanent Secretary in the Civil Service and currently Rector of the University of the Arts, supported Lloyd's argument:

There is much evidence – especially in the press – of lazy, complacent and arrogant practice and the consequence of this is the parallel universe to which Lloyd refers.

Richard Eyre, the stage and screen director, observed:

Journalists often regard Daniel Ellsberg's maxim – 'all leaders lie and it's our duty to expose their lies' – as a vindication of, at least, deviousness and, at worst, blackmail, while blinding themselves to the fact zealous exposure of lies isn't always the same thing as revelation of the truth. And the motives of individual journalists are at least as venal and self-interested as those who they are indicting . . .

Anthony Sampson, who reviewed all these responses to Lloyd's critique, concluded:

Most respondents think [that Lloyd is right], and there can be no doubt about the genuine anguish of many distinguished people who feel aggrieved or simply resigned to the misrepresentations of the press.

So is the press malign and determined to distort perceptions of those in power? David Leigh, also of *The Guardian*, writing 'from the front line', as it were, contributes a powerful defence of the toiling hack. From his own experience he argues:

▶

... when a journalist asks members of British institutions uncomfortable questions about what is going on, they respond with more or less polished evasions or with downright lies. They employ expensive PR teams to paint pictures that drift artistically away from reality. They try to intimidate with their lawyers. They conceal what they can and what they can't conceal, they distort.

He argues that all people in power are prone to this tendency: dictatorships try to suppress all dissent but democracies are not saved by elections every five years but by 'free speech coupled with a network of civic agencies which are truculent and unfettered. It's important that the various media behave as countervailing powers in a democracy; in fact it's absolutely necessary.' He went on to suggest that our leaders are often 'quite deranged'. Leigh concludes that on balance journalists do a necessary job pretty well but their performance is marred and debased by the fact that there is 'a race to the bottom in a declining market' and that it is true that 'some newspaper owners and newspaper people are venal, vain, cynical, sycophantic, low minded, partisan, unscrupulous or vindictive.' In *The Times* a few weeks earlier (8 December 2004), Simon Jenkins anticipated much of Leigh's case, writing that 'The British press is the most reptilian in the world', adding that 'it needs to be', given the weakness of Parliament in calling Blair to account and the way his government used spin to obfuscate every move it made.

Peter Oborne's critique of 'Manipulative Populism'

The well-known columnist, author and broadcaster Oborne, wrote a swingeing attack on the 'supplanting of parliamentary democracy' ... 'a regime of media hype, spin doctors and skullduggery' (*The Triumph of the Political Class*). He recalls that Stanley Baldwin and Clem Attlee were prime ministers who worked through their ministers – who are the people who actually wield the legal power of government – and parliament. It followed that the Chief Whip was the person on whom the PM relied most heavily for support in his political battles.

But no more: the arrival of the 'celebrity prime minister' by which Oborne seems to mean Tony Blair (he doesn't mention Thatcher), has seen the emphasis shift to the chief spin doctor; he expresses this by reference to the eclipse of the fictional Francis Urquart – the epicene villain of Dobbs' *House of Cards* by the fictional Malcolm Tucker, the foul-mouthed hero-villain of Armando Ianucci's *The Thick of It* and *In the Loop*.

All the same black arts are at work; however, the battlefield has changed. Urquhart applied himself to parliament, Tucker bypassed the traditional institutions of the state and was only concerned with the media and its other methods of control: access, favouritism, information and the creation of an elite corps of client journalists.

Oborne recalls Brown's promise to:

'bring back cabinet government, respect civil service impartiality, restore the primacy of parliament and to abandon the dark political arts at which the team of political assassins around Blair had so excelled.'

However, Brown did none of these things and Cameron's appointment of Andy Coulson – former editor of *The News of the World* – does not suggest any real change if a new regime enters Downing Street. Oborne also explains that the elevation of Campbell and Coulson is due not necessarily to mere media strategies, but to the new nature of the media. It is now so all-encompassing, such a constant and demanding presence that it has become the instrument of a new kind of politics. Parliament is supposed to be the body which ultimately determines policy and decisions but the media is now so powerful it can apply a range of influences: certainly delays, sometimes vetos as well as urge courses of action. Oborne cites the vivid phrase coined by Anthony Barnett to describe this new way in which we are governed: 'manipulative populism'.

■ The mass media and the theory of pluralist democracy

If the mass media have such a transforming impact on politics, then how have they affected the fabric of British democracy? It all depends on what we mean by democracy. The popular and indeed 'official' view is that our elected legislature exerts watchdog control over the executive and allows a large degree of citizen participation in the process of government. This pluralist system provides a free market of ideas and a shifting, open competition for power between political parties, pressure groups and various other groups in society. Supporters of the present system claim that not only is it how the system ought to work (a normative theory of government) but it is, to a large extent, also descriptive: this is how it works in practice.

According to this view, the media play a vital political role:

1 They report and represent popular views to those invested with decision-making powers.

2 They inform society about the actions of government, educating voters in the issues of the day. The range of newspapers available provides a variety of interpretations and advice.

3 They act as a watchdog of the public interest, defending the ordinary person against a possibly over-mighty government through their powers of exposure, investigation and interrogation. To fulfil this neutral, disinterested role it follows that the media need to be given extensive freedom to question and publish.

This pluralist view of the media's role, once again both normative and descriptive, has been criticised under the following points.

Ownership and control influence media messages

Excluding the BBC, the media organisations are substantially part of the business world and embrace profit making as a central objective. This argument has more force since, following Murdoch's smashing of the trade union stranglehold over the press through his 'Wapping' revolution, newspapers now make substantial profits. This fact alone severely prejudices media claims to objectivity in reporting the news and reflecting popular feeling. In recent years ownership has concentrated markedly. About 80 per cent of newspaper circulation is in the hands of four conglomerates: Associated Newspapers, owned by the Rothermere family and controlling the *Daily Mail* and the *Mail on Sunday*; the Mirror Newspaper Group, owning the *Mirror*, *Sunday Mirror* and *Sunday People*; United Newspapers, owning the *Express*, the *Sunday Express*,

the *Star* and the *Standard*; and News International, owning *The Times*, *Sunday Times*, *News of the World* and the *Sun*. These latter-day press barons and media groups also own rafts of the regional press and have strong television interests: Murdoch, for example, owns Sky Television. Following the imprisonment of Conrad Black, the *Daily Telegraph* and *Sunday Telegraph* titles were taken over by the financier Barclay Brothers.

Nor is the press especially accountable: the Press Council used to be a powerful and respected watchdog on newspaper editors, but it has tended to acquiesce meekly in the concentration of ownership on the grounds that the danger of monopoly control is less unacceptable than the bankruptcy of familiar national titles. Moreover, since the *Sun* has regularly flouted its rulings, the council has lost even more respect and has been unable, for example, to prevent the private lives of public figures being invaded by tabloid journalists to an alarming degree.

BIOGRAPHY

Sir Christopher Meyer, Chairman of the Press Complaints Commission (1944–)

Oxbridge-educated Meyer is a career diplomat who stepped in to take over the PCC chair when Lord Wakeham became enmired in the 2002 Enron scandal. He served in Moscow, Brussels, Bonn and Washington and is fluent in all the relevant languages. In the 1980s, he was the chief Foreign Office spokesman under Geoffrey Howe and then took over as chief press officer. It is said that Meyer was pivotal in building a good relationship between Blair and Bush in the wake of the latter's controversial election – though much of this could be explained by good personal chemistry. In 2005 he published memoirs entitled *DC Confidential* which distributed insights into the way in which Blair operated (not good on detail), Prescott (poor on expressing himself), Jack Straw ('more to be liked than admired') and sundry other ministers whom he described as 'pygmies'. Apart from these personal swipes, however, there was little of substance in the book and Meyer survived calls for him to resign his PCC post.

Television evinces a much clearer distinction between ownership and control and fits more easily into the pluralist model. The BBC, of course, is government-owned, and in theory at least its board of governors exercises independent control. Independent television is privately owned, and this ownership is becoming more concentrated, but the Independent Broadcasting Authority (IBA) uses its considerable legal powers under the 1981 Broadcasting Act to ensure 'balance' and 'due accuracy and impartiality' on sensitive political issues. This is not to say that television can be acquitted of the charge of bias – as we shall see below – but merely that television controllers are forbidden by law to display open partisanship and that those people who own their companies cannot insist on particular editorial lines.

News values are at odds with the requirements of a pluralist system

In order to create profits media organisations compete for their audiences, with the consequent pursuit of the lowest common denominator in public taste. In the case of the tabloids this means the relegation of hard news to inside pages and the promotion to the front page of trivial stories such as sex scandals, royal family gossip and the comings and goings of soap opera stars. The same tendency has been apparent on television, with the reduction of current affairs programmes, their demotion from peak viewing times and the dilution of news programmes with more 'human interest' stories. As a result of this tendency it can be argued that the media's educative role in a pluralist democracy is being diminished. Some would go further, however, and maintain that the dominant news values adopted by the media are in any case inappropriate for this role. The experience of successful newspapers has helped to create a set of criteria for judging newsworthiness that news editors in all branches of the media automatically accept and apply more or less intuitively. The themes to which the public are believed to respond include:

1 *Personalities*: People quickly become bored with statistics and carefully marshalled arguments and relate to stories that involve disagreement, personality conflicts or interesting personal details.

2 *Revelations*: Journalist Nicholas Tomalin once defined news as the making public of something that someone wished to keep secret. Leaked documents, financial malpractice and sexual peccadilloes, e.g. the revelation that John Major had a four-year affair with Edwina Currie, are assiduously reported and eagerly read.

3 *Disasters*: The public has both a natural and a somewhat morbid interest in such matters.

4 *Visual back-up*: Stories that can be supported by good photographs (or film footage on TV) will often take precedence over those that cannot be so supported.

It is commonly believed that newspapers which ignore these ground rules will fail commercially and that current affairs television which tries too hard to be serious will be largely ignored and described, fatally, as 'boring'. There is much evidence to suggest that these news values are based on fact: that, perhaps to our shame, these are the themes to which we most readily respond. However, it does mean that the vast media industry is engaged in providing a distorted view of the world via its concentration on limited and relatively unimportant aspects of social reality.

'Tabloidisation' of television

Studies have shown the reduction of peak time current affairs television since the 1980s and some have argued there has been a progressive 'dumbing down' of the medium. Possible explanations for this, offered by Leach *et al.* (2003, pp. 164–5), are that:

1 Television competition has taken its cue from print journalism where falling sales have induced a 'race to the bottom'.

2 Newspapers are chasing younger readers and hope the snappy, abbreviated style, peppered with items about celebrities and the like, will prove attractive to this demographic.

3 Rupert Murdoch's influence of the mass media. For example, when Elvis Presley died *The Times* did not cover the funeral in 1977 as it was deemed inappropriate but after Murdoch took over in 1981 two journalists were sent to cover Bob Marley's last rites.

4 Increased competition from satellite and cable plus Internet-carried material has forced more populist policies.

BOX 8.2   IDEAS AND PERSPECTIVES

Bias, broadcasting and the political parties

Harold Wilson was notoriously paranoid about the media and believed that not only the press but also the BBC was 'ineradicably' biased against him, full of 'card carrying Tories', in the words of Michael Cockerell. Perhaps it is being in government that explains it, as in the 1980s it was Margaret Thatcher and her 'enforcer' Norman Tebbit who seemed paranoid. He launched ferocious attacks on the corporation, calling it 'the insufferable, smug, sanctimonious, naive, guilt-ridden, wet, pink, orthodoxy of that sunset home of that third-rate decade, the sixties'.

Answering questions in the House can be stressful amid all the noise, but ultimately the barbs can be ignored and the questions avoided easily. But on radio or television well-briefed interviewers can put politicians on the spot. This is why ministers of both parties have complained so vehemently about *Today* presenter John Humphrys and *Newsnight*'s Jeremy Paxman. Cockerell explains that Humphrys is not a 'politically motivated questioner; his aim is to strip away the public relations gloss and to use his own sharp teeth to counter pre-rehearsed soundbites' (*Guardian*, 28 May 1996).

This probably gets to the heart of the perennial conflict between politicians and the media. Politicians in power ideally would like to control the media – Mrs Thatcher once said she did not like short interviews but would like instead to have four hours of airtime on her own – and resent the criticism that they receive from journalists and interviewers. In a pluralist democracy it is indeed the job of the media to make government more accountable to the public, and perhaps it is when politicians do not like it that the media are doing their jobs most effectively.

The lobby system favours the government of the day

The pluralist model requires that the media report news in a truthful and neutral way. We have already seen that ownership heavily influences the partisanship of the press, but other critics argue that the lobby system of political reporting introduces a distortion of a different kind. Some 150 political journalists at Westminster are known collectively as 'the lobby'. In effect, they belong to a club with strict rules whereby they receive special briefings from government spokesmen in exchange for keeping quiet about their sources. Supporters claim that this is an important means of obtaining information that the public would not otherwise receive, but critics disagree. Anthony Howard, the veteran political commentator, has written that lobby correspondents, rather like prostitutes, become 'clients' or otherwise 'instruments for a politician's gratification' (Hennessy 1985: 9). The charge is that journalists become lazy, uncritical and incurious, preferring to derive their copy from bland government briefings – often delivered at dictation speed.

Television companies are vulnerable to political pressure

Ever since the broadcasting media became an integral part of the political process during the 1950s, governments of all complexions have had uneasy relationships with the BBC, an organisation with a worldwide reputation for excellence and for accurate, objective current affairs coverage. Margaret Thatcher, however, took government hostility to new lengths; indeed, 'abhorrence of the BBC appeared for a while to be a litmus test for the Conservativeness of MPs' (Negrine 1995: 125). Governments seek to influence the BBC in three major ways. First, they have the power of appointment to the corporation's board of governors. The post of chairman is especially important; Marmaduke Hussey's appointment in 1986 was believed to be a response to perceived left-wing tendencies (according to one report, he was ordered by Norman Tebbit's office to 'get in there and sort it out – in days and not months'). Second, governments can threaten to alter the licence system (although former Home Secretary Willie Whitelaw knew of no occasion when this threat had been used): Margaret Thatcher was known to favour the introduction of advertising to finance the BBC, but the Peacock Commission on the financing of television refused to endorse this approach. Third, government's attempt to exert pressure in relation to particular programmes – often citing security reasons. The range of disputes between the Thatcher governments and the BBC is unparalleled in recent history. In part this was a consequence of a dominant, long-established and relatively unchallenged Prime Minister as well as Thatcher's determination to challenge the old consensus – she long suspected that it resided tenaciously within the top echelons of the BBC.

Marxist theories of class dominance

The Glasgow University Media Group

On the basis of their extensive programme analyses, the Glasgow University Media Group suggest that television coverage of economic news tends to place the 'blame for society's industrial and economic problems at the door of the workforce. This is done in the face of contradictory evidence, which when it appears is either ignored [or] smothered' (1976: 267–8). Reports on industrial relations were 'clearly skewed against the interests of the working class and organised labour . . . in favour of the managers of industry'. The Glasgow research provoked a storm of criticism. In 1985, an academic counterblast was provided by Martin Harrison (1985), who criticised the slender basis of the Glasgow research and adduced new evidence that contradicted its conclusions. The Glasgow research is often cited in support of more general theories on how the media reinforce, protect and advance dominant class interests in society. Variations on the theme were produced by Gramsci, in the 1930s by the Frankfurt School of social theorists and in the 1970s by the sociocultural approach of Professor Stuart Hall (for detailed analysis see McQuail 1983: 57–70; Watts 1997), but the essence of their case is summed up in Marx's proposition that 'the ideas of the ruling class are in every epoch the ruling ideas'. He argued that those people who own and control the economic means of production – the ruling class – will seek to persuade everyone else that preserving status quo values and institutions is in the interests of society as a whole.

The means employed are infinitely subtle and indirect, via religious ideas, support for the institution of the family, the monarchy and much else.

Inevitably the role of the mass media, according to this analysis, is crucial. Marxists totally reject the pluralist model of the media as independent and neutral, as the servant rather than the master of society. They see the media merely as the instrument of class domination, owned by the ruling class and carrying their messages into every home in the land. It is in moments of crisis, Marxists would claim, that the fundamental bias of state institutions is made clear. In 1926, during the General Strike, Lord Reith, the first Director General of the BBC, provided some evidence for this view when he confided to his diary, 'they want us to be able to say they did not commandeer us, but they know they can trust us not to be really impartial'.

Which of the two models better describes the role of the media in British society? From the discussion so far, the pluralist model would appear inadequate in a number of respects. Its ability to act as a fair and accurate channel of communication between government and society is distorted by the political bias of the press, the lobby system, news values and the tendency of television to reflect consensual values. Moreover, the media are far from being truly independent: the press is largely owned by capitalist enterprises, and television is vulnerable to government pressure of various kinds. Does this mean that the dominance model is closer to the truth? Not really.

1   As former editor of ITN News, David Nicholas, observes (Tyne Tees TV, April 1986), 'trying to manipulate the news is as natural an instinct to a politician as breathing oxygen', but because politicians try does not mean that they always succeed. People who work in the media jealously guard their freedom and vigorously resist government interference.

2   The media may tend to reflect consensual views, but this does not prevent radical messages regularly breaking into the news – sometimes because they accord with news values themselves. Television also challenges and criticises the status quo: for example, at the humorous level in the form of *Bremner, Bird and Fortune* and *The Thick of It* and at the serious level in the form of the BBC's regular *Panorama* programme.

3   Programmes such as *Rough Justice* and *First Tuesday* in the past have shown that persistent and highly professional research can shame a reluctant establishment into action to reverse

Table 8.4 Summary table to show 'democrativeness' of media elements

Democratic criteria	Media and democrative tendency[c,d,e]				
	Broadsheets	Tabloids	Radio	BBC	Commercial TV
Easily accessible (for target audience)	+	+	+	+	+
Varied and plentiful	+	+	+	+	+
Concentration of ownership	−	−	−	+	−
Reliable factually	+	−	+	+	+
High-value political content	+	−	0	−	+
Accountability 1[a]	+	−	+	−	+
Accountability 2[b]	−	−	−	−	−
Low bias	0	−	+	+	+

[a] Accountability 1 = tendency for the media element to facilitate democracy.
[b] Accountability 2 = degree of accountability of medium to public.
[c] + = high tendency to encourage democracy.
[d] − = low tendency to encourage democracy.
[e] 0 = neutral effect (i.e. '0' is given for BBC radio as most of its five channels are music-based, and '0' for the bias of broadsheets as they tend to take give space to alternative opinions to their editorials).
Source: B. Jones (2000) 'Media and Government' in R. Pyper and L. Robins (eds) United Kindom Governance. Reprinted by permission of Palgrave Macmillan

injustices – as in the case of the Guildford Four, released in 1989 after fifteen years of wrongful imprisonment.

4 News values do not invariably serve ruling-class interests, otherwise governments would not try so hard to manipulate them. And even the most serious of the quality newspapers will join the feeding frenzy of a scandal like the one which submerged David Blunkett in 2004, once they deem the appropriate point has been reached.

Each model, then, contains elements of the truth, but neither comes near the whole truth. Which is the nearer? The reader must decide; but despite all its inadequacies and distortions the pluralist model probably offers the better framework for understanding how the mass media interact with the British political system. Table 8.4 reveals the complexity of the argument: some elements fit neatly into a supporting role, while others do not.

■ Language and politics

All this modern emphasis on technology can obscure the fact that in politics language is still of crucial importance. Taking the example of Northern Ireland, we have seen how the precise meaning of

words has provided a passionate bone of contention. When the IRA announced its ceasefire in 1994, its opponents insisted it should be a 'permanent' one. However, the paramilitary organisation did not wish to abandon its ability to use the threat of violence as a negotiating counter and refused to comply, insisting that its term 'complete' ceasefire was as good as the British government needed or would in any case get. Gerry Adams, president of the political wing of the IRA, Sinn Fein, had a similar problem over his attitude towards bombings. His close contact with the bombers made it impossible for him to condemn the bombing of Manchester in June 1996, so he used other less committing words like 'regret' or 'unfortunate'. Another aspect is tone of voice, which can bestow whole varieties of meaning to a statement or a speech. Sir Patrick Mayhew, for example, John Major's Northern Ireland Secretary, specialised in being 'calm'.

I went to the CBI conference in Birmingham to hear the Prime Minister speak, and there on a giant TV screen . . . was our very own Big Brother. This Big Brother smiles a lot in a self deprecating kind of way. He uses 'um' and 'well' as a rhetorical device, to convince us he's not reading out a prepared text, but needs to pause to work out exactly what he means. There is a prepared text of course but he adds to it phrases such as 'I really think' and 'you know I really have to tell you' and 'in my view'. This is the new oratory. The old politicians told us they were right, and that there was no room for doubt, the new politician is not telling us truths, but selling us himself . . . His message is that you should take him on trust; you should believe him because you love him.

Simon Hoggart, 'Commons Sketch: Blair lays on the therapy for the terracotta army', the *Guardian*, 3 November 1999. © Guardian Newspapers Limited, reprinted with permission

■ Media and the Internet

1 *Information*: It is now possible to download immense amounts of up-to-date information about political issues via the Internet.

2 *E-mail*: It is possible to communicate with politicians and the politically active all over the world, extending enormously the scope of political action.

3 *Interactive democracy*: By being hooked up to the Internet, it might be possible for politicians or government in democracies to seek endorsement for policies directly from the people. This would have all kinds of drawbacks, e.g. it could slow down the political process even more than at present in developed countries; it could give a platform to unsavoury messages like racism and power-seeking ideologues; it might enthrone the majority with a power it chooses to abuse. But these opportunities exist, and it is virtually certain that they will be experimented with if not adopted in the near future.

4 *Blogs*: It is now possible for anyone to set up their own website and issue opinions and information to the world on a regular basis. In the year 2005 it was calculated that 80,000 weblogs (blogs) were created and their rate of increase has now become exponential. Many younger people now use such sources as a matter of course, and some – like the US Drudge Report – break new stories or influence election campaigns. Fareed Zakaria offers this insight into the implications of the revolution currently taking place (see also Box 8.4):

Today's information revolution has produced thousands of outlets for news that make central control impossible and dissent easy. The Internet has taken this process another huge step forward, being a system where, in the columnist Thomas Friedman's words, 'Everyone is connected but no one is in control.'

Zakaria (2004)

However, the Internet still has some way to go before the existing media are usurped. Most blogs are manned by one or two people only; they do not have the same income as mainstream media; their scoops are still rare and often confined to fringe issues and political gossip. But, as Box 8.3 below suggests, in the USA things have maybe the locus of power is shifting much faster than in the UK.

5 *Mobile phones*: Virtually everyone now owns a mobile phone and this fact, together with the onrush of technology, has produced the transmission of more and more different types of information via their tiny screens. Some political parties have issued text messages to phone owners, but in 2006 more possibilities were opened up by the mobile provider which announced the results of an experiment whereby television had been broadcast direct to mobile phone subscribers. Despite the smallness of the screens, the trial was declared successful with thousands of mobile owners watching several hours of television a week – though most of it at home rather than on the move. Inevitably news and political content will in future be imbibed via this unlikely route and will become yet another facet of the political media.

BOX 8.3   The Huffington Post

Starting as a blog run by Arriana Huffington, Greek-born Oxbridge-educated and oil millionaire divorcee, the 'HuffPo' is making waves in the States. This is partly because its owner, once the scourge of the right, has swung to the left and now champions Obama. Moreover, while print journalism licks its wounds at redundancies and closures, the liberal blog had just announced, in April 2009, a $1.7m fund to help fill the gap left by the disappearing investigative news teams. The rise of the blog has been astonishing:

The fund also signals the website's ambition to move to a more central position in the media landscape – it began to call itself an 'internet newspaper' last year. April 2009 may well be seen as the moment the Huffington Post came of age. The HuffPo's rise has been impressive. Less than four years old and with fewer than 60 staff (including seven news reporters), it is now a competitor to the New York Times, *158 years old and with more than 1,000 journalists. According to the ratings website Comscore, in February the HuffPo drew more than a third of the* Times's *traffic: 7.3 million unique users to 18.4 million.*

Ed Pilkington, *Guardian, Media Guardian*, 6 April 2009

If the Drudge Report and the HuffPo as well as others continue to grow and the mainstream to contract, it might not be long before the new technology totally transforms the world of news reporting and commentary.

Political bloggers were delighted on 11 April 2009 when popular blogger Guido Fawkes received a link highly embarrassing to the government. It seemed that Damian McBride, a close aide of Gordon Brown, had been planning, with Derek Draper (former aide to Peter Mandelson) to launch a Labour blog which would disseminate smear stories (flagrant and untrue) damaging to the Conservatives. McBride resigned on 11 April, a day which might well mark a further shift in UK political communication from mainstream to cyberspace. But this day is still a long, long way off in the UK; most political blogs are one-man operations, even the big ones, like Iain Dale's Diary, Conservative Home and Guido Fawkes. All three of these, incidentally, are on the right; the left have not really begun to fire properly in the blogosphere.

BOX 8.4   BRITAIN IN CONTEXT

The media

The nature of the media in any country is usually a reflection of its political character. Democracies believe in freedom of speech and hence in open media, though politicians in democracies seek constantly to manipulate the media to their own advantage. In authoritarian systems the media are usually heavily controlled in terms of what newspapers can print or broadcasters can say on air.

The media in the UK play a similar role to those in the USA. The major difference is that in the latter, candidates can buy airtime to show their own political ads and to issue 'attack ads' to weaken opposing candidates. As such ads are very expensive, this

gives an advantage to campaigns which are well funded. Indeed, many candidates in the US and incumbent legislators, governors and so forth, spend much of their energies raising campaign cash. The phenomenon of 'spin doctors' was more or less invented in the US where sculpting messages or media images for mass consumption has been something of a growth industry; they have since been disseminated worldwide to wherever democratic elections are regularly held. Much campaign output is either 'semi-mediated' like the presidential debates or 'mediated' in news broadcasts, but in the latter case candidates and their aides have become clever in gaining favourable media attention.

Many media critics claim that in the US the media favour the right in that they reflect and reinforce attitudes wholly accepting of the status quo. They point to Fox News, owned by Rupert Murdoch, which arguably leans towards a Bush interpretation of issues and news stories. As in the UK debate, others deny such bias and argue the media are essentially free. But this argument attains a worldwide dimension when ownership of the media is examined. Huge media conglomerates like Murdoch's News Corporation or Berlusconi's Mediaset control media in other countries and there is concern that some political control is thereby connected. Murdoch, for example, broadcasts satellite television into China and has agreed to some censorship controls demanded by the government of that country.

China has also sought to censor one of the fastest growing media forms: communication via the Internet. Here it is the search engine company, Google, which has attracted criticism for agreeing to controls over its activities in China. But such control cannot stop the burgeoning spread of such communication, especially the 'blogosphere'.

Blogs are online logs or diaries which are essentially forms of personal websites. They can be purely individual and carry all kinds of information from the person concerned – for example, 'I got up this morning and worked in the garden for two hours', about a business venture, about musical enthusiasms, about political issues, or, like the most successful and much visited ones, about celebrity gossip.

Writing in *The Guardian* on 9 February 2006, Charles Arthur reported that the blogosphere was 60 times its size of three years earlier and was doubling in size every five months; 75,000 are created every day and over 13 million were still active three months after their creation. Quite where this explosion of Internet communication will lead is unclear. It could prove to be a force for subversion – chipping away at the base of the status quo in a number of countries. Or it could be the object of government censorship in some countries, with governments hunting down these individuals hunched in front of their flickering screens. Or it could be neither and merely take its place as yet another logical element of globalisation.

Chapter summary

The spoken voice was the main form of political communication until the spread of newspapers in the nineteenth century. Broadcasting introduced a revolution into the way politics is conducted as its spread is instant and its influence so great. New political actors have emerged specialising in the media, and politicians have learned to master their techniques. Press news values tend to influence television also, but the latter is more vulnerable to political pressure than the already politicised press. Class dominance theories suggest that the media are no more than an instrument of the ruling class, but there is reason to believe that they exercise considerable independence and are not incompatible with democracy.

Discussion points

- Should British political parties be allowed to buy political advertising on television?

- Has televising Parliament enhanced or detracted from the efficacy of Parliament?

- Does television substantially affect voting behaviour?

- Do the media reinforce the political status quo or challenge it?

- Should interviewers risk appearing rude when confronting politicians?

- How important have blogs become in disseminating news and comment?

Further reading

A useful but now dated study of the media and British politics is Negrine (1995). Budge *et al.* (2007) provide two excellent chapters (13 and 14). The two most readable studies of leadership, the media and politics are both by Michael Cockerell (Cockerell 1988; Cockerell *et al.* 1984). Bruce (1992) is excellent on the behaviour of politicians in relation to the media. Blumler and Gurevitch (1995) is an essay on the crisis of communication for citizenship and as such is an interesting source of ideas. See Jones (1993) on the television interview. The most brilliant and funny book about the press is Chippendale and Orrie's history of the *Sun* (1992).

Bibliography

Barnett, S. and Gaber, I. (2001) *Westminster Tales: The 21st Century Crisis in Political Journalism* (Continuum).

Bilton, A., Bennett, K., Jones, P., Skinner, D., Stanworth, M. and Webster, A. (1996) *Introductory Sociology*, 3rd edn (Macmillan).

Blumler, J.G. and Gurevitch, M. (1995) *The Crisis of Public Communication* (Routledge).

Blumler, J.G. and McQuail, D. (1967) *Television in Politics* (Faber and Faber).

Blumler, J.G., Gurevitch, M. and Ives, J. (1978) *The Challenge of Election Broadcasting* (Leeds University Press).

Bruce, B. (1992) *Images of Power* (Kogan Page).

Budge, I., Crewe, I., McKay, D. and Newton, K. (2007) *The New British Politics* (Longman).

Chippendale, P. and Orrie, C. (1992) *Stick it Up Your Punter* (Mandarin).

Cockerell, M. (1988) *Live from Number Ten* (Faber and Faber).

Cockerell, M., Walker, D. and Hennessy, P. (1984) *Sources Close to the Prime Minister* (Macmillan).

Cohen, N. (1999) *The Observer*, 24 October 1999.

Cronkite, W. (1997) *A Reporter's Life* (Knopf).

Denver, D. (1992) *Elections and Voting Behaviour*, 2nd edn (Harvester Wheatsheaf).

Donovan, P. (1998) *All Our Todays: Forty Years of the Today Programme* (Arrow).

Fowler, N. (1991) *Ministers Decide: A Memoire of the Thatcher Years* (Chapmans).

Franklin, B. (1999) *Tough on Sound-bites, Tough on the Causes of Sound-bites: New Labour News Management* (Catalyst Pamphlet).

Geddes, A. and Tonge, J. (1997) *Labour's Landslide* (Manchester University Press).

Glasgow University Media Group (1976) *Bad News* (Routledge and Kegan Paul).

Gould, P. (1999) *The Unfinished Revolution* (Abacus).

Green, J. (1982) *Book of Political Quotes* (Angus and Robertson).

Harrison, M. (1985) *TV News: Whose Bias* (Hermitage, Policy Journals).

Hennessy, P. (1985) *What the Papers Never Said* (Political Education Press).

Hoggart, S. (1999a) 'Commons Sketch: Blair lays on the therapy for the terracotta army', *The Guardian*, 3 November 1999.

Hoggart, S. (1999b) 'Commons Sketch: no joke for No. 10 when Hague gag hits the target', *The Guardian*, 11 November 1999.

Ingham, B. (2003) 'The wages of spin', *Sunday Times*, 16 March (adapted from The *Wages of Spin*, John Murray, 2003).

Jones, B. (1993) '"The pitiless probing eye": politicians and the broadcast political interview', *Parliamentary Affairs*, January.

Jones, B. (2000) 'Media and government', in R. Pyper and L. Robins (eds) *United Kingdom Governance* (Palgrave Macmillan).

King, A. (ed.) (1997) *New Labour Triumphs: Britain at the Polls* (Chatham House).

Leach, R. *et al.* (1998) *British Politics* (Palgrave).

Lloyd, J. (2004) *What the Media are Doing to Our Politics* (Constable).

Marr, A. (1999) 'And the news is . . . electric', *The Observer*, 17 October.

McQuail, D. (1983) *Mass Communication Theory: An Introduction* (Sage).

Mullin, C. (2009) *A View from the Foothills* (Profile Books).

Negrine, R. (1995) *Politics and the Mass Media*, 2nd edn (Routledge).

Newton, K. (1992) 'Do voters believe everything they read in the papers?', in I. Crewe, P. Norris, D. Denver and D. Broughton (eds) *British Elections and Parties Yearbook* (Harvester Wheatsheaf).

Oborne, P. (2007) *The Triumph of the Political Class* (Simon & Schuster).

Ornstein, N. and Mann, T. (2000) *The Permanent Campaign, and its Future* (AET).

O'Rourke, P.J. (1992) *Parliament of Whores* (Picador).

Sevaldsen, J. and Vardmand, O. (1993) *Contemporary British Society*, 4th edn (Academic Press).

Seyd, P. and Whiteley, P. (1992) *Labour's Grass Roots* (Clarendon Press).

Seymore-Ure, C. (1974) *The Political Impact of the Mass Media* (Constable).

Watts, D. (1997) *Political Communication Today* (Manchester University Press).

Whale, J. (1977) *The Politics of the Media* (Fontana).

Wring, D. and Deacon, D. (2005) 'The election unspun' in A. Geddes and J. Tonge, *Britain Decides* (Palgrave).

Zakaria, F. (2004) *The Future of Freedom* (Norton).

Useful websites

UK Media Internet Directory: Newspapers: www.mcc.ac.uk/jcridlan.htm

Daily Telegraph: www.telegraph.co.uk
The Independent: www.independent.co.uk
The Times: www.the-times.co.uk
Guardian: www.guardian.co.uk
The Economist: www.economist.co.uk
BBC Television: www.bbc.co.uk
BBC charter review: www.bbc.charterreview.org.uk
ITN: www.itn.co.uk
CNN: www.cnn.com

Blog sites

http://skipper59.blogspot.com/ (run by the author of this chapter)
http://5thnovember.blogspot.com/
http://normblog.typepad.com/
http://samizdata.net/blog/
http://chickyog.blogspot.com/
http://oliverkamm.typepad.com/

Topic 7:
Policy Process

The policy-making process

Bill Jones

Bill Jones

Learning objectives

- To define policy in government.
- To encourage familiarity with the most popular models of policy making.
- To examine the notion of the policy process.
- To give some examples of questionable policy making.

From Chapter 21 of *Politics UK*, 7/e. Bill Jones and Philip Norton. © Pearson Education 2001–2010. All rights reserved.

Introduction

This chapter examines the anatomy of policy and policy making in central government, focusing on its stages together with some theories relating to the process before concluding with a look at two case studies where outcome failed to match expectations and one of a policy currently in the making. Accordingly the chapter delves briefly into the complex area of policy studies, an area that has attracted attention, because it deals with political outcomes and draws together so many elements, embodying so much of the political universe: process, influence, power and pressure as well as the impact of personality. Consequently, policy studies has emerged as a kind of sub-discipline with some claim to be a focus for a social science approach to human interaction involving such subjects as psychology, sociology, economics, history, philosophy and political science. Policy studies was essentially born in the USA, so much of it focuses on American examples and policy environments; but more generally it draws on public policy in Western liberal democracies as a whole. The Bibliography provides an introduction to some of the voluminous literature in the field.

■ How policy is made

Policy can be defined as a set of ideas and proposals for action culminating in a government decision; to study policy, therefore, is to study how decisions are made. Government decisions can take many forms: Burch (1979: 108) distinguishes between two broad kinds, as follows:

1 Rules, regulations and public pronouncements (e.g. Acts of Parliament, Orders in Council, White Papers, ministerial and departmental circulars).

2 Public expenditure and its distribution: the government spends some £500 billion per annum, mostly on public goods and services (e.g. educa-tion, hospitals) and transfer payments (e.g. social security payments and unemployment benefit).

Figure 21.1 portrays the government as a system that has as its input political demands together with resources available and its 'output' as the different kinds of government decision. The latter impact on society and influence future 'inputs', so the process is circular and constant.

Both Burch and Wood (1990) and Jordan and Richardson (1987) review a number of different analyses as 'models': possible or approximate versions of what happens in reality. Eight of these are summarised below. For a fuller account of the available models, see Parsons (1995), John (1998), Hill (2000) and Dorey (2006).

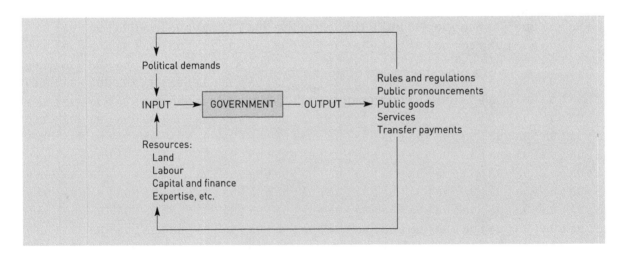

Figure 21.1 The policy process
Source: Burch (1979)

■ Models of policy making

1 *The conventional model*: This is the 'official' explanation of policy making found in Central Office of Information publications and the utterances of civil servants in public (though seldom in private). This maintains that Parliament represents and interprets the public will through its representatives, who support government ministers, who formulate executive policies, which are thereupon faithfully and impartially implemented by civil servants. The notion that a 'thin red line' of democracy connects voters with civil servants via the nominee of a political party in Parliament strikes many as tenuous but this is the officially sanctioned theory of how policy is made.

2 *The ruling-class model*: This is effectively the Marxist assertion, that those empowered with taking key decisions in the state – civil servants and politicians – subscribe consciously or unconsciously to the values of the dominant economic class, the property-owning upper middle classes. It follows that 'the executive of the modern state is but a committee for managing the common affairs of the whole bourgeoisie' (Marx and Engels 1848). According to this view, most policy outputs will have the effect of protecting dominant group interests. It also assumes that the superstructure of democracy is all false, hiding the true 'hegemony' of the economic class. Ralph Miliband (1969) provides a good analysis of this approach (though, ironically, two of his sons are now key people in this very system); for a summary of the argument see John (1998), Chapter 5.

The following two models attribute decisive importance to differing elements within the political system.

3 *The pluralist model*: This is often associated with the US political scientist Robert Dahl. It assumes that power is dispersed within society to the various interest groups that constitute it – business, labour, agriculture, and so forth – and that they can 'make themselves heard effectively at some crucial stage in the process of decision' (Jordan and Richardson 1987: 16). According to this view, interest groups interact and negotiate policy with each other in a kind of free market, with government acting as a more or less neutral referee.

4 *Corporatism*: This is associated with the work of Philippe Schmitter and is offered as an alternative to pluralism. This model perceives an alliance between ministers, civil servants and the leaders of pressure groups in which the last are given a central role in the policy-making process in exchange for exerting pressure upon their members to conform with or accept government decisions. In this view, therefore, interest groups become an extension – or even a quasi-form – of government. Corporatism has also been used pejoratively by British politicians of the left (Benn), right (Thatcher) and centre (Owen) to describe the decision-making style of the discredited 1974–9 Labour government.

The next two models ascribe key importance to two specific elements of the system.

5 *The party government model*: The stress here is on political parties and the assertion that they provide the major channel for policy formulation. Some, like Wilensky (1975), regard 'politics' as peripheral to the formation of policy, while others, like Castles (1989) maintain that the agenda is shaped by the processes of liberal democracy (Parsons 1995: section 2.11).

6 *The Whitehall model*: This contends that civil servants either initiate major policy or so alter it as it passes through their hands as to make it substantially theirs – thus making them the key influence on policy. Allison (1971) argued that bureaucracies do not meekly do the bidding of elected masters but are fragmented, competing centres of power: in John's words, 'Policy often arrives as the outcome of an uncoordinated fight between government bureaus' (John 1998: 44). Ministers discuss possible future actions with their very experienced and able advisers. If a trusted senior civil servant advises against a new initiative, this is bound to give the minister pause for more thought and adjustments might be made or the idea might even be dropped completely. Whitehall is not just 'in the loop' of policy making, *it is an essential part* of this loop.

The final two theories concentrate upon the way in which decision makers set about their tasks.

7 *Rational decision making*: This approach assumes that decision makers behave in a logical, sequential fashion. Accordingly, they will identify their objectives, formulate possible strategies, think through their implications and finally

choose the course of action that on balance best achieves their objectives. This approach is consistent with the traditional model in that civil servants undertake the analysis and then offer up the options for popularly elected politicians to take the decisions (see Parsons 1995: section 3.4; John 1998: Chapter 6).

8 *Incrementalism*: This approach, associated with the hugely influential work of Charles Lindblom, denies that policy makers are so rational and argues that in practice they usually try to cope or 'muddle through'. They tend to start with the status quo and make what adjustments they can to manage or at least accommodate new situations. In other words, policy makers do not solve problems but merely adjust to them. The case of privatisation argues against this 'adjusting' approach in that when Nigel Lawson came to consider it in the early 1980s the cupboard, in terms of relevant files and experience, was totally bare. Instead, Conservative ministers had to devise wholly new approaches and, whatever one's views on the outcome, it is perhaps to their credit that – even allowing for a determined Prime Minister and a large majority – they succeeded in a government culture so resistant to radical innovation.

It is clear that most of these models are basically descriptive, while others, like the rational choice and conventional models, are also partially prescriptive – they offer an ideal approach as to how policies should be made – but cannot necessarily tell us how decisions are actually made.

It is also obvious that echoing somewhere within each approach is the ring of truth. It would not be too difficult to find examples in support of any of the above models. The truth is that policy making is such a protean, dense area of activity that it is extremely difficult to generalise and be accurate in all cases. Nevertheless, the search for valid statements is worth the effort, otherwise our political system will remain incomprehensible. We will therefore look at the process in greater detail in a search for some generally true propositions about it.

■ The policy cycle

If they agree on nothing else, policy study scholars seem to agree that policy making can be understood better as a cycle; a problem arrives on the agenda and is processed by the system until an answer is found. Analyses of the cycle can be quite sophisticated. Hogwood and Gunn (1984) discern a number of stages: deciding to decide (issue search and agenda setting); deciding how to decide; issue definition, forecasting; setting objectives and priorities; options analysis; policy implementation, monitoring and control; evaluation and review; and policy maintenance, succession or termination. However, Lindblom disagrees. He argues that 'Deliberate or orderly steps . . . are not an accurate portrayal of how the policy process actually works. Policy making is, instead, a complexly interactive process without beginning or end' (Lindblom and Woodhouse 1993: 11, quoted in Parsons 1995: 22). However, policy studies can appear overly abstract and removed from reality at times; for the limited purposes of this chapter, three easily understood stages will suffice: initiation, formulation and implementation. These are considered below but first a brief look at how 'problems' come to be defined as such and how they come to be seen as requiring solutions.

'Social construction' of problems

This concept appears in Dorey (2006: 8–11) and relates to the evolving nature of things requiring action. In the nineteenth century women were denied certain basic rights and could even be beaten or raped by their husbands. It has taken a long while but societal values have changed so that women have acquired the vote and legal protection against what is now seen as abuse. Similarly homosexuals – once persecuted and imprisoned – are now allowed to be themselves outside the reach of the criminal law. Attitudes towards legal drug use (alcohol, nicotine) and illegal use (cannabis, heroin, cocaine) are also in a constant state of change and influence related frameworks (for example, smoking is now seen as seriously unhealthy and is banned in workplaces).

Dorey also points out how wider values and ideological changes influence political action. Poverty was once not seen as a problem – prosperity was a personal responsibility – but by the twentieth century Liberal ideology was becoming the new orthodoxy; tax funded state assistance began to be introduced to alleviate problems of old age, illness and unemployment. Moreover, the extension of the vote to lower socio-economic strata, meant 'inaction' – which favoured employers and owners of property – was no longer so easy to maintain.

Agenda setting

John Kingdon (1995, see Dorey 2006: 27–31) perceived it necessary for three 'streams' to conjoin for an item to be added to public policy: the recognition of something as a problem (problem stream); the identification of possible solutions (policy stream); and the requisite opportunities – time, accession to power of a party prepared to act and so forth (political stream). For example, poverty was not seen as a legitimate concern of government until Liberalism and Socialism emerged to suggest it might be and no action was taken until the Liberal and Labour parties gained power for periods in the twentieth century.

Policy initiation

Agenda setting

Each government decision has a long and complex provenance, but all must start somewhere. It is tempting to think that they originate, eureka-like, in the minds of single individuals, but they are more often the product of debate or a general climate of opinion involving many minds. Policy initiatives, moreover, can originate in all parts of the political system. Setting the political agenda is a curiously elusive process. Items can be deliberately introduced by government, and clearly it has many routes available to it, e.g. Tony Blair in the summer of 1999 announcing in an interview that fox hunting really *would* be banned; or Blair again, announcing, in the wake of the 'cash for peerages' scandal in March 2006, that greater transparency would be introduced regarding loans to political parties. The media too have enormous power to set the agenda: Michael Buerk's reports from Ethiopia detailing a scale of famine that touched the nation and initiated assistance; Alan Milburn, in an interview on 9 April 2006, refusing to say he would not be a candidate for the leadership when Blair stood down.

Figure 21.2 depicts six groups of possible policy initiators placed on a continuum starting from the periphery and moving in towards the nerve centre of government in No. 10. The figure uses the idea of 'distance from the centre', capturing the truth that the routes into policy making are many and varied (see also Parsons 1995: section 2.4).

General public

The public's role in policy making is usually limited to (the democratically vital function of) voting for a particular policy package at general elections. They do have other occasional opportunities, however, for example the referendums on the EC and Scottish and Welsh devolution in the 1970s, and pressures can be built up through lobbying MPs, as when, in the mid-1980s, Sir Keith Joseph was forced to withdraw his proposals to charge parents for a proportion of

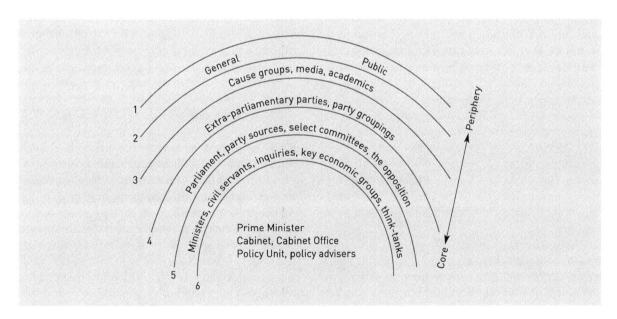

Figure 21.2 Policy initiatives

their children's university tuition fees. Occasionally, events occur that create widespread public concern, and governments often take action in the wake of them. For example, legislation on dogs was enacted after a spate of attacks by dogs on children one summer in the 1980s, and handguns were banned after the Dunblane shootings of March 1996. In many cases – as in the two just cited – such precipitate action, in reaction to the sudden rousing of public opinion, proves to be poorly framed and receives much criticism. In more recent years, public opinion has been roused by the proposed fox hunting ban and the war in Iraq in spring 2003. Both attracted huge demonstrations in London; in the former case they had some observable effect in delaying and altering proposed measures, but in the latter case Tony Blair carried on, convinced that he was right, and ignored the public outcry. However, the repercussions and damage of ignoring public and party opposition may take years to make themselves felt; what is without doubt is that Blair paid a heavy price in political support for ignoring the Iraq outcry.

Cause groups, media and academic experts

Many cause groups (see also Chapter 10) operate in the 'wilderness' – their values antithetical to government and not listened to – and many also stay there, but some do influence public opinion and decision makers and after years of struggle achieve action on issues such as abortion, capital punishment and the environment. Others achieve success on specific issues after an extended period of campaigning, such as Des Wilson's 1960s and 1970s campaign to reduce lead in petrol. Some groups achieve success via a single well-publicised event such as the Countryside Alliance's march on the Labour Party conference in 1999, which caused the government to postpone action on fox hunting during the coming session (despite Blair's assurances that he would act). Certain policy 'environments' will include a bewildering array of pressure groups, all of which seek to lean on the policy-making tiller. Local government associations, for example, are particularly important in areas like education, housing and social services.

Media coverage heavily affects the climate in which policy is discussed, and important policy proposals occasionally emerge from television programmes, newspaper editorials, articles in journals and so forth. One editorial on its own would have little effect, but a near consensus in the press might well stimulate action. Occasionally ideas are picked up from individual journalists – Mrs Thatcher used to be advised regularly by right-wing journalists such as Woodrow Wyatt, Paul Johnson and Simon Heffer. Other media figures who used to be consulted regularly on policy matters by Margaret Thatcher included the press magnates Rupert Murdoch and Conrad Black. Murdoch was also rumoured to advise Blair whenever he chose to visit Downing Street and where, because of his massive media clout, he was assured of a warm welcome. One commentator even argued Murdoch was virtually an additional member of the Cabinet (Wilby 2006). We also know that a wide range of influential people were regularly invited to dine with the Blairs at the PM's official rural retreat, Chequers, and almost certainly dinner-table conversation occasionally results in some kind of action. Lord Levy, a tennis partner of Tony Blair, eventually found himself acting as Blair's emissary to the Middle East and later as a key fund raiser (in March 2006 controversially so, when the 'loans for peerages' row erupted) for the Labour Party.

Occasionally the media provide crucial information. The classic example of this was in 1987, when Nigel Lawson, as Chancellor, denied entry to the ERM by prime ministerial veto, had tried to achieve his object by other means, namely manipulating the value of the pound to shadow that of the deutschmark. When *Financial Times* journalists interviewed Margaret Thatcher, they questioned her about this policy. She denied any knowledge of it but when they produced definitive evidence in the form of charts she accepted, somewhat surprised, that they were correct, and the stage was set for the mammoth argument that resulted in Lawson's damaging resignation two years later and the beginning of the end of her reign in No. 10 (for more on the media and agenda setting, see Parsons 1995: section 2.3).

All these agencies in the 'outer rim' (see Figure 21.2) interact to provide that intangible climate of discussion that encourages the emergence of certain proposals and inhibits others. Each policy environment has its own climate created by its specialist press, pressure groups, academics, practitioners and the like, who frequently meet in conferences and on advisory committees. Specific policy environments therefore exist in their 'own' world but also exist in a wider, overarching reality – e.g. an economic recession, an overseas war – which sets limits to and influences policy content.

However, an interesting feature of these peripheral bodies is that from time to time they are blessed

BIOGRAPHY

David Hume (1711–73)

Scottish philosopher and historian. Studied in Edinburgh – where his depressive temperament meant it took time for him to settle – but went to live in France, where he wrote his *Treatise on Human Nature* (1739). He questioned the validity of principles, which he described as 'artificial', and challenged the notion of natural law as well as the social contract ideas of Hobbes, Locke and Rousseau. Hume was bitterly disappointed when his opus failed to make much impact, but his *Essays Moral and Political* (1743), produced shortly afterwards, were an instant success and confirmed his reputation as one of the founding, and greatest, British empiricist philosophers of his age.

with favour, their arguments listened to, their proposals adopted, their leaders embraced by government and given advisory or even executive status. It is almost as if, godlike, the government has reached down and plucked them up to place them – albeit temporarily – on high.

Part 2 of this book explained how policy emerged out of an ideological framework and pointed out how academics, philosophers and other thinkers had contributed towards these frameworks. The most obvious influences on the Left would include Karl Marx, R.H. Tawney, Harold Laski, William Beveridge and, incomparably in the economic sphere, J.M. Keynes. Right-wing writers would include figures such as David Hume and Michael Oakeshott and (on economics from the 1970s onwards) the two overseas academics Friedrich Hayek and Milton Friedman. Academics specialising in specific policy areas such as transport, housing, criminology and so forth also regularly come up with proposals, some of which are taken up or drawn upon. John Major welcomed the views of the so-called 'seven wise men'

Lord Anthony Giddens, Blair's sociologist guru on Third Way thinking
Source: Press Association Images / Associated Press

BIOGRAPHY

Michael Oakeshott (1901–90)

Conservative philosopher. Educated at Cambridge, where he taught until 1949. *Experience and its Modes* (1933) was his first notable work. His writings lie within the pragmatic, sceptical traditions of Conservative thinking. He did not believe the purpose of politics was to achieve any particular end; rather, he saw the politicians' role as guiding the ship of state, enabling people to live their lives. He was a professor at the London School of Economics from 1950 to 1969.

(selected academics) on economic policy. Blair and Brown established a formal committee called the Monetary Policy Committee comprising academics and financial experts who every month advise the Bank of England on interest rates. On other occasions, academics can suddenly be welcomed in by leading figures in government, as when sociologist Anthony Giddens was used by Blair as a kind of 'guru' regarding the formulation of 'Third way' thinking.

Extra-parliamentary parties and party groupings

Both the Labour and Conservative extra-parliamentary parties find it easier to influence their respective leaders in opposition than in government. As Chapter 10 noted, Labour's system of internal democracy gave a substantial policy-making role to the trade unions, the National Executive Committee and the party conference during the 1930s and up until the 1970s (New Labour somewhat emasculated conference during and since the 1990s). The Conservative Party is far less democratic, but conference can set the mood for policy formulation, the research department can initiate important proposals, and the Advisory Committee on Policy did much to reformulate the main outlines of Conservative policy in the late 1970s.

Party groupings – many of which have contacts with Parliament – can also exert influence. The Fabian Society, founded in 1884, has long acted as a kind of left-wing think tank (see Box 21.1), and in the 1980s the once left-wing Labour Coordinating Committee was influential in advising Neil Kinnock

as he shifted Labour's policies towards the centre. Similarly, the No Turning Back Group in the Conservatives sought to keep the party on the right-wing track indicated by their heroine Margaret Thatcher, both before and after her fall from power, and it took the 'Cameron uprising' in the autumn of 2005 to remove what many perceived as its dead hand. The Institute for Public Policy Research (IPPR) has established itself over the past decade as a kind of Blairite think tank, constantly on hand to feed in relevant ideas and research findings.

Parliament

The role of Parliament in initiating policy can be considered under two headings: party sources and party groups, and non-party sources. In government, parliamentary parties have to work through their backbench committees, although individual MPs seek to use their easy access to ministers to exert influence and press their own solutions. One Conservative MP, David Evans, pulled off the remarkable coup of convincing his Prime Minister that the identity card system introduced by Luton Town Football Club should be compulsorily introduced nationwide. His success was short-lived: the scheme was dropped in January 1990 (though it did not die – see the section on identity cards towards the end of this chapter).

The Opposition is concerned to prepare its policies for when and if it takes over the reins of government. Neil Kinnock wrested future policy making out of the party's NEC with his policy review exercise (1987–9), involving leading members of his frontbench team in the process. However, the Opposition also has to make policy 'on the hoof' in reaction to political events. It is their function and in their interests to oppose, to offer alternatives to government – but this is not easy. Opposition spokesmen lack the detailed information and support enjoyed by government; they need to react to events in a way that is consistent with their other policy positions; they need to provide enough detail to offer a credible alternative, yet avoid 'host-ages to fortune' and closing options should they come to power. The Conservatives after 1997 found it hard to perform as an effective opposition, through splits in their ranks and uncertain leadership. Most commentators judged that this was not good for the health of the nation's democracy; the election of the young and dynamic new leader, David Cameron, in December 2005 transformed this situation. Unsurprisingly,

BOX 21.1 IDEAS AND PERSPECTIVES

Think tanks

Mrs Thatcher regained her momentum partly because she discovered 'Thatcherism': a new set of ideas comprising the abolition of constraints in the economy, privatising state-owned enterprises and reform of the public sector. They were provided by the intelligentsia of the 'New Right', many of them working through think-tanks (*The Economist*, 18 November 1992).

After the demise of Thatcher in 1990, these American-style independent hot-houses of ideas receded. The Centre for Policy Studies (CPS) used to issue a report every fortnight, but with Major in power rather than its original patron, its output slowed to zero. The output of the Adam Smith Institute (ASI), once a pioneer in privatisation ideas, also slowed and with Blair in power it was reduced to producing a complimentary report on his first 200 days. The Institute for Economic Affairs (IEA) was the oldest right-wing think tank, but it also curtailed its activities once Thatcher had gone. It also has to be said that the disaster of the 'poll tax', a product of the ASI, contributed to their declining respect. And the splits did not help: Graham Mather left the IEA to form his own European Policy Forum, while David Willetts at the CPS left after criticism to become an MP and director of the Social Market Foundation.

Labour has been relatively light on think tanks, but the Fabian Society, set up by the Webbs in 1884, has effectively been a highly influential think tank for over 100 years. It still exists with an impressive membership from the public and the parliamentary party. It organises seminars and conferences and keeps up a good flow of pamphlets and serious studies, a post-1997 one being the work of a certain Tony Blair. In addition, at the current time there is the Institute for Public Policy Research (IPPR), which has produced a number of New Labour studies. Demos – initially headed by Geoff Mulgan before he became a No. 10 adviser is now led by Tom Bentley. Are think tank personnel merely seeking to enter politics and become MPs? According to Tom Clougherty, the young director of the ASI, during a student study group visit in March 2009, his role gave him far more influence than any MP might exert. Certainly many think tank personnel have made the journey into senior advisory or ministerial positions, for example David Miliband (IPPR), John Redwood (Centre Policy Studies) and Geoff Mulgan (Demos) (see Dorey 2006: 19–26)

he initially poured energy into changing the unpopular image and 'brand' of his party, and his policy statements were little more than statements of intent, designed to drag the party into the middle ground on social justice and the environment. Creating detailed policies, announced Oliver Letwin in April 2006, would take another eighteen months of focused effort. Received wisdom for oppositions is that such exercises are best left until close to the election; an abiding problem for oppositions is that any good ideas they might come up with can be stolen by government and represented as its own.

Party groups (some of which have membership outside Parliament) such as the Bow Group, Monday Club, Tribune and Campaign Group can all have peripheral – but rarely direct – influence on policy making.

The seventeen departmental select committees regularly make reports and recommendations, some of which are adopted. Most experts agree that these committees are much more important now that their proceedings can be televised, especially the Treasury Committee which summoned so many senior finance people for interrogation in the wake of the banking collapse in 2008. Most reports represent cross-party consensus on specific issues but others, such as the Social Services Committee, once chaired by the much admired (and briefly a minister) Frank Field, can offer wide-ranging and coherent alternatives to government policy. Individual MPs probably have a better chance of influencing specific, usually very specific, policy areas through the opportunities available to move private members' bills (see Chapter 15).

Failure to utilise the policy-making machinery provided by the governing party can lead to dissent. In May 2003, certain Labour MPs were complaining that the Prime Minister, set on ignoring Parliament, was now introducing policy – especially that relating to universities – that had originated wholly in his own office and not at all in the governing party. Party critics claimed 'top-up fees' in higher education in the autumn of 2003 was the product of Downing Street adviser Andrew Adonis – appointed and not elected, of course. After a cliff-hanging process of accommodation by the government of these internal criticisms, the bill eventually became an act on 27 January 2004 by a majority of only five. Adonis was later elevated to the peerage and made schools minister after the 2005 election.

Ministers, departments, official inquiries and 'think tanks'

Strong-minded ministers will always develop policy ideas of their own either as a reflection of their own convictions or to get noticed and further their ambitions. Michael Heseltine, in the wake of the Toxteth troubles, probably shared both motivations when he submitted a paper to the Cabinet called 'It Took a Riot', proposing a new and un-Thatcherite approach to inner city regeneration: the policy was not accepted by Cabinet but was partially implemented in Merseyside, though not elsewhere. Such major initiatives are not the province of civil servants, but through their day-to-day involvement in running the country they are constantly proposing detailed improvements and adjustments to existing arrangements. Such initiatives are not necessarily the preserve of senior officials: even junior officers can propose changes that can be taken up and implemented.

A Royal Commission can be the precursor to major policy changes (for example, the Redcliffe–Maud Royal Commission on Local Government, 1966–9), but Margaret Thatcher was not well disposed towards such time-consuming, essentially disinterested procedures – she always felt she knew what needed doing – and during the 1980s none was set up. Major, however, set up the Royal Commission on Criminal Justice, and Blair the Royal Commission on the House of Lords in 2000 chaired by Lord Wakeham. He has also initiated scores of task forces and inquiries to prepare the ground for new legislation. Departments regularly establish their own inquiries, often employing outside experts, which go on to make important policy recommendations.

Right-wing think tanks were especially favoured by Margaret Thatcher (see Box 21.1). *The Economist* (6 May 1989) noted how she spurned Oxbridge dons – the traditional source of advice for No. 10 – and suggested that 'the civil service is constitutionally incapable of generating the policy innovation which the prime minister craves'. Instead, as a reforming premier she instinctively listened to the advice of 'people who have been uncorrupted by the old establishment'. Think tank advice was often channelled to Margaret Thatcher via the No. 10 Policy Unit. Their radical suggestions acted as a sounding board when published and helped to push the climate of debate further to the right. If new ideas are received in a hostile fashion, ministers can easily disavow them. The 'privatisation' of government advice in the form of think tanks was a striking feature of Margaret Thatcher's impact upon policy making. The Institute for Public Policy Research (IPPR) has established itself over the past decade as a kind of Blairite think tank, constantly on hand to feed in relevant ideas and research findings (see Box 21.1).

Prime Minister and Cabinet

This is the nerve centre of government, supported by the high-powered network of Cabinet committees, the Cabinet Office, the No. 10 Policy Unit and policy advisers. After a period of ten years in office, it is likely that any Prime Minister will dominate policy making. Chapter 17 made it clear that while many sought to whisper policy suggestions in her ear, Margaret Thatcher's radical beliefs provided her with an apparently full agenda of her own. The evidence of her extraordinary personal impact on major policy areas is plain to see: privatisation, trade union legislation, the environment, the exchange rate, sanctions against South Africa, the poll tax and Europe – the list could go on. However, she was also unusual in taking a personal interest in less weighty matters such as her (ill-starred) attempt to clean up litter from Britain's streets following a visit to litter-free Israel. Harold Wilson saw himself as a 'deep lying halfback feeding the ball forward to the chaps who score the goals'. Thatcher was not content with this role: she wanted to score the goals as well. Wilson also said that a Prime Minister governs by 'interest and curiosity': Thatcher had insatiable appetites in both respects and an energy that enabled her to feed them to a remarkable degree. Under her, assisted by her own relentless energy and a constitution that delivers so much power to the executive, the office of Prime Minister took on a policy-initiating role comparable, perhaps, with that of the US President. John Major was also exceptionally hard-working, as premiers must be, but he was happy to delegate more than his predecessor and to listen to voices around the Cabinet table, especially that of his powerful deputy, Michael Heseltine. Blair proved to be a premier more in the Thatcher mould, bypassing Cabinet and making decisions in small groups of close advisers (allegedly sitting on the sofa in No. 10 Downing Street), especially his 'kitchen cabinet', which originally included Alastair Campbell, Jonathan Powell and, more often than not, unelected aides rather than elected politicians (see Chapter 17). Blair continued the 'presidentialising' tendency in British politics, dominating the spotlight of national attention and conducting a very personal style of government. The decision to back George W. Bush in his assault on Iraq in 2003 was very much the result of Blair's own passionate determination that this policy was the morally correct one. In her evidence to the Foreign Affairs Select Committee on 17 June 2003, Clare Short claimed a 'shocking collapse in proper government procedure' in that all the main decisions were made by Blair and a small unelected entourage of Blair, Alastair Campbell, Lady (Sally) Morgan, Jonathan Powell and adviser David Manning. Throughout the process, Foreign Secretary Jack Straw had been a mere 'cypher'. Gordon Brown claimed he would seek a return to more traditional policy-making but in practice – for example over the 2008 economic crisis – this did not appear to be the case (see Box 21.2 later in this chapter).

The concept of the core executive

This approach to understanding the nerve centre of British government has come into its own in recent years as it provides a clearer picture of how decision-making occurs while supplying a number of useful correctives to more traditional thinking (for a fuller discussion see Chapter 17). The basic idea of the core executive is that decision making takes place at the highest level, constituted by a body of leading figures drawn, depending on the issue, from the Prime Minister's Office, the Cabinet and Cabinet Office plus the head officials of the departments concerned with the particular issue. This is a more helpful concept in that it reduces the notion of a simple hierarchy and replaces the idea of a tip to the pyramid with that of a halo or circle of key people. This is also useful in that it avoids the diversion of the difference between the political and administrative, the minister and civil servant. Anyone who has been involved in policy making will describe how civil servants – in theory policy 'eunuchs' who merely stand by loyally while politicians undertake this democratically driven function – participate in its evolution as centrally as any politician. And the same goes, in recent years, for the top political advisers like Alastair Campbell. It also embraces the idea of a permanent core of central 'players' on the policy-making stage plus a regular cast who visit according to the issue on the agenda. One of the best short accounts of the core executive – Moran (2005), *Politics and Governance in the UK* – elaborates usefully on the modern PM's office:

The details [of the PM's Office] constantly change, partly because prime ministers constantly worry about whether they are being adequately served, and partly because life at the centre has a frenetic, hothouse quality: little empires are constantly being built (and dismantled) as different people struggle for the ear of the prime minister and for their own personal advancement. The atmosphere is rather like that of the court of a monarch, where the skill lies in catching the ear and the eye of the powerful one.

Moran (2005: 118)

So private secretaries will process the information and paper which goes before the top person; combinations of civil servants and political advisers will feed in policy advice; and the press office will seek to ensure that what disseminates out to the wider political system, and beyond that to voters themselves, is formulated – with great sensitivity and sophistication – in a way which will advance policy objectives and not undermine them.

From this brief and admittedly selective description it is clear that:

- Policy can be initiated at both the micro and macro levels from within any part of the political system, but the frequency and importance of initiatives grow as one moves from the periphery towards the centre.

- Even peripheral influences can be swiftly drawn into the centre should the centre wish it.

- Each policy environment is to some extent a world unto itself with its own distinctive characteristics.

- The core executive, comprising the system's top decision makers, will be complicit in formulating high policy and directing it outwards and downwards to the relevant parts of the government machine.

Higher education policy making, for example, will include, just for starters, the Prime Minister, the Cabinet, the No. 10 Policy Unit, plus senior officials from Education (the core executive) assisted by think tanks, numerous parliamentary and party committees, more middle-ranking officials from the Departments of Education and Employment, the Treasury, the funding councils for the universities, the Committee of Vice-Chancellors and Principals, the University and College Union and other unions, and *The Times Higher Education Supplement*, together with a galaxy of academic experts on any and every aspect of the subject. Downing Street policy – not just the PM but his network of aides and advisers – is now of key importance in this high-profile policy area.

Policy formulation

Once a policy idea has received political endorsement it is fed into the system for detailed elaboration. This process involves certain key players from the initiation process, principally civil servants, possibly key pressure group leaders and outside experts (who usually are also political sympathisers) and, usually at a later stage, ministers. In the case of a major measure, there is often a learning phase in which civil servants and ministers acquaint themselves with the detail of the measure: this may require close consultation with experts and practitioners in the relevant policy environment. The measure, if it requires legislation, then has to chart a course first through the bureaucracy and then the legislature.

The bureaucratic process

This will entail numerous information-gathering and advisory committee meetings and a sequence of coordinating meetings with other ministries, especially the Treasury if finance is involved. Some of these meetings might be coordinated by the Cabinet Office, and when ministers become involved the measures will be progressed in Cabinet committees and ultimately full Cabinet before being passed on

to parliamentary counsel, the expert drafters of parliamentary bills.

The legislative process

As Chapters 15 and 16 explained, this process involves several readings and debates in both chambers. Studies show that most legislation passes through unscathed, but controversial measures will face a number of hazards, which may influence their eventual shape. Opposition MPs and peers may seek to delay and move hostile amendments, but more important are rebellions within the government party: for example, determined backbench Labour opposition to the university top-up fees legislation in January 2004 produced a series of amendments to the measure which made the original proposal almost unrecognisable – though such examples are rare. The task of piloting measures through the legislature falls to ministers, closely advised by senior officials, and this is often when junior ministers can show their mettle and make a case for their advancement.

From this brief description it is clear that four sets of actors dominate the policy formulation process: ministers, civil servants, pressure group leaders and an array of experts appropriate to the subject. Some scholars calculate that the key personnel involved in policy formulation might number no more than 3,500. As in policy initiation, Margaret Thatcher also played an unusually interventionist role in this process. Reportedly she regularly called ministers and civil servants into No. 10 to speed things up, shift developments on to the desired track or discourage those with whom she disagreed. It would seem that Tony Blair was in the same mould and maybe more so, raging in public and private at the inertia of the public sector and the more general 'forces of conservatism' he criticised at the 1999 Bournemouth party conference. Dynamic politicians like Thatcher and Blair become impatient at the slowness with which the wheels of government turn and so seek to catalyse its progress through personal interventions. In her resignation speech Clare Short, who resigned in May 2003 over the role of the UN in reconstructing Iraq, bitterly attacked Blair's centralisation of policy making in a fashion which was still valid in 2006:

I think what's going on in the second term in this government, power is being increasingly centralised around the prime minister and just a few advisers, ever increasingly few. The Cabinet is now only a 'dignified'

Genghis the Tory. Riddell suggests right-wing forces exist behind Cameron
Source: Copyright © Chris Riddell. From the *Observer*, 30 August 2009. Reproduced with permission from Guardian Newspapers Limited

part of the constitution. It's gone the way of the Privy Council. Seriously, various policy initiatives are being driven by advisers [in No. 10] who are never scrutinised, never accountable.

Lord Butler of Brockwell, former Cabinet Secretary, was a well-known sceptic of Blair's methods involving political aides and meetings on the Number 10 sofa. His July 2004 *Review of Intelligence on Weapons of Mass Destruction*, arising from the decision to invade Iraq alongside US forces, contained a section on the machinery of government. In it the report cited evidence from two former Cabinet members who 'expressed their concern about the informal nature of much of the Government's decision-making process, and the relative lack of use of established Cabinet Committee machinery' (pp. 146–7). Specifically, the report pointed out that from April 2002 to the outbreak of hostilities, the Defence and Overseas Policy Committee did not meet once, yet there were 'some 25 meetings attended by key Ministers, officials and military officers most closely involved [who] provided the

framework of discussion and decision making within Government'.

Policy implementation

It is easy to assume that once the government has acted on something or legislated on an issue it is more or less closed. Certainly the record of government action reveals any number of measures that have fulfilled their objectives: for example, the Attlee government wished to establish a National Health Service and did so; in the 1980s, Conservative governments wished to sell off houses to council tenants and did so. But there are always problems that impede or sometimes frustrate implementation or that produce undesired side effects. Between legislation and implementation many factors intervene. Jordan and Richardson (1982: 234–5) quote the conditions that Hood suggests need to be fulfilled to achieve perfect implementation:

1   There must be a unitary administrative system rather like a huge army with a single line of

309

authority. Conflict of authority could weaken control, and all information should be centralised in order to avoid compartmentalism.

2　The norms and rules enforced by the system have to be uniform. Similarly, objectives must be kept uniform if the unitary administrative system is to be really effective.

3　There must be perfect obedience or perfect control.

4　There must be perfect information and perfect communication – as well as perfect coordination.

5　There must be sufficient time for administrative resources to be mobilised.

To fulfil wholly any, let alone all, of these conditions would be rare indeed, so some degree of failure is inevitable with any government programme. Examples are easy to find.

Education

The 1944 Education Act intended that the new grammar, technical and secondary modern schools were to be different but share a 'parity of esteem'. In practice this did not happen: grammar schools became easily the most prestigious and recruited disproportionately from the middle classes: the government could not control parental choice. To remedy this, comprehensive schools were set up in the 1950s and 1960s, but it was the middle-class children who still performed best in examinations. Reformers also neglected one crucial and in retrospect blindingly obvious factor: comprehensive schools recruit from their own hinterlands, so inner-city schools draw children from predominantly working-class areas with a culture tending to produce lower educational standards, while suburban schools are drawn from more middle-class families who place a high value on education and whose children consequently achieve higher standards. The government made policy on the basis of inadequate information and awareness.

Poll tax

The euphemistically named 'community charge' – known as the 'poll tax' – was the brainchild variously of right-wing think tanks, Kenneth Baker, William Waldegrave and others (although following its collapse most people were keen to disclaim parentage – political failures, unsurprisingly, are always

'orphans'). The rationale behind it was logical; local taxes – the 'rates' – were based on property but penalised the wealthy, who paid more on big properties. However, over half were either exempted or received rebates yet still enjoyed the benefits of local services; consequently they had no reason to vote for lower rates and were not 'accountable' for them in the opinion of Conservatives like Thatcher, a keen supporter of the scheme. The new tax was to be a flat-rate one and payable by all to some degree, even students and the unemployed. The obvious unfairness of taxing the poor as heavily as the rich was widely recognised, even by Conservative voters. Yet Thatcher's personal support, defiant style and the pusillanimous nature of many MPs and ministers – Michael Portillo informed conference that he was not daunted but 'delighted' to be placed in charge of it – let a clearly flawed law onto the statute book. In March 1990, polls showed a huge majority opposed it and on 7 April a riot erupted in London. When John Major succeeded Thatcher he quickly replaced the measure with one more closely resembling the old property-based rates, and the heat soon left the issue of local government finance (for more on the poll tax, see Chapter 19). Programme failure also often results from the operation of constraints that constantly bear upon policy makers.

Constraints upon policy makers

Financial resources

Policy makers have to operate within available financial resources, which are a function of the nation's economic health at any particular time, and the willingness of key decision makers, especially in the Treasury, to make appropriate provision from funds available to government.

Political support

This is initially necessary to gain endorsement for a policy idea, but support is also necessary throughout the often extended and complex policy-making process. Lack of it, for example, characterised the tortured birth of the poll tax as well as its ignominious demise. Support at the political level is also crucial, but it is highly desirable within the bureaucracy and elsewhere in the policy environment. Resistance to policies can kill them off *en route*, and anticipated resistance is also important; as Jordan and Richardson (1982: 238) hypothesised: 'There are probably more policies which are never introduced because of the anticipation of resistance, than policies which have failed because of resistance.' Some departments now seek to gauge levels of popular support through the use of focus groups, a technique borrowed from commercial and political marketing (see Chapter 18 and below).

Competence of key personnel

An able, energetic minister is likely to push policy measures through; a weak minister is not. Civil servants are famously able in Britain, but even they need to work hard to be up to the task of mastering rapidly the detail of new measures; their failure will impede the progress of a measure and limit its efficacy. Tony Blair has created (maybe necessary) waves in the Civil Service by emphasising the primacy of 'delivery'. Civil servants must be able to achieve practical things as well as advise ministers.

Time

New legislative initiatives need to carve space out of a timetable so overcrowded that winners of Private Members' ballots are lobbied by departments themselves to adopt bills awaiting parliamentary consideration. Moreover, the whole system is arguably over-centralised and, some would say, chronically overloaded.

Timing

Measures can fail if timing is not propitious. Just after a general election, for example, is a good time to introduce controversial measures. Margaret Thatcher, it will be recalled, was unable to secure the sale of British Leyland to an American company in the spring of 1986 because she had lost so much support over the Westland episode.

Coordination

Whitehall departments divide up the work of government in a particular way: proposals that fall between ministries are often at a disadvantage, and the job of coordinating diverse departments is not, in the view of critics, managed with particular efficiency. Burch (1979: 133) also notes that:

Too often policy making becomes a conflict between departments for a share of the limited resources available. This is ... especially true of expenditure politics
when departments fight for their own corner at the cost of broader policy objectives.

Personality factors

Key decision makers are not as rational as perhaps they ought to be. They might have personal objectives – ambition, desire for image and status, and rivalries – which lead them to oppose rather than support certain policy objectives. The best recent examples concern rows between Prime Ministers and their Chancellors: Margaret Thatcher and Nigel Lawson in the late 1980s; Blair and Brown clashed bitterly over very many issues, for example entering the single currency – the euro, Blair was enthusiastic and Chancellor Brown cautious to the point of applying a veto to such a move.

Geographical factors

A bias in favour of the south-east is often detectable in government policies – for example, in the granting of defence contracts – partly because decision makers in our centralised system live in the home counties, partly because the south-east has a more buoyant economy and partly as a result of political factors: this after all is the heartland of the traditional party of government. (For a subtle and controversial analysis of territorial politics in the UK, see Bulpitt [1983].)

International events

The increasing interdependence of the large economies has made events such as the quadrupling of oil prices in the early 1970s major constraints upon policy making. In some cases these constraints are formal, as when the International Monetary Fund attached strict public expenditure conditions to its 1976 loan to Callaghan's Labour government. Political events such as the Falklands War can clearly have an enormous impact upon major policy areas, while the 1989 revolutions in the communist countries changed the whole context within which foreign policy is formulated. The greatest perturbations in the present century were caused initially by the terrorist attacks of 11 September 2001 followed by the successive US-led wars in Afghanistan and Iraq.

The influence of Europe

Treaty obligations and the growing power of Community institutions have imposed increasingly

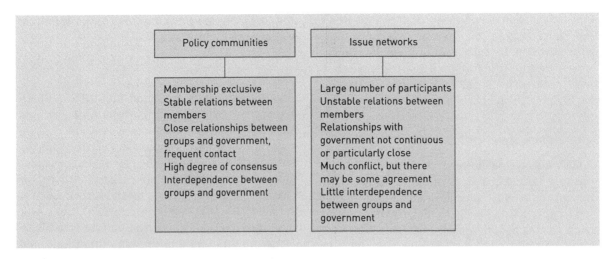

Figure 21.3 Policy networks
Source: Baggott (1995: 24)

powerful constraints upon the freedom of action that British policy makers have enjoyed (see Chapter 27). British policy making is now well embedded into the Brussels machinery with senior civil servants constantly travelling on the shuttle to Brussels, Strasbourg and Luxembourg.

Policy networks

Jordan and Richardson (1987) argued that policy making in Britain is not uniform; every aspect has its own specific characteristics. They lay less stress on manifestos or the activities of Parliament but point to the mass of interconnecting bodies that have an interest in the policy area: the 'policy community'.

To some extent this is a theory about how interest groups interact with government to help formulate policy. Access to the policy community is restricted to actors prepared to play the game: act constitutionally, accept that the government has the last word, keep agreements and make reasonable demands. These rules automatically exclude radical groups with high-profile campaigning styles in most cases, although the accession to power of a radical political message can alter this, as in the case of Thatcherism. To exercise real clout, a group has to become an 'insider' (see Chapter 10). Communities have a core and a periphery – rather like that suggested in Figure 21.3 – with the stable core continuously involved in the policy process and a secondary group, less stable in membership, involved from time to time but lacking the resources to be in the core.

Professor Rod Rhodes developed this idea but saw that often the policy community was not cohesive or sharply defined; he began to discern a more fragmented and more accessible form: a 'policy network' with a very large and constantly changing membership, often with conflicting views. Baggott's diagram (Figure 21.3) shows the contrast between the two ideas with some clarity. Baggott (1995: 26) criticises the approach for not explaining the provenance of the networks and over-concentrating on the group–government nexus to the exclusion of the broader political environment.

Comprehensive political marketing

Jennifer Lees-Marchment wrote a book in 2001 which argued that marketing had become so all-pervasive in modern politics that politicians now 'design' policies for the electoral market and then deliver them once in power. She claims parties no longer dispense 'grand ideologies' striving to convert voters to their faiths. Instead they have adjusted to the way we now vote: instrumentally, expecting parties to deliver on promises made in the marketplace of election campaigns. She argued that initially Labour was 'product-based' in the early 1980s when it persisted in selling something no one wanted. The result was failure. Then the party tried a 'sales-oriented' approach, improving its campaigning capacity through advertising, direct mailings and so forth. The result was better but still not enough to win. Then, as New Labour, it began to listen to 'market' demands via focus groups and polls, and fashioned a 'product' the market, i.e. voters, really wanted. The result was the 1997 landslide. The thesis has been criticised as showing politics as devoid of real passion, or any meaning at all; but the analysis is sufficiently acute for much of it to emit the ring of truth.

■ Case studies in policy making

This chapter concludes with two case studies: an examination of policy formulation and implementation in the Millennium Dome; and the ongoing issue of identity cards.

The Millennium Dome

A Conservative project

The provenance of this idea is to be found in John Major's 1992 administration: to celebrate the new millennium in a way that would capture the imagin-

ations of the British people, rather as the Festival of Britain had done in 1951. The Millennium Commission was set up in 1993 and received substantial funding from the National Lottery. Various ideas were mooted to celebrate the event, some located outside the capital – one in Birmingham being the strongest rival to the London region. Michael Heseltine was keen on an exhibition based on the site of an old gasworks on the Greenwich peninsula on the prime meridian (0 degrees longitude). He became the driving force behind it, being appointed to the Millennium Commission when it was set up in 1994 and continuing in this role after becoming Deputy Prime Minister in 1995. In 1996, he set up a Cabinet subcommittee to progress the idea and to raise capital from bankers and businessmen. Crick (1997: 430) tells how the DPM bullied and twisted arms, holding a series of weekly breakfast meetings to ensure that the project would be embraced by the government. The problem was that financing the project was very problematic, more so than the rejected Birmingham option. However, Heseltine was

Finding a use for the Millennium Dome continues to prove difficult
Source: Copyright © Chris Riddell. From the *Observer*, 10 September 2000. Reproduced with permission from Guardian Newspapers Limited

totally committed to the idea and steamrolled the doubters. In 1997, it seemed that the forthcoming election might imperil the project, so he personally lobbied Blair before the election (Heseltine 2000: 513) and won his agreement to continue with it (should he win the election), subject to a review.

New Labour adopts the Dome

New Labour considered the Dome in an early Cabinet. Blair, it seemed, was uncertain and dithered for a month over a decision. Peter Mandelson, grandson of Herbert Morrison, architect of the 1951 Festival, was the chief proponent of the project but was opposed by Gordon Brown, who scorned such PR approaches and was worried that the Treasury would have to bail out a possible failure. With a week to go, 'the costings were dubious; the sponsorship was absent; the contents were vague when not non-existent' (Rawnsley 2000: 54). Moreover, the press was mostly derisive and other ministers were highly sceptical, including Chris Smith, Frank Dobson (who said that the Dome should be 'fired into outer space'), Clare Short and David Blunkett. However, Blair was taken by Mandelson's flamboyant vision of a huge, symbolic, all-inclusive dome to celebrate the 'rebirth of Britain under New Labour'. It seems that the initial doubts of John Prescott had been won over by the regeneration aspects of the scheme. At a pre-Cabinet meeting on 19 June 1997, moreover, he insisted that abandonment of the project at this early stage would make them look 'not much of a government'. When Blair had to leave the meeting early, Prescott took over and faced so much criticism that he dared not take a vote. Instead, 'Tony wants it' was enough for the project to be approved. Blair chose to ignore the Dome's critics in the press, Parliament and Cabinet and to press on with the (destined) national 'folly'.

In a *Guardian* article (13 May 2003) following her resignation as International Development Secretary, Clare Short recalled the decision on the Dome being taken:

We went around the table and everyone spoke. I remember Donald Dewar saying you could have a party and free drink for everyone in the country and still save a lot of money. Then Tony said 'I've got to go' and went out and announced we were going ahead with the dome. John Prescott was left there to sum up and that's how we learned that Cabinet government was coming to an end.

Short added that this was too often the way in which bad decisions were taken.

The Dome

The structure was designed by the Richard Rogers Partnership and became the world's largest dome, covering, remarkably, nearly 20 acres. It was divided into six zones for the purposes of the exhibition, including a Learning Zone, a Body Zone, a Talk Zone and a Faith Zone. Mandelson was the first minister to be in charge of the project, Blair's former flatmate Lord Falconer the next in line. Jenny Page, a former civil servant, was made chief executive of the government-owned Millennium Experience Company. In 1997, the first of many public controversies was caused when Stephen Bayley, the somewhat volatile consultant creative director, resigned. Critics fastened onto the lateness of the project and the inaccessibility of the site plus the paucity of displays to fill the vast new arena. Mandelson's visit to Disneyland in January 1998 gave out all the wrong signals. Through the fog of government pronouncements the press delightedly began to discern something decidedly pear-shaped. Mandelson's 'it's going to knock your socks off' merely added fuel to negative expectations. The cost soon escalated from £200 million closer to £1 billion, and the undoubted quality of the Dome's structure – completed, astonishingly, on time – did not silence the critics, many of whom were invited to the opening celebration on New Year's Eve 1999. The evening's performances were rated as good but, by the greatest ill fortune, transport to the Dome broke down and huge crowds of key opinion formers were left waiting for three hours at a freezing East London station during which they sharpened their pens and then dipped them in vitriol for the next day's papers. Even New Labour's spin machine could not save the Dome from a comprehensive panning.

From then on it was downhill. The exhibitions were open to the public for the space of a year, and to meet financial targets twelve million members of the public were expected to pay the £20 entrance fee. However, actual attendance figures were half that, and while most who visited claimed that it was value for money, a vociferous minority insisted that it was not. Rawnsley comments acidly that 'The Dome was the vapid glorification of marketing over content, fashion over creation, ephemera over achievement . . . It was a folie de bombast' (2000: 327–30). Even a Dome supporter, Polly Toynbee in the *Guardian*, had to confess that it was 'a lemon'. Within weeks, the Dome had to be subsidised with a further £60 million of lottery money. In February

Jenny Page resigned, to be replaced by a Frenchman from Eurodisney, Pierre-Yves Gerbeau. The press assiduously reported the poor attendance and the breakdowns. In May, the chairman of the Millennium Company resigned. Poor 'Charlie' Falconer – the fall guy once Mandelson had departed – was forced to sustain a false enthusiasm for an unconscionable period. Eventually, the government came to sell the structure but found few takers. In the end, it gave the building away – in exchange for a share of putative profits – to a company which successfully turned it into a venue for rock concerts. A 'vacuous temple to political vanity' (Rawnsley 2000: 331) had lost the nation a sum of money that could have built many schools and hospitals.

What went wrong?

- *Icon politics*: The government opted for a vanity project with little focus or meaning. Moran (2001) calls this 'icon politics', projects chosen merely for their symbolic significance. Inevitably it was decided by those occupying the inner sanctum of government – it was intended to be Blair's opening manifesto ploy in his re-election campaign.

- *Entertainment ill-suited to government*: The project was entertainment-based, and governments are not designed or equipped to succeed in such a fickle area. Desperate attempts to please a huge audience almost inevitably turned into banality; whatever the media advisers might have sought to feed to the nation, no amount of spin could change this.

- *Financial warnings*: From early days, warnings regarding uncertain finances were ignored.

- *Cabinet doubts* were voiced but overruled because of the iconic significance of the project. Fear of damaging criticism from the Opposition meant that such high-level criticism failed to enter the public domain.

- *Abandonment* of the project at an early stage might have minimised the damage but the government – Blair to the fore – determined not to admit defeat and to brazen out the hurricane of flak.

All these factors contributed to the digging of an ever deeper hole by the government: a classic case of policy making gone horribly wrong.

Postscript: a happier ending?

The future of the Dome itself hung in the balance for a while. John Prescott was associated with a scheme inspired by billionaire Philip Anshcutz to turn it into a mega casino but opposition to such establishments eventually scuppered it. The US businessman was behind Meridian Delta, the company which bought the Dome in 2001. If permission can be obtained, part of the Dome is still in theory available for a super casino but the rest of it has been converted into a leisure facilities centre and an arena for music concerts. Bon Jovi provided the opening concert in June 2007 but the O_2 arena has now become a well-recognised facility, meaning that not all of the Millennium Dome concept has crumbled into dust and ridicule.

Identity cards

This second case study is different because it is an ongoing policy issue which will not be finally resolved for some years yet. This policy saga – for that is what it has become – first entered the public domain in February 2002 when David Blunkett, the then Home Secretary, announced an 'entitlement card' to prevent benefit fraud and deter terrorism. The idea soon attracted vitriolic criticism for its estimated cost of over a billion pounds and its erosion of civil liberties. In consequence the idea was repackaged to be introduced in stages with a full decision on a compulsory scheme delayed until 2013. Many suggested the idea should be dropped, but instead of dropping the scheme after the 2005 election it was submitted to Parliament at the end of June. This time, however, the card was to include biometric information relating to the subject's face, fingerprints and iris; it was passed on its second reading but the government's slimmed majority was further reduced by rebels – mostly from the left-wing Campaign Group – to a mere thirty-one. In the *Guardian* on 28 June 2005 Martin Kettle discussed objections by David Davis, Charles Clarke's Conservative Shadow Home Secretary, who had suggested that the idea had to pass the test of four questions:

1   Will it work to achieve its stated goals? Certainly it would help prevent benefit and identity fraud but few believe, even in government, that it would deter terrorists, producing an (at best) opaque case for the innovation in the first place. Debates in the Lords during January made the

case seem more 'dubious' the longer they continued, according to the *Guardian* on 18 January 2006. In a letter to the same paper on 23 January 2006, the minister in charge, Tony McNulty, argued that the card would be a major blow against financial and benefit fraud: 'linking a unique biometric to personal data means people have control over access to their details'.

2   Is the government capable of introducing such a system? IT-based schemes have turned out to be notoriously difficult to introduce successfully and huge amounts had been wasted by the NHS on new data processing which had proved calamitous, as had the tax credit scheme which had resulted in huge overpayments being claimed back from recipients.

3   Is it cost-effective? Initial estimates of the cost exceeded £1 bn but that soon tripled, with the

government's best estimate of the cost to the public of the card – in combination with a passport – being £93 per person. Over half of respondents to an ICM poll supported the scheme at such a price in June 2005. The Home Office calculated the cost at £6 bn over ten years, but a careful study by the LSE placed the total cost at £19 bn or even £24 bn. While rebutting the LSE estimate as absurd, the government resisted giving detailed costings on the grounds that such commercially sensitive information would prevent the public from receiving the best possible deal when contracts were issued. Lord Crickhowell in the Lords debate inevitably accused the government of offering the taxpayer a 'pig in the poke'.

4   Can civil liberties be safeguarded? The Information Commissioner, Richard Thomas, thinks

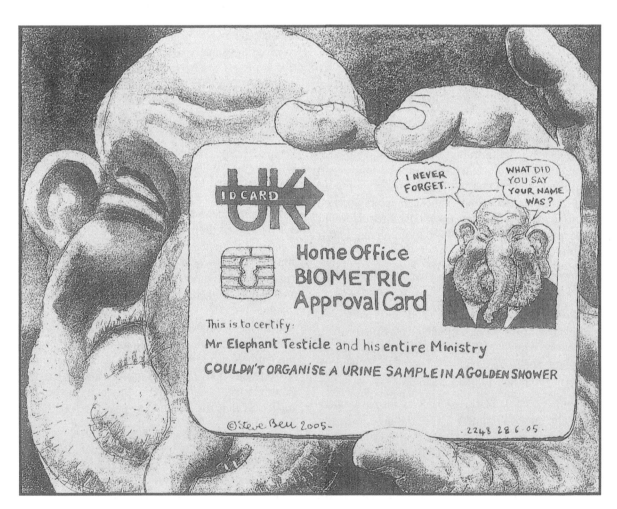

Steve Bell's caustic view on Charles Clarke's plans for ID cards
Source: Copyright © Steve Bell. From the *Guardian*, 28 June 2005. Reproduced with permission

not. He addressed the Home Affairs Select Committee in June 2004 and confessed himself 'increasingly alarmed' by the plan. He did not see a 'sufficient rationale' for recording for the whole population: their name, address, date of birth, gender, nationality and biometric details from finger and eye scans. The idea had 'potential for significant detrimental impact on the day-to-day lives of individuals'.

So, ID cards appear to be too expensive, too riskily experimental, and far too dangerous a violation of civil liberties. But the government – convinced that these judgements will all be proved wrong – was determined to push through a 'flagship' piece of legislation. On 29 March 2006 votes in both Houses appeared to end the conflict between the two Houses. Despite the opposition of the Liberal Democrats, the measure was passed in the House of Lords 287–60. MPs later approved it 301–84. From 2008 everyone renewing a passport will be issued an ID card and have their details placed on the National Identity Register. Through a legislative compromise, people will have the right, until 2010 not to be given a card; however, they will still have to pay for one and have their details placed on the NIR. Anyone seeking a passport after 2010 will be obliged to have an ID Card.

However, 'implementation' is subject to all kinds of pressures as we have seen. Public support for the idea was damaged by the loss of 25 million names by HMRC in November 2007. In March 2008 the Home Office announced that as a result of this loss plans had been put back by two years to 2012. In November it was announced that foreign nationals living in UK could apply for identity cards at a variety of centres thoughout the country. Eventually all foreign nationals will have to have such cards and by 2015 90 per cent will have been issued with one. In March 2008 the Home Office announced future plans on ID cards.

From 2011–12 everyone over 16 who applies for a passport will have fingerprints and facial scans added to a National Identity Register. From 2010 students will be encouraged to acquire ID cards. The aim was that everyone would eventually carry an ID card and the government hoped the nation would come to accept this as normal, just as it is in other European countries. However, the Conservatives and Liberal Democrats were strongly opposed on civil liberties grounds and when they formed their coalition after the May 2010 election, their Queen's Speech contained an 'Identity Documents Bill' to cancel the programme and destroy all data on the national identity register. So this substantial piece of policy making had a somewhat tortured history and fell at the last through that oldest of democratic reasons: the election of a new government.

BOX 21.2 BRITAIN IN CONTEXT

Policy making in the USA

Each political system produces different patterns of policy making. To some extent this is a direct reflection of system 'mechanics', but political culture and personalities as well as international factors often play important roles. So we see that in the USA, policy emerges via a route very different from that in the UK. At heart the British Prime Minister dominates the executive, like the President, but as long as his party is behind him, he also dominates the legislature. The US chief executive, however, is separately elected and has responsibility for initiating and implementing policy: on the face of it a more powerful figure. However, the US system is complex with myriad checks and balances.

The President is Head of State, Commander in Chief of the Armed Forces, Chief Appointing Officer, Chief Diplomat and, effectively, Chief Legislator. The President can veto any Congressional bill with which he disagrees; in addition to this he has responsibility for the successful implementation of policy. But these powers are balanced by the sole ability of Congress to declare war, the requirement for many appointments to be confirmed by the Senate, the need for a two-thirds majority to ratify treaties, the power of Congress over the making of new laws and the raising of revenue, the ability of Congress to override the veto with a two-thirds majority, and the ability of Congress to impeach the President for 'high crimes and misdemeanors'.

The President faces substantial foreign policy constraints from the Senate, made even more restrictive after the War Powers Act in 1973 in the wake of the Vietnam War. He has more freedom of action domestically but cannot set interest rates and is dependent on Congress for revenue. For a long time after the Constitution deemed that Congress would check the President, Congress was perceived as the more powerful institution, but in 1933 Roosevelt successfully extended presidential powers in a bid to overcome the problems created by the Depression. Since then the relationship has ebbed and flowed. Presidential success is crucially dependent on the President's ability to negotiate successfully with Congress; he often has to persuade dissident legislators from his *own* party to give him the support he needs to push measures through; party discipline is nowhere near as strong as in the UK. Congress may also, of course, be of a different political complexion, as Clinton found to his cost towards the end of his time in power.

The President appoints Cabinet members to lead departments but shares one much criticised feature of British politics: he tends to rely a great deal on personal aides and advisers. Both Thatcher and Blair were criticised for allowing their 'kitchen cabinets' to assume too much power, as did Nixon, Carter, Reagan and Clinton. George Bush Jr has also attracted some criticism but has perhaps tended to give secretaries of state like Rumsfeld and Rice relatively more room in which to operate. So a constant tension exists between departments and White House advisers as to whom the President listens and whose advice he follows.

The President has two other powerful weapons at his disposal. Firstly, he can appoint to the Supreme Court judges who tend to reflect his political views, thus influencing the context in which laws will be made over the next two to three decades. Secondly, he has unrivalled access to public opinion which he uses to encourage or even bully Congress into passing his laws. Roosevelt, when negotiating with unsympathetic Congressional leaders, used to glance meaningfully at the microphone placed on his desk in the Oval Office – it often did the trick. Public opinion is a constant resource available to the President as voters can be thus mobilised to put pressure on Congress to follow the presidential lead. This explains why presidential ratings are often taken more seriously in the US than those of the Prime Minister in the UK.

Chapter summary

Policy can be defined as either rules and regulations or public expenditure and its distribution. There are various theories about or models of policy making, including the pluralist, corporatist, ruling-class and Whitehall models, plus the rational choice and incrementalist perspectives on decision making. Policy can be seen to pass through three stages: initiation, formulation and implementation. 'Core' decision makers have a constant control of the process, but elements from the 'periphery' are brought in from time to time. The concept of policy networks is useful in analysing policy making. Extra-parliamentary parties and think tanks can have considerable influence, depending on the issue and the situation. Implementation can be very difficult and result in policy objectives being missed or even reversed. Policy makers face many restraints upon their actions, including timing, coordination and international events.

Discussion points

- Which model of policy making seems closest to reality?

- Should there be more popular control over policy making?

- How persuasive is Lindblom's theory of incrementalism?

- What lessons can be learned from the process whereby the Millennium Dome project brought into being?

Further reading

Building on the foundation texts of Lasswell, Simon, Lindblom, Etzioni, Dror and Wildavsky, the field of policy studies has spawned a substantial literature over the past forty years or more. In recent decades, Burch and Wood (1990) and Ham and Hill (1993) have provided good introductions to the denser studies available. Hogwood and Gunn (1984) is well written and interesting, as is Jordan and Richardson (1987). For an up-to-date and penetrating analysis see Smith (1993). The best comprehensive study of policy studies used to be Wayne Parsons' *Public Policy* (1995), but that role has been thankfully superseded by Peter Dorey's excellent shorter and more accessible *Policy Making in Britain*. Peter John's *Analysing Public Policy* (1998) and Michael Hill's *The Policy Process in the Modern State* (2000) are both short, competent, clear, though now slightly dated treatments. For a very good shorter introduction to the topic, Moran's *Politics and Governance in the UK* (2005: 412–50) has not been bettered.

Bibliography

Allison, G.T. (1971) *The Essence of Decision: Explaining the Cuban Missile Crisis* (Little, Brown).

Ashbee, E. and Ashford, N. (1999) *US Politics Today* (Manchester University Press).

Bachrach, P.S. and Baratz, M.S. (1970) *Power and Poverty, Theory and Practice* (Oxford University Press).

Baggott, R. (1995) *Pressure Groups Today* (Manchester University Press).

Bulpitt, J. (1983) *Territory and Power in the United Kingdom* (Manchester University Press).

Burch, M. (1979) 'The Policy Making Process', in B. Jones and D. Kavanagh (eds) *British Politics Today* (Manchester University Press).

Burch, M. and Wood, B. (1990) *Public Policy in Britain*, 2nd edn (Martin Robertson).

Butler, Lord of Brockwell (2004) *Review of Intelligence on Weapons of Mass Destruction*, HC898, July.

Castles, F. (1982) *The Impact of Parties* (Sage).

Castles, F. (1989) *The Comparative History of Public Policy* (Oxford University Press).

Crick, M. (1997) *Michael Heseltine* (Hamish Hamilton).

Dorey, P. (2006) *Policy Making in Britain* (Sage).

Downs, A. (1957) *An Economic Theory of Democracy* (Harper & Row).

Easton, D. (1965) *A Framework for Political Analysis* (Prentice Hall).

Etzioni, A. (1964) *A Comparative Analysis of Complex Organisations* (Prentice Hall).

Etzioni, A. (1968) *An Active Society: A Theory of Societal and Political Processes* (Free Press).

Franklin, B. (1998) *Tough on Soundbites, Tough on the Causes of Soundbites, Catalyst paper* 3 (Catalyst).

Hague, R., Harrop, M. and Breslin, S. (1998) *Comparative Government and Politics* (Macmillan).

Ham, C. and Hill, M. (1993) *The Policy Process in the Modern Capitalist State* (Harvester Wheatsheaf).

Heseltine, M. (2000) *Life in the Jungle: My Autobiography* (Coronet).

Hill, M.J. (ed.) (1993) *New Agendas in the Study of the Policy Process* (Harvester Wheatsheaf).

Hill, M. (2000) *The Policy Process in the Modern State* (Prentice Hall).

Hogwood, B. (1992) *Trends in British Public Policy* (Open University Press).

Hogwood, B. and Gunn, L.A. (1984) *Policy Analysis in the Real World* (Oxford University Press).

Jessop, B. (1990) *State Theory: Putting Capitalist States in Their Place* (Polity Press).

John, P. (1998) *Analysing Public Policy* (Pinter).

Jones, B. (1986) *Is Democracy Working?* (Tyne Tees TV).

Jordan, G. and Richardson, J.J. (1982) 'The British Policy Style or the Logic of Negotiation', in J.J. Richardson (ed.) *Policy Styles in Western Europe* (Allen & Unwin).

Jordan, G. and Richardson, J.J. (1987) *Governing Under Pressure* (Martin Robertson).

Lee, G. (1989) 'Privatisation', in B. Jones (ed.) *Political Issues in Britain Today*, 3rd edn (Manchester University Press).

Lees-Marchment, J. (2001) *Political Marketing and British Political Parties: The Party's Just Begun* (Manchester University Press).

Lindblom, C.E. (1959) 'The Science of Muddling Through', *Public Administration Review*, Vol. 19.

Lindblom, C.E. and Woodhouse, E.J. (1993) *The Policy Making Process*, 3rd edn (Prentice Hall).

Marx, K. and Engels, E. (1848) *The Communist Manifesto* (Oxford University Press).

McKay, D. (2001) *American Politics and Society* (Blackwell).

Miliband, R. (1969) *The State in Capitalist Society* (Weidenfeld & Nicolson).

Moran, M. (2001) 'Not Steering but Drowning: Policy Catastrophes and the Regulatory State', *Political Quarterly*, Autumn, pp. 414–27.

Moran, M. (2005) *Politics and Governance in the UK* (Palgrave).

National Audit Office, *The Millennium Dome: report by the Comptroller and Auditor General*, HC936 1999–2000, accessible at www.open.gov.uk/nao

Naughtie, J. (2001) *The Rivals* (Fourth Estate).

Parsons, W. (1995) *Public Policy* (Edward Elgar).

Platt, S. (1998) *Government by Task Force*, Catalyst paper 2 (Catalyst).

Rawnsley, A. (2000) *Servants of the People* (Hamish Hamilton).

Rawnsley, A. (2010) *The End of the Party: The Rise and Fall of New Labour* (Viking).

Rowlands, D. and Pollock, A. (2004) 'Choice and Responsiveness for Older People in the "Patient Centred" NHS', *British Medical Journal*, January.

Schmitter, P.C. (1979) 'Still the Century of Corporatism', in P.C. Schmitter and G. Lembruch (eds) *Trends Towards Corporatist Intermediation* (Sage).

Schnattschneider, E.E. (1960) *The Semisovereign People* (Holt, Reinhart & Winston).

Simpson, D. (1999) *Pressure Groups* (Hodder & Stoughton).

Smith, M. (1993) *Pressure, Power and Policy* (Harvester Wheatsheaf).

Watts, D. (2003) *Understanding US/UK Government and Politics* (Manchester University Press).

Wilby, P. 'Rupert Murdoch is Effectively a Member of Blair's Cabinet', *The Guardian*, 1 July 2006.

Wildavsky, A. (1979) *Speaking the Truth to Power* (Little, Brown).

Wilensky, H. (1975) *The Welfare State and Equality* (University of California Press).

Useful websites

Fabian Society: www.fabian-society.org.uk

Demos: www.demos.co.uk

Catalyst: www.catalystforum.org.uk

10 Downing Street: www.number10.gov.uk

Anti-ID Card Group: www.no2id.net

Topic 8:
Prime Minister and Cabinet

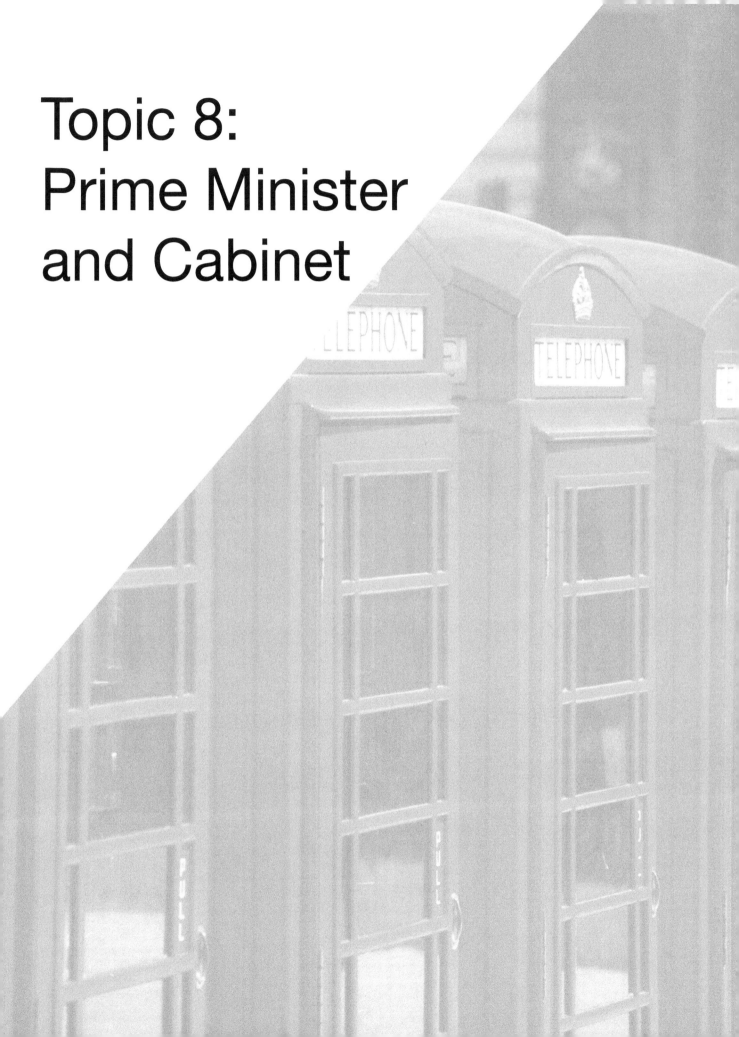

The Prime Minister, the Cabinet and the core executive

We have seen that the British constitution gives exceptional power to governments. Since the Prime Minister is the most powerful member of the Cabinet, and the Cabinet is effectively the governing committee of the country, this small group comprises the most powerful people in Britain. The way they work together and with a small core of other political influentials raises a host of important and controversial questions about the British system of government. Has the office of Prime Minister (PM) been transformed from the traditional 'first among equals' into a powerful political executive akin, in many ways, to a president? Or is the Cabinet still the effective centre of all important decision making? How do the prime ministerial styles of Thatcher, Major and Blair compare, and what effect does this have on the fate of their governments? How is the work of Prime Minister and Cabinet organised, and how do they relate to the broader apparatus of government?

The chapter is divided into seven main sections. They describe how the machinery of government works at this, the highest level of government, and how different officials and agencies interact in the decision-making process. The chapter focuses on:

- the Prime Minister
- the Cabinet
- the Cabinet, departments and joined-up government
- the eternal political triangle: departments, Cabinet and Prime Minister
- prime ministerial styles: Thatcher, Major, Blair
- prime ministerial versus Cabinet government
- the core executive.

The Prime Minister

Prime Minister

The head of the executive branch of government and chair of the Cabinet.

Since Britain has no written constitution, the powers and duties of the **Prime Minister** are neither clearly defined nor legally limited. They have evolved according to historical circumstances since 1721 when Robert Walpole started to create what is now regarded as the modern prime ministerial role. Since then there have been 51 prime ministers (post-war premiers are listed in Table 5.1), each exercising authority in different ways. Consequently, it is difficult to say exactly what the job of the PM is. As one incumbent (Herbert Asquith, prime minister 1908–16) remarked, it is 'what the office holder chooses and is able to make of it'. It is clear

Table 5.1 Post-war prime ministers

Prime Minister	Dates	Party
Clement Attlee	1945–51	Labour
Sir Winston Churchill	1951–5	Conservative
Sir Anthony Eden	1955–7	Conservative
Harold Macmillan	1957–63	Conservative
Sir Alec Douglas-Home	1963–4	Conservative
Harold Wilson	1964–70	Labour
Edward Heath	1970–4	Conservative
Harold Wilson	1974–6	Labour
James Callaghan	1976–9	Labour
Margaret Thatcher	1979–90	Conservative
John Major	1990–7	Conservative
Tony Blair	1997–	Labour

that the Prime Minister is the head of government at home (the monarch is the head of state), and the political representative of the country abroad, but this job description hides a multitude of responsibilities and powers. Among other things, the Prime Minister:

- Decides the number and nature of Cabinet and government posts and who is to fill them. This requires restructuring the Cabinet and its membership from time to time.

- Chairs Cabinet meetings, manages their agendas and discussion, calls on speakers, sums up discussion, and directs the writing of minutes.

- Decides the number and nature of Cabinet committees, subcommittees and ministerial groups, and appoints their chairs and members. Chairs some of the most important committees.

- Oversees the armed forces and security services.

- Manages relations between the Cabinet and the wider world of Parliament, the media, other countries, and international organisations – far and away the most important being the EU.

- Manages the flow of government information to the outside world.

- Answers formal questions in the House of Commons (Prime Minister's Questions – PMQs).

- Approves senior positions in the Civil Service and the diplomatic service. Recommends senior appointments in the Church of England, the judiciary, the Privy Council, quangos and other civil positions.

- Has a hand in the honours list.

- Dissolves Parliament before calling an election.

- Takes the lead in crises of government and the governing party.

- Leads the governing party and maintains contact with its MPs and party headquarters.

- Maintains contact with heads of other states as necessary.

- Keeps watch on the broad political agenda and the course of government.

BRIEFINGS

5.1 A day in the life of the Prime Minister

07.00	Wake
07.30	Family breakfast
08.00	Go over the day's diary with PM Office staff
08.30	Briefing meeting on political issue of the day
09.00	Meeting with No. 10 staff on education
10.00	Meeting on election reform
10.30	Briefing on PM Question Time
10.45	Visit the secretariat in the PM's Office
11.45	Briefing on freedom of information seminar
12.00	Seminar on freedom of information (Salad/sandwich lunch)
13.15	Interview with journalist
14.15	Seminar with policy advisers
15.15	Meeting with foreign head of state
16.00	Meeting with national politician
16.30	Meeting with top civil servant
17.00	Meeting with Cabinet colleague
17.30	Meeting with Cabinet colleague
18.00	Meeting about Cabinet committee business
19.30	Private dinner/family time
22.00	House of Commons vote/read official documents
23.00	Sleep

Note: Based on different sources.

Even this list, long though it is, does not capture the staggering range and responsibilities of the Prime Minister. Being head of government involves many tasks ranging from formal representation of the nation and crisis management at home and abroad, to guiding the daily work of the government and maintaining contact with senior figures in the government, Parliament and Civil Service at home, and senior statesmen abroad. This means constant travel, a ceaseless round of meetings, an endless chain of decision making, and incessant public appearances. The job is as demanding as it is difficult and as Tony Blair has put it: 'nothing prepares you for the difficulty of being prime minister'.

Margaret Thatcher, stormbird of British politics

It is clear, even from recent history, that prime ministers bring very different qualities, aptitudes and interests to the job. Margaret Thatcher was possibly the most memorable prime minister of the post-war period, unique in many respects. Though no feminist, she is the only woman to have held the post. But she was perhaps better known as a woman with a mission – to regenerate Britain – with a force and energy that stirred strong feelings of love or loathing.

From lower-middle-class origins (her father was a shopkeeper, but mayor of his town of Grantham) she went from the local grammar school to a chemistry degree at Oxford, followed by a law qualification. She was elected to Parliament in 1959, and within 11 years was minister of education in the Heath government of 1970.

Two events precipitated her break with the 'social democratic consensus' that had prevailed since the war. One was the election defeat of the Conservative government in 1974, following strike action by trade unions. The other, her conversion to free market policies on the grounds that government failure was due to 'overloading' the state with too much taxation and responsibility.

Winning the 1979 general election as the result of a general distaste for trade union action in the 'winter of discontent', she set out on a radical campaign to 'get government off the backs of the people' by cutting taxation and public services, reducing government regulation and privatising state enterprises. Her three successive general election victories (1979, 1983, 1987) had a lot to do with her forceful and dynamic politics, which seemed to make her political position impregnable, in spite of an increasingly autocratic style. When this led to the hugely unpopular poll tax (see Chapter 12) and open hostility with the Europhiles in her own party (see Chapter 8) her Cabinet dumped her for fear of losing the 1992 general election. She was the longest serving Prime Minister for 150 years and was replaced in No. 10 by John Major in 1990.

John Major: overreaction to Thatcher?

John Major came from a poor London family. The son of a circus performer and manufacturer of garden gnomes, he left grammar school at 16 with almost no qualifications, but rose rapidly through banking, a short period of local government experience, to election as a Conservative MP in 1979 – the year that Thatcher came to power. He was favoured by her during the 1980s precisely because he had no connections with the traditional Conservative grandees. Ten years after his election, Thatcher made him Foreign Secretary, and in short order he became Leader of the House, Deputy Prime Minister, and Chancellor of the Exchequer. He replaced Thatcher as Prime Minister in 1990.

Although a Thatcher supporter in the 1980s, he rapidly distanced his government from hers by abolishing the poll tax, taking up a more pro-European political stance, and adopting a radically different political style. He replaced the autocracy of the Thatcher era with something more collegial and unassuming. He succeeded in winning the 1992 election as a result but immediately ran into serious trouble when a mismanaged currency crisis forced the pound out of the European Monetary System. Government infighting over Europe, and a growing national concern over government 'sleaze' added to his reputation for being a weak and ineffective leader, and he was defeated spectacularly in the general election of 1997 by Blair and New Labour.

Tony Blair and New Labour

Blair and Major form a striking contrast in style and background: Major came from an underprivileged background, while Blair shares an exclusive background with many Conservative MPs. Born in Edinburgh in 1953, the son of a barrister and lecturer, Blair attended Fettes public school, went on to Oxford to study law and began a barrister's practice in London. He was attracted to Labour by his Christian Socialist beliefs and after winning his first parliamentary election in 1983 rose as fast as Major through his party ranks to a shadow Cabinet post in 1988. When John Smith, the Labour leader, died suddenly in 1994 Blair stepped into his shoes and immediately set about changing the Labour Party along lines already initiated by his predecessors Kinnock and Smith.

Under the slogan 'New Labour, New Britain', Blair led Labour away from its policies of nationalisation, high taxation, universal welfare benefits, alignment with the trade unions and 'Old Labour'. In their place he put centrist ('Third Way') policies – cautious economics, low taxation, a leaning towards free markets, and support for the EU. He loosened Labour's close ties to the unions, and introduced the most modern of public relations systems. He abolished Labour's Clause 4, which committed the party to public ownership, but emphasised the importance of high-quality education ('education, education, education'), and changed its image on law and order. As opposition spokesman on home affairs he caught the head-lines and outflanked a startled Conservative government by claiming to be 'tough on crime, tough on the causes of crime'.

By taking the centre ground, he was able to maximise Labour's advantage over an unpopular and factious Conservative government in the mid-1990s, and was elected as Prime Minister by a landslide in 1997. Labour had been in opposition for 18 years. At 43 he was the youngest Prime Minister in almost 200 years, and the first to have a child born at No. 10 Downing Street for 150 years. Blair's goal in 1997, however, was not one term in office (five years) but at least three in order to complete his programme of reforms. New Labour started cautiously, adopting the outgoing Conservative government's budget, but engaged in an ambitious pro-gramme of constitutional reform (see the previous chapter). The result was another landslide win in 2001, and a more modest victory in 2005.

Freedom and constraint on PM power: hiring and firing

The great diversity of prime ministerial styles is not surprising given the lack of constitutional rules about their role and their wide range of powers. There is plenty of room to exercise their personal strengths and weaknesses. But personal charac-teristics are not the only thing that matter here. In their daily working life prime ministers are also limited by the force of circumstances. To illustrate this we will focus on the power to hire and fire members of the Cabinet and the government, partly because it is so important, and partly because it illustrates the powers and limitations of the office very well.

In theory, prime ministers have a free hand to decide how large or small their Cabinets are. In practice there are natural limits to Cabinet size. It is presently 23 strong, with another 1 'in attendance', but it has been as small as 16, and during the war Churchill's Cabinet had 10 members. For the most part, however, much less than 15 is too small to cover all the important aspects of modern government, and much more than 25 is too large for an effective committee. Most recent prime ministers have settled for a cabinet of 20–23.

In theory, prime ministers can merge or divide Cabinet posts in any way they want. The present Cabinet combines responsibility for Scotland with transport, and Wales and Northern Ireland go together. Culture goes with media and sport, and education is joined with skills. There is one post with no specific departmental duties (Minister without Portfolio). In practice, however, some Cabinet posts are more or less fixed – Chancellor of the Exchequer, Home Secretary, Foreign Secretary, and education, health, social services, transport, the environment, Scotland, Wales and Northern Ireland must be represented in one form or another.

In theory, prime ministers can fill Cabinet posts as they wish. In practice, they may be severely restricted in their choice:

- The convention is that most Cabinet members, and especially the most import-ant ones, must be answerable to, and therefore members of, the House of Commons. This has 646 members.

- In single-party governments Cabinet members must be drawn from the majority party – usually between 330 and 400 individuals.

- Some powerful figures virtually select themselves for high office – Blair must find Cabinet places for Prescott, Brown and Straw.

- Other posts must be filled from a small pool of possibilities – the Welsh or Scottish offices are normally filled by Welsh and Scottish MPs.

- Some MPs are ruled out of holding government positions. Blair is unlikely to be able to reappoint Blunkett, Mandelson or Byers, if the question ever arose.

- The Cabinet should be a balance of men and women, maturity and promise, different political factions (left and right, Europhiles and Europhobes). The PM must take care to keep the government together and not leave out a potentially disruptive faction.

- Having filled Cabinet posts, the PM must fill more than 100 other government posts, most of them from a total pool of not much more than 300 members of the parliamentary party.

Once the political has-beens, the never-will-bes and those with difficult histories have been ruled out, the Prime Minister may be left with rather little choice. This is not to say that the PM has no room for manoeuvre. Some powerful political figures have been kept out of the Cabinet by their prime minister, or out of the Cabinet post they really wanted. Thatcher and Blair have contrived to put their own supporters into important government positions, and Cabinet sackings, promotions and reshuffles are fairly frequent as prime ministers try to balance the demands of political circumstances and groups jockeying for power. Equally, two very successful post-war prime ministers, Macmillan and Thatcher, seem to have signalled weakness rather than strength when they engaged in major Cabinet reshuffles in 1962 and 1989. Both were soon out of power.

In sum, the PM's powers to hire and fire government members are, as are many other functions of the office, a mixture of surprising freedom and constraint. There is often little choice, and some ministers choose themselves by virtue of their political position and stature. At the same time some PMs have juggled the careers of powerful people and have shaped governments to their own taste.

The Prime Minister's Office

We have emphasised the enormous number of prime ministerial tasks, and the extreme pressures of the job, but the PM does not carry this burden alone. He is supported by a staff of about 45–50 senior officials, and a total staff of over 200 in the Prime Minister's Office. Some are Civil Service appointments, others are purely political. Numbers in the Office are steadily rising and its organisation constantly changing, but the work centres around the following:

- The Policy Directorate, which has a staff of about 30, and includes the PM's private office (led by a Chief of Staff) and the Policy Directorate, which deals with short-term policy issues.

- The Strategy Unit, with a staff of 60 working on long-term issues of policy and implementation.

- Communications. Not just the Prime Minister's but *all* government press releases and briefing documents flow through this office. The Prime Minister's press secretary is very influential, therefore (think Alastair Campbell).

- Political operations – the management and development of the government's political strategy. This is directed by a Labour Party appointee who is paid by the party.

■ Government relations – the management and development of the PM's relations with the government agencies of central, regional and local government.

The Prime Minister's Office works closely with the Cabinet Office (see below), and with the Whip's Office in Parliament (see Chapter 18), and has close and constant contact with all the main executive agencies and government departments in Whitehall, including the Deputy Prime Minister's Office, which was created in 2002 and has a staff of its own. Under Blair, the PM's Office, the Cabinet Office and the Deputy Prime Minister's Office have become, in effect, a single, centralised executive office.

The kitchen cabinet

This is not the end of the story. Prime ministers often gather around them a collection of personal friends and advisers they can trust. They are often private individuals, not government officials, but they have direct access ('face time') to the PM. They are often resented by 'regular' politicians and civil servants, although one can appreciate the PM's need for advice he can trust from outside official circles. Thatcher and Blair seem to have made extensive use of their **kitchen cabinets**, but Major relied more on the official Cabinet. Being a closed and constantly informal circle of associates, friends and insiders, the composition of the kitchen cabinet is a matter of speculation and, in any case, it probably changes quite quickly according to circumstances.

Kitchen cabinet

The loose and informal policy advice group that prime ministers may collect around them, and that may include politicians, public officials and private citizens.

The Cabinet

Cabinet

The committee of the leading members of the government who are empowered to make decisions on behalf of the government.

The **Cabinet** must not be confused with the government. There are usually 20–25 Cabinet members but more than 110 people in the government, including Cabinet ministers and others who attend Cabinet, junior ministers (27), parliamentary under-secretaries and private secretaries (37), whips (23) and law officers (3). Most Cabinet members are drawn from the House of Commons because of the convention that they should be accountable to the elected chamber of government, but some come from the Lords. Most Cabinet members are ministers who run Whitehall departments (Table 5.2).

The Cabinet, like the Prime Minister's Office, has changed over time. Churchill had only 10 members in his wartime Cabinet, and experimented with 16 'overlords' in 1951. The experiment did not last long and the Cabinet soon returned to its normal size. Whatever its size and composition, the Cabinet is the central committee of government. Its main purposes are as follows:

■ to take major government decisions and approve government policy

■ to reconcile the responsibilities of ministers to their individual departments with their responsibilities to the government as a whole

■ to resolve any differences between ministers acting in their departmental capacities.

The Cabinet coordinates the policies of Whitehall departments and directs the work of government as a whole. As such it is the 'central committee' of the government executive, and it either discusses and makes important decisions, or ratifies the decisions of Cabinet committees. In doing so it is supposed to follow the principle of collective responsibility.

Table 5.2 Cabinet members, 5 May 2006

Name	Office
Tony Blair	Prime Minister, First Lord of the Treasury, and minister for the Civil Service
John Prescott	Deputy Prime Minister and First Secretary of State
Gordon Brown	Chancellor of the Exchequer
Margaret Beckett	Secretary of State for Foreign and Commonwealth Affairs
John Hutton	Secretary of State for Work and Pensions
David Miliband	Secretary of State for Environment, Food and Rural Affairs
Douglas Alexander	Secretary of State for Transport and Secretary of State for Scotland
Des Browne	Secretary of State for Defence
Jack Straw	Leader of the House of Commons and Lord Privy Seal
Patricia Hewitt	Secretary of State for Health
Alastair Darling	Secretary of State for Trade and Industry
Tessa Jowell	Secretary of State for Culture, Media and Sport
Jacqui Smith	Chief Whip (Parliamentary Secretary to the Treasury)
John Reid	Secretary of State for the Home Department
Peter Hain	Secretary of State for Northern Ireland, and Secretary of State for Wales
Hazel Blears	Minister without Portfolio and Labour Party chairman
Baroness Amos	Leader of the House of Lords and Lord President of the Council
Lord Falconer of Thoroton	Secretary of State for Constitutional Affairs and Lord Chancellor
Hilary Benn	Secretary of State for International Development
Alan Johnson	Secretary of State for Education and Skills
Ruth Kelly	Secretary of State for Communities and Local Government, and Minister for Women
Hilary Armstrong	Minister for the Cabinet Office and for Social Exclusion (and Chancellor of the Duchy of Lancaster)
Stephen Timms	Chief Secretary to the Treasury
Also attending the Cabinet	
Lord Grocott of Telford	Lords Chief Whip and Captain of the Gentlemen at Arms

Source: www.pm.gov.uk

Collective responsibility

> **Collective responsibility**
>
> The principle whereby decisions and policies of the Cabinet are binding on all members of the government, who must support them in public, to maintain a united front, or resign their government post.

As a collective decision-making body the Cabinet is bound by the principle of 'collective responsibility'. It may be the centre of acute conflict in the privacy of the Cabinet room, but it must present a united front in public. As the nineteenth-century prime minister, Lord Melbourne, said: 'It doesn't matter what we say as long as we all say the same thing.' Cabinet discussions are secret (members sign the Official Secrets Act) and, to preserve the appearance of unanimity, the prime minister sums up the mood of the meeting, which adds to the PM's power. Votes in Cabinet are rare and usually reserved for special decisions, such as that of going to war with Argentina over the Falklands.

The nature of collective responsibility is changing. Originally applied only to the Cabinet, it now covers all government members. Between 1994 and 1997 the Labour Party also extended it to members of its shadow Cabinet. In contrast, the government suspended collective responsibility in 1975 and 1977 over the issue of the European Union. In 1994 a Cabinet minister, Michael Portillo, made thinly veiled criticisms of the Cabinet's European policy, but was not disciplined in public. Some ministers have also circumvented collective responsibility by leaking documents. The principle of collective responsibility, it seems, is now applied more broadly but also more weakly.

Cabinet committees

Established during the crisis years of the Second World War as a way of doing Cabinet work quickly and efficiently in small groups, Cabinet committees now play an important part in government. According to Cabinet Office information: 'Both Committees and Subcommittees act by implied devolution of authority from the Cabinet and their decisions therefore have the same formal status as decisions of the full Cabinet.' This means that committee decisions do not need Cabinet agreement or ratification.

The prime minister decides the number, terms of reference, membership and chairs of committees (Table 5.3). Most are composed of Cabinet members, but some include junior ministers and senior civil servants. There are five main kinds of committees dealing with Cabinet business in the present system:

- **Full Cabinet committees** dealing with the most important areas of government, such as defence and overseas policy, domestic affairs and schools policy. They are normally chaired by the prime minister or the Cabinet minister responsible for the area. In 2006 there were 30 full Cabinet committees.

- **Sub-committees** covering a narrower range of issues than their full committee. There were 18 of these in 2006.

- **Miscellaneous groups** concerned with specific tasks and usually having a short life span.

Table 5.3 Examples of Cabinet committees

Cabinet committees change over time, and miscellaneous groups often have a short life, but the following illustrates their work:

Committee on Constitutional Affairs – Chaired by the Lord Privy Seal and Leader of the House of Commons, this has 19 members, all drawn from the government. Its terms of reference are 'To consider strategic issues relating to the Government's constitutional reform policies including House of Lords reform and issues arising from devolution to Scotland, Wales and Northern Ireland.' It has three sub-committees covering electoral policy, freedom of information and parliamentary modernisation.

Committee on defence and overseas policy – Chaired by the Prime Minister with the Foreign Secretary as deputy chair, this has a membership of eight government members, with other ministers, the heads of the intelligence agencies and the Chief of Defence Staff invited to attend as necessary. Its terms of reference are 'To set strategies for the Government's defence and overseas policy.' It has four sub-committees covering international terrorism, protective security and resilience, Iraq, and conflict prevention and reconstruction.

Committee on European policy – Chaired by the foreign secretary this committee has 22 members, with other ministers and staff of the United Kingdom's permanent representative to the European Union (see Chapter 8) invited to attend as necessary. Its terms of reference are 'To determine the United Kingdom's policies on European Union issues, and to oversee the United Kingdom's relations with other member states and principal partners of the European Union.' It has no sub-committees.

Ministerial committee on influenza pandemic planning – A miscellaneous group chaired by the secretary of state for health with 16 government members, and other ministers and officials of the security and intelligence services, government communications, medical and scientific staff, and the devolved authorities of Scotland, Wales and Northern Ireland invited to attend as required.

Source: Government web sites

- **Consultative committees** are attended by Cabinet members and outside officials who meet to ensure a proper discussion of matters of common interest. Consultative committees are not bound by collective responsibility and they are consultative not executive bodies.

- **Official committees** shadow their Cabinet equivalents and are staffed by officials (mainly civil servants from Whitehall departments). They usually meet before their equivalents in order to identify possible problems and clarify key issues.

Committees, sub-committees and miscellaneous groups were much used by Thatcher to bypass formal discussion in her full Cabinet. She could fill them with her own nominees and so get her own way. John Major's more consensual style resulted in more discussion in full Cabinet. Blair comes between Major and Thatcher: on some matters he seems to push his own initiatives through ad hoc committees; on others he has used short meetings of his full Cabinet. One of the most interesting Blair initiatives was the Joint Consultative Committee with the Liberal Democratic Party (JCC). Although the work of the committee was suspended in 2001, it was important because it broke the constitutional convention that government committees were composed only of government members. It provided a political device to put pressure on traditionalists within the Cabinet who opposed change, as well as being a way of isolating the Conservative opposition.

The Cabinet Office

The Cabinet Office is a nerve centre of government. It supports and services the work of the Cabinet and its committees by timetabling meetings, preparing agendas and documents, drafting and circulating minutes, and following up decisions. The Office also plays a major part in coordinating the policies of government and Whitehall departments, analysing policy options, working out how best to deliver government policy, and then driving them through to the point of delivery. It consists of about 30 sections run by 50 senior officials and civil servants, and employs more than 2,000 staff. The secretariat is so important that its head, the secretary of the Cabinet, is the country's senior civil servant. The Cabinet secretary is in daily contact with the Prime Minister and Cabinet members, attends Cabinet meetings (although not for party political items) and some Cabinet committees. The Cabinet Office now works so closely with the Prime Minister's and Deputy Prime Minister's Offices that all three have become virtually one single operation.

The Cabinet, departments and joined-up government

The Cabinet has many responsibilities and roles. Politically, it must decide government policy and what legislation to put before Parliament. Administratively, it must ensure the efficient and effective functioning of government departments. Collectively, it must resolve disputes between departments, political factions and individual ministers. These functions overlap, of course, with those of the prime minister, which is why Cabinet and prime ministers and their respective Offices must collaborate so closely.

As the highest committee of government, the Cabinet is especially important for making final decisions that cannot be made elsewhere, either because they are so important or because they are points of acute conflict. Sometimes this conflict is a matter of ideology and principle (joining the euro, banning fox hunting, war in Iraq) and sometimes it is more organisational, involving the interests of the ministries and departments of government. The Cabinet is the place to resolve such conflicts, either in committee or around the large table in the Cabinet room.

Even if there is no conflict, policies still have to be coordinated, and coordination is extremely difficult to achieve in modern, large-scale government. On the one hand, the operations of the state are so huge that they must be broken up into manageable parts and organisations that are run by people with specialised abilities and knowledge. On the other hand no government service or policy area is an island on its own. All are related to others. Building a motorway affects the environment, has an impact on agriculture and consequences for other forms of transport, and costs money that could be spent on other services. One of the most difficult problems of government is being caught between the incompatible demands of departmentalisation and specialisation and the need to coordinate very complex policy issues across a large number of separate organisations. As the government machinery becomes larger, more complex and more specialised, the more important it is to create coordinated government, but the more difficult to do so.

Blair first used the term joined-up government when he launched the Social Exclusion Unit in 1997, as part of the Prime Minister's Office. Since then, joined-up government has risen and fallen in the political agenda. At first it was much discussed and different organisations and procedures were set up to achieve it, most of them within the Prime Minister's Office. Many have been subsequently reorganised, merged, downgraded or quietly dropped. The term 'joined-up government' is not often heard nowadays, either because it has become incorporated into standard thinking about public policy or, more likely, because it is a good idea that is extremely hard to implement. It is now mainly the responsibility of the Office of the Deputy Prime Minister. We will return to the subject in Chapter 7.

The eternal political triangle

Decision making within the Cabinet rests on three important principles, which often conflict with each other:

1. **Departmental autonomy** Whitehall departments are among the largest organisations in the country, and most ministers spend most of their time running them. This requires departmental autonomy, partly because different departments deal with different policy areas – education, defence, transport, health – and partly because they have their own practices, cultures and operating procedures. Ministers must defend their departments against other departments and fellow ministers. Indeed, the more effectively they do this, the greater their political reputation and the higher they are likely to rise up the greasy pole of politics. It is the job of the Cabinet to resolve inter-departmental disputes.

Cabinet collegiality

The feeling among Cabinet members that they must act closely and cooperatively together, even when they conflict over policy issues and departmental interests.

2. **Cabinet collegiality** At the same time the Cabinet must be a collegial body capable of resolving conflict and making collective decisions. Whatever their rivalries, Cabinet members must form a united front, and to do this they must have the chance of discussing issues.

3. **Prime ministerial authority** Prime ministers are leaders. Even the most powerful and ambitious ministers want the prime minister to lead the Cabinet, the party and the country. Besides, ministers are often so overburdened by their departmental duties that they have little time for general policy issues. The prime minister must try to hold all the many reins of government, rise above conflict in Cabinet, and settle disputes authoritatively. In this sense the PM is not a colleague of Cabinet members, but their boss.

The three principles do not always fit well together. Departmental autonomy clashes with collegiality when ministers fight, as they must, for money and their policies. Too little discussion and consultation undermines Cabinet collegiality. A dominant prime minister can easily undermine collegiality, and one who interferes with departmental affairs too much will erode autonomy. Conversely, a weak prime minister will not control departmental and personal rivalries. A good PM must know when to talk or listen, when to lead or follow, when to control or delegate. In short, a good PM balances the demands of autonomy, collegiality and leadership. It is an exceedingly difficult and delicate task, and there are recent examples of it going badly wrong, as we will now see.

Prime ministerial styles

Thatcher as Prime Minister

When Thatcher came to power in 1979 she seemed to be a strong and dynamic leader who could take charge of government and reverse national decline. The Falklands War strengthened popular belief in her leadership qualities. Yet when she lost power in 1990, as the longest serving Prime Minister of the century, she was widely seen as dogmatic and autocratic. For much of her time in Downing Street she dominated the government and stretched prime ministerial authority to its limits. She was an ambitious and driving force, but she also intervened too much in the departmental affairs of her ministers, and undermined Cabinet collegiality with her critical style.

The poll tax is a case in point. This policy to shift local taxation from a graduated property tax to a flat-rate tax on individuals was described as the worst idea in the world, and there was little government or even Cabinet support for it, but Thatcher pushed it through Parliament, forcing her colleagues to support it publicly against their own judgement. Its unpopularity was one of the more important factors leading to the Cabinet forcing her from office. Other examples of her leadership style are listed in Briefing 5.2. In general, Thatcher placed the principle of prime ministerial authority way above departmental autonomy and Cabinet collegiality – the eternal triangle was balanced on one corner, so it fell over.

Major as Prime Minister

Major adopted a more collegial and consensual style (see Briefing 5.3). Initially this succeeded in healing political wounds and unifying the government. He also came out of the Gulf War (1991) with much respect as a political leader. Yet after a while his quiet and unassuming style was described as 'grey', dithering and ineffective. His Cabinet was described as a collection of 'political chums', and was accused of being 'in office but not in power'. Intense conflicts about economic policy, social policy and the EU surfaced. The government appeared weak, divided and directionless. In the end, the eternal triangle of Major's Cabinet was balanced on departmental autonomy, so it toppled over.

Blair as Prime Minister

In the first years of his administration Tony Blair combined some of the best characteristics of Thatcher's dynamism and leadership with Major's informal and unassuming style. He managed to combine two contradictory tendencies:

BRIEFINGS

5.2 Prime ministerial style: Thatcher

- Ensured that 'dries' (right-wing free marketeers) dominated her Cabinets and committees.
- Sacked 12 Cabinet ministers, 1979–90.
- Reduced the frequency of Cabinet and committee meetings. Wilson's annual average of Cabinet meetings was 59, Thatcher's was 35.
- Greater use of ad hoc committees and the kitchen cabinet. It is said that some of her ministers knew nothing about some ad hoc committees, although they made important decisions.
- Intervened a great deal in departmental affairs.
- Publicly criticised some of her ministers, or used leaks against them, but strictly enforced collective responsibility.
- Started Cabinet discussions by stating her own views, rather than listening and summing up.
- Did not consult her Cabinets about some major policy decisions (e.g. the banning of trade unions from Government Communications Headquarters (GCHQ) in 1984).
- Appointed weak ministers who could be controlled.
- Kept some major issues off Cabinet agendas. Michael Heseltine claimed this as the reason for his resignation in 1986.
- Attended parliamentary debates less frequently than any other modern prime minister.

BRIEFINGS

5.3 Prime ministerial style: Major

- Made more use of the Cabinet, less of committees.
- More emphasis on Cabinet collegiality and consensus, less on leadership.
- A greater mix of opinion in the Cabinet, especially wets and dries, Europhiles and Eurosceptics.
- Greater openness in government.
- Less intervention in departmental affairs.
- Lapses of collective responsibility: Portillo's veiled criticism of the government in 1994 went publicly unchecked.

1. He has further centralised the Labour Party and imposed unprecedented discipline on it, reversing some traditional policies (Clause 4, public spending) with little debate and a great show of unanimity. He gradually appointed more of his supporters to senior positions. He reduced the number and length of Cabinet meetings, working (as did Thatcher) through Cabinet committees. He greatly increased the size and power of the Prime Minister's Office. His unprecedented popularity in the country, until Iraq, enhanced his leadership. In short, he is strong on prime ministerial authority.

2. In the earlier years he had the full support of the Cabinet on many of the most controversial policies, such as taxing and spending, and Scottish and Welsh devolution, and kept his Cabinet colleagues together by approaching some controversial issues (the EU, the euro, electoral reform) slowly and cautiously. Although said to be a control freak, he allows some of his senior Cabinet colleagues much autonomy – especially Gordon Brown on economic matters. In short, he has been strong on departmental autonomy and Cabinet collegiality.

Plate 5.1 The war on terrorism results in more power being accumulated in the hands of the government. Here 'King' Tony Blair receives a grovelling courtier

Source: Cartoon Stock

Until the early years of his second term in government, at least, Blair's Cabinet was generally a good balance of the three principles of prime ministerial authority, departmental autonomy and Cabinet collegiality. An extremely popular prime minister for an unprecedented period, Blair then gained a reputation for too personal a leadership style (the 'Tony Show') involving a few favoured advisers ('Tony's cronies') rather than wide discussion, and government by spin-doctor. He came to be personally identified with some unpopular policies (Iraq, close alignment with Bush, foundation hospitals, top-up fees and the Education Bill of 2006). The political triangle has shifted from a balance of elements towards too much prime ministerial authority.

BRIEFINGS

5.4 Prime ministerial style: Blair

- Took on major agenda and policy-setting powers of the government and made it clear that he would not tolerate dissent either from his Cabinet or from the Parliamentary Labour Party.

- Reduced the number, length and documentation of Cabinet meetings (it meets for about an hour) using committees and sub-committees more. The number and length of Cabinet meetings rose slightly in 2004–5, but is still low by historical standards.

- Employed increasing numbers of personal advisers. Major had 8. In 2005 Blair had 28.

- Had adopted an informal style of decision making ('sofa government') based on 'bi-laterals' (meetings between him and one other person). Policy on Iraq seems to have been largely formulated in private meetings with President Bush, and he promised a referendum on the EU constitution in 2004 without discussing it with Cabinet colleagues. The Butler Report (2004) on intelligence on weapons of mass destruction was critical of the 'informality and circumscribed character of Government procedures' and the risks it presents for informed, collective political judgement.

- Spends even less time than Thatcher in the Commons, more and more on public speeches, press conferences and international high-level meetings.

- Allows considerable discretion to strong Cabinet ministers (Gordon Brown, Jack Straw and David Blunkett), provided their policies are broadly in line with government policy.

- Is careful to keep the Cabinet united on potentially divisive issues – Europe, the euro, electoral reform, Lords reform – but Iraq may have been an exception.

- Carefully cultivates his leadership image and places great importance on media management and 'message discipline' (centralising all government communications in his own Office and repeating the same theme many times).

- At the same time, he has an open and informal prime ministerial style – 'Call me Tony'; refusing to wear a morning coat at the Queen Mother's funeral.

Who governs: Cabinet or Prime Minister?

Prime ministerial government

The theory that the office of the Prime Minister has become so powerful that he or she now forms a political executive similar to that of a president.

A classic and long-running debate about British government revolves around the question of whether the power of the prime minister has increased relative to the Cabinet. It is said that the PM is no longer 'first among equals' but a dominant political executive, and the result is not Cabinet, but **prime ministerial government**. The Cabinet, once said to be the 'efficient secret of government' because it, and not the Commons, made decisions, is now a 'dignified' part of government that hides the real power of a presidential prime minister. This assertion dates back at least to Churchill's war government, but it surfaces again whenever forceful prime ministers emerge – Macmillan, Wilson, Thatcher and Blair. The 'controversy' that follows summarises some views on the matter.

Prime ministerial government

The argument that we have prime ministerial government is found in John Mackintosh's *The British Cabinet* and Richard Crossman's introduction to the 1960 edition of Bagehot's *The English Constitution*. Both claim that the British Prime Minister is now so powerful that the office is more akin to that of a president. Key decisions are made by the PM, plus a few powerful members of the Cabinet, the government and the kitchen cabinet. Key Cabinet committees are under prime ministerial control, with the Cabinet often only a rubber stamp, or not consulted at all. The prime minister directs the entire flow of government information and dominates relations between the Cabinet and the wider world. The overall result is said to be executive democracy or leadership democracy rather than parliamentary democracy.

Cabinet government

Cabinet government

The theory that the Cabinet, not the Prime Minister, forms a collective political executive that constrains the power of the Prime Minister to the role of 'first among equals'.

This school of thought argues that the political system limits the PM's power and ensures that the Cabinet forms a collective political executive. In the short run, PMs may be formidable, but in the long run they depend on Cabinet and party support, and most important matters will have to be agreed by Cabinet. Since the power of the Cabinet rests on the support of the majority party in the House of Commons it must, to some extent, reflect its political complexion. This, in turn, places constraints on the power of both the PM and the Cabinet, and ensures a degree of accountability of the political executive to the majority party in the Commons.

335

BRIEFINGS

5.5 Cabinet, Cabinet committees and other executive meetings, 1950–2000

Cabinet Since the 1950s the number and duration of Cabinet meetings has steadily declined, from about 100 a year to about 40. Under Blair they rarely last for more than 60 minutes.

Cabinet committees Between 1970 and 2000 the number of Cabinet committee meetings fell more than 50 per cent.

Other meetings Since 1979, and especially under Blair since 1997, business has increasingly been handled by:

- ad hoc meetings of senior ministers
- kitchen cabinet meetings
- bilateral meetings between the PM and favoured friends and colleagues.

CONTROVERSY

Prime ministerial or Cabinet government?

Prime ministerial government

- The powers of the Prime Minister are considerable.
- There are no constitutional limits to the power of the Prime Minister.
- The fusion of the executive and the legislative branches of government gives the Prime Minister direct influence over both.
- One-party government and strict party discipline ensure the power of the Prime Minister over the governing party in Parliament.
- The apparatus of Whitehall government is hierarchically organised with the Prime Minister at the peak and in control.
- The office of the PM accumulates power over time, ratcheting up with each new incumbent. Wartime conditions gave Churchill special powers that were expanded by strong successors: Attlee, Macmillan, Wilson, Thatcher, Blair.
- The Prime Minister is at the centre of mass media attention. This gives the PM power over government colleagues.
- The Prime Minister represents the country in international meetings (often widely covered in the mass media).
- The Prime Minister's Office and the Cabinet Office are increasingly linked under the direction of the Prime Minister.
- All government communication with the media is increasingly controlled by the PM's Office.

Cabinet government

- Modern government is now so complicated and demanding that one person cannot possibly control all key decisions.
- Important political factions in the party need to be represented in the Cabinet if confidence in the Prime Minister is to be maintained.
- The Prime Minister has powerful and ambitious rivals for office. Some, but not all, may be ignored. Blair cannot keep Brown out of a senior Cabinet position.
- Ministers can use the weapon of resignation against the Prime Minister (Nigel Lawson in 1989, Sir Geoffrey Howe in 1990), although it may do the minister more harm than the Prime Minister in the short term.
- Politics is a hard and ruthless game. PMs need to be constantly watchful and careful, listening carefully to advice from all quarters – party whips, the Prime Minister's Office and advisers, commissions and committees of enquiry, Whitehall staff, the media, and especially friends and advisers who speak their minds.
- The media can be a powerful critic of the Prime Minister. Douglas-Home, Wilson, Heath and Major were weakened by a hostile press.
- Powerful PMs have been driven from office by Cabinet colleagues – notably Macmillan and Thatcher.

Cabinet or prime ministerial government?

There is no question that the British Prime Minister holds one of the most powerful political offices in the western world. What is not clear, however, is whether there is a trend towards greater prime ministerial power:

1. There is nothing new about powerful prime ministers – British history is full of them from the very first, Sir Robert Walpole, to Thatcher and Blair.

2. Strong prime ministers, such as Churchill, Macmillan and Thatcher, have often been followed by weaker ones, such as Eden, Douglas-Home and Major.

3. Relations between the Prime Minister and Cabinet members are largely secret, although surrounded by rumour and hearsay. It is difficult to know what really goes on, and difficult to draw firm conclusions about prime ministerial or Cabinet government.

4. It is often assumed that there must be rivalry and competition between the PM and leading Cabinet members, where there may actually be agreement and unity. Blair and Brown have often been presented (by the media looking for

CONTROVERSY

Prime ministerial or Cabinet government? What commentators say

It is no exaggeration to declare that the British premiership has turned not into a British version of the American presidency, but into an authentically British presidency.

M. Foley, 'Presidential politics in Britain', *Talking Politics*, **6** (3), 1994, p. 141

Cabinet does not make all the decisions but it does make all the major ones, and it sets the broad framework within which more detailed policies are initiated and developed.

M. Burch, 'Prime minister and cabinet: an executive in transition', in R. Pyper and L. Robins (eds), *Governing the UK in the 1990s*, London: Macmillan, 1995, p. 103

The prime minister is the leading figure in the Cabinet whose voice carries most weight. But he is not the all-powerful individual which many have recently claimed him to be. His office has great potentialities, but the use made of them depends on many variables – the personality, the temperament, and the ability of the prime minister, what he wants to achieve and the methods he uses. It depends also on his colleagues, their personalities, temperaments and abilities, what they want to do and their methods.

G. W. Jones, 'The prime minister's power', in A. King (ed.), *The British Prime Minister*, London: Macmillan, 2nd edn, 1985, p. 216

Centralisation of power in the hands of one person has gone too far and amounts to a system of personal rule in the very heart of our parliamentary democracy.

Tony Benn, 'The case for a constitutional premiership', in A. King (ed.), *The British Prime Minister*, London: Macmillan, 2nd edn, 1985, p. 22

The prime minister leads, guides and supports his team, but relies upon their energies and expertise, just as they in turn rely upon his leadership ... The relationship is subtle and variable, but essentially it is one of mutual reliance. A strong prime minister needs strong ministers.

S. James, *British Cabinet Government*, London: Routledge, 1992, pp. 133–4

The more I've been here, the clearer it's become to me that Cabinet government is a reality; let's say that the power of departments and departmental ministers is strong ... I should perhaps add that this is the way this prime minister, in particular, likes to work ... He's a conciliator and therefore goes with the grain of the system of Cabinet government, rather than against it.

1993 interview with senior civil servant, quoted in C. Campbell and G. K. Wilson, *The End of Whitehall*, Oxford: Blackwell, 1995

trouble) as locked in battle. In fact, in the earlier years they often seemed to be close colleagues.

5. The memoirs of leading political figures, as well as commentators outside the system, are frequently contradictory.

In short, the controversy about whether we have prime ministerial or Cabinet government seems to be unresolvable. Consequently, political scientists have turned to a different way of analysing the political executive, using the concept of the 'core executive'.

The core executive

Frustrated by endless controversy about whether we have prime ministerial or Cabinet government, some political scientists have pointed out that both are embedded in a wider network of power relations that spread well beyond Downing Street and the Cabinet room. Increasingly during the twentieth century, and especially under Thatcher and Blair, the power of the political executive has been strengthened and centralised, and its tentacles of power have stretched out to other influential bodies, agencies, committees and individuals in Whitehall and Westminster. This network of power and influence at the apex of government has been termed 'the core executive'. It consists of the following:

- the prime minister, leading members of the Prime Minister's Office, and the more influential members of the prime minister's kitchen cabinet

- the Cabinet and its main committees, leading members of the Cabinet Office, and the more influential ministerial advisers

- the most senior officials in Whitehall departments, agencies and other bodies (e.g. the Bank of England and the main security and intelligence organisations)

- the individuals and organisations that circle around the Prime Minister, the Cabinet and those who serve them

- some members of the House of Commons and the Lords – government whips and a few chairs of Commons committees.

The advantage of focusing on the core executive is that it avoids the old and (some claim) sterile argument about prime ministerial versus Cabinet government to focus on the broader picture of decision-making power and influence. It sees power at the pinnacle of the British state less as the tip of a hierarchical pyramid formed by a few organisations, and more as a complex network of people and bodies in constant interaction and exerting mutual influences. However, the concept has three main problems as an analytical tool in political science.

Numbers

How many people are included in the core executive – 50, 100, 500, 1,000, 5,000, or more? The core executive most certainly includes the 'big beasts' of the Cabinet, but should we also include a few of the most influential junior ministers, and if so how many – 5, 10, or 20? Almost certainly the core executive includes the most important Cabinet committees, but should we also include some important subcommittees as well? Which ones and how many? Almost certainly the core executive includes the most influential people in the Prime Minister's Office, but is this 10, 20, 40, or 60 people? We should also include some of the most influential members of the kitchen cabinet, but who? Then there are the most important senior mandarins in Whitehall, but who? Discussions of the core executive are often rather vague about exactly which offices or people are involved and even about approximate numbers and offices.

Changing circles of power

The answer to the numbers problem is that a lot depends on the particular issue under discussion. The core executive may change its composition according to issues, circumstances and times. A small circle made strategic decisions about the Falklands and Gulf Wars, including senior military chiefs; a larger circle is likely to influence the decision on whether or not to join the euro (excluding military chiefs but including senior staff of the Bank of England and Treasury). Some people and institutions are involved in only one decision, others are involved in a few or many issues, but not all. A very few are involved in all major policy decisions. But this answer simply raises the problem: if different individuals and bodies are influential on different key issues, then the composition of the core executive will change from one issue to the next. If the head of the armed forces is involved in crucially important decisions about Iraq but not about the euro, the Education Bill, hospital trusts or constitutional reform, is he a member of the core executive or not? Or is he sometimes a member and sometimes not? In this case, is there any such thing as the core executive at all? Are we back to identifying the prime minister, the Cabinet, and a handful of senior staff members in the PM's Office and Cabinet Office as the inner core of power because it is involved in almost all key decisions, with constantly changing outer circles of lesser power circling around it? But if these are constantly changing and with lesser power, are they really part of the core executive – or only sometimes?

What does the concept of the core executive explain?

The concept of the core executive is useful in directing attention to the wide network of power and influence at the highest level of government, but it does not help much to answer important questions about who wields power, why, in whose interests, and to what effect? Why are some institutions, groups and individuals more powerful than others? And under what sorts of circumstances? How and why do they come to be powerful? How do they exercise their power, and in whose interests? Core executive theory does little to answer these questions and we have to turn to substantive theories such as class, pluralist, elite and bureaucratic theories as explanations, which is what we will do in following chapters.

Summary

- There is no question that the British Prime Minister has considerable power. A series of strong prime ministers since 1940 testifies to the fact.

- Neither is there much doubt that the Cabinet can be a powerful body. It reasserted its power over Thatcher in 1990, and it is not a body that even an authoritative leader such as Blair can take for granted.

■ An effective political executive rests on the three principles of Cabinet collegiality, departmental autonomy and prime ministerial authority. If these are unbalanced the system will not work effectively.

■ The power of the Prime Minister relative to the Cabinet has swung substantially from one prime minister to the next, and within the term of office of the same PM. Thatcher started in a more collegial mode than she ended. Major's Cabinet started collegially but ended divided. In his earlier years at No. 10 Blair managed to blend prime ministerial authority, departmental autonomy and Cabinet collegiality. Later his style emphasised prime ministerial authority more heavily.

■ Consequently there is much evidence to support both the theory of prime ministerial government and that of Cabinet government.

■ Some political scientists have stopped arguing about prime ministerial versus Cabinet government to focus on the much wider network of power and authority relations found in the core executive. There are many indications that the power of the core executive has been increased and centralised, especially under Thatcher and Blair.

MILESTONES

1721	Robert Walpole acknowledged as the first Prime Minister
1735	Walpole makes 10 Downing Street his official residence
1782	Resignation of the Lord North government on the principle that collective Cabinet responsibility links the Prime Minister with his Cabinet
1914–18	Lloyd George's wartime Cabinet has fewer than 10 members
1916	Lloyd George creates the Cabinet Office
1922	Prime Minister Bonar Law creates a peacetime Cabinet with only 16 people
1931	Appointment of the first Prime Minister's press officer
1937	First statutory reference to the Office of Prime Minister in the Ministers of the Crown Act
1940–5	Wartime emergency gives Churchill great powers as Prime Minister. The modern Cabinet committee system created. The wartime Cabinet had 10 or fewer members
1945–51	Attlee (Deputy Prime Minister under Churchill) continues as a strong leader
1951	Churchill's short-lived experiment with 16 'overlords'
1962	Macmillan's 'night of the long knives' – a Cabinet reshuffle that replaced almost half the members
1964	Wilson creates a Political Office in 10 Downing Street. Ministers allowed their own special advisers
1970	Central Policy Review Staff (CPRS) created by Heath. Super-ministries created: the Department of Trade and Industry, and the Department of the Environment
1974	Wilson sets up first PM's Policy Unit
1975	Collective responsibility suspended during the EC referendum. Collective responsibility again suspended over the issue of the voting system to be used in EC elections
1979	Thatcher starts process of expanding and strengthening the Prime Minister's Office. Gives special role to the PM's press secretary
1983	Thatcher abolishes the CPRS. Cabinet secretary becomes head of the Civil Service
1989	Thatcher shuffles 62 government positions. Lawson (the Chancellor of the Exchequer) resigns from government, criticising Thatcher's leadership and her economic advisers
1990	Sir Geoffrey Howe resigns from the Cabinet, criticising Thatcher's leadership. Thatcher's domination of the government contributes to her downfall. Major introduces a more collegial style of Cabinet government

▶

Milestones in British constitutional development continued

1992	Information about Cabinet committees made public for the first time
1994	Michael Portillo ignores the principle of collective Cabinet responsibility with criticisms of the government's EU policy
1994–7	Principle of collective responsibility applied to Labour's shadow Cabinet
1997	Blair's new Cabinet includes a predominance of strong party notables but marked by consensus on central policies. PM's Office expanded and strengthened
2002	Office of Deputy Prime Minister created
2002–5	The work of the Prime Minister's Office, the Deputy Prime Minister's Office and the Cabinet Office gradually merged to form an executive office.

Essays

1. Discuss the claim that Thatcher's period in office provides clear evidence of prime ministerial government, Major's clear evidence of Cabinet government, and Blair's clear evidence of both.

2. How useful do you find the concept of the 'core executive' in the analysis of British government?

Projects

1. Read this chapter carefully and pick out the bodies, agencies and offices that contribute most to the centralisation of executive power in British government. Explain how they do so, and say whether such centralisation is inevitable.

2. Read carefully through this chapter and make a note of the different bodies, agencies and committees that can help to produce joined-up government, and those which are more likely to produce fragmented government.

Further reading

A short up-to-date book is S. Buckley, *The Prime Minister and Cabinet* (Manchester: The Politics Association, 2006). Longer and older books are S. James, *British Cabinet Government* (London: Routledge, 1998) and G. Thomas, *The Prime Minister and Cabinet Today* (Manchester: Manchester University Press, 1998). A. King (ed.), *The British Prime Minister* (London: Macmillan, 2nd edn, 1985) is the classic collection of readings, and a useful collection of articles on the core executive is contained in R. A. W. Rhodes and P. Dunleavy (eds), *Prime Minister, Cabinet and Core Executive* (London: Macmillan, 1995). The most recent and complete study of Blair as prime minister is A. Seldon and D. Kavanagh (eds), *The Blair Effect 2001–5* (Cambridge: Cambridge University Press, 2005).

Recent articles include M. Burch and I. Holliday, 'The Blair government and the core executive', *Government and Opposition*, **39** (1), 2004, pp. 1–21; M. Rathbone, 'The British cabinet', *Talking Politics*, **16** (1), September 2003, pp. 36–9; M. Garnbett, 'Still first among equals?', *Politics Review*, **14** (4), April 2005, pp. 2–5; P. Riddell, 'Prime ministers and Parliament', *Parliamentary Affairs*, **57** (4), 2004, pp. 814–29.

The classic works on Cabinet and prime ministerial government are J. Mackintosh, *The British Cabinet* (London: Stevens, 1962) and R. Crossman, 'Introduction' to W. Bagehot, *The English Constitution* (London: Fontana, 1963).

Useful web sites on the core executive

Hot links to these sites can be found on the CWS at www.pearsoned.co.uk/budge.

Key sites for the core executive are those of 10 Downing Street (www.number-10.gov.uk) and the Cabinet Office (www.cabinet-office.gov.uk) and the Office of the Deputy Prime Minister at www.odpm.gov.uk.

The web sites for the key Whitehall departments within the core executive are the Treasury (www.hm-treasury.gov.uk), the Foreign Office (www.fco.gov.uk), the Home Department (www.homeoffice.gov.uk) and the Department for Constitutional Affairs (www.lcd.gov.uk). Others may be accessed through links within the Cabinet Office web site (www.cabinet-office.gov.uk).

In addition, three sites with information about Thatcher, Major and Blair as prime ministers is available on: www.margaret-thatcher.com; www.johnmajor.co.uk; and http://www.biogs.com/blair.

Ministries, ministers and mandarins: central government in Britain

Ministers in charge of government departments must work very closely with the civil servants who administer their departments. Ministers, of course, are elected politicians, but civil servants are non-political, permanent and appointed officials – bureaucrats, in other words. There are hundreds of thousands of civil servants, ranging from filing clerks to a small number of very senior administrators who are often referred to as 'mandarins', after the top civil servants of ancient China. The implication is that British mandarins are also highly trained, exceptionally able, totally dedicated and no less inscrutable than their Chinese counterparts. This chapter is concerned with the relationship between government ministers and the highest mandarin level of the Civil Service. The next chapter will look more broadly at the general workings of the administrative machinery of the state.

The relationship between ministers and top civil servants is crucial to the modern state. It is the government departments that actually produce public services – health, education, public transport, national defence – and it is the mandarins, not ministers, who have specialist knowledge and experience of how to run the huge organisations that deliver these services. In theory, ministers have the political function of making public policy, and mandarins the administrative task of advising on policy matters and implementing whatever ministers decide. In practice, it is impossible to draw such a simple distinction between the role of the minister and the top civil servants.

For this reason, the relationships between ministers and mandarins are both important and complex, and raise all sorts of issues. What is the proper relationship between ministers and mandarins? Should civil servants be responsible to the public, to Parliament, or only to their ministers? Should ministers be responsible for everything their civil servants do? Do civil servants really run the country? How has the relationship between ministers and mandarins changed since the Whitehall reforms of the 1980s and 1990s? What special features has New Labour brought to Whitehall operations?

This chapter examines:

- departments and ministries of Whitehall

- ministerial roles and responsibilities

- ministers and civil servants

- mandarin power?

- politicisation of the Civil Service?

- New Labour and the mandarins.

Departments and ministries of Whitehall

The central administration of Britain, like that of almost all other countries, is organised into separate departments or ministries (there is no real distinction between the two). There are about 70 of these. Cabinet ministers head 17 of the major ministries (Table 6.1).

Both the number and nature of ministries may change – just as Cabinet posts change – when the government reorganises departments. A huge ministry was created in 1997 dealing with regional and local government, housing and planning, social exclusion, and regeneration and neighbourhood development. But it was too large for effective coordination and was split up after the election of 2001. A department concerned with constitutional affairs is a new development, and in the latest Cabinet Welsh and Scottish affairs are combined with other jobs because the creation of the two regional authorities has reduced the workload in London.

The most important department is the Treasury, because it manages the national economy and controls the spending of other government departments. Its Comprehensive Spending Review (CSR – introduced by Gordon Brown) requires departments to justify their spending plans for a rolling three-year period. The Treasury used to have a limited coordination role, but the CSR gives it greater powers to control spending and direct future spending plans for Whitehall as a whole – another example of the centralisation of executive power and of the attempt to create joined-up government. The next CSR is planned for 2007.

BRIEFINGS

6.1 British central administration

Whitehall   The area of central London, close to Westminster, where the main ministries and their offices are located. Hence 'Whitehall' is often used as a symbolic term for central bureaucracy and the Civil Service.

Civil servant   A servant of the Crown (in effect of the government) who is employed in a civilian capacity (i.e. not a member of the armed forces), and who is paid for wholly and directly from central government funds (not by local government, agencies, nationalised industries or quangos).

Mandarin   A term given to the thousand or so top civil servants who have regular, personal contact with ministers and act as policy advisers. They are collectively known as the Senior Civil Service, and consist mainly of permanent secretaries (the senior civil servant in each department), under-secretaries and deputy secretaries. They constitute not much more than about 0.2 per cent of all civil servants.

Mandarin power   The theory that top civil servants exert a powerful influence over government policy making because of their ability, experience, expertise, training and special knowledge. One version of the theory claims that civil servants, not ministers, run the country.

Minister   There are more than 110 members of the government, including Cabinet ministers and those who attend the Cabinet, ministers of state and parliamentary under-secretaries of state (PUSS – or 'pussies' for short), down to the lowest rank of (unpaid) parliamentary secretaries. Collectively the last three are known as junior ministers. They usually look after the work of a particular part of their department, under the general direction of their senior minister. As government has grown so has the number of junior ministers – from 23 in 1945 to 89 in 2006.

Ministerial responsibility   The principle that ministers are responsible to Parliament for their own and their department's actions. In theory ministers take responsibility for administrative failure in their department, and for any individual injustice it may cause, whether they are personally involved or not.

Special adviser   Special advisers are not civil servants but political appointees who are either policy experts or general political advisers to ministers.

Table 6.1 Major departments and ministries of central government

Department	Main functions	Planned expenditure 2007/8 (£ million)	Web address
Department for Constitutional Affairs	Upholding justice, rights and democracy	3,856	http://www.dca.gov.uk
Department for Culture, Media and Sport (DCMS)	Museums, galleries, libraries, arts, sport, heritage, media, tourism, national lottery	1,668	http://www.culture.gov.uk
Home Department	The internal affairs of England and Wales (justice, crime and victims, security, passports and immigration, police, prisons, public safety, drugs, science research and statistics)	9,437	http://www.homeoffice.gov.uk
Department of Health (DH)	Health, welfare and well-being	92,621	http://www.dh.gov.uk
Foreign and Commonwealth Office	Foreign affairs and policy, relations with the Commonwealth	1,606	http://www.fco.gov.uk
Department for Transport (DfT)	The transport system	8,056	http://www.dft.gov.uk
Department for education and skills (DfES)	Education and training	23.8	http://www.dfes.gov.uk
Department of Trade and Industry (DTI)	Trade, industry, productivity	6,733	http://www.dti.gov.uk
Department for Environment, Food, and Rural Affairs (Defra)	Farming and fisheries, food and drink, horticulture, animal welfare, environment, rural affairs	3.4	http://www.defra.gov.uk
HM Treasury	The UK economy, tax, work, welfare, public spending and services, enterprise and productivity	Not appropriate	http://www.hm-treasury.gov.uk
Northern Ireland Office	Northern Ireland	8,391	http://www.nio.gov.uk
Privy Council Office	The exercise of prerogative powers, the affairs of chartered bodies (institutions, charities, companies), final Court of Appeal for the Commonwealth countries who choose to use it	724	http://www.privy-council.org.uk
Wales Office	Represents Welsh interests in Westminster, liaising with the devolved administration in Wales	8,766	http://www.walesoffice.gov.uk
Scotland Office	Represents Scottish interests in Westminster, liaising with the devolved administration in Scotland	17,644	http://www.scotlandoffice.gov.uk
Department for Work and Pensions (DWP)	Work, unemployment, disabled people, pensions	7,449	http://www.dwp.gov.uk
Department for International Development (DfID)	International aid and development	5,288	http://www.dfid.gov.uk
Ministry of Defence (MoD)	Defending the UK, international peace and security	33,457	http://www.mod.uk
Office of Deputy Prime Minister	Communities and local government	5,125	http://www.communities.gov.uk
Cabinet Office	Supports the prime minister and Cabinet, coordinating the policy and operations of government	2,154	http://www.cabinetoffice.gov.uk

Note: Because of departmental reorganisation not all figures are available.
Source: www.cabinet-office.gov.uk and HM Treasury *Public Expenditure Statistical Analysis 2005*, London, Table 4.1. Reproduced under the terms of the Click-Use Licence

Ministries are sometimes conglomerates of responsibilities that have grown up rather haphazardly. The most obvious example of this is the Home Department, which has retained all the activities of government that have not been hived off to more specialist ministries. Most ministries, however, focus on one policy area, such as foreign and commonwealth affairs, transport, health, trade and industry, defense, and education (see Table 6.1).

This focus contributes to the development of a 'departmental view', adding to the clash of views and adversarial nature of decision making in the Cabinet. Clearly, having a department charged with one service – transport, health or education – means that it will press its special interests and opinions. Departments have developed their own cultures and views of how best to do things over their decades of operations. Since no ministry has total control of everything it does, each has to cooperate or conflict with others from time to time according to circumstances, and there are often clashes between the departments with conflicting interests, particularly between spending departments fighting for a larger slice of the cake. If they cannot resolve their differences they may take their struggles right up to the Cabinet if necessary.

To understand the subtle and complex nature of this struggle for policy supremacy between ministers and departments we must first consider: (a) the general structure of ministries and departments; and (b) the enormous dependence of politicians on civil servants that this structure creates, a dependence that is quite notable in the British system, though not unique to it.

Ministry structure

Each major department is run by a senior minister or secretary of state, who usually holds a Cabinet seat. To try to keep pace with the huge increase in government work, post-war governments have appointed increasing numbers of junior ministers. In 2006 the Blair government consisted of the following:

- 23 Cabinet ministers (plus 1 more who attended Cabinet meetings), most of whom were department heads

- 27 ministers of state, who are usually responsible for specific aspects of their department's work

- 35 parliamentary under-secretaries of state, and parliamentary private secretaries (PPSs) who assist ministers.

The more important the department, the more senior and junior ministers it has. The Treasury has two Cabinet seats (the Chancellor and the Chief Secretary to the Treasury) and three ministers of state, but the Welsh Office has a Cabinet minister (shared with Northern Ireland) and a parliamentary under-secretary. Figure 6.1 shows the structure of a typical department. Many Cabinet ministers have served an apprenticeship by rising through the ranks of the government from parliamentary secretaries (unpaid ministerial bag carriers), often in a range of different departments.

Ministers are, legally speaking, powerful agents of government in the sense that most Acts of Parliament empower them – not the Prime Minister, the Cabinet, or senior civil servants – to do certain things. For this reason ministers are also formally responsible for what goes on in their department, and are answerable to Parliament for all that the department does in their name. Since government departments are among the largest organisations in the country, this is a huge responsibility.

Figure 6.1 Structure of a typical Whitehall department

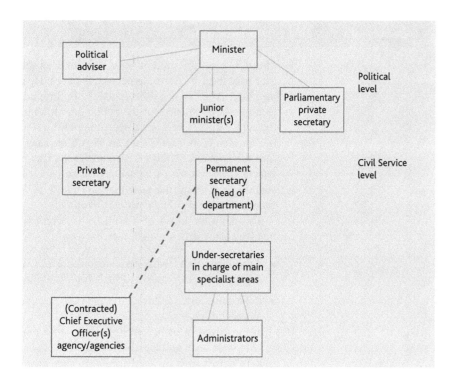

Plate 6.1 Aerial view of Whitehall looking towards the Houses of Parliament

Source: Alamy/Andrew Holt

Ministerial roles and responsibilities

Ministers have an incredibly busy and crowded schedule. In an average day a minister may meet with mandarins to talk about departmental matters, attend a press meeting, travel to a public function, be briefed about parliamentary business, receive a deputation from the public or a foreign government, attend a political meeting, a dinner, or a late-night sitting of the House of Commons, and then work late into the night on a dispatch box full of papers to be read in time for an early start the next day. Ministers also attend the Cabinet and its committees, travel to Brussels and to their parliamentary constituencies, and attend party meetings and conference. During the year they are likely to have to handle time-consuming departmental and political crises as well.

The daily workload of a minister is varied and crushingly heavy because it involves many different activities:

- **Administration**   Ministers are responsible for the daily operations of their department and for cases of maladministration.

- **Policy making**   Ministers set the policy of their department and are involved in general government policy making in the Cabinet and its committees. They are involved in many meetings with other ministers whose business overlaps with their own, and they have to fight for their department and its resources in the Cabinet.

- **Politics**   Ministers are accountable to Parliament, and attend its sessions to answer questions, speak in debates, vote and pilot legislation through Parliament. They also have party meetings and constituencies to nurse.

- **Public relations**   Ministers meet the media regularly to explain departmental policy and further their own careers. They keep up a demanding schedule of travel around the country to dinners, conferences, meetings and openings of various kinds. They meet deputations from interest groups, and receive a huge volume of mail.

- **The EU**   Many ministers read mountains of documents, attend innumerable meetings, and travel thousands of miles on EU business.

Ministers are mostly drawn from the approximately 300–400 people who get elected to Parliament for the majority party. In spite of the huge demands and complexity of their jobs, members of the House of Commons have no special background or training to prepare them for ministerial work. Not one of the members of the Labour government elected in 1997, and out of power for the previous 18 years, had ever held a government job.

Moreover, ministers usually spend little time in any one department before being moved in a government reshuffle. On average they spend two years in one job before switching to another. Between 1945 and 2003 there were 28 ministers of education, each lasting, on average, barely more than two years in office. One, Kenneth Clarke, was Chancellor of the Duchy of Lancaster, and secretary for health and then education, and home secretary, all within a six-year period, before becoming chancellor of the exchequer in 1993, a post he held until 1997. It is said to take over a year to master the work of a department, and at least another year to make any sort of impact on it, by which time ministers have often moved to another job.

Ministerial responsibility

Untrained and inexperienced though they may be, ministers are responsible to Parliament, and can be forced to resign if they or their departments perform badly.

BRIEFINGS

6.2 Ministerial responsibility: what they say

The individual responsibility of ministers for the work of their departments means that they are answerable to Parliament for all their department's activities. They bear the consequences for any failure in administration, any injustice to an individual or any aspect of a policy that may be criticised in Parliament, whether personally involved or not.

Central Office of Information, *The British System of Government*, HMSO: London, 1994, p. 42

The evidence of this study destroys the Crichel Down Affair as the key example of ministerial responsibility. The true convention regarding ministerial resignations is hang on for as long as you can. How long a minister can hang on depends upon his or her stock of political capital.

Keith Dowding, *The Civil Service*, London: Routledge, 1995, p. 169

Ministerial responsibility

The principle whereby ministers are responsible to Parliament for their own and all their department's actions. In theory, ministers are responsible for administrative failure in their department, and for any injustice it may cause, whether they are personally responsible or not.

According to convention they bear responsibility for administrative failure in their departments, for any injustices it may cause, and for general policy failures, whether or not they are personally responsible. In theory, ministers are responsible for everything that goes on in their departments. The classic example is the famous Crichel Down affair of 1954 when the minister of agriculture, Sir Thomas Dugdale, resigned because of departmental maladministration about which he knew nothing.

In theory, the convention of **ministerial responsibility** is a cornerstone of the British constitution because it is the basis of government accountability to Parliament, and hence the main mechanism for holding ministers responsible for their actions. In practice, however, ministerial responsibility does not work this way. Since the Second World War, no minister has resigned because of Civil Service mistakes. Table 6.2 shows that most ministers resign for personal reasons (sex scandals or drunken driving) or because of an error in their ministerial role (the Falklands in 1982, or salmonella in 1988). Even the much-quoted precedent of Crichel Down can be explained in terms of the minister losing backbench support, rather than taking responsibility for Civil Service errors.

There are many more recent examples of ministers hanging on to their posts in spite of departmental failures. To take just one small policy area as an example – that of prison escapes – we find four recent cases of ministers refusing to take responsibility for departmental failures: in 1983 (Secretary of State for Northern Ireland, James Prior), 1991 (Home Secretary, Kenneth Baker) and 1994 and 1995 (Home Secretary, Michael Howard).

There are six main reasons why the convention of ministerial responsibility is not always followed in practice:

1. Conventions are by definition not legally binding, but depend on the willingness of politicians to abide by them.

2. Ministers cannot possibly know everything about their huge departments or be held responsible for every one of its actions. It is estimated that they usually know little more than 1 per cent of departmental matters.

3. While ministers are supposed to resign because of 'failure' or 'injustice', or 'criticism' in Parliament, these are difficult terms to define. In any case, ministers are continuously criticised in Parliament, where there is a continual background of ritual catcalls for resignations.

Table 6.2 Some ministerial resignations and their causes

Year	Minister	Cause of resignation
1982	Nicholas Fairbairn (solicitor-general for Scotland)	Private life and handling of a departmental matter
1982	Lord Carrington (Foreign Secretary), Humphrey Atkins (Lord Privy Seal), Richard Luce (Minister of State, Foreign Office)	Failure to take due note of warnings that Argentina was planning a Falklands invasion
1985	Cecil Parkinson (Transport Secretary)	Private life, the Sara Keays affair
1986	Leon Brittan (Secretary of Trade and Industry)	Leaking official documents about the sale of Westland Helicopters
1986	Michael Heseltine (Defence Secretary)	Disagreement with Cabinet over sale of Westland Helicopters
1988	Edwina Currie (Under-Secretary of State, Health)	Claimed (correctly) that British eggs are infected with salmonella and forced to resign
1990	Patrick Nicholls (Under-Secretary of State, Environment)	Drunken driving
1992	David Mellor (National Heritage minister)	Private life and acceptance of hospitality from businessmen lobbying government
1993	Michael Mates (Minister of State, Northern Ireland)	Relations with Asil Nadir, businessman who jumped bail in a fraud trial
1994	Tim Yeo (Minister of State, Environment)	Private life and illegitimate child
1994	Lord Caithness (Minister of State, Transport)	Private life
1994	Tim Smith (Under-Secretary of State, Northern Ireland)	Accepted cash for asking parliamentary questions
1994	Neil Hamilton (Under-Secretary, Corporate Affairs)	Cash for questions
1995	Allan Stewart (Under-Secretary, Scotland)	Waving pickaxe at anti-road demonstrators
1995	Charles Wardle (Under-Secretary, Industry and Energy)	Opposition to government's immigration policy
1995	Robert Hughes (Parliamentary Secretary)	Private life
1996	David Willetts (Parliamentary Secretary)	Secretly directing Conservative members of Privileges Committee when he was a whip
1998	Ron Davies (Secretary of State for Wales)	Private life
1998	Peter Mandelson (Minister without Portfolio)	Conduct in office – undeclared personal loan from Paymaster-General, and Hinduja passport affair
1998	Geoffrey Robinson (Paymaster-General)	Conduct in office – personal loan to Peter Mandelson
2000	Peter Kilfoyle (Under-secretary of State, Defence)	Disagreement with government policy
2001	Keith Vaz (Minister of State for Europe, Foreign Office)	Misconduct (technically did not resign as a minister but was reshuffled out of office after suspension from the Commons for misconduct)
2002	Stephen Byers (Transport Secretary)	Various transport problems, especially Railtrack, plus behaviour of special advisers
2002	Estelle Morris (Education Secretary)	Various problems concerning schools' policy, especially controversy over A-level results – exacerbated by negative media coverage
2003	Robin Cook (Leader of the House of Commons) John Denham (Minister of State, Home Office)	Disagreement with government policy (Iraq)
2003	Clare Short (Minister for International Development)	Disagreement with government policy (Iraq)
2003	Alan Milburn (Health Secretary)	To spend more time with family
2004	Beverley Hughes (Immigration Minister)	Visa irregularities
2004	David Blunkett (Home Secretary)	Fast tracking nanny's visa
2004	Andrew Smith (Secretary of State for Work and Pensions)	To spend more time with work and constituency following rumours that he would be dropped from the Cabinet
2005	David Blunkett (Minister for Work and Pensions)	Not following procedures for former ministers taking private sector work

4. A minister who should resign may be protected by his or her Cabinet colleagues for political reasons, although in different circumstances the same minister might be sacrificed to public opinion for the same failing. Sometimes governments make a political gesture and find a scapegoat, and sometimes they close ranks to protect themselves.

5. The creation of Whitehall agencies with a degree of independence from ministers (Chapter 7) makes it more difficult to distinguish between the policy failures of ministers and the bureaucratic failures of agencies. Each side can blame the other.

6. When there is such a rapid turnover of ministers, is it fair to blame one for problems that may have been inherited from a predecessor?

As a result the convention of ministerial responsibility is vague, and mainly results in resignation where ministers have lost the support of their government colleagues and/or their party backbenchers.

Ministers and civil servants

Civil servant

A servant of the Crown (i.e. the government) who is employed in a civilian capacity (i.e. not a member of the armed forces) and who is paid wholly and directly from central government funds (not local government, nationalised industries or quangos).

Mandarins

The comparatively small number (about 1,000) of very senior civil servants who have close and regular contact with ministers in their capacity as policy advisers.

Civil Service impartiality

The principle whereby civil servants should be politically neutral and serve their Cabinet ministers regardless of which party is in power and of what they may personally feel about their minister's policies.

Senior and junior ministers constitute a thin political layer of elected politicians superimposed on top of a large army of appointed **civil servants**. At the head of each army division is a permanent secretary who, as the equivalent of the chief executive officer of the department, oversees its daily administration, acts as a policy adviser to the minister, and as the channel of communication between the minister and the layers of officials below. In the post-war years permanent secretaries were powerful figures, and they still constitute an important part of the core executive. However, the Civil Service is now less hierarchical and more flexible than it was. Ministers have a much wider range of contacts and methods of working within their departments than before. So permanent secretaries may not be such powerful gatekeepers nowadays.

Nevertheless, British ministers are dependent on their career civil servants to a degree that is unusual in western democracies. In many countries incoming ministers bring with them a new team of political appointees to serve as senior administrators and policy advisers. This team may leave when a new minister takes over, especially if a new party or coalition comes to power. This is not how things work in the United Kingdom, where civil servants are permanent. Ministers have little control over the selection of the permanent officials with whom they have to work so closely. The idea is that British civil servants are professional and highly trained administrators who are appointed and promoted according to ability and experience, not according to their politics. Only if 'things don't work out' between a minister and his senior officials can the minister demand changes of staff, but there are limits to how many changes can be made. Ministerial dependence on permanent officials will be heightened if he or she is new to the department – as they often are when they are members of a new government, or when they have just been moved as part of a government reshuffle. To make things work effectively and efficiently between elected politicians and their top-flight permanent officials – the **mandarins** – both ministers and civil servants must play special and carefully defined roles in the policy making and administration of the state.

The civil servant's role

The civil servant's role has four main features: **impartiality**, **anonymity**, permanence and confidentiality:

BRIEFINGS

6.3 Civil Service impartiality and anonymity

In the determination of policy the civil servant has no constitutional responsibility or role distinct from that of the minister. It is the civil servant's duty... to give the minister honest and impartial advice, without fear or favour, and whether the advice accords with the minister's views or not... When, having been given all the relevant information and advice, the minister has taken a decision, it is the duty of civil servants loyally to carry out the decision with precisely the same energy and goodwill, whether they agree with it or not.

Civil Servants and Ministers: Duties and Responsibilities, London: HMSO, 1986, pp. 7–8

The Civil Service as such has no constitutional personality or responsibility separate from the duly constituted Government of the day... The duty of the individual civil servant is first and foremost to the Minister of the Crown who is in charge of the department in which he or she is serving.

The Armstrong Memorandum, *Civil Service Management Code*, Issue 1, London: HMSO, 1993, paras 3–4 (Sir Robert Armstrong, Cabinet secretary, 1979–88, and head of the Civil Service, 1981–8)

Although my generation of civil servants has been brought up to regard every act taken by an official as an act in the name of the Minister, our successors may... have to be prepared to defend in public, and possibly without the shield of ministerial protection, the acts they take.

Sir D. Wass, 'The public sector in modern society', *Public Administration*, **61** (1), 1983, p. 12 (Sir Douglas Wass, Permanent Secretary at the Treasury, 1974–83, and joint head of the Civil Service, 1981–3)

- **Osmotherly Rules**   A set of rules for the guidance of officials appearing before House of Commons select committees and designed to protect the principle of Civil Service impartiality, anonymity and confidentiality.

- **The Armstrong Memorandum**   The official statement on the duties and responsibilities of civil servants, including their role in relationship to ministers.

Civil Service anonymity

Civil servants are the confidential advisers of ministers and must not be asked questions about politically controversial matters or the policy advice they give.

Osmotherly Rules

A set of rules, named after their author, Edward Osmotherly of the Civil Service Department, for the guidance of civil servants appearing before Commons select committees and designed to protect Civil Service impartiality, anonymity and secrecy.

1. **Impartiality**   Civil servants must serve their political masters – their ministers – and be strictly impartial about party politics and ministerial policies. They must not enter the political fray. For their part, ministers must not ask civil servants to perform political tasks. Appointments and promotion in the Civil Service should not involve political considerations, or be affected by a change of government. According to the Osmotherly Rules, Commons committees must not ask civil servants 'questions in the field of political controversy'.

2. **Anonymity**   Civil servants are anonymous. They should give their minister their best policy advice without fear or favour, but it is for the minister to defend department policy in public. The Osmotherly Rules state that parliamentary committees must not ask questions about the conduct of particular civil servants or about the advice they give to ministers.

3. **Permanence**   Unlike the system in many other countries, top British civil servants do not change with a change of government. Impartiality and anonymity should mean they serve whichever party is in power to the best of their ability and whatever their own political opinions or department views.

4. **Confidentiality**   The advice civil servants give their ministers is confidential, and the Osmotherly Rules and Armstrong Memorandum state that they cannot be asked to reveal their advice in public. Civil servants sign the Official Secrets Act.

Plate 6.2 The drive to reduce red tape and bureaucracy has, according to some commentators, resulted in an increase in red tape and bureaucracy

Source: Cartoon Stock

Events in the 1980s and 1990s, however, suggest that these four principles have been changed under the pressure of political events:

- **Impartiality and the Tisdall affair** In 1983 the civil servant Sarah Tisdall was sentenced at the Old Bailey to six months in prison for leaking information about the arrival of Cruise missiles at Greenham Common. She believed her defence secretary was avoiding ministerial accountability. Her case raises the question of whether the Civil Service should carry out all ministerial directives, even those they feel are morally or legally dubious. Is their first duty to the public interest, or to their minister?

- **The Ponting affair** Clive Ponting was a civil servant who was prosecuted in 1985 for releasing secret information suggesting that the battleship *Belgrano* was sunk during the Falklands War for political reasons, and not for military ones as claimed by the government. He argued that civil servants have a duty to the public interest that might, under certain circumstances, require them to 'go public'. The judge instructed the jury to find him guilty, on the grounds that ministers should judge what is in the public interest, but the jury acquitted him.

- **The 'arms to Iraq' affair** The Scott Inquiry into the arms to Iraq affair (where the Conservative government had secretly relaxed the rules on exporting arms to Iraq in the 1980s) found that ministers had asked civil servants to help them misinform Parliament and the public, and that civil servants seemed to have colluded with them.

- **Anonymity** An inquiry into the collapse of Vehicle and General Insurance in 1971 placed the blame on named officials. An inquiry following the Westland Helicopters affair in 1986 criticised five named civil servants for their role in leaking a letter, and another, Sir Robert Armstrong, the Cabinet secretary, for failing to take disciplinary action against them. In recent times the anonymity of civil servants has been increasingly difficult to maintain, as the media, political memoirs and official inquiries have publicised Civil Service and ministerial conduct. In 2006 a row blew up about the ruling of the information commissioner that the names of civil servants must not be deleted from documents released to the public under the Freedom of Information Act.

■ **Permanence**   Civil servants are also now less permanent than they used to be. The chief executive officers in charge of executive agencies are on fixed-term contracts (see Chapter 7).

In sum, the theory and practice of the Civil Service role are not the same thing, and the practice has changed in recent decades under the pressures of modern government.

Mandarin power?

In theory, ministers are the elected politicians who make public policy; civil servants provide policy advice and carry out ministerial orders and administer the decisions. Civil servants are 'on tap, but not on top', as the saying goes. In practice, it is impossible to draw a clear distinction between policy and administration. Policy inevitably involves administrative questions. For example, the poll tax, whether or not it was a good idea in principle, was difficult and expensive to implement and might have been rejected on administrative grounds alone. Administration often involves important policy issues, and policy involves important administrative matters. A series of administrative decisions about how to run a policy programme can easily affect its basic rationale.

Consequently, the roles of ministers and their Whitehall staff are blurred. Where the minister's job ends and the permanent secretary's begins is not at all clear. As Sir Humphrey, the caricature of the archetypal mandarin, says in the TV programme *Yes, Minister* with deliberate obscurity and ambiguity:

> I do feel that there is a real dilemma here, in that while it has been government policy to regard policy as the responsibility of ministers, and administration as the responsibility of officials, questions of administrative policy can cause confusion between the administration of policy and the policy of administration, especially where the responsibility for the administration of the policy of administration conflicts or overlaps with the responsibility for the policy of the administration of policy.
>
> J. Lynn and A. Jay, *Yes, Minister*, London: BBC, 1982, p. 176

Mandarin power/ dictatorship of the official

The theory that, no matter which party forms the government, civil servants will exert a powerful influence over government, or even control it, because of their ability, experience and expertise.

The overlap of policy and administration is not just of theoretical interest. It has important implications for the power potential of Whitehall mandarins.

According to the German sociologist Max Weber permanent officials, especially civil servants, hold the reins of power in the modern bureaucratic state. 'For the time being', he wrote, 'the **dictatorship of the official**, not that of the worker, is on the march.' His argument for making this claim was that permanent officials have the training, the ability and the experience that enables them to control or manipulate their nominal political masters. Officials are full time, experienced and highly trained professionals picked for their special ability; politicians are part time, often inexperienced amateurs who are elected from the general population.

There are many arguments for and against Weber's startling claim when we apply it to the British Civil Service. But for every argument in favour of **mandarin power** there seems to be another contradicting it. While the arguments do not necessarily cancel each other out, we have to turn to other ways of trying to resolve the controversy. One obvious way is to call on the evidence of insiders who know the Whitehall and Westminster 'village' well, and one obvious place to search is the growing body of political memoirs of ministers and mandarins who have written about their personal experiences. Unfortunately, these are also inconclusive. Not only is the evidence anecdotal and patchy, but for every minister – Benn, Castle,

CONTROVERSY

Mandarin or ministerial power? The theory

Mandarin power

Numbers

About 1,000 civil servants have a direct input into the policy-making process compared with about 60 ministers and junior ministers

Time

Civil servants are full time; ministers divide their time between many activities

Permanence and experience

Civil servants are permanent; ministers are temporary; civil servants often have many years' experience; ministers have few (if any)

Ability and training

Top civil servants are exceptionally able, usually with excellent educational qualifications. Ministers are untrained and not elected for their educational qualifications

Monopoly of advice and information

Ministers are heavily dependent on their civil servants for policy advice. This is a uniquely British situation, as elsewhere they take independent policy advisers in with them, as a matter of course

Tricks of the trade

Civil servants may use tricks of the trade: putting important documents at the bottom of the dispatch box; concealing major policy issues in long, complex reports; giving ministers little time for decisions; selective use of facts; getting other departments to intervene in matters of mutual interest

The departmental view versus vague party platforms

Departments have a comprehensive policy view; ministers have sketchy guidance from their party manifesto

Civil Service ambition

Those at the top of the Civil Service hierarchy are able and ambitious. Some ministers are weak, appointed because they can be controlled by Cabinet colleagues

Civil Service empire building

Civil servants are ambitious for their departments: they want to build empires

Evidence

It is not difficult to draw up a long list of ministers who were run by their departments

Ministerial power

The boss

Numbers may not count for much when ministers can use their legitimate power to overrule civil servants

Time is not the essence

It does not take a good minister long to come to grips with the essentials of policy decisions

Permanence and experience

Some ministers take charge of their department quickly: a few have much government experience if their party has been in power for some time

All amateurs

Civil servants are generalists, not specialists, and have no more professional training for their job than ministers. Some ministers are exceptionally able

Outside advice

Ministers are not totally dependent on civil servants or advice; they have their own (non-Civil Service) advisers, professionals, the party, pressure groups, academics and the media

Ministerial experience

It does not take ministers long to learn these tricks and ways of countering them. They have tricks of their own, and may be able to make life difficult for non-compliant civil servants

Cabinet and party backing

Ministers can use the party election manifesto and the weight of Cabinet opinion to force (if necessary) civil servants to accept a policy

Personality

Ministers are not famous for being shy and uncertain; many have great ambition, confidence and force of character to drive their will

Professional ethos

The Civil Service has a strong and well-developed ethos or ethic of serving ministers to their best ability

Evidence

It is not difficult to draw up a long list of ministers who ran their departments

355

CONTROVERSY

Mandarin or ministerial power? Some insider evidence

The trouble with the Civil Service is that it wants a quiet life. The civil servants want to move slowly along the escalator towards their knighthood and retirement and they have no interest whatsoever in trying to develop new lines of activity.

Tony Benn, *Out of the Wilderness, Diaries 1963–1967*, London: Arrow Books, 1987, p. 195

I believe that civil servants like to be under ministerial control. There is nothing they dislike more than to have a minister whom they feel is weak, who does not know his mind and who wants to leave it all to them ... What they like is to have a minister who knows a policy he wants to pursue.

Edward Heath, quoted in Peter Barberis (ed.), *The Whitehall Reader*, Buckingham: Open University Press, 1996, p. 83

Even at the ODM [Ministry of Overseas Development] I remember Andy Cohen, the Permanent Secretary, trying to wear me down ... He would be in my office about seven times a day saying, 'Minister, I know the ultimate decision is yours but I would be failing in my duty if I didn't tell you how unhappy your decision makes me.' Seven times a day. One person [the Minister] against the vast department.

Barbara Castle, *Mandarin Power*, quoted in Barberis, op. cit., p. 66

Ministers set the policy agenda, often with help from officials, and make decisions within it. They seek, and officials offer, advice within the framework of the policy agenda.

Lord Burns, permanent secretary of the Treasury, 1991–8, quoted in Kevin Theakston (ed.), *Bureaucrats and Leadership*, Basingstoke: Palgrave Macmillan, 2000, p. 40

I think the minister who complains that his civil servants are too powerful is either a weak minister or an incompetent one.

Denis Healey, quoted in Barberis, op. cit., p. 81

Already I realise the tremendous effort it requires not to be taken over by the Civil Service. My Minister's room is like a padded cell ... there is a constant preoccupation to ensure that the Minister does what is correct.

Richard Crossman, *The Diaries of a Cabinet Minister*, vol. 1, London: Hamilton and Cape, 1975, pp. 21–2

Broadly speaking, I would say that it is quite untrue to believe that Whitehall, if you are firmly committed to anything, would try to stop you doing it.

Richard Crossman, *Socialism and Affluence: Four Fabian Papers*, London: Fabian Society, 1967, p. 80

We concentrate on what *can* happen, not what *ought* to happen.

Sir Brian Cubbon (permanent secretary of the Northern Ireland Office, 1978–88), 'The duty of the professional', in R. Chapman (ed.), *Ethics in Public Service*, Edinburgh: Edinburgh University Press, 1993, p. 10

Only bad ministers blame the Civil Service, because only bad ministers let themselves be dominated by the Civil Service.

Gerald Kaufman, 'How to be a minister', *Politics Review*, **7** (1), 1997, p. 13

Crossman – claiming that civil servants were unhelpful or obstructive, there is another – Wilson, Carrington, Heath, Healey and Crossman – saying that they are professionals who can be controlled. Crossman appears to disagree with himself, so he appears in both lists.

If neither abstract argument nor insider evidence offers a conclusive answer to the controversy about mandarin power, perhaps the most significant evidence is provided by developments under Thatcher and Major. Their governments reformed the Civil Service structure and mode of operation in fundamental ways and, moreover, won big battles against determined opposition from almost all sections of Whitehall. This constitutes clear evidence that British civil servants can be brought under government control, if the government is determined to push its reforms through. Whatever may have been the case before 1979, Whitehall mandarins were not 'on top' in the 1980s and early 1990s when they had to submit to reforms they strongly disliked. In fact in this period, far from being too strong, civil servants were criticised at the time for being too weak and compliant, and giving in to ill-thought-out and hastily implemented government plans. Indeed it was even argued that the Civil Service had abandoned its traditional political neutrality to become a political tool of the government. The same complaint was raised a decade later by the Hutton Inquiry (http://www.the-hutton-inquiry.org.uk/index.htm) and the Butler Report of 2004 (http://www.butlerreview.org.uk), when it was asked whether the intelligence community was too sensitive to what the government wanted to hear and presented evidence to suit it.

Politicising the Civil Service: what price the code of ethics?

Since the 1980s the problem has not been that civil servants use their powers for their own purposes but, on the contrary, that the government has used civil servants for its own party political purposes. Critics argue that the Civil Service has been increasingly politicised by the Thatcher and Blair governments. There is some evidence for this view, although much of it is anecdotal and it is very difficult to know what actually has happened given the private and secret nature of most government business at this very high level. However, the Scott Inquiry (see above) showed that politicians had used civil servants to perform political tasks. It is also claimed that civil servants such as Sarah Tisdall, Clive Ponting and Dr David Kelly breached the Civil Service code by engaging in politics. After much pressure, the government accepted a formal code of ethics drafted by the Treasury and Civil Service Select Committee of the House of Commons dealing with the roles and responsibilities of civil servants. It came into effect in January 1996. An appeals procedure was set up for civil servants who felt under pressure to compromise their political neutrality, and a Propriety and Ethics Team was also created to give advice on ethical issues involving the Civil Service and the Cabinet.

There is continuing disquiet about dangers to the traditional role of the Civil Service. In 2003 the Committee on Standards in Public Life called for a Civil Service Act to place the Civil Service on a statutory footing. The Public Administration Committee of the House of Commons published its own draft Bill in 2004 and meanwhile the Civil Service Commissioners warned against the further politicisation of the Civil Service. With some reluctance, it seems, the government published a draft Bill in 2006 to regulate the appointment, duties and conduct of civil servants and special advisers.

New Labour and the mandarins

The Thatcher/Major Conservative governments were in power for 18 years. In that time they reshaped almost every aspect of government policy, appointed almost every senior civil servant, tried to remodel large parts of the Whitehall machinery, and did their best to instil a Thatcherite culture in Whitehall. As a result, some observers in 1997 suggested that the Blair government would need to clean-sweep the top levels of the Civil Service and replace it with its own people. No such thing happened, and the transfer of power from Conservative to Labour government was relatively uneventful, with the exception of a few minor 'hiccups'. Many top

Task forces

Task forces are usually small, official groups set up to do a particular and fairly limited job (write a report, investigate an issue or event), and dissolved when they have completed the task.

information officers (spin doctors) in Whitehall were replaced, but they held politically sensitive posts. In large part the Civil Service adapted to its new political masters. However, the Blair government has done two things to change working patterns in Whitehall: it has significantly enlarged and strengthened the role of special advisers, and it has created a large number of **task forces**.

Special advisers

The Civil Service once enjoyed a virtual monopoly as advisers to ministers. This was partly because British parties do little planning about how to turn their vague campaign promises into specific policies. For example, Richard Crossman, a new minister in 1964, noted with dismay in his diary that the file at Labour's headquarters on one of its longest standing policy commitments was almost empty. 'Think tanks' (outside centres providing policy advice) are relatively new in Britain, and limited in numbers and resources. Policy working groups in the main parties are relatively weak, and policy recommendations of parliamentary select committees (Chapter 18) often ignored. Thus, the first port of call for a minister in need of advice was, until recently, their senior civil servants. This has changed as governments become aware of their dependence on the mandarins, even though they did not appoint them in the first place.

A response to this has been the appointment of special advisers from outside the Civil Service. These are not new to British government, but their numbers have increased in the past 10–15 years. Compared with the 46 special advisers in Major's government there are now more than 75, with some 26 in the Prime Minister's and Deputy Prime Minister's Offices.

Special advisers are temporary civil servants and bound by the Civil Service code. But, unlike regular civil servants, they do not need to be appointed on merit or to be politically neutral. Most departments have no more than two special advisers but there are exceptions. The Department for Education and Skills and the Office of the Deputy Prime Minister have had more. Special advisers are paid out of public funds, and in 2004/5 cost £5.5 million.

There are two kinds of special advisers. The first are policy experts with specialist knowledge, and the second are political advisers (not a Civil Service function) who think generally about political tactics and strategy for their minister and the government. Many are on part-time or short-term contracts. As outsiders who are answerable only to the minister who employs them, they are independent of the civil servants. On the one hand, special consultants give the government a greater range of advice and greater freedom of action; on the other, they may undermine the traditional role of senior civil servants. Moreover, there has been a crossing of lines between the Civil Service, the government and the political parties, a trend further complicated by the fact that a few special advisers have the power to give orders to civil servants. This was part of the controversy about how one special adviser, Alastair Campbell, might have 'sexed-up' an intelligence report on Iraqi weapons of mass destruction.

The role and powers of special advisers continues to concern the Committee on Standards in Public Life, which points out that mixing special advisers' advice with that of civil servants effectively prejudices the objectivity and neutrality of civil servants. The advice of some special advisers has also been controversial. Jo Moore's email on the day of the 11 September 2001 attacks on the United States to her minister, Steven Byers, contributed to both of them losing their jobs. She wrote: 'It's now a very good day to get out anything we want to bury. Councillors' expenses?' This piece of special advice was followed by announcing two rather small changes to local government expenses.

Task forces

A second notable change in Whitehall since 1997 is the growth of task forces, ad hoc advisory groups and review bodies. Collectively these three fall into the broader category of non-departmental public bodies (NDPBs). They are appointed by ministers but work at arm's length with a degree of independence from government. They are usually appointed to carry out very specific tasks and have a limited lifespan. Members of the bodies are usually people in public, business and professional life, who are appointed for their specialist knowledge and skills. In 2005 there were 458 such groups in central government, ranging from the Food in Schools Management Group and the Employers Task Force on Pensions to the Expert Group on Mental Health in Prisons and the Music Industry Forum.

Such groups can ignore the traditional Whitehall approach to problems by getting outside experts to search for new and pragmatic solutions to government problems. For example, National Health Service task forces, composed of medical professionals and patients, can explore ways to improve the service. Other groups are set up because there is little expertise on a subject in Westminster or Whitehall, such as the group that reported on Near Earth Objects (asteroids and comets) that threatened the globe. Task forces are also good at cutting across departmental boundaries, and hence can help joined-up government, except that they add yet another layer and type of public body to the system, and hence can fragment it as well.

The problem with such groups is that they undermine the policy advice role of civil servants, and they bypass the traditional Whitehall structures of departmental and inter-departmental committees. There is such a large number and bewildering variety of them, and such a rapid turnover, that they are difficult to keep track of and are accountable only to their minister. They are yet another influence that encourages government to fragment and fly off in many directions.

Summary

- In theory, ministers are responsible for policy and civil servants for administration, but in practice no clear line can be drawn between policy and administration.

- In theory, ministers are responsible to Parliament for their own actions and those of their departments and civil servants. In practice, the principle of ministerial responsibility is often breached.

- In theory, civil servants are impartial, anonymous, permanent, and protected by secrecy. In practice, all four features of the civil servant's role have been undermined in recent years.

- The old controversy about mandarin power is unlikely to be resolved, because arguments are inconclusive and insider evidence is contradictory. However, it is clear that politicians wielded decisive power over their mandarins in the 1980s and 1990s when the Thatcher and Major governments implemented sweeping reforms of Whitehall.

- After much pressure, the government published its Civil Service Bill in 2006, but its increasing use of special advisers and task forces has tended to undermine the traditional policy adviser role of senior civil servants and bypass normal departmental methods of policy making.

- Critics of the Whitehall system claim that the doctrines which are supposed to regulate ministerial and Civil Service relationships are more mythical than real. They argue for clearer and firmer rules, especially on the role of Civil Service and special advisers, and for better procedures to protect civil servants from ministers who try to use them for political purposes.

MILESTONES

Milestones in relationships between ministers and mandarins in the post-war period

Nineteenth century	The modern principles of Civil Service permanence, neutrality and anonymity become established along with ministerial responsibility
1954	Crichel Down affair. Secretary of State for Agriculture, Sir Thomas Dugdale, resigns because of maladministration in his department. Later research suggests that he was forced from office because he lost backbench support
1955	Creation of junior minister posts (to fill in for ministers away from London)
1964	Junior ministers given specific departmental responsibilities. Named Ministry of Aviation officials blamed for excessive profits paid in defence contracts to Ferranti Ltd for Bloodhound missiles
1968	Foreign Office officials named by Commons select committee for failure to compensate British victims of the Nazis (the Sachsenhausen case)
1971	Collapse of Vehicle and General Insurance Co. A named civil servant is blamed, but the minister, John Davies, does not resign
1973	Cabinet Office sets up its European Secretariat to coordinate departmental policy on the EEC
1976	Publication of Osmotherly Rules, guiding officials and politicians involved in the proceedings of Commons committees
1983	Sarah Tisdall jailed for leaking documents about the siting of Cruise missiles on Greenham Common
1984–5	Ponting trial. Clive Ponting had leaked documents showing the political motives for sinking the Argentine cruiser, *Belgrano*, in the Falklands War with the loss of 700 lives. Acquitted by jury against judge's instructions
1985	Armstrong Memorandum on the duties and responsibilities of civil servants
1986–7	Westland Helicopters affair. Colette Bowes, a civil servant, publicly identified for leaking a secret letter on the instruction of her minister, Sir Leon Brittan, who then resigned
1987	A revised version of the Armstrong Memorandum
1995–6	Scott Report into 'arms for Iraq' (also known as the Matrix Churchill affair) finds that the government had used civil servants to try to suppress embarrassing information at a trial on grounds of 'national security'
1996	Civil Service code comes into effect
1997	Smooth transfer of power from Conservatives to Labour after May general election
1997–2005	Growing numbers of special advisers and task forces used in Whitehall
2004	Butler Report raises concerns about government decision making and the role of special advisers.
2006	The issue of Civil Service confidentiality clashes with Freedom of Information requirements about the release of official documents that name civil servants. Consultation on a new Civil Service code

Essays

1. Argue the case for and against a permanent layer of civil servants at the top of Whitehall departments.

2. In what ways, and for what reasons, has the role of Whitehall mandarins changed in the last 30 years?

3. Are ministers really responsible to Parliament in their departmental capacities?

Projects

1. Playing the roles of a minister and a permanent secretary, argue the case for and against special advisers and task forces in central government.

2. Find out what you can from newspaper reports about any cases involving ministerial responsibility (e.g. Sir Thomas Dugdale and the Crichel Down affair, 1954; Norman Lamont and the withdrawal of the pound sterling from the EMS in 1992; James Prior, Kenneth Baker and Michael Howard and prison escapes in 1983, 1991, 1994 and 1995; Stephen Byers, transport and the Millennium Dome, 2002; and Keith Vaz and misconduct, 2002) What, if anything, do these case histories tell us about ministerial responsibility?

Further reading

General accounts of the Civil Service can be found in R. Pyper, *The British Civil Service* (London: Prentice-Hall/Harvester Wheatsheaf, 1995), and K. Theakston, *The Civil Service Since 1945* (Oxford: Blackwell, 1995). Longer, but very readable, is P. Hennessy, *Whitehall* (London: Secker & Warburg, 1989), and a more advanced text is K. Dowding, *The Civil Service* (London: Routledge, 1995). For a useful set of insider views on the relationships between ministers and mandarins, see P. Barberis (ed.), *The Whitehall Reader* (Buckingham: Open University Press, 1996). The same book has a section on Civil Service loyalties, responsibilities and ethics. An excellent account of the decline of the Whitehall Model based on extensive interviews is Colin Campbell and Graham K. Wilson, *The End of Whitehall: Death of a Paradigm* (Oxford: Blackwell, 1995).

Shorter and more recent articles on the Civil Service are T. Butcher, 'The Civil Service under New Labour', *Politics Review*, **11** (3), 2002, pp. 29–31; R. Pyper, 'Ministers, civil servants and advisers', in J. Fisher, D. Denver and J. Benyon (eds), *Central Debates in British Politics* (Harlow: Pearson, 2003); and R. Pyper, 'Politics and the Civil Service' *Politics Review*, September 2005, pp. 17–21. For recent and general overviews, see K. Jenkins, 'Parliament, government and the Civil Service', *Parliamentary Affairs*, **57** (4), 2004, pp. 800–13 and A. Gray and B. Jenkins, 'Government and administration: public service and public servants', *Parliamentary Affairs*, **58** (2), 2005, pp. 230–47.

Useful web sites on ministries, ministers and mandarins

Hot links to these sites can be found on the CWS at www.pearsoned.co.uk/budge.

A good way to start your research on the structure of ministries and departments is to visit the Cabinet Office web site www.cabinet-office.gov.uk and the direct government web site on http://www.direct.gov.uk where you will find a comprehensive description of the ministerial network and the organisation of the Civil Service. Web site addresses for Whitehall departments are listed in Table 6.1.

The official reference point for the Civil Service is their home page www.civilservice.gov.uk. In addition there are various sites where the functioning of the Civil Service is scrutinised. The FDA is the trade union and professional body for Britain's senior public servants (www.fda.org.uk). Using their search engine enables access to a variety of reports and articles on the Civil Service. Useful information is also available on www.epolitix.com (here again we recommend you use their search engine) and the Study of Parliament Group at www.spg.org.uk.

Topic 9:
Parliament

The House of Commons

Philip Norton

Learning objectives

- To explain the importance of the House of Commons in terms of its history and its functions.

- To identify and assess the means available to Members of Parliament to fulfil those functions.

- To describe and analyse pressures on the House and proposals for reform.

- To identify different approaches to parliamentary power.

Introduction

The House of Commons has evolved over seven centuries. At various times, it has played a powerful role in the affairs of the nation. Its most consistent activity has been to check the executive power. Its power has been limited by royal patronage and, more recently, by the growth of parties. It nonetheless remains an important part of the political process. It has to give its assent to measures of public policy. Ministers appear before it to justify their actions. It remains an arena for national debate and the clash of competing party views. It provides an important institutional constraint on the actions of government. However, its capacity to fulfil its functions has been the subject of debate. Criticism has led to various demands for change.

■ Origins of Parliament

Parliament has its origins in the thirteenth century. It was derived not from first principles or some grand design but from the King's need to raise more money. Its subsequent development may be ascribed to the actions and philosophies of different monarchs, the ambitions and attitudes of its members, external political pressures and prevailing assumptions as to the most appropriate form of government. Its functions and political significance have been moulded, though not in any consistent manner, over several hundred years.

Despite the rich and varied history of the institution, two broad generalisations are possible. The first concerns Parliament's position in relation to the executive. Parliament is not, and never has been on any continuous basis, a part of that executive. Although the Glorious Revolution of 1688 confirmed the form of government as that of 'parliamentary government', the phrase, as we have seen already (Chapter 13), means government through Parliament, not government by Parliament. There have been periods when Parliament has been an important actor in the making of public policy, not least for a period in the nineteenth century, but its essential and historically established position has been that of a reactive, or policy-influencing, assembly (Box 15.1; see Mezey 1979; Norton 2005); that is, public policy is formulated by the executive and then presented to Parliament for discussion and approval. Parliament has the power to amend or reject the policy placed before it, but it has not the capacity to substitute on any regular basis a policy of its own. Parliament has looked to the executive to take the initiative in the formulation of public policy, and it continues to do so.

The second generalisation concerns the various tasks, or functions, fulfilled by Parliament. Parliament is a multifunctional body. Not only does it serve as

BOX 15.1 IDEAS AND PERSPECTIVES

Types of legislature

- *Policy-making legislatures*: These are legislatures that not only can modify or reject measures brought forward by the executive but also can formulate and substitute policy of their own (e.g. the US Congress).
- *Policy-influencing legislatures*: These are legislatures that can modify and sometimes reject measures brought forward by the executive but lack the capacity to formulate and substitute policy of their own (e.g. UK Parliament, German Bundestag).
- *Legislatures with little or no policy effect*: These are legislatures that can neither modify nor reject measures brought forward by the executive, nor formulate and substitute policies of their own. They typically meet for only a short period each year to give formal approval to whatever is placed before them (e.g. former legislatures of Eastern European communist states, such as East Germany).

a reactive body in the making of public policy, it also carries out several other tasks. Its principal tasks were established within the first two centuries of its development. In the fourteenth century, the King accepted that taxes should not be levied without the assent of Parliament. The giving of such assent was variously withheld until the King responded to petitions requesting a redress of grievances. At the same time, Parliament began to take an interest in how money was spent and began to look at the actions of public servants. It became, in a rather haphazard way, a body for the critical scrutiny of government.

■ The development of Parliament

Knights and burgesses were summoned in the thirteenth century in order to give assent to the King's decision to raise extra taxes. They joined the King's court, comprising the leading churchmen and barons of the realm. In the fourteenth century, the summoning of knights and burgesses became a regular feature of those occasions when the King summoned a 'parliament'. At various times during the century, the knights and burgesses sat separately from the churchmen and barons, so there developed two chambers – the Commons and the Lords.

The House of Commons became more significant in subsequent centuries. It was an important political actor during the Tudor reigns of the sixteenth century and a powerful opponent of the Stuart monarchs, who asserted the divine right of kings to rule in the seventeenth. Clashes occurred between Parliament and Charles I – leading to the beheading of the King and a short-lived period of republican government under Oliver Cromwell – and, later, between Parliament and James II. The fleeing of James II in 1688 allowed leading parliamentarians to offer the throne to James's daughter and son-in-law (Mary and William) on Parliament's terms, and the supremacy of Parliament was established. Henceforth, the King could not legislate – or suspend laws – without the assent of Parliament.

Parliament nonetheless continued to look to the executive power – initially the King, and later the King's ministers assembled in Cabinet – to take the initiative in formulating measures of public policy. When measures were laid before Parliament, assent was normally forthcoming. In the eighteenth century, royal influence was employed, either directly or through the aristocratic patrons of 'rotten boroughs',

to ensure the return of a House favourable to the ministry. This influence was broken in the nineteenth century. The 1832 Reform Act enlarged the electorate by 49 per cent and abolished many, although not all, rotten boroughs. The effect of the measure was to loosen the grip of the aristocracy on the House of Commons and to loosen the grip of the monarch on the choice of government. The last time a government fell for want of the monarch's confidence was in 1834. MPs entered a period when they were relatively independent in their behaviour, being prepared on occasion to oust ministers and sometimes governments (as in 1852, 1855, 1856 and 1866) and to amend and variously reject legislation. Except for the years from 1841 to 1846, party ties were extremely loose.

This so-called **golden age** was to prove short-lived. At that time, there was little public business to transact and what there was of it was reasonably easy to comprehend. Members were not tied overly to party and could make a judgement on the business before them. The consequence of the 1867 Reform Act, enlarging the electorate by 88 per cent, and of later Acts reducing corrupt practices, was to create an electorate too large, and too protected by the law, to be 'bought' by individual candidates. Extensive organisation was necessary to reach the new voters, and organised political parties soon came to dominate elections. For a winning party to govern effectively, its members in the House of Commons needed to be united, and by the end of the century cohesive party voting was a feature of parliamentary life. Party influence thus succeeded royal patronage in ensuring the assent of MPs for measures brought forward by ministers of the crown.

The effect on Parliament of the rise of a mass electorate was profound. Governments came to be chosen by the electorate, not – as had occasionally happened in preceding years – by the House of Commons. Popular demands of government engendered not only more measures of public policy, but more extensive and complex measures. By the turn of the century, Parliament lacked the political will and the institutional resources necessary to subject increasingly detailed government bills to sustained and effective scrutiny. Albeit in a somewhat different form to earlier centuries, executive dominance had returned.

For the House of Commons, though, the developments of the nineteenth century served to confirm it as the pre-eminent component of the Crown-in-Parliament. The Glorious Revolution had established

Parliament's supremacy over the King. The rise of the democratic principle in the nineteenth century established the supremacy of the elected House over the unelected. The House of Commons was clearly a representative chamber in that it was freely elected and in that its members were returned to defend and pursue the interests of electors (see Chapter 16). The House of Lords could claim to be representative in neither sense. The subordinate position of the House of Lords was confirmed by statute in the Parliament Act of 1911.

The position so established in the nineteenth century continued into the twentieth. The House of Commons remained – and remains – the dominant chamber in a Parliament dominated by party, with the initiative for measures of public policy resting with the Cabinet and with a party majority in the House ensuring the passage of those measures.

That sets the historical context. What, then, is the contemporary position of the House of Commons? What are the essential characteristics of the House – its members and its procedures? What functions does it fulfil? What tools does it have at its disposal to fulfil them? And to what extent have developments in recent years strengthened or weakened its capacity to carry out those functions?

■ The House of Commons

The size of the House of Commons has varied over time, ranging in the twentieth century from a high of 707 seats (1918–22) to a low of 615 (1922–45). The number was reduced in 1922 because of the loss of (most) Irish seats; it has varied in postwar years

and from 1945 to 1974 stood at 630; because of the increase in the size of the population, it was increased in 1974 to 635, in 1983 to 650, in 1992 to 651 and in 1997 to 659. In 2001, there was the first reduction since 1922: the number of seats in Scotland went down from 72 to 59 to take account of the fact that Scotland had its own parliament. As a result, the number of seats in the 2005 Parliament was 646. The number is set to increase to 650 in the Parliament of 2010.

Elections

The maximum life of a parliament is five years. Between 1715 and 1911, it was seven years. Members (MPs) are returned for single-member constituencies. These have been the norm since the Reform Act of 1885, although twelve double-member constituencies survived until the general election of 1950. The method of election employed is the 'first-past-the-post' system, with the candidate receiving the largest number of votes being declared the winner. This again has been the norm since 1885, although not until the general election of 1950 (with the abolition of university seats, for some of which a system of proportional representation was used) did it become universal. All seats nowadays are contested by two or more candidates. Again, this is a relatively recent development. In elections before 1945 a significant fraction of members – an average of 13 per cent – were returned unopposed. As late as the 1951 election, four Ulster Unionist MPs were returned in uncontested elections.

Each constituency comprises a defined geographical area, and the MP is returned to represent all citizens living within that area. (University seats

---

BOX 15.2   IDEAS AND PERSPECTIVES

The atmosphere of the House

By the standards of the Palace of Westminster, the House of Commons (Figure 15.1) is not a particularly ornate chamber. Relatively new compared with the rest of the Palace – rebuilt after being destroyed on 10 May 1941 by enemy bombing – it has a fairly functional feel to it. When it was rebuilt, there was a change in the style but not in the size. This meant that it was too small to accommodate every member. This has proved to be beneficial on two counts. First, on the rare occasions that the House is full, it conveys a sense of theatre: some members sit on the steps in the aisles, some crowd around the Speaker's chair, some stand in packed ranks at the bar of the House. Tension rises as the Prime Minister, or another senior minister, closes for the government and the Speaker rises to put the question. Members then troop into the voting lobbies either side of the chamber. If the outcome of the vote is uncertain, the tension is

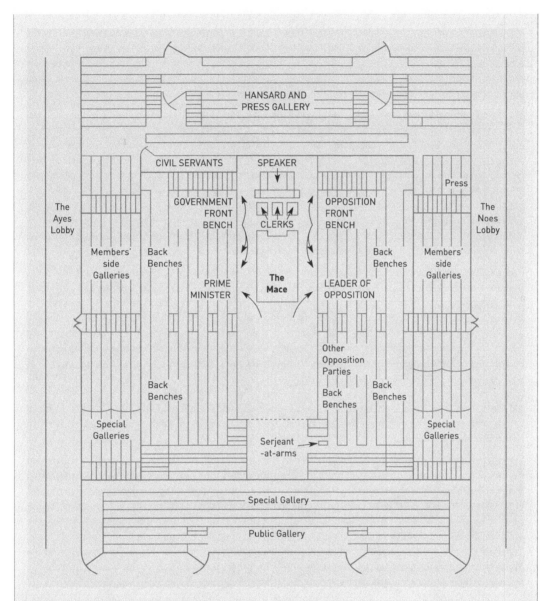

Figure 15.1 House of Commons seating plan

close to unbearable. After ten to fifteen minutes – sometimes longer – the tellers return and those representing the winning side line up on the right at the table, facing the Speaker. Once those on the winning side realise they have won, a massive cheer goes up. The most dramatic vote of recent history was on 28 March 1979, when the Labour government lost a vote of confidence by one vote. There have been dramatic votes in the twenty-first century when the Labour government has come close to defeat, as on the second reading of the Education Bill in 2003 – even the government whips were not sure who had won – or the the occasions when it was defeated: in 2005 on a provision to allow 90-day detention without trial and in 2009 on the resettlement rights in the UK of former Gurkha soldiers.

The second reason why the small chamber is better than a larger one is simply because such dramatic occasions are rare. Most of the time the chamber is notable for the rows of empty green benches as a handful of MPs sit around listening – or half-listening, or whispering to a neighbour – as one of their number delivers a speech from notes, sometimes quite copious notes. The chamber looks cavernous on such occasions. With a much larger chamber, the sheer emptiness of the place would be overwhelming.

The empty green benches are more apparent now than in previous decades. It is common to lament a fall in attendance. Most MPs have other things to do. There is little vital business in the chamber and now-adays there are very few members who will attract a crowd when they speak: the big speakers of yesteryear are either dead (Enoch Powell, Edward Heath, Robin Cook, Michael Foot), departed (Tony Benn) or in the House of Lords (Michael Heseltine, Margaret Thatcher). A change in the hours of sittings, allowing MPs to get away early on a Thursday evening, coupled with a tendency to schedule less im-portant business for a Thursday, has meant that for some MPs it is now virtually a three-day week. They arrive in Westminster on the Monday – sometimes late in the day – and depart on Thursday. Neither parliamentary party meets now on a Thursday; indeed, very few meetings are organised on a Thursday. Most are now crowded into the day on Tuesday or Wednesday.

Proceedings in the chamber can be lively during Question Time, but even during that attendance – other than for Prime Minister's Questions – can be pretty poor. During debates, the proceedings can be notably dull. The government front bench will have one or two ministers listening, taking notes as necessary for the purpose of replying at the end. A government whip will be perched further along the bench, keeping an eye on proceedings, taking notes and liaising with the Chair about business. Their opposite numbers will be on the Opposition front bench. Notes or signals will variously pass between the whips, followed sometimes by a meeting behind the Speaker's Chair to fix some deal. Some MPs will wander in, look at what is going on and then depart. Some take their seats, stay a few minutes and go. A few will spend some time in the chamber and occasionally intervene to make a point. Some MPs (such as Labour MP Dennis Skinner) are regulars in the chamber, but they are the exceptions. Each tends to have a particular place where they like to sit, so even if there is plenty of space close to where they enter the chamber they move to the spot they are familiar with.

Visitors to the public gallery may be disappointed by the small number of MPs in the chamber, but at least nowadays the proceedings are easier to follow than they have ever been. One can work out the actual order of business in the chamber from the Order Paper, nowadays simplified to indicate the actual order of business. MPs still refer to one another in the third person and by constituency, but whenever an MP rises to speak or intervene the occupant of the Chair calls out the MP's name. Some exchanges can be enlightening as well as entertaining, but they tend to be exceptional. Proceedings tend to be predictable. Tensions can rise in an ill-tempered debate, and all the diplomatic skills – or disciplinary powers – of the Speaker or Deputy Speaker may be necessary to restore order. Some MPs try to get around the rules by raising partisan points on bogus points of order, much to the despair of the Speaker.

There are the exceptional debates, not just those when the chamber is packed but when an issue comes up in which some MPs have a genuine interest and of which they have some expert knowledge. On those occasions, those listening learn something and the minister takes the speeches seriously. One rough measure of how seriously the speech is being taken is the number of notes that pass between the minis-ter and the civil servants in the official box.

For members of the public, proceedings are not only easier to follow than before but they are also now permitted to take notes. One inconvenience, however, is that they now sit behind a screen to watch MPs at work. The screen was installed for reasons of security – not so much to protect ordinary MPs but rather the Prime Minister and members of the Cabinet – and serves as a reminder of the difficult times in which public figures have to operate.

were exceptional: the constituencies comprised graduates of the universities, regardless of where they were living.) Constituency boundaries are at present drawn up and revised regularly by independent Boundary Commissions (one covering each country – England, Scotland, Wales and Northern Ireland); each commission is chaired formally by the Speaker of the House of Commons, although the essential work of leadership is undertaken by a deputy, who is a judge. Under existing legislation, boundary reviews are required every eight to twelve years. The commissions are enjoined to produce constituencies within each country of roughly equal size (in terms of the number of electors), although as far as possible retaining existing county and natural boundaries. An Electoral Commission, created by the 2000 Act, reports on elections and referendums, oversees the registration of, and donations to, political parties, and seeks to raise public awareness of elections.

Members

Although the House may constitute a representative assembly in that it is freely elected and MPs are returned to defend and pursue the interests of constituents, it is not a representative assembly in being typical of the socio-economic population that elects it. The members returned to the House are generally male, middle-class and white. These characteristics have been marked throughout the twentieth century. The House has tended to become even more middle-class in the years since 1945. Before 1945, and especially in the early years of the century, the Conservative ranks contained a significant number of upper-class and upper middle-class men of private means, while the parliamentary Labour Party (the PLP) was notable for the number of MPs from manual working-class backgrounds: they constituted a little over half of the PLP from 1922 to 1935 and before that had been in an overwhelming majority (Rush 1979: 69–123). Since 1945, the number of business people on the Conservative benches has increased, as has the number of graduates, often journalists or teachers, on the Labour benches.

The shift in the background of Conservative MPs since 1945 is reflected in education as well as occupation. In 1945, just over 83 per cent of Conservative MPs had been educated at public schools – 27 per cent at Eton. Almost two-thirds – 65 per cent – had been to university, with half having gone to Oxford or Cambridge. Sixty years later – in the

Table 15.1 University-educated MPs, 2005 (%)

Party	University (all)	Oxford and Cambridge
Labour	64	16
Conservative	81	43
Liberal Democrat	79	31

Source: B. Criddle (2005) 'MPs and candidates', in D. Kavanagh and D. Butler (eds) *The British General Election of 2005*. Reproduced with permission of Palgrave Macmillan

parliament elected in 2005 – 60 per cent were public-school educated, with just under 8 per cent having been at Eton; 81 per cent had been at university, the proportion having gone to Oxford or Cambridge comprising 43 per cent (see Table 15.1). The party has witnessed, particularly in the general elections in and since 1979, a growing number of newly elected candidates who have gone to state schools and then gone on to Oxbridge or some other university. The underlying trend continues to be for the proportion of university-educated MPs to be greater among the new intake of MPs than among the parliamentary party as a whole, and for a university education to be more prevalent among MPs than among unsuccessful candidates. The trend also continues of new MPs being less likely to have attended Eton than Conservative MPs as a whole. In the 2005 general election, 'the new Conservative intake was less elitist with fewer than half from private schools and fewer with the elitist pedigree of "public school and Oxbridge" – only 22 per cent of newcomers compared to 35 per cent in the entire Parliamentary Party' (Criddle 2005: 165–6). The members of the parliamentary party are not socially typical, but they are somewhat more middle-class than the members elected in the years before 1979.

On the Labour side, the notable change in educational background has been the rise in the number of graduates. In 1945, just over one-third of Labour MPs (34 per cent) had been to university. By 1970, just over half of the PLP were university graduates. In the parliaments of Labour governments from 1997 onwards, approximately two out of every three Labour MPs had been to university, though the figure dipped slightly in 2005. In 1997 the figure was 66 per cent, in 2001 it was 67 per cent and in 2005 it was 64 per cent (Table 15.1). Most of these were graduates of universities other than Oxford and Cambridge. The percentage of Oxbridge-educated Labour MPs has shown little change – the percentage educated at Oxbridge in 2005 (16 per cent) was almost identical to that of 1945.

These figures reflect the growing middle-class nature of the PLP. The percentage of manual workers in the party declined in each successive parliament until 1974, increased in 1979 and 1983, but then dropped back in subsequent elections. Only 17 per cent of new Labour MPs in 1992 were drawn from manual backgrounds. It declined further in subsequent elections, reaching its lowest percentage ever – 10 per cent – in 2005; only two of the new intake in 2005 came from a manual background. 'Labour MPs', as Byron Criddle noted in his analysis of the 2005 Parliament, 'were increasingly drawn from the ranks of professional politicians, who dominated the new intake and who had come to rival the weight of the teaching profession' (Criddle 2005: 166).

Indeed, there is something of a convergence between members on both sides in terms of education and background. Of new MPs elected to the House of Commons, the vast majority – on both sides of the House – are university-educated, and a large proportion drawn not only from some middle-class occupation but from an occupation that is in the domain of politics or communication. Teachers, journalists and political staffers have been notable among the new intake of Labour MPs in and since 1997; just over 20 per cent of Labour MPs returned in 2005 had been academics or teachers. Business and the professions continue to dominate on the Conservative benches, though 17 per cent of the Tory MPs elected in 2005 had been political organisers, publishers or journalists.

This convergence also reflects the growth of the 'career politician' – the individual who lives for politics, who seeks entry to the House of Commons as early as possible and who seeks to stay in the House for as long as possible, ideally holding government office along the way (King 1981; Riddell 1993). Career politicians are contrasted with old-style MPs, who used to make a mark in other fields before becoming involved in politics and who could – and variously did – leave the House of Commons to pursue some other interest (for example, heading a major company or the family firm). The old-style members may have been ambitious in terms of government office, but they recognised that there was more to life than politics. For career politicians, politics is their life. The career politician has always existed in British politics, but their numbers have grown in recent years. They often (though not in all cases) hold a job in an area related to politics before

seeking election. The consequence of the growth of the career politician is something we shall consider later.

Where there is a difference between the two sides is in terms of council experience and in terms of gender. Labour MPs are more likely to have served as local councillors. Of the new MPs elected in 1997, almost two-thirds of Labour MPs had served as councillors, compared with one-quarter of Conservative MPs. The new but relatively small Labour intake of 2001 also included a number of long-standing councillors, especially in safe Labour seats (Criddle 2002: 192). There are also many more women sitting on the Labour benches than on the Conservative (and Liberal Democrat) benches.

Women became eligible to sit in the House only in 1918. The number elected since then has been small. Between 1918 and 1974, the total number of women elected to the House was only 112 (including Countess Markievicz, the first woman elected but who, as a Sinn Fein candidate, did not take her seat). In the 1983 general election, 23 women were elected to the House; in 1987 the figure was 41 and in 1992 it was 60, still less than 10 per cent of the membership. The Labour Party in 1993 adopted a policy of all-women short lists in a number of constituencies in order to boost the number of female Labour MPs. Although the policy was struck down by an employment tribunal in 1996 on the grounds that it breached sex discrimination legislation, this did not affect seats where female candidates had already been selected. As a result, a record number of female Labour MPs were elected in 1997: no less than 101, 64 of them elected for the first time. Labour replaced all-women short lists with 50–50 short lists (half of the candidates female, the other half male) but this failed to push up the number of women candidates. In the 2001 election, the number of women MPs dropped to 118. However, more were adopted for safe seats in the subsequent Parliament and in 2005 the number increased to an all-time high of 128, just under 20 per cent of the total.

The number of women MPs on the Labour benches is more marked than on the benches of other parties. Although Conservative leaders have encouraged local parties to adopt female candidates, very few have done so. The result has been a notable disparity between the parties (see Table 15.2). In 2005, seventeen women were elected as Conservative MPs, three more than in 1997; although a record number, it still represented less than 9 per cent of

Table 15.2 Women elected to Parliament, 2005

Party	Number of women MPs (2001 figure in parentheses)	
Labour	98	(95)
Conservative	17	(14)
Liberal Democrat	10	(5)
SNP	0	(1)
United Ulster Unionists	1	(1)
Democratic Unionists	1	(1)
Sinn Fein	1	(1)
Other	0	(0)
Total	128	118

Source: From B. Criddle (2005) 'MPs and candidates', in D. Kavanagh and D. Butler (eds) *The British General Election of 2005*, p. 159. Reproduced with permission of Palgrave Macmillan

the parliamentary party. The Liberal Democrats have also had problems in getting more women elected; in 2005 they managed to double – from five to ten – the number of female MPs; again, an all-time high but one that represented only 16 per cent of Liberal Democrat MPs. The percentage of women MPs in the House of Commons in recent parliaments remains low compared to some other countries – especially the Nordic countries – but it is now above the average for national parliaments. Data compiled by the Inter-Parliamentary Union show that in 2005 the UK ranked fifty-first out of 187 national parliaments in terms of the proportion of women members.

The number of non-white MPs remains very small. For most of the twentieth century there were none at all. The first non-white MP was elected in 1892: Dadabhai Naoroji, an Indian, was elected as Liberal MP for Finsbury Central. Another Indian was elected as a Conservative three years later. A third sat from 1922 to 1929. There was then a 58-year gap. In 1987, four non-white MPs were elected. In 1992 the number increased to six (five Labour and one Conservative) and in 1997 to nine (all Labour), including the first Muslim MP and two Sikhs. In 2001, the figure reached twelve, again all sitting on the Labour benches (although the Conservatives did have one MP who was Anglo-Indian). In 2005, the number increased to fifteen, with thirteen on the Labour benches (four of them Muslims) and the Conservatives now having two MPs from ethnic backgrounds – one black and one Asian. The fifteen represent 2.3 per cent of MPs – another all-time high – but still less than half

of what would correspond to the proportion in the population.

One reason for the persistence of white, male MPs is the length of time that MPs typically serve in the House. Some MPs sit for thirty or forty years. In the 2005–10 Parliament, the Father of the House of Commons (the longest continuously serving MP), Labour MP Alan Williams, had been first elected in 1964. Another MP was elected in 1959 but did not have continuous service, losing his seat in 1964 and being returned for another in 1966. Seven MPs – including well-known figures such as Kenneth Clarke, John Prescott and Dennis Skinner – had served continuously since 1970. A typical member sits for about 20 years. Given the growth in the number of career politicians, it is unlikely that this figure will decrease; if anything, the reverse. Even if parties are keen to replace existing MPs with candidates from a wider range of backgrounds, the opportunity to replace them does not necessarily come up very quickly. The length of service of legislators is a particular feature of the British House of Commons: MPs tend to serve as members longer than legislators in other comparable legislatures (see Table 15.3). Even in the 1997 general election, which – as a result of a massive swing to the Labour party – brought in a record number of new MPs (no fewer than 253), more than 60 per cent of MPs had served in the previous parliament. More than 30 MPs had first been elected to parliament in 1970 or earlier. However, the figures suggest that even when the

Table 15.3 Average length of legislative service, 1994

Country	Average length of service (years)
Canada	6.5
France	7
Denmark	7.8
Germany	8.2
Israel	11
USA (Senate)	11.1
USA (House)	12.2
New Zealand	13.1
Japan	15
United Kingdom	20

Source: A. Somit and A. Roemmele (1995) 'The victorious legislative incumbent as a threat to democracy', *Legislative Studies Newsletter*, Vol. 18, No. 2, July. Reproduced by permission of A. Somit

opportunity exists to select a new candidate, local parties tend to select candidates in the same mould as their predecessors.

Members are paid an annual salary, but until 1912 they received no payment at all. Since then, they have been paid, but on a relatively modest basis. In 1954, for example, the salary was £1,250 and in 1964 it was increased to £3,250. In January 1996, an MP's salary was £34,086, fairly modest by international comparison – legislators in Italy, the USA, France and Germany were all paid considerably more (more than twice as much in Italy and the USA) – and by comparison with higher levels of management in the UK. (Ministers receive higher salaries.) In July 1996, MPs voted to increase their salaries by 26 per cent, to £43,000. The increase was controversial, and unpopular, but it still left MPs lagging behind the salaries of members of other comparable legislatures. The salary has increased since and, in April 2009, it was set at £64,766.

Since the 1960s, parliamentary facilities have also improved. In the mid-1960s, an MP was guaranteed only a locker in which to keep papers and received no allowance, whether for hiring a secretary or even to cover the cost of telephone calls. If an MP was lucky enough to have an office, it was usually shared with several other MPs. A secretary had to be paid out of the MP's own pocket. A secretarial allowance (of £500) was introduced in 1969. This allowance evolved into an office cost allowance, allowing an MP to hire one and sometimes two secretaries and in most cases a research assistant (more often than not, part-time). In 1999, the office cost allowance stood at £50,264. In 2001, the House agreed to a new system. The office cost allowance was split into two: a staff cost allowance and an incidental expenses provision. Each MP could claim a staff cost allowance, enabling them to employ up to the equivalent of three full-time staff, but with the staff paid centrally by the House authorities and on agreed rates with standard contracts. In 2008, the figure was increased to the equivalent of 3.5 staff. Each MP can also claim a further £20,000 towards incidental expenses. MPs can claim travel expenses and, for those living outside London (and thus having to maintain two homes), an additional costs allowance – known since 2009 as a personal additional accommodation expenditure – up to £24,222 (2009–10 figures). MPs with inner London constituencies receive a small London supplement. The additional cost allowance, as we shall see, became highly controversial in 2009 when details of claims made by MPs were published. A communications allowance was also introduced in 2007, 'to assist in the work of communicating with the public on parliamentary business'. It was initially set at £10,000 but was increased in 2008 to £10,400 and frozen at that figure until 2011.

The physical space available to MPs has also increased. Buildings close to the Palace of Westminster – including the former Scotland Yard buildings in Derby Gate, known as the Norman Shaw Buildings – were acquired for parliamentary use. More recently, buildings in Parliament Street – between Whitehall and Parliament Square – were taken over and redeveloped, retaining the exterior but with a modern and integrated complex of offices inside. They have the address of 1 Parliament Street. To these has been added a major purpose-built parliamentary building, known as Portcullis House, in Bridge Street, just across the road from the Clock Tower housing Big Ben and linked to the Palace by an underground passage. With the completion of Portcullis House, which includes rooms for committee meetings as well as suites of offices for MPs, each MP now has an office.

Sittings of the House

The House to which Members are returned meets annually, each parliamentary session running usually now from November to November. There is a long summer recess, but the session is not prorogued (formally adjourned) until shortly after the House returns in the autumn; that allows the House to meet and deal with bills which have not completed their passage. The effect of prorogation is to kill off unfinished public business; any bills that have not received the Royal Assent fall, though there is now provision for some bills to be carried over from one session to another. In the event of a general election being called, Parliament is dissolved, cutting short the session. If a general election is held in the spring, the new session will usually be a long one, running from the sitting of the new House through to the November of the following year.

The House usually sits for more than 150 days a year, a not unusual number compared with some other legislatures, such as those of the USA, Canada and France, although considerably more than most other legislatures. What makes it distinctive is the number of hours for which it sits: it sits usually for more than 1,200 hours a year. The figures for the period from 2001 to 2008 are given in Table 15.4. In

Table 15.4 The House of Commons: length of sittings, 2001–8

Session	Number of sitting days	Number of hours sat	Average length of sitting day
2001–2[a]	201	1,297	7 hours 40 minutes
2002–3	162	1,287	7 hours 57 minutes
2003–4	157	1,215	7 hours 44 minutes
2004–5[b]	65	535	8 hours 14 minutes
2005–6[a]	208	1,572	7 hours 33 minutes
2006–7	146	1,119	7 hours 40 minutes
2007–8	165	1,306	7 hours 55 minutes

[a] Long session following a spring general election.
[b] Short session, because of the calling of a general election.
Source: From the *House of Commons Sessional Information Digests, 2001–8*. © Parliamentary Copyright 2008. Parliamentary copyright material is reproduced with the permission of the Controller of Her Majesty's Stationery Office (HMSO) on behalf of Parliament

previous parliaments, the sittings were sometimes longer, averaging nearly 1,500 hours in non-election sessions in the 1987–92 parliament. Other elected chambers are not able to compete with these figures.

Until 1999, the House sat at 2.30 p.m. on the first four days of the week and at 9.30 a.m. on Fridays. On the first four days, it usually rose by 10.30 p.m. In an experiment started in 1999, it started meeting at 11.30 a.m. on Thursdays (rising earlier in the evening, usually by 7.00 or 8.00 p.m.). In 2002, the House agreed to meet at 11.30 a.m. on Tuesdays and Wednesdays as well, with the House rising by 7.00 p.m. (by 6.00 p.m. on Thursdays). The new sitting times took effect in 2003. However, they did not prove popular with all MPs (especially with MPs living long distances from London) and in 2005 the House voted to revert to a 2.30 p.m. start on a Tuesday, though agreeing to sit at 10.30 a.m. on a Thursday. The House thus has an uneven pattern of sitting times: 2.30 p.m. on Monday and Tuesday, 11.30 a.m. on Wednesday, 10.30 a.m. on Thursday, and (if sitting) 9.30 a.m. on Friday. Sittings may, in certain circumstances, be extended in order to transact particular business. Late or all-night sittings variously take place to get through the remaining stages of a bill. (If the House has an all-night sitting and is still sitting when the new day's sitting is scheduled to commence, then the business for that next day falls.) Late-night sittings became rare in the 1992–7 parliament but were employed again following the return of a Labour government in 1997 in order to get some of its major legislation through. On Fridays, when **private members' bills** are normally discussed, the House rises at 3.00 p.m. To give

MPs more time to be in their constituencies, the House does not sit every Friday: ten Fridays each session are designated as non-sitting Fridays.

As a result of a change agreed by the House in 1999, there is also a 'parallel chamber', or 'main committee', allowing MPs to meet and discuss issues separate from the main chamber (see Box 15.3). This allows for non-contentious issues to be debated. Meetings are held in the Grand Committee Room, just off Westminster Hall, and are known formally as meetings in Westminster Hall. The topics covered on Tuesdays and Wednesdays each week are proposed by private Members; the Thursday sitting is given over to a debate on a subject of general interest or a select committee report. All MPs can attend – as in the main chamber – although in practice few do so.

Functions

The principal function of the House is often seen as involvement in law making. It is, after all, classified as a legislature and the name means carrier, or giver, of law. In practice, as we have seen, the House essentially responds to the measures that the government brings forward. Furthermore, much of the time of the House is given over to business that has nothing directly to do with legislation. Question Time is now an established feature of the House. It is not part of the legislative process. When the House debates the economy or the government's industrial policy, those debates are not parts of the formal legislative process. The House has an important role to play in the legislative process, but it is clearly not its only role.

BOX 15.3 IDEAS AND PERSPECTIVES

The Grand Committee is located just off Westminister Hall.
Source: Copyright © Adam Woolfitt / Corbis

Meetings in Westminster Hall

In December 1999, the House of Commons introduced a new form of meeting – meetings in Westminster Hall. These enable MPs to meet separately from the main chamber, and the gathering is sometimes described as a parallel chamber. (The parallel chamber is modelled on Australian experience.) Meetings in Westminster Hall are open to all MPs. They can come in as they can in the main chamber. The principal differences between the main chamber and the room used for the parallel chamber are of size and structure. The room used – the Grand Committee Room, located just off the cavernous Westminster Hall – is much smaller than the chamber of the House of Commons. (For part of 2006 another room was used while the Grand Committee Room was redeveloped.) It also differs in structure. MPs sit at desks arranged in a semicircle around a raised dais. The desks are fixed and have desktop microphones. Meetings are presided over by a Deputy Speaker or one of the MPs on the Chairmen's Panel (senior MPs who are drawn on in order to chair standing committees) and are usually used for discussing non-contentious business. Votes cannot be held. Meetings now take place from 9.30 a.m. to 2.00 p.m. on Tuesdays, from 9.30 to 11.30 a.m. and from 2.30 to 5.00 p.m. on Wednesdays, and from 2.30 to 5.30 p.m. on Thursdays. On Tuesdays and Wednesdays, there are short debates on topics raised by individual members. Thus, for example, on Tuesday 14 July 2009, the topics debated were healthcare services in Shropshire, rail service on the East Coast mainline, HM Prison Wellingborough, government funding for local authority support for adults with learning difficulties, and the effect on communities of government policy on gypsies and travellers. The following day, topics included abortion law in Northern Ireland, combat stress and the NHS, and local authorities' role in promoting apprenticeships. Thursday sittings are given over to debates on general topics or select committee reports. Thus, on Thursday 16 July 2009, the report of the Communities and Local Government Committee on 'Housing and the Credit Crunch', and the government's response to it, were debated. Attendance at meetings is low – usually a handful of MPs – not dissimilar to the chamber itself when private members' motions are taken.

The creation of the parallel chamber was controversial. Supporters see it as a way of allowing issues, for which there would otherwise be no time in the chamber, to be discussed. Most Conservative MPs voted against setting it up because they feared it would serve to distract attention from the chamber and absorb MPs' energies on minor issues. In the event, meetings of the new body have proved low-key, attracting virtually no media attention (the inaugural meeting was effectively ignored) and very little attention on the part of MPs. The chamber was initially employed on an experimental basis, but MPs subsequently voted to make it permanent. It was not seen as damaging to the main chamber and back-benchers have found it useful as a means of raising issues that they might not have the opportunity to raise in the main chamber. Each debate brings an issue to the attention of government, with a junior minister replying. The proceedings are published in *Hansard*.

The principal functions of the House can be grouped under four headings: those of legitimisation, recruitment, scrutiny and influence, and expression. Several other functions can be identified (see Norton, 2005) but these can largely be subsumed under these four broad headings.

Legitimisation

The primary purpose for which the representatives of the counties and boroughs (the communes) were first summoned was to assent to the King's demand for additional taxes. Subsequently, their assent also came to be necessary for legislation. The House has thus been, since its inception, a legitimising body.

The House fulfils the task of 'manifest legitimisation', that is, the overt, conscious giving of assent. In the UK the function has two elements: the giving of assent to bills and to requests for supply (money) and the giving of assent to the government itself. The government depends on the confidence of the House of Commons for its continuance in office. If the House withdraws its confidence, then by convention the government resigns or requests the dissolution of Parliament.

The House proceeds on the basis of motions laid before it: for example, to give a bill a second reading or to express confidence in the government. By approving such motions, the House gives its formal – manifest – assent. Members may vote on motions. The Speaker of the House asks those supporting the motion to say 'aye', those opposing to say 'no'. If no dissenting voices are heard, the Speaker declares that 'the ayes have it'. If some MPs shout 'no' and persist then members divide (that is, vote). A simple majority is all that is necessary. (This is subject to two basic requirements: that at least forty MPs – a quorum – are shown by the division to be present and that, in voting on a closure motion, at least 100 MPs have voted in favour.) Members vote by trooping through two lobbies, known as the division lobbies (an 'aye' lobby and a 'no' lobby), where they are counted and their names recorded. The result of the vote is then announced in the chamber.

It is this accepted need for the House to confer legitimacy through giving its assent that constitutes the basic power of the House in relation to government. Initially, the knights and burgesses summoned to the King's court were expected to give assent. Gradually, members began to realise that, as a body, they could deny assent to supply and later to legislation. This formed the basis on which they could ensure the effective fulfilment of other functions. It remains the basis of the power of the House of Commons. Without the assent of the House, no measure can become an Act of Parliament. The contemporary point of contention is the extent to which the House is prepared to use its power to deny assent. Critics contend that the effect of the growth of party and hence party cohesion has largely nullified the willingness of the House to employ it.

The House also fulfils what Robert Packenham has termed the function of 'latent legitimisation'. According to Packenham, this derives from the fact that 'simply by meeting regularly and uninterruptedly, the legislature produces, among the relevant populace and élites, a wider and deeper sense of the government's moral right to rule than would otherwise have obtained' (Packenham, in Norton 1990: 87). However, it can be argued that such activity is necessary but not sufficient to generate such an underlying sense of legitimacy. Latent legitimacy can be said to derive from the House fulfilling the other functions expected of it (Norton 2005: 10).

Given that Parliament not only sits regularly but has fulfilled a range of tasks expected of it for a considerable period of time, it is arguably a much stronger agent of latent legitimisation than many other legislatures. It would seem plausible to hypothesise that the function is weaker in a political system in which the legislature is a recent and conscious creation of resuscitation by the prevailing regime and fails to carry out tasks expected of it by the people.

Recruitment

Ministers are normally drawn from, and remain within, Parliament. The situation is governed solely by convention. There is no legal requirement that a minister has to be an MP or peer.

The practice of appointing ministers from those who sit in Parliament derives from expediency. Historically, it was to the King's benefit to have his ministers in Parliament, where they could influence, lead and marshal support for the crown. It was to the benefit of Parliament to have ministers who could answer for their conduct. An attempt was made early in the eighteenth century to prevent ministers from sitting in Parliament, but the legislation was superseded by another law allowing the practice to continue (Norton 2005: 43).

The convention that ministers be drawn from and remain within Parliament – predominantly now, by convention, the House of Commons – is a strong one inasmuch as all ministers are currently MPs or peers. It is extremely rare for a minister to be appointed who does not sit in either House and even rarer for that person to remain outside Parliament while in office: the person is either elevated to the peerage (nowadays the most used route) or found a safe seat to contest in a by-election. On occasion, one of the Scottish law officers – the Solicitor General for Scotland – was appointed from the ranks of Scottish lawyers and remained outside Parliament, but that was the exception that proves the rule. The post ceased to be part of the UK government following devolution.

The relationship between the House and ministers is governed by convention. Under the convention of individual ministerial responsibility, ministers are answerable to the House for their own conduct and that of their particular departments. Under the convention of collective ministerial responsibility, the Cabinet is responsible to the House for government policy as a whole. It is this latter convention that requires a request for the dissolution of Parliament or the resignation of the government in the event of the House passing a **motion of no confidence** in the government.

The fact that ministers remain in Parliament clearly has a number of advantages to government. Things have not changed that much from earlier centuries in that ministers can use their positions to lead and marshal their supporters. Ministers themselves add notably to the voting strength of the government, the so-called 'payroll vote' in the House. Just over eighty ministers serve in the Commons and just over twenty in the Lords. With ministers' unpaid helpers – parliamentary private secretaries – added to the number, the payroll vote usually comprises a third or more of the MPs sat on the government side of the House. The government thus has a sizeable guaranteed vote to begin with. Party loyalty – and ambition for office – usually ensures that the votes of **backbenchers** follow those of ministers.

The convention that ministers be drawn from the ranks of parliamentarians has certain advantages for Parliament. It ensures that members are close to ministers, both formally and informally. Ministers can be questioned on the floor of the House; members can waylay them in the corridors and the division lobbies for private conversations. The fact that ministers remain as members of the House means that they retain some affinity with other members. MPs elevated to ministerial office retain their constituency duties.

Above all, though, the convention renders the House of Commons powerful as a recruiting agent. The route to ministerial office is through Parliament. In some other systems, the legislature is but one route to the top. In the USA, for example, there are multiple routes: cabinet ministers – and presidents – can be drawn from the ranks of business executives, academics, state governors, former army officers and lawyers. The US Congress enjoys no monopoly on recruitment to executive office. In the UK, Parliament does have such a monopoly. Parliament is the exclusive route for those intending to reach the top of the political ladder. Those aspiring to ministerial office thus have to seek election to the House of Commons (or hope – often in vain – for a peerage) and have to make their mark in the House. The House also serves as an important testing ground for potential ministers and, indeed, for those on the ministerial ladder (see Norton 2005: 50–2). A poor performance at the despatch box can harm a minister's chances of further promotion. A con-

sistently poor performance can result in the minister losing office. Conversely, a bravura performance at the despatch box may save a minister who is under pressure to go. For ambitious politicians, the chamber matters.

Scrutiny and influence

Scrutiny and influence are essentially conjoined functions. The House subjects both the measures and the actions of government to scrutiny. It does so through various means: debate, questioning and committee deliberations. If it does not like what is before it, it can influence the bill or the policy under consideration. It may influence solely by the force of argument. It may influence by threatening to deny assent (that is, by threatening to defeat the government). Ultimately, it may actually refuse its assent, denying the government a majority in the division lobbies.

These two functions are central to the activity of the House and absorb most of its time. Government business enjoys precedence on most days. The House spends most of its time discussing legislation and the policy and actions of ministers. Although the dominance of *party* has ensured that normally the government is assured a majority in divisions, the party *system* helps to ensure that government is subject to critical scrutiny from opposition parties in the House. The procedures of the House are premised on the existence of two principal parties, with each having the opportunity to be heard. Membership of all committees of the House replicates party strength on the floor of the House, thus ensuring that the opposition has an opportunity to offer critical comments and to force government to respond at all stages of the parliamentary process.

Furthermore, scrutiny and influence may also take place outside, or despite, the context of party. MPs sit for particular constituencies. Although elected on a party label, they are nonetheless expected to ensure that government policy does not damage constituency interests. They may also be influenced by moral and religious views that ensure they pay careful attention to bills and government policies that run counter to their personal convictions. They may also listen to bodies outside Parliament – charities, consumer groups, professional organisations, companies – that have a particular interest in, or knowledge of, the subject under debate.

However, the extent to which the House actually fulfils these functions is a matter of dispute. Critics contend that the government stranglehold, via its party majority, ensures that the House is denied the means for sustained and effective scrutiny, and that, inasmuch as it may exert some limited scrutiny, that scrutiny is not matched by the capacity to influence government. MPs may consider and find fault with a particular measure but not then prove willing to use their power to amend or reject it.

Expression

The House serves not one but several expressive functions. Members serve to express the particular views and demands of constituents. An individual constituent or a group of constituents may be affected adversely by some particular policy or by the actions of some public officials. Constituents may feel that a particular policy is bad for the constituency or for the country. Contacting the local MP will usually result in the MP passing on the views to the relevant minister and may even result in the member raising the issue on the floor of the House. The pursuit of such cases by MPs ensures that they are heard and their points considered by ministers.

MPs also express the views of different groups in society as a whole. A range of issues that do not fall within the ambit of party politics are taken up and pursued by private members. MPs may express the views of organised interests, such as particular industries or occupations. They may express the views of different sectors of society, such as students or the elderly. Many will give voice to the concerns of particular charitable, religious or moral groups. For example, some MPs press for reform of the laws governing abortion, some want to liberalise the laws concerning homosexuality, and some want to strengthen the laws on road safety. These issues can be pursued by MPs through a number of parliamentary procedures (see Cowley 1998). In some cases, members table amendments to government bills. Another route is through the use of private members' bills. Although the more contentious the issue, the less likely the bill is to be passed, the debate on the bill serves an important function: it allows the different views to be expressed in an authoritative public forum, heard by the relevant minister and open to coverage by the mass media.

MPs, then, serve to express the views of constituents and different groups to the House and to government. MPs may also serve to express the views of the House and of government to constituents and organised groups. The House may reach a decision on a particular topic. Members may then fulfil an important role in explaining why that decision was taken. Members individually may explain decisions to constituents. **Select committees** of the House may, in effect, explain particular policies through their reports, which are read not just by government but also by groups with a particular interest in the committee's area of inquiry. The House thus has a tremendous potential to serve several expressive functions. The extent to which it does so is a matter of considerable debate. MPs have limited time and resources to pursue all the matters brought to their attention. The attention given to their activities by the media and by government may be slight. Many groups may bypass Parliament in order to express their views directly to ministers. Furthermore, it is argued, the views expressed by MPs on behalf of others are drowned out by the noise of party battle. By limiting the resources of the House and by keeping information to itself, the government has limited the capacity of the House to arm itself with the knowledge necessary to raise support for public policies.

These are the most important functions that may be ascribed to the House. The list is not an exhaustive one. Other tasks are carried out by the House. These include, for example, a disciplinary role (punishing breaches of privilege and contempt) and a small quasi-judicial role, primarily in dealing with private legislation (legislation affecting private interests, not to be confused with private members' legislation). Other functions often ascribed to the House can, as we have explained, be subsumed under the four main headings we have provided. However, two other functions, identified by Walter Bagehot in *The English Constitution* in 1867, have been lost by the House. One, the 'elective' function – that is, choosing the government – was held only briefly during the nineteenth century. Before then it was a function exercised by the monarch. Since then, it has passed largely, although not quite exclusively, to the electorate. The electorate chooses a government on a regular basis at general elections. The House retains the power to turn a government out through passing a motion of no confidence; but it is not a power it has exercised regularly – in the past century, it was used only in 1924 and 1979, opposition parties combining to turn out a minority government.

The other function is that of legislating. Initially, the need for the House to give its assent was transformed by members into the power to initiate measures, first through the presentation of petitions to the crown and later through the introduction of bills. This power was important in the nineteenth century, when the House could be described as sharing the legislative power with government. Even so, its exercise was limited. Most legislation introduced into the House was private legislation. Since then, public legislation has expanded as parties have become more powerful. Parties have ensured that the power to formulate – to 'make' – legislation rests with government, with the House then giving its assent. In so far as the House has retained a residual legislative power, it is exercised through the medium of private members' legislation. However, even that legislative power can be described now as one shared with government. Since 1959, no private member's bill that has been the subject of a vote at second reading (the debate on principle) has made it to the statute book without government providing time for it.

■ Scrutiny and influence

The functions that the House retains can be described as modest but appropriate to a reactive legislature. They have developed over time. But how well are they currently carried out? The principal functions of the House in relation to the executive are those of scrutiny and influence. The means available to the House to fulfil those functions are also at the disposal of members for expressing the views of their constituents and of wider interests. They can be grouped under two headings: legislation and executive actions.

Legislation

For Parliament, the legislative process constitutes the consideration of a bill once it has been formally introduced. However, in recent years, some bills have been published in draft form and considered by a committee prior to formal introduction (Kennon 2004; Hansard Society 2004; Constitution Committee 2004; Norton 2005: 75–7). From 1997–8 to 2006–7, fifty-eight bills were published in draft and thus available for some pre-legislative scrutiny (Constitution Committee 2008: 6). The number peaked in the 2003–4 session, when 12 bills were published in draft, representing one in three of government bills for the session. Such scrutiny

enables members to examine and comment before the government has decided on the final wording, and hence may be more willing to make changes before it commits itself to the measure. Despite considerable time pressures, bills subject to pre-legislative scrutiny have been variously amended as a result of recommendations by the committees considering them (Norton 2005: 77). The committees engaging in such scrutiny have normally been departmental **select committees**.

When a bill is formally introduced into Parliament, it has to go through a well-established process involving debate and consideration in committee. About 30–40 per cent of the time of the House is taken up with debate on bills. In the 2007–08 session, for example, it was 38 per cent (see Table 15.5). The bulk of this time is given over to government bills. (Private members' legislation usually occupies just under, or occasionally just over, 5 per cent of time on the floor of the House.) Every bill has to go through three 'readings' plus a committee and (usually) a report stage. The stages are shown in Table 15.6.

The first reading marks the formal introduction. No debate takes place. Indeed, at this stage there is not even a printed bill. All that is read out is the bill's title. Following first reading, the bill is printed. The second reading comprises a debate on the principle of the measure. Most government bills will be allocated a half or a full day's debate for second reading. Major bills, especially of constitutional significance, may be given two or more days for debate. In the 1997–2001 Parliament, for example, the bills providing for devolution to Scotland and Wales, for an elected Greater London Authority, and for removal of most hereditary peers from membership of the House of Lords were each accorded a two-day debate.

The debate itself follows a standard pattern: the minister responsible for the bill opens the debate, explaining the provisions of the bill and justifying its introduction. The relevant shadow minister then makes a speech from the opposition front bench, outlining the stance of the opposition on the bill. After these two frontbench speeches, most members present tend to leave the chamber, usually leaving a small number of MPs to listen to the remaining speeches. Backbenchers from both sides of the House are then called alternately, plus usually a member from one or more of the minor parties, and the debate is then wound up with speeches from the opposition and government front benches. (The

Table 15.5 Time spent on the floor of the House, 2007–8

Business	Total time spent (hours : minutes)
Addresses, including debate on Queen's Speech	37.42
Government bills	
Second reading	116.01
Committee of the whole House	79.20
Report	116.06
Third reading	15.40
Lords amendments	38.29
Allocation of time orders (including programme motions)	7.14
Private members' bills (including ten-minute rule bills)	74.47
Government motions	
EC documents	5.35
Business motions	10.36
General	64.35
Opposition motions	125.22
Private Members' motions (substantive)	2.54
Adjournment	
Government debates	99.16
Topical debates	35.42
Last day before recess	16.12
Daily half-hour debates (at end of business)	82.40
Standing Order No. 24 debate (emergency debate)	3.14
Estimates	19.21
Money resolutions	0.22
Ways and Means resolutions (including Budget debate)	24.31
Statutory instruments	27.38
Question Time (including topical questions)	142.14
Urgent Questions	1.16
Statements (including business statements)	106.33
Miscellaneous	32.20
Daily prayers	13.25
Total	**1306.31**

Source: House of Commons Sessional Information Digest, 2007–08. © Parliamentary Copyright 2008. Parliamentary copyright material is reproduced with the permission of the Controller of Her Majesty's Stationery Office (HMSO) on behalf of Parliament

House tends to fill up again for the winding-up speeches.) If the bill is contested, the House then divides. Debates, though not always predictable in content, are generally so in outcome: only three times in the past 100 years has the government lost a vote on second reading (in 1924, 1977 and 1986). Speeches on occasion may influence some votes, even whole debates, but they are exceptional. A government sometimes loses the argument but not usually the vote.

Once approved in principle, the bill is then sent to committee for detailed scrutiny. Some bills, because of their constitutional significance or because of the need for a speedy passage, will have their committee stage on the floor of the House. In most sessions the number is very small. The majority of bills, though, are sent to a **public bill committee**. Up to 2006, bills were sent to standing committees. Standing committees were introduced in 1882 and became the norm in 1907. Despite the name, they were 'standing' only in name (Standing Committee A, Standing Committee B etc.): their membership changed for each bill. The committees were limited not only by the fact that there was no permanent membership but by their inability to take evidence. Witnesses could not be summoned and written evidence received. The committees could only consider the bills before them. They proceeded by way of discussing amendments to clauses before agreeing the clauses. Each committee was structured like the chamber in miniature; one side facing the other, with ministers, shadow ministers and whips among the membership and with debate following party lines. Government backbenchers were encouraged to keep quiet to facilitate the passage of the bill and opposition MPs encouraged to speak in order to challenge the government. Government defeats in committee were rare.

Because of the limitations of standing committees, their utilisation came in for considerable criticism. In 2006, following a report from the Select Committee on the Modernisation of the House of Commons, the House agreed a new procedure: the public bill committee (PBC). In dealing with private members' bills and certain other bills, they are similar to the old standing committees. However, they differ significantly in respect of Government bills that have been introduced in the Commons and have been subject to a programme motion (stipulating the times at which stages have to be completed), but which have not had pre-legislative scrutiny (in other words, been before an evidence-taking committee):

Table 15.6 Legislative stages

Stage	Where taken	Comments
First reading	On the floor of the House	Formal introduction: no debate
Second reading	On the floor of the House[a]	Debate on the principle
[Money resolution	On the floor of the House	Commons only]
Committee	In public bill committee in the Commons unless House votes otherwise (certain bills taken on the floor of the House); in Grand Committee or on the floor of the House in the Lords	Considered clause by clause; amendments may be made
Report[b]	On the floor of the House	Bill reported back to House; amendments may be made
Third reading	On the floor of the House	Final approval: no amendments possible in the Commons
Lords (or Commons) amendments	On the floor of the House	Consideration of amendments made by other House

[a] In the Commons, non-contentious bills may be referred to a committee.
[b] If a bill is taken in committee of the whole House in the Commons and no amendments are made, there is no report stage.

in dealing with these bills, public bill committees are empowered to take both oral and written evidence. Within the time it has to consider a bill, the committee can determine what proportion of sittings will be devoted to taking evidence. In its evidence-taking, a committee is supported by the Scrutiny Unit, a body of specialists employed by the House, which also prepares briefing material for the committee.

In the first two sessions of their operations (2006–07, 2007–08), 17 bills were sent to evidence-taking public bill committees for their committee stage. Out of a total of 199 sittings by the committees, 50 of them were devoted to taking evidence. In addition, 411 written pieces of evidence were accepted (Levy 2009: 26). As the use of public bill committees has developed, so MPs have tended to be better informed and more willing to engage in debating the provisions of the bill. As Jessica Levy has noted, 'Along with introducing the practice of direct questioning of witnesses (and the minister) in place of probing amendments, PBCs have proved more efficient than their standing committee predecessors' (Levy 2009: 49).

However, PBCs also have similarities with their predecessor standing committees. Each committee comprises between 16 and 50 members, though the norm is to appoint close to the minimum, other than for big bills like the Finance Bill. The membership is appointed anew for each bill. The membership thus lacks a corporate ethos. Each committee is chaired by a member of the Chairmen's Panel, whose role is

to preside in a manner similar to the Speaker; there is thus no leadership of the committee as a collective body. The membership reflects the party composition of the House, and ministers, shadow ministers and **whips** are appointed, with the government whips present to ensure, as in the chamber, that the government gets its business. One of the biggest constraints remains one of time. Committees are under pressure because of the number of bills introduced each session and the need to get them through usually by the end of the session. Several committees may therefore be appointed at roughly the same time. The need to get the business transacted by a stipulated date limits the time available to hear witnesses and, equally importantly, digest what they have to say in time to influence debate on the amendments moved in committee.

After the committee stage, a bill returns to the House for the report stage. This provides an opportunity for the House to decide whether it wishes to make any further amendments and is often used by the government to introduce amendments promised during committee stage, as well as any last-minute (sometimes numerous) amendments of its own. There is, though, no report stage if a bill has been taken for its committee stage on the floor of the House and been passed without amendment.

There then follows the bill's third reading, when the House gives its final approval to the measure. Such debates are often short. If the bill is not contentious, there may be no debate at all. As can be seen from Table 15.5, debate on third reading occupies relatively little time. On completion of its third reading, the bill then goes to the House of Lords and, if the Upper House makes any amendments, the bill then returns to the Commons for it to consider the amendments. In most cases, the amendments are accepted. If not, the House of Lords usually gives way, though sometimes only after considerable behind-the-scenes negotiations. Once both Houses have approved the bill, it then goes to the Queen for the Royal Assent. Once that assent is given, then that, as far as Parliament is concerned, concludes the legislative process.

The process is fairly well established but much criticised (see, e.g., Brazier 2004), not only because of the inefficiencies of the committee procedure but also because of the time constraints imposed by government. In the past, after considerable time had been taken up by opposition MPs debating the early clauses of a bill in committee, the governments would resort to a timetable, or guillotine, motion, imposing a timetable for the remaining provisions of a bill. Guillotine motions had been variously employed since 1887 but their increased use in the last quarter of the twentieth century attracted frequent condemnation. Because of the criticism, the two principal parties agreed in 1994 to a voluntary timetabling of bills. This meant that each bill was subject to an agreed timetable from the beginning, thus avoiding the need for a guillotine to be introduced at a later stage. However, this agreement was not sustained in the new parliament returned in May 1997 and the Labour government variously resorted to the use of the guillotine, or what were termed programme motions, to get measures through. In 2000–1, new standing orders were introduced for programming motions, and programming is now a common and much disputed feature of business. Programme motions differ from the previous use of the guillotine in that they are introduced and agreed by the House following the second readings of bills. Most government bills are now subject to such motions. The most stringent part of programming tends to be for consideration of Lords amendments, where it is not uncommon for a programme motion to stipulate that debate on the amendments, however many or important they are, is limited to one hour.

Bills thus follow a fairly predictable route. There are some variations: some non-contentious bills, for example, can be sent to a second reading committee, thus avoiding taking up valuable debating time on the floor of the House. Private members'

bills are also treated differently, primarily in terms of timetabling. They have to go through all the stages listed, but time for their consideration on the floor of the House is extremely limited. Each session a ballot is held and the names of twenty private members are drawn. They are then entitled to introduce bills during the Fridays allocated to such bills, but only about the top half-dozen are likely to achieve full debates.

Bills constitute primary legislation. They often contain powers for regulations to be made under their authority once enacted. These regulations – known as delegated or secondary legislation and usually taking the form of what are termed statutory instruments – may be made subject to parliamentary approval. (Under the affirmative resolution procedure, the regulation must be approved by Parliament in order to come into force; under the negative resolution procedure, it comes into force unless Parliament disapproves it.) Some regulations, though, only have to be laid before the House and others do not even have to be laid.

Given the growth of delegated legislation in post-war years – sometimes more than 1,500 statutory instruments are introduced in a session – the House has sought to undertake scrutiny of it (Norton 2005: 91–3). Detailed, and essentially technical, scrutiny is undertaken by a Select Committee on Statutory Instruments. However, there is no requirement that the government has to wait for the committee to report on a regulation before bringing it before the House for approval, and on occasion – although not frequently – the government will seek approval before a regulation has been considered by the committee. Time for debate is also extremely limited, and much delegated legislation is hived off for discussion in a standing committee on delegated legislation. There is also a separate committee and procedure for dealing with regulatory reform orders, enabling primary legislation imposing a regulatory burden to be changed by order. There are also separate committees and procedures for dealing with draft European legislation: it is considered by a European Scrutiny Committee and, if recommended for debate, is discussed normally by one of three European committees.

Executive actions

Various means are employed to scrutinise and to influence the actions of government. These same means can be and usually are employed by MPs

House of Commons in session
Source: Corbis / Bettmann

to express the views of constituents and different interests in society. The means essentially are those available on the floor of the House (debates and Question Time), those available on the committee corridor (select committees) and those available off the floor of the House (early day motions, correspondence, the parliamentary commissioner for administration, party committees and all-party groups). Some individually are of limited use. It is their use in combination that can be effective in influencing government.

Debates and Question Time

Most of the time of the House is taken up debating or questioning the actions of government. *Debates* take different forms. They can be on a substantive motion (for example, congratulating or condemning the policy of the government on a particular issue) or, in order to allow wide-ranging discussion (especially on a topic on which the government may have no fixed position), on an adjournment motion ('That this House do now adjourn'). For example, prior to the Gulf War at the beginning of 1991, the situation

in the Persian Gulf was debated on an adjournment motion. After military action had begun, the House debated a substantive motion approving the action. Adjournment debates under this heading can be described as full-scale adjournment debates. They are distinct from the half-hour adjournment debates that take place at the end of every sitting of the House. These half-hour debates take the form of a backbencher raising a particular issue and the relevant minister then responding. After exactly half an hour, the debate concludes and the House adjourns.

Debates are initiated by different bodies in the House. Most motions introduced by government are to approve legislation. However, the government occasionally initiates debates on particular policies. These can range from major issues of public policy, such as war in Iraq in 2003, to debate on essentially parliamentary matters, such as select committee nominations and the installation of the security screen in the public gallery. More frequently, debates are introduced by opposition parties. Twenty days each year are designated as opposition days. On seventeen of these twenty days, the motion (or motions – a day's debate can be split into two) is chosen by the Leader of the Opposition. On the remaining three days, the topic is chosen by the leader of the third-largest party in the House (the Liberal Democrats). One or two additional days are usually found for other parties. There are also three estimates days each session, the choice of estimate for debate being made by a select committee of the House: the Liaison Committee, comprising the MPs who chair other select committees.

A recent innovation – introduced in 2007 – is the topical debate. Each week, a ninety-minute debate is held on a topical issue, of local, national or international importance suggested by an MP. Subjects are suggested by members to the Leader of the House – by letter, e-mail or in questions to the Leader on the weekly business statement (mostly the last of these) – and the Leader announces which topic has been selected. On 14 May 2009, for example, the topical debate was on Sri Lanka and on 4 June 2009 it was on 'The Economy: Supporting Business'.

Private members are also responsible for initiating the topics in the daily half-hour adjournment debates: on three days a week (four, if sitting on a Friday), members are selected by ballot, and on one the Speaker chooses the member. These backbenchers' occasions provide opportunities to raise essentially non-partisan issues, especially those of concern to constituents. Although such debates are poorly attended, they allow members to put an issue on the public record and elicit a response from government.

The half-hour adjournment debates involve a backbencher raising an issue, sometimes one or two other backbenchers making quick contributions, and then a response from a minister. Full-scale half-day or full-day debates initiated by government or opposition resemble instead the practice adopted in second reading debates. There are speeches from the two front benches, followed by backbench speeches alternating between the two sides of the House, followed by winding-up speeches from the front benches and then, if necessary, a vote. The term 'debate' is itself a misnomer. Members rarely debate but rather deliver prepared speeches, which often fail to take up the points made by preceding speakers. Members wishing to take part usually inform the Speaker in advance and can usually obtain some indication from the Speaker if and when they are likely to be called. There is a tendency for members not to stay for the whole debate after they have spoken. Members, especially backbenchers,

frequently address a very small audience – sometimes no more than half a dozen MPs. There is a prevailing view in the House that attendance has dropped over recent years. MPs now have offices they can spend time in. There are competing demands on their time, and as the outcome of most votes is predictable – and members know perfectly well how they intend to vote – there appears little incentive to spend time in the chamber. Major set-piece debates – as on a motion of confidence – and a debate in which the outcome is uncertain can still attract a crowded chamber, some members having to sit on the floor or stand at the bar of the House in order to listen to the proceedings. Occasionally a particularly good speaker, such as former Conservative leader William Hague, may attract members into the chamber. Such occasions are exceptional. On most days, MPs addressing the House do so to rows of empty green benches.

Debates take place on motions. However, there is one form of business taken on the floor of the House that departs from the rule requiring a motion to be before the House. That is *Question Time*. This takes place on four days of the week – Monday to Thursday – when the House is sitting. It is the first substantive order of business once the House sits: it commences once prayers and some minor business – announcements from the Speaker, certain non-debatable motions concerning private legislation – are completed. It concludes exactly one hour after the House has commenced sitting.

Question Time itself is of relatively recent origin (see Franklin and Norton 1993). The first recorded instance of a question being asked was in the House of Lords in 1721, and the first printed notice of questions to ministers was issued in 1835. Question time itself – a dedicated slot under the heading of 'Questions' on the order paper – dates from 1869. The institution of a dedicated slot for Prime Minister's Questions is of even more recent origin, dating from July 1961. From 1961 to 1997, the Prime Minister answered questions for fifteen minutes on two days of the week (Tuesday and Thursday). In May 1997, the new Labour Prime Minister, Tony Blair, changed the procedure, answering questions for thirty minutes once a week on a Wednesday.

The practice of asking questions is popular with MPs, and the demand to ask questions exceeds the time available. Members are thus restricted in the number they can put on the order paper: no more than one to any one department on any day and no more than two in total on the day. (It is thus possible to have a question to the department answering before Prime Minister's Questions and one to the Prime Minister.) Questions can be tabled up to three working days in advance (four for those to the secretaries of state for Northern Ireland, Scotland and Wales) and are selected by a random physical and computer shuffle. Questions must be precisely that – statements and expressions of opinion are inadmissible – and each must be on a matter for which the minister has responsibility. There is also an extensive list of topics (including arms sales, budgetary forecasts and purchasing contracts) on which government will not answer questions. Ministers may also decline to answer on grounds of 'disproportionate cost'. At the end of 2008, the cost of answering an oral question was estimated to be £410. If the cost of answering a particular question was calculated to be £750 or more, then the minister may decline to answer.

The normal practice of tabling questions seeking answers to clear and specific questions tabled in advance was complemented in 2007 by the introduction of a new type of question. Towards the end of questions to a particular department, there are now 'topical questions'. These are not dissimilar to Prime Minister's Questions in that a member asks a minister an 'open' question – 'If he will make a statement on his departmental responsibilities' – and then supplementary questions can be on any aspect of the responsibilities of the department. The procedure enables questions to be raised that are current and provides an opportunity for opposition members to test ministers to ensure that they are fully briefed on issues affecting their departments.

Ministers answer questions on a rota basis, most ministries coming up on the rota every five weeks. The larger departments, such as the Treasury, are each allocated a full question time. Smaller departments are allocated only part of a question time (some may get 30 minutes, or even 10 minutes.) All questions tabled by members used to be printed on the order paper, a practice that was costly and largely pointless. The number tabled often ran into three figures, but the number of questions actually answered in the time available was usually fewer than 20. Following changes approved by the House in 1990, only the top 25 – fewer if the department is not taking up the whole of Question Time – are now printed.

The MP with the first question rises and says 'Question Number One, Mr Speaker' and then sits down. The minister rises and replies to the question.

The MP is then called to put a follow-up – or 'supplementary' – question, to which the minister responds. Another member may then be permitted by the Speaker to put another supplementary. If an opposition **frontbencher** rises, he or she has priority. During Prime Minister's Question Time, the Leader of the Opposition is frequently at the despatch box and is permitted up to six interventions (and the leader of the Liberal Democrats three). The Speaker decides when to move on to the next question.

During an average session, about 2,000 to 3,000 questions will receive an oral answer. In the 2007–8 session, for example, the number was 2,645 (out of 5,151 that were published on the order paper). With supplementaries included, the figure is nearer 7,000: in 2007–8 it was 6,760.

Question Time is not the only opportunity afforded to MPs to put questions to ministers. Members can also table questions for written answer. These provide an opportunity to elicit more detailed answers than can be obtained through an oral question and are particularly useful for obtaining data from departments. The questions, along with ministers' answers, are published in *Hansard*, the official record of parliamentary proceedings. There is no limit on the number of written questions that an MP can table. The average MP tables just over 100 a session. Exceptionally, some members table well in excess of 1,000. The number tabled each year has risen over the decades (see Franklin and Norton 1993: 27). By the 1990s, some sessions saw more than 40,000 questions being tabled. This figure has been far exceeded in the twenty-first century. In the 2007–8 session, the number was 78,508.

Question Time itself remains an important opportunity for backbenchers to raise issues of concern to constituents and to question ministers on differing aspects of their policies and intentions. However, it has become increasingly adversarial in nature, with opposition frontbenchers participating regularly – a practice that has developed over the past 30 years – and with questions and supplementaries often being partisan in content. Some members view the proceedings, especially Prime Minister's Question Time, as a farce. However, it remains an occasion for keeping ministers on their toes (figuratively as well as literally), and it ensures that a whole range of issues is brought to the attention of ministers. It also ensures that much material is put on the public record that would not otherwise be available.

Select committees

The House has made greater use in recent years of select committees, appointed not to consider the particular details of bills (the task of public bill committees) but to consider particular subjects assigned by the House. Historically, they are well-established features of parliamentary scrutiny. They were frequently used in Tudor and Stuart parliaments. Their use declined in the latter half of the nineteenth century, the government – with its party majority – not looking too favourably on bodies that could subject it to critical scrutiny. For most of the twentieth century, the use of such committees was very limited. The position changed in the 1960s and, more dramatically, in the 1970s.

The House has a number of long-standing select committees concerned with its privileges and internal arrangements. However, for the first half of the twentieth century, the House had only two major select committees for investigating the policy or actions of government: the Public Accounts Committee (PAC) and the Estimates Committee. Founded in 1861, the PAC remains in existence and is the doyen of investigative select committees. It undertakes post hoc (i.e. after the event) scrutiny of public expenditure, checking to ensure that it has been properly incurred for the purpose for which it was voted. The Estimates Committee was first appointed in 1912 for the purpose of examining ways in which policies could be carried out cost-effectively. In abeyance from 1914 to 1921 and again during the Second World War, it fulfilled a useful but limited role. It was abolished in 1971 and replaced by an Expenditure Committee with wider terms of reference.

The PAC and Estimates Committees were supplemented in the 1940s by a Select Committee on Statutory Instruments and in the 1950s by one on nationalised industries. There was a more deliberate and extensive use of select committees in the latter half of the 1960s, when the Labour Leader of the House, Richard Crossman, introduced several reforms to try to increase the efficiency and influence of the House. A number of select committees were established, some to cover particular policy sectors (such as science and technology) and others particular government departments (such as education). One was also appointed to cover the newly created Parliamentary Commissioner for Administration (PCA), better known as the ombudsman. However, the experience of the committees did not meet the expectations of their supporters. They suffered from limited resources, limited attention (from backbenchers, government and the media), limited powers (they could only send for 'persons, papers and records' and make recommendations), the absence of any effective linkage between their activities and the floor of the House, and the lack of a coherent approach to, and coverage of, government policy. Some did not survive for very long. The result was a patchwork quilt of committees, with limited coverage of public policy.

Recognition of these problems led to the appointment in 1976 of a Procedure Select Committee, which reported in 1978. It recommended the appointment of a series of select committees, covering all the main departments of state, with wide terms of reference and with power to appoint specialist advisers as the committees deemed appropriate. It also recommended that committee members be selected independently of the whips, the task to be undertaken by the Select Committee of Selection, the body formally responsible for nominating members. At the beginning of the new parliament in 1979, the Conservative Leader of the House, Norman St John-Stevas, brought forward motions to give effect to the Procedure Committee recommendations. By a vote of 248 to 12, the House approved the creation of the new committees. Initially, twelve were appointed, soon joined by committees covering Scottish and Welsh affairs. In the light of their appointment, various other committees were wound up. The PAC and the Committee on the Parliamentary Commissioner were retained. In 1980, a Liaison Select Committee, comprising predominantly select committee chairmen, was appointed to coordinate the work of the committees.

The fourteen new committees began work effectively in 1980. Their number has fluctuated since, usually reflecting changes in departmental structure. Committees were also added to cover sectors or departments not previously covered, notably science and technology and, in 1994, Northern Ireland. In the parliament returned in 1997, sixteen departmental select committees were appointed. The number increased in the following parliament after changes in the structure of departments and by the end of the parliament eighteen were in existence: they were reappointed in the 2005 parliament. As a result of further changes in departments, the number increased to nineteen. There also exists the Committees on Arms Export Control (formerly known as the Quadripartite Committee), comprising four departmental select committees (defence, foreign affairs, international development, and business, innovation and skills) which meet on occasion in order to examine strategic export controls. There are also several non-departmental select committees. These comprise principally 'domestic' committees – such as the Committee on Standards and Privileges and the Finance and Services Committee – but they also include investigative committees, such as the PAC, Environmental Audit, Public Administration, European Scrutiny and Statutory Instruments Committees, and regional committees. In 2009, nine regional committees were appointed to examine the regional strategies and the work of the regional bodies for the regions of England.

The nineteen departmental select committees in existence at the end of 2009 are listed in Table 15.7. Each committee is established 'to examine the expenditure, administration and policy' of the department or departments it covers and of associated public bodies. As can be seen from the table, a committee has usually eleven, thirteen or fourteen members. The chairmanships of the committees are shared between the parties – usually in rough pro-portion to party strength in the House – although committee members are responsible for electing one of their own number from the relevant party to the chair. This power vested in committee members has variously resulted in the election of independent-minded chairmen, such as Nicholas Winterton (Conservative chairman of the Health Committee, 1991–2), Frank Field (Labour chairman of the Social Security Committee, 1990–7), Chris Mullin (Labour chairman of the Home Affairs Committee, 1997–9 and 2001–3) and Gwyneth Dunwoody (Labour chairman of the Transport Sub-Committee 1997–2002, Transport Committee 2002–2008).

Each committee has control of its own agenda and decides what to investigate. It has power to take evidence, and much of its time is spent questioning witnesses. Each committee normally meets once a week when the House is sitting in order to hold a public, evidence-taking session. Members sit in a horseshoe shape, MPs sitting around the horseshoe – not necessarily grouped according to party – with the witness or witnesses seated in the gap of the horseshoe. Each session will normally last between one and two hours.

Table 15.7 Departmental select committees, 2009

Committee (number of members in parenthesis)	Chairman
Business, Innovation and Skills (11)	Peter Luff (Con)
Children, Schools and Families (14)	Barry Sheerman (Lab)
Communities and Local Government (11)	Dr Phyllis Starkey (Lab)
Culture, Media and Sport (11)	John Whittingdale (Con)
Defence (14)	Rt Hon. James Arbuthnot (Con)
Energy and Climate Change (14)	Elliot Morley (Lab)
Environment, Food and Rural Affairs (14)	Rt Hon. Michael Jack (Con)
Foreign Affairs (14)	Mike Gapes (Lab)
Health (11)	Rt Hon. Kevin Barron (Lab)
Home Affairs (14)	Rt Hon. Keith Vaz (Lab)
International Development (11)	Rt Hon Malcolm Bruce (Lib Dem)
Justice (14)	Rt Hon Sir Alan Beith (Lib Dem)
Northern Ireland Affairs (13)	Sir Patrick Cormack (Con)
Science and Technology (13)	Phil Willis (Lib Dem)
Scottish Affairs (11)	Mohammad Sarwar (Lab)
Transport (11)	Louise Ellman (Lab)
Treasury (14)	Rt Hon. John McFall (Lab)
Welsh Affairs (11)	Dr Hywel Francis (Lab)
Work and Pensions (11)	Terry Rooney (Lab)

Committee practices vary. Some hold long-term inquiries, some go for short-term inquiries, and some adopt a mixture of the two approaches. Some will also summon senior ministers for a single session just to review present policy and not as part of a continuing inquiry. The Chancellor of the Exchequer, for example, appears each year before the Treasury Committee for a wide-ranging session on economic policy. Although committees cannot force ministers to attend, the attendance of the appropriate minister is normally easily arranged. So, too, is the attendance of civil servants, although they cannot divulge information on advice offered to ministers or express opinions on policy: that is left to ministers. Attendance by ministers and civil servants before committees is regular and frequent, although most witnesses called by committees represent outside bodies. In investigating a particular subject, a committee will call as witnesses representatives of bodies working in the area or with a particular expertise or interest in it. Figure 15.2 shows but part of the agenda of select committee meetings and witnesses in a typical week.

At the conclusion of an inquiry, a committee draws up a report. The report is normally drafted by the committee clerk – a full-time officer of the House – under the guidance of the chair. It is then discussed in private session by the committee. Amendments are variously made, although it is relatively rare for committees to divide along party lines. Once agreed, the report is published. The committees are prolific in their output. From their creation in 1979 through to the summer recess in 2004, they published a total of 1,932 reports. Among the subjects being examined in 2009 were the banking crisis, housing finance, teacher training, global security, carbon budgets, the future of aviation, alcohol, the cocaine trade, the Department of International Development's programme in Nigeria, students and universities, and policing and justice in Northern Ireland. Most reports embody recommendations for government action. Some of the recommendations are accepted. Others become subject to the 'delayed drop' effect: the government rejects or ignores a report but several years later, without necessarily acknowledging the work of the committee, implements some of the recommendations. Overall, only a minority of the recommendations emanating from committees will be accepted immediately and acted on by government. A more common response is to note a recommendation or to say that it is under review.

A select committee has no formal powers to force the government to take any action on a report. All that the government is committed to do is to issue a written response to each report within 60 days of the report being published. The target is not always met.

The departmental select committees, like the House itself, are multifunctional. They serve several purposes. They have added considerably to the store of knowledge of the House. They provide an important means for specialisation by members. They serve an important expressive function. By calling witnesses from outside groups, they allow those groups to get their views on the public record. The evidence from witnesses is published. Reports are published in paper form and on the Internet (www.parliament.uk, see under 'committees'). More time is now devoted to committee reports as a result of various Thursdays being devoted to debating them in Westminster Hall. The committees may take up the cases espoused by some of the groups, ensuring that the issue is brought onto the political agenda. The reports from the committees are read and digested by the groups, thus providing the committees with the potential to serve as important agents for mobilising support. Above all, though, the committees serve as important means for scrutinising and influencing government, especially the former. Ministers and civil servants know they may be called before committees to account for their actions. Committee sessions allow MPs to put questions to ministers in greater detail than is possible on the floor of the House. They give MPs the only opportunity they have to ask questions of officials. Not only will poor performances be noted – not least by the media – but also poor answers may attract critical comment in the committee's report. No minister or official wishes to be seen squirming in the face of difficult questions.

Select committees have thus developed as a major feature of parliamentary activity, with most MPs viewing that activity in a positive light. Their purview now even encompasses the Prime Minister. Prior to 2002, Prime Minister Tony Blair had refused requests to appear before the Public Administration Select Committee, citing the fact that his predecessors had not appeared before select committees. In 2002, he reversed his stance and agreed to appear before the Liaison Committee to answer questions. His first appearance, for two-and-a-half hours, took place on 16 July. It is now standard practice that the prime minister appears before the committee twice a year.

Tuesday 14 July 2009

Treasury

Subject: Appointment of Adam Posen to the Monetary Policy Committee, Bank of England

Witnesses: Adam Posen, External Member of the Monetary Policy Committee, Bank of England

Environmental Audit

Subject: Carbon Budgets

Witnesses: Sir David King, Director, and Dr Cameron Hepburn, Senior Research Fellow, Smith School of Enterprise and the Environment, University of Oxford; Professor Paul Ekins, Professor of Energy and Environment Policy, King's College London; Professor David MacKay, Professor of Natural Philosophy, Department of Physics, Cavendish Laboratory, University of Cambridge

Business and Enterprise

Subject: Exporting out of recession

Witnesses: Lord Davies of Abersoch CBE, Minister for Trade and Investment, Department for Business, Innovation and Skills, and Gareth Thomas MP, Minister of State, Department for International Development

Culture, Media and Sport

Subject: Press standards, privacy and libel

Witnesses: To be confirmed

Defence

Subject: ISTAR

Witnesses: Air Vice-Marshal Carl Dixon OBE, Capability Manager (Information Superiority), Air Commodore N J Gordon MBE, Air Officer ISTAR in Headquarters 2 Group, and Brigadier Kevin Abraham, Director Joint Capability, Ministry of Defence

Home Affairs

Subject: (i) The Work of Europol; (ii) The Cocaine Trade

Witnesses: (i) Rob Wainwright, Director, Europol (ii) Mitch Winehouse

Welsh Affairs

Subject: Ports in Wales

Witnesses: Paul Clark MP, Parliamentary Under-Secretary of State, Department for Transport; Ieuan Wyn Jones AM, Deputy First Minister and Minister for the Economy and Transport, Welsh Assembly Government

Joint Committee on Human Rights

Subject: Business and Human Rights

Witnesses: Rt Hon Michael Wills MP, Minister of State, Ministry of Justice, Ian Lucas MP, Parliamentary Under-Secretary of State, Department for Business, Innovation and Skills, and Rt Hon Lord Malloch-Brown KCMG, Minister for Africa, Asia and the UN, Foreign and Commonwealth Office

Home Affairs

Subject: The work of the Home Office

Witnesses: Rt Hon Alan Johnson MP, Secretary of State for the Home Department

Justice

Subject: Constitutional Reform and Renewal

Witnesses: Rt Hon Jack Straw MP, Secretary of State for Justice and Lord Chancellor

Figure 15.2 Meetings of select committees

Despite these various strengths and advances, limitations remain. Membership has usually been determined by the whips, though in 2010 the House voted for members to be elected by the House. The committees have limited powers and limited resources. They have the time and resources to investigate only a small number of issues. The number of reports they issue exceeds the time available on the floor of the House or in Westminster Hall to debate them. Most reports will not be mentioned on the floor of the House or even read by most MPs. Government is committed to providing a written response to committee reports but under no obligation to take action on the recommendations made in those reports. And although ministers and officials appear before committees, they do not necessarily reveal as much as the committees would like. Although the committees constitute a major step forward for the House of Commons, many MPs would like to see them strengthened.

Early day motions

Of the other devices available to members, early day motions (EDMs) are increasingly popular, although of limited impact. A member may table a motion for debate 'on an early day'. In practice, there is invariably no time to debate such motions. However, they are printed and other MPs can add their names to them. Consequently, they are used as a form of parliamentary notice board. If a motion attracts a large number of signatures, it may induce the government to take some action or at least to pause, or it may seriously embarrass the government. This happens occasionally. An EDM in 2002–3 expressing concern over possible military action against Iraq attracted the signatures of more than 150 Labour MPs, seen as a signal that the government might run into substantial opposition on its own side if it were pre-cipitate in agreeing to use force to topple the Iraqi regime; the government subsequently suffered the largest rebellious vote by backbenchers in the postwar era. Such occasions, though, are rare. EDMs are more often used for fulfilling a limited expressive function, allowing members to make clear their views on a range of issues, often reflecting representations made to them by people and groups outside the House. Examples of such EDMs are illustrated in Figure 15.3. The range of topics is extremely broad and the number of motions tabled an increasingly large one, exacerbated by motions unrelated to public policy, for example,

congratulating particular sporting teams or individuals on their achievements.

In the 1970s and 1980s, about 300–400 EDMs were tabled each year. In the 1990s, the number each year exceeded 1,000. In the 1992–7 parliament, a total of 7,831 were tabled – an average of just over 1,500 a session. The number dipped in the 1997–2001 parliament, when 3,613, an average of just over 900 a year, were submitted, but increased notably in the 2001–5 parliament when MPs put in a total of 6,767 – an average of 1,691 a session. The number has increased substantially since then, with over 2,000 a session being submitted. In the long 2005–06 session, 2,924 were tabled, in 2006–07 it was 2,385 and in 2007–08 the figure was 2,727. The consequence of excessive use of EDMs is that their value as a means of indicating strength of opinion on an issue of political significance is devalued. Their utility, which was always limited, is thus marginal, although not non-existent. Each is studied by the relevant government department and they still give MPs the opportunity to put issues of concern on the public record. An EDM which attracts more than 300 signatures – which rarely happens – will get noticed. Most of the rest will not.

Correspondence

The means so far considered have been public means by which MPs can scrutinise government and make representations to it. However, a number of private means exist, two official and two unofficial. One official means is through corresponding with ministers. Since the 1950s, the flow of letters to MPs from constituents and a range of organisations (companies, charities and the like) has grown enormously. The flow increased significantly in the 1960s and increased dramatically in subsequent decades. In the late 1960s a typical MP would receive something in the region of 2,000 to 3,000 items of mail every year. In 2008, 4.1 million items of mail were delivered to the Palace of Westminster, 85 per cent of them going to the House of Commons: that averages out at nearly 5,500 items of mail per MP. The usual method for an MP to pursue a matter raised by a constituent is by writing to the relevant minister, usually forwarding the letter from the constituent. At least 10,000 to 15,000 letters a month are written by MPs to ministers.

For an MP, writing to a minister is one of the most cost-effective ways of pursuing constituency casework (see Norton and Wood 1993: Chapter 3). A letter invites a considered, often detailed response, usually free of the party pressures that prevail in the chamber; by being a private communication, it

Asterisk figures show number of MPs to have signed the motion. The first six names to sign (the sponsors) are always listed, followed by the names of the latest Members to sign.

97 FLOOD MANAGEMENT   3:12:08
Miss Anne McIntosh
Mr Peter Ainsworth
Mr James Paice
Bill Wiggin
Mr Simon Burns
Mr David Drew
                                                                                        * 64

   Dr Julian Lewis
That this House notes the devastation caused by recent flooding and the institutional confusion and chaos that was exposed; regrets that responsibility for surface water flooding remains unclear, with no single body in charge; and urges the Government to bring responsibility for flood management under the remit of one body at the earliest opportunity.

113 PROVISION OF PUBLIC LAVATORIES   4:12:08
Tim Farron
Peter Bottomley
Dr Evan Harris
Mr Mike Hancock
Jeremy Corbyn
Mr David Drew
                                                                                        * 31

   Patrick Mercer
That this House believes that the provision of public lavatories is a vital public service and notes with regret the closure of public lavatories over recent years; recognises that these closures have a particular impact on older and disabled people and those with young families; and calls on the Government to make the necessary resources available to enable local authorities to provide public lavatories.

As an Amendment to Tim Farron's proposed Motion (Provision of Public Lavatories):
Bob Spink
Frank Cook
Mr Andy Reed
                                                                                        * 3

Line **5**, at end add 'and calls on local authorities which are considering closures of public lavatories to fully consult residents before any decisions are taken.'
                                                                            8:12:08 (a1)

174 FIREFIGHTER SAFETY   8:12:08
Mr Andrew Dismore
Mr Michael Clapham
John McDonnell
Mr David Drew
Ian Stewart
Mr Martin Caton
                                                                                        * 142

Mr Robert Marshall-Andrews   Steve Webb   Derek Twigg
Jim Sheridan
That this House notes the recent increased number of firefighter deaths highlighted in the Fire Brigades Union report In the Line of Duty; further notes the lack of safety-critical operational guidance for fire authorities highlighted in that report, and the absence of a properly resourced national body with overall responsibility for recording and investigating firefighter deaths and other serious incidents; and calls for work to be commenced with stakeholders leading to the creation of such a body with responsibility for developing and agreeing safety-critical operational guidance arising from those investigations.

258 ANIMAL TESTING AND HOUSEHOLD CLEANING PRODUCTS   11:12:08
Bob Russell
Mr Adrian Sanders
Mr David Drew
John McDonnell
Mr Andrew Dismore
David Simpson
                                                                                        * 115

   Mr Anthony Wright
That this House supports the campaign of the British Union for the Abolition of Vivisection to end the suffering of animals in tests for household cleaning products and their ingredients; and urges the House of Commons Commission to demonstrate support for this initiative by ensuring that cleaning products used throughout the parliamentary estate have been certified as not tested on animals.

Figure 15.3 Examples of early day motions to show how MPs use this device to draw attention to particular issues, July 2009

avoids putting a minister publicly on the defensive. Ministers are thus more likely to respond sympathetically in the use of their discretion than is the case if faced with demands on the floor of the House. Furthermore, there is no limit on the number of letters an MP can write, and those letters can usually be dictated at a time of the member's choosing. Letters from MPs to ministers are accorded priority in a department – each is circulated in a special yellow folder – and have to be replied to by a minister. If a letter fails to obtain the desired response, the member has the option of then taking the matter further, either by seeing the minister or by raising the matter publicly on the floor of the House.

Correspondence is a valuable and efficient means of ensuring that a matter is considered by a minister. A great many letters on a particular problem can alert a minister to the scale of that problem and produce action. Letter writing is also a valuable means of fulfilling an expressive function. Most constituents who write do so to express a particular viewpoint or in order to obtain an authoritative explanation of why some action was or was not taken; only a minority write to try to have a particular decision changed. Writing to the MP is a long-established, and now much used, means for citizens to have some input into the political process. Nonetheless, corresponding with ministers has a number of limitations (see Norton 2005: Chapter 9). MPs are not always well versed in the subjects raised with them by constituents. Some lack sufficient interest, or knowledge of the political system, to pursue cases effectively. Increasingly, they have difficulty finding the time to deal with all the matters raised by them.

Parliamentary commissioner for administration

Since the late 1960s, MPs have had another option at their disposal in pursuing particular issues raised by constituents. The Parliamentary Commissioner for Administration – or ombudsman – was established under an Act of 1967 to investigate cases of maladministration within government. The term 'maladministration' essentially covers any error in the way a matter is handled by a public servant: it does not extend to cover the merits of policies. The ombudsman considers only complaints referred by MPs: a citizen cannot complain directly. The Commissioner enjoys some protection in office in that he or she can only be removed by an address by both Houses of Parliament to the crown. (The first

female ombudsman – Ann Abraham – was appointed in 2002.) She has a relatively modest staff of just over fifty. She can summon papers and take evidence under oath. When an inquiry is completed, she sends a copy to the MP who referred the case as well as to the relevant department. Her recommendations are normally acted on. However, she labours under a number of limitations: she has a limited remit, limited resources and limited access to certain files – she has no formal powers to see Cabinet papers. Perhaps most notably, she has no powers of enforcement. If she reports that officials have acted improperly or unjustly in the exercise of their administrative duties, it is then up to government to decide what action to take in response; if it fails to act, the only remaining means available to achieve action is through parliamentary pressure.

The number of cases referred to the ombudsman has increased over the years. Most complaints are deemed not to fall within her remit. In 2008–09, 79 per cent of complaints received were not properly made or were premature. In the year, 401 cases for investigation were accepted. The Departments attracting the most parliamentary complaints were the Department of Work and Pensions, the Home Office, and HM Revenue and Customs. Many are not taken forward and in other cases inquiries are undertaken to see whether the body that is the subject of the complaint wishes to take action that meets with the approval of the complainant. This frequently happens. Although the relevant departments usually act on the ombudsman's recommendations – a failure to do so is rare – the government has since 2002 twice rejected recommendations that certain factual information should be released under the Code of Practice on Access to Government Information, in 2005 rejecting the findings in a case where some applicants to a scheme to compensate people interned by the Japanese in the Second World War were excluded because they or their parents were not born in the United Kingdom, and in 2006 rejecting the findings in a case on the handling of pension schemes.

The ombudsman reports to the Public Administration Committee in the Commons which can then pursue any matters that have not been resolved satisfactorily. In December 2005, for example, it held a hearing on the report concerning the treatment of those interned by the Japanese who were denied compensation. In appearing before the committee, the relevant minister announced that the issue was being urgently reviewed.

The Commissioner thus serves a useful service to MPs – and their constituents – but constitutes something of a limited last resort and one that has no direct powers of enforcement. MPs prefer to keep casework in their own hands and pursue it with government directly. For most members, the preferred device for pursuing a matter with a minister remains that of direct correspondence.

Party committees

An important unofficial means of scrutinising and influencing government is that of party committees. These are unofficial in that they are committees of the parliamentary parties and not officially constituted committees of the House.

Each parliamentary party has some form of organisation, usually with weekly meetings of the parliamentary party. The two largest parties – Conservative and Labour – have traditionally had a sufficient number of members to sustain a series of committees. Conservative backbench committees were first established in the 1920s and established a reputation for being politically powerful (Norton 1979, 1994). The committees had elected officers and usually met weekly to discuss forthcoming business and topics of interest, often with invited speakers. Any Tory MP could attend and if a controversial issue attracted a large audience, it signalled to the whips that there was a problem. However, the early 1990s witnessed a decline in attendance at meetings – members had many competing demands on their time – and the massive decline in the number of Conservative MPs in the 1997 general election meant that the party had insufficient numbers to maintain the committees on the scale of previous decades. As a result, the number of committees was scaled down and in 2003 a new practice instituted, with four omnibus committees sharing the same time slot and meeting on a rota basis.

Labour backbench committees traditionally lacked the clout of Conservative committees, but in the 1992–7 parliament the standing orders of the Parliamentary Labour Party (PLP) were changed in order to enhance the consultative status of the committees. Since 1997, Labour ministers have consulted with backbench committees, some achieving a reputation for being assiduous in doing so. The committees also serve another purpose: they allow MPs to specialise in a particular subject. They enable an MP, through serving as officer of a committee, to achieve some status in the parliamentary party. This is often especially helpful to new members, giving them their first opportunity to make a mark in parliamentary life. It may also serve as a way of getting noticed for the purpose of being promoted to ministerial office. However, despite their attraction to MPs and their influence within party ranks, the committees have to compete for the attention of members – there are many other demands on members' time.

All-party groups

All-party groups, like party committees, are not formally constituted committees of the House. They are formed on a cross-party basis, with officerships being shared among members of different parties. They have proved particularly popular in recent decades. In 1988 there were 103 all-party subject groups. The number has grown massively since. By 2009, the number had grown to 430. (There are also 140 country groups, each bringing together MPs – and peers – with a special interest in the country or territory concerned.) Some of the groups, known as all-party parliamentary groups, are confined to a parliamentary voting membership; some – known as associate parliamentary groups – include non-parliamentarians. The subjects covered by these groups are diverse, including, for example, AIDS, alcohol abuse, boxing, compassion in dying, electoral reform, folk arts, gas safety, girl guiding, hill farming, Irish in Britain, Islam, prison health, rowing, and tourism. Some exist in name only. Others are active in discussing and promoting a particular cause, some pressing the government for action. Among the more influential are the disability group, the long-established parliamentary and scientific committee, and the football group, which has been active in influencing policy on such issues as safety in sports grounds. The breast cancer group has been especially active in raising parliamentary awareness of the condition. Many of the all-party groups have links with relevant outside bodies – about two-thirds receive support, usually administrative, from interest groups (Norton 2005: 128) – and can act as useful means of access to the political process for such groups. Like party committees, all-party groups have to compete with the other demands made on MPs' time.

In combination, then, a variety of means are available to MPs to scrutinise and influence government and through which they can serve to make known the views of citizens. The means vary in effectiveness and viewed in isolation may appear of little use. However, they are not mutually exclusive, and MPs will often use several of them in order to pursue a particular issue. An MP may write privately to a minister and, if not satisfied with the response, may table a question or seek a half-hour adjournment debate. In order to give prominence to an issue, a member may table an EDM, speak in debate and bombard the minister with a series of written questions. The most effective MPs are those who know how to use these means in combination and – on occasion – which ones to avoid.

■ Members under pressure

MPs are called on to carry out the tasks of the House. As we have seen, the resources available to them to carry out those tasks have increased in recent years. MPs have more resources than before. They have a better salary than before, and they have office and support facilities far in excess of those available to their predecessors. However, the demands on the typical MP have increased massively in recent decades, on a scale that far surpasses the increase in the resources available to deal with them. The increase in demands on MPs' time can be ascribed to four sources: public business, organised interests, constituents and MPs themselves.

Public business

The volume of business has increased in recent decades. This is particularly pronounced in terms of legislation. The number of bills introduced by the government is nowadays not much greater than it was in earlier decades. What has increased is the volume. Bills are much longer than they used to be. They are also more complex. Before 1950, no more than 1,000 pages of public Acts were passed each year. Before 1980, no more than 2,000 pages were passed each year. Since 1980, the figure has usually been in excess of 2,500 pages and on occasion has surpassed 3,000 pages. Since 2000, some bills have been so big that they have had to be published in two parts. This increased volume places a significant strain on parliamentary resources. Most bills go to public bill committees. The longer and more complex the bill, the more time it needs in committee. The Education Reform Bill in 1987–8 received more parliamentary time (200 hours) than any other

postwar measure. Given that several public bill committees will normally be in existence at the same time – bills frequently go for committee consideration at the same time in the session – there is a tremendous strain on the finite resources of MPs, in terms of both their number and the time they have at their disposal.

In addition to the greater volume of public legislation, there is also the burden of other business. This includes, for example, having to scrutinise EU legislation, a task that falls principally on the European Scrutiny Committee (which considers all EU documents submitted to the House) and three European committees, responsible for discussing documents that the House considers worthy of further consideration. It also includes the work of the select committees. As can be calculated from Table 15.7, the departmental select committees take up the time of 237 MPs. Committee work, which often requires reading a substantial amount of paperwork submitted by witnesses and outside bodies, can be time-consuming. Some of the material can be detailed and complex. All this work – in terms of both the European committees and the departmental select committees – represents a relatively recent increase in the workload of MPs; there were no European committees prior to the 1970s and, as we have seen, only a few investigative select committees. Then there are the other select committees, both investigative and domestic. Some MPs can be appointed to serve on three or four separate committees.

Organised interests

MPs have always been subject to lobbying by outside groups – groups wanting members to push for a particular outcome in terms of public policy. However, that lobbying has become pronounced in recent decades (Norton 2005: Chapter 10). Since 1979, organised interests – firms, charities, consumer groups, professional bodies, pressure groups – appear to have 'discovered' Parliament. Government appeared to adopt more of an arm's-length relationship with outside bodies. The departmental select committees came into being and provided particular targets for organised interests. The 1970s had also seen something of a growth in the voting independence of MPs. As a consequence of these several developments, the House of Commons looked far more attractive than ever before to organised interests wanting to influence public policy (Rush 1990; Norton 1999a). One survey of organised interests found that three-quarters had 'regular or frequent contact with one or more Members of Parliament' (Rush 1990: 280). Of the groups that had such contact, more than 80 per cent had asked MPs to table parliamentary questions, and almost 80 per cent had asked MPs to arrange meetings at the House of Commons. Over half had asked MPs to table amendments to bills and to table a motion. It is common to hear MPs in debates refer to material they have received from interest groups (see Norton 2005: 201). This contact between organised interests and MPs has a number of beneficial consequences. Among other things, Members are provided with advice and information that can prove useful in questioning government and in raising new issues. However, it also has some negative consequences. One is the demand on MPs' time. One survey of 248 MPs in 1992 found that on average an MP spent over three-and-a-half hours a week meeting group representatives (Norris 1997: 36–7). Further time is taken up by acting on the requests of such groups and by reading and, if necessary, responding to the mass of material that is mailed by the groups. MPs now have difficulty coping with the sheer volume of lobbying material that is sent to them.

Constituents

Organised interests have been responsible for a marked increase in the mailbag of MPs. So too have constituents. We have touched already on the volume of mail received in the House of Commons in the twenty-first century. For the MP, constituency work takes priority and can occupy a large portion of the day in dictating replies to constituents' letters. It can also occupy most of every weekend, through both appearances at constituency functions and holding constituency surgeries – publicly advertised meetings at which constituents can see the MP in private to discuss particular concerns.

When an MP receives a letter from a constituent that raises a particular grievance (failure to receive a particular state benefit, for example) or issue of public policy, the MP will normally pursue the matter with the government through writing to the relevant minister. Ministers answer in the region of 250,000 letters a year, mostly from MPs.

The burden of constituency demands continues to increase, and MPs have difficulty finding the time to cope with constituency demands and the demands of public business (see Norton and Wood 1993; Norton 2005: 189–91). By 1996 it was estimated that MPs devoted almost 40 per cent of their time to constituency business (Power 1996: 14). The problem is particularly acute for MPs with constituencies close to Westminster: constituents expect them to find the time to be at constituency events, even when the House is sitting. The burden has also increased as constituents – as well as pressure groups – have made increasing use of e-mail. In 2002, the Information Committee of the Commons reported that 10–20 per cent of an MP's correspondence might be received electronically, a figure which it noted was set to climb. E-mail is quick as well as cheap – unlike letters, no stamps are required. MPs are not only recipients of communications but are themselves generators of communications to constituents. Apart from particular correspondence, this may take the form of newsletters and, increasingly, websites. Most MPs have websites and some engage in interactive dialogue through the use of blogs (see Norton 2007). A number also now use Twitter.

MPs themselves

MPs are also responsible for adding to their own burden and to that of the resources of the House. As we have seen, recent years have seen the growth of the career politician. There is a greater body of members who are keen to be re-elected and to achieve office. They are keen to be noticed in the House. Achieving a high profile in the House helps them to be noticed locally. This may help, albeit at the margins, with re-election (see Norton and Wood 1993) and, indeed, may help with reselection by the local party. It is also considered necessary for the purposes of promotion, given the growing number of career politicians and hence the more competitive parliamentary environment. The tendency of the career politician is to table as many questions as is permissible: research assistants will variously be asked to come up with suitable drafts (see Franklin and Norton 1993). The career politician will try to intervene as often as possible in the chamber and will table early day motions to raise issues. There is also likely to be an allied tendency to attract media attention, not least with frequent press releases.

All these pressures add up to create a particular burden for MPs. Surveys by the senior salaries review body have shown that, over the decades, the amount of time devoted to parliamentary duties has increased. One study in the 1990s suggested that MPs typically work in excess of a seventy-hour week. It is difficult for MPs to keep pace with all the demands made of them. Their resources have improved in recent years, and they have been aided considerably by new technology, but the resources have not kept pace with the demands made of members. For many MPs, it is a case of running in order to stand still. For others, it is a case of slipping backwards. There is a particularly important conflict between trying to find time for constituency work and finding time for dealing with public business in the House (Norton and Wood 1993; Norton 2005: 189–91). So long as constituency work takes priority, then the time needed for public business is under particular pressure.

■ The House under pressure

The fact that MPs work hard for their constituents is frequently acknowledged by constituents. Assessments of the role of the local MP tend to be positive (twice as many people saying the local MP did a good job as the proportion saying the MP did a bad

job) and consistent, having shown little change over a number of years. However, the view held by citizens about the House of Commons appears more ambivalent, certainly more volatile, than the views they hold of the local MP. The proportion of people thinking that the House of Commons is doing a good job has varied over the years, sometimes quite substantially. In a 1991 MORI poll, for example, 59 per cent of those questioned thought that Parliament worked well or fairly well. Four years later, in 1995, that figure had gone down to 37 per cent. The number saying it worked fairly or very badly increased from 16 to 38 per cent. Since then, as shown in Table 15.8, the proportion saying it works well has increased slightly, but then slipped back before slumping in May 2009 to 20 per cent. The percentage fairly or very dissatisfied reached an unprecedented 63 per cent. Whereas the preceding polls had shown more people giving a positive than a negative response (albeit at times only just), the difference in 2009 was minus 43 per cent.

What, then, might explain why attitudes towards Parliament are not more positive? The House of Commons has seen major changes in recent decades. Some of these changes, such as the creation of the departmental select committees, have reinforced

Table 15.8 Views on the efficacy of Parliament 1995–2009
Q Are you satisfied or dissatisfied with the way that Parliament works?

	21 April–8 May 1995* %	17–21 August 2000* %	9–15 May 2001** %	6–17 December 2003 %	23–28 November 2006 %	29–31 May 2009*** %
Very satisfied	2	4	4	1	2	2
Fairly satisfied	32	39	41	35	33	18
Neither satisfied nor dissatisfied	27	19	16	27	24	11
Fairly dissatisfied	22	21	19	23	24	30
Very dissatisfied	9	8	11	9	9	33
No opinion	8	10	9	5	8	6
Satisfied	34	43	45	36	35	20
Dissatisfied	31	29	30	32	33	63
Net satisfied	+3	+14	+15	+4	+2	−43

*In 1995 and 2000, asked as 'To what extent are you satisfied or dissatisfied with the way each is doing its job these days? The way Parliament works'
**In 2001, asked as 'To what extent are you satisfied or dissatisfied with the way each is doing its job these days? The way the Westminster Parliament works'
***In 2009, asked as 'Q To what extent are you satisfied or dissatisfied with the way each is doing its job these days? The Westminster Parliament'
Source: Ipsos MORI

the capacity of the House to fulfil a number of its functions. However, other changes – internal as well as external to the House – have served to challenge its public standing and its capacity to fulfil the tasks expected of it. These can be summarised under the headings of partisanship, executive dominance, the creation of other policy-making bodies, and sleaze.

Partisanship

The clash between the parties is a characteristic of British political life. It is a long-standing feature of the House of Commons. There is a perception that, in recent years, it has become more intense. This is reflected, for example, in the nature of Prime Minister's Question Time, where the desire for partisan point-scoring has largely squeezed out genuine attempts to elicit information (see Franklin and Norton 1993). However, perhaps most importantly of all, partisanship is now more publicly visible. The introduction of the television cameras to the Commons means that, in a single news broadcast covering the House, more people will see the House in that single broadcast than could ever have sat in the public gallery of the House. Although there is general support for broadcasting proceedings among public and politicians, the focus on the chamber has tended to encourage a negative perception. A 1996 MORI poll revealed a very clear perception of politicians engaged in negative point-scoring (Table 15.9). As the author of a 1999 Hansard Society study of the broadcasting of Parliament noted, 'The overwhelming perception of parliamentarians as point-scoring, unoriginal and dogmatically partisan can not be blamed entirely on negative reporting by journalists. If one purpose of broadcasting Parliament was to allow people to judge it for themselves, the low esteem MPs are held in by the public has not been elevated by ten years of live exposure' (Coleman 1999: 21). When people see the House on television, they see either a largely empty chamber – MPs are busy doing things elsewhere – or a body of baying MPs, busy shouting at one another and cheering their own side. That is particularly noticeable at Prime Minister's Question Time. One Gallup poll in 1993 found that 82 per cent of those questioned agreed that what took place 'sounds like feeding time at the zoo'. As Peter Riddell noted of Prime Minister's Question Time, 'no other aspect of parliamentary life generates more public complaints' (*The Times*: 4 April 1994). For MPs who want to win the next election, supporting their own side in the cham-

Table 15.9 Perceptions of MPs

Response	%
Q. When you hear politicians from different parties on radio and television, do you have the impression that they are mainly concerned with reaching agreement or are they mainly concerned with scoring points off each other?	
Reaching agreement	3
Scoring points	93
Don't know	4
Q. When you hear politicians on television or radio, do you feel that they fairly often break new ground, or do you almost always feel you've heard it all before?	
New ground	4
Heard it before	92
Don't know	4
Q. When you hear politicians on television or radio, do you feel that they are usually saying what they believe to be true, or are they usually merely spouting the party line?	
Truthful	6
Party line	88
Don't know	6

Source: From S. Coleman (1999) *Electronic Media, Parliament and the Media*, p. 20. Reproduced with permission from the Hansard Society

ber takes precedence over maintaining public trust in the institution (see Norton 1997: 365). Given that the television coverage focuses on the chamber and not on the committee work of the House, the enduring perception that viewers have is of a House of noisy, point-scoring MPs, contributing little new to political debate.

Executive dominance

There has been a perception of a growth in executive dominance in the UK (see Allen 2001). The effect of this, it is argued, is a greater marginalisation of Parliament. Party dominates the House, and this stranglehold has been exacerbated as more and more power has been concentrated in Downing Street. This perception of executive dominance was marked when Margaret Thatcher occupied Downing Street and was revived under the premiership of Tony Blair. The extent to which Parliament is marginalised has been the subject of academic debate, but the perception of a peripheral legislature resonates with

Table 15.10 Perceptions of parliamentary control over government: Parliament does not have sufficient control over what the government does

	1991 (%)	1995 (%)	2000 (%)
Strongly agree	10	13	21
Tend to agree	40	39	32
Neither agree nor disagree	19	21	20
Tend to disagree	20	15	8
Strongly disagree	3	3	4
No opinion	9	9	15

Sources: MORI state of the nation poll 1995, ICM Research state of the nation poll 2000. Copyright © Ipsos MORI, reproduced with permission

the public. The MORI state of the nation polls in the 1990s and in 2000 found a growing body of respondents who believed that Parliament did not have sufficient control over what the government does (Table 15.10). By the mid-1990s, a majority of respondents – 52 per cent – agreed with the statement that Parliament does not have sufficient control over what the government does. Only 18 per cent disagreed. This perception appears to have been reinforced under the Labour government of Tony Blair. As can be seen from Table 15.10, by 2000 the biggest change was in the percentage of respondents who agreed 'strongly' with the statement.

The popular perception of Labour MPs slavishly voting as they are told was encapsulated by a *Guardian* cartoon showing a Labour MP holding an electronic voting device displaying two options: 'Agree with Tony [Blair]' and 'Strongly Agree with Tony'. As research by Philip Cowley (2002, 2005) and Cowley and Stuart (2008) has shown, this perception is overstated. The Blair and Brown governments have faced unprecedented rebelliousness from backbenchers. The three most notable occasions have been: in 2002 when 122 Labour MPs voted against government policy on Iraq, the biggest rebellion on foreign policy faced by any Labour government; in 2005 when the Blair government suffered its first defeat on a whipped vote, MPs voting down a government proposal to allow detention without charge for ninety days; and in 2009 when the Brown government was defeated on the rights of former Gurkha soldiers to settle in Britain. Labour MPs have been willing to vote against the government to a degree not popularly recognised. However, the perception of executive dominance persists – the Prime Minister governing with little regard to Parliament – and it remains the case that the government will almost always get its way in a parliamentary vote. The defeat in 2005 was

the first in more than 2,000 votes to take place in the Commons since the Labour government was returned in 1997. There remains a popular view of a House of Commons that it is not calling government to account. The House is weak in the face of a strong executive.

Creation of other policy-making bodies

The capacity of the House to fulfil its functions is undermined not only by executive domination of the House but also by the creation of other policy-making bodies. Even if MPs had the political will to determine outcomes, their capacity to do so is now limited by the seepage of policy-making powers to other bodies. There are three principal bodies or rather three collections of bodies involved: the institutions of the EU, the courts and the devolved assemblies.

The effect of membership of the European Union will be touched on in Chapter 27. We shall return to its legal implications in Chapter 20. Membership has served to transfer policy competences in various sectors to the institutions of the European Union: they have increased in number with subsequent treaty amendments. Other than being able, under the Lisbon Treaty, to challenge a proposal on the grounds that it breaches subsidiarity, parliament has no formal role in the law-making process of the EU. It seeks to influence the British minister prior to the meeting of the relevant Council of Ministers, but – if qualified majority voting (QMV) is employed – the minister may be outvoted. There is nothing that Parliament can do to prevent regulations having binding effect in the UK or to prevent the intention of directives from being achieved.

The courts have acquired new powers as a result of British membership of the EU as well now as a consequence of the incorporation of the European Convention on Human Rights (ECHR) into British law and as a consequence of devolution. The effect of these we shall explore in greater depth in Chapter 20. Various disputed issues of public policy are now resolved by the courts, which have the power to suspend or set aside British law if it conflicts with EU law. The courts are responsible for interpreting the provisions of the ECHR. The courts are also responsible for determining the legal limits established by the Acts creating elected bodies in Scotland, Wales and Northern Ireland. The capacity of the House of Commons to intervene or to overrule the courts is now effectively limited.

The devolution of powers to elected assemblies in different parts of the United Kingdom also limits the decision-making capacity of Parliament. Parliament is not expected to legislate on matters devolved to the Scottish Parliament. The Scottish Parliament has been given power to legislate in areas not reserved under the Scotland Act and has also been given power to amend primary legislation passed by Parliament. The powers of the National Assembly for Wales have been extended under the terms of the Government of Wales Act 2006. The creation of a power-sharing Northern Ireland Assembly in 2007 has also resulted in a shift of power from Westminster to Stormont. The scope of decision making by Parliament is thus constricted.

Sleaze

Throughout the twentieth century, there were various scandals involving politicians accepting illicit payments in return for some political favour. In the 1970s and 1980s, there was criticism of MPs for accepting payment to act as advisers to lobbying firms or hiring themselves out as consultants. One book, published in 1991, was entitled *MPs for Hire* (Hollingsworth 1991). At the time it was published, 384 MPs held 522 directorships and 452 consultancies. In 1994, the issue hit the headlines when a journalist, posing as a businessman, offered twenty MPs £1,000 each to table parliamentary questions. Two Conservative MPs did not immediately say no to the offer. The story attracted extensive media coverage. The two MPs were briefly suspended from the service of the House. The story was further fuelled later in the year when *The Guardian* claimed that two ministers had, when backbenchers, accepted money to table questions; one, Tim Smith, then promptly resigned as a minister and the other, Neil Hamilton, was eventually forced to leave office. The furore generated by the stories led the Prime Minister, John Major, to establish the Committee on Standards in Public Life, under a judge, Lord Nolan. In 1995, the House accepted the recommendations of the committee about payment from outside sources, though not without opposition from some Conservative Members. MPs went further than the committee recommended in deciding to ban any paid advocacy by MPs: members cannot advocate a particular cause in Parliament in return for payment. Members were also required to disclose income received from outside bodies that is paid to them because they are MPs (for example, money from a company for advice on how to present a case to government). The House also approved the recommendation to establish a

code of conduct and appoint a Parliamentary Commissioner for Standards to ensure that the rules are followed. The code was subsequently drawn up and agreed. It is accompanied by a guide to the rules of the House relating to members' conduct.

The effect of the 'cash for questions' scandal was reflected in opinion polls. In a 1985 MORI poll, 46 per cent thought that 'most' MPs made a lot of money by using public office improperly. In 1994, the figure was 64 per cent, and 77 per cent agreed with the statement that 'most MPs care more about special interests than they care about people like you'. Continuing allegations of breaches of the rules after the return of a new government in 1997 did nothing to help Parliament's reputation (see Doig 2001, 2002). However, what was to precipitate the slump in the reputation in the House of Commons in 2009 was a scandal over MPs' expenses. The House in 1971 introduced an additional cost allowance to assist MPs with maintaining a second home. Initially a modest sum, the amount that an MP representing a seat outside London could claim had reached £24,222 for 2009–10. Though the amount claimable was known, details about claims were not made public. In 2009, details were to be released under the Freedom of Information Act, but the *Daily Telegraph* got hold of advance and unexpurgated copies of the claims made by MPs and published details over a number of weeks. Publication of details of some of the claims – most prominently for a duck house, clearing a moat, in two instances claiming for mortgages that had already been paid off, and in another claiming for, even though not having, a second home – led to a public scandal. There was public dissatisfaction with the ease with which MPs could claim money for a whole range of items (furniture, household goods and repairs, food), often without receipts, and, in effect, supplement their salaries. The scandal led to the police investigating the actions of some MPs (such as those claiming to cover non-existent mortgages) and to the Speaker of the House of Commons, Michael Martin, resigning: he had resisted attempts to make public details of the claim and was the target of much of the criticism of how the House had responded to the crisis. Several MPs that had made claims that attracted particular public opprobrium announced that they would not be seeking re-election; some Labour MPs were brought before a party 'star chamber' and told that they would not be permitted to stand again as Labour candidates. The Government achieved enactment of the Parliamentary Standards

Act 2009, transferring responsibility for policing and paying allowances to an independent body. The Committee on Standards in Public Life was given responsibility for making other recommendations to address the problem. The public reaction was unprecedented in living memory, resulting in a marked collapse in trust in the House of Commons and leaving MPs unsure of how to respond.

■ Pressure for change

These variables combine to produce a House of Commons that is under pressure to restore public confidence and to fulfil effectively the functions ascribed to it. There are various calls for reform of the House in order to address both problems. However, there is no agreement on what should be done. Even in the wake of the scandal over MPs' expenses in 2009, not all those demanding reform are agreed on the scale of the problem, and they come up with very different proposals for reform. There are, put simply, three principal approaches to reform. Each derives from a particular perception of the role of the House of Commons in the political system. They can be related very roughly to the three types of legislature identified at the beginning of the chapter.

1 *Radical*: The radical approach wants to see Parliament as a policy-making legislature. Parliament is seen as weak in relation to the executive – and is seen to be getting weaker. Reform of the House of Commons within the present constitutional and political framework is deemed inadequate to the task. Without radical constitutional reform, the House of Commons will remain party-dominated and under the thumb of the executive. To achieve a policy-making legislature, the radical approach not only supports reform within the institution but also wants major reform of the constitution in order to change fundamentally the relationship between Parliament and government. Such change would include a new electoral system as well as an elected second chamber. As such, this radical approach can be seen to fit very much within the liberal approach to the constitution (see Chapter 13). The most extreme form of this view advocates a separation of powers, with the executive elected separately from the House of Commons. Only with radical

reform, it is argued, can high levels of public trust in Parliament be achieved.

2 *Reform*: This approach wants to strengthen the House of Commons as a policy-influencing body, the onus for policy-*making* resting with government but with the House of Commons having the opportunity to consider policy proposals in detail and to influence their content. As such, it falls very much within the traditional approach to constitutional change (see Chapter 15), although it is not exclusive to it. Traditionalists, for example, can find common cause with adherents to the socialist approach in respect of some reforms. Even adherents of the liberal approach will support reform, although arguing that it does not go far enough. (For traditionalists, reform is both necessary and sufficient. For liberals, it is necessary but not sufficient.) Reformers favour structural and procedural changes within the House. They want to strengthen committees. They want more time for legislative scrutiny. Given the collapse in trust in the Commons, they also want to enhance the relationship between Parliament and the public, with greater scope for members of the public to make their views known, for example through e-petitions and online consultations. Reducing the size of the House was also seen as making more efficient use of resources, not least through reducing the pressure created by members themselves. The sorts of reforms that are advocated are listed in Table 15.11.

3 *Leave alone*: This approach, as the name suggests, opposes change. It is the stance of a High Tory (see Chapter 13) although it is not exclusive to the High Tory approach. Some Labour MPs have opposed reform, wanting to retain the chamber as the central debating forum. Those who support this stance stress the importance of the chamber as the place where the great issues of the day are debated. Committees and greater specialisation detract from the fulfilment of this historical role, allowing MPs to get bogged down in the detail rather than the principle of what is proposed by government. Providing MPs with offices takes them away from the chamber. Although not quite envisaging a House with little or no policy effect, advocates of this approach see the role of the House as one of supporting government. They emphasise that there is no great public demand for change, with scandals such as those of MPs' expenses in 2009 constituting, in their view,

Table 15.11 Reform of the House of Commons: proposals to strengthen the House

- Make pre-legislative scrutiny the norm by publishing all bills, before their introduction into Parliament, in draft form and allowing select committees to study them.
- Require each bill at some stage during its passage to be subject to examination by an evidence-taking committee.
- Create more time for evidence-taking by public bill committees.
- Make greater use of online consultations for select committee inquiries.
- Give departmental select committees an annual research budget (Banham 1994: 50, suggested £2 million a year for each committee).
- Create new procedures for examining delegated legislation and give the House the power to amend statutory instruments.
- Give select committees, and the Speaker, powers to summon ministers.
- Introduce e-petitions and establish a petitions committee to consider issues of importance raised by the public.
- Reduce the number of MPs, creating a smaller and more professional House.

essentially transient and ultimately marginal events. Most people want a government that can govern, and the House of Commons is there to support that government in carrying out the programme it laid before the electors.

For radicals, the contemporary emphasis on constitutional reform gives them hope that their stance may be vindicated. The creation of new elected assemblies in Scotland, Wales and Northern Ireland – both elected for fixed terms – will, they hope, act as a spur to radical change in England. Not only do these parts of the UK have their own elected assemblies, they also have electoral systems that are different to that employed for the House of Commons. With the use also of different electoral systems for the Greater London Assembly and the European Parliament, the House of Commons remains the only legislative body in the UK elected by the first-past-the-post system. Those who adopt this radical stance view electoral reform as a crucial mechanism for revitalising the House of Commons.

For reformers, reform constitutes a practical as well as a desirable option. They point to what has happened in recent years as well as to various reform tracts identifying the case for further change. The introduction of the departmental select committees in 1979 showed what could be achieved in strengthen-

ing Parliament as a policy-influencing legislature. Some reforms have been carried out since 1997 as a consequence of reports issued by the Select Committee on Modernisation of the House of Commons (see Brazier *et al.* 2005). These have included the creation of the 'parallel chamber' in Westminster Hall, the creation of public bill committees, the election by the House of members of select committees and the introduction of regular post-legislative review. More modest changes have included the introduction of payment for those who chair both select and public bill committees.

Reformers want to see more significant changes, and recent years have seen the publication of various reform tracts, including the reports of the Conservative Party's Commission to Strengthen Parliament (the Norton Report) 2000, the Hansard Society's Commissions on Parliamentary Scrutiny (the Newton Report) 2001 and on the Communication of Parliamentary Democracy (the Puttnam Report) 2005, as well as reports from the Modernisation Committee in the Commons and the Constitution Committee in the House of Lords. The Constitution Committee's report, *Parliament and the Legislative Process* (2004), advocated not only reform of the legislative process, but also more extensive pre-legislative and post-legislative scrutiny. The report has led to the introduction of post-legislative review as a standard procedure, most Acts to be reviewed three to five years after enactment.

Those who want to leave the House of Commons alone take heart from the fact that they frequently succeed, not least by default (see Norton 1999b). Many ministers are not too keen on any significant reform that will strengthen the capacity of Parliament to criticise government or prevent it having its way. They want Parliament to expedite government business, not have it delayed. Robin Cook, when he was Leader of the House (2001–3), had notable difficulty in carrying his colleagues with him in pursuing a reform agenda. The whips have proved reluctant to see change and in 2002 were accused of encouraging Labour MPs not to agree to all the recommendations of the Modernisation Committee. Also, MPs – once a parliament is under way – become too tied up with the day-to-day demands of constituency work and public business to stand back and address the issue of parliamentary reform. The 'leave alone' tendency may not be strong in its advocacy but can be quite powerful in achieving the outcome it wants.

Parliamentary reform has been a feature of debates over the past forty years. However, the problem in achieving reform is the classic one. Most MPs are elected to support the party in government. At the same time, they are members of a body that is supposed to subject to critical scrutiny the very government they are elected to support. Are they going to vote to strengthen the House of Commons if the effect is to limit the very government they were elected to support? The options are not necessarily mutually exclusive – reformers argue that good government needs an effective Parliament – but perceptions are all-important. If ministers think a strengthened Parliament is a threat, will they not be inclined to call on their parliamentary majority to oppose it? In those circumstances, backbenchers may have to choose between party and Parliament. Some recent reforms have been important, but none challenges the basic capacity of government to get its way. At the end of the day, the government achieves passage of its measures.

■ Explaining Parliamentary power

As is apparent from the figures in Tables 15.8 and 15.10, as well as the demands for reform made by observers and many politicians, there is a widespread perception that Parliament is not doing as good a job as it should be doing. The House of Commons is seen as weak in the face of executive dominance. Yet Parliament has survived for several centuries; it is at the heart of our political system. Just how powerful is it? On the face of it, not very, yet much depends on how power is defined. There are different approaches. The three principal approaches derive from explaining the capacity to affect outcomes in terms of observable decision making (the pluralist approach), non-decision making (deriving from élite theory) and institutional constraints (Norton 2005).

Decision making

This approach focuses on how issues are resolved once they are on the political agenda. Once a government brings forward a proposal, what difference does Parliament make to it? Does the measure emerge in the form in which the government introduced it or at least in the form it wants it? From this perspective, Parliament exercises some power, but it is limited. Parliament has the coercive capacity to say 'no' to government. Legislation is dependent

on the assent of Parliament. If MPs vote down a bill, then it cannot proceed. However, as we have seen, the use of this coercive capacity is rare. MPs also have a persuasive capacity: that is, they may induce government not to proceed with a measure (or to change it) even though it has the option of proceeding. Ministers may be persuaded by the force of argument, by a desire to maintain goodwill on the part of their own supporters, by the desire to avoid embarrassing publicity (the public appearance of a divided party), or by the threat of defeat. Even with large majorities in the 1997 and 2001 parliaments, Labour ministers occasionally made concessions to their own backbenchers. Thus, for example, Jack Straw as Home Secretary made changes to the Criminal Justice (Terrorism and Conspiracy) Bill as well as to the Immigration and Asylum Bill in order to assuage the criticisms of Labour MPs (Cowley 2002: 32, 52–4). When one Labour MP opposed to provisions for incapacity benefit embodied in a welfare bill went to see the then Social Security Secretary, Alistair Darling, he was asked 'What's your price?' (Cowley 2002: 47). This persuasive capacity became more pronounced in the 2005–10 parliament, when – with a reduced overall majority – the threat of defeat became more potent.

MPs thus have the capacity to affect the outcome of measures, but that capacity is extremely limited. Most bills will clear the Commons in the form they were introduced or at least in the form preferred by government. Amendments made in response to backbench pressure – or from members of other parties – are few and far between. Concessions are occasionally offered in order to ensure that enough MPs are prepared to vote for the bill. Ministers generally opt for the minimum they can get away with in terms of concessions; in the 1997–2001 parliament, for example, negotiations 'rarely yielded anything that discontented backbenchers wanted' (Cowley 2002: 180). The House of Commons *can* make a difference and occasionally the difference is significant and high-profile, but on the whole it is usually at the margins. From this perspective, Parliament is not a particularly powerful body and certainly not as powerful as many would wish it to be.

Non-decision making

Non-decision making is the capacity to keep certain things off the political agenda. The pluralist, or decision making, approach is concerned with outcomes once an issue is on the agenda. The élitist, or non-decision making approach, focuses on how issues get on to the agenda in the first place. Non-decision making is when an issue is kept off the agenda. In élite theory, there is a body that acts as a gate-keeper, ensuring that certain fundamental matters never become the subject of political debate. Parliament is not seen as part of such an élite, but the concept of non-decision making is relevant in so far as it relates to anticipated reaction. An issue may be kept off the political agenda because those responsible for agenda setting realise that it would encounter significant and possible fatal opposition. There may be occasions, therefore, when the government decides not to bring forward a bill because it does not believe it could get it through Parliament. On occasion, the adverse reaction may be so obvious that ministers do not even need to discuss it. As a consequence, there are obvious problems in detecting instances of non-decision making. There have been cases, though, where a government has been known not to proceed with a measure because of anticipated reaction. When she was Prime Minister, Margaret Thatcher once said that she had not been as radical in economic policy as she would have liked: the reason, she said, was because she would not have been able to get the approval of Parliament. That may have been a post hoc rationalisation for not being more radical rather than the actual reason, but it points to the potential power of Parliament.

Anticipation of how MPs may behave thus has some influence on government. It is a feature not confined to the UK. As Cox and Morgenstern (2002: 446) have observed, 'the venerable "rule of anticipated reactions" makes even primarily reactive legislatures . . . relevant'. If government becomes too extreme, then Parliament may act to constrain it. Knowing that, government avoids the extremes. As such, Parliament is powerful, though the number of occasions when ministers have actually contemplated introducing a measure but then decided not to because of anticipated parliamentary reaction is likely to be very small. Given the problems of identifying non-decision making, that can only be surmised, but the existence of overall majorities for government and the willingness of MPs to vote loyally with their party make it plausible.

Institutional constraints

The institutional approach is not so much concerned with the substance of a measure but rather with the institutional structures and norms that determine how an issue is resolved. Here the concern is not with how MPs behave – whether they vote for a bill or not – but with the rules (and the acceptance of those rules) that determine how a bill becomes law. However large the government's parliamentary majority, it cannot simply get all the measures it wants passed by Parliament within a matter of days or weeks. Each bill, as we have seen, has to go through a set procedure. There are several stages each bill has to go through and there are gaps between each stage. As we have seen, there is limited parliamentary time available. The finite number of MPs available to serve on public bill committees may be seen as a problem for Parliament but it also limits the number of bills that can be considered at the same time. Government thus has to consider which bills it wishes to introduce each year. There is not sufficient parliamentary time to deal with all the bills it would like to introduce and only a minority of bills put forward by departments are accepted for introduction in a particular session. Even then, there is the problem of miscalculation and a bill may not get through in the time available. A bill is more likely to fail because of misjudgements about timing (or the calling of a general election, prematurely bringing a Parliament to an end) than it is because MPs have voted it down.

From this institutional perspective, Parliament is a notably powerful body. For bills to become law and be enforced by the courts, they have to be assented to by Parliament. There is no alternative process. The parliamentary *process* is thus crucial and that process is governed by a large body of often complex rules. The book embodying all the rules and precedents, known as *Erskine May* (the name of the clerk who first produced it in the nineteenth century), runs to more than 1,000 pages. Though the House of Commons is master of its procedure, and the government could use its majority to change the rules (and sometimes does), it cannot embark on wholesale change. Ministers are not procedural experts – they rely on the clerks, who are politically neutral – and the House proceeds on the basis of a common acceptance of the rules. There is a general acceptance that government is entitled to get its business done and the opposition is entitled to be heard.

Parliament thus functions on the basis of a consensus on the rules. If government tried to manipulate the rules excessively in its favour, opposition parties may refuse to continue playing by those rules. There is thus what has been termed an 'equilibrium of legitimacy' (Norton 2001a: 28), each side accepting the legitimacy of the other in what it seeks to do. That acceptance allows the process to function effectively. It is an acceptance that underpins the institutional power of Parliament. It is an acceptance that shapes ministers' behaviour. Bills have to be drawn up in a particular form for introduction to Parliament. Ministers are not only drawn from Parliament – and remain constituency MPs – they also have to appear in Parliament to justify their measures and their policies and to answer MPs' questions. There is no legal requirement for ministers to turn up at Question Time to answer questions, but the accepted rules of procedure ensure that they do. Whether they like it or not, Parliament shapes what they do. As an *institution*, Parliament is a powerful body.

BOX 15.4 BRITAIN IN CONTEXT

Ancient and large, but not unusual

The Westminster Parliament is distinctive because of its longevity. It is one of the oldest parliaments in the world. However, in terms of its place in the political system – especially in its relationship to the executive – it is not unusual. Of the types of legislature identified in Box 15.1, it is the first – that of *policy-making legislatures* – that is notable for not being a crowded category. Of national legislatures, only the US Congress has occupied the category for any continuous period of time. It is joined by the state legislatures of the USA and a few legislatures of more recent creation.

The category of *policy-influencing legislatures* is the crowded category and encompasses most legislatures in western Europe and the Commonwealth. It has also been swelled by the changes in the legislatures of the new democracies of southern, central and eastern Europe: previously they occupied the third category, that of *legislatures with little or no policy effect*, but – with democratisation– they have now moved up to occupy the second or even (sometimes briefly) the first category. The third category is now largely confined to dictatorships and one-party states, where legislatures exist for the purpose of giving assent to whatever is placed before them.

Within the category of policy-influencing legislatures, the UK Parliament is not ranked in the top reaches of the category; that is, there are other legislatures that utilise more extensively the capacity to amend or reject measures brought forward by the executive. The Italian parliament and the Scandinavian legislatures are among the strongest legislatures in the category. Westminster, and other Westminster-style legislatures, has less impact on public policy by virtue of the fact that it exists in a Cabinet-centred, two-party system, where the parties compete for the all-or-nothing spoils of electoral victory under a first-past-the-post electoral system. Continental parliamentary systems, utilising different electoral systems, place more stress on coalitions, with parliaments operating through committees on a more consensual basis.

The UK Parliament, however, is not seen as the weakest legislature in the category of policy-influencing legislatures. In western Europe, the weakest in this category are the French and Irish parliaments.

The categories identified in Box 15.1 cover legislatures in relation to public policy. Most legislatures fulfil a range of other functions. The UK Parliament is distinctive, but not unique, for the emphasis that its members give to constituency work. In common with other parliamentary – as opposed to presidential – systems, it serves as the route for advancement to executive office. It shares many of its functions with other policy-influencing legislatures. As with many other legislatures, it is under threat from the expansion of executive power. Where it is distinctive is in terms of its size. There are more than 1,400 parliamentarians (MPs and peers) at Westminster, making the UK Parliament the largest in the democratic world. (The US Congress, by contrast, has a total of 535 members; some legislatures in small states have fewer than 100 members.) Both chambers, in terms of sitting hours, are also among the busiest legislative chambers in the world.

Chapter summary

Parliament is an institution at the heart of the British political system. The principal role of the House of Commons is one of scrutinising government. Various means are available to MPs to undertake this role. Those means have been strengthened in recent years but have made only a modest contribution to improved scrutiny. Members and the House have been subject to pressures that have made it difficult for MPs to fulfil their jobs effectively. Some politicians see no need for change. Others advocate reform of the House, some through radical constitutional change, others through reform from within the institution. Inertia may prevent reform being achieved, but the issue is on the political agenda.

Discussion points

■ What are the most important functions of the House of Commons?

■ What purpose is served by select committees? Should they be strengthened?

■ Should, and can, the House of Commons improve its scrutiny of government legislation?

■ Is the increase in the constituency work of MPs a good or a bad thing?

■ Will reforming the practices and procedures make any difference to public perceptions of the House of Commons?

■ What should be done to restore public confidence in the House of Commons?

■ What would *you* do with the House of Commons – and why?

Further reading

The most recent texts on Parliament, useful for the student, are Riddell (2000), Rush (2005), Norton (2005), and Rogers and Walters (2006). Riddell analyses the pressures faced by Parliament. Rogers and Walters offer a good overview of Parliament, especially its procedures. Rush and Norton are designed for student use, the latter analysing Parliament from different theoretical perspectives and examining the relationship of Parliament to the citizen as well as to government. There is also a wide range of essays, by practitioners and academics, on different aspects of Parliament in Baldwin (2005).

The socio-economic background of MPs is covered by Rush (2001) and the behaviour of MPs in recent parliaments by Cowley (2002, 2005). The largely neglected relationship of Parliament to pressure groups is the subject of Rush (1990) and the report of the Public Administration Committee (2008). Parliamentary questions are considered extensively in Franklin and Norton (1993) and briefly in Giddings and Irwin (2005). The Procedure Committee of the House of Commons has also published a number of reports on parliamentary questions: the most recent, on written questions, was published in 2009 (Procedure Committee 2009a). MPs' constituency service is covered in Norton and Wood (1993), Power (1998) and Chapter 9 of Norton (2005). Parliamentary scrutiny of executive agencies is the subject of Giddings (1995). The relationship of Parliament to the law is discussed in Oliver and Drewry (1998). The relationship of Parliament to the European Union is covered comprehensively in Giddings and Drewry (2004). Many of these books are the products of research by study groups of the Study of Parliament Group (SPG), a body that draws together academics and clerks of Parliament. A reflective set of essays, by members of the SPG, on parliamentary change and the issues facing Parliament in the twenty-first century is to be found in Giddings (2005). The relationships of Parliament to the European Union, government, pressure groups and citizens are put in comparative context in Norton (1996), Norton (1998), Norton (1999a) and Norton (2002) respectively.

A critique of Parliament's scrutiny of the executive is to be found in Weir and Beetham (1999). On parliamentary reform since 1900, see Kelso (2009). On proposals for reform of the House of

Commons, see the Commission to Strengthen Parliament (2000), Norton (2001b), the Hansard Society Commission on Parliamentary Scrutiny (2001), the Constitution Committee of the House of Lords (2004), Brazier (2004) and the Modernisation Committee of the House of Commons (2006, 2007). On the proposal for e-petitioning of Parliament, see the Procedure Committee (2009b), On the consequences of attempts at modernisation, see Brazier *et al.* (2005).

Bibliography

Allen, G. (2001) *The Last Prime Minister* (Graham Allen).

Baldwin, N.D.J. (ed.) (2005) *Parliament in the 21st Century* (Politico's).

Banham, J. (1994) *The Anatomy of Change* (Weidenfeld & Nicolson).

Brand, J. (1992) *British Parliamentary Parties* (Oxford University Press).

Brazier, A. (2004) 'Standing Committees: Imperfect Scrutiny', in A. Brazier (ed.) *Parliament, Politics and Law Making* (Hansard Society).

Brazier, A., Flinders, M. and McHugh, D. (2005) *New Politics, New Parliament?* (Hansard Society).

Coleman, S. (1999) *Electronic Media, Parliament and the Media* (Hansard Society).

Commission to Strengthen Parliament (2000) *Strengthening Parliament* (Conservative Party).

Constitution Committee, House of Lords (2004) *Parliament and the Legislative Process*, 14th Report, Session 2003–4, HL Paper 173–I (The Stationery Office).

Constitution Committee, House of Lords (2008) *Pre-Legislative Scrutiny in the 2006–07 Session*, Session 2007–08, HL Paper 43 (The Stationery Office).

Cowley, P. (ed.) (1998) *Conscience and Parliament* (Cass).

Cowley, P. (2002) *Revolts and Rebellions* (Politico's).

Cowley, P. (2005) *The Rebels* (Politico's).

Cowley, P. and Norton, P. (1996) *Blair's Bastards* (Centre for Legislative Studies).

Cowley, P. and Stuart, M. (2008) 'A Rebellious Decade: Backbench Rebellions under Tony Blair,

1997–207', in M. Beech and S. Lee (eds) *Ten Years of New Labour* (Palgrave Macmillan).

Cox, G.W. and Morgenstern, S. (2002) 'Epilogue: Latin America's Assemblies and Proactive Presidents', in S. Morgenstern and B. Nacif (eds) *Legislative Politics in Latin America* (Cambridge University Press).

Criddle, B. (1992) 'MPs and Candidates', in D. Butler and D. Kavanagh (eds) *The British General Election of 1992* (Macmillan).

Criddle, B. (1997) 'MPs and Candidates', in D. Butler and D. Kavanagh (eds) *The British General Election of 1997* (Macmillan).

Criddle, B. (2002) 'MPs and Candidates', in D. Butler and D. Kavanagh (eds) *The British General Election of 2001* (Macmillan).

Criddle, B. (2005) 'MPs and Candidates', in D. Kavanagh and D. Butler (eds) *The British General Election of 2005* (Palgrave Macmillan).

Doig, A. (2001) 'Sleaze: Picking up the Threads or "Back to Basics" Scandals?', *Parliamentary Affairs*, Vol. 54, No. 2.

Doig, A. (2002) 'Sleaze Fatigue in "the House of Ill-repute"', *Parliamentary Affairs*, Vol. 55, No. 2.

Drewry, G. (ed.) (1989) *The New Select Committees*, revised edn (Oxford University Press).

Franklin, M. and Norton, P. (eds) (1993) *Parliamentary Questions* (Oxford University Press).

Giddings, P. (ed.) (1995) *Parliamentary Accountability* (Macmillan).

Giddings, P. (ed.) (2005) *The Future of Parliament* (Palgrave Macmillan).

Giddings, P. and Drewry, G. (eds) (2004) *Britain in the European Union* (Palgrave).

Giddings, P. and Irwin, H. (2005) 'Objects and Questions', in P. Giddings (ed.) *The Future of Parliament* (Palgrave Macmillan).

Griffith, J.A.G. and Ryle, M. (1989) *Parliament* (Sweet & Maxwell).

Hansard Society (1993) *Making the Law: Report of the Commission on the Legislative Process* (Hansard Society).

Hansard Society (2004) *Issues in Law-Making 5. Pre-Legislative Scrutiny* (Hansard Society).

Hansard Society Commission on the Communication of Parliamentary Democracy, *Members Only?* (Hansard Society).

Hansard Society Commission on Parliamentary Scrutiny (2001) *The Challenge for Parliament:*

Making Government Accountable (Vacher Dod Publishing).

Hollingsworth, M. (1991) *MPs for Hire* (Bloomsbury).

Kennon, A. (2004) 'Pre-legislative Scrutiny of Draft Bills', *Public Law*, Autumn, pp. 477–94.

Kelso, A. (2009) *Parliamentary reform at Westminster* (Manchester University Press).

King, A. (1981) 'The Rise of the Career Politician in Britain – and its Consequences', *British Journal of Political Science*, Vol. 11.

Levy, J. (2009) *Strengthening Parliament's Powers of Scrutiny?* (The Constitution Unit, University College London).

Mezey, M. (1979) *Comparative Legislatures* (Duke University Press).

Modernisation of the House of Commons Select Committee (2006) House of Commons, *The Legislative Process*, First Report, Session 2005–06, HC 1097 (The Stationery Office).

Modernisation of the House of Commons Select Committee (2007) House of Commons, *Revitalising the Chamber: The Role of the Backbench Member*, First Report, Session 2006–07, HC 337 (The Stationery Office).

Norris, P. (1997) 'The Puzzle of Constituency Service', *The Journal of Legislative Studies*, Vol. 3, No. 2.

Norton, P. (1979) 'The Organization of Parliamentary Parties', in S.A. Walkland (ed.) *The House of Commons in the Twentieth Century* (Oxford University Press).

Norton, P. (ed.) (1990) *Legislatures* (Oxford University Press).

Norton, P. (1993) *Does Parliament Matter?* (Harvester Wheatsheaf).

Norton, P. (1994) 'The Parliamentary Party and Party Committees', in A. Seldon and S. Ball (eds) *Conservative Century: The Conservative Party since 1900* (Oxford University Press).

Norton, P. (ed.) (1996) *National Parliaments and the European Union* (Cass).

Norton, P. (1997) 'The United Kingdom: Restoring Confidence?', *Parliamentary Affairs*, Vol. 50, No. 3.

Norton, P. (ed.) (1998) *Parliaments and Governments in Western Europe* (Cass).

Norton, P. (1999a) 'The United Kingdom: Parliament Under Pressure', in P. Norton (ed.) *Parliaments and Pressure Groups in Western Europe* (Cass).

Norton, P. (1999b) 'The House of Commons: The Half Empty Bottle of Reform', in B. Jones (ed.) *Political Issues in Britain Today*, 5th edn (Manchester University Press).

Norton, P. (2001a) 'Playing by the Rules: The Constraining Hand of Parliamentary Procedure', *The Journal of Legislative Studies*, Vol. 7.

Norton, P. (2001b) 'Parliament', in A. Seldon (ed.) *The Blair Effect* (Little, Brown).

Norton, P. (ed.) (2002) *Parliaments and Citizens in Western Europe* (Cass).

Norton, P. (2004) 'Parliament and Legislative Scrutiny: an Overview of Issues in the Legislative Process', in A. Brazier (ed.) *Parliament, Politics and Law Making* (Hansard Society).

Norton, P. (2005) *Parliament in British Politics* (Palgrave Macmillan).

Norton, P. (2007) 'Four Models of Political Representation: British MPs and the Use of ICT', *The Journal of Legislative Studies*, Vol. 13.

Norton, P. and Wood, D. (1993) *Back from Westminster* (University Press of Kentucky).

Oliver, D. and Drewry, G. (eds) (1998) *The Law and Parliament* (Butterworth).

Power, G. (1996) *Reinventing Westminster* (Charter 88).

Power, G. (1998) *Representing the People: MPs and their Constituents* (Fabian Society).

Procedure Committee, House of Commons (1990) *The Working of the Select Committee System*, Session 1989–90, HC 19 (HMSO).

Procedure Committee, House of Commons (2009a) *Written Parliamentary Questions*, Third Report, Session 2008–09, HC 859 (The Stationery Office).

Procedure Committee, House of Commons (2009b) *e-Petitions: Call for Government Action*, Second Report, Session 2008–09, HC 493 (The Stationery Office).

Public Administration Committee, House of Commons (2008) *Lobbying: Access and Influence in Whitehall*, First Report, Session 2008–09, HC 36–I (The Stationery Office).

Riddell, P. (1993) *Honest Opportunism* (Hamish Hamilton).

Riddell, P. (2000) *Parliament Under Blair* (Politico's).

Rogers, R. and Walters, R. (2006) *How Parliament Works*, 6th edn (Longman).

Rush, M. (ed.) (1979) 'Members of Parliament', in S.A. Walkland (ed.) *The House of Commons in the Twentieth Century* (Oxford University Press).

▶

Rush, M. (1990) *Pressure Politics* (Oxford University Press).

Rush, M. (2001) *The Role of the Member of Parliament Since 1868* (Oxford University Press).

Rush, M. (2005) *How Parliament Works* (Manchester University Press).

Somit, A. and Roemmele, A. (1995) 'The Victorious Legislative Incumbent as a Threat to Democracy: a Nine Nation Study', *American Political Science Association: Legislative Studies Section Newsletter*, Vol. 18, No. 2, July.

Weir, S. and Beetham, D. (1999) *Political Power and Democratic Control in Britain* (Routledge).

Guide to parliamentary committees: www.parliament.uk/about/how/committees.cfm

Factsheets: www.parliament.uk/parliamentary_ publications_and_archives/factsheets.cfm

Parliamentary education service: www.parliament.uk/education/index.htm

Register of Members' Interests: www.publications. parliament.uk/pa/cm/cmregmem.htm

Hansard: www.publications.parliament.uk/pa/cm/ cmhansrd.htm

Other related websites

Commission to Strengthen Parliament (the Norton Report): www.conservatives.com/pdf/norton.pdf

Hansard Society for Parliamentary Government: www.hansard-society.org.uk

Useful websites

Parliamentary websites

Parliament: www.parliament.uk

Parliamentary Committees: www.parliament.uk/ business/committees.cfm

The House of Lords

Philip Norton

Learning objectives

- To describe the nature, development and role of the House of Lords.

- To identify the extent and consequences of fundamental changes made to the House in recent years.

- To assess proposals for further change to the second chamber.

Introduction

The House of Lords serves as the second chamber in a **bicameral legislature**. The bicameral system that the United Kingdom now enjoys has been described as one of asymmetrical bicameralism. That is, there are two chambers, but one is politically inferior to the other. The role of the second chamber in relation to the first moved in the twentieth century from being co-equal to subordinate. As a subordinate chamber, it has carried out tasks that have been recognised as useful to the political system, but it has never fully escaped criticism for the nature of its composition. It was variously reformed at different times in the twentieth century, the most dramatic change coming at the end of the century. Debate continues as to what form the second chamber should take in the twenty-first century.

The House of Lords is remarkable for its longevity. What makes this longevity all the more remarkable are two features peculiar to the House. The first is that it has never been an elected chamber. The second is that, until 1999, the membership of the House was based principally on the hereditary principle. The bulk of the membership comprised **hereditary peers**. Only at the end of the twentieth century were most of the hereditary peers removed. The removal of the hereditary peers was not accompanied by a move to an elected second chamber. Whether the United Kingdom is to have an elected or unelected second chamber remains a matter of dispute. It perhaps says something for the work of the House of Lords that the contemporary debate revolves around what form the second chamber should take rather than whether or not the United Kingdom should have a second chamber.

What, then, is the history of the House of Lords? How has it changed over the past century? What tasks does it currently fulfil? And what shape is it likely to take in the future?

■ History

The House of Lords is generally viewed by historians as having its origins in the Anglo-Saxon *Witenagemot* and more especially its Norman successor, the *Curia Regis* (Court of the King). Two features of the King's *Curia* of the twelfth and thirteenth centuries were to remain central characteristics of the House of Lords. One was the basic composition, comprising the **lords spiritual** and the **lords temporal**. At the time of the Magna Carta, the *Curia* comprised the leading prelates of the kingdom (archbishops, bishops and abbots) and the earls and chief barons. The main change, historically, was to be the shift in balance between the two: the churchmen – the lords spiritual – moved from being a dominant to being a small part of the House. The other significant feature was the basis on which members were summoned. The King's tenants-in-chief attended court because of their position. Various minor barons were summoned because the King wished them to attend. 'From the beginning the will of the king was an element in determining its make up' (White 1908:

299). If a baron regularly received a summons to court, the presumption grew that the summons would be issued to his heir. A body thus developed that peers attended on the basis of a strictly hereditary dignity without reference to tenure. The result was to be a House of Lords based on the principle of heredity, with writs of summons being personal to the recipients. Members were not summoned to speak on behalf of some other individuals or bodies. Any notion of representativeness was squeezed out. Even the lords spiritual – who served by reason of their position in the established Church – were summoned to take part in a personal capacity.

The lack of any representative capacity led to the House occupying a position of political – and later legal – inferiority to the House of Commons. As early as the fifteenth century, the privilege of initiating measures of taxation was conceded to the Lower House. The most significant shift, though, took place in the nineteenth century. As we have seen (Chapter 15), the effect of the Reform Acts was to consign the Lords to a recognisably subordinate role to that of the Commons, although not until the passage of

The statue of Richard the Lionheart stands outside the entrance to the House of Lords
Source: One-Image Photography / Alamy

the Parliament Act of 1911 was that role confirmed by statute. Under the terms of the Act, the House could delay a non-money bill for no more than two sessions, and money bills (those dealing exclusively with money, and so certified by the Speaker) were to become law one month after leaving the Commons whether approved by the House of Lords or not. Bills to prolong the life of a parliament, along with delegated legislation and bills originating in the House of Lords, were excluded from the provisions of the Act. The two-session veto over non-money bills was reduced to one session by the Parliament Act of 1949.

The subordinate position of the House of Lords to the House of Commons was thus established. However, the House remained a subject of political controversy. The hereditary principle was attacked by those who saw no reason for membership of the second chamber to be determined by accident of privileged birth. It was attacked as well because the bulk of the membership tended to favour the Conservative cause. Ever since the eighteenth cen-

tury, when William Pitt the Younger created peers on an unprecedented scale, the Conservatives enjoyed a political ascendancy (if not always an absolute majority) in the House. In other words, occupying a subordinate position did not render the House acceptable: the composition of the House, however much it was subordinated to the Commons, was unacceptable. There were some attempts in the period of Conservative government from 1951 to 1964 to render it more acceptable, not by removing hereditary peers or destroying the Conservative predominance but rather by supplementing the existing membership with a new type of membership. The Life Peerages Act 1958 made provision for people to be made members for life of the House of Lords, their titles – and their entitlement to a seat in the House of Lords – to cease upon their death. This was designed to strengthen the House by allowing people who objected to the hereditary principle to become members. Following the 1958 Act, few hereditary peerages were created. None was created under Labour governments, and only one

Conservative Prime Minister, Margaret Thatcher, nominated any (and then only three – Harold Macmillan, who became the Earl of Stockton; George Thomas, former Speaker of the House of Commons; and William Whitelaw, her Deputy Prime Minister). The 1963 Peerages Act made provision for hereditary peers who wished to do so to disclaim their titles. Prior to 1999, these were the most important measures to affect the membership of the House. Although both measures – and especially the 1958 Act – had significant consequences, pressure continued for more radical reform. In 1999, acting on a commitment embodied in the Labour manifesto in the 1997 general election, the Labour government achieved passage of the House of Lords Act. This removed from membership of the House all but ninety-two of the hereditary members. The effect was to transform the House from one composed predominantly of hereditary peers to one composed overwhelmingly of **life peers**. However, the removal of the hereditary peers was seen as but one stage in a process of reform. The House of Lords created by their removal was deemed to be an interim House, to remain in place while proposals for a second stage of reform were considered. The issue of what should constitute the second stage of reform has proved highly contentious.

Membership

Until the passage of the House of Lords Act, which removed most hereditary peers from membership, the House of Lords had more than 1,000 members, making it the largest regularly sitting legislative chamber in the world. Its size was hardly surprising given the number of peers created over the centuries by each succeeding monarch, although the largest increase was in the twentieth century. In 1906, the House had a membership of 602. In January 1999, it had 1,296. Of those, 759 were hereditary peers. (The figure includes one prince and three dukes of the blood royal.) The remaining members comprised 485 life peers, 26 peers created under the Appellate Jurisdiction Act 1876 (the law lords, appointed to carry out the judicial business of the House) and 26 lords spiritual (the 2 archbishops and 24 senior bishops of the Church of England). With the removal of all but 92 of the hereditary peers, the House remains a relatively large one. In the immediate wake of the removal of the hereditary peers, the

House had 666 members. With new creations and deaths, the figure has fluctuated since, but with a clear upward trajectory. By July 2009, there were 739 members. (Though, of these, 12 were on leave of absence, 2 were suspended until the end of the session and 1 was disqualified while serving as an MEP.) Of these 739, 598 were life peers created under the provisions of the 1958 Act.

The membership of the House has thus been affected dramatically by the 1958 Life Peerages Act and the 1999 House of Lords Act. In many respects, the former made possible the latter, creating a new pool of members who could serve once hereditary peers were removed. Indeed, the creation of life peerages under the 1958 Act had a dramatic effect on the House in terms both of composition and activity. The impact of the 1999 Act will be considered in greater detail later.

Composition

In terms of composition, the 1958 Act made possible a substantial increase in the number of Labour members. Previously, Labour members had been in a notable minority. In 1924, when Labour first formed a minority government, the party had only one supporter in the Upper House. The position changed only gradually. In 1945, there were 18 Labour peers. Forty-four Labour peers were created in the period of Labour government from 1945 to 1951, but their successors did not always support the Labour Party. By 1999, there were only 17 hereditary peers sitting on the Labour benches. Life peerages enabled Labour's ranks to be swelled over time. Prominent Labour supporters who objected to hereditary peerages were prepared to accept life peerages, so various former ministers, ex-MPs, trade union leaders and other public figures were elevated to the House of Lords. At the beginning of 1999, there were more than 150 life peers sitting on the Labour benches. Apart from former ministers and MPs, they included figures such as the broadcaster Melvyn Bragg, film producer David Puttnam, crime writer Ruth Rendell, and TV presenter, professor and doctor Robert Winston. Further creations helped bring the number above 200 and by December 2005 there were 210 Labour peers as against 207 Conservatives. A combination of more Labour creations and the death of a number of Conservative peers has further widened the gap.

Table 16.1 Composition of the House of Lords, July 2009

By party

Party	Life Peers	Hereditary: elected by party	Hereditary: elected office holders	Hereditary: * royal office holder	Bishops	Total
Conservative	145	39	9	0	0	193
Labour	211	2	2	0	0	215
Liberal Democrat	66	3	2	0	0	71
Cross-bench	169	29	2	2	0	202
Bishops	0	0	0	0	26	26
Other**	15	2	0	0	0	17
Total	606	75	15	2	26	724

NB Excludes 12 Members who are on leave of absence, 2 who are suspended and 1 disqualified as an MEP

By type	Men	Women	Total
Archbishops and bishops	26	0	26
Life Peers under the Appellate Jurisdiction Act 1876	22	1	23
Life Peers under the Life Peerages Act 1958	452	146	598
Peers under House of Lords Act 1999	90	2	92
Total	590	149	739

* These are: The Marquess of Cholmondeley, Lord Great Chamberlain (Crossbench), The Duke of Norfolk, Earl Marshal (Crossbench)

** These are:

Non-affiliated – L. Archer of Weston-Super-Mare; L. Black of Crossharbour; L. Brabazon of Tara; B. Clark of Calton; B. Ford; B. Hayman, Lord Speaker; L. Jacobs; L. Kalms; L. Roper; L. Smith of Finsbury; L. Triesman; L. Watson of Invergowrie; B. Young of Old Scone

L. Pearson of Rannoch: UKIP; L. Willoughby de Broke: UKIP; L. Stevens of Ludgate: Conservative Independent; L. Stoddart of Swindon: Independent Labour

Source: www.parliament.uk

The creation of life peers from 1958 onwards served to lessen the party imbalance in the House. In 1945, Conservative peers accounted for 50.4 per cent of the membership. In 1998, the figure was 38.4 per cent (Baldwin 1999). Before 1999, the second-largest category in the House comprised those peers who choose to sit independently of party ranks and occupy the cross-benches in the House. At the beginning of 1999 – that is, in the pre-reform House – the state of the parties was Conservative 473, Labour 168, Liberal Democrats 67 and cross-benchers 322. This left in excess of 250 other peers who did not align themselves with any of these groupings. The effect of the removal of most hereditary peers in 1999 was to create greater equality between the two main parties, leaving the balance of power being held by the cross-benchers and the Liberal Democrats. The composition of the House, in July 2009, is given in Table 16.1.

The creation of life peers drawn from modest backgrounds has also served to affect the social profile of the membership. Hereditary peers were typically drawn from the cream of upper-class society. Life peers were drawn from a more diverse social background. However, even with the influx of life peers, the membership remained, and remains, socially atypical. Life peerages are normally conferred on those who have achieved some particular distinction in society, be it social, cultural, sporting, economic or political. By the time the recipients have achieved such a distinction, they are, by definition, atypical. There was therefore little chance of the House becoming socially typical. Members of the House are drawn notably from backgrounds in the law, the Civil Service and the teaching profession, these three categories accounting for nearly 40 per cent of the membership (Criddle *et al.* 2005: 34–5). The next largest category – accounting for just nearly 5 per cent of the membership – is that of trade union officials. The House is also atypical in terms of age and gender. Given that peerages tend to be given to those who have already achieved something in life and that they entail service for life, it is not surprising that the average age of the membership is 68. It is rare for people to be made life peers while in their 20s or 30s. Television mogul Lord Alli (born 1964) was elevated to the peerage in 1998 at the age of 34.

The Chamber of the House of Lords
Source: Rolf Richardson / Alamy

Lawyer and Conservative Party vice-chair Baroness Warsi (b. 1971) became a peer in 2007 at the age of 36. The hereditary peerage produced some young peers, succeeding their fathers at an early age, but they were small in number and largely disappeared as a result of the House of Lords Act, though not entirely: in 2009, of the ten youngest peers, five were hereditary peers. One of them, Lord Freyberg (born 1970), entered the House at the age of 23. Women, who were first admitted to the House under the provisions of the 1958 Life Peerages Act, also constitute a minority of the membership, but a growing one. In 1990, there were 80 women in the House, constituting 7 per cent of the membership. The removal of a large number of – overwhelmingly male – hereditary peers and the creation of more women life peers has meant that the number, and proportion, of women peers has increased notably. In July 2009, there were 149 women peers, constituting just over 20 per cent of the membership. Of these, all bar two held life peerages. Recent years have seen several black and Asian peers created, although they constitute a small proportion of the total. There are also a number of openly gay peers, including Lord Alli, Cabinet minister Lord Mandelson, former cabinet minister Lord Smith of Finsbury, and former head of BP Lord Brown of Maddingley.

There has been another consequence of life peerages in terms of the membership of the House. It has brought into the House a body of individuals who are frequently expert in a particular area or have experience in a particular field. This claim is not exclusive to life peers – some hereditary peers are notable for their expertise or experience in particular fields – but it is associated predominantly with them. This has led to claims that when the House debates a subject, however arcane it may be, there is usually one or more experts in the House to discuss it (Baldwin 1985). Thus, for example, in a short debate on the contribution of science, technology and engineering to the United Kingdom, held on 4 June 2009 and introduced by the President of the Environment Industries Commission, the speakers included the President of the Royal Society; a research neuroscientist and director of the Royal Institution of the UK; the honorary chairman of Cambridge University's technology transfer office and director of several high-technology companies; the director of the Warwick Manufacturing Group at Warwick University; the chairman of the Foundation for Science and Technology; and a peer who had spent more than 20 years in consulting engineering as an engineering designer and 25 years as an engineering journalist. The minister replying to the debate was himself a former development engineer with a PhD in robotics who had chaired the BioIndustry Association. This claim to expertise in many fields is often contrasted with membership of the House of Commons, where the career politician – expert in the practice of politics – dominates. The body of expertise and experience serves, as we shall see, to bolster the capacity of the House to fulfil a number of its functions.

■ Activity

The creation of life peers also had a dramatic effect on the activity of the House. In the 1950s, the House met at a leisurely pace and was poorly attended. Peers have never been paid a salary and many members, like the minor barons in the thirteenth century, found attending to be a chore, sometimes an expensive one: the practice, as in the thirteenth century, was to stay away. The House rarely met for more than three days a week, and each sitting was usually no more than three or four hours in length. For most of the decade, the average daily attendance did not reach three figures. Little interest was shown in its activities by most of its own members; not surprisingly, little interest was shown by those outside the House.

This was to change significantly in each succeeding decade (see Figure 16.1). Life peers were disproportionately active. Although they constituted a minority of the House, they came to constitute a

Session	Average daily attendance
2002–03	362
2003–04	368
2004–05	388
2005–06	403
2006–07	415
2007–08	413

Figure 16.1 Average daily attendance in the chamber, 2002–2008

Source: House of Lords (2008) *The Work of the House of Lords 2007–08*. © Parliamentary copyright 2008. Parliamentary copyright material is reproduced with the permission of the Controller of Her Majesty's Stationery Office (HMSO) on behalf of Parliament

majority of the most active members of the House. The effect of the increasing numbers of life peers was apparent in the attendance of members. Peers attended in ever greater numbers and the House sat for longer. Late-night sittings, virtually unknown in the 1950s and for much of the 1960s, became regular features. In the 1980s and 1990s, the average daily sitting was six or seven hours. By the end of the 1980s, more than 800 peers – two-thirds of the membership – attended one or more sittings each year and, of those, more than 500 contributed to debate. By the time of the House of Lords Act in 1999, the House was boasting a better attendance in the chamber than the House of Commons. The effect of the 1999 Act was to result in a House in which the active members dominated. Although the membership halved in 1999, the daily attendance hardly changed. Whereas the average daily attendance figure for 1992–3 constituted just under one-third of the membership, that for the post-reform 2003–4 session constitutes more than half. In the 2003–4 session, 50 per cent of the members attended 65 per cent or more of the sittings – a remarkable achievement given that many members had full-time posts outside the House, attending in order to give the benefit of their expertise. The House now witnesses an average daily attendance that exceeds 400 (Figure 16.1).

One other consequence of the more active House was that the number of votes increased. They were few and far between in the 1950s, about ten to twenty a year. By the 1980s and 1990s, the figure was usually closer to 200. The political composition of the House meant that a Labour government was vulnerable to defeat. In the period of Labour government from 1974 to 1979, the government suffered 362 defeats at the hands of the House of Lords. However, Conservative governments were not immune. The preponderance of Conservative peers did not always translate into a majority for a Conservative government. In the period of Conservative government from 1979 to 1997, ministers suffered just over 250 defeats in the House. The government was vulnerable to a combination of opposition parties, the cross-benchers and, on occasion, some of its own supporters. The Labour government elected in 1997 was vulnerable to defeat, at least for the first two sessions, because of the large number of Conservative peers. Since the removal of most hereditary peers in 1999, it cannot be defeated by the Conservatives alone but is vulnerable to defeat because of a combination of opposition parties or

of the opposition and cross-benchers or of all the opposition parties and a preponderance of cross-benchers. From 1997 through to May 2009, the government suffered 489 defeats; of these, 419 took place in the post-1999 reformed House. A future Conservative government will be as vulnerable to the same combination of forces as the Labour government; as such, both parties now enjoy equality in the House.

The House also became more visible to the outside world. In 1985, television cameras were allowed to broadcast proceedings. There was a four-year gap before the televising of Commons proceedings began: in those four years, the House of Lords enjoyed exclusive television coverage. In the 1990s, the House was also ahead of the House of Commons in appointing an information officer and seeking to ensure better public understanding of its role and activities. The Information Office of the House has been highly active in disseminating information about the work of the House, generating booklets and information packs for which the House of Commons has no equivalent.

■ Procedures

The House differs significantly from the Commons not only in its size, composition and remuneration (peers can claim allowances to cover travel, accommodation, subsistence and some secretarial support, but they still receive no salary) but also in its procedures. The presiding officer of the House, who sits on the Woolsack, has no powers to call peers to speak or to enforce order. The maintenance of the rules of order is the responsibility of the House itself, although peers usually look to the Leader of the House to give a lead. Peers wishing to speak in a set-piece debate, such as a second reading debate, submit their names in advance (they can now do so electronically), and a list of speakers is circulated shortly prior to the debate. Peers then rise to speak in the order on the list. At other times, as in Question Time, if two peers rise at the same time, one is expected to give way. (If neither does so, other peers make clear their preference as to who should speak by shouting out the name of the person they wish to hear.) If a speaker strays from what is permissible, other peers shout 'Order'. If a speaker goes on for too long, it is always open to another peer to rise and call attention to the fact (a task normally undertaken by the government whip on duty) or, in extreme cases, to move the motion 'That the noble peer be no longer heard', but this is a device rarely employed. The Lords remains a more chamber-oriented institution than the Commons, although – as we shall see – it is making more use of committees than before. Although the House votes more frequently than it used to, the number of divisions in the Lords is fewer than in the Commons. (There will usually be about three times as many votes each year in the Commons as in the Lords.) This in part reflects the recognition by peers of the political predominance of the elected chamber. Peers are often reluctant to press issues to a vote and rarely do so on the principle of a measure. By virtue of an agreement reached between the two party leaders in the Lords in 1945, the House does not divide on the second reading of any bill promised in the government's election manifesto and, by extension now, any bill appearing in the government's programme for the session. This is known as the Salisbury convention, named after the Conservative leader in the Lords who enunciated it.

There are also two other features where it differs from the Commons and which enhance its capacity to affect the outcome of legislation. First, the House discusses all amendments tabled to bills. In the Commons, the chair selects only a limited number for debate. Second, there are no timetable (guillotine) motions. Debate continues so long as peers wish to speak. There are also considerable opportunities for peers to raise issues in the House. Some debates are time-limited (although not the committee and report stages of bills) and a fifteen-minute time limit operates for backbench speeches in set-piece debates. Peers keep their speeches even shorter if a great many of them sign up to speak in a time-limited debate. Time limits force peers to think about what they want to say and to ensure that they focus on the main points. The results tend to be a series of short, informed and often highly educative speeches.

■ Functions

The debate about reform of the House of Lords has focused largely, though not wholly, on its composition. The functions of the House – the tasks that it carries out – have not generated as much controversy. There has been a wide body of agreement that the functions it fulfilled in the twentieth century, and continues to fulfil in the twenty-first, are appropriate to a second chamber. As we shall see, this view is not necessarily held by all those expressing views on the House of Lords. Nonetheless, the view has tended to predominate among those engaged in the debate, including the government of the day. The functions are broadly similar to those of the Commons but not as extensive. The extent to which they differ derives from the fact that politically the House is no longer co-equal with the Commons.

Legitimisation

The House fulfils the functions of both manifest and latent legitimisation, but on a modest scale. It is called upon to give the seal of approval to bills, but if it fails to give that approval, it can be overridden later by the House of Commons under the provisions of the Parliament Acts. Only in very rare circumstances – as in the case of a bill to lengthen the life of a parliament, secondary legislation or (somewhat more significantly) bills originating in the Lords – is its veto absolute. By virtue of being one of the two chambers of Parliament and by fulfilling the functions it does effectively, the House may have a limited claim to fulfilling a function of latent legitimisation. It is a long-established part of the nation's constitutional arrangements. However, such a claim is offset by the House having no claim to being a representative assembly – neither speaking for particular bodies in society nor being socially typical – and by its limited legislative authority. A claim to traditional authority has been superseded by a claim to specialised knowledge, the House being able to draw on experience and expertise in considering the measures before it, but that 'technocratic' legitimacy is not on a par with the legitimacy of the elected chamber.

Recruitment

The House provides some of the personnel of government. As we have seen (Chapter 9), ministers are drawn from Parliament and, by convention, predominantly now from the elected House.

The Prime Minister appoints a number of ministers from the Upper House primarily for political and managerial reasons. Although the government is normally assured of getting its bills through the House, it is not necessarily guaranteed getting them through in the form it wants them. It is therefore prudent to have ministers in the Lords in order to explain bills and to marshal support. In addition, the House provides a pool from which the Prime Minister can draw in order to supplement ministers drawn from the Commons. The advantage offered by peers is that, with no constituency responsibilities, they are able to devote more time to ministerial work than is the case with ministers who do have constituency duties. It also has the advantage of widening the pool of talent available to the Prime Minister. Someone from outside Parliament can be elevated to the peerage at the same time as being appointed to government office. Both Tony Blair and his successor, Gordon Brown, made use of this power to enhance the ranks of their ministerial team, each bringing in a range of people from industry (Lord Sainsbury, Lord Simon of Highbury, Lord Jones of Birmingham, Baroness Vadera), the law (Lord Falconer of Thoroton), broadcasting (Lord MacDonald of Tradeston, Lord Carter of Barnes), the health service (Lord Darzi), finance (Lord Myners, Lord Davies of Abersoch), the military (Admiral Lord West), the EU (Lord Mandelson, Baroness Kinnock), the UN (Lord Malloch-Brown) as well as some Downing Street advisers (Baroness Morgan of Huyton, Lord Adonis), to serve as ministers.

Ministerial appointments in the Lords have also enabled women politicians to be promoted. Five women have served as Leaders of the House of Lords (Baroness Young 1981–2, Baroness Jay 1998–2001, Baroness Amos 2003–07, Baroness Ashton 2007–08, and Baroness Royall 2008–). Of the ministers in the Lords in mid-2009, approximately one-third were women. Baroness Amos was the first black woman to serve in the Cabinet. Baroness Scotland was the first woman and first black person to serve as Attorney General.

However, the number of ministers appointed in the Lords is relatively small. At least two peers have traditionally served in the Cabinet (Lord Chancellor and Leader of the House) but usually no more than four. Four is a rarity and two, until 2005, the norm. Under the Constitutional Reform Act 2005, the Lord Chancellor need no longer be a peer; Jack Straw was the first MP to be appointed to the post. There is thus now only the Leader of the House who sits automatically in the Cabinet. However, there have been occasions when a peer has been appointed to head a department. Gordon Brown appointed two peers to head departments: Business Secretary Lord Mandelson and Transport Secretary Lord Adonis. Usually about 20 other ministers are drawn from the Lords, supplemented by eight whips (including the Chief Whip). The number of ministers does not match the number of ministries, with the result that the whips have to take on responsibility for answering for particular departments – another difference from the House of Commons, where the whips have no responsibility for appearing at the despatch box. A frequent speaker at the despatch box is the government deputy chief whip, who often represents one or more senior departments without a junior minister. Even with a small number of posts to be filled, governments have on occasion had difficulty in finding suitable peers for ministerial office. It used to be the case that Conservative governments had sometimes to draw on young hereditary peers. Labour governments were limited by the relatively small number of Labour peers. The creation of life peerages in recent years, quantitatively and qualitatively, has widened the pool of talent. Both sides have tended to use the Whips' Office as a training ground for substantive ministerial office.

Scrutiny and influence

It is in its remaining functions that the House of Lords is significant. The House performs an important role as an agent of scrutiny and influence. The House does not undertake the task of scrutiny on behalf of constituents, as peers have none. Rather, the House undertakes a more general task of scrutiny. Three features of the House render it particularly suitable for the detailed scrutiny of legislation. First, as an unelected House, it cannot claim the legitimacy to reject the principle of measures agreed by the elected House. Thus, basically by default, it focuses on the detail rather than the principle. Second, as we have noted already, its membership includes people who have distinguished themselves in particular fields – such as the sciences, the law, education, business, industrial relations – who can look at relevant legislation from the perspective of practitioners in the field rather than from the perspective of elected party politicians. And, third, the House has the time to debate non-money bills in more detail than is usually possible in the Commons – as we have seen, there is no provision for a guillotine, and all amendments are discussed. The House thus serves as an important revising chamber, trying to ensure that a bill is well drafted and internally coherent. In order to improve the bill, it will often make amendments, most of which will be accepted by the Commons. In terms of legislative scrutiny, the House has thus developed a role that is viewed as complementary to, rather than one competing with (or identical to), that of the Commons.

The value of the House as a revising chamber is shown by the number of amendments it makes to legislation. Most of these are moved by the government itself, but a significant proportion of these are amendments promised by government in response to comments made by backbench members. Each session, the House will typically agree 1,000 to 4,000 amendments to bills. (In the 1999–2000 session, the number of amendments made totalled 4,761, constituting an all-time record.) In the 2007–08 session, of 7,259 amendments that were tabled, 2,625 were agreed (House of Lords 2008).

Even these figures do not do justice to the scrutiny undertaken by the Lords. The scrutiny is frequently constructive and is acknowledged as such by the government. Thus, for example, during the 1998–9 session, 108 non-government amendments were moved to the Access to Justice Bill. Of these, 71 received a ministerial response that was positive. The responses were important not only for their number but also for their range: they included promising to consider points raised in debate (28 occasions), accepting the principle of an amendment (21 occasions) and promising to draw a point to the attention of those responsible for drafting the bill (three occasions) (Norton 1999). Ten amendments were accepted as they stood. The constructive work undertaken by the House was conceded by the Lord Chancellor, Lord Irvine of Lairg, at the conclusion of the bill's passage through the House. The importance of these figures lay not only in the number of constructive responses from government but also in the fact that it is difficult to envisage scrutiny in the House of Commons producing such a response.

This role in scrutinising legislation – in so far as it constitutes a 'second look' at legislation – is of special importance given that it has been characterised as one of the two core functions of the House (Norton 1999), meaning that it is a function that is particular to the House as the second chamber. It is not a function that the House of Commons can carry out, since it is difficult if not impossible for it to act as a revising chamber for its own measures; that has been likened to asking the same doctor for a second opinion. The role of the House as a revising chamber is thus offered as being central to the case for retaining a second chamber. It is also the role that occupies the most time in the House: usually about 50 to 60 per cent is devoted to considering legislation.

The House also scrutinises, and on occasion influences, government policy. Peers can debate policy in a less partisan atmosphere than the Commons and are not subject to the constituency and party influences that dominate in the elected House. They are therefore in a position to debate issues of public policy that may not be at the heart of the partisan battle and which, consequently, receive little attention in the Commons. Given their backgrounds, peers are also often – although not always – able to debate public policy from the perspective of those engaged in the subject. The House is able to debate higher education, for example, with considerable authority. The Lords contains several distinguished academics and members with experience in higher education (university chancellors, vice-chancellors and pro-vice-chancellors, masters of university colleges, peers who have chaired HE funding bodies, led inquiries into higher education, and former secretaries of state for education); although the House of Commons contains some former university lecturers, it does not have members with the same experience and status in education as those in the Upper House.

Expression

The House, like the Commons, also fulfils a number of expressive functions. It can bring issues onto the political agenda in a way not always possible in the Commons. MPs are wary of raising issues that may not be popular with constituents and that have little salience in terms of party politics. Peers are answerable to no one but themselves. They can raise whatever issues they feel need raising. The House may thus debate issues of concern to particular groups in society that MPs are not willing to address. Formally, it is not a function the House is expected to fulfil. Indeed, according to *Erskine May*, the parliamentary 'bible' on procedure, Lords may indicate that an outside body agrees with the substance of their views, but they should avoid creating an impression that they are speaking as representatives of outside bodies. Thus, not only is the House not a representative assembly, it should avoid giving the impression of being one! In practice, peers take up issues that concern them, often alerted to the issue by outside bodies. Peers are frequently lobbied by outside organisations. One extensive survey in the 1990s found that half of the groups surveyed were in touch with peers at least once a month, and almost one in five were in contact on a weekly basis (Baggott 1995: 93, 164). Each peer receives letters each year usually running into four figures, most from outside organisations. Some groups write to ask peers to move amendments to bills, some merely keep members informed of what is happening with the organisation, and some are keen that peers raise issues with government, if necessary on the floor of the House. Some peers are particularly active in raising the concerns of particular groups, such as farmers, the disabled, the terminally ill, or the people of Zimbabwe, or pursuing very particular issues, such as railways, the effects of smoking or the upkeep of war graves.

The House also has the potential to express views to citizens and influence their stance on public policy. The function is limited by the absence of any democratic legitimacy, the capacity to influence deriving from the longevity of the House and its place as one of the two chambers of Parliament, as well as from the authority of the individual peers who may be involved. However, the scope for fulfilling this function is somewhat greater than in the House of Commons, simply because more time is available for it in the House of Lords. Between 20 and 30 per cent of the time of the House is given over each session to debates on motions tabled by peers: about 20 per cent of time is given over to general debates, and between 4 and 10 per cent of the time is given over to questions for short debate (QSDs), each lasting for 60 or 90 minutes.

Other functions

To these functions may be added a number of others, some of which are peculiar to the Upper House. Foremost among these historically has been the judicial function. The House until 2009 constituted the highest court of appeal within the United Kingdom. Although formally a function residing in the House as a whole, in practice it was carried out by a judicial committee comprising twelve **law lords** – judges specially appointed to the House to enable it to fulfil its judicial role – and peers who have held high judicial office. The law lords, though members of the House, avoided speaking on any matters that may be deemed partisan or involve measures on which they may later have had to adjudicate in a judicial capacity. They also normally abstained from voting, though on occasion a law lord voted on

an issue that had been the subject of a free vote. However, this long-standing judicial function ceased to reside in the House in 2009, when a new supreme court, created under the Constitutional Reform Act 2005, came into being (see Chapter 13) and the law lords moved from the Palace of Westminster to form the justices of the new court.

Like the Commons, the House also retains a small legislative role, primarily in the form of private members' legislation. Peers can introduce private members' bills, and a small number achieve passage, but it is small – even compared with the number of such bills promoted by MPs. The introduction of such bills by peers is more important in fulfilling an expressive function – allowing views on the subject to be aired – than in fulfilling a legislative role. Time is normally found to debate each private member's bill and, by convention, the government – even if opposed to the measure – does not divide against it. Among contentious issues raised by such bills has been that of decriminalising the actions of those seeking to assist terminally ill individuals who wish to bring their lives to an end (assisted dying). The Assisted Dying Bill introduced by Lord Joffe in the 2004–05 session helped ensure that the issue was discussed and enabled people with views on the issue to make them known. The time given to private members' legislation is important but not extensive: as in the Commons, it occupies usually less than 5 per cent of the time of the House.

The House is also ascribed a distinct role, that of a constitutional safeguard. This is reflected in the provisions of the Parliament Acts. The House, as we have noted, retains a veto over bills to extend the life of a parliament. It is considered a potential brake on a government that seeks to act in a dictatorial or generally unacceptable manner: hence it may use its limited power to amend or, more significantly, to delay a bill. In practice, though, the power is a limited one, as well as one not expected to require action by the House on any regular basis. The House lacks a legitimate elected base of its own that would allow it to act, on a substantial and sustained basis, contrary to the wishes of an elected government. Even so, it constitutes the other core function of the House in that it is a function that the House alone, as the second chamber, can fulfil: the House of Commons cannot act as a constitutional check upon itself.

In combination, these various functions render the House a useful body – especially as a revising chamber and for raising and debating issues on which peers are well informed – but one that is clearly subordinate to the elected chamber. The fact that the House is not elected explains its limited functions; it is also the reason why it is considered particularly suited to fulfil the functions it does retain.

■ Scrutiny and influence

The means available to the House to fulfil the tasks of scrutiny and influence can be considered, as with the Commons, under two heads: legislation and executive actions. The means available to the House are also those available to fulfil its expressive functions.

Legislation

As we have seen, 50 to 60 per cent of the time of the House is given over to legislation. Bills in the Lords have to go through stages analogous to those in the House of Commons. There are, though, differences in procedure. First readings are normally taken formally, but there have been rare occasions when they have been debated: on four occasions (in 1888, 1933, 1943 and 1969) first readings were actually opposed. Second readings, as in the Commons, constitute debates on the principle of the measure. However, votes on second reading are exceptionally rare. Because of the Salisbury convention, the House does not vote on the second reading of government bills. A vote may take place if, as exceptionally happens, a free vote is permitted. This happened in 1990 on the War Crimes Bill and in 1999 on the Sexual Offences (Amendment) Bill to lower the age of consent for homosexual acts to 16. Both bills had been passed by large majorities in the House of Commons but both were rejected, on free votes, in the House of Lords. Both occasions were exceptional. Both measures were later enacted under the provisions of the Parliament Act.

The main work of the House takes place at committee and report stages. For some bills, the committee stage is actually dispensed with. After second reading, a motion may be moved 'That this Bill be not committed' and, if agreed to, the bill then awaits third reading. This procedure is usually employed for supply and money bills when there is no desire to present amendments. For those bills that do receive a committee stage, it is taken either on the floor of the House or in grand committee. Virtually all bills used to be taken on the floor of the House, but now in order to ensure that the House continues to examine all bills in detail, several are considered in grand committee.

The grand committee is, in effect, something of a parallel chamber. It comprises all members of the House and can meet while the House is in session. In practice, attendance is relatively small – comprising those with a particular interest in the measure – permitting sessions to be held in the Moses Room, an ornate committee room just off the Peers' Lobby. In 2007–08, 13 bills were considered in grand committee. Votes cannot take place in grand committee, so amendments can only be accepted if no member objects. (If objection is made, the matter has to be held over to report stage.) Of 1,769 amendments moved in grand committee in 2007–08, 357 were accepted.

More recently, the House has also experimented with sending a bill to a special procedure public bill committee, which is empowered to take oral and written evidence. Of longer standing is the power to refer a bill, or indeed any proposal, to a select committee for detailed investigation. It is a power that has been utilised when it has been considered necessary or desirable to examine witnesses and evidence from outside bodies. Between 1972 and 1991, seven bills were sent to select committees. All bar one of the bills were private members' bills. More recently, select committees have been appointed to consider a major government bill (the Constitutional Reform Bill) and a Private Member's Bill (the Assisted Dying for the Terminally Ill).

Committee stage in the Lords differs notably from committee stage in the Commons. In the Lords, all amendments tabled are debated and – whether on the floor or in Grand Committee – any peer can attend the proceedings. All peers with an interest or expertise in a measure can thus take part, be it for the whole of the committee stage or on particular amendments of interest to them. There is thus the potential for a more thorough consideration than is possible in the Commons. The emphasis is on ensuring that the bill is well drafted and coherent.

Report and third reading provide further opportunities for consideration. Again, all amendments tabled are debated. Report may be used by government to bring forward amendments promised at committee stage and also to offer new amendments of its own. It is also an opportunity for members to return to issues that received an inadequate response by government at committee stage (although amendments rejected by the House at committee stage cannot again be considered). It is also possible for amendments to be made at third reading, and this opportunity is variously employed. The motion for third reading is put formally and agreed to and then amendments are taken. Once they have been dealt with, the motion 'That the Bill do now pass' is put. The result is that some bills, especially large or contentious bills, can and do receive a considerable amount of attention at different stages in the House of Lords.

Executive actions

As in the House of Commons, various means are available for scrutinising the actions of the executive. The principal means available on the floor of the House are those of debate and questions. Off the floor of the House, there are select committees and, at the unofficial level, party meetings.

Debates

Debates, as in the Commons, take place on motions. These may express a particular view, or they may take the form of either 'take note' motions or motions calling for papers. 'Take note' motions are employed in order to allow the House to debate reports from select committees or to discuss topics on which the government wishes to hear peers' views: ministers use 'take note' motions rather than motions calling for papers because with the latter they are responsible for supplying the papers being called for. Motions calling for papers are used by backbenchers to call attention to a particular issue; at the end of the debate it is customary to withdraw the motion, the purpose for which it was tabled – to ensure a debate – having been achieved.

All peers who wish to speak in debate do so, and there is a greater likelihood than in the Commons that the proceedings will constitute what they purport to be: that is, debates. Party ties are less rigid than in the Commons, though nonetheless still strong (see Norton 2003), and peers frequently pay attention to what is being said. Although the order in which peers speak is determined beforehand, it is common practice for a peer who is speaking to give way to interventions. Within the context of the chamber, the chances of a speech having an impact on the thought and even the votes of others are considerably greater than in the more predictable

Lower House. Indeed, it is not unknown for peers when, uncertain as to how to vote, to ask 'what does X think about it?'.

One day each week, up until the Whit recess, is given over to two general debates. (The debate day used to be Wednesday but in 2005 the House agreed to change it to Thursday.) Once a month, the debates are determined by ballot. Peers wishing to have debates submit motions which then appear on the order paper and two are drawn at random by the clerk on a set day. The topics on the remaining debate days are allocated to each of the parties in turn and to the cross-benchers. The two debates last up to a total of five hours. The balloted debates are automatically each of two-and-a-half hours in length. On the party days, the time, within the five-hour maximum, is varied depending on the number of speakers. These general debates are occasions for issues to be raised by backbenchers rather than frontbenchers. The purpose of each short debate is to allow peers to discuss a particular topic rather than to come to a conclusion about it. Topics discussed tend to be non-partisan, and the range is broad. On 21 May 2009, for example, Lord Dixon-Smith moved a motion to call attention to the changes required of society to meet the 2050 carbon dioxide emissions target set by the Climate Change Committee and Lord Moynihan moved a motion to call attention to the impact of disease on the British bee population, the spread of the varroa mite and the consequences for the pollination of crops and fruit. Both motions provided the opportunity for interested peers to offer their views and for ministers to explain the government's position and to reveal what proposals were under consideration by the relevant department. The time devoted to each debate is divided equally among the number of backbench speakers (the opener and the minister replying have fixed time limits) and, in the event of many peers wishing to speak, the time available to each may be as little as four or five minutes.

Questions

Questions taken on the floor in the Lords are of two types: oral questions and questions for short debate (QSD). (Lords may also table questions for written answer, and nowadays they do so in increasing numbers: often more than 5,000 a session.) Oral questions are taken in Question Time at the start of each sitting: the House sits at 2.30 p.m. on Monday and Tuesday, 3.00 p.m. on Wednesday and 11.00 a.m. on

NOTICES AND ORDERS OF THE DAY

Tuesday 28 April 2009 at 2.30pm
Lord Collins of Mapesbury *will be introduced as a Lord of Appeal in Ordinary*

*Oral questions, 30 minutes

*Lord Dykes to ask Her Majesty's Government when they next expect to hold discussions on climate change issues with the Czech Presidency of the European Union.

*Baroness Warsi to ask Her Majesty's Government what is their position on polygamous marriage in the United Kingdom.

*Lord James of Blackheath to ask Her Majesty's Government what controls they will apply to ensure that Scottish banks printing money do not do so at a level that would disproportionately favour the Scottish economy.

*Lord Dubs to ask Her Majesty's Government how many homeowners will be helped by the recently announced Homeowners Mortgage Support Scheme; and what is the forecast cost of it.

Health Bill [HL] Report [Lord Darzi of Denham] *11th Report from the Joint Committee on Human Rights*

Baroness Howells of St Davids to ask Her Majesty's Government what steps they will take to ensure that the United Nations can act in accordance with the objectives outlined in the preamble to the Charter of the United Nations. *(Dinner break business, 1 hour)*

In the Moses Room at 3.30pm

Perpetuities and Accumulations Bill [HL] Second Reading Committee [Lord Bach]

The following two motions are expected to be debated together:

European Communities (Definition of Treaties) (United Nations Convention on the Rights of Persons with Disabilities) Order 2009 Consideration in Grand Committee [Lord McKenzie of Luton] *10th Report from the Joint Committee on Statutory Instruments*

Lord Lester of Herne Hill to move that the Grand Committee do consider the Report of the Joint Committee on Human Rights on the United Nations Convention on the Rights of Persons with Disabilities: Reservations and Interpretative Declaration (12th Report, HL Paper 70).

Figure 16.2 House of Lords order paper: in the House of Lords, questions are addressed to Her Majesty's Government and not to a particular minister

Thursday. (If sitting on a Friday, it sits at 10.00 a.m. but no questions are taken.) Question Time lasts for up to a maximum of 30 minutes and no more than four questions may be taken. Questions are similar to those tabled for oral answer in the Commons, although – unlike in the Commons – they are addressed to Her Majesty's Government and not to a particular minister (see Figure 16.2). Also, there is no departmental rota: the questions may be to different departments. A question to an environment minister, for example, may be followed by one to a defence minister. A peer rises to ask the question appearing in his or her name on the order paper, the relevant minister (or whip) replies for the government, and then supplementary questions – confined to the subject of the original question – follow. This procedure, assuming the maximum number of questions is tabled (it usually is), allows for seven to eight minutes for each question, the peer who tabled the motion by tradition being allowed to ask

the first supplementary. Hence, although Question Time is shorter than in the Commons, the concentration on a particular question is much greater and allows for more probing.

At the end of the day's sitting, or during what is termed the 'dinner hour' (when the House breaks in mid-evening from the main business), there is also usually a QSD (as, for example, Baroness Howell's question shown in Figure 16.2). If taken during the dinner hour, debate lasts for a maximum of 60 minutes. If taken as the last business of the day, it lasts for a maximum of 90 minutes. Peers who wish to speak do so – signing up in advance – and the appropriate minister replies to the debate. The advantages of QSDs are similar to those of the half-hour adjournment debates in the Commons, except that in this case there is a much greater opportunity for other members to participate. It is not unknown for the number of speakers to run into double-figures. The topics are generally varied and non-partisan. On

12 May 2009, for example, Lord Rodgers of Quarry Bank raised the role of privy counsellors; the following evening, Lord Jones of Cheltenham asked what assessment the Government had made of the future of St Helena, and the following night Lord Richard asked whether the Government would accord formal recognition to the men and women of Bomber Command during the Second World War.

Committees

Although the House remains a chamber-oriented institution, it has made greater use in recent years of committees. Apart from a number of established committees dealing, for example, with domestic function of the House, it has variously made use of ad hoc select committees. Some ad hoc committees have been appointed to consider the desirability of certain legislative measures. A number have been appointed to consider issues of public policy. (Some are also appointed to deal with essentially internal matters, such as the speakership of the House.) The House has also made use of its power to create sessional select committees, i.e. committees appointed regularly from session to session rather than for the purpose of one particular inquiry. The House has

three long-established committees with reputations as high-powered bodies. They have been joined by three more, plus a joint committee.

The most prominent of the established committees is the *European Union Committee* (known, until 1999, as the European Communities Committee). Established in 1974, it undertakes scrutiny of draft European legislation, seeking to identify those proposals that raise important questions of principle or policy and which deserve consideration by the House. All documents are sifted by the chairman of the committee – who also holds the formal and salaried position of deputy chairman of committees – with those deemed potentially important being sent to a subcommittee. The committee works through seven subcommittees (see Table 16.2), each subcommittee comprising two or more members of the main committee and several co-opted members. In total, the subcommittees draw on the services of 70 to 80 peers. Each subcommittee covers a particular area. Subcommittee E, for example, deals with law and institutions. Members are appointed on the basis of their particular expertise. Subcommittee E includes some eminent lawyers – it was, until 2009, chaired by a law lord – as well as members who have experience of government. A subcommittee, having

Table 16.2 Committees in the House of Lords, July 2009

Name of Committee	Chairman
Communications	Rt Hon. Lord Fowler (Con)
Constitution	Rt Hon. Lord Goodlad (Con)
Delegated Powers and Regulatory Reform	Lord Godhart QC (Lib Dem)
Economic Affairs	Lord Vallance of Tummel (Lib Dem)
Subcommittee on the Finance Bill	Lord Vallance of Tummel (Lib Dem)
European Union Committee	Rt Hon. Lord Roper (Non-affiliated)
Subcommittees:	
A. Economic and financial affairs, and international trade	Baroness Cohen of Pimlico (Lab)
B. Internal market	Rt Hon. Lord Freeman (Con)
C. Foreign affairs, defence and development policy	Lord Teverson (Lib Dem)
D. Environment and agriculture	Lord Sewel (Lab)
E. Law and institutions	Rt Hon. Lord Mance (Law Lord)
F. Home affairs	Rt Hon. Lord Jopling (Con)
G. Social policy and consumer affairs	Baroness Howarth of Breckland (Cross-bench)
Merits of Statutory Instruments	Lord Filkin (Lab)
Science and Technology	Lord Sutherland of Houndwood (Cross-bench)
[Joint Committee on Human Rights	Andrew Dismore MP (Lab)]

had documents referred to it, can decide that the document requires no further consideration, or can call in evidence from government departments and outside bodies. If it decides that a document requires further consideration, then it is held 'under scrutiny' – that is, subject to the scrutiny reserve. The government cannot, except in exceptional circumstances, agree to a proposal in the Council of Ministers if it is still under scrutiny by Parliament.

Written evidence to a subcommittee may be supplemented by oral evidence and, on occasion (though not often), a minister may be invited to give evidence in person. The subcommittees prepare reports for the House (in total, about 20 to 30 a year), including recommendations as to whether the documents should be debated by the House. (About 2 per cent of the time of the House is taken up debating EU documents, usually on 'take note' motions.) The EU Committee has built up an impressive reputation as a thorough and informed body, issuing reports that are more extensive than its counterpart in the Commons, and which are considered authoritative both within Whitehall and in the institutions of the EU. The House, like the chambers of other national legislatures, has had no formal role in the European legislative process (see Norton 1996) and so has no power, other than that of persuasion, to affect outcomes. The significance of the reports, therefore, has tended to lie in informing debate rather than in changing particular decisions (Norton 2005: 153).

The *Select Committee on Science and Technology* was appointed in 1979 following the demise of the equivalent committee in the Commons. (The Commons committee has since been re-created.) The remit of the committee – 'to consider science and technology' – is wide, and its inquiries have covered a broad range. The committee is essentially non-partisan in approach and benefits from a number of peers with an expertise in the subject. Recent chairmen have included the President of the Royal Academy of Engineers and a former rector of the Imperial College of Science, Technology and Medicine. For its inquiry into pandemic influenza in 2005 it co-opted Lord May, the President of the Royal Academy (a former chief scientific adviser to the government), and Lord Soulsby of Swaffham Prior, President of the Royal Institute of Public Health (and previously a professor of parasitology). In recent sessions it has investigated genomic medicine, nanotechnologies and food, pandemic influenza, personal Internet security, science and

technology research funding priorities, systematics and taxonomy, and waste reduction. The committee has raised issues that otherwise might have been neglected by government – and certainly not considered in any depth by the Commons – and various of its reports have proved influential (see Grantham 1993; Hayter 1992).

The *Delegated Powers and Regulatory Reform Committee*, previously known as the Delegated Powers and Deregulation Committee, looks at whether powers of delegated legislation in a bill are appropriate and makes recommendations to the House accordingly (see Himsworth 1995). It also reports on documents under the Regulatory Reform Act 2001, which allows regulations in primary legislation to be removed by secondary legislation. The committee has established itself as a powerful and informed committee, its recommendations being taken seriously by the House and by government. Indeed, it is standard practice for the government to accept its recommendations. At report stage of the Access to Justice Bill in February 1999, for example, the government moved 34 amendments to give effect to the recommendations of the committee.

These committees have been supplemented by three more. The *Constitution Committee* was established in 2001 to report on the constitutional implications of public bills and to keep the operation of the constitution under review. It regularly issues reports on the constitutional implications of bills and has published major reports on, among other topics, the process of constitutional change, devolution, inter-institutional relations in the UK, the regulatory state, Parliament and the legislative process, the surveillance state, and the relations between Parliament, the executive and the courts. The *Economic Affairs Committee* was also appointed in 2001. It has published reports on banking supervision and regulation, the impact of economic sanctions, the current state of monetary policy, apprenticeship, and the state of the British economy. It has also established a subcommittee to consider the annual Finance Bill. The *Communications Committee* is the most recent of the sessional committees, having been appointed in 2007. It succeeded an ad hoc committee on the BBC Charter Renewal. Since its creation, it has undertaken a number of in-depth studies, publishing reports on the chairmanship of the BBC, the ownership of the news, government communications, and public service broadcasting.

As a consequence of the passage of the Human Rights Act 1998, the two Houses have also created a

Joint Committee on Human Rights. The committee is chaired by an MP, but it follows Lords procedures. It has six members drawn from each House. It considers matters relating to human rights and has functions relating to remedial orders (bringing UK law into line with the European Convention on Human Rights) under the 1998 Act. Its main task is reporting to the House on bills that have implications for human rights. It was particularly influential, for example, in reporting on the Anti-Terrorism, Crime and Security Bill in 2001. In the light of the committee's report, and pressure from members in both chambers, the government agreed to make changes to the bill.

These permanent committees are variously supplemented by ad hoc committees, appointed to consider particular issues. Committees reporting in the twenty-first century have covered the monetary policy committee of the Bank of England (2001), stem cell research (2002), the crash of Chinook helicopter ZD576 (2002), animals in scientific procedures (2002), religious offences (2003), the Constitutional Reform Bill (2004), the Assisted Dying for the Terminally Ill Bill (2005), the speakership of the House (2006), economic regulators (2007), intergovernmental organisations (2008), and the Barnett Formula (2009). Most of these attracted considerable media attention. The report on the Chinook helicopter crash was debated in both Houses. Various ad hoc joint committees have also been appointed to consider draft bills; one was also appointed to consider the conventions applying to the Lords.

The committees thus constitute a valuable and growing supplement to the work undertaken on the floor of the House. They allow the House to specialise to some degree and to draw on the expertise of its membership, an expertise that cannot be matched by the elected House of Commons. Like select committees in the Commons, the committees choose their own topics of inquiry. However, unlike the Commons committees, there is no government majority. A typical 12-member committee will comprise four Labour peers, four Conservatives, two Liberal Democrats and two cross-benchers. The composition in terms of expertise and political affiliation encourages a notable bipartisan approach.

The committees also fulfil an important expressive function. They take evidence from interested bodies – the submission of written evidence is extensive – thus allowing groups an opportunity to get their views on the public record. Given the expertise of the committees, reports are treated as weighty documents by interested groups; consequently, the committees enjoy some capacity to raise support for particular measures of public policy. Committees also have the capacity to elicit a government response at the despatch box as well as in writing. The government provides a written response to each committee report – agreeing in 2005 to do so within two months, bringing it into line with the Commons – but if the committee recommends that a report be debated in the House, then time is found to debate it. The House has agreed that such debates should be in prime time, but this is not always possible to achieve.

Party meetings

The parties in the Lords are organised, with their own leaders and whips. Even the cross-benchers, allied to no party, have their own elected leader (known as the convenor) and circulate a weekly document detailing the business for the week ahead. (They even have their own website: www.crossbenchpeers.org.uk.) However, neither the Conservative nor the Labour Party in the Lords has a committee structure. Instead, peers are able to attend the Commons backbench committees or policy group meetings, and a number do so. Any attempt at influence through the party structure in the Lords, therefore, takes the form of talking to the whips or of raising the issue at the weekly party meeting.

Party meetings, as well as those of cross-bench peers, are held each week. (The meeting day has changed in recent years, following changes to the arrangement of business in the House.) Such meetings are useful for discussing future business as well as for hearing from invited speakers. For example, in meetings of the Association of Conservative Peers (ACP) – the Lords equivalent to the 1922 Committee – the business usually comprises a short talk by a member of the executive of the 1922 Committee about developments in the Commons, the Chief Whip announcing the business for the following week, and a discussion on a particular issue or a talk from a frontbencher or expert on a particular subject. When a major bill is coming before the House, the relevant member of the Shadow Cabinet (or, if in government, minister) may be invited to attend, along with a junior spokesperson, to brief peers on the bill. Sometimes party meetings have the characteristics of a specialist committee, since often peers with an expertise in the topic will attend and question the speaker. For a minister or shadow minister, or even an expert speaker, the occasion may be a testing one, having to justify a measure or proposal before an often well-informed audience.

Party meetings are useful as two-way channels of communication between leaders and led in the Lords and, in a wider context, between a party's supporters in the Lords and the leadership of the whole party. Given the problems of ensuring structured and regular contact between whips and their party's peers, the party meetings provide a useful means of gauging the mood of the regular attenders. They are also useful ways of enhancing communication with the Commons, former MPs often being active in the membership. In 2009, both the main party groups were chaired by ex-MPs.

■ Reform: stage one

Demands for reform of the House of Lords were a feature of both the late nineteenth century and the twentieth. As the democratic principle became more widely accepted in the nineteenth century, so calls for the reform of the unelected, Conservative-dominated House of Lords became more strident. Conservative obstruction of Liberal bills in the 1880s led the Liberal Lord Morley to demand that the Upper House 'mend or end', an approach adopted as Liberal policy in 1891. In 1894, the Liberal conference voted in favour of abolishing the Lords' power of veto. When the Lords rejected the Budget of the Liberal government in 1909, the government introduced the Parliament Bill. Passed in 1911, the preamble envisaged an elected House. An inter-party conference in 1918 proposed a scheme for phasing out the hereditary peers, but no time was found to implement the proposals. A 1948 party leaders' conference agreed that heredity alone should not be the basis for membership. Again, no action was taken. In 1969, the Parliament (No. 2) Bill, introduced by the Labour government led by Harold Wilson, sought to phase out the hereditary element. The bill foundered in the House of Commons after encountering opposition from Conservative MPs, led by Enoch Powell, who felt it went too far, and from Labour MPs, led by Michael Foot, who believed it did not go far enough. The willingness of the House of Lords to defeat the Labour government in the period from 1974 to 1979 reinforced Labour antagonism.

In 1983, the Labour Party manifesto committed the party to abolition of the Upper House. Under Neil Kinnock (leader 1983–92) this stance was softened. In its election manifesto in 1992, the party advocated instead an elected second chamber. This was later amended under Tony Blair's leadership to a two-stage reform: first, the elimination of the hereditary element; and, second and in a later Parliament, the introduction of a new reformed second chamber. The Liberal Democrats favoured a reformed second chamber – a senate – as part of a wider package of constitutional reform. Charter 88, the constitutional reform movement created in 1988 (see Chapter 13), included reform of the Upper House 'to establish a democratic, non-hereditary second chamber' as a fundamental part of its reform programme.

The Labour manifesto in the 1997 general election included the commitment to reform in two stages. 'The House of Lords', it declared, 'must be reformed. As an initial, self-contained reform, not dependent on further reform in the future, the rights of hereditary peers to sit and vote in the House of Lords will be ended by statute.' That, it said, would be the first step in a process of reform 'to make the House of Lords more democratic and representative'. A committee of both Houses of Parliament would be appointed to undertake a wide-ranging review of possible further change and to bring forward proposals for reform.

The Labour victory in the 1997 general election provided a parliamentary majority to give effect to the manifesto commitment. However, anticipating problems in the House of Lords, the government delayed bringing in a bill to remove hereditary peers until the second session of the parliament. The bill, introduced in January 1999, had one principal clause which ended membership of the House of Lords on the basis of a hereditary peerage. It was passed by the House of Commons by a large majority. In the House of Lords, peers adhered to the Salisbury convention and did not vote on second reading. However, they subjected it to prolonged debate at committee and report stage. In the Lords, an amendment was introduced – and accepted by the government – providing that 92 peers should remain members of the interim House. The 92 would comprise 75 chosen by hereditary peers on a party basis (the number to be divided according to party strength among hereditary peers), 15 to be chosen by all members of the House for the purpose of being available to serve the House, for example as

Deputy Speakers, and the Earl Marshal and the Lord Great Chamberlain, in order to fulfil particular functions associated with their offices. The government had indicated in advance that it would accept the amendment, on condition that the Lords did not frustrate passage of the bill. Although the House made various other amendments to the bill, against the government's wishes, the bill made it eventually to the statute book. All bar the 92 hereditary peers exempted by the Act ceased to be members at the end of the session. When the House met for the state opening of Parliament on 17 November 1999, it was thus a very different House from that which had sat only the week before. It was still a House of Lords, but instead of a House with a membership based predominantly on the heredity principle, it was now primarily an appointed House, the bulk of the members being there by virtue of life peerages.

■ Reform: stage two

After the return of the Labour government in 1997, opponents criticised ministers for not having announced what form stage two of Lords reform would take. The government responded by appointing a Royal Commission on Reform of the House of Lords to consider reform in the light of other constitutional developments while having regard to the need to maintain the Commons as the pre-eminent chamber. The Commission, chaired by a Conservative peer, Lord Wakeham (a former Leader of both the House of Commons and the House of Lords), was appointed at the beginning of 1999 and was required to report by the end of the year. It held a number of public meetings in different parts of the country and completed its report by the end of 1999: it was published in January 2000.

In its report, *A House for the Future* (Cmd 4534), the Royal Commission recommended a House of 550 members, with a minority being elected. It identified three options for the size of the elected element:

1 *Option A*: 65 elected members, the 'election' taking place on the basis of votes cast regionally in a general election.

2 *Option B*: 87 elected members, directly elected at the same time as elections to the European Parliament.

3 *Option C*: 195 elected members, elected by proportional representation at the same time as European Parliament elections.

Under options B and C, a third of the members would be elected at each European Parliament election. A majority of the members of the Commission favoured option B. It was proposed that the regional members – whatever their number and method of selection – should serve for the equivalent of three electoral cycles and that the appointed members should serve for fixed terms of 15 years. Under the proposals, existing life peers would remain members of the House.

The Commission's report was extensive, but the reaction to it focused on its recommendations for election. Supporters of an appointed second chamber felt that it went too far. Supporters of an elected second chamber argued that it did not go far enough. Many critics of the report felt that at least 50 per cent of the members should be elected. The report did not get a particularly good press.

Although not well received by the press, the Commission's report was received sympathetically by the government. Following its 1997 manifesto commitment, it sought to set up a joint committee of both Houses, but the parties could not agree on what the committee should do. The Labour manifesto in the 2001 general election committed the government to completing reform of the House of Lords: 'We have given our support to the report and conclusions to the report of the Wakeham Commission, and will seek to implement them in the most effective way possible.' In November 2001, the government published a White Paper, 'Completing the Reform', proposing that 20 per cent of the members be elected. It invited comments, and the reaction it got was largely unfavourable. In a debate in the House of Commons, many Labour MPs argued that the White Paper did not go far enough. Both the Conservative and Labour parties supported a predominantly elected second chamber. The Public Administration Committee in the Commons issued a report, *The Second Chamber: Continuing the Reform*, arguing that, on the basis of the evidence it had taken, the 'centre of gravity' among those it had consulted was for a House with 60 per cent of the membership elected. An early day motion favouring a predominantly elected second chamber attracted the signatures of more than 300 MPs.

Recognising that its proposals were not attracting sufficient support in order to proceed, the government decided to hand over responsibility to Parliament itself. It recommended, and both Houses agreed to, the appointment of a joint committee. After meeting twice, the committee issued a short report explaining how it intended to proceed. It indicated that it would proceed in two stages. The first would involve looking at all the existing evidence and outlining options for the role and composition of the second chamber. The second would involve seeing whether the opinions expressed by both Houses on the options could be brought closer to one another, if not actually reconciled. The committee would then address more detailed matters, along with any outstanding issues concerning the functioning of Parliament and any constitutional settlement that might be necessary in determining the relations of the two Houses. 'The Committee believes that such a settlement would need to be robust, practical and command broad support in Parliament and beyond if it is to have any chance to endure.'

The committee completed the first stage of its work at the end of 2002, when it published a report addressing functions and composition. It argued that the existing functions of the House were appropriate. On composition, it listed seven options – ranging from an all-appointed to an all-elected House – and recommended that each House debate the options and then vote on each one. Both Houses debated the joint committee's report in January 2003. Opinion in the Commons was divided among the several options. Opinion in the Lords was strongly in favour of an all-appointed House. On 4 February, both Houses voted on the options. MPs voted down the all-appointed option but then proceeded to vote down all the remaining options favouring partial or total election (see Maclean *et al.* 2003; Norton 2004). (An amendment favouring unicameralism was also put and defeated.) Peers voted by a three-to-one majority in favour of the all-appointed option and, by a similar margin, against all the remaining options. Of the options, that of an all-appointed chamber was the only one to be carried by either House. The outcome of the votes in the Commons was unexpected – commentators had expected a majority in favour of one of the options supporting election (the vote on 80 per cent of members being elected was lost by three votes) – and it was widely assumed in the light of the votes that there was little chance of proceeding with moves towards a second stage of reform involving election (see Norton 2004: 195–7).

Instead, the government decided to introduce a bill to remove the remaining hereditary peers from the House of Lords, establish a statutory appointments commission and provide that peers could be expelled if convicted of an offence subject to a certain term of imprisonment. However, the government abandoned the idea when it failed to craft an amendment-proof bill: it feared that MPs might try to amend it by introducing provisions for election. Some parliamentarians sought to keep the issue on the political agenda. The debate divided between those who were interested in reforming the powers of the Upper House and those who wanted to change its composition.

Labour peers in the Lords established a working party to review the powers, procedures and conventions of the House. Its report, published in 2004, favoured a new Parliament Act, embodying a time limit for bills in the Lords (and for bills starting life in the Lords to be brought within the scope of the Act), as well as a codification of conventions (Labour Peers Group 2004). The recommendations received a mixed response from peers, but in replying the Lord Chancellor, Lord Falconer, indicated sympathy with the argument for putting a time limit on bills in the Lords.

The debate then switched to those who favoured a reform of the composition of the House. In 2005, five prominent MPs – including former Conservative Chancellor Ken Clarke and former Labour Foreign Secretary Robin Cook – published a reform tract, *Reforming the House of Lords*, in which they argued the case for a 350-member second chamber, with 70 per cent elected, the elected members serving for the equivalent of three parliaments and with one-third of the membership being renewed at each general election (Clarke *et al.* 2005). Led by Liberal Democrat Paul Tyler, they introduced a private member's bill, the Second Chamber of Parliament Bill, designed to give effect to their recommendations. The bill made no progress.

Labour's 2005 election manifesto showed that the government was drawn more to a reform of powers than a major change in composition. Declaring that a reformed Upper House 'must be effective, legitimate and more representative without challenging the primacy of the House of Commons', it said that, following a review by a committee of both Houses, 'we will seek agreement on codifying the key conventions of the Lords, and developing alternative forms of scrutiny that complement rather than replicate those of the Commons; the review should also explore how the upper chamber might offer a better route for public engagement in scrutiny and policy making.' It also committed the party to legislate to place 'reasonable limits on the time bills spend in the second chamber – no longer than 60 sitting days for most bills'. The paragraph dealing with composition was short: 'As part of the process of modernisation, we will remove the remaining heredi-tary peers and allow a free vote on the composition of the House.'

In the new 2005 parliament, a joint committee on conventions was appointed – it essentially endorsed the existing conventions, but made clear they would not necessarily be able to survive any substantial reform of the House – and the Government published another white paper on Lords reform (HM Government 2007), this time indicating a preference for a House with 50 per cent of the members elected and 50 per cent appointed. In March 2007, both Houses were again invited to vote on various options. Peers repeated their votes of 2003, voting by three-to-one in favour of an appointed House and against all the other options. However, on this occasion, MPs voted in favour of an 80 per cent elected House (by 305 votes to 267) as well as for a wholly elected House (by 337 votes to 224), though the majority for a wholly elected House was inflated by a substantial number of Labour MPs who opposed an elected House voting for the option in order to sabotage election: they reasoned that the Government would find unaccept-able a wholly elected House.

The Government responded by establishing a group of leading members of each party to discuss ways of implementing the decision of the Commons. The outcome was a white paper in July 2008 (Ministry of Justice 2008) which identified different options but which produced little by way of concrete recommendations: Justice Secretary Jack Straw conceded in the foreword that it was not 'a final blueprint for reform'. It was announced that the white paper would be debated in both Houses before the end of the session. The White Paper evoked a largely apathetic response and was over-shadowed by a range of other contentious issues. The debates in the two chambers never materialised. The government conceded that it would not be possible to legislate in that Parliament in order to create an elected chamber.

Various participants in the debate on the future of the House noted that the House of Lords that followed the Parliament Act of 1911 had been intended as an interim House until legislation could be passed to provide for a more democratic chamber. That interim House lasted for nearly 90 years. Some wondered whether the interim House that existed following the passage of the House of Lords Act might not now last a similar period of time.

■ The future of the second chamber?

The question of what to do with the House of Lords has thus been a notable item on the political agenda. Given that the removal of hereditary peers from membership of the House was intended as the first stage in a two-stage process, the future shape of the House remains a matter of debate. What are the options?

In the period leading up to the reform of the House in 1999, four approaches to reform were identified (Norton 1982: 119–29). These were known as the four Rs – retain, reform, replace or remove altogether. With some adaptation, they remain the four approaches following the passage of the House of Lords Act.

Retain

This approach favours retaining the House as a non-elected chamber. It argues that the interim House, comprising predominantly life peers, is preferable to an elected or part-elected chamber. The House, it is argued, does a good job. It complements the elected House in that it carries out tasks that are qualitatively different from those of the House of Commons. It is able to do so because its members offer particular expertise. By retaining a House of life peers, one not only creates a body of knowledge and experience, one also creates a body with some degree of independence. The cross-benchers in the House hold the balance of power and are able to judge matters with some degree of detachment. If the House were to be elected, it would have the same claim to democratic legitimacy as the Commons and would either be the same as the Commons – thus constituting a rubber-stamping body and achieving nothing – or, if elected by a different method or at different times, have the potential to clash with the Commons and create stalemate in the political system. Election would challenge, not enhance, the core accountability of the political system (see Norton 2007). Who would electors hold accountable if two elected chambers failed to reach agreement?

This approach has been taken by a number of MPs and peers, indeed by a clear majority of peers. Support for the retain option has also taken organisational form. In 2002, a campaign to argue the case against an elected second chamber was formed within Parliament. Led by an MP (Sir Patrick Cormack, Conservative MP for Staffordshire South) and a peer (this writer), it attracted a growing body of cross-party support in both Houses (Norton 2004). The group argued for some change, including closing off the by-election provision for peers, enabling peers to apply for permanent leave of absence, and putting the Lords appointments commission on a statutory basis – and supported a private member's bill to implement these changes, introduced by one of its supporters, Lord Steel of Aikwood; though not making much progress, the Bill garnered cross-party support and influenced the Government to introduce similar provisions in its Constitutional Reform and Governance Bill in 2009 though the provisions failed to be enacted. The changes advocated by the group were designed to strengthen, not destroy, the existing appointed House. For it, appointment was fundamental to maintaining the existing value of the House. It believes the House adds value to the political process; a partly or wholly elected House it views as value detracting.

Reform

This approach, advocated by the Royal Commission, favours some modification to the interim House, although retaining what are seen as the essential strengths of the existing House. It acknowledges the value of having a membership that is expert and one that has a degree of independence from government. At the same time, it argues that a wholly appointed chamber lacks democratic legitimacy. Therefore it favours a mix of appointed and elected members. The advantages of such a system were touched on in the government's 1998 White Paper, Modernising Parliament (pp. 49–50): 'It would combine some of the most valued features of the present House of Lords with a democratic basis suitable for a modern legislative chamber.' The extent of the mix of nominated

and elected members is a matter of some debate. Some would like to see a small proportion of members elected. The Royal Commission, as we have seen, put forward three options. The government, in its 2001 White Paper, recommended that 20 per cent of the membership be elected and in 2007 increased this to 50 per cent. Some reformers favour an indirect form of election, members serving by virtue of election by an electoral college comprising, say, members of local authorities or other assemblies.

Replace

This approach favours doing away with the House of Lords and replacing it with a new second chamber. Some wish to replace it with a wholly elected house. Election, it is contended, would give the House a legitimacy that a nominated chamber, or even a part-elected chamber, lacks (see Box 16.1). That greater legitimacy would allow the House to serve as a more effective check on government, knowing that it was not open to accusations of being undemocratic. It would have the teeth that the House of Lords lacks. Government can ignore the House of Lords: it could not ignore an elected second chamber. If members were elected on a national and regional basis, this – it is argued – would allow the different parts of the United Kingdom (Scotland, Wales, Northern Ireland and the English regions) to have a more distinct voice in the political process. This stance is taken by a number of organisations, including the Liberal Democrats and Unlock Democracy. Both favour an elected senate. It is also the stance taken by a former Labour Leader of the House of Lords, Lord Richard (see Richard and Welfare 1999) and, as we have seen, by some senior MPs (Clarke et al. 2005). It is also the stance taken by the Labour government following the vote of the House of Commons in 2007.

Others who favour doing away with the House of Lords want to replace it not with an elected chamber but with a chamber composed of representatives of different organised interests – a **functional chamber**. This, it is claimed, would ensure that the different groups in society – trade unions, charities, industry, consumer bodies – had a direct input into the political process instead of having to lobby MPs and peers in the hope of getting a hearing. The problem with this proposal is that it would prove difficult to agree on which groups should enjoy representation in the House. Defenders of the existing House point out that there is extensive de facto functional

---

BOX 16.1   DEBATE

An elected second chamber

The case for

- Democratic – allows voters to choose members of the chamber.
- Provides a limit on the powers of the first chamber.
- Provides an additional limit on the powers of government.
- Gives citizens an additional channel for seeking a redress of grievance or a change of public policy.
- Can be used to provide for representation of the different parts of the United Kingdom.
- Confers popular legitimacy on the chamber.

The case against

- Rids the second chamber of the expertise and the experience provided by life peers.
- Undermines accountability – who should electors hold accountable if the second chamber disagrees with the first?
- Superfluous if dominated by the same party that has a majority in the first chamber.
- Objectionable if it runs into frequent conflict with the popularly elected first chamber.
- Will not be socially representative – election tends to favour white, middle-aged and male candidates – and would thus, in any event, simply replicate the House of Commons.
- May prevent the elected government from being able to implement its manifesto commitments.
- Legitimacy of the political process will be threatened if conflict between the two chambers produces stalemate or unpopular compromise policies.

---

representation in any event, with leading figures in a great many groups having been ennobled.

There is also a third variation. Anthony Barnett and Peter Carty of the think-tank Demos have made the case for a second chamber chosen in part by lot (see also Barnett 1997). In evidence to the Royal Commission in 1999, they argued that people chosen randomly would be able to bring an independent view.

We want 'People's Peers' but they must come from the people and not be chosen from above, by an official body. It is possible to have a strong non-partisan element in the Second Chamber, and for this to be and to be seen to be democratic and lively.

The principle of public participation, they argued, should be extended to the national legislature.

Remove altogether

Under this approach, the House of Lords would be abolished and not replaced at all. Instead, the UK would have a **unicameral legislature**, the legislative burden being shouldered by a reformed House of Commons. Supporters of this approach argue that

there is no case for an unelected second chamber, since it has no legitimacy to challenge an elected chamber, and that there is no case for an elected second chamber, since this would result in either imitation or conflict. Parliament should therefore constitute a single chamber, like legislatures in Scandinavia and New Zealand. The House of Commons should be reformed in order that it may fulfil all the functions currently carried out by the two chambers.

Opponents of this approach argue that a single chamber would not be able to carry the burden, not least given the volume of public business in a country with a population of 60 million, many times larger than New Zealand and the Scandinavian countries with unicameral legislatures. Furthermore, they contend, the House of Commons could not fulfil the task of a constitutional safeguard, since it would essentially be acting as a safeguard against itself. Nor would it be an appropriate body to undertake a second look at legislation, since it would not be able to bring to bear a different point of view and different experience from that brought to bear the first time around.

Although abolition has on occasion attracted some support – including, as we have seen, at one point from the Labour Party – it is not an approach that has made much of the running in recent debate. It did, though, attract 163 votes when MPs voted on it in March 2007.

Polls reveal that opinion on the Lords is mixed. Supporters of change cite opinion polls showing that most respondents generally favour the reform or replace options, though with no clear majority for either. In a MORI poll in 1998, 24 per cent of respondents wanted to replace the House with a new second chamber elected by the public; 23 per cent wanted to replace it with a part-elected, part-nominated chamber; 20 per cent wanted to leave the House as it was (with the passage of the 1999 Act their preferred option fell by the way); 13 per cent favoured removing hereditary peers and having new peers nominated by government; and only 12 per cent favoured abolition. In a December 2001 ICM/ Democratic Audit poll, 27 per cent favoured a wholly elected House, 27 per cent a House with most members elected, 14 per cent a House with a minority of members elected and 9 per cent a wholly appointed House. (Abolition was not offered as an option.) Almost a quarter of the respondents gave a 'don't know' response.

Supporters of an appointed chamber cite polls which show that people view the work of the House of Lords in a positive light and do not regard reform as a priority for government. An ICM poll for the think tank *Politeia* in March 2005 found that 72 per cent of respondents thought that the House of Lords did a very or fairly good job; only 23 per cent thought that it did a fairly bad or very bad job. A similarly large majority – 71 per cent – thought that the House provided an effective check on the power of the government. Almost two-thirds – 63 per cent – believed that the powers of the Lords should not be reduced. Though there may be support for change, it appears not to be very deep: 59 per cent of those questioned agreed that reform of the Lords was not a priority for the next five years.

A 2007 Ipsos MORI poll carried out for the Constitution Unit at University College London also revealed that members of the public believed that in determining the legitimacy of the Lords, trust in the appointments process was most important (76 per cent listed it as very important), followed by the House considering legislation carefully and in detail (73 per cent), members being experts in their field (54 per cent), and the House acting in accordance with public opinion (53 per cent). Having some members elected by the public came fifth in the list of priorities. When asked to select the two most important factors, election again came fifth. Those who claimed to be knowledgeable about Parliament ranked the inclusion of elected members even lower still (Russell 2007: 6). The survey also found that a slightly higher proportion of the public consider the House of Lords is carrying out its policy role well than say the same about the Commons. As Meg Russell concluded:

Contrary to expectations, given widespread support for elected members in many earlier surveys, this factor is not considered important in comparison with other factors such as careful legislative scrutiny, trust in appointments, and listening to public opinion. Even when offered two choices about what matters, relatively few members of the public pick election, with more supporting the factors already mentioned or inclusion of independent members . . . However, there is concern about the way in which members of the House of Lords are chosen. One solution to this problem is clearly to introduce elections for the upper house. But our results suggest that a reform to the appointments process might actually have more widespread support.

Russell (2007: 8)

The debate continues. The options in terms of the contemporary debate are those of retain, reform, replace or remove altogether. Each, as we have seen, has its proponents. The arguments for and against an elected chamber are considered in Box 16.1. The battle to determine the future shape of the second chamber continues. No side has emerged triumphant.

BOX 16.2 IDEAS AND PERSPECTIVES

The atmosphere in the House

The House of Lords is stunning in its grandeur. For some, it is awe-inspiring; for others, it is suffocating. The House combines crown, Church and a chamber of the legislature. The magnificent throne dominates the chamber. On entering the chamber, a peer bows to the cloth of estate – just above the throne – as a mark of respect. (Unlike the Commons, there is no bowing when leaving the chamber.) Look up and you see the magnificent stained glass windows. Look down and you see the red benches of a debating chamber. The House combines symbolism with the efficiency of a working body. From the bar of the House you see the throne: lower your eye-line and you see the laptop computer on the table of the House. The clerks sit in their wigs and gowns, using the laptop as well as controlling the button for resetting the digital clocks in the chamber.

On Mondays to Thursdays, the benches are usually packed for the start of business. The combination of increasing attendance and a relatively small chamber means that peers often have to get in early to get their preferred spot on the benches. (Unlike the Commons, one cannot reserve a seat in advance.) The Lord Speaker's procession mirrors that of the Speaker of the House of Commons in its pomp and dignity. Peers bow as the mace passes. Once the Lord Speaker has taken her place on the Woolsack, prayers are said. Once these are over, members of the public are admitted to the gallery and other peers come into the chamber. At the start of Question Time, the Clerk of the Parliaments, sitting bewigged at the table, rises and announces the name of the peer who has the first question on the Order Paper. The peer rises and declares, 'I beg leave to ask the question standing in my name on the Order Paper'. The answering minister rises to the despatch box and reads out a prepared response. The peer rises to put a supplementary, followed later by others. If two peers rise at the same time, one is expected to give way; otherwise, as a self-regulating chamber, it is members who decide – usually by calling out the name of the peer they wish to hear, or else by shouting 'this side', indicating that the last supplementary was put by someone on the other side of the House. If neither gives way, the Leader of the House usually intervenes, but the Leader can be overruled by the House. Normally, good manners prevail.

Peers take a lively interest in questions. There are approximately seven or eight minutes available for each question. If time on a question goes beyond that, peers shout 'next question'. Ministers need to be well briefed. It is usually obvious when ministers are out of their depth or have been caught out. Question Time can be educational. The topics are diverse and usually there is knowledge on the part of questioners and ministers. If a minister runs into trouble, the fact that the chamber is packed adds to the tension. Question Time can also be funny. When a minister, questioned about the use of mobile 'phones on aeroplanes, faced a supplementary about the perils of mobile telephones 'on terra firma', he did not hear the full supplementary and had to ask a colleague. Realising he had taken some time to return to the despatch box, he rose and said: 'I am sorry My Lords, I thought terra firma might be some obscure airline!' On another occasion, a question about the safety of a female chimpanzee that had been mistreated received a very detailed answer, which included the facts – as I recall – that the chimp was now in a sanctuary with other chimps, that the group was led by a male of a certain age and that the chimp was enjoying herself. Whereupon the redoubtable Baroness Trumpington got to her feet and declared: 'My Lords, she is better off than I am!'

The House of Lords is a remarkably egalitarian institution: members are peers in the true sense. The atmosphere of the House can be tense, sometimes exciting – the results of votes are frequently uncertain – and occasionally a little rough. Maiden speeches, given priority in debates and heard in respectful silence (peers cannot enter or leave the chamber while they are taking place), can be nerve-wracking, even for the most experienced of public speakers. Most of the time the House has the feel of what it is: a working body, engaged in debate and legislative scrutiny. The emphasis is on constructive debate and revision. Partisan shouting matches are rare. At times, especially at the committee stage of bills, attendance can be small, the main debate taking place between the two front benches, but the effect of the probing from the opposition benches ensures that ministers have to offer informed responses. Notes frequently pass from civil servants in the officials' box to the minister at the despatch box. The quality of ministers can be very good. Ministers who are well regarded and who take the House seriously can rely on the occasional indulgence of the House if they make a slip. The responsibilities of some ministers mean that they spend a great deal of time in the chamber. In the 2005–6 session, the Home Office minister, Baroness Scotland, was regularly at the despatch box, taking bills through the House, as was the constitutional affairs minister, Baroness Ashton of Upholland. In 2004, Baroness Scotland was voted peer of the year by the Political Studies Association, and in the 2005 *House Magazine* Parliamentary Awards ceremony, Baroness Ashton was voted minister of the year.

The only way to appreciate the atmosphere, and the productive nature of the House, is to be there. One certainly cannot glean it from television – the House is squeezed out by the Commons – or from the official report. *Hansard* is good at tidying up speeches, correcting grammar and titles. The tidying up can also have the effect of sanitising proceedings. During the passage of the Access to Justice Bill, Conservative Baroness Wilcox – a champion of consumers – moved an amendment dealing with consumer affairs. The Lord Chancellor, to the delight – and obvious surprise – of Lady Wilcox, promptly accepted the import of the amendment. Lady Wilcox rose and exclaimed 'Gosh. Thanks'. This appeared in *Hansard* as 'I thank the noble and learned Lord. He has pleased me very much today'! When the House collapses in laughter – as it did after the minister's terra firma remark or Baroness Trumpington's intervention – this either appears in *Hansard* as 'Noble Lords: Oh!' or else is ignored. No, one definitely has to be there to appreciate the atmosphere.

BOX 16.3 BRITAIN IN CONTEXT

A distinctive second chamber

The House of Lords is distinctive as a second chamber because of its existence as a second chamber, its membership and its size.

It is distinctive, but far from unique, in existing as a second chamber; that is, as part of a bicameral legislature. Almost two-thirds of countries have unicameral legislatures (Massicotte 2001). Bicameral legislatures are, however, common in Western countries, especially larger ones, and in federal systems.

It is distinctive, but again not unique, in that its members are appointed rather than elected. (It was unique in the period up to 1999, when most of its members served in the House by virtue of having inherited their seats; no other major national legislature had a chamber based on the hereditary principle.) Of the 66 second chambers that exist, 17 use appointment as the predominant method of selection: the most prominent in the Western world are the UK and Canada. Of the remaining countries with second chambers, 27 employ direct election as the predominant method of selection; the rest employ indirect election or some other method of selection (Russell 2000: 29–32).

The House of Lords is unusual in that it has no fixed membership – the membership varies as some members die and others are appointed at different times. Members are also exceptional in terms of their tenure. Though it is common for members of second chambers to serve longer terms than members of the first chamber, no other chamber is based predominantly on life membership. In the House of Lords, all members serve for life other than the Lords Spiritual, who cease to be members when they retire as Archbishops or Bishops. The House is remarkable also in terms of its size. Whereas it is common for second chambers to have a smaller membership than the first, the House of Lords is larger than the first and, indeed, has a claim to be the largest second chamber in the democratic world; the House of Commons has a claim to be the largest first chamber. Together, they form the largest legislature in the democratic world.

Chapter summary

The House of Lords serves as a notable body of scrutiny – both of legislation and of public policy – and as a body for giving expression to views that otherwise would not be put on the public record. As such, it adds value to the political process. The fact that it is not elected means that it has limited significance as a body for legitimising government and measures of public policy and as a body through which politicians are recruited to ministerial office. The fact that it is not elected also makes it a target of continuing demands for reform.

The question of what to do with the House of Lords has been a matter of debate for more than a century. The election of a Labour government in 1997, committed to reform of the House, brought it to the forefront of debate. The removal in 1999 of most hereditary peers from membership fundamentally changed the composition of the House. It became a chamber composed overwhelmingly of life peers. For some, that was a perfectly acceptable chamber. For others, it was not. The House of Lords serves not only as a forum to discuss political issues. It is itself a political issue. That is likely to remain the case.

Discussion points

■ What are the principal functions of the House of Lords? Are they appropriate functions for a second chamber of Parliament?

■ Does the House of Lords do a better job than the House of Commons in scrutinising government legislation? If so, why?

■ Should the institutions of the European Union pay attention to reports from the House of Lords?

■ Was the government right to get rid of most hereditary peers from the House of Lords? Should it have got rid of all of them?

■ Would a reform of the appointments process to the House of Lords be preferable to having an elected House?

■ What would you do with the House of Lords – and why?

Further reading

The main text on the House of Lords is Shell (2007). Crewe (2005) constitutes a fascinating anthropological study. On the work of the House, see also Part IV of Blackburn and Kennon (2003), Chapter 6 of Baldwin (2005), Norton (2005) passim. On peers' voting behaviour, see Norton (2003) and the work produced by the Constitution Unit at University College London (www.ucl.ac.uk/constitution-unit/research/parliament/house-of-lords.html). On the House prior to the reform of 1999 see Shell and Beamish (1993) and Dickson and Carmichael (1999), the latter providing useful material on the House in both its political and judicial roles.

On Lords reform, see Kent (1998), Tyrie (1998), Richard and Welfare (1999), the Report of the Royal Commission on the Reform of the House of Lords, A House for the Future (2000), the Government White Paper, The House of Lords: Completing the Reform (2001), the report from the Public Administration Select Committee, The Second Chamber: Continuing the Reform (2002), Norton (2004), Shell (2004), Clarke et al. (2005), Norton (2007), HM Government (2007), Ministry of Justice (2008), and Tyrie, Young and Gough (2009). Morrison (2001), Chapter 5, offers an overview enriched by extensive interviews. Useful comparative information is to be found in Russell (2000). There is also valuable material on the website of the Royal Commission, www.archive.official-documents.co.uk/document/cm45/4534/4534.htm

Bibliography

Baggott, R. (1995) Pressure Groups Today (Manchester University Press).

Baldwin, N.D.J. (1985) 'The House of Lords: Behavioural Changes', in P. Norton (ed.) *Parliament in the 1980s* (Blackwell).

Baldwin, N.D.J. (1999) 'The Membership and Work of the House of Lords', in B. Dickson and P. Carmichael (eds) *The House of Lords: Its Parliamentary and Judicial Roles* (Hart Publishing).

Baldwin, N.D.J. (ed.) (2005) *Parliament in the 21st Century* (Politico's).

Barnett, A. (1997) *This Time: Our Constitutional Revolution* (Vintage).

Blackburn, R. and Kennon, A. (2003) *Griffith and Ryle on Parliament: Functions, Practice and Procedures*, 2nd edn (Sweet & Maxwell).

Clarke, K., Cook, R., Tyler, P., Wright, T. and Young, G. (2005) *Reforming the House of Lords* (The Constitution Unit).

Constitution Unit (1996) *Reform of the House of Lords* (The Constitution Unit).

Constitutional Commission (1999) *The Report of the Constitutional Commission on Options for a New Second Chamber* (Constitutional Commission).

Crewe, E. (2005) *Lords of Parliament* (Manchester University Press).

Criddle, B., Childs, S. and Norton, P. (2005) 'The Make-up of Parliament', in P. Giddings (ed.) *The Future of Parliament* (Palgrave Macmillan).

Dickson, B. and Carmichael, P. (eds) (1999) *The House of Lords: Its Parliamentary and Judicial Roles* (Hart Publishing).

Drewry, G. and Brock, J. (1993) 'Government Legislation: An Overview', in D. Shell and D. Beamish (eds) *The House of Lords at Work* (Oxford University Press).

Grantham, C. (1993) 'Select Committees', in D. Shell and D. Beamish (eds) *The House of Lords at Work* (Oxford University Press).

Hayter, P.D.G. (1992) 'The Parliamentary Monitoring of Science and Technology', *Government and Opposition*, Vol. 26.

Himsworth, C.M.G. (1995) 'The Delegated Powers Scrutiny Committee', *Public Law*, Spring.

HM Government (2007) *The House of Lords: Reform*, Cm 7072 (The Stationery Office).

House of Lords: Completing the Reform (2001) Cmd 5291 (The Stationery Office).

House of Lords (2006) *House of Lords Annual Report and Accounts 2005–06*. (The Stationery Office).

House of Lords (2008) House of Lords: Public Bill Sessional Statistics for Session 2007–08 (Public and Private Bills Office, House of Lords).

House of Lords Information Office (2005) *The Work of the House of Lords* (House of Lords).

Kent, N. (1998) *Enhancing Our Democracy* (Tory Reform Group).

Labour Peers Group (2004) *Reform of the Powers, Procedures and Conventions of the House of Lords* (Labour Peers Group).

Maclean, I., Spirling, A. and Russell, M. (2003) 'None of the Above: the UK House of Commons Vote Reforming the House of Lords, February 2003', *Political Quarterly*, Vol. 74.

Massicotte, L. (2001) 'Legislative Unicameralism: A Global Survey and a Few Case Studies', *The Journal of Legislative Studies*, Vol. 7, No. 1, pp. 151–70.

Ministry of Justice (2008) *An Elected Second Chamber: Further reform of the House of Lords*, Cm 7438 (The Stationery Office).

Modernising Parliament: Reforming the House of Lords (1999) Cm 4183 (The Stationery Office).

Morrison, J. (2001) *Reforming Britain: New Labour, New Constitution?* (Reuters/Pearson Education).

Norton, P. (1982) *The Constitution in Flux* (Basil Blackwell).

Norton, P. (ed.) (1996) *National Parliaments and the European Union* (Cass).

Norton, P. (1999) 'Adding value to the political system', submission to the Royal Commission on the House of Lords.

Norton, P. (2003) 'Cohesion Without Voting: Party Voting in the House of Lords', *The Journal of Legislative Studies*, Vol. 9.

Norton, P. (2004) 'Reforming the House of Lords: A View from the Parapets', *Representation*, Vol. 40.

Norton, P. (2005) *Parliament in British Politics* (Palgrave Macmillan).

Norton, P. (2007) 'Adding Value? The Role of Second Chambers', *Asia Pacific Law Review*, Vol. 15.

Patterson, S.C. and Mughan, A. (eds) (1999) *Senates: Bicameralism in the Contemporary World* (Ohio State University Press).

Public Administration Select Committee (2002) *The Second Chamber: Continuing the Reform*, Fifth Report, Session 2001–2002, HC 494-I (The Stationery Office).

Richard, Lord and Welfare, D. (1999) *Unfinished Business: Reforming the House of Lords* (Vintage).

Royal Commission on the Reform of the House of Lords (2000) *A House for the Future*, Cm 4534 (The Stationery Office).

Rush, M. (ed.) (1990) *Parliament and Pressure Politics* (Clarendon Press).

Russell, M. (2000) *Reforming the House of Lords: Lessons from Overseas* (Oxford University Press).

Russell, M. (2007) 'Peers and Public Attitudes to the Contemporary House of Lords', www.ucl.ac.uk/constitution-unit/files/research/parliament/lords/survey-results2007.pdf.

Shell, D. (1983) 'The House of Lords', in D. Judge (ed.) *The Politics of Parliamentary Reform* (Heinemann).

Shell, D. (2004) 'The Future of the Second Chamber', *Parliamentary Affairs*, Vol. 57.

Shell, D. (2005) 'The House of Lords: A Chamber of Scrutiny', in P. Giddings (ed.) *The Future of Parliament* (Palgrave Macmillan).

Shell, D. (2007) *The House of Lords* (Manchester University Press).

Shell, D. and Beamish, D. (eds) (1993) *The House of Lords at Work* (Oxford University Press).

Tyrie, A. (1998) *Reforming the Lords: A Conservative Approach* (Conservative Policy Forum).

Tyrie, A., Young, G. and Gough, H. (2009) *An Elected Second Chamber: A Conservative View* (The Constitution Unit).

White, A.B. (1908) *The Making of the English Constitution 1449–1485* (G.P. Putnam).

Useful websites

Parliamentary websites

Cross-bench peers: www.crossbenchpeers.org.uk

Government Whips' Office: www.lordswhips.org.uk (provides details on future business, including speakers)

House of Lords: www.parliament.uk/lords/index.cfm

House of Lords Select Committees: www.parliament.uk/business/committees/ld_select.cfm

The Work of the House of Lords: www.parliament.uk/documents/upload/HoLwork.pdf

What Lords do: www.parliament.uk/about/how/members/lords.cfm

Reform

HM Government, *The House of Lords: Reform*: www.official-documents.gov.uk/document/cm70/7027/7027.pdf

Ministry of Justice, *An Elected Second Chamber: Further reform of the House of Lords*: www.official-documents.gov.uk/document/cm74/7438/7438.pdf

Report of the Royal Commission on the Reform of the House of Lords (Wakeham Commission): www.archive.official-documents.co.uk/document/cm45/4534/contents.htm

Unlock Democracy: www.unlockdemocracy.org.uk/

And another thing . . .

Managing the Cabinet's big beasts

Andrew Heywood

All too often the Cabinet in the UK is portrayed as a single, collective force – something that Prime Ministers try to subdue and control for fear of succumbing to it. This, indeed, is the conventional image of the political executive as a battle ground between the personal power of the Prime Minister and the collective weight of the Cabinet. Prime Ministers exert influence to the extent that they are able to emancipate themselves from the constraints of Cabinet collegiality. However, in many, perhaps most, circumstances this image is misleading. Despite the fact that, thanks to collective responsibility, the Cabinet ministers stand or fall together, the Cabinet usually acts more as a collection of individuals than as a single collective force. The Prime Minister has no single relationship with the Cabinet, but rather a series of individual relationships with some 20 to 23 ministers. Most of these ministers, most of the time, can nevertheless be treated (should the Prime Minister so wish) with cavalier disregard. Quite simply, they need the Prime Minister much more than the Prime Minister needs them. The same, however, cannot be said about the Cabinet's major figures – its 'big beasts'.

Who are the Cabinet's big beasts? What is it that distinguishes the big beasts from, if you like, the small ducks? Three key factors stand out. First, big beasts have a significant power base within the party. They enjoy support within the parliamentary party, among backbenchers and, in all likelihood, among ministerial colleagues inside and outside the Cabinet, as well as in the party more widely. This means that they will be influential players in any future power struggle within the party, and may even be leadership contenders themselves. Second, big beasts are figures of a certain public standing. They not only attract media attention and have high

name-recognition, but also command a measure of public respect as 'Cabinet heavyweights', usually linked to perceived competence and a record of policy success. This means that their fate – their rise or their fall – has an electoral impact on the government itself.

Third, big beasts *project* themselves as big beasts. They develop and sustain independent political identities, albeit within the confines of Cabinet collegiality and party unity. Big beasts not only possess political leverage, but are also willing to use it. In other words, objective and subjective factors need to coincide. A prominent Cabinet minister who distinguishes himself or herself by scrupulous loyalty towards the Prime Minister – such as William (Willie) Whitelaw, home secretary and Deputy Prime Minister in Thatcher's first government, 1979–83 – is not a big beast. As Thatcher later, and gratefully, put it, 'Every Cabinet needs a Willie'. By the same token, political projection is not enough in itself if party and electoral leverage wane. For instance, John Prescott, Deputy Prime Minister under Blair, 1997–2007, probably ceased to be a big beast once Blair had secured a second landslide election victory in 2001, as this demonstrated the declining significance of the left-wing and trade union elements within the party that tended to identify with Prescott as the leading survivor of 'old' Labour.

Ultimately, a big beast is a minister whose resignation would seriously weaken the Prime Minister, either or both by undermining party support or by damaging the Prime Minister's public image. This does not, however, mean that big beasts are necessarily threats to, still less rivals of, the Prime Minister. Indeed, big beasts may benefit prime ministers as well as constrain them. No Prime Minister wants to be seen to preside over a Cabinet of min- nows. To some extent, the standing of the Prime Minister is a reflection of the talent and ability in his or her Cabinet, so long as, of course, unity and loy- alty are maintained. The key point, though, is that the loyalty and support of Cabinet heavyweights cannot be taken for granted: it must be worked for; big beasts must be 'managed'. But what does this mean? Balance-of-power theorists in international relations helpfully distinguish between two types of behaviour that subordinate states adopt in relation to dominant states. They may either 'band- wagon' (that is, side with a stronger power in the hope of increasing security and influence, meaning that they 'jump on the bandwagon') or 'balance' (that is, oppose or challenge a stronger or rising power for fear of leaving themselves exposed). In short, Prime Ministers manage the Cabinet's big beasts by encouraging them to 'bandwagon' rather than 'balance'.

The classic strategy for ensuring the loyalty of Cabinet heavyweights, inclining them towards 'bandwagoning' behaviour, is through patronage and preferment. Big beasts do not become big beasts because they hold senior Cabinet posts; they hold senior Cabinet posts because they are big beasts. Senior appointments work in two ways. In the first place, they prevent a potentially dangerous 'gap' opening up between a minister's Cabinet rank and his or her sense of their own importance. Non- preferment risks encouraging ministers to 'balance' by manoeuvring against the Prime Minister, either in pursuit of their own leadership ambitions or in the belief that their careers would prosper better under an alternative leader.

The second, and vital, consideration is that senior appointments ensure that big beasts are forced to remain politically 'close' to the Prime Minister. Ministers who hold senior posts – especially those of Chancellor of the Exchequer, Foreign Secretary and Home Secretary – are not only forced into closer and more regular contact with the Prime Minister (even perhaps being drawn into the Prime Minister's inner circle), but their greater public prominence also leaves very little scope for disloyalty. For senior- ranking ministers, open criticism of the Prime Minister is unthinkable, and even the hint of 'manoeuvrings' against the premier is likely to damage the minister concerned every bit as much as the Prime Minister. Nevertheless, patronage is the beginning of the process of managing big beasts, not the end. Prime Ministers must also be astute enough to recognise when big

beasts need to be 'stroked' and when they need to be 'checked', as both strategies have their pitfalls. This is best illustrated by when things go wrong.

Margaret Thatcher claimed in her memoirs that she had been toppled by a 'Cabinet coup' (Thatcher 1993). In fact, the bulk of her Cabinet only advised her in a series of individual meetings in November 1990 to withdraw her candidacy in the second ballot of the Conservative Party's leadership election once her failure to secure victory in the first ballot had demonstrated that she was doomed to defeat. Nevertheless, the Cabinet did play a role in this process, but more through individual actions rather than collective ones. The preconditions for Thatcher's downfall were laid by three senior-level resignations from her Cabinet – those of the Defence Secretary Michael Heseltine in 1986, the Chancellor of the Exchequer Nigel Lawson in 1989, and the Deputy Prime Minister Geoffrey Howe in 1990. The cumula- tive impact of these resignations was to expose key policy divisions in the Conservative Party and the government (particularly over Europe) and to damage Thatcher's reputation and public standing. Together with unpopular policies such as the 'Poll Tax', they contributed to the developing impression that the Prime Minister had become an electoral liability.

Heseltine, Lawson and Howe were certainly more dangerous outside of the cabinet than they had been inside. The party leadership election in 1990 was precipitated by a challenge by Michael Heseltine, very publicly supported by Lawson and Howe – something that would have been impossible had they remained in the Cabinet. What is more, each of the resignations was avoidable, as each stemmed from a failure to 'stroke' a big beast who was in danger of 'balancing' rather than 'bandwagoning'. Heseltine resigned over the Westland Affair when he believed that the Prime Minister had sided with his rival, Leon Brittan; Lawson resigned over a policy clash with the Prime Minister's economic advisor, Alan Walters, who she continued to back; and Howe resigned over Thatcher's unilateral asser- tion that the UK would never enter a single European currency.

The relationship between Prime Minister Tony Blair and his Chancellor Gordon Brown offers a par- ticularly instructive example of the successes and failures of managing big beasts. Aside from specula- tion about a possible deal in 1994 that allowed Blair to challenge for the leadership of the party while Brown stood aside, in return for a promise by Blair to step aside in favour of Brown in due course,

Blair's treatment of Brown bears all the classic hallmarks of a 'stroking' approach. As, with Blair, one of the two leading figures in the 'new' Labour project, an effective shadow Chancellor and the architect of Labour's 1997 landslide election victory, Brown was duly, and predictably, rewarded with control over the Treasury. Once the Prime Minister had consolidated 'new' Labour's control over key areas of policy making, it is no exaggeration to suggest that, for Blair, cabinet management largely boiled down to managing Gordon Brown. He did this consistently by encouraging 'bandwagoning' rather than 'balancing', allowing Brown, for instance, to build up an unprecedented power base in the Treasury which enabled him to exert control over large swathes of domestic policy. Brown came to operate almost as a 'second' Prime Minister responsible for domestic affairs.

This strategy proved to be highly effective for most of Blair's first two terms, even ensuring Brown's full and open support for the deeply controversial decision in 2003 to invade Iraq. Brown's backing for the policy helped to consolidate Cabinet support and at least reduced hostility to it on the Labour backbenches. Brown's 'bandwagoning' benefited both himself and the Prime Minister. However, as the Blair premiership extended, after 2005, into its third term, the drawbacks of 'stroking' became increasingly apparent. Brown's public prominence, his standing in the party and his power base in the Treasury, to say nothing of his record of policy success (based on years of stable economic growth), fuelled his ambitions as well as those of Brownite elements within the government and party who were increasingly frustrated by Blair's long tenure. In other words, 'stroking' strategies had ultimately produced a 'balancing' response. At the same time, however, precisely the same factors effectively ruled out a shift at this stage to a 'checking' strategy, in which Brown may have been marginalised, demoted or even sacked. The result of this was that Blair stood down as Prime Minister in June 2007 without having served his promised full third term

and against a backdrop of barely concealed hostility between Blairites and Brownites, which damaged the images of both the outgoing and the incoming Prime Minister.

There are signs, nevertheless, that big beasts may be a species in decline. The Blair cabinets of 1997–2007 contained but a single, genuine big beast, while the Brown Cabinet after 2007 arguably contained none. By contrast, Harold Wilson's Cabinets in the 1960s featured such heavyweights as Anthony Crosland, Dennis Healey, Roy Jenkins and Dick Crossman. Where have all the big beasts gone? They appear to have succumbed to the changing nature of political careers and to the changing character of political parties. The trend in favour of 'career politicians', whose main, and sometimes only, professional experience has been within, or related to, the Westminster jungle, is certainly part of the explanation. Working outside of Westminster, especially in senior positions – in academic life, business, law, journalism, the trade unions, the civil service or wherever – gave politicians wider skills, knowledge and experience, making them, somehow, figures of greater substance. Similarly, as programmatic, mass-membership political parties have given way to modern 'catch-all' parties, political careers are increasingly built on the basis of presentational qualities and televisual skills, discouraging rising politicians from taking up 'serious' ideological stances and relieving them of the need to cultivate support within the factions and tendencies of the party. However, if the conveyer belt that produces big beasts now functions less reliably, much of the texture and vibrancy of cabinet government will be lost. It might also mark the point at which the task of checking Prime Ministerial power passed finally from the Cabinet to the electorate.

Reference

Thatcher, M. (1993) *The Downing Street Years* (HarperCollins).

Topic 10:
Devolution

Devolution

Russell Deacon

Learning objectives

- To define devolution and note the various devolutionary models.

- To explain the background and role of nationalism and the subsequent drive towards political devolution within the UK.

- To cover the story of how devolution evolved across the United Kingdom and Northern Ireland.

- To assess some of the key events and developments in devolutionary politics in the first decade of devolution.

- To explore some of the major impacts on the politics of the UK from the advent of devolution.

From Chapter 12 of *Politics UK*, 7/e. Bill Jones and Philip Norton. © Pearson Education 2001–2010. All rights reserved.

Introduction

The topic of devolution is not as modern as it may sound. It has dominated politics at various periods over the last 120 years, causing wars, the splitting of political parties and the downfall of governments. Since wide-scale political devolution arrived in the United Kingdom and Northern Ireland, at the end of the last century, the whole nature of British politics itself has undergone an evolutionary change. As the media in the United Kingdom tends to be dominated by that based around London, many people may not be aware of the extent of the changes to our political system or the variation in policy output over the last decade.

What then is devolution? At a basic level, devolution is simply the devolving of powers from the centre to the periphery. Importantly, this does not involve transferring sovereignty from Westminster, which therefore makes it distinctly different from federalism. In the case of the United Kingdom devolution therefore means transferring powers from Westminster and Whitehall to the devolved bodies and administrative offices across the United Kingdom. The process of devolution can be categorised as three discrete processes:

1 *Administrative*: The process by which power is transferred to allow specific functions to be carried out.

2 *Executive*: The process by which power is transferred to enable policy decisions to be made.

3 *Legislative*: The process by which the power to make laws is conferred on another body.

The United Kingdom and Northern Ireland has had administrative devolution for over a century. This expanded over time so that by the 1990s it covered all of the UK. Executive and legislative devolution, outside of Northern Ireland, however, are of a more recent occurrence. This type of devolution has had a far greater impact on the politics of the UK. It is this sort of devolution (often referred to as political devolution) that is examined in this chapter.

■ Theory

In 2005, Jennifer Todd, drawing upon the work of around twenty of the most prominent academics who had commented on devolution since the mid-1970s, highlighted three models of territorial politics which provide us with a way to assess devolutionary change.

The first model is that of 'state realism'. Within this model the state has adapted its state power and state sovereignty to take account of changing political realities. This new form of devolution is therefore simply the older dual polity whereby the centre allowed a certain practical autonomy on local issues to its peripheries, while retaining control over high politics. Under this model, however, the divide between the centre and the periphery is not clear-cut and therefore the older 'mainframe' of the unitary state may be under intolerable strain and crack.

The second model considers devolution to be driven by 'European regionalism'. This model indicates that nations within the UK move from 'state-centred' to 'European-determined linkage politics'. This means that within a European context, nations such as Scotland, Wales and Northern Ireland need the UK Parliament less and less as they are able to interact directly with the European Union without needing to go through Westminster. In turn, the European Union and European Commission require regions or nations in order to determine their policy output, such as the establishment of European regional development funding or support for cultural and linguistic policies. In the case of the United Kingdom part of this packaging involves the identification and recognition of the constituent nations.

The final model sees devolution as a 'renewal of imperial legacies'. Here the Westminster government, just as it did with its colonies in the last century, transfers more and more sovereignty and powers to the devolved nations. The strategy behind this is that in time they will become dominions independent in their own right. Those advocating this model point to Northern Ireland as an example of this. Here the Westminster government would be glad to be rid of its responsibilities for this troubled province. The main drawback to this theory, however, is that all mainstream British political parties constantly advocate their commitment to maintaining the union.

■ Nationalism and the drive towards political devolution

Nationalism in the United Kingdom is normally related to those groups that believe that either the nation or a putative nation is at the centre of a political system of government. Due to the fact that political boundaries in the British Isles have been fairly constant for the last five centuries, national identities have had time to develop and take firm, historical root. Even in Ireland, where the political boundaries were only firmly established in 1922, the national identity focuses on whether its citizens feel themselves to be Irish or British Irish nationals. And each side forms its own brand of nationalism, accordingly.

One of the common misconceptions of both academics and historians is to label only those groups that desire independence for their own nation, such as Plaid Cymru in Wales or the Scottish National Party in Scotland. This extends to *Mebion Kernow* in Cornwall or, in the case of Ireland, desiring union with another nation, either the Irish Republic or the UK. As many of us know nationalism in the British Isles is both wider and more complex than this. In the nineteenth century the Liberal Prime Minister, William Gladstone, was the originator of 'Home Rule – all round'; meaning in essence devolution for all of the nations of the British Isles. After this was defeated by the Liberal Unionists, who split from their own party and the Conservatives' liberal nationalism emerged once more in Scotland and Wales in the late Victorian and Edwardian era. The Young Scot's Society and *Cymru Fydd* (Wales to be) were both Liberal Party nationalist movements that pursued devolutionary policies which sought to place their own nations at the centre of their own political systems. Nationalism has continued in the Liberal Party and subsequently in the Liberal Democrat Party with a desire for a federal system of government for

the United Kingdom. Within the Labour Party, initially supportive of devolution, this desire was much reduced, particularly after the Russian Revolution and the First World War produced left-wing proponents who advocated the need for international socialism. It nevertheless maintained a distinct presence within the Labour Party from then on, despite the strong unionist tendency that existed in the Labour Party after the First World War. British and English nationalism have been ever-present in the Conservative party. There have even on occasions been elements of support for Scottish nationalism within the party. This, however, was never the case in Wales and for most of its history the Conservative Party has remained staunchly unionist there (British nationalist).

In Ireland, nationalism has always been viewed from a different perspective when compared to perceptions in England, Wales and Scotland. This is the nationalism which on both sides had blood on its hands, through centuries of religious warfare and rebellions against the British crown. This did not occur anywhere else in Great Britain after the last Jacobean revolt in Scotland in 1745. Firstly, Irish nationalism simply and unwaveringly demanded home rule. As this desire was rejected, so Irish nationalism became more violent. Irish nationalism then developed into Catholic nationalism pursuing the ideal of a united and independent Ireland. This was in turn countered by Protestant nationalism (Unionism) which sought to keep Ireland within the United Kingdom. The two then opposed each other in a bloody Irish civil war that lasted nearly the whole of the twentieth century.

In Wales and Scotland a new type of nationalism developed in the years before the Second World War. This was the nationalism of independence rather than home rule. By the end of the century, it would eclipse the nationalism which exists within the three mainstream UK parties. In 1925, Plaid Cymru was formed and then in 1934 the Scottish Nationalist Party (SNP) was created. Both had had their origins in other nationalist organisations but it was these parties that came to represent the mainstream independence nationalism of their respective nation states. Political scientists, however, do not always refer directly to them as nationalist parties. This label they reserve for those anti-immigrant parties, normally on the far political right such as the BNP. Instead Plaid Cymru and the SNP are referred to by them as ethnoregionalist parties. This means that they represent a specific regional/national group within a larger nation state, in this context the Welsh and the Scottish peoples in the United Kingdom. In the political world and in the media, however, they remain defined as nationalist parties but students of politics should be aware there is a clear distinction between nationalist and ethnoregionalist parties. Having stated this, however, they are still referred to by their commonly known label – 'nationalist party' in this chapter.

While in Northern Ireland the nationalist parties displaced the mainstream British political parties this has never been the case in Scotland or Wales. Here, for decades after their foundation, both Plaid Cymru and the SNP struggled to make any political progress. It was only with Plaid Cymru's by-election win in Carmarthen in 1966 and the SNPs similar by-election win in Hamilton in 1967 that the modern period of Scottish and Welsh nationalism associated with a drive towards independence started. This nationalist impact was seen to be so sudden and potentially damaging electorally to the Labour Party, which traditionally relied on their Scottish and Welsh seats to counteract the Conservatives' majority of the English seats, that they set up a Royal Commission under Lord Kilbrandon to examine the issue of devolution. When Lord Kilbrandon reported back in 1973 it was to a Conservative government under Edward Heath. It was some five years later, under the Labour government of James Callaghan and after much political turmoil, that the referendums on Scottish and Welsh devolution were held. The devolution referendum was defeated in Wales, in 1979, and in Scotland an insufficient majority was gained to carry it forwards. The Labour government then fell due to a vote of no confidence, being the first government to fall on an issue of devolution since Gladstone's Liberal government had split on Irish Home Rule almost a century before.

Two months later, that year, in the general election the Conservatives won and the pro-devolution Liberals, Plaid Cymru and the SNP lost between them 13 of their 29 MPs. The SNP was reduced from 11 to just two seats in the process. The victorious Conservatives had honed their campaigning skills in the Scottish and Welsh elections and increased their seats in these nations at the pro-devolutionists' expense. The new government under Margaret Thatcher was unashamedly pro-unionist. A month after their victory the Conservatives reversed the devolutionary mechanisms. The political fortunes of the pro-devolutionists were now put on hold for two decades.

Ireland

The historical events that resulted in the formation of the province of Northern Ireland (Ulster) fill many volumes. Bearing this in mind, the historical elements so instrumental in understanding the politics of Northern Ireland can only be touched upon here. Ulster has been a constant reminder of the British Isles' violent, sectarian and turbulent past transported into modern times. The religious wars between Catholics and Protestants that faded from the British mainland more than four centuries ago have yet to die in Northern Ireland. Politics there today therefore remains almost totally divided between political parties which were formed on a religious basis. The Catholic nationalists are republicans who seek a union with the Catholic Irish Republic, while the Protestants seek to maintain the union with the protestant United Kingdom (unionists). The only party that is non-sectarian is the 'Alliance Party', which is linked to the British Liberal Democrats but attracting only marginal support in Northern Ireland. In short, therefore after the Anglo-Irish Treaty of 1922, Northern Ireland broke away from Southern Ireland (Eire) and from then onwards has developed a separate political identity. It was given its own Parliament, known by the place in which it was prominently located – Stormont. Until 1972 Stormont ran the province, with near autonomy, as part of the United Kingdom with its own prime minister, the last being Brian Faulkner.

Stormont, however, was a Protestant-controlled Parliament that supported the mechanisms of a Protestant state which maintained a strict segregation similar to that between black and white citizens in the southern United States until the late 1960s. The Catholics, inspired by the American black civil rights movement, sought their own civil rights during the 1960s, mainly through their own political party called the Social Democratic and Labour Party (SDLP). This movement was heavily resisted by the Stormont government and enforced by the almost exclusively Protestant-manned Royal Ulster Constabulary (RUC) and their auxiliary policemen (B Specials). This produced a situation that got ever more violent and started a period known as 'the Troubles'. At its height in 1972, 467 people were killed, 323 of them civilians. The atrocities of that year became infamous in Irish history and included events such as: Bloody Sunday, Bloody Friday, McGurk's Bar, Kelly's Bar, Callender Street and

Abercorn. For the next three-and-a-half decades, while the British Army and Royal Ulster Constabulary fought the IRA, and the various other paramilitary organisations, the politicians (sometimes closely connected to paramilitaries, in particular Sinn Fein with the IRA) British and Irish Prime Ministers and the occasional American President, tried every 'carrot and stick' method they could conceive of to end the Troubles.

The current Northern Ireland peace process began with the signing of the Good Friday Agreement (named after the day on which it was signed) and its subsequent approval by a Northern Ireland referendum in May 1998. This created the devolved Northern Ireland Assembly, which officially started in December 1999. Because of the previous problems with Northern Ireland politics, such as the gerrymandering of boundaries, the Assembly's elections were under STV, the most proportional system possible. The Good Friday Agreement meant that all of the main political parties would in future have to power share in any Northern Ireland government. The largest political party would take the First Minister post and the second largest that of Deputy First Minister. But within a short space of time the peace process ground to a halt once more. A row in February 2000 between the political parties over weapons decommissioning led to a four-month suspension of the Assembly.

A further crisis came in July 2001 when David Trimble, the Assembly's first minister and leader of the moderate Ulster Unionist Party (UUP), resigned out of frustration at the IRA's failure to decommission their weapons. He returned later that year when the IRA began to put its 'weapons beyond use'. The Northern Ireland Assembly then resumed business for a short period. Then, in July 2002 the IRA made an unprecedented apology for 'non-combatant' deaths. But Mr Trimble resigned again three months later after the discovery of incriminating documents in Sinn Fein's offices. Britain then resumed direct rule of Northern Ireland with the Prime Minister postponing the next Assembly elections until November 2003. In these elections, the more radical unionist Ian Paisley's Democratic Unionist Party (DUP) – which opposed the Good Friday agreement – displaced the UUP as the biggest party in the Assembly. At the same time, Sinn Fein replaced the moderate SDLP as the main Catholic (republican) party. As the rest of British politics was moving towards the political centre, Northern Ireland's was moving to the political extremes.

For a long while after the elections there was stalemate once more. In December 2004, remarkably, it seemed as though Mr Paisley might become the new First Minister, with Sinn Fein's Martin McGuinness (the former head of the IRA) as Deputy First Minister. But a bank raid and a brutal murder, both blamed on the IRA, wrecked the deal.

In Britain's general election in May 2005, the Democratic Unionists gained parliamentary seats at Mr Trimble's expense, and Sinn Fein escaped punishment for the IRA's misdemeanours by also increasing their share of the vote. But the British government's hasty welcome to the IRA's promise in July 2005 to 'end the armed campaign' enraged Unionists and pushed them further away from cooperation. Consequently, there was no devolved Assembly between the 2003 and 2007 elections. When the 2007 Northern Ireland Assembly elections occurred, the DUP and Sein Fein were now the main political parties in Northern Ireland (Table 12.1). It would therefore only be with their cooperation that Northern Ireland's Assembly would restart. Political progress was now stuck on the thorny issue of law and order in Northern Ireland. By now, the RUC had been disbanded and replaced with the Police Service of Northern Ireland (PSNI), which had a much larger number of Catholic officers in it. Yet this still lacked the required Republican support, something that was essential for Ulster's future.

In January 2007 Sinn Fein voted to support policing in Northern Ireland for the first time in the party's history. This broke the political log jam and enabled the DUP to remove a vital political barrier and join government with them. At the same time Tony Blair was using the 'stick' of introducing water charges for Northern Ireland, which all Northern Irish parties opposed, and Gordon Brown, then

Table 12.1 Northern Ireland Assembly results 1998–2007 (108 seats)

Party	1998	2003	2007
Social Democratic and Labour Party (SDLP)	24	18	16
Ulster Unionist Party (UUP)	28	30 (33)*	18
Democratic Unionist Party (DUP)	20	27 (24)*	36
Sinn Fein	18	24	28
Alliance	6	6	7
Others	12	3	3

* Three UUP defections to the DUP

Chancellor, offered the 'carrot' of £1bn extra funding if an Executive was formed. The strategy worked and the DUP leader Ian Paisley, at the age of 81, now saw his moment in history and finally joined with his lifelong republican foes in a joint administration. He became the First Minister and Martin McGuiness the Deputy First Minister. It seemed as though the threat of the gun had finally been removed from Northern Irish politics.

Then in May 2008 Northern Ireland got a new First Minister – Peter Robinson, the long-time deputy leader of the DUP, acceded, as Ian Paisley stood down. Sinn Fein then refused to nominate Martin McGuiness as Deputy First Minister unless the DUP agreed to the devolution of justice. Gordon Brown intervened and Gerry Adams was called to Number 10 to try and make a compromise. Between May and November the Executive did not meet and during this period the image of devolution took a nosedive with the general public. An accommodation was eventually reached in which the DUP agreed with Sinn Fein to make the police answerable to an Irish justice minister in time but both Sinn Fein and the DUP ruled themselves out of this post. The issue on policing was only resolved after another lengthy period of political posturing which also at one stage involved the temporary resignation of Peter Robinson, albeit on unrelated issues connected to a financial scandal involving his wife. Devolution in Northern Ireland always appears to be on a knife edge, the key issues contributing to this instability are as follows:

- There still remain a number of problems in Northern Irish politics which could cause the process to break down at any time.
- Some paramilitaries such as the Real and Continuity IRA continue to mount operations. Their actions, or those of the security services in seeking to tackle them, cause tensions among Unionists and Republicans which could split the Assembly once more.
- Some DUP members such as the MEP Jim Allister remain anti-power sharing and are still popular among their party and the public. Their views could once more stop power sharing. In addition much of the DUP's own membership and support base remain opposed to power sharing.
- The DUP's decision to back Labour in the 42-day detention of terror suspects in the Westminster Parliament's 2008 vote made the Ulster Unionists oppose the detention period and join with traditional forces, the Conservatives. They now field joint candidates' in Westminster general elections,

resulting in the Conservatives no longer being able to remain neutral from Northern Irish politics.
- The southern Irish political party Fianna Fail now has a grassroots organisation in Northern Ireland particularly in South Armagh. The involvement of southern Irish political parties in Northern Irish politics remains something of an unknown quantity.

Scotland

Scotland, Wales and England became joined at the start of the seventeenth century. In March 1603 the English Queen Elizabeth I died and King James of Scotland became king of England and Ireland. This happened in a smooth transition of power quite different from most previous changes of monarch in both Scotland and England. James now concentrated his reign in England and for the rest of his life he only visited Scotland once, in 1617. This showed the start of a transition of power to England that went on for the next century.

When the Scottish Parliament was abolished with the Act of Union in 1707, the event was described by the Scottish Lord Chancellor, James Ogilvy, as like the 'end of an old song'. Yet the distinctive tune of Scotland and Scottishness did not end with the demise of its parliament. The Scottish church, education and legal systems remained separate from those in England and Wales. From 1885 onwards there was also a separate government department and minister for Scotland. Unlike the positions of Northern Ireland and Wales there was never any doubt over Scotland's existence as a country separate from England. Over time much of the government's business in Scotland was transferred from London to the Scottish Office in Edinburgh. From 1926 the Scottish Secretary also sat in the Cabinet. Therefore by the time the Second World War arrived, the Scottish Office already represented a substantial devolved administrative department.

For the first seven decades of the twentieth century there were sporadic attempts to push forward political devolution for Scotland among all of the parties in Scotland. This was strongest in the Scottish Liberals and the Scottish National Party (SNP) but there were also politicians in the Labour and Conservative (Unionist Party) who supported political devolution. They were, however, kept in check by a far more powerful unionist tendency in their respective parties that endured in Labour's case into the late 1970s and in the Conservatives into the late 1990s. The rise of the SNP as a political threat to Labour, in particular, and the recommendations of the Kilbrandon Commission in 1973 which led in turn to the failed devolution referendum of 1979. Albeit a referendum was won but failed to reach a vital 40 per cent threshold of the total Scottish population needed to vote in favour of a Scottish Parliament. In the event only 36 per cent of the total electorate had voted 'Yes'. During this period some interesting questions were raised in respect of Scottish devolution that were never effectively answered, see Box 12.1.

The 1980s and 1990s saw a succession of unionist Thatcherite Scottish secretaries who proved both unpopular and a boom for Scottish nationalism. The introduction of the hugely controversial and unpopular community charge (poll tax) in Scotland, a year before it occurred in England, also fuelled the feeling that the nation had become something of a testing ground for Thatcherism. Attempts by the last Conservative Scottish Secretary, Michael Forsyth, to increase and improve administrative devolution, while also giving a greater role to Westminster's Scottish Committees, did little to reduce the public and political mood for increased political devolution. From the mid-1980s onwards poll after poll indicated that the Scottish population wanted a Scottish par-

liament, and as time went on, this idea became more rather than less popular.

In March 1989 the Scottish Labour and Liberal Democrat Parties, together with a number of minor parties, trade unions, the churches and civil organisations formed the Scottish Constitutional Convention. As the body was only concerned with political devolution rather than independence, the SNP refused to join it. John Smith, George Robertson and Donald Dewar for the Labour Party and David Steel and Jim Wallace for the Scottish Liberal Democrats were the key political figures behind the move towards a Scottish parliament. The Convention published its report setting out the ground for a proportionally elected primary law-making and tax-raising Scottish parliament in November 1995 entitled *Scotland's Parliament, Scotland's Right*. With the Conservatives and Unionists totally removed from Scottish Westminster politics after the 1997 general election, a referendum was held in the September which saw a massive majority in favour of a Scottish Parliament (of those who voted 74.3 per cent were for the Parliament and 60.2 supported tax raising powers). The combined anti-devolutionist forces of both Scottish Labour

BOX 12.1   Scottish influence on UK politics and the West Lothian question

From the introduction of the *Authorised King James's Version of the Bible* (1611), the standard text for the Church of England for more than 250 years, to the succession of Scottish Prime Ministers such as Sir Henry Campbell Bannerman, Ramsey MacDonald, Andrew Bonar Law, Sir Alex Douglas Hume and Gordon Brown, Scottish influence on British politics has been substantial. There have been an even greater number of Scottish Cabinet ministers at Westminster and leaders of other British political parties such as the Liberals/Liberal Democrats (four of their seven postwar leaders). Yet the Scottish influence hasn't always been welcomed. In 1978 the anti-devolutionist Scottish Labour MP Tam Dalyell posed what became known as the West Lothian question. This concerned what right he had to vote on laws related to England and Wales, when English and Welsh MPs could not vote on issues related to West Lothian. This was because they are devolved from the Westminster Parliament to the Scottish Parliament. This issue

has remained contentious to this day. It even concerned Gordon Brown, the Prime Minister, as his Kirkcaldy and Cowdenbeath constituency is in Scotland. This means that he is unable to vote on devolved issues in Scotland. In January 2004 the government only won a vote on top-up fees for England by the use of its Scottish MPs, Gordon Brown being one of these. This had also happened before on the creation of foundation hospitals, despite the fact that the Scottish Parliament had decided not to introduce these fees itself.

In 2005 the number of Scottish MPs at Westminster was reduced from 72 to 57, as part of the attempts to address the situation. This, however, didn't end the problem only reduce it. None of the three main political parties would end the right of Scottish MPs to vote on English bills. The Conservatives, however, plan to end Scottish MPs' right to take part in and vote on the line-by-line consideration of English parliamentary bills.

and Conservative MPs present in 1979 had now gone, which was reflected in the size of the 'Yes' vote.

Financially, the Scottish Parliament still relies on Westminster for its annual block grant and does not have significant tax-raising powers. It can raise income tax levels by up to 3 pence in the pound. This limits its autonomy for fiscal spending and this limited variation in income tax has only been suggested once. This was by the SNP government in 2007 when they suggested raising it in order to introduce a local Scottish income tax to replace the local government council tax. The SNP, however, dropped the idea in the face of fierce business opposition, pressures from Westminster and by the actual practicality of the three pence rise being insufficient to fund a replacement to council tax.

The first Scottish elections were on 6 May 1999 and saw a turnout of 58 per cent. Some 73 Members of the Scottish Parliament (MSPs) were elected by the traditional Westminster style first-past-the-post system and an additional 56 MSPs elected through AMS (the proportional electoral additional member system), in eight Scottish regions. The results were significant because:

- These were the first elections to a Scottish Parliament in three centuries.

- No one party gained a majority, which was not unexpected from the new proportional election, therefore a coalition government would operate in future.

- It saw the UK's first Green Party parliamentarian, on the regional list for the Lothians.

- The first Scottish Militant Party member was also elected – Tommy Sheridan – in the Glasgow region.

- The rebel Labour MP Denis Canavan was elected in Falkirk West. He had been deselected by his own party, then stood against them and won. His success would encourage other Labour members not selected to do the same, not only in Scotland but also in Wales and London.

After the election was held, the process of forming the first Scottish government for almost three centuries occurred. The government in Scotland was initially referred to as 'The Scottish Executive' but is now widely known as 'The Scottish Government'. It is legally separate from the legislature and similar to the position in the Westminster Parliament. No one political party has every gained an overall majority at a Scottish Parliamentary election, see Table 12.2. Therefore after the 1999 and 2003 Scottish elections it was a Labour–Liberal Democrat coalition which formed and signed a four-year cooperation agreement in each instance. The first was called *Partnership for Scotland* followed by the unimaginatively titled *A Partnership for a Better Scotland* in August 2003.

Labour's Donald Dewar became the first politician to take the title of First Minister in Scotland and the Scottish Liberal Democrats' Jim Wallace, was his deputy. Dewar, who was seen as one of the 'fathers of Scottish devolution' died suddenly of a brain haemorrhage on 11 October 2000. He was replaced by Henry McLeish in April 2001. McLeish, however, resigned on 8 November 2001 due to the so-called 'Officegate' expenses row, which centred on the sub-letting of his constituency office in Glenrothes. He, in turn, was replaced by the the Motherwell and Wishaw Member of the Scottish Parliament, Jack McConnell. For the next five-and-a-half years the Scottish coalition executive worked effectively together through a series of policy and

Table 12.2 Scottish general election parliamentary elections results 1999–2007

Party	1999 Constituency	1999 List	2003 Constituency	2003 List	2007 Constituency	2007 List
Labour	53	3	46	4	37	9
Scottish National Party	7	28	9	18	21	26
Conservative and Unionist	0	18	3	15	4	13
Scottish Liberal Democrat	12	5	13	4	11	5
Scottish Green Party	0	1	0	7	0	2
Scottish Socialists	0	1	0	6	0	0
Independents	1	0	2	1	1	0
Others	0	0	0	1	0	0

Holyrood, seat of the Scottish Parliament, cost ten times the original estimate, a worthwhile investment?
Source: PA Wire / Empics

legislative changes which saw Scotland pursuing significantly different policies to those in England. The problems over the introduction of university tuition fees with both sides taking differing views (Labour for them, Scottish Liberal Democrats against) led to an independent commission being established that determined in favour of them not being introduced. The new Parliament building at Holyrood also became something of a scandal, costing ten times its original estimate. Both the architect Enric Miralles and the First Minister Donald Dewar who had been responsible for the original proposals, however, were dead by the time Lord Fraser's inquiry into the building had been undertaken.

From the outset the Scottish Parliament had been established with the power to create its own (primary) laws. This meant that laws could be made in three different ways: namely via Executive Bills, Committee Bills and MSP's Bills. The vast majority of legislation, as with the Westminster Parliament, is through Executive Bills. These Acts have helped provide Scotland with laws as diverse as those giving free long-term care for the elderly to those abolishing fox hunting and establishing STV as a method of election for Scottish local government.

Whereas the 2003 Scottish general election had been significant for continuing the Lab–Lib coalition government and widening the number of political parties present in the Parliament to six political parties, the 2007 election saw an end to this. In that election the SNP gained 20 seats. Its leader, Alex Salmond, returned to the Parliament after a four-year gap during which he had been leading his party at Westminster. The SNPs' gains had been at the expense of the other political parties, in particular the minority parties who had lost 12 of their 14 MSPs. The Conservatives and Labour, however, would not consider going into coalition with the SNP. The Scottish Liberal Democrats also refused to join them in coalition, due to their stance on not supporting a pro-independence party. The SNP formed a minority government with Scottish Green Party support but still 16 seats short of a majority. The centrepiece of the SNP government's programme is its commitment to having a referendum on independence, its so-called 'National Conversation' (see Box 12.3). There was, however, already a debate on Scotland's devolved future. This had arrived following a debate in the Scottish Parliament on 6 December 2007 where those developing it had resolved to set up an independently chaired commission to review devolution in Scotland. This was under Sir Kenneth Calman, Chancellor of the University of Glasgow. The remit of the Commission on Scottish Devolution was:

To review the provisions of the Scotland Act 1998 in the light of experience and to recommend any changes to the present constitutional arrangements that would enable the Scottish Parliament to serve the people of Scotland better, improve the financial accountability of the Scottish Parliament, and continue to secure the position of Scotland within the United Kingdom.

The Commission had the subsequent endorsement of the Scottish Secretary and UK Westminster government in March 2008. While it consulted, the SNP government rose in the opinions polls to as high as 48 per cent in August 2007 and constantly above Labour's share of around 30 per cent. In July 2008, the party triumphed in the by-election in Glasgow East, one of Labour's safest seats, by 365 votes and in the process overturned a Labour majority of 13,507 to win with a swing of 22.54 per cent. It seemed as though the SNP would sweep all before them. The arrival of the credit crunch, however, and subsequent discrediting of the Scottish banks and building societies, including Alex Salmond's former employer, the Royal Bank of Scotland, led to a fall in the SNPs fortunes. In November 2008 Labour won the Glenrothes by-election, with a comfortable majority of 6,737 over the SNP. The constituency bordered Gordon Brown's own seat and therefore the result acted as something of a boost to his own flagging status as Prime Minister. After this victory

the distance between the SNP and Labour in the Scottish opinion polls showed the SNP still to be ahead but often only by one or two per cent. Ten years after devolution had arrived, Scotland once more was very much a two-party dominated system albeit with Labour or the SNP having to find another party in order to gain absolute power.

When the Calman Commission reported back in June 2009 it indicated that after 10 years Scottish devolution could be declared to be a 'success'. In declaring this Calman also recommended that it should further evolve and that Holyrood should take charge over much more of its own revenue raising. In future half the income tax raised in Scotland as well as stamp duty, landfill tax and air passenger duty would be collected by the Scottish government and form a third of its budget. The Calman Commission also said the Scottish Parliament should control other areas such as national speed limits, drink-driving laws and airgun legislation. While the SNP Government criticised Calman for not giving the Scottish Parliament full fiscal powers the other political parties welcomed its recommendation as naturally extending devolution. With a Westminster election on the horizon the Scottish Parliament then set about seeing how Calman could be implemented in practice. Shortly after this the SNP Justice Secretary Kenny MacAskill freed the terminally-ill Lockerbie bomber Abdelbasset Ali al-Megrahi in August, on compassionate grounds. This caused a storm of protest across the political spectrum but in particular in the United States, from President Obama downwards. On 2 September 2009 the SNP was overwhelmingly defeated in a vote on its handling of Ali al-Megrahi's release. Although the SNP continued as a minority government it was felt that Scotland's international standing had been damaged and that the lessons of the Ali al-Megrahi affair would have to be looked at carefully if Scotland was ever itself to become an independent sovereign nation.

Wales

Prior to the Acts of Union between 1536–42 under Henry VIII, Wales was not one nation but a patchwork quilt of crown lands and Marcher lordships. Therefore, until Welsh nationalism emerged in the latter half of the nineteenth century, Wales had been integrated closely into England. To all intents and purposes Wales ceased to be a nation and instead became a series of counties almost fully assimilated into England. During the late nineteenth century the Liberal Prime Minister William Gladstone was the first British leader to accept that Wales was a nation distinct from England. Liberal MPs such as Tom Ellis and David Lloyd George pushed forward Welsh nationalism and consequently the Liberal governments between 1905 and 1916 saw the establishment of many of the trappings of nationhood including a National Library and National Museum.

Despite the founding of Plaid Cymru (Party of Wales) in 1925, Welsh nationalism at a Parliamentary level remained mainly in the Welsh Liberal or Liberal National Party. The Labour Party, which under the Merthyr Tydfil MP Keir Hardie (1900–1916), had been pro-devolution after the First World War, turned almost against it. Those few Labour MPs who were pro-devolution did so against a rising tide of unionism. Nevertheless, despite this strong unionist stance, Jim Griffith, the deputy leader of the Labour Party, who was pro-devolution was able to persuade Harold Wilson and the wider Labour Party to establish both a Welsh Office and a Welsh Secretary in the Cabinet in 1964. This began a period of significant executive devolution in Wales.

The Conservatives in Wales always remained hostile to Welsh devolution with no significant figure emerging as pro-Welsh devolution, during the twentieth century. Thus with the vast majority of Welsh MPs being hostile or indifferent to Welsh devolution and the Welsh Liberals disappearing to just one MP (Emlyn Hooson) by 1966, Welsh nationalism was only reignited in 1966 when the Plaid Cymru President and their political hero, Gwynfor Evans, was elected to Carmarthen in 1966. From now on Plaid Cymru was seen as a direct threat to the Labour Party in Wales and they realised they had to do something to combat the appeal of the rising nationalist tide. As we noted earlier this resulted in the establishment of the Kilbrandon Commission in 1968 and the subsequent failure of the St David's Day devolution referendum in 1979. The referendum had only

occurred in the first place because of the minority Labour government's reliance on Welsh Liberal and Plaid Cymru MPs to stay in power.

A few months after the referendum result, a general election saw Margaret Thatcher's Conservative government elected which then controlled politics in Wales for the next 18 years. Although they always remained against political devolution, the various Conservative Welsh Secretaries enhanced administrative devolution. This included establishing the use of the Barnett formula (Box 12.2) which determined government funding for Wales, the extension of devolved powers in Wales and the reforming of Welsh local government into a system of 22 unitary authorities. Only Nicolas Edwards (1979–87), the first of the Thatcher–Major period Welsh Secretaries, however, was actually a Welsh MP. During the last ten years of Conservative rule in Wales therefore the succession of Welsh Secretaries with English constituencies, including Peter Walker, John Redwood and William Hague, fuelled resentment of a new era of English colonialism by 'unaccountable quasi colonial governors' who ruled via a series of unelected quangos. During this period the Welsh Labour Party continued to win the majority of Welsh seats but remained powerless against their Conservative foes. This was enough to persuade many within the Labour Party to support devolution and therefore by the general election of 1997, the party had become committed to introducing an elected Welsh Assembly in its first term.

When the Labour Party included an element of proportional representation in its plans (the additional member system), it was enough to persuade Plaid Cymru and the Welsh Liberal Democrats to endorse their plans in the referendum. With the Conservatives routed in the 1997 general election, losing all of their Welsh seats, and the Labour anti-devolution MPs silenced there was no effective opposition to the 'Yes' campaign. This helped them

BOX 12.2 Barnett formula

The Barnett formula was brought in as a funding mechanism for the devolved administrations prior to their expected arrival in 1979. The funding formula from the Westminster government to the proposed devolved bodies was established by Joel Barnett, then the Labour Chief Secretary to the Treasury. It was based loosely on the population sizes of Scotland, Wales and England (10:5:85). The Barnett Formula remains controversial, in that various political parties state that it is either too generous or not generous enough and needs revision. Despite these claims the Barnett Formula has only undergone slight alterations since it was introduced in 1979.

Rt Hon Ron Davies (1946–)

Secretary of State for Wales 1997–98, leader of the Wales Labour Party 1998. At the age of 24 leader of Bedwas and Machen Urban District Council, youngest in the UK. Elected MP for Caerphilly in 1983 and joined the Opposition front bench in 1987 as Agriculture spokesman. Shadow Welsh Secretary from October 1992. Drew up most of the Welsh devolution policy and successfully led the 'Yes for Wales' referendum. Regarded as the 'father of Welsh devolution'. He resigned as Welsh Secretary and the Welsh Labour leader in 1998, after a sexual scandal on Clapham Common. Elected as the Assembly Member for Caerphilly in 1999 he resigned from that position in 2003 after another sexual scandal. In 2008, he was elected as an Independent councillor and then served as a Cabinet Member in the Plaid Cymru-led Caerphilly County Council. In the process he became the first New Labour Cabinet member to serve the cause and policy aims of another political party. Davies' evolution from New Labour Cabinet Member and 'father of devolution' to Council Cabinet Member of Plaid Cymru-led council in ten years is perhaps one of the most unusual changes in career path in Welsh political history.

win a narrow victory, by just 6,721 votes (0.3 per cent of the total vote). Wales was then given a national assembly of some 60 elected members (40 constituency members and 20 proportional members – list members). This assembly, unlike that in Scotland and Northern Ireland, would only have the power to amend secondary, rather than to originate its own primary legislation.

The Labour leader, Ron Davies, who led the 'Yes' campaign did not become the First Secretary (changed in 2001 to First Minister) as envisaged. Davies had been forced to resign and so a new leader was needed (see Biography). Thus when the dust settled after the 1999 Welsh Assembly elections it was Alun Michael, Ron Davies replacement as Welsh Secretary, and Tony Blair's loyal right-hand man in Wales who became the First secretary. He had won a controversial Labour party election competition against Rhodri Morgan to become Davies' replacement. Michael led a minority government in the Welsh Assembly and had initially refused to go into coalition with the Welsh Liberal Democrats, preferring to govern alone. As his party lacked a majority by three seats, it was only a matter of time before they were defeated. This came over a vote of 'no confidence' concerning his ability to gain matched-funding from the Westminster government's Treasury to secure European Objective One funding to Wales. Gordon Brown, then Chancellor, did not give his support in time and Michael resigned. He was replaced by Rhodri Morgan in an unelected leadership contest. Morgan then gained the required finance from the Treasury

and formed a coalition government with the Welsh Liberal Democrats led by Michael German.

The Lab–Lib Welsh Assembly coalition (2000–2003) was significant for five main things:

1 It gave both Wales and the Liberal Democrats their first taste of coalition government since 1945. In the process it showed that coalition government could be stable and that the identity of those political parties within it could remain distinct.

2 It revitalised the Welsh Assembly government's policy outputs by introducing a raft of Welsh policies such as limitation on top-up fees for students and free entry to museums that could be seen to be distinctly Welsh.

3 It started the process of changing the Assembly from one based on the vision of a corporate body, in which the opposition and government were both members of the legislature, to develop into one where the Assembly Members were divided into the executive and legislature.

4 The Assembly became a truly bilingual institution, whereby its business was conducted through both Welsh and English, led by the Presiding Officer – Lord Elis Thomas (the former leader of Plaid Cymru and Chairman of the Welsh Language Board).

5 It established a number of commissions which examined controversial aspects of Welsh Assembly coalition policy. The Rees Commission, for instance, provided a compromise solution

of student tuition fees, and the Sunderland Commission looked at the future of Welsh local government. It was the Richard Commission (chaired by the Labour Peer Lord Ivor Richard) which was established to examine the Assembly's current powers and the adequacy of its electoral systems.

The 2003 Welsh Assembly elections had seen Labour gain exactly half of the Assembly seats with the opposition gaining the other half. Lord Dafydd Elis Thomas immediately accepted the Presiding Officer's post once more. He had been the Presiding Officer (the Assembly's equivalent of the House of Commons Speaker) in the 1999–2003 Assembly. As the Presiding Officer can only vote in the Assembly's plenary sessions as a casting vote in the event of a tie, Thomas's decision meant that Labour now had an effective majority of one. They did not need to form a coalition. Rhodri Morgan was once more elected the First Minister and the Assembly set out to follow a Labour policy agenda, which, among other things, included the abolition of prescription fees in Wales.

When the Richard Commission reported back, it was after the Lab–Lib Coalition government had finished. They recommended that the Assembly be given full law-making powers and that it increase the number of Assembly Members to 80, to be elected by STV. Richard also recommended that the Welsh Assembly be formally divided on a parliamentary legislature and executive basis. While the Labour Party was happy to accept the last recommendation, it did not want to accept the first two. Therefore the electoral arrangements were ignored and the law-making powers were reduced to a complicated staged implementation of primary powers which still had to go through Westminster.

At the start of 2005, amid much controversy about rising costs, as it had risen in price from £12 million to £24 million pounds, the Assembly moved into a purpose-built legislative chamber on Cardiff Bay's waterfront. Then in May the Labour Assembly Member Peter Law contested his own Bleanau Gwent seat against the official Labour 'all-women shortlist' candidate. Law won the seat but in the process was expelled from the Labour Party. The Labour Party was now in a minority in the Assembly but limped on in government for the next two years suffering a number of defeats and having to come to 'arrangements' with the other political parties in order to get their policies and budget through. This provided an important reminder to the Labour Party of the instability of one-party minority government.

The 2007 Assembly elections, now entitled the 'Welsh General Election' once again saw no one party gain a majority, with Labour remaining the largest party but with five seats short of a majority (see Table 12.3). It was then a whole month before the parties fully examined the various possible combinations possible and the result was somewhat of a surprise for everyone including the political parties themselves. Labour joined together with its bitter political foe, Plaid Cymru, in what was termed the Red–Green Alliance (Red being the colour of Labour and Green that of Plaid Cymru). Rhodri Morgan once more became the first Minister and Plaid Cymru's leader Ieuen Wyn Jones the Deputy Minister. At the centre of the agreement between the parties was the establishment of another commission – the All Wales Convention – to examine how the proposed referendum in Wales on obtaining full primary law making would be best won. The Commission was chaired by the former British Ambassador to the United Nations, Sir Emyr Jones Parry. The desire for full law-making powers in Wales has risen over 2007, 2008 and 2009 (see Table 12.4).

Initially, the Labour government in Westminster under Tony Blair had tried to control the policy outputs of the Welsh Assembly. Over time, however, this desire to control had diminished and Wales was allowed very much to go its own way. Here Labour

Table 12.3 Welsh Assembly election results 1999–2007

Year	Constituency 1999	List 1999	Constituency 2003	List 2003	Constituency 2007	List 2007
Labour	27	1	30	0	24	2
Plaid Cymru	9	8	5	7	7	8
Conservatives	1	8	1	10	5	7
Welsh Liberal Democrats	3	3	3	3	3	3
Independents/others	0	0	1	0	1	0

BOX 12.3 Independence

Whereas there are no political parties advocating independence for Northern Ireland, there are those who advocate it for Wales, Scotland and even England. In a BBC Wales/ICM poll on 24 February 2009, some 13 per cent of Welsh people supported an independent Wales either inside or outside of the European Union. In similar polls in 1997, this figure had stood at 14.1 per cent and in 2003 at 13.9 per cent. Even in Plaid Cymru opinion is split as to whether the party should pursue independence or not. This is not the case in Scotland, however. Here the SNP, as the government there have committed themselves to bringing forward a Referendum Bill in 2010, offering the options of the status quo, enhanced devolution or full independence. The process leading up to this has been entitled the 'National Conversation'. All of the main UK parties reject independence for Scotland, although in May 2008, Labour's former Scottish leader Wendy Alexander backed a referendum while Gordon Brown did not.

In November 2006, an ICM opinion poll for the *Sunday Telegraph* set the desire for independence among Scots at 52 per cent. By February 2009, however, it was down to 33 per cent, indicating the changeability on the issue. The more surprising element of the *Sunday Telegraph* poll was the fact that 48 per cent of English voters also wanted complete independence from the rest of the UK. This is also the view of the English National Party which frequently contests elections, albeit with little success, with English independence as its central policy agenda.

Table 12.4 The desire to see primary law-making powers for Wales

Institution	2007	2008	2009
In favour of turning assembly into full law-making parliament	47	49	52
Against turning assembly into full law-making parliament	44	42	39
Don't know	9	9	9

Source: BBC Wales/ICM polls, June 2007, February 2008, February 2009

Table 12.5 Who has the most influence on Wales?

Institution	1999	2003	2009
Assembly government	26	22.4	40
UK Government	25	57.9	29
Local councils	7	15	15
European Union	37	4.7	8
Don't know	6	0	7

Sources: 1999 poll *The Economist* Newspaper Limited, London (6 November 1999); 2003 poll Richard Commission; 2009 poll, BBC Wales/ICM poll (24 February 2009)

worked with both the Welsh Liberal Democrats and later Plaid Cymru to pursue agreed policy agendas in a way that was still alien to the Labour governments of Westminster. The ten years of Welsh devolution had also shown that there was a demand from within the Welsh Assembly and across the Welsh public for greater devolution. This, however, had been resisted and limited by the more unionist elements within the Welsh Labour Party rather than the British Labour Party in the ways it had previously used. The Welsh Labour MPs, conscious of their loss of power and status, continued to resist further advances in devolution. Yet the demands for increased powers remained solid in Wales and it is therefore likely that the Welsh Assembly will develop into a Parliament more similar to the Scottish model. By 2009 opinion polls were already indicating that the Welsh people thought that the Welsh Assembly government had the greatest influence on their lives, itself an indication of just how much it had embedded itself into Welsh life (Table 12.5).

■ Devolution and the European Union (EU)

Jennifer Todd's models of devolution, cited at the start of this chapter, see devolution in the UK in part as a need to adapt to the EU's desire of 'European regionalism'. In turn, opinion polls across the United Kingdom have sometimes stated that the EU is the most important influential political institution on their lives (see Table 12.5). The level of trust in the EU across the UK has also increased over time. The *Eurobarometer*, that judges public

Table 12.6 Interest in EU affairs in the devolved nations/region

	Wales	Scotland	Northern Ireland	Greater London	UK average
Interested/fairly interested in European affairs	54.7	53.7	54.9	59.2	52.8
Voted in the last European elections	33.5	39.2	48.3	34.4	33.8
Believe that the EU should take a role in tackling:					
Climate change	86.1	81.2	83	79.3	80.4
Terrorism	92.2	86.3	86.3	83.4	85.6
Protecting human rights	88.4	88.6	85	86.7	84.8

Source: Eurobarometer (2007) Attitudes towards the EU in the United Kingdom, FlashEurobarometer 207, May 2007

opinion across the EU, has indicated that the awareness and interest in the EU among the devolved nations is considerably higher than the UK average, see Table 12.6.

Prior to political devolution to the non-English nations in the United Kingdom, there were three territorial departments' (Northern Ireland, Scottish and Welsh Offices) connections to the European Commission. This was mainly through four different processes:

1 The direct links and setting up of administrative processes required by the process of administering the Common Agricultural Policy and the European structural funds (European Social Fund and European Regional Development Funds).

2 The establishment of or support of territorial offices in Brussels, such as the Wales Information Centre. These acted as information gathering and lobbying organisations.

3 The secondment of territorial departments' civil servants to the European Commission and UKrep (the United Kingdom's Embassy to the European Commission).

4 The territorial departments' ministers attending Council of Ministers meetings and their inclusion in the Westminster government's Cabinet European Committee.

The EU referred to the territorial departments when they existed and later on to the English Regional Assemblies as sub-national authorities (SNAs). As those SNAs that covered the territorial departments gained political devolution the Westminster government committed itself to include them in the EU policy process. Although the UK government was keen to retain a single UK position on all EU issues, it did allow the non-English devolved bodies con-

siderable access to the UK's EU policy-making mechanisms. It also allowed Scotland and Northern Ireland primary legislative competence over those areas of responsibilities that had been devolved which were affected by EU policy. Wales, lacking the primary legislative powers, did not gain this same responsibility.

The relationship between the three devolved bodies and the Westminster government was developed through an inter-administration memorandum of understanding (MoU) in 2001 between the Office of the Deputy Prime Minister, then John Prescott, and the three devolved bodies. The MoU laid down a concordat for coordinating EU policy across the United Kingdom. In essence, the relationship meant that the Westminster government allowed the devolved bodies full integration into the process provided that the devolved bodies respected the confidentiality of the process and kept any discussions concerning this EU policy process within the designated processes. It took some while for the Whitehall Departments to fully remember that they had a duty to consult about relevant EU issues with the devolved bodies. Ultimately, as the UK lacks a constitutional court to resolve differences, the devolved SNAs can only get their own EU policy desires satisfied by successfully lobbying the Westminster government. As we saw earlier, this happened in Wales in 2000 when the Assembly successfully lobbied the Westminster government for additional resources to match-fund EU structural funds. This was too late, however, to save the career of the Labour First Secretary, Alan Michael, who lost a vote of no confidence over this issue.

The main area of access to and influence on EU policy making therefore remains the Westminster government. The SNAs also have a representation of the EU's Committee of the Regions which represents all 74 for the EUs designated regions. This body

457

acts a mechanism for the regions to influence overall policy. All of the political devolved SNAs have offices in Brussels to serve as their eyes and ears with the Commission and Parliament. These offices, however, are not used on the whole to bypass the Westminster government but instead to act as an additional resource and information gatherer for each body. Officially therefore, the UK government regards them as part of the extended UKrep family rather than as independent agencies and they have consequently been given the requisite diplomatic status.

There are a number of differing characteristics of the devolved bodies and EU policy making. As the UK has what is known as asymmetrical (unequal) devolution and differing national interests or attitudes to the EU, policy creation differs. Thus, whereas fishing is an important issue in Scottish–EU relations, it is of little importance in Wales. Whereas the issue of ensuring that the European Parliament accepts Welsh as a fully recognised language is important to Wales–EU relations but acknowledges it is of no importance to the other devolved nations. At the same time the Westminster government will also often listen more to the opinions of one nation it regards as having more expertise in that area. Asymmetrical devolution also means that the English regions do not have the same impact on the EU process as do the other three nations. Within the SNAs, also the specific attention paid to EU issues varies. Therefore despite the fact that the Mayor of London is responsible for administering the European Structural Funds there is no specific committee on the GLA to scrutinise European issues directly. Instead it goes through the other committees. The case is similar in the Northern Ireland Assembly. Scotland and Wales, however, have both committees and ministers responsible for EU policy making.

The devolved bodies have also been able to interpret EU policies according to their own criteria, on occasions, setting the rules even if they have not been sanctioned by the European Commission. In February 2009, for instance, the Northern Ireland Assembly allocated farm modernisation payments on a 'first come, first served' basis which saw thousands of farmers waiting outside the Department of Agriculture's offices for days. Although the European Commission stated the projects should only get funding on 'objective criteria, rather than a first come, first served basis', the Northern Ireland Assembly still interpreted matters in its own way. This has caused considerable confusion which may not have occurred had there existed a centralised UK policy.

■ England and its regions

England under the flag of St George is seen from the outside as being one homogenous nation. There are, however, strong regional identities which politicians can only ignore at their peril. People in numerous English towns, cities and councils have their own distinct identities as strong as any national ones. Politicians have been long aware of this English regional distinctiveness which is particularly acute in counties such as Cornwall and Yorkshire and cities such as Liverpool, Manchester and London. Politicians, however, have been split as to how to deal with the distinctiveness. Over the last decade they have sought to tackle it by supporting it with regional political and administrative devolution. They have embraced local identity through the local government authority reorganisation with the re-establishment of old counties such as Rutland and old county borough councils such as Reading and Oxford. Unionists within both the Labour and Conservative parties, however, have sought to have minimum English regional identity and instead retain a strong unitary parliament in Westminster.

The origins of English devolution go back to a Speaker's conference in 1920 which decided the best solution to the problems of the devolutionary pressures in Ireland was 'Home Rule all round' for all of the British Isles nation states. The Labour and Conservative governments of that period did not agree with this notion, however and devolution of administrative power in England made slow progress. In the 1930s came the embryos of devolved government from the Special Areas Act 1934 which classified specific areas of the England according to their economic deprivation. Then during the Second World War England was divided into regional government areas for defence and other administrative purposes under regional governors. In the 1960s, the Regional Economic Planning Councils and Regional Economic Planning Boards were set up under Harold Wilson's Labour government. In the 1970s the Kilbrandon Commission had suggested regional elected authorities for England but the measure had not gone forward after the failure of Scottish and Welsh devolution in 1979. Then, under Margaret Thatcher's Conservative government, Urban Development Corporations were set up in the 1980s. All devolved some elements of administrative power from Whitehall to the regions but the boundaries of the different organisations often did not coincide. At the same time the Thatcher government had become increasingly frustrated by the Labour-controlled metropolitan authorities and the Greater London Council (led by Ken Livingstone) acting as alternative centres of power and undermining their own administration. They therefore abolished them all in 1986 leaving the large English metropolitan areas without an elected layer of government to control cross-borough activities.

Implementing the so-called 'European regionalism' model of devolution, it was the arrival of the EU's reforms to its Structural Funds (which provide economic assistance to specified regions) that required set and administratively integrated regional offices. Therefore in 1994, under Prime Minister John Major, the ten Government Offices of the Regions were established with the purpose of bringing together those elements of central government that needed to be integrated in order to make use of the EU's structural funds. When Labour came into power they turned these Government Offices into Regional Development Agencies which had Regional Chambers (RCs) above them. The RCs in the English regions were made up of appointed local government councillors, people from business and industry and other notables. When they were established at the start of the century it was thought that this would be a temporary measure and that in time they would replaced by democratically elected members. In the event this did not occur and they were in time disbanded. The thrust beyond English devolution in Tony Blair's government came almost wholly from John Prescott, the Deputy Prime Minister. English devolution fell under his direct remit.

When Jack Straw had been the Labour Home Secretary in charge of the devolutionary process at the start of New Labour's 1997 term in office, he had defined what was called 'the triple lock' on the progress of English political devolution. This stated that if an English region wanted political devolution:

- They would have to petition to become a directly elected assembly.

- Parliament would have to legislate for this.

- The electorate in the region would have to approve these measures in a referendum.

With Wales, Scotland and then Northern Ireland gaining devolution, England became one of the few countries in Europe without a form of regional government. This changed marginally in 2000 when a referendum was passed which established an elected mayor for London and an elected London Regional Authority, see Box 12.4. This did not apply for the rest of England, however. Prescott was therefore keen to see this spread to other English regions even if it didn't comply with Jack Straw's triple lock. Opinion polls had indicated that there was a demand for English regional government. This was highest in the north-east and north-west. In 2002 Prescott brought out the White paper: Your Region, Your Choice: Revitalising the English Regions which was followed by the White paper Your Region, Your Say. This set out the case for elected regional chambers in the English regions but not all at once, instead, it would be a step-by-step approach with the regions with the strongest identity going first. The Regional Assemblies (Preparations) Act 1993 went through Westminster and it was then planned to hold postal referendums in the north-west, north-east and Yorkshire and Humberside. Problems with postal voting during the European elections in June 2004 meant that the referendum on English devolution was scaled down to just one region – the north-east – and on 4 November 2004 a referendum was held there.

Support for the concept of a regional assembly in the north-east failed by almost five to one. The two 'No' campaigns, which ran there, had successfully defeated the 'Yes' campaign on similar issues to those that had resulted in the Welsh people rejecting their Assembly referendum in 1979. These revolved around the perception that they didn't want any more politicians, the assembly wasn't powerful enough, their regional identity wasn't strong enough, most Labour and Conservative politicians remained against it, as did local government which feared being scrapped.

The negative vote in the north-east in effect killed off English devolution. The Regional Chambers were scrapped although the RDAs were kept. Government ministers were now allocated to the nine English regions to run the RDAs. The Westminster Parliament set up eight English Regional Select Committees on an experimental basis in November 2008 to monitor the ministers and the RDAs. As part of the national strategy on the recession Gordon Brown also linked the RDAs and their government ministers into a Regional Economic Council to help plan government strategy. There were, however, no plans to make this an elected body, although the Conservatives still plan an English-only voting Parliament for Westminster.

BOX 12.4   Personality politics: The Mayor of London

There is one area of England that does have its own devolved government. That is London, with the Greater London Authority (GLA). The GLA is made up of a directly elected mayor and a separately elected authority. The Mayor of London controls a number of the capital's major public bodies. He sets the budget for the Metropolitan Police Service (MPS), Transport for London (TfL), The London Fire and Emergency Planning Authority (LFEPA), the London Development Agency (LDA) and the Greater London Authority (GLA).

Even before its inception the position of elected mayor of the authority became one of personality politics. Ken Livingstone, the former Labour leader of the GLC saw himself as the rightful heir to the mayor of the GLA. He was not selected by Labour in its controversial selection contest and then stood and won as an Independent against the official Labour candidate. For the next eight years Livingstone ran London with both success and personal controversy, often in the process ignoring the role of the GLA as a scrutinising body. It was Livingstone who introduced the successful traffic congestion charge and also helped gain the Olympics for London in 2012.

Livingstone was defeated in 2008 by a Conservative politician as colourful in character as himself, Boris Johnson. The former MP for Henley-on-Thames and editor of *The Spectator*, Johnson had established a reputation for political mishaps and general buffoonery. Nevertheless this only added spice to his appeal as a candidate and he was duly elected by a majority of 139,772 votes.

The London-based media had engaged with the London mayoral election to a degree unparalleled in British politics, outside of the British general elections. Combined with the Conservative candidate victory this now enthused the Conservative party to introduce elected mayors across England. This was despite the fact that Labour's plans to introduce elected mayors had already widely failed and the Conservatives themselves had scrapped the metropolitan counties in the 1980s when council leaders such as Ken Livingstone had been seen to challenge their authority in central government.

Table 12.7 Public spending as share of GDP UK countries and London 2006

Nation/region	2005–06
United Kingdom	43.0%
England	40.9%
London	33.4%
Wales	62.4%
Scotland	54.9%
Northern Ireland	71.3%

Source: Office for National Statistics, 2008

Table 12.8 GDP per inhabitant UK countries and London 2006

Nation/region	GDP per inhabitant (euros)	GDP as a percentage of the EU average
United Kingdom	32,000	120.4
London	52,900	198.8
Wales	24,000	90.4
Scotland	30,800	115.9
Northern Ireland	26,000	97.1

Source: *Eurostat*, February 2009 (there is no separate figure for England)

■ Conclusions on devolution

After a decade of devolution in the United Kingdom we can conclude that it has had a number of impacts on the British political system. The foremost of these are:

■ Devolution has not helped the nations and regions of the regions converge (Tables 12.7 and 12.8). Disparities have remained as wide as under the strictly unionist state.

■ The constituent parts of the United Kingdom have not broken away from each other as was predicted by the anti-devolutionists. Even in Scotland where the SNP has pursued this policy it still looks fairly remote. The Union therefore has remained intact.

- Most of the political parties who are represented in the devolved bodies are not happy with the status quo. There have therefore been constant revisions and proposals for revisions of the constitutional devolution settlements.

- No one political party has ever gained the majority of the seats in a devolved government election. Coalition government and/or electoral pacts have become the norm now outside of Westminster politics. The Scottish Parliament and Northern Ireland Assembly have for their entire existence consisted of coalition governments. The Welsh Assembly has consisted of coalition governments for two of its three terms. This has moved the devolved governments and British politics closer to the European style of politics.

- The stability of the executives in Scotland and Wales has proved that proportional representation does not lead to unstable government, as has always been claimed would be the case, if it was introduced in Westminster.

- A whole new generation of young and female politicians who would have been unable to progress through the existing political system to Westminster have emerged. This has greatly reduced the gender imbalance in British politics. At the same time there has been the opportunity for the advancement of minor parties such as the Greens that have not been represented at Westminster thereby increasing the diversity of the political system.

- The quality of the elected representatives to the devolved institutions, however, has not always been of the level expected at the outset of devolution. Sometimes these have been unfavourably compared with those going to Westminster. This has led to accusations that devolved institutions have had to make do with 'second eleven' with the 'first eleven' going to Westminster. Many of those elected come from a local government,

public services or political party administrative background. What is forgotten, however, is that there are also equally poor Westminster MPs but because the media highlights only the most able Westminster politicians the poorer ones tend to go unnoticed.

- Relations between central and devolved governments have seen minimal change from pre-devolution arrangements for dealing with Scottish, Welsh and Northern Irish matters, relying on departmental concordats, bilateral and informal links largely among officials and not ministers. As a result the constitutional deadlock, also widely predicted, between the centre and devolved government has not occurred.

- With a lack of their own tax-raising powers, the devolved institutions are still under the considerable influence of Whitehall, the Chancellor of the Exchequer and the Treasury. Frustrations over the adequacy of the Barnett Formula remain, with non-English nations requiring greater funding. In time, however, particularly this may change. This is especially true in Scotland with the Calman Report advocating much larger tax-raising power there.

- Policy and service differences between the devolved nations and England have intensified, particularly in certain aspects of healthcare. This has caused regional jealousy and animosity to occur.

- Not all politicians at Westminster have been prepared to accept the devolution in their own political powers and there often remains resistance or hostility to losing these powers. This has become most apparent in Wales as the nation moves towards a referendum on gaining full primary law-making powers for its Assembly. While most Assembly Members support the transfer of powers, most Westminster MPs do not.

- Personality politics, particularly in London, has caught the attention of the media creating unprecedented interest in devolved politics.

Chapter summary

At the start of this chapter we looked at Todd's three models of devolution. The type of devolution in Britain appears to have occurred along a version of Todd's 'state realism' model, within elements of the 'European regionalism' model. Devolution has resulted in modest and incremental change, with some minimal adaptations to cope with the demands devolution has created, in both Westminster and Whitehall. Westminster still maintains a strong legislative role in the devolved nations. This is true even in Scotland where the Sewell convention enables Westminster to legislate for devolved matters with the Scottish Parliament's consent. Westminster maintains a strong presence over taxation, international affairs, commerce and the economy and many social welfare issues. At the same time the Home Civil Service remains loyal to no single devolved government but instead to the crown. The much heralded break up of the United Kingdom therefore seems not a great deal closer than it was when the devolution process started in 1997, despite the threat of an independence referendum in Scotland. Relations between the devolved institutions and the Westminster government have also remained good even when there has been a difference of party political government in Scotland and Westminster. The fiscal restraint caused by the banking crisis and the role of a future Conservative government in its relationship with the devolved institutions may test this relationship once more. At the moment though it appears that devolution has been a further stage of political evolution rather than the revolution some sceptics predicted.

Discussion points

■ How have the policy differences affected the lives of the citizens in the respective nation states in terms of issues such as education and health?

■ Has devolution resulted in the end of the concept of Britishness?

■ Why do you think that English nationalism still remains a relatively minor political force?

■ Have the London-based political parties fully accepted their lack of control over events in the devolved nations?

■ Has devolution caused British politics to become more European and less Anglo-Saxon in nature?

■ What will be the likely shape of devolution by 2020?

Further reading

Those who wish to have brief overall picture of devolution and its developments should read

Devolution in the United Kingdom by Russell Deacon and Alan Sandry. A more comprehensive coverage of devolution can be found in *Devolution in Britain Today* by Russell Deacon. Those students who wish to examine the devolved politics of a particular region or nation now have a wealth of texts to choose from, including official publications and reports of the devolved bodies themselves. Edinburgh University Press, Manchester University Press and the University of Wales Press specialise in these, as do Welsh Academic Press. In particular, the reports produced by the Institute of Welsh Affairs and The Constitution Unit of the University of London are particularly useful.

Bibliography

Bulmer, Simon, Burch, Martin, Hogwood, Patricia and Scott, Andrew 'UK Devolution and the European Union: A Tale of Cooperative Asymmetry?', *Publius: The Journal of Federalism*, Vol. 36, No. 1, pp. 75–93.

Deacon, Russell (2002) *The Governance of Wales: The Welsh Office and the Policy Process 1964–99* (Welsh Academic Press).

Deacon, Russell (2006) *Devolution in Britain Today* (Manchester University Press).

Deacon, Russell and Sandry, Alan (2007) *Devolution in the United Kingdom* (Edinburgh University Press).

Devine, Tom (ed.) (2008) *Scotland and the Union 1707–2007* (Edinburgh University Press).

Eurobarometer (2007) Attitudes towards the EU in the United Kingdom, FlashEurobarometer 207, May 2007.

McEvoy, Joanne (2008) *The Politics of Northern Ireland* (Edinburgh University Press).

Osmond, John (2007) *Crossing the Rubicon: Coalition Politics Welsh Style* (Institute of Welsh Affairs).

Palmer, Rosanne (2008) *Devolution, Asymmetry and Europe: Multi-Level Governance in the United Kingdom* (Peter Lang).

Todd, Jennifer (2005), 'A New Territorial Politics in the British Isles?' in John Coakely, Brigid Laffan and Jennifer Todd, *Renovation Or Revolution? New Territorial Politics in Ireland and the United Kingdom* (University College Dublin Press).

And another thing . . .

The great parliamentary expenses crisis

Chris Mullin, MP

'THEY'RE ALL AT IT,' screamed the front page of the *Daily Mirror* over a story about MPs allowances.

Actually, we're not. The only place where I have ever worked where they were 'all at it' was Mirror Group Newspapers in the 1970s where, at the end of my first week, my expense claim was rejected by the man who was supposed to vouch for its accuracy on the grounds that it was so low that it would be an embarrassment to my colleagues.

I was then treated to a lesson in how to construct a fraudulent expense claim which, when no one was looking, I threw away.

One is not obliged, however, to believe every tabloid lie to recognise that MPs have brought much of their current travail upon themselves. It has been obvious for years that the system of remuneration and allowances is deeply flawed, that there have been wholesale abuses and that many opportunities for reform have been either avoided or actively resisted.

The flaws are threefold. First, to the huge embarrassment of many of us, we get to decide how much we should receive in pay and allowances. This has been justified on the grounds that Parliament is sovereign and, therefore, even though the issue is referred to the Senior Salaries Review Body, it is up to us to decide whether or not to accept their recommendations. So far as salaries are concerned, MPs have, in recent years at least, been generally restrained, often voting for lower than recommended increases in keeping with government pay policy. There have been notable exceptions, however. In 1996 MPs voted by a large majority (some of us were opposed) to award themselves a whopping 26 per cent pay increase.

So far as allowances are concerned, we have been generous to ourselves. In 2001 we voted through (again some of us, I am glad to say, voted against) an outrageous 42 per cent increase in the Additional Costs Allowance that enables those of us who represent constituencies beyond commuting distance of Westminster to maintain a second home, either in London or the constituency. From that moment onwards it became a target to be aimed at, rather than recompense for expenses legitimately incurred.

The second major flaw is that there has been no effective system of audit. For years officials of the House of Commons Fees Office encouraged Members to maximise their claims, rather than regulating how the allowances were spent. When I was first elected and for many years afterwards, it was not uncommon for a Member asking for advice to be told, 'it's your money, spend it as you see fit'. Some members came to regard the allowance as an extension of their salary, simply dividing the maximum amount claimable by 12 and claiming in monthly instalments, without ever being asked to provide any serious evidence of outgoings. Gradually, in recent years, the rules have been tightened, but old habits die hard.

Third, there was an absence of transparency and, therefore, no pressure on Members to justify their use of public money. When the Freedom of Information Act became law in 1999, it took a while for MPs to grasp the likely consequences. But the consequences were foreseeable. As long ago as May 2002 the then Leader of the House, Robin Cook, remarked presciently that 'few members have yet tumbled to the juggernaut heading their way'. How right he was.

Once the penny did drop, instead of cleaning up the system, the House of Commons authorities moved heaven and earth to avoid having to comply. The whips on both sides conspired to introduce a Private Members' Bill that would have exempted

MPs from the provisions of the Act. In fairness, it must be said that many Members refused to go along with this and as a result the proposed bill was swiftly abandoned.

By now requests for information were flooding in from journalists and members of the public. The House authorities initially responded by publishing headline figures for different categories of each MP's expenses. At the same time the rules were tightened, requiring the provision of receipts – but only for expenditure over £250. Unsurprisingly, this did not satisfy inquirers, whose appetite had by now been whetted by attempts to avoid disclosure. Unwisely, the House authorities chose to resist, employing lawyers to argue that the limited disclosure already conceded was sufficient to meet the demands of the Freedom of Information Act. Needless to say the Information Commissioner, Richard Thomas, was having none of this. Neither were the judges who, in due course, ruled that MPs should have to account in full for their use of public money.

At which point the House authorities caved in and agreed to provide full details of expenses claims for each of the previous four years, minus addresses and personal details such as bank account numbers and credit card details. It was a massive task. More than a million documents had to be scanned and MPs were given a chance to comment and to suggest deletions. While this was underway, someone apparently stole the computer disc containing the unedited details and sold it to the *Daily Telegraph* for a six-figure sum.

The results were devastating. For day after relentless day the *Telegraph* published details of some of the more exotic claims for the maintenance and repairs of swimming pools, tennis courts and even a moat. Home Secretary Jacqui Smith's husband was found, unknown to her, to have claimed for the hire of a pornographic video; more seriously she was found to be claiming the second home allowance against her family home. She was not the only one.

A new phenomenon – which quickly became known as 'flipping' – was identified. Some MPs, it appeared, were changing homes frequently in order to exploit to the full the second home allowance. Some were, at the same time, temporarily designating second homes as principal residences in order to avoid Capital Gains Tax when they sold up. Several were found to be claiming for mortgages that no longer existed. One was found to be claiming for a home on the south coast, over 100 miles from her constituency.

Almost immediately heads began to roll. Several ministers – including the Home Secretary – resigned or stepped down voluntarily from the government. Half a dozen Tory grandees who had been using the second homes allowance to maintain their country estates announced that they would not be contesting the next election. A number of Labour MPs announced – or were instructed by their party to announce – that they, too, would not be seeking re-election. One stood down immediately, triggering a by-election.

Party leaders vied with each other to demonstrate to an outraged public that they were dealing firmly with miscreants. Gordon Brown publicly disowned a member of his Cabinet who had avoided paying Capital Gains Tax. The Labour Party set up a 'Star Chamber' to deal with the most blatant examples of abuse. Tory leader David Cameron ordered the worst offenders in his party to repay excess claims – he himself repaid the cost of trimming the wisteria (Tory excesses were so much more elegant than Labour's) on his constituency residence and some of the big Tory offenders were simply ordered to announce that they would not contest the next election or face expulsion. One of Cameron's close aides, Andrew McKie, was among the casualties, along with his wife, Julie Kirkbride. Not to be outdone, the Liberal leader Nick Clegg called for constituents to be given the right to recall, mid-term, misbehaving MPs.

On 19 May 2009, the scandal consumed its most prominent victim. The Speaker, Michael Martin, announced his retirement. Fairly or unfairly, Speaker Martin had become widely regarded as an obstacle to reform and in the end pressure on him to stand down became irresistible.

The tabloids were in heaven. Tabloid journalism requires a constant supply of victims, be they misbehaving footballers, errant soap stars or dodgy politicians – and here, courtesy of the *Telegraph*, was an unlimited supply. Even the most minor infringements suddenly became front page news.

The political impact was considerable. For the first time opinion polls rated MPs as lower in public esteem than even the bankers who had brought the world economy to the brink of destruction. All the main parties were contaminated, but Labour came off worst, partly because it was the governing party and it happened on their watch. The impact was reflected in the results of European elections in June 2009 when the Labour vote all but collapsed. Even the Tories, who had been riding high in the opinion polls, did not do particularly well. The beneficiaries were fringe parties, unrepresented at Westminster: the United Kingdom Independence Party, the Greens and – ominously – the British National Party.

The impact on the self-confidence of the political classes was devastating. For weeks the House of Commons was traumatised as members sat around awaiting the call from the *Daily Telegraph*. An unprecedented number of sitting Members, innocent and guilty alike, decided to stand down come the election. The damage to politics in general and the democratic process as a whole is incalculable.

As for the future, the key reforms have already been made. Transparency and proper audit will ensure that the abuses of the past can never be repeated. The damage to the political system as a whole will, however, take much longer to repair.

Chris Mullin was the MP for Sunderland South from 1987 to 2010. In 2009 he published a volume of diaries entitled *A View From the Foothills*. Two further volumes are in the pipeline.

Index

Page references followed by "f" indicate illustrated figures or photographs; followed by "t" indicates a table.

A

Access channels
    mass media and, 277-286
Advisory committees, 302
Anarchism, 33, 70
Aristotle, 2
Attlee, Clement, 45
Authoritarian
    regimes, 33
    state, 32-33
Authoritarian governments
    political parties in, 136, 455
Authoritarian regimes
    democracy and, 33
Authoritarian systems
    assemblies in, 401

B

Bagehot, Walter, 378
Bank of England, 61, 137, 304, 389, 426
Basic rights, 300
Bicameralism, 410
Bourgeoisie, 9
Brown, Gordon, 23, 45-46, 148, 160, 206, 275, 307, 418, 447-449

C

Cabinet
    coalition, 32, 58, 66, 217-218, 450
    minority, 21, 58, 217, 314, 378, 415, 452-455
    principle, 10-11, 167, 366, 417-419
Callaghan, James, 62, 446
Chirac, Jacques, 11
Citizen participation, 286
Civil liberties, 70, 315-317
Clegg, Nick, 32, 135, 209, 465
Cold War, 33, 50, 137
Colonialism, 453
Committee(s)
    advisory, 303-304
Common market, 45
Commonwealth, 44, 389
Communist
    bloc, 51, 76
    Europe, 9, 21, 49-50, 75, 311
    rule, 19, 50, 365
    system, 19, 49, 74-75, 310-311
Communist Party(ies)
    In Eastern Europe, 51
Competitive parties
    elections and, 140, 163, 282, 369, 446
    in government, 4, 27, 161, 278, 304, 402, 426, 455
Concordat, 457
Conservative Party
    in Britain, 6-7, 18, 50-51, 71, 146, 153-154, 276, 311-312, 393, 462-463
    in France, 303
Conservatives
    in Germany, 157
Constitutional
    council, 29, 215, 425, 450
    crisis, 30, 147, 388, 462
    monarchy, 69
    reform, 30-32, 143, 167-168, 216-217, 378, 417-418
    rules, 71, 144, 216, 399, 416, 458
Corporatism, 54, 299
Crosland, Anthony, 27, 441
Crown
    British, 69, 162-165, 216, 391, 444-446

D

Democracy
    parliamentary, 5-6, 27, 48, 73, 135, 153, 285, 305, 401-402
    participatory, 27
    presidential, 150, 292, 318
    representative, 7, 47, 74, 134, 160, 432
    socialist, 26-27, 53-54, 73-75, 152, 163, 400
Downing Street, 220-221, 285, 302, 397, 418

E

East Germany
    Communist Party of, 58
    interest groups, 312
    party system, 146
Economy
    women and, 41
economy and
    International Monetary Fund, 74, 311
Electoral College, 136, 431
Electoral systems, 134, 401, 455
Empire(s)
    German, 54
    Soviet, 45
England
    cabinet, 10, 22, 57, 167, 368, 426, 448-449
    civil service, 10, 42, 413, 462
    European Union, 20, 152, 167-168, 444
    House of Commons, 41, 164, 216, 369-370, 411-412, 455
    House of Lords, 167, 368, 411-413
    political participation, 136
    prime minister, 9, 20, 61-62, 155, 216, 304, 368, 412, 445-447
Ethnic
    nationalism, 115
European Union (EU)
    constitution, 23-24, 44, 318, 400-401, 424, 462
    Council of Ministers, 398, 425, 457
    creation of, 20, 138, 285, 386, 412-413
    European Economic Community (EEC), 167
    European Parliament, 41, 137, 156, 401, 428, 458
    Parliament of, 365
    political parties, 34, 67, 133-134, 161, 286, 365, 441, 444-445
    Presidency, 423
    public opinion, 45-46, 156, 318

F

Falklands War, 20, 311
Fascism, 33, 54, 66
Federal systems, 435
Federalism, 444
First world, 42, 74, 445
France
    local, 42, 169-170, 302, 370
    Parliament and, 370
    Revolution of, 112
    Senate, 371
Friedman, Milton, 9, 20, 303
Fundamentalism, 150

G

Germany
    Bundestag, 364
    welfare state, 31-32
Gorbachev, Mikhail, 51
Gorbachev, Mikhail S., 51
Government power(s)
    abuses of, 466
    bureaucracy and, 148, 308
    cabinet and, 57, 307, 366
    separation of, 70, 400
    spending by, 143, 163

Green party

    in Scotland, 146-148, 156, 366, 445-446
    in the European Union, 406

H

Head of state, 155, 317
Hobbes, Thomas, 8
Human rights
    abuses, 70
Hussein, Saddam, 3

I

Immigration
    new, 21-25, 55, 69, 209-210
India
    mixed economy, 73-74
    population, 42
    women in, 41-42
Industrial democracies, 201
Industrial policy, 373
Interest aggregation, 241
Interest articulation, 241
Interest group systems
    pluralist, 285-290, 299, 402
Interest groups
    institutional, 136, 364, 425
Internationalism, 47, 74
Islam, 76, 393

K

Kyoto Protocol, 49

L

Liberal democracy, 76-77, 160, 299
Liberals, 9, 20, 69, 155, 216, 282, 400, 446
Locke, John, 69, 154

M

MacMillan, Harold, 19, 412
Major, John, 9, 20-21, 61, 161, 287, 303, 399, 459
Michels, Robert, 7
Mixed economy, 18, 66-67
Monarchs, 6, 70, 364-365
Muhammad, 58

N

Nationalism, 8, 33, 54, 443
Nationalist parties, 445-446
Nation-state, 47
New Politics, 29, 406
New social movements, 230-233, 263
Number of political parties, 451

O

Obama, Barack, 49
Ombudsman, 386
Open primaries, 162

P

Party families, 130
Party system(s)
    fragmented, 68, 299
    two-party, 145-146, 159-160, 404, 452
Peak association, 233
Personal rule, 337
Plurality system, 175
Poland
    corporatism, 262-263
    unions, 261-263
Policy implementation, 300
Policymaking
    and government, 237
Political class, 45, 285
Political cleavages, 111
Political exploitation, 22

Political freedom, 112
Political participation, 136
Political parties
    centrist, 139
    extremist, 58, 206
    leftist, 119
Political party(ies)
    discipline and, 49
Political rights, 39
Political system(s)
    functions and, 364, 429
Ponting, Clive, 353
Populism, 136
Power-sharing, 399
Proportional representation, 134, 158, 366, 428,
        453
Protestant, 445-446
Public goods, 3, 298

R
Redistribution of wealth, 24, 73
Referendum, 23, 148, 159, 218-222, 446-447
Regime(s)
    constitutional, 389
Regulatory state, 425
Representative democracy, 47, 74, 134
Rule of law, 18

S
Salmond, Alex, 451
Scottish National Party, 146, 158, 212, 445
Smith, Adam, 20, 71, 305
Social democratic parties, 108
Social trust, 226
Socialism, 17, 49, 68, 145, 301, 445
Sri Lanka, 384
Stalin, Joseph, 50
Supranational, 148

T
Taliban, 31
Thatcher, Margaret, 17-20, 44-45, 66-67, 167, 214,
        278-279, 302, 368, 412, 446
Thatcherism, 19-21, 53, 66, 143, 312, 449
Third World, 10
Totalitarian, 54
Treaty
    of Rome, 45

U
Ukraine, 50
Unemployment
    high, 42, 72
    insurance, 62, 73
United Kingdom
    committees in, 424
    executive agencies and, 327
    Whitehall and, 372
United States
    amendments to, 419-420
    blanket, 58
    conservatives and, 452
    judiciary, 6
    pressure groups and, 286, 405

V
Vietnam War, 318
Voting turnout, 202, 256

W
Wales
    Welsh Assembly, 134-135, 157, 389, 453-456
Welfare state, 18-20, 44, 66, 320
Whip, 214, 285, 417
Wilson, Harold, 62, 155, 279, 306, 427, 453

Z
Zimbabwe, 420